STUDENT-DRIVEN, FACU

THE MGMT SOLUTION

Visually Engaging Textbook

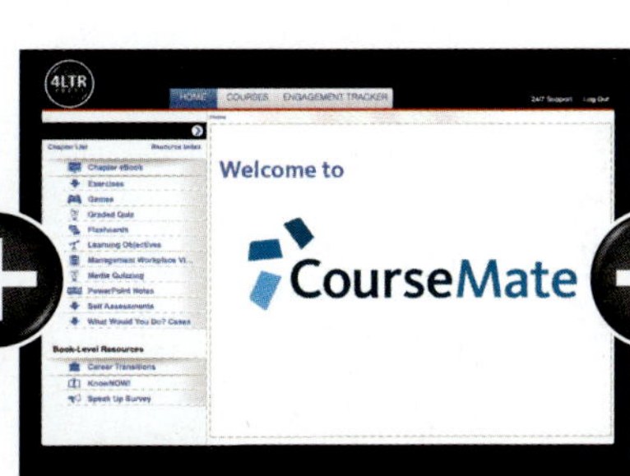

Online Study Tools

Tear-out Review Cards

Special Note To Students

It is important to begin reading this text with one thing in mind: *This business course does not have to be difficult*. We have done everything possible to eliminate the problems that students encounter in a typical class. All the features in each chapter have been evaluated and recommended by instructors with years of teaching experience. In addition, business students were asked to critique each chapter component. Based on this feedback, the text includes the following features:

- *Learning objectives* appear at the beginning of each chapter.
- *Inside Business* is a chapter-opening case that highlights how successful companies do business on a day-to-day basis.
- *Margin notes* are used throughout the text to reinforce both learning objectives and key terms.
- *Boxed features* highlight how both employees and entrepreneurs can be successful.
- *Spotlight* features highlight interesting facts about business and society and often provide a real-world example of an important concept within a chapter.

Interactive Ebook

STUDENT RESOURCES:

- Flashcards
- Interactive ebook
- Audio chapter summaries
- Games
- Cases and exercises
- Media quizzes
- Videos
- PowerPoint slides

INSTRUCTOR RESOURCES:

- Instructor's manual
- PowerPoint slides
- Test bank
- Instructor prep cards

Students sign in at **www.nelsonbrain.com**

Instructors sign in at **www.nelson.com/login**

"The online learning is great and the review cards in the back make test review easy!"

– Kyle McConnell, Fanshawe College

NELSON EDUCATION

MGMT, Second Canadian Edition
by Chuck Williams, Terri Champion, and Ike Hall

Vice President, Editorial Higher Education:
Anne Williams

Acquisitions Editor:
Alwynn Pinard

Marketing Manager:
Dave Stratton

Developmental Editors:
Roberta Osborne, Luciano Nicassio, Renae McCann

Photo Researcher and Permissions Coordinator:
Jessie Coffey

Senior Content Production Manager:
Natalia Denesiuk Harris

Production Service:
Integra

Copy Editor:
Matthew Kudelka

Proofreader:
Integra

Indexer:
Ursula Acton

Design Director:
Ken Phipps

Managing Designer:
Franca Amore

Interior Design:
Kyle Gell Design

Cover Design:
Trinh Truong

Cover Image:
Mel Curtis/Getty Images

Compositor:
Integra

Printed and bound in the United States of America
1 2 3 4 16 15 14

For more information contact Nelson Education Ltd., 1120 Birchmount Road, Toronto, Ontario, M1K 5G4. Or you can visit our Internet site at http://www.nelson.com

Library and Archives Canada Cataloguing in Publication Data

Williams, Chuck, 1959–, author

MGMT / Chuck Williams, Terri Champion, Ike Hall. — Second Canadian edition.

Includes bibliographical references and index.
ISBN 978-0-17-666224-0 (pbk.)

1. Management—Textbooks. I. Hall, Ike, author II. Champion, Terri, 1965–, author III. Title.

HD31.W51675 2014 658
C2013-907277-2

ISBN-13: 978-0-17-666224-0
ISBN-10: 0-17-666224-3

Brief Contents

Top to bottom: AlexAranda/Shutterstock.com; Slavoljub Pantelic/Shutterstock.com; iodrakon/Shutterstock.com; Lambros Kazan/Shutterstock.com; Alvov/Shutterstock.com

Contents

AlexAranda/Shutterstock.com (top); Pressmaster/Shutterstock.com (bottom)

Pavel L Photo and Video/Shutterstock.com

Andy Dean Photography/Shutterstock.com (top); Slavoljub Pantelic/Shutterstock.com (bottom)

Pojoslaw/Shutterstock.com (top); Monkey Business Images/Shutterstock.com (bottom)

wavebreakmedia/Shutterstock.com (top); Lambros Kazan/Shutterstock.com (bottom)

Maxim Petrichuk/Shutterstock.com

Igor Dutina/Shutterstock.com (top); Alvov/Shutterstock.com (bottom)

Hamara/Shutterstock.com (top); Claudio Bravo/Shutterstock.com (bottom)

Management

LEARNING OUTCOMES

LO1 Describe what management is.

LO2 Explain the four functions of management.

LO3 Describe different kinds of managers.

LO4 Explain the major roles and subroles that managers perform in their jobs.

LO5 Explain what companies look for in managers.

LO6 Discuss the top mistakes that managers make in their jobs.

LO7 Describe the transition that employees go through when they are promoted to management.

LO8 Explain how and why companies can create competitive advantage through people.

What Is Management?

Management issues are fundamental to any organization: How do we plan to get things done, organize the company to be efficient and effective, lead and motivate employees, and put controls in place to make sure our plans are followed and our goals are met? Good management is basic to starting a business, growing a business, and maintaining a business once it has achieved some measure of success.

To understand how important *good* management is, think about this mistake. Managers at Dunkin' Donuts Canada were accused of making critical management errors that severely affected the chain's Quebec operation. Their accusers were a group of franchisees who sued the company for what they saw as poor management. The franchisees blamed Dunkin' Donuts management for making poor marketing decisions that failed to protect and enhance the brand in the face of rising competition, and for persuading franchisees to buy into a new business strategy that ultimately failed. The company saw the number of Dunkin' Donut locations in Quebec decline rapidly, from 250 in 1995 to 115 in 2003 and down to 11 by 2012. The Quebec Superior Court agreed with the franchisees and awarded them over $16 million in damages.[1]

Ah, bad managers and bad management. Is it any wonder that Canadian companies pay consultants nearly $10 billion a year for advice on basic management issues such as how to lead people effectively, organize a company efficiently, and manage large-scale projects and processes?[2] This textbook will help you understand some of the basic issues that management consultants help companies resolve. (And it won't cost you billions of dollars.)

LO1 Management Is ...

Many of today's managers got their start working on the factory floor, clearing dishes off tables, helping customers fit a suit, or wiping up a spill in aisle. Similarly, lots of you will start at the bottom and work your way up. There's no better way to get to know your competition, your customers, and your business. But whether you begin your career at the entry level or as a supervisor, your job is not to do the work but to help others do theirs. **Management** is getting work done through others. Canadian businessman and television personality Jim Treliving is co-owner and co-chairman of the Boston Pizza chain and the T&M Group of Companies, with an impressive portfolio of businesses that generate over $1 billion in sales annually. Jim started out as an RCMP officer but later traded in his uniform to become a Boston Pizza franchisee in Penticton, British Columbia. Working hands-on in the business, Jim learned how to manage and run a successful franchise, balancing two important management concepts—efficiency and effectiveness. He and his partner George Melville eventually purchased the entire Boston Pizza chain in 1983 and began expanding the brand across Canada; in the process, they began growing their own group of companies. According to Jim, "behind every great company, is a great team." Jim's entrepreneurial spirit coupled with his skills in strategic planning and marketing have served him well; however, when asked to explain his success, he explains, "I think it's managing people. I think I get along with people well. I can understand people. I can read people fairly decently." A testament to Jim's belief in the value of good management, Boston Pizza has appeared on Canada's Best Managed Companies list numerous times. In 2008, Boston Pizza became a member of the Platinum Club, having won the Best Managed award for six consecutive years.[3]

Management getting work done through others

Efficiency getting work done with a minimum of effort, expense, or waste

Effectiveness accomplishing tasks that help fulfill organizational objectives

Jim Treliving's experience with Boston Pizza suggests that managers have to be concerned with efficiency and effectiveness. **Efficiency** is getting work done with minimal effort, expense, or waste. How does the Shouldice Hospital in Toronto perform more than 7,500 hernia surgeries a year on patients from all over the world even though it employs only 10 full-time surgeons? The Shouldice Hernia Centre, founded in 1945, is a testament to the principles of efficiency and productivity. Both were hallmarks of Frederick Taylor's theory of scientific management. The hospital has 5 operating theatres, 89 hospital beds, and a staff of 160, all of them focused on providing an extremely specialized high-quality and high-volume service. A well-organized admissions screening and scheduling system allows for efficient management of demand and capacity, and the delivery system allows for maximum patient involvement to ensure efficiency and low cost. The facility encourages exercise and rapid recovery—there are no TVs or telephones in patient rooms, but there *are* 23 acres of gardens for patients to stroll in. The centre's results are impressive—at Shouldice, the chances of complication are 0.5 percent and the chances of recurrence after hernia repair average less than 1 percent. Compare this to the average in North America for recurrence after hernia repair, which is 10 percent. In addition, recovery times and costs are lower compared to other hospitals and clinics.[4]

Overall, efficiency is an important focus for individual organizations and for Canada as a whole, given that labour productivity is tied to a country's economic success and standard of living. You'll learn more about labour productivity in Chapter 18 on managing service and manufacturing operations.

Efficiency alone is not enough to ensure success. Managers must also strive for **effectiveness**, which means accomplishing tasks that help fulfill organizational objectives such as customer service and satisfaction. Wal-Mart's new computerized scheduling system is an example of efficiency and effectiveness. It used to take Wal-Mart a full day to schedule the weekly shifts for a single store. Now, Wal-Mart's computerized system calculates the schedules for 1.3 million workers in one day. The same system measures trends in store sales and customer

Planning (management functions) determining organizational goals and a means for achieving them

Organizing deciding where decisions will be made, who will do what jobs and tasks, and who will work for whom

traffic so that Wal-Mart can have more employees on the job whenever its stores are busy. Tests in 39 stores indicated that 70 percent of customers reported improved checkout times and service using this scheduling system.[5]

LO2 Management Functions

Henri Fayol, the managing director (CEO) of a large steel company in the early 1900s, was one of the founders of the field of management. You'll learn more about Fayol and management's other key figures when you read about the history of management in Chapter 2. Based on his 20 years as a CEO, Fayol argued that "the success of an enterprise generally depends much more on the administrative ability of its leaders than on their technical ability."[6] For example, although John Riccitiello, CEO of Electronic Arts (EA), the world's leading computer game developer, considers himself to be a serious "gamer," his business experience prior to joining EA included management positions at Sara Lee Corporation, Wilson Sporting Goods, PepsiCo, Inc., and The Clorox Company. Riccitiello's ability to run a company that competes in a fast-paced and rapidly changing industry has more to do with his management capabilities than with his technical knowledge of how to design or produce video games.[7]

Managers need to perform five managerial functions in order to succeed, according to Fayol: planning, organizing, coordinating, commanding, and controlling.[8] Most management textbooks today have updated this list by dropping the coordinating function and referring to Fayol's commanding function as "leading." Thus, Fayol's management functions are known today in this updated form: planning, organizing, leading, controlling. Studies indicate that managers who perform these management functions well are more successful, gaining promotions for themselves and profits for their companies. One study has found that the more time CEOs spend planning, the more profitable their companies are.[9] A 25-year study at AT&T found that employees with better planning and decision-making skills were more likely to be promoted into management jobs, to succeed as managers, and to be promoted into upper levels of management.[10] The evidence is clear. Managers at all levels of an organization serve their companies well when they plan, organize, lead, and control. (That's why this book is organized around the functions of management outlined in Exhibit 1.1.)

*Now let's take a closer look at each of the management functions: **2.1 planning, 2.2 organizing, 2.3 leading,** and **2.4 controlling.***

2.1 Planning

Planning involves determining organizational goals as well as means for achieving them. As you'll learn in Chapter 5, planning is one of the best ways to improve performance. It encourages people to work harder, to work hard for extended periods, to engage in behaviours directly related to accomplishing goals, and to think of better ways to do their jobs. But most important, companies that plan have larger profits and faster growth than companies that don't plan.

Exhibit 1.1 The Four Functions of Management

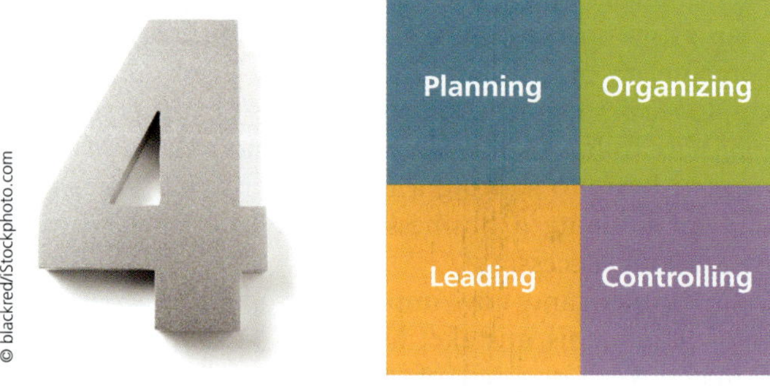

© blackred/iStockphoto.com

For example, the question "What business are we in?" is at the heart of strategic planning, which you'll learn about in Chapter 6. If you can answer the question "What business are we in?" in two sentences or less, chances are you have a very clear plan for your business. Christine Day, CEO of Vancouver-based athletic apparel company lululemon athletica, inc., knows precisely what business her company is in: "creating components for people to live a longer, healthier, more fun life."[11] The same is true for Google. Even though the company makes money selling search-based Internet advertising, Google says it is not in the advertising business but in the business of organizing the world's information.[12] Not only can you search Google for websites, images, books, scholarly articles, and shopping opportunities, but you can also organize your personal life using Google's calendar, e-mail, photo, and document sharing, and feed reader applications. Even Google's $1.65 billion purchase of YouTube adheres to the business Google is in by helping users access and organize video content.

You'll learn more about planning in Chapter 5 on planning and decision making, Chapter 6 on organizational strategy, Chapter 7 on innovation and change, and Chapter 8 on global management.

2.2 Organizing

Organizing is deciding where decisions will be made, who will do what jobs and tasks, and who will work for whom in the company. Imagine the massive effort that faced the Vancouver Organizing Committee for the 2010 Olympic and Paralympic Winter Games (VANOC). The International Olympic Committee announced on July 2, 2003, that VANOC would be tasked with the enormous challenge of organizing this global event, which over 17 days would bring to Vancouver more than 6,850 athletes and officials from more than 80 countries, along with 10,000 media representatives and 2.3 million visitors. Organizing efforts encompassed new sports facilities and venues, major transportation infrastructure projects, housing accommodations (including the Olympic

Athletes Village), event ticket sales, the planning of the opening and closing ceremonies, medal presentations, retail merchandise sales, security measures, and the coordination of more than 50,000 workers and volunteers. To make Vancouver 2010 a reality, VANOC needed to administer a budget of $580 million for capital infrastructure from the federal and provincial governments and a further $1.76 billion operating budget funded by television revenues, ticket sales, corporate sponsorships, and private contributions. Construction cost overruns and a global economic downturn presented major challenges to VANOC's operating budget and were a cause for concern. But there was also plenty of good news: event ticket sales were oversubscribed, the sports venues were completed ahead of schedule, and major transportation projects—including rapid transit service between downtown Vancouver and the airport—were fully operational three months earlier than anticipated. There is no doubt that it took an incredible amount of organizational effort to host an international event of this calibre. With the world watching, VANOC put on an event that made Canadians proud.[13]

You'll learn more about organizing in Chapter 9 on designing organizations, Chapter 10 on managing teams, Chapter 11 on managing human resources, and Chapter 12 on managing individuals and a diverse workforce.

2.3 Leading

Our third management function, **leading**, involves inspiring and motivating employees to work hard to achieve organizational goals. John Stanton, founder and president of the Edmonton-based Running Room chain of retail stores, which cater to running and fitness enthusiasts alike, knows how important leadership is to building a successful company. Since opening his first store in 1984, Stanton's company has grown into North America's largest specialty retailer of sporting goods, apparel, and footwear, with stores from coast to coast. He credits much of his success to his original vision for the company, which hasn't changed much over the years—locate stores near parks, trails, and post-run meeting places like cafés; provide specialized knowledge and technical expertise on shoe selection as well as health and nutrition; offer running clinics and weekly runs for everyone from beginners to avid runners and marathoners; and promote a lifestyle of wellness and community. Much of Running Room's success in achieving this vision can be attributed to Stanton himself, who spends about 300 days a year on the road, visiting Running Room stores and participating in numerous charity runs and marathons across North America. All of this allows him to stay up to date on the needs of his consumers and staff. Examples of his approachable and accessible leadership style are found throughout the company: his e-mail address is posted on the company website; he acts as the voice of the company's voice-mail receptionist; and he utilizes a company-wide computer network that allows store employees to stay connected with one another and with head office. The results speak for themselves: the Running Room boasts an employee turnover rate that is half the industry average. It was voted one of Canada's Best Managed Companies in 2007 and 2010 and continues to expand in both Canada and the United States.[14]

Leading inspiring and motivating workers to work hard to achieve organizational goals

Controlling monitoring progress toward goal achievement and taking corrective action when needed

You'll learn more about leading in Chapter 13 on motivation, Chapter 14 on leadership, and Chapter 15 on managing communication.

2.4 Controlling

The last function of management, **controlling**, involves monitoring progress toward goal achievement and taking corrective action when progress isn't being made. The basic control process involves setting standards to achieve goals, comparing actual performance to those standards, and then making changes to return performance to those standards.

Mike Duke, Wal-Mart's CEO, runs the world's largest company, which rings up $410 billion a year in annual sales (a figure that will be even larger by the time you read this). Duke, an engineer by education, is well known for being organized and meticulous in his attention to detail. He maintains a red folder for each of the executives who reports to him (eight in all). On the outside of each folder, his assistant writes the executive's name and the time of Duke's next meeting with him. Each folder contains a set of goals, problems, and follow-up items related to that manager's responsibilities. For example, the folder for Brian Cornell, who runs Sam's Club, Wal-Mart's discount warehouse chain, contains recent sales figures, a question that Duke has regarding the strategy Sam's is using to purchase real estate for new locations, and an e-mail from a Sam's Club member who wrote to Duke complaining that the Member's Mark facial tissue (a private brand sold by Sam's) gets stuck in the box and doesn't pull out easily. Regarding the tissue, Duke said, "Brian's team identified that as a real problem. And I said, 'Great, now that we've identified the problem, when are we going to solve it?'

AlexAranda/Shutterstock.com

Top managers executives responsible for the overall direction of the organization

And I keep this in here until Brian tells me it's solved. It's a follow-up mechanism."[15]

You'll learn more about the control function in Chapter 16 on control, Chapter 17 on managing information, and Chapter 18 on managing service and manufacturing operations.

What Do Managers Do?

Not all managerial jobs are the same. The demands and requirements placed on the CEO of Sony are significantly different from those placed on the manager of your local Wendy's restaurant. However, managers at all levels have a role to play in terms of the core management functions of planning, organizing, leading and controlling.

LO3 Kinds of Managers

As shown in Exhibit 1.2, there are four kinds of managers, each with different jobs and responsibilities: ***3.1 top managers, 3.2 middle managers, 3.3 first-line managers, and 3.4 team leaders.***

3.1 Top Managers

Top managers hold positions like chief executive officer (CEO), chief operating officer (COO), chief financial officer (CFO), and chief information officer (CIO), and are responsible for the overall direction of the organization. Top managers have the following responsibilities.[16] First, they are responsible for creating a context for change. In many large corporations it is not uncommon for a CEO to be fired because he or she failed to move fast enough to effect significant change. In fact, the most critical time for a CEO is the first 100 days. This indicates that more

Exhibit 1.2 What the Four Kinds of Managers Do

Jobs	Responsibilities
Top Managers CEO, CIO, COO, Vice President, CFO, Corporate Heads	change commitment culture environment
Middle Managers General Manager Plant Manager Regional Manager Divisional Manager	resources objectives coordination subunit performance strategy implementation
First-Line Managers Office Manager Shift Supervisor Department Manager	nonmanagerial worker supervision teaching and training scheduling facilitation
Team Leaders Team Leader Team Contact Group Facilitator	facilitation external relationships internal relationships

EDHAR/Shutterstock.com

YanLev/Shutterstock.com

ColorBlind Images/Blend Images/Jupiterimages

Marcin Balcerzak/Shutterstock.com

and more organizations today are expecting to see results quickly and that they use the first few months of a top manager's tenure as a means of determining whether that person will succeed.[17] In both Europe and the United States, 35 percent of all CEOs are eventually fired because of their failure to successfully change their companies.[18] Creating a context for change includes forming a long-range vision or mission for the company.

Once that vision or mission is set, the second responsibility of top managers is to develop employees' commitment to and ownership of the company's performance. That is, top managers are responsible for creating employee buy-in. Third, top managers must create a positive organizational culture through language and action. Top managers impart company values, strategies, and lessons through what they do and say to others both inside and outside the company. Above all, no matter what they communicate, it's critical for CEOs to send and reinforce clear, consistent messages.[19] A former *Fortune* 500 CEO said, "I tried to [use] exactly the same words every time so that I didn't produce a lot of, 'Last time you said this, this time you said that.' You've got to say the same thing over and over and over."[20]

Finally, top managers are responsible for monitoring their business environments. This means that they must closely monitor customers' needs, competitors' moves, and long-term business, economic, and social trends. *You'll read more about business environments in Chapter 3.*

3.2 Middle Managers

Middle managers hold positions like plant manager, regional manager, or divisional manager. They are responsible for setting objectives consistent with top management's goals and for planning and implementing subunit strategies for achieving those objectives.[21] One specific middle management responsibility is to plan and allocate resources to meet objectives.

Middle managers managers responsible for setting objectives consistent with top management's goals and for planning and implementing subunit strategies for achieving these objectives

A second major responsibility is to coordinate and link groups, departments, and divisions within a company. The use of just-in-time inventory practices to keep inventory costs at the lowest level possible is an important business practice that has become a mainstay of the North American automotive industry. For this practice to succeed, parts and supplies must be shipped in a timely manner to allow plant managers to reach production objectives and targets. However, since September 11, 2001, border wait times have increased, which has left plant managers dealing with frustrating delays, rescheduling of production runs, and increased costs. It is estimated that delays at the Canada–US border have increased production costs for new vehicles by $800 per unit.[22]

Why Middle Managers May Be the Most Important People in Your Company

A study conducted by Wharton Management professor Ethan Mollick may change the way the business community views middle managers. According to Mollick, middle managers are often overlooked even though they play a large role in a firm's performance, particularly in industries that are innovative and knowledge-intensive such as computer games, software, and biotech. Middle managers in these industries often have key roles related to project management and responsibilities that include resource allocation, supervision of others, meeting deadlines, and fostering an innovative environment. In fact, in the computer game industry, "success ... relies not just on managers in charge of innovation, but also in project managers capable of organizing dozens of programmers and coordinating budgets that often reach into the tens of millions of dollars." In addition, although top management plays a major role in setting the overall vision and direction of a company, "they don't have a big part in deciding which individual projects are selected and how they are run. At least for the computer game industry—and no doubt lots of knowledge-based industries—it is all about the middle managers."

Source: E. Mollick, "People and Process, Suits and Innovators: The Role of Individuals in Firm Performance," March 1, 2011. Available at SSRN: http://ssrn.com/abstract=1630546 or http://dx.doi.org/10.2139/ssrn.1630546; E. Mollick, "Why Middle Managers May Be the Most Important People in Your Company" May 25, 2011 in *Knowledge@Wharton* at http://knowledge.wharton.upenn.edu/article.cfm?articleid=2783, accessed November 30, 2012.

First-line managers managers who train and supervise the performance of nonmanagerial employees who are directly responsible for producing the company's products or services

Team leaders managers responsible for facilitating team activities toward accomplishing a goal

A third responsibility of middle management is to monitor and manage the performance of subunits and of individual managers. Canada's upscale menswear retail chain, Harry Rosen Inc., invested in a customized software system to help sales associates better manage customer relationships. The system enables them to view customer preferences and buying history; it also helps develop marketing campaigns targeted to individual customer preferences. The system also provides management with important real-time information and sales reports, which are used to evaluate storewide and individual sales associate performance. As a result, management is able to assess how stores and associates are performing in terms of key performance indicators, thereby ensuring that the Harry Rosen quality and brand image is maintained.[23]

Finally, middle managers are responsible for implementing the changes or strategies generated by top managers. Wal-Mart's strategy reflects its mission, "Saving people money so they can live better." When Wal-Mart began selling groceries in its new 18,500-square-metre supercentres, it made purchasing manager Brian Wilson responsible for buying perishable goods more cheaply than Wal-Mart's competitors. When small produce suppliers had trouble meeting Wal-Mart's needs, Wilson worked closely with them and connected them to RetailLink, Wal-Mart's computer network, "which allows our suppliers immediate access to all information needed to help run the business." Over time, these steps helped the produce suppliers reduce costs and deliver the enormous quantities of fresh fruits and vegetables that Wal-Mart's Supercenters need.[24]

3.3 First-Line Managers

First-line managers hold positions like office manager, shift supervisor, or department manager. The primary responsibility of first-line managers is to manage the performance of the entry-level employees who are directly responsible for producing a company's goods and services. First-line managers are the only managers who don't supervise other managers. The responsibilities of first-line managers include monitoring, teaching, and short-term planning.

First-line managers encourage, monitor, and reward the performance of their workers. They also teach entry-level employees how to do their jobs. Damian Mogavero's company, Avero LLC, helps restaurants analyze sales data for each member of a restaurant's wait staff. Restaurant managers who use the data, says Mogavero, will often take their top-selling server to lunch each week as a reward. The best managers, however, will also take their poorest-selling servers out to lunch to talk about what they can do to improve their performance.[25]

First-line managers also make detailed schedules and operating plans based on middle management's intermediate-range plans. By contrast to the long-term plans of top managers (three to five years out) and the intermediate plans of middle managers (6 to 18 months out), first-line managers engage in plans and actions that typically produce results within two weeks.[26] Consider the typical convenience store manager (e.g., 7-Eleven), who starts the day by driving past competitors' stores to inspect their gasoline prices and then checks the outside of his or her store for anything that might need maintenance, such as burned-out lights or signs, or restocking, like windshield washer fluid and paper towels. Then comes an inside check, where the manager determines what needs to be done for that day. (Are there enough coffee and donuts for breakfast? enough sandwiches for lunch?) Once the day is planned, the manager turns to weekend orders. After accounting for the weather (hot or cold) and the sales trends at the same time last year, the manager makes sure the store will have enough beer, soft drinks, and Sunday papers on hand. Finally, the manager looks 7 to 10 days ahead for hiring needs. Because of strict hiring procedures (basic math tests, background checks, and so on), it can take that long to hire new employees. Said one convenience store manager, "I have to continually interview, even if I am fully staffed."[27]

3.4 Team Leaders

The fourth kind of manager is the team leader. This relatively new kind of management job developed as companies shifted to self-managing teams, which by definition have no formal supervisor. In traditional management hierarchies, first-line managers are responsible for the performance of nonmanagerial employees and have the authority to hire and fire workers, make job assignments, and control resources. In this new structure, the teams themselves perform nearly all of the functions performed by first-line managers under traditional hierarchies.[28]

Team leaders thus have a different set of responsibilities than traditional first-line managers.[29] **Team leaders** are primarily responsible for facilitating team activities toward accomplishing a goal. This doesn't mean that team leaders are responsible for team performance. They aren't. The team is. Team leaders help their team members plan and schedule work, learn to

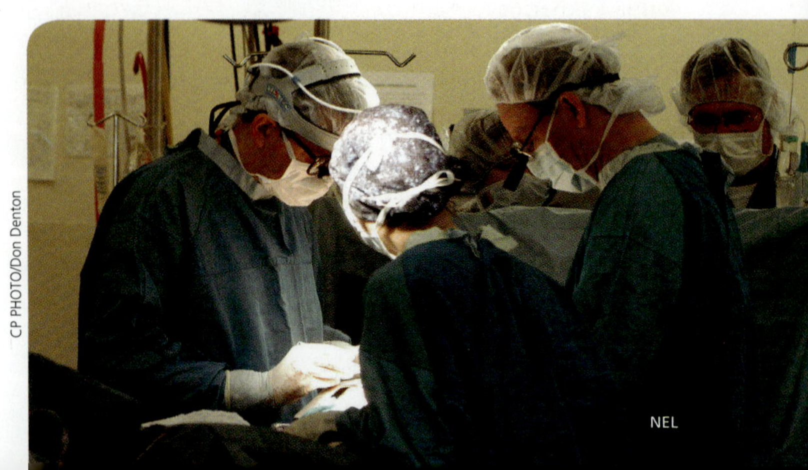
CP PHOTO/Don Denton

solve problems, and work effectively with one another. Management consultant Franklin Jonath says: "The idea is for the team leader to be at the service of the group. It should be clear that the team members own the outcome. The leader is there to bring intellectual, emotional, and spiritual resources to the team. Through his or her actions, the leader should be able to show the others how to think about the work that they're doing in the context of their lives."[30]

Relationships among team members and between different teams are crucial to good team performance and must be well-managed by team leaders. Getting along with others is much more important in team structures because team members can't get work done without the help of their teammates. For example, studies have shown that it's not the surgeon but the interactions between the surgeon and all operating room team members that determine surgical outcomes. When team members like nurses, technicians, and other doctors find it difficult to speak up or voice a concern in the operating room, serious mistakes can occur no matter how talented the surgeon. Consequently, many surgeons now are using "safety pauses" to better involve members of their surgical teams. The surgeon will pause, ask if anyone has concerns, and address them if need be at that time. Studies show that safety pauses reduce errors, such as operating on the wrong leg or beginning surgery with key surgical instruments missing.[31]

Team leaders are also responsible for managing external relationships, acting as the bridge or liaison between their teams and other teams, departments, and divisions in a company. For example, if a member of Team A complains about the quality of Team B's work, Team A's leader needs to initiate a meeting with Team B's leader. Together, these team leaders are responsible for getting members of both teams to work together to solve the problem. If it's done right, the problem is solved without involving company management or blaming members of the other team.[32]

A team leader's job involves a different set of skills than traditional management jobs typically do. For example, a Hewlett-Packard ad for a team leader position says: "Job seeker must enjoy coaching, working with people, and bringing about improvement through hands-off guidance and leadership."[33] Team leaders who fail to understand how their roles are different from those of traditional managers often struggle in their jobs. A team leader at Texas Instruments reacted with skepticism to his initial experience with teams: "I didn't buy into teams, partly because there was no clear plan on what I was supposed to do ... I never let the operators [team members] do any scheduling or any ordering of parts because that was mine. I figured as long as I had that, I had a job." After shifting jobs, however, he learned the difference in approach in a setting where members of the team took turns at the leadership role. He eventually became a consultant to help team leaders develop their skills and solve problems.[34]

You will learn more about teams in Chapter 10.

LO4 Managerial Roles

Although all four types of managers engage in planning, organizing, leading, and controlling, if you were to follow them around during a typical day on the job, you would probably not use these terms to describe what they actually do. Rather, what you'd see are the various *roles* managers play. Henry Mintzberg studied several CEOs over the course of a week, analyzing their mail, their conversations, and their actions. He concluded that managers fulfill three major roles while performing their jobs:[35]

- interpersonal roles
- informational roles
- decisional roles

In other words, managers talk to people, gather and give information, and make decisions. Furthermore, as shown in Exhibit 1.3, these three major roles can be subdivided into 10 subroles. *Let's examine each major role—**4.1 interpersonal, 4.2 informational,** and **4.3 decisional roles**—and the 10 subroles.*

4.1 Interpersonal Roles

More than anything else, management jobs are people-intensive. Estimates vary with the level of management, but most managers spend between two-thirds and four-fifths of their time in face-to-face communication with others.[36] If you're a loner, or if you consider dealing with people a pain, then you may not be cut out for management work. In fulfilling the interpersonal role of management, managers perform three subroles: figurehead, leader, and liaison.

Exhibit 1.3 Mintzberg's Managerial Roles

Interpersonal Roles
- Figurehead
- Leader
- Liaison

Informational Roles
- Monitor
- Disseminator
- Spokesperson

Decisional Roles
- Entrepreneur
- Disturbance Handler
- Resource Allocator
- Negotiator

Top to bottom: EDHAR/Shutterstock.com; R. Gino Santa Maria/Shutterstock.com; © Tuomas Kujansuu/iStockphoto.com

Source: Reprinted by permission of *Harvard Business Review* (an exhibit) from "The Manager's Job: Folklore and Fact," By Mintzberg, H. *Harvard Business Review*, July-August 1975.

Figurehead role the interpersonal role managers play when they perform ceremonial duties

Leader role the interpersonal role managers play when they motivate and encourage workers to accomplish organizational objectives

Liaison role the interpersonal role managers play when they deal with people outside their units

Monitor role the informational role managers play when they scan their environment for information

Disseminator role the informational role managers play when they share information with others in their departments or companies

Spokesperson role the informational role managers play when they share information with people outside their departments or companies

In the **figurehead role**, managers perform ceremonial duties like greeting company visitors, speaking at the opening of a new facility, or representing the company at a community luncheon to support local charities. In the **leader role**, managers motivate and encourage workers to accomplish organizational objectives. Vancouver-based Mountain Equipment Co-op (MEC) is an outdoor recreation retail chain known for its unique retail format. Customers are offered a lifetime membership and a share of the company for a one-time payment of five dollars. Their unique approach fits well with the culture set by MEC's leaders, who make corporate social responsibility—in particular, ethical sourcing and sustainability—a top priority, and who focus strongly on employee motivation. MEC provides employees with onsite yoga classes, shower facilities for bicycle commuters, outdoor patio areas with lounge chairs and barbeques, a climbing wall, and a sign-out system where employees can borrow outdoor equipment. Employees can listen to music at work, bring pets to work when needed, participate in after-work bike rides and company running teams, and receive tuition subsidies for courses taken at outside institutions that support ongoing career development. The company's culture and its leadership approach explain why MEC was selected as one of Canada's Top 100 Employers for 2010.[37]

In the **liaison role**, managers deal with people outside their units. Studies consistently indicate that managers spend as much time with outsiders as they do with their own subordinates and their own bosses.[38]

4.2 Informational Roles

Not only do managers spend most of their time in face-to-face contact with others, but they also spend much of it obtaining and sharing information. Indeed, Mintzberg found that the managers in his study spent 40 percent of their time giving and getting information from others. In this regard, management can be viewed as processing information, gathering information by scanning the business environment and listening to others in face-to-face conversations, processing that information, and then sharing that information with people inside and outside the company. Mintzberg described three informational subroles: monitor, disseminator, and spokesperson.

In the **monitor role**, managers scan their environment for information, actively contact others for information, and, because of their personal contacts, receive a great deal of unsolicited information. Besides receiving firsthand information, managers monitor their environment by reading local newspapers and national papers like the *Globe and Mail* to keep track of customers, competitors, and technological changes that may affect their businesses. Nowadays, managers can also take advantage of electronic monitoring and distribution services that track the news wires for stories related to their businesses.

Because of their numerous personal contacts and their access to subordinates, managers are often hubs for the distribution of critical information. In the **disseminator role**, managers share the information they have collected with their subordinates and others in the company. There will never be a complete substitute for face-to-face dissemination of information. Yet technology is changing how information is shared and collected. Although the primary methods of communication in large companies are e-mail and voice mail, managers are also using company intranets, online video, blogs, podcasts, and wikis to communicate internally with employees. Managers are also beginning to realize the value of social networking technologies like Facebook and Twitter to disseminate information internally. Vancouver-based lululemon athletica uses Twitter, Facebook, blogging, and Flickr to help maintain open lines of communication with employees in their 170-plus stores across North America and Australia. Carolyn Coles, lululemon's online community manager, explains that social networking "helps to keep everyone connected at every level and empowered, and really elevates internal conversation."[39]

In contrast to the disseminator role, in which managers distribute information to employees inside the company, in the **spokesperson role**, managers share information with people outside their departments and

MGMT**FACT**

Connect to Your Business

These services deliver customized electronic newspapers that include only stories on topics the managers specify:

- Canadian News Wire (CNW) (http://www.newswire.ca) connects organizations to relevant news and information, including social media releases that allow multimedia content.
- Globe Investor (http://www.theglobeandmail.com/globe-investor) offers up-to-date financial news and articles on stock trends.
- Canadian Press (http://www.thecanadianpress.com), in addition to being a multimedia real-time news agency, provides subscribers with news alerts to developing stories related to a specific company and/or industry.
- Business Wire (http://www.businesswire.com) monitors and distributes daily news headlines from major industries.

AP Photo/Paul Sakuma, File

companies. One of the most common ways CEOs serve as spokespeople for their companies is at annual meetings with company shareholders or the board of directors. CEOs also serve as spokespersons to the media when their companies are involved in major news stories. The late Steve Jobs, founder and former CEO of Apple, used his platform as company spokesperson to communicate the Apple vision to customers and competitors alike. He was famous for his new product launch presentations, carefully planning and rehearsing his speeches to capture attention and create excitement among industry experts, Apple fans, potential customers, the media, and the business community at large. At the launch of the iPhone in 2007, Jobs described the device as a "revolutionary and magical product that is literally 5 years ahead of any other mobile phone."[40]

4.3 Decisional Roles

Mintzberg found that obtaining and sharing information is not an end in itself. Obtaining and sharing information with people inside and outside the company is useful to managers because it helps them make good decisions. According to Mintzberg, managers engage in four decisional subroles: entrepreneur, disturbance handler, resource allocator, and negotiator.

In the **entrepreneur role**, managers adapt themselves, their subordinates, and their units to change. Ontario's Lakeport Brewing Corp. was struggling to survive in the extremely competitive beer industry when Teresa Cascioli was brought in as manager to try and salvage a company that was in deep financial trouble. Cascioli's strategy of expanding the product line, redesigning the packaging and labels, switching to a can format, and—more important—reducing the price of a case of beer to $24 or a buck a beer (the lowest legal price in Ontario), was considered by many in the industry to be brash and full of risk, considering that Lakeport had been started as a premium brewery. But her gamble paid off—the company's market share began to rise as a result of her innovative discount strategy, and eventually the brewery became the fourth-largest in the province and the sixth-largest in Canada.[41]

Entrepreneur role the decisional role managers play when they adapt themselves, their subordinates, and their units to change

Disturbance handler role the decisional role managers play when they respond to severe problems that demand immediate action

In the **disturbance handler role**, managers respond to pressures and problems so severe that they demand immediate attention and action. Managers often play the role of disturbance handler when the board of a failing company hires a new CEO to turn the company around. After Ford Motor Company's market share shrank from 25 to 16 percent and the company lost $7 billion in nine months, Alan Mulally came from Boeing to become Ford's new CEO. Mulally quickly arranged $23.5 billion in financing to cover the losses and introduced a plan to cut costs by reducing the number of cars Ford produces, standardizing the use of shared parts across Ford vehicles, and laying off half of Ford's 82,000 factory workers.[42]

Antena/Jupiterimages

Resource allocator role the decisional role managers play when they decide who gets what resources

Negotiator role the decisional role managers play when they negotiate schedules, projects, goals, outcomes, resources, and employee raises

Technical skills the specialized procedures, techniques, and knowledge required to get the job done

In the **resource allocator role**, managers decide who will get what resources and how much of each resource they will get. Hoping to revive sales of its luxury cars, top managers at General Motors acted as resource allocators by redirecting long-term investment of $4 billion to the company's Cadillac brand. Put in perspective, that means that executives invested nearly 10 percent of GM's total capital budget in a division that accounted for only 4 percent of GM sales.[43]

In the **negotiator role**, managers may negotiate schedules, projects, goals, outcomes, resources, and employee raises. After years of lawsuits, it took only two days for the new CEO of EMI Group Ltd., which owns the rights to sell Beatles music, to negotiate a deal to make the legendary band's music available for sale at Apple's iTunes store. Although surviving members Paul McCartney and Ringo Starr, and the widows of John Lennon and George Harrison, have veto rights over how the music is distributed, in the end they agreed to allow digital downloads of the band's music. Just two months after the negotiation, 5 million Beatles songs and 2 million Beatles albums had been sold and downloaded via iTunes.[44] As shown by EMI's experience, negotiating is a key to success and a basic part of managerial work.

Justin Sullivan/Getty Images News

What Does It Take to Be a Manager?

> *I didn't have the slightest idea what my job was. I walked in giggling and laughing because I had been promoted and had no idea what principles or style to be guided by. After the first day, I felt like I had run into a brick wall. (Sales Representative #1)*
>
> *Suddenly, I found myself saying, boy, I can't be responsible for getting all that revenue. I don't have the time. Suddenly you've got to go from [taking care of] yourself and say now I'm the manager, and what does a manager do? It takes a while thinking about it for it to really hit you ... A manager gets things done through other people. That's a very, very hard transition to make. (Sales Representative #2)*[45]

The above statements come from two star sales representatives, who, on the basis of their superior performance, were promoted to the position of sales manager. As their comments indicate, at first they did not feel confident about their ability to do their jobs as managers. Like most new managers, these sales managers suddenly realized that the knowledge, skills, and abilities that led to success early in their careers (and were probably responsible for their promotion into management) would not necessarily help them succeed as managers. As sales representatives, they were responsible for managing only their own performance. But as sales managers, they were now directly responsible for supervising all of the sales representatives in their sales territories. Furthermore, they were now directly accountable for whether those sales representatives achieved their sales goals.

If performance in nonmanagerial jobs doesn't necessarily prepare you for a managerial job, then what does it take to be a manager?

LO5 What Companies Look for in Managers

When companies look for employees who would be good managers, they look for individuals who have technical skills, human skills, conceptual skills, and the motivation to manage.[46] Exhibit 1.4 shows the relative importance of these four skills to the jobs of team leaders, first-line managers, middle managers, and top managers.

Technical skills are the specialized procedures, techniques, and knowledge required to get the job done. For the sales managers like the ones quoted earlier, technical

Exhibit 1.4 Management Skills

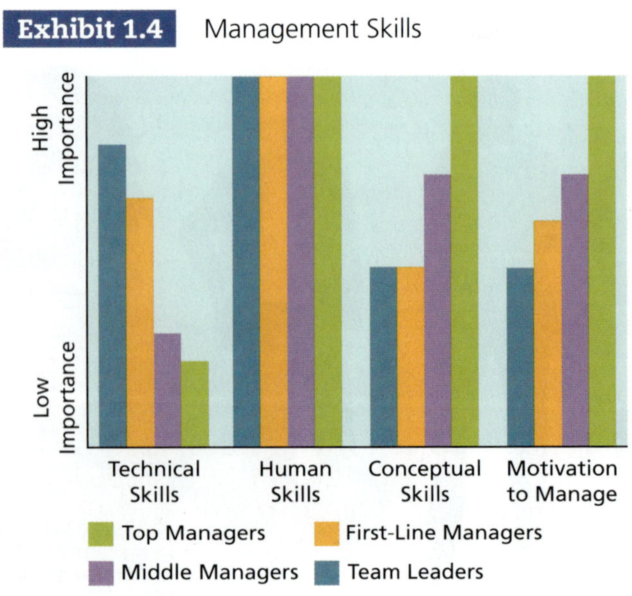

Hans Bjurling/Getting Images

skills include the ability to find new sales prospects, develop accurate sales pitches based on customer needs, and close the sale. For a nurse supervisor, technical skills would include being able to insert an IV or operate a crash cart if a patient goes into cardiac arrest.

Technical skills are most important for team leaders and lower level managers because it is they who supervise the workers who produce products or serve customers. Team leaders and first-line managers need technical knowledge and skills to train new employees and help employees solve problems. Technical knowledge and skills are also needed to troubleshoot problems that employees can't handle. Technical skills become less important as managers rise through the managerial ranks, but they are still important.

Human skills can be summarized as the ability to work well with others. Managers with people skills work effectively within groups, encourage others to express their thoughts and feelings, are sensitive to others' needs and viewpoints, and are good listeners and communicators. Human skills are equally important at all levels of management, from first-line supervisors to CEOs. However, because lower level managers spend much of their time solving technical problems, upper-level managers may actually spend more time dealing directly with people. On average, first-line managers spend 57 percent of their time with people, but that percentage increases to 63 percent for middle managers and 78 percent for top managers.[47]

Conceptual skills include the ability to see the organization as a whole, to understand how the different parts of the company affect one another, and to recognize how the company fits into or is affected by elements of its external environment such as the local community, social and economic forces, customers, and the competition. Good managers must be able to recognize, understand, and reconcile multiple complex problems and perspectives. In other words, managers have to be smart! In fact, intelligence makes so much difference to managerial performance that managers with above-average intelligence typically outperform managers of average intelligence by approximately 48 percent.[48] Clearly, companies need to be careful to promote smart workers into management. Conceptual skills increase in importance as managers rise through the management hierarchy.

Good management involves much more than intelligence, however. For example, making the department genius a manager can be disastrous if that genius lacks technical skills, human skills, or one other factor known as the motivation to manage. **Motivation to manage** is an assessment of how motivated employees are to interact with superiors, participate in competitive situations, behave assertively toward others, tell others what to do, reward good behaviour and punish poor behaviour, perform actions that are highly visible to others, and handle and organize administrative tasks. Managers typically have a stronger motivation to manage than their subordinates, and managers at higher levels usually have a stronger motivation to manage than managers at lower levels. Furthermore, managers with a stronger motivation to manage are promoted faster, are rated as better managers by their employees, and earn more money than managers with a weak motivation to manage.[49]

Human skills the ability to work well with others

Conceptual skills the ability to see the organization as a whole, understand how the different parts affect one another, and recognize how the company fits into or is affected by its environment

Motivation to manage an assessment of how enthusiastic employees are about managing the work of others

LO6 Mistakes Managers Make

It is generally accepted that good management will enhance organizational performance, and that some managers are better than others. However, reaching a consensus on what makes a good manager is more challenging than determining what makes for a *bad* manager. For that reason, one way to understand what it takes to be a good manager is to look at the common mistakes managers make. In other words, we can learn just as much from what managers *shouldn't* do as from what they *should* do.

Several studies of US and British managers have compared "arrivers," or managers who made it all the way to the top of their companies, with "derailers," or managers who were successful early in their careers but were knocked off the fast track by the time they reached the middle to upper levels of management.[50] The researchers found that there were only a few differences between arrivers and derailers. For the most part, both groups were talented and both groups had weaknesses. But what distinguished derailers from arrivers was that derailers possessed two or more fatal flaws with respect to the way that they managed people. Although arrivers were by no means perfect, they usually had no more than one fatal flaw or had found ways to minimize the effects of their flaws on the people with whom they worked.

The most common mistake made by derailers was being insensitive to others, through their abrasive, intimidating, and bullying management style. The authors of

Ten Mistakes Managers Make

1. Specific business problems
2. Insensitivity (abrasive, intimidating, bully)
3. Cold, aloof, arrogant
4. Betrayed trust
5. Overmanaging, failing to delegate
6. Overly ambitious
7. Failed to staff effectively
8. Unable to think strategically
9. Unable to adapt to a boss with a different style
10. Overly dependent on an advocate or mentor

Source: M.W. McCall, Jr., and M. M. Lombardo, "What Makes a Top Executive?" *Psychology Today*, February 1983, 26–31.

Shutterstock/Konstantin Sutyagin

one study described a manager who walked into his subordinate's office and interrupted a meeting by saying, "I need to see you." When the subordinate tried to explain that he was not available because he was in the middle of a meeting, the manager barked, "I don't give a damn. I said I wanted to see you now."[51] Not surprisingly, only 25 percent of derailers were rated by others as being good with people compared to 75 percent of arrivers.

Another common mistake made by derailers is betraying a trust. Betraying a trust doesn't necessarily mean being dishonest. Instead, it means making others look bad by not doing what you said you would do when you said you would do it. That mistake, in itself, is not fatal because managers and their workers aren't machines. Tasks go undone in every company every single business day. There's always too much to do and not enough time, people, money, or resources to do it. The fatal betrayal of trust is failing to inform others when things will not be done on time. This failure to admit mistakes, quickly inform others of the mistakes, take responsibility for the mistakes, and then fix them without blaming others distinguished the behaviour of derailers from that of arrivers.

John Lund/Blend Images/Getty Images

Derailers also make the mistake of being overly political and ambitious. Managers who always have their eye on their next job rarely establish more than superficial relationships with peers and coworkers. In their haste to gain credit for successes that will be noticed by upper management, they make the fatal mistake of treating people as though they don't matter. An employee with an overly ambitious boss described him this way: "He gave me a new definition of shared risk: If something I did was successful, he took the credit. If it wasn't, I got the blame."[52]

Lastly, a fatal mistake often made by derailers is being unable to delegate, build a team, and staff effectively. Many derailed managers are unable to make the most basic transition to managerial work: to quit being hands-on doers and start getting work done through others. When managers meddle in decisions that their subordinates should be making—when they can't stop being doers—they alienate the people who work for them. According to Richard Kilburg of Johns Hopkins University, when managers interfere with workers' decisions, "You ... have a tendency to lose your most creative people. They're able to say, 'Screw this. I'm not staying here.'"[53] As well, because they are trying to do their subordinates' jobs in addition to their own, managers who fail to delegate will not have enough time to do anything well.

LO7 The Transition to Management: The First Year

Studies show that most derailment occurs following a management transition to a position with greater responsibility and greater scrutiny. In *Becoming a Manager: Mastery of a New Identity,* Harvard Business School professor Linda Hill followed the development of 19 people in their first year as managers. Her study found that becoming a manager produced a profound psychological transition that changed the way these managers viewed themselves and others. As shown in Exhibit 1.5, the evolution of the managers' thoughts, expectations, and realities over the course of their first year in management reveals the magnitude of the changes they experienced.

Exhibit 1.5 Stages in the Transition to Management

MANAGER'S INITIAL EXPECTATIONS	AFTER SIX MONTHS AS A MANAGER	AFTER A YEAR AS A MANAGER
JAN FEB MAR	APR MAY JUN	JUL AUG SEP OCT NOV DEC
Be the boss	Initial expectations were wrong	No longer "doer"
Formal authority	Fast pace	Communication, listening, & positive reinforcement
Manage tasks	Heavy workload	Learning to adapt to and control stress
Job is not managing people	Job is to be problem solver and troubleshooter for subordinates	Job is people development

Source: L.A. Hill, *Becoming a Manager: Mastery of a New Identity* (Boston: Harvard Business School Press, 1992).

Initially, the managers in Hill's study believed that their job was to exercise formal authority and to manage tasks—basically being the boss, telling others what to do, making decisions, and getting things done. In fact, most of the new managers were attracted to management positions because they wanted to be in charge. Surprisingly, the new managers did not believe that their job was to manage people. The only aspects of people management mentioned by the new managers were hiring and firing.

After six months, most of the new managers had concluded that their initial expectations about managerial work were wrong. Management wasn't just about being the boss, making decisions, and telling others what to do. The first surprise was the fast pace and heavy workload involved. Said one manager: "This job is much harder than you think. It is 40 to 50 percent more work than being a producer! Who would have ever guessed?" The pace of managerial work was startling, too. Another manager said: "You have eight or nine people looking for your time ... coming into and out of your office all day long." A somewhat frustrated manager declared that management was "a job that never ended ... a job you couldn't get your hands around."

Informal descriptions like this are consistent with studies indicating that the average first-line manager spends no more than two minutes on a task before being interrupted by a request from a subordinate, a phone call, or an e-mail. The pace is somewhat less hurried for top managers, who spend an average of nine minutes on a task before having to switch to another. In practice, this means that supervisors may perform 30 different tasks per hour, while top managers perform seven different tasks per hour, with each task typically different from the one that preceded it. A manager described this frenetic level of activity: "The only time you are in control is when you shut your door, and then I feel I am not doing the job I'm supposed to be doing, which is being with the people."

The other major surprise after six months on the job was that the managers' expectations about what they should do as managers were very different from their subordinates' expectations. Initially, the managers defined their jobs as helping their subordinates perform their jobs well. For the managers, who still defined themselves as doers rather than managers, assisting their subordinates meant going out on sales calls or handling customer complaints. But when the managers "assisted" in this way, their subordinates were resentful and viewed their help as interference. The subordinates wanted their managers to help them by solving problems they themselves couldn't solve. Once managers realized this distinction, they embraced their role as problem solvers and troubleshooters. They could then help without interfering with their subordinates' jobs.

After a year on the job, most of the managers thought of themselves as managers and no longer as doers. In making the transition, they finally realized that people management was the most important part of their job. One manager summarized the lesson that had taken him a year to learn: "As many demands as managers have on their time, I think their primary responsibility is people development. Not production, but people development." Another indication of how much their views had changed was that most of the managers now regretted the rather heavy-handed approach they had used in their early attempts to manage their subordinates. "I wasn't good at managing ... so I was bossy like a first-grade teacher." "Now I see that I started out as a drill sergeant. I was

Shutterstock/Pablo H Caridad

Top managers spend an average of 9 minutes on a given task before having to switch to another.

Lane Oatey/Blue Jean Images/Getty Images

inflexible, just a lot of how-to's." By the end of the year, most of the managers had abandoned their authoritarian approach for one based on communication, listening, and positive reinforcement.

Finally, after beginning their year as managers in frustration, the managers came to feel comfortable with their subordinates, with the demands of their jobs, and with their emerging managerial styles. While being managers had made them acutely aware of their limitations and their need to develop as people, it also provided them with an unexpected reward of coaching and developing the people who worked for them. One manager said: "I realize now that when I accepted the position of branch manager that it is truly an exciting vocation. It is truly awesome, even at this level; it can be terribly challenging and terribly exciting."

Why Management Matters

It is generally accepted that good management will enhance organizational performance and that some managers are better than others. "When managers fail, it costs time and resources to recruit, select, and train new ones. Also there are hidden costs associated with 'golden parachutes,' lost intellectual and social capital, missed business objectives and destroyed employee morale."[54] A study of senior human resource executives estimated the cost of derailment to be between $750,000 and $1,500,000 per senior manager.[55]

"Managerial incompetence also has serious moral implications because bad managers cause great misery for their subordinates."[56] Organizational climate surveys routinely show that about 75 percent of working adults report that the most stressful aspect of their job is their immediate boss.[57] Overall, research findings link employee stress to bad managers and even go so far to infer that "bad managers are a major health hazard; they impose enormous medical costs on society, and degrade the quality of life of many people."[58] The bottom line, so to speak, is that organizations that practise good management principles provide a healthier and more positive work environment for their employees, which can lead to enhanced organizational performance.

LO8 Competitive Advantage through People

In his books *Competitive Advantage through People* and *The Human Equation: Building Profits by Putting People First,* Stanford University business professor Jeffrey Pfeffer contends that what separates top-performing companies from their competitors is the way they treat their workforces—in other words, their management style.[59]

Pfeffer found that managers in top-performing companies used ideas like employment security, selective hiring, self-managed teams and decentralization, high pay contingent on company performance, extensive training, reduced status distinctions (between managers and employees), and extensive sharing of financial information to achieve financial performance that, on average, was 40 percent higher than that of other companies. These ideas, which are explained in detail in Exhibit 1.6, help organizations develop workforces that are smarter, better trained, more motivated, and more committed than their competitors' workforces. And—as indicated by the phenomenal growth and return on investment earned by these companies—smarter, better trained, and more committed workforces provide superior products and services to customers. Those customers then keep buying and, by telling others about their positive experiences, bring in new customers.

According to Pfeffer, companies that invest in their people also create long-lasting competitive advantages that are difficult for other companies to duplicate. The importance of employee management is particularly critical during tough economic times, when morale and employee engagement often experience a downturn. This is often reflected in the bottom line. The president of HiringSmart Canada believes that "engagement is the single most reliable indicator of business performance. The more engaged a group of people is, the more emotional skin they have in the game [and] the more committed they are to generating results." High levels of employee engagement can be a valuable competitive advantage to management, which is why management must identify and recruit high-potential employees and utilize best-management practices in order to hold on to them.[60]

In terms of the relationship between people management and financial performance, results from a 2002 study that included 750 companies in Canada, the United States, and Europe showed a positive correlation between a company's human capital practices and financial results. Companies that utilized superior human resources practices generated a 64 percent total return to shareholders (TRS) over a five-year period, compared to 21 percent TRS for companies with weak HR practices.[61]

To determine how investing in people affects stock market performance, researchers matched companies on *Fortune* magazine's list of "100 Best Companies to Work for in America" with companies that were similar in industry, size, and—this is key—operating performance. Both sets of companies were equally good performers; the key difference was how well they treated their employees.

Exhibit 1.6 Competitive Advantage through People: Management Practices

1. *Employment security*—Employment security is the ultimate form of commitment companies can make to their workers. Employees can innovate and increase company productivity without fearing the loss of their jobs.
2. *Selective hiring*—If employees are the basis for a company's competitive advantage, and those employees have employment security, then the company needs to aggressively recruit and selectively screen applicants in order to hire the most talented employees available.
3. *Self-managed teams and decentralization*—Self-managed teams are responsible for their own hiring, purchasing, job assignments, and production. Self-managed teams can often produce enormous increases in productivity through increased employee commitment and creativity. Decentralization allows employees who are closest to (and most knowledgeable about) problems, production, and customers to make timely decisions. Decentralization increases employee satisfaction and commitment.
4. *High wages contingent on organizational performance*—High wages are needed to attract and retain talented workers and to indicate that the organization values its workers. Employees, like company founders, shareholders, and managers, need to share in the financial rewards when the company is successful. Why? Because employees who have a financial stake in their companies are more likely to take a long-run view of the business and think like business owners.
5. *Training and skill development*—Like a high-tech company that spends millions of dollars to upgrade computers or research and development labs, a company whose competitive advantage is based on its people must invest in the training and skill development of its people.
6. *Reduction of status differences*—A company should treat everyone, no matter what the job, as equals. There are no reserved parking spaces. Everyone eats in the same cafeteria and has similar benefits. The result: improved communication as employees focus on problems and solutions rather than on how they are less valued than managers.
7. *Sharing information*—If employees are to make decisions that are good for the long-run health and success of the company, they need to be given information about costs, finances, productivity, development times, and strategies that was previously known only by company managers.

Source: J. Pfeffer, *The Human Equation: Building Profits by Putting People First* (Boston: Harvard Business School Press, 1996.)

In 2012, *Fortune* once again ranked Google as America's Best Company to Work For.

THE CANADIAN PRESS/Frank Gunn

For both sets of companies, the researchers found that employee attitudes such as job satisfaction changed little from year to year. The people who worked for the "100 Best" companies were consistently much more satisfied with their jobs and employers year after year than were employees in the matched companies. More important, those stable differences in employee attitudes were strongly related to differences in stock market performance. Over a three-year period, an investment in the "100 Best" companies would have resulted in an 82 percent cumulative stock return compared to just 37 percent for the matched companies.[62] This difference is remarkable given that both sets of companies were equally good performers at the beginning of the period.

Finally, research also indicates that managers have an important effect on customer satisfaction. Many people find this surprising. They don't understand how managers, who are largely responsible for what goes on inside the company, can affect what goes on outside the company. They wonder how managers, who often interact with customers under negative conditions (e.g., when customers are angry or dissatisfied), can actually improve customer satisfaction. It turns out that managers influence customer satisfaction through employee satisfaction. When employees are satisfied with their jobs, their bosses, and the companies they work for, they provide much better service to customers.[63] In turn, customers are more satisfied, too.

You will learn more about the service–profit chain in Chapter 18 on managing service and manufacturing operations.

2

History of Management

LEARNING OUTCOMES

LO1 Explain the origins of management.

LO2 Explain the history of scientific management.

LO3 Discuss the history of bureaucratic and administrative management.

LO4 Explain the history of human relations management.

LO5 Discuss the history of operations, information, systems, and contingency management.

It took 20,000 workers 23 years to complete this pyramid; more than 8,000 were needed just to quarry the stones and transport them.

In the Beginning

Each day, managers are asked to solve challenging problems and are given only a limited amount of time, people, or resources. Yet it's still their responsibility to get things done on time and within budget. Tell today's managers to "reward workers for improved production or performance," "set specific goals to increase motivation," or "innovate to create and sustain a competitive advantage," and they'll respond, "Of course, who doesn't know that?" A mere 125 years ago, however, business ideas and practices were so different that today's widely accepted management ideas would have been as self-evident as space travel, cellphones, and the Internet. In fact, management jobs and management careers did not exist 125 years ago, so management was not yet a field of study. If there were no managers 125 years ago, but you can't walk down the hall today without bumping into one, where did management come from?

LO1 The Origins of Management

Although we can find the seeds of many of today's management ideas throughout history, not until the last two centuries did systematic changes in the nature of work and organizations create a compelling need for managers.

Let's begin our discussion of the origins of management by learning about ***1.1 management ideas and practice throughout history*** *and* ***1.2 why we need managers today.***

1.1 Management Ideas and Practice Throughout History

Examples of management thought and practice can be found throughout history.[1] For example, the Egyptians recognized the need for planning, organizing, and controlling; for submitting written requests; and for consulting staff for advice before making decisions. The practical problems they encountered while building the Great Pyramids no doubt led to the development of these management ideas. The enormity of the task they faced is evident in the pyramid of King Khufu, which contains 2.3 million blocks of stone. Each block had to be quarried, cut to a precise size and shape, cured (hardened in the sun), transported by boat for two or three days, moved onto the construction site, numbered to identify where it would be placed, and then shaped and smoothed so that it would fit perfectly into place. It took 20,000 workers 23 years to complete this pyramid; more than 8,000 were needed just to quarry the stones and transport them.[2]

1.2 Why We Need Managers Today

Working from 8 a.m. to 5 p.m., coffee breaks, lunch hours, crushing rush hour traffic, and punching a time clock are things we associate with today's working world. But for most of history, people didn't commute to work. Work usually occurred in homes or on farms. Even most of those who didn't earn their living from agriculture didn't commute to work. Blacksmiths, furniture makers, leather-goods makers, and other skilled tradespeople and craft workers, who formed trade guilds (the predecessors of labour unions) in England as early as 1093, typically worked out of shops in or next to their homes.[3] Likewise, until the late 1800s, cottage workers worked with one another out of small homes that were often built in semicircles. A family in each cottage would complete a different production step, and work passed from one cottage to the next until production was complete. With small, self-organized work groups, no commute, no bosses, and no common building, there wasn't a strong need for management.

During the Industrial Revolution (1750–1900), however, jobs and organizations changed dramatically.[4] First, the availability of power (steam engines and, later, electricity) made it possible for poorly paid unskilled labourers running machines to replace highly paid skilled artisans, who in the past had made entire goods themselves by hand. This new mass production system was based on a division of labour: each worker, interacting with a machine, performed a separate, highly specialized task that was but a small part of all the steps required to make a given manufactured good. With workers focusing on their individual tasks, managers were needed to coordinate the different parts of the production system and to optimize its overall performance. Productivity skyrocketed at companies that understood this. At Ford Motor Company, where the assembly line was developed, the time required to assemble a car dropped from 12.5 man hours to just 93 minutes.[5]

Second, instead of being performed in fields, homes, or small shops, jobs were carried out in large, formal organizations where hundreds if not thousands of people worked under one roof.[6] In 1913, Henry Ford employed 12,000 people just at his Highland Park, Michigan, factory. With individual factories employing so many workers under one roof, companies had a strong need to impose order and structure. For the first time, they needed managers who knew how to organize large groups, work with employees, enforce rules, and make good decisions.

Skilled tradesmen or craftsmen often worked out of their homes or cottages, completing one element of a production process and then passing the work on to the next cottage.

© Topfoto/GetStock.com

WitR/Shutterstock.com

Scientific management thoroughly studying and testing different work methods to identify the best, most efficient way to complete a job

The Evolution of Management

Before 1880, business educators taught only basic bookkeeping and secretarial skills, and no one published books or articles about management.[7] Today, you can turn to dozens of academic journals, hundreds of business school and practitioner journals, and thousands of books and articles if you have a question about management. In the next four sections, you will learn about other important contributors to the field of management and how their ideas have shaped our current understanding of management theory and practice.

LO2 Scientific Management

Bosses, who were hired by the company owner or founder, used to make decisions by the seat of their pants—haphazardly, without any systematic study, thought, or collection of information. Little thought was given to worker motivation, for the boss dictated how fast and how hard the worker toiled. With no incentives for bosses and workers to cooperate, both groups played the system, trying to take advantage of each other. Moreover, each worker did the same job in his or her own way with different methods and different tools. In short, there were no procedures for standardizing operations and no standards by which to judge whether performance was good or bad; nor was there any follow-up to determine whether productivity or quality actually improved when changes were made.[8]

This all changed with the advent of **scientific management**, which involved the thorough study and testing of different work methods to identify the best, most efficient ways to complete a job.

*Let's find out more about scientific management by learning about **2.1 Frederick W. Taylor, the father of scientific management, 2.2 Frank and Lillian Gilbreth and motion studies,** and **2.3 Henry Gantt and his Gantt charts.***

2.1 Father of Scientific Management: Frederick W. Taylor

Frederick W. Taylor (1856–1915), the father of scientific management, began his career as a worker at the Midvale Steel Company. He was later promoted to patternmaker, supervisor, and then chief engineer.

Prior to the Scientific Management movement, there were no procedures to standardize operations, no standards by which to judge whether performance was good or bad, and no follow-up to determine whether productivity or quality actually improved when changes were made.

Douglas Miller/Hulton Archive/Getty Images

At Midvale, Taylor was deeply affected by his three-year struggle to get the men who worked for him to do, as he called it, "a fair day's work." As soon as he became the boss, "the men who were working under me ... knew that I was onto the whole game of **soldiering**, or deliberately restricting output [to one-third of what they were capable of producing]."[9]

Taylor tried everything he could think of to improve output. By doing the job himself, he showed workers that it was possible to produce more output. He hired new workers and trained them himself, hoping they would produce more. But "very heavy social pressure" from the other workers kept them from doing so. Pushed by Taylor, the workers began breaking their machines so that they couldn't produce. Taylor responded by fining them every time they broke a machine and for any violation of the rules, no matter how small, such as being late to work. Tensions became so severe that some of the workers threatened to shoot him.

The remedy that Taylor eventually developed was scientific management. The goal of scientific management was to use systematic study to find the optimal means of doing each task. To do that, managers had to follow the four principles shown in Exhibit 2.1. First, they had to "develop a science" for each element of work. That meant they had to study it. Analyze it. Determine the optimal means to do the work. For example, one of Taylor's controversial proposals at the time was to give rest breaks to factory workers doing physical labour. We take breaks for granted today, but factory workers in Taylor's day were expected to work without stopping.[10] Through systematic experiments, he showed that frequent rest breaks greatly increased daily output.

Second, managers had to scientifically select, train, teach, and develop workers to help them reach their full potential. Before Taylor, supervisors often hired on the basis of favouritism and nepotism. Who you knew was often more important than what you could do. By contrast, Taylor instructed supervisors to hire "first class" workers on the basis of their aptitude to do a job well. For similar reasons, he also recommended that companies train and develop their workers—a rare practice at the time.

Soldiering when workers deliberately slow their pace or restrict their work outputs

The third principle instructed managers to cooperate with employees to ensure that the scientific principles were actually implemented. As Taylor knew from experience, workers and management more often than not viewed each other as enemies. Taylor said: "The majority of these men believe that the fundamental interests of employees and employers are necessarily antagonistic. Scientific management, on the contrary, is founded on the firm conviction that the true interests of the two are one and the same. Prosperity for the employer cannot exist through a long term of years unless it is accompanied by prosperity for the employee. Moreover, it is possible to give the workman what he most wants—high wages—and the employer what he wants—a low labour cost—for his manufactures."[11]

The fourth principle of scientific management was to divide the work and the responsibility equally between management and workers. Prior to Taylor, workers alone were held responsible for productivity and performance. But, said Taylor, "almost every act of the workman should be preceded by one or more preparatory acts of the management which enable him to do his work better and quicker than he otherwise could."[12]

Taylor believed that these principles could be used to determine a "fair day's work," that is, what an average worker could produce at a reasonable pace, day in and day out. Once that was determined, it was management's responsibility to pay workers fairly for that fair day's work. In essence, Taylor was trying to align management and employees so that what was good for employees was also good for management. In this way, he felt, workers and managers could avoid the conflicts he had experienced at Midvale Steel. According to Taylor, one of the best ways to align management and employees was to offer incentives to motivate workers. In particular, he believed in piece-rate incentives in which work pay was directly tied to how much workers produced.

Taylor remains a controversial figure among some academics, but his key ideas have stood the test of time.[13]

Exhibit 2.1 Taylor's Four Principles of Scientific Management

First:	Develop a science for each element of a man's work, which replaces the old rule-of-thumb method.
Second:	Scientifically select and then train, teach, and develop the workman, whereas in the past he chose his own work and trained himself as best he could.
Third:	Heartily cooperate with the men so as to ensure all of the work being done is in accordance with the principles of the science that have been developed.
Fourth:	There is an almost equal division of the work and the responsibility between the management and the workmen. The management take over all the work for which they are better fitted than the workmen, while in the past almost all of the work and the greater part of the responsibility were thrown upon the men.

Source: F.W. Taylor, *The Principles of Scientific Management* (New York: Harper, 1911).

Nayashkova Olga/Shutterstock.com

Want Fries with That?

Don't think scientific management has much to do with today's work life? Think again: about the last time you were at the store and the clerk said, "Have a nice day." Service providers—particularly at restaurants—use scripts to ensure that employees are following the "one best way" of interacting with the customers. McDonald's uses a speech-only script (workers must say, "May I help you, ma'am?" instead of "Can I help someone?"). Drive-thru employees at Taco Bell are trained to use only one greeting, "Hi, how are you today?" and never to say, "Hi, how are you?" or "Welcome to Taco Bell." At Olive Garden, workers must greet the table within thirty seconds of arrival; take the drink order within three minutes; suggest five items while taking the order; and check back with the table three minutes after the food arrives.

Source: A. Scharf, "Scripted Talk: From 'Welcome to McDonald's' to 'Paper or Plastic?' Employers Control the Speech of Service Workers," *Dollars & Sense*, September-October 2003, 35; McCann, "Have a Nice Day and an Icy Stare," *Marketing Week*, 2 September 2004, 27.

Motion study breaking each task or job into its separate motions and then eliminating those that are unnecessary or repetitive

Time study timing how long it takes good workers to complete each part of their jobs

2.2 Motion Studies: Frank and Lillian Gilbreth

The husband-and-wife team of Frank and Lillian Gilbreth are best known for their use of motion studies to simplify work.

Frank Gilbreth (1868–1924) began his career as an apprentice bricklayer. While learning the trade, he noticed the bricklayers using three different sets of motions—one to teach others how to lay bricks, a second to work at a slow pace, and a third to work at a fast pace.[14] Wondering which was best, he studied the various approaches and began eliminating unnecessary motions. For example, by designing a stand that could be raised to waist height, he eliminated the need for a bricklayer to bend over to pick up each brick. When lower-paid workers placed all the bricks with their most attractive side up, bricklayers no longer wasted time turning a brick over to find it. By mixing a more consistent mortar, bricklayers no longer had to tap each brick numerous times to put it in the right position. Together, Gilbreth's improvements raised productivity from 120 to 350 bricks per hour and from 1,000 bricks to 2,700 bricks per day.

As a result of this experience with bricklaying, Gilbreth and his wife Lillian developed a long-term interest in using motion study to simplify work, improve productivity, and reduce the level of effort required to safely perform a job. **Motion study** broke each task or job into separate motions and then eliminated those that were unnecessary or repetitive. Because many motions were completed very quickly, the Gilbreths used motion picture films—a relatively new technology at the time—to analyze jobs. Most film cameras, however, were hand-cranked and thus variable in their film speed, so Frank Gilbreth invented the microchronometer, a large clock that could record time to 1/2000th of a second. By placing the microchronometer next to the worker in the camera's field of vision, the Gilbreths could use film to detect and precisely time even the slightest, fastest movements. Motion study typically yielded production increases of 25 to 300 percent.

© Christine Balderas/iStockphoto.com

> Taylor was trying to align management and employees so that what was good for employees was also good for management.

Frederick W. Taylor also strove to simplify work, but he did so by managing time rather than motion.[15] Taylor developed time study to put an end to soldiering and to determine what could be considered a fair day's work. **Time study** worked by timing how long it took a "first-class man" to complete each part of his job. A standard time was established after allowing for rest periods, and a worker's pay increased or decreased depending on whether the worker exceeded or fell below that standard.

Lillian Gilbreth (1878–1972) was also an important contributor to management. When Frank died in 1924, she continued the work of their management consulting company (which they had shared for over a dozen years) on her own. Lillian was particularly concerned with the human side of work and was an early contributor to the field of industrial psychology. She established ways to improve office communication, incentive programs, job satisfaction, and management training. Her work also convinced the government to enact laws regarding workplace safety, ergonomics, and child labour.

2.3 Charts: Henry Gantt

Henry Gantt (1861–1919) was first a protégé and then an associate of Frederick Taylor. Gantt is best known for the Gantt chart, but he also made significant contributions to management with respect to the training and development of workers. As shown in Exhibit 2.2 on page 24, a **Gantt chart** visually indicates which tasks must be completed at which times in order to complete a project. It accomplishes this by showing time in various units on the *x*-axis and tasks on the *y*-axis. For example, Exhibit 2.2 shows that the following tasks must be completed by the following dates: in order to start construction on a new company headquarters by the week of November 18, the architectural firm must be selected by October 7, the architectural planning done by November 4, permits obtained from the city by November 11, site preparation finished by November 18, and loans and financing finalized by November 18. Although simple and straightforward, Gantt charts were revolutionary in the era of seat-of-the-pants management because of the detailed planning information they provided to managers. The use of Gantt charts is so widespread today that nearly all project management software and computer spreadsheets have the capability to create charts that track and visually display the progress being made on a project.

Gantt chart a graphic chart that shows which tasks must be completed at which times in order to complete a project or task

Gantt, along with Taylor, was one of the first to urge companies to train and develop their workers.[16] In his work with companies, he found that workers achieved their best performance levels if they were trained first. At the time, however, supervisors were reluctant to teach workers what they knew for fear they could lose their jobs to more knowledgeable workers. Gantt overcame the supervisors' resistance by rewarding them with bonuses for properly training all of their workers. Gantt's approach to training was straightforward: "(1) a scientific investigation in detail of each piece of work, and the determination of the best method and the shortest time in which the work can be done. (2) A teacher capable of teaching the best method and the shortest time. (3) Reward for both teacher and pupil when the latter is successful."[17]

LO3 Bureaucratic and Administrative Management

The field of scientific management focused on improving the efficiency of manufacturing facilities and their workers. At about the same time, equally important ideas about bureaucratic and administrative management were developing in Europe. German sociologist Max Weber presented a new way to run entire organizations in *The Theory of Economic and Social Organization* (1922). Henri Fayol,

Exhibit 2.2 Gantt Chart for Starting Construction on a New Headquarters

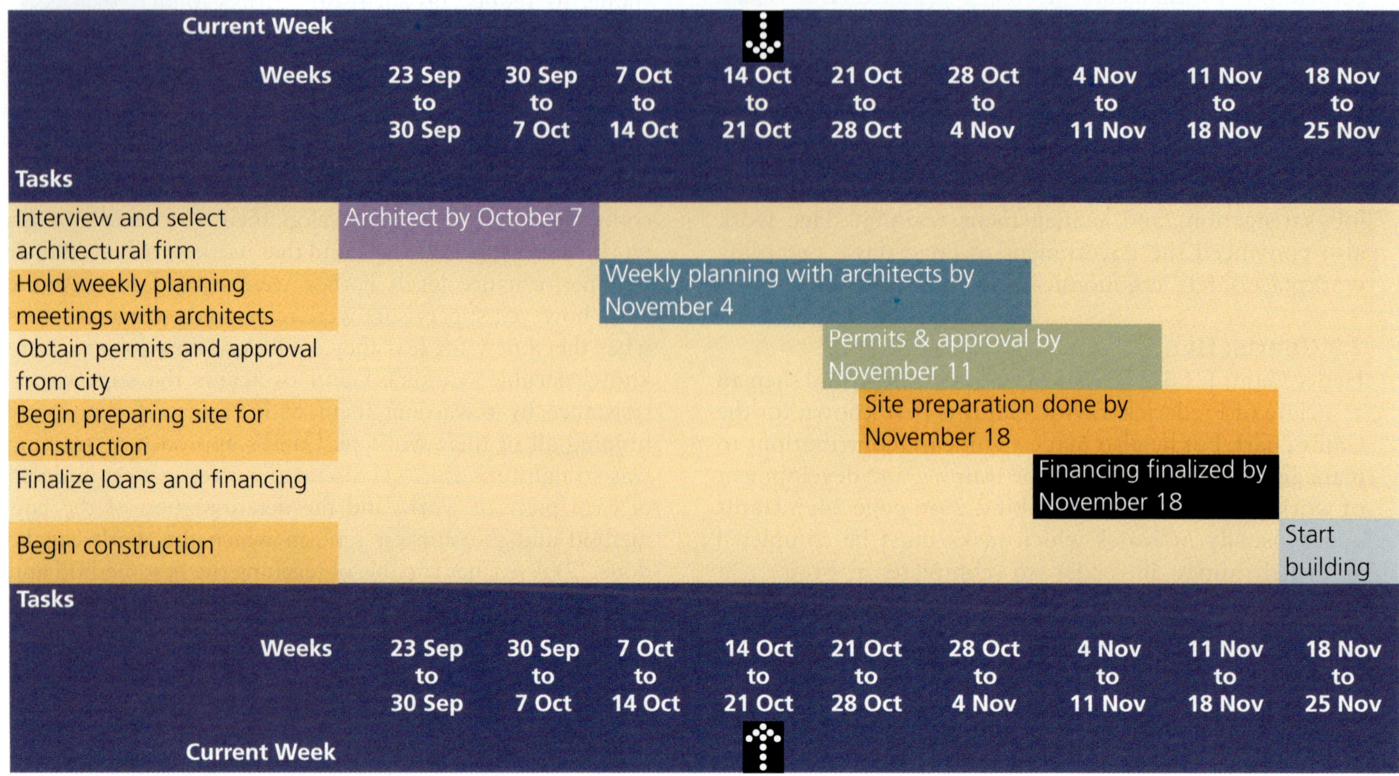

Bureaucracy the exercise of control on the basis of knowledge, expertise, or experience

an experienced French CEO, published his ideas about how managers should do in their jobs in *General and Industrial Management* (1916).

*Let's find out more about Weber's and Fayol's contributions to management by learning about **3.1 bureaucratic management** and **3.2 administrative management.***

3.1 Bureaucratic Management: Max Weber

Today, when we hear the term *bureaucracy,* we think of inefficiency and red tape, incompetence and ineffectiveness, and rigid administrators blindly enforcing nonsensical rules. When German sociologist Max Weber (1864–1920) first proposed the idea of bureaucratic organizations, however, these problems were associated with monarchies and patriarchies rather than bureaucracies. In monarchies, where kings, queens, sultans, and emperors ruled, and patriarchies, where wise men, councils of elders, or male heads of extended families ruled, the top leaders typically achieved their positions by virtue of birthright. Similarly, promotion to a prominent position of authority was based on who you knew (politics), on who you were (heredity), or on tradition.

An organization's rules and procedures should apply to all members regardless of their position or status.

It was against this historical background that Weber proposed the then new idea of bureaucracy. According to Weber, **bureaucracy** is "the exercise of control on the basis of knowledge."[18] Rather than ruling by virtue of favouritism or personal or family connections, people in a bureaucracy would lead by virtue of their rational-legal authority—in other words, their knowledge, expertise, or experience. Furthermore, the aim of bureaucracy is not to protect authority but to achieve an organization's goals in the most efficient way possible.

Exhibit 2.3 shows the seven elements that, according to Weber, characterize bureaucracies. First, instead of hiring people because of their family or political connections or personal loyalty, they should be hired because their technical training or education qualifies them to do the job well. Second, along the same lines, promotion within the company should no longer be based on who you know or who you are (heredity), but on your experience or achievements. And to further limit the influence of personal connections in the promotion process, *managers* rather than organizational owners should decide who gets promoted. Third, each position or job should be viewed as part of a chain of command that clarifies who reports to whom throughout the organization. Those higher in the chain of command have the right, if they so choose, to give commands, take

A bureaucracy is known for adhering to strict reporting relationships and recording rules, regulations, and policies to ensure consistency throughout the organization.

© Mark Evans/iStockphoto.com

action, and make decisions concerning activities occurring anywhere below them in the chain. Fourth, to increase efficiency and effectiveness, tasks and responsibilities should be separated and assigned to those best qualified to complete them. Fifth, an organization's rules and procedures should apply to all members regardless of their position or status. Sixth, to ensure consistency and fairness over time and across different leaders, all rules, procedures, and decisions should be recorded in writing. Finally, to reduce favouritism, "professional" managers rather than company owners should manage or supervise the organization.

Weber's ideas about bureaucracy represented a tremendous improvement. They supplanted favouritism with fairness, the goal of personal gain with the goal of efficiency, and traditions or arbitrary decision making with logical rules and procedures.

Today, however, after more than a century of experience, we recognize that bureaucracy has its limitations. In bureaucracies, managers are sup-posed to influence employee behaviour by fairly rewarding or punishing employees for compliance or noncompliance with organizational policies, rules, and procedures. In reality, though, most employees would argue that bureaucratic managers emphasize punishment for noncompliance much more than reward for compliance. Ironically, bureaucratic management was created to prevent just this type of managerial behaviour.

3.2 Administrative Management: Henri Fayol

Though his work was not translated and widely recognized until 1949, Henri Fayol (1841–1925) was as important a contributor to the field of management as Frederick Taylor. Taylor's ideas changed companies from the shop floor up; Fayol's ideas, which were shaped by his experience as a managing director (CEO), generally changed companies from the board of directors down. Fayol is best known for developing 5 functions of managers and 14 principles of management.

The formative events in Fayol's business career came during his 20-plus years as the managing director (CEO) of a steel company that owned several coal and iron ore mines and employed 10,000 to 13,000 workers. Fayol was initially hired by the board of directors to shut the "hopeless" steel company down. But after "four months of reflection and study," he presented the board

Exhibit 2.3 Elements of Bureaucratic Organizations

Qualification-based hiring:	Employees are hired on the basis of their technical training or educational background.
Merit-based promotion:	Promotion is based on experience or achievement. Managers, not organizational owners, decide who is promoted.
Chain of command:	Each job occurs within a hierarchy, the chain of command, in which each position reports and is accountable to a higher position. A grievance procedure and a right to appeal protect people in lower positions.
Division of labour:	Tasks, responsibilities, and authority are clearly divided and defined.
Impartial application of rules and procedures:	Rules and procedures apply to all members of the organization and will be applied in an impartial manner, regardless of one's position or status
Recorded in writing:	All administrative decisions, acts, rules, or procedures will be recorded in writing.
Managers separate from owners:	The owners of an organization should not manage or supervise the organization.

Source: M. Weber, *The Theory of Economic and Social Organization*, trans. A. Henderson & T. Parsons (New York: The Free Press, 1947), 329–334.

Integrative conflict resolution an approach to dealing with conflict in which both parties deal with the conflict by indicating their preferences and then working together to find an alternative that meets the needs of both

with a plan, backed by detailed facts and figures, to save the company. With little to lose, the board agreed. Fayol then began turning the company around by obtaining supplies of key resources such as coal and iron ore; using research to develop new steel alloy products; carefully selecting key subordinates in research, purchasing, manufacturing, and sales and then delegating responsibility to them; and cutting costs by moving the company to a better location closer to key markets. Looking back 10 years later, Fayol attributed his and the company's success to changes in management practices.

Based on his experience as a CEO, Fayol argued that "the success of an enterprise generally depends much more on the administrative ability of its leaders than on their technical ability."[19] And, as you learned in Chapter 1, managers need to perform five managerial functions if they are to be successful: planning, organizing, coordinating, commanding, and controlling.[20] Most management textbooks have dropped the coordinating function and now refer to Fayol's commanding function as "leading"; thus, these functions are commonly listed today as planning (determining organizational goals and a means for achieving them), organizing (deciding where decisions will be made, who will do what jobs and tasks, and who will work for whom), leading (inspiring and motivating workers to work hard to achieve organizational goals), and controlling (monitoring progress toward goal achievement and taking corrective action when needed). In addition, according to Fayol, effective management is based on the 14 principles listed in Exhibit 2.4.

LO4 Human Relations Management

As we have seen, scientific management focuses on improving efficiency; bureaucratic management focuses on using knowledge, fairness, and logical rules and procedures; and administrative management focuses on how managers should do in their jobs. The human relations approach to management focuses on people. This approach to management sees people not simply as extensions of machines but as valuable organizational resources in their own right. Human relations management holds that people's needs are important and understands that their efforts, motivation, and performance are affected by the work they do and by their relationships with their bosses, coworkers, and work groups. In other words, efficiency alone is not enough. Organizational success also depends on treating workers well.

*Find out more about human relations management by reading about **4.1 Mary Parker Follett's theories of constructive conflict, 4.2 Elton Mayo's Hawthorne studies, and 4.3 Chester Barnard's theories of cooperation and acceptance of authority.***

4.1 Constructive Conflict: Mary Parker Follett

Mary Parker Follett (1868–1933) was a social worker who, after 25 years of working with schools and nonprofit organizations, began lecturing and writing about management and working extensively as a consultant for business and government. Many of today's "new" management ideas can be traced clearly to her work.

Follett is known for developing ideas regarding constructive conflict, also called cognitive conflict (see Chapter 5 on decision making and Chapter 10 on teams). Unlike most people, then and now, who view conflict as bad, Follett believed that conflict could be beneficial. She said that conflict is "the appearance of difference, difference of opinions, of interests. For that is what conflict means—difference." She went on to say: "As conflict—difference—is here in this world, as we cannot avoid it, we should, I think, use it to work for us. Instead of condemning it, we should set it to work for us. Thus we shall not be afraid of conflict, but shall recognize that there is a destructive way of dealing with such moments and a constructive way."[21]

Follett believed that the best way to deal with conflict was not domination, where one side wins and the other loses, nor was it compromise, where each side gives up some of what they want; rather, it was integration. Instead of one side dominating the other or both sides compromising, the point of **integrative conflict resolution** is to have both parties indicate their preferences and then work together to find an alternative that meets the needs of both. Follett wrote that "integration involves invention, and the clever thing is to recognize this, and not to let one's thinking stay within the boundaries of two alternatives which are mutually exclusive."

Follett also believed that authority flows from job knowledge and experience rather than position. Leadership involves setting the tone for the team rather than being aggressive and domineering, which may be harmful. Control, by contrast, should be based on facts, information, and coordination. In the end, Follett's contributions added significantly to our understanding of the human, social, and psychological sides of management. Peter Parker, the former chairman of the London School of Economics, said about Follett: "People often puzzle about who is the father of management. I don't know who the father was, but I have no doubt about who was the mother."[22]

4.2 Hawthorne Studies: Elton Mayo

Australian-born Elton Mayo (1880–1948) is best known for his role in the famous Hawthorne Studies at the Western Electric Company in Chicago between 1924 and 1932. Although Mayo didn't join the studies until 1928, he played a significant role thereafter, writing about the results in his book, *The Human Problems of an Industrial Civilization*.[23] The first stage of the Hawthorne Studies investigated the effects of lighting levels and incentives on employee productivity in the Relay Test Assembly

Exhibit 2.4 Fayol's 14 Principles of Management

1 **Division of work**
Increase production by dividing work so that each worker completes smaller tasks or job elements.

2 **Authority and responsibility**
A manager's authority, which is the "right to give orders," should be commensurate with the manager's responsibility. However, organizations should enact controls to prevent managers from abusing their authority.

3 **Discipline**
Clearly defined rules and procedures are needed at all organizational levels to ensure order and proper behaviour.

4 **Unity of command**
To avoid confusion and conflict, each employee should report to and receive orders from just one boss.

5 **Unity of direction**
One person and one plan should be used in deciding the activities to be used to accomplish each organizational objective.

6 **Subordination of individual interests to the general interest**
Employees must put the organization's interests and goals before their own.

7 **Remuneration**
Compensation should be fair and satisfactory to both the employees and the organization; that is, don't overpay or underpay employees.

8 **Centralization**
Avoid too much centralization or decentralization. Strike a balance depending on the circumstances and employees involved.

9 **Scalar chain**
From the top to the bottom of an organization, each position is part of a vertical chain of authority in which each worker reports to just one boss. For the sake of simplicity, communication outside normal work groups or departments should follow the vertical chain of authority.

10 **Order**
To avoid conflicts and confusion, order can be obtained by having a place for everyone and having everyone in his or her place; in other words, there should be no overlapping responsibilities.

11 **Equity**
Kind, fair, and just treatment for all will develop devotion and loyalty. This does not exclude discipline, if warranted, and consideration of the broader general interest of the organization.

12 **Stability of tenure of personnel**
Low turnover, meaning a stable workforce with high tenure, benefits an organization by improving performance, lowering costs, and giving employees, especially managers, time to learn their jobs.

13 **Initiative**
Because it is a "great source of strength for business," managers should encourage the development of initiative, or the ability to develop and implement a plan, in others.

14 **Esprit de corps**
Develop a strong sense of morale and unity among workers that encourages coordination of efforts.

Sources: H. Fayol, *General and Industrial Management* (London: Pittman & Sons, 1949); M. Fells, "Fayol Stands the Test of Time," *Journal of Management History* 6 (2000): 345–360; C. Rodrigues, "Fayol's 14 Principles of Management Then and Now: A Framework for Managing Today's Organizations Effectively," *Management Decision* 39 (2001): 880–889.

Pressmaster/Shutterstock.com

Room, where workers took approximately a minute to put "together a coil, armature, contact springs, and insulators in a fixture and secure the parts by means of four machine screws."[24] Two groups of six experienced female workers, five to do the work and one to supply needed parts, were separated from the main part of the factory by a 10-foot partition and placed at a standard work bench with the necessary parts and tools. Over the next five years, the experimenters introduced various levels and combinations of lighting, financial incentives, and rest pauses (work breaks) to study the effect on productivity. Curiously, production levels increased whether the experimenters increased or decreased the lighting, paid workers based on individual production or group production, or increased or decreased the number and length of rest pauses. The question was: Why?

Mayo and his colleagues eventually concluded that two things accounted for the results. First, substantially more attention was being paid to these workers than to workers in the rest of the plant. Mayo wrote: "Before every change of program [in the study], the group is consulted. Their comments are listened to and discussed; sometimes their objections are allowed to negate a suggestion. The group unquestionably develops a sense of participation in the critical determinations and becomes something of a social unit."[25]

For years, the Hawthorne Effect has been *incorrectly* defined as increasing productivity by paying more attention to workers.[26] But it is not simply about attention from management. This effect cannot be understood without giving equal importance to the "social units," which became intensively cohesive groups. Mayo wrote: "What actually happened was that six individuals became a team and the team gave itself wholeheartedly and spontaneously to cooperation in the experiment. The consequence was that they felt themselves to be participating freely and without afterthought, and were happy in the knowledge that they were working without coercion from above or limits from below."[27]

Women in the Relay Assembly Test Room, ca. 1930. Western Electric Company Hawthorne Studies Collection. Baker Library Historical Collections, Harvard Business School.

For the first time, human factors related to work were found to be more important than the physical conditions or design of the work. The increased attention from management and the development of cohesive work groups together led to significantly higher job satisfaction and productivity. In short, the Hawthorne Studies found that workers' feelings and attitudes affected their work.

The next stage of the Hawthorne Studies was conducted in the Bank Wiring Room, where

> *the group consisted of nine wiremen, three solderers, and two inspectors. Each of these groups performed a specific task and collaborated with the other two in completion of each unit of equipment. The task consisted of setting up the banks of terminals side-by-side on frames, wiring the corresponding terminals from bank to bank, soldering the connections, and inspecting with a test set for short circuits or breaks in the wire. One solderman serviced the work of the three wiremen.*[28]

While productivity increased in the Relay Test Assembly Room no matter what the researchers did, productivity dropped in the Bank Wiring Room. Again, the question was why.

Mayo and his colleagues found that different group dynamics were responsible. The workers in the Bank Wiring Room had been an existing work group for some time and had already developed strong negative norms that governed their behaviour. For instance, despite a group financial incentive for production, the group members decided they would wire only 6,000 to 6,600 connections a day (depending on the kind of equipment they were wiring), well below the production goal of 7,300 connections that management had set for them. Individual workers who worked at a faster pace were socially ostracized from the group, or "binged" (hit on the arm), until they slowed their work pace. The group's behaviour was reminiscent of the soldiering that Frederick Taylor had observed.

In the end, the Hawthorne Studies demonstrated that the workplace was more complex than previously thought, that workers were not just extensions of machines, and that financial incentives weren't necessarily the most important motivator for workers. Thanks to Mayo and the Hawthorne Studies, managers better understood the effect that group social interactions, employee satisfaction, and attitudes had on individual and group performance.

4.3 Cooperation and Acceptance of Authority: Chester Barnard

Like Henri Fayol, Chester Barnard (1886–1961) had experience as a top executive that shaped his views of management. Barnard began his career as an engineer and went on to become president of a telephone company.

Tough Jobs

During the early twentieth century, labour unrest, dissatisfaction, and protests (some of them violent) were widespread in North America, Europe, and Asia. On May 1, 1919, Winnipeg's building and metal workers went on strike over wages; soon after, they were joined by a number of other labour and trade unions, who walked off the job; this in turn caused a groundswell of demonstrations and riots known as the Winnipeg General Strike. Working conditions contributed to the unrest. Millions of workers in large factories were toiling at boring, repetitive, unsafe jobs for low pay. Employee turnover was high, and absenteeism was rampant. It's not surprising that Mayo's ideas became popular during this period.

Foote Collection, Winnipeg Free Press

Organization a system of consciously coordinated activities or forces created by two or more people

Barnard's ideas, published in his classic book, *The Functions of the Executive,* influenced companies from the board of directors down. He is best known for his ideas about cooperation and the acceptance of authority.

Barnard proposed a comprehensive theory of cooperation in formal organizations. He defined an **organization** as a "system of consciously coordinated activities or forces of two or more persons." In other words, organization occurs whenever two people work together for some purpose, whether it be classmates working together to complete a class project, Habitat for Humanity volunteers donating their time to build a house, or managers working with subordinates to reduce costs, improve quality, or increase sales. Why did Barnard place so much emphasis on cooperation? Because cooperation is *not* the normal state of affairs: "Failure to cooperate, failure of cooperation, failure of organization, disorganization, disintegration, destruction of organization—and reorganization—are characteristic facts of human history."[29]

According to Barnard, the extent to which people willingly cooperate in an organization depends on how workers perceive executive authority and whether they're willing to accept it. Many managerial requests or directives occupy a *zone of indifference* in which acceptance of managerial authority is automatic. For example, if your boss asks you for a copy of the monthly inventory report, and compiling and writing that report is part of your job, you think nothing of the request and automatically send it. In general, people will be indifferent to managerial directives or orders if they (1) are understood, (2) are consistent with the purpose of the organization, (3) are compatible with the people's personal interests, and (4) can actually be carried out by those people. Acceptance of managerial authority (i.e., cooperation) is not automatic, however. Ask people to do things contrary to the organization's purpose or to their own benefit and they'll put up a fight. While many people assume that managers have the authority to do whatever they want, Barnard, referring to the "fiction of superior authority," believed that workers ultimately *grant* managers their authority.

LO5 Operations, Information, Systems, and Contingency Management

In this last section, we review four other significant historical approaches to management that have influenced how today's managers produce goods and services on a daily basis, gather and manage the information they need to understand their businesses and make good decisions, understand how the different parts of the company work together as a whole, and recognize when and where particular management practices are likely to work.

*To better understand these ideas, let's learn about **5.1 operations management, 5.2 information management, 5.3 systems management,** and **5.4 contingency management.***

5.1 Operations Management

In Chapter 18, you will learn about *operations management*, which involves managing the daily production of goods and services. In general, operations management uses a quantitative or mathematical approach to find ways to increase productivity, improve quality, and manage or reduce costly inventories. The most commonly used operations management tools and methods are quality control, forecasting techniques, capacity planning, productivity measurement and improvement, linear programming, scheduling systems, inventory systems, work measurement techniques (similar to the Gilbreths' motion studies), project management (similar to Gantt's charts), and cost–benefit analysis.[30]

Today, with these tools and techniques, we take it for granted that manufactured goods will be made with standardized, interchangeable parts; that the design of those parts will be based on specific, detailed plans; and that manufacturing companies will aggressively manage inventories to keep costs low and increase productivity. These key elements of operations management have some rather strange origins: guns, geometry, and fire.

Beginning in the 1500s, skilled craftsmen made the lock, stock, and barrel of a gun by hand. After each part was made, a skilled gun finisher assembled the parts into a complete gun. But the gun finisher did not simply screw the different parts of a gun together, as is done today. Instead, each handmade part required extensive finishing and adjusting so that it would fit together with the other handmade gun parts. Hand fitting was necessary because, even when made by the same skilled craftsman, no two parts were alike. Today, we would say that these parts were low quality because they varied so much from part to part.

All of this changed in 1791 when the US government, worried about a possible war with France, ordered 40,000 muskets from private gun contractors. Because each handmade musket was unique, a replacement part had to be handcrafted if a part broke. One contractor, Eli Whitney (who is better known for his invention of the cotton gin), determined that if gun parts were made accurately enough, guns could be made with standardized, interchangeable parts. So he designed machine tools that allowed unskilled workers to make each gun part the same as the next. In 1801, he demonstrated the superiority of interchangeable parts to President-elect Thomas Jefferson by quickly and easily assembling complete muskets from randomly picked piles of musket parts. Today, most products are manufactured using standardized, interchangeable parts.

Once standardized, interchangeable parts became the norm and could be made from design drawings alone, manufacturers ran into a costly problem that they had never encountered before: too much inventory. *Inventory* is the amount and number of raw materials, parts, and finished products that a company has in its possession. A solution to this problem was found in 1905 when the Oldsmobile Motor Works in Detroit burned down. Management rented a new production facility to get production up and running as quickly as possible after the fire. But because

DreamPictures/Shannon Faulk/Blend Images/Getty Images

the new facility was much smaller, there was no room to store large stockpiles of inventory. Therefore, the company made do with what it called "hand-to-mouth inventories," in which each production station had only enough parts on hand to do a short production run. Since all of its parts suppliers were close by, Oldsmobile could place orders in the morning and receive them in the afternoon (even without telephones), just as with today's computerized, just-in-time inventory systems. So, contrary to common belief, just-in-time inventory systems were not invented by Japanese manufacturers. Rather, they were invented out of necessity a century ago because of a fire.

5.2 Information Management

For most of recorded history, information was expensive, difficult to obtain, and slow to spread. Documents were written by hand. Books and manuscripts were extremely labour-intensive and therefore expensive. Although letters and other such documents were relatively easy to produce, transporting the information in them relied on horses, foot travellers, and ships.

Consequently, throughout history, organizations have pushed for and quickly adopted new information technologies that reduce the cost and/or increase the speed with which they can acquire, retrieve, and communicate information. The first technologies to truly revolutionize the business use of information were paper and the printing press. In the 14th century, water-powered machines were created to pulverize rags into pulp for making paper. Paper prices quickly dropped by 400 percent. Less than a half-century later, Johannes Gutenberg invented the printing press, which reduced the cost and time needed to copy written information by 99.8 percent. In 15th-century Florence, Italy, a scribe charged one florin (an Italian unit of money) to hand-copy one document page. By contrast, a printer could set up and print 1,025 copies of the same document for just three florins.

What Gutenberg's printing press did for publishing, the manual typewriter did for daily communication. Before 1850, most business correspondence was written by hand and copied using the letter press. With the ink still wet, the letter was placed in a tissue paper book. A hand press was then used to squeeze the book and copy the still-wet ink onto the tissue paper. By the 1870s, manual typewriters had made it cheaper, easier, and faster to produce and copy business correspondence. Of course, in the 1980s, slightly more than a century later, typewriters were replaced by personal computers and word processing software for identical reasons.

Finally, businesses have always looked for information technologies that speed access to timely information. The Medici family, which opened banks throughout Europe in the early 1400s, used posting messengers to keep in contact with their more than 40 branch managers. The post

System a set of interrelated elements or parts that function as a whole

Subsystems smaller systems that operate in the context of a larger system

Synergy when two or more subsystems working together can produce more than they can working apart

Closed systems systems that can sustain themselves without interacting with their environment

Open systems systems that can sustain themselves only by interacting with their environment, on which they depend for their survival

Contingency approach holds that there are no universal management theories and that the most effective management theory or idea depends on the kinds of problems or situations that managers are facing at a particular time and place

messengers, who predated the US Postal Service Pony Express by 400 years, could travel 90 miles per day, twice what average riders could cover, because the Medicis were willing to pay for the expense of providing them with fresh horses. The need for timely information also led companies to quickly adopt the telegraph in the 1860s, the telephone in the 1880s, and, of course, Internet technologies in recent years.

5.3 Systems Management

Today's companies are much larger and more complex. They most likely manufacture, service, *and* finance what they sell. They also operate in a complex, fast-changing, competitive, global environment that can quickly turn competitive advantages into competitive disadvantages.

How can managers make sense of this complexity both within and outside their organizations? One way to deal with organizational and environmental complexity is to take a systems view of organizations.[31] A **system** is a set of interrelated elements or parts that function as a whole. Rather than viewing one part of an organization as separate from the other parts, a systems approach encourages managers to complicate their thinking by looking for connections between the different parts of the organization. Indeed, one of the more important ideas in the systems approach to management is that organizational systems are composed of parts or **subsystems**, which are simply smaller systems within larger systems. Subsystems and their connections matter in systems theory because they make it possible for managers to create synergy. **Synergy** occurs when two or more subsystems working together can produce more than they can working apart. In other words, synergy occurs when 1 + 1 = 3.

Exhibit 2.5 illustrates how the elements of systems management work together. **Closed systems** can function without interacting with their environments; however, nearly all organizations should be viewed as **open systems** that interact with their environments and depend on them for survival. Therefore, rather than viewing what goes on within the organization as separate from what goes on outside it, the systems approach encourages managers to look for connections between the different parts of the organization and the different parts of its environment.

A systems view of organizations offers several advantages. First, it forces managers to view their organization as part of and subject to the competitive, economic, social, technological, and legal/regulatory forces in their environment.[32] Second, it also forces managers to be aware of how the environment affects specific parts of the organization. Third, because of the complexity and difficulty of trying to achieve synergies between different parts of the organization, the systems view encourages managers to focus on better communication and cooperation within the organization. Finally, an organization's survival depends on making sure that it continues to satisfy critical environmental stakeholders such as shareholders, employees, customers, suppliers, governments, and local communities.

5.4 Contingency Management

Earlier you learned that the goal of scientific management was to use systematic study to find the one best way of doing each task and then use that one best way everywhere. The problem, as you may have gathered from reading about the various approaches to management, is that no one in management seems to agree on what that one best way is. In fact, there isn't *one* best way. More than a century of management research has shown that there are clear boundaries or limitations to most management theories and practices. None of them are universal. Any given theory or practice may work much of the time, but none of them work all the time. How, then, is a manager to decide what theory to use? Well, it depends on the situation. The **contingency approach** to management states that there are no universal management theories and that the most effective management theory or idea depends on the kinds of problems or situations that managers or organizations are facing at a particular time.[33]

A practical implication of the contingency approach is that management is much harder than it looks. In fact, because of the clarity and obviousness of management

The cash register, invented in 1879, kept sales clerks honest by recording all sales transactions on a roll of paper securely locked inside the machine. But managers soon realized that its most important contribution was better management and control of their business. For example, department stores could track performance and sales by installing separate cash registers in the food, clothing, and hardware departments.

Cash Management

Exhibit 2.5 The Organization as an Open System

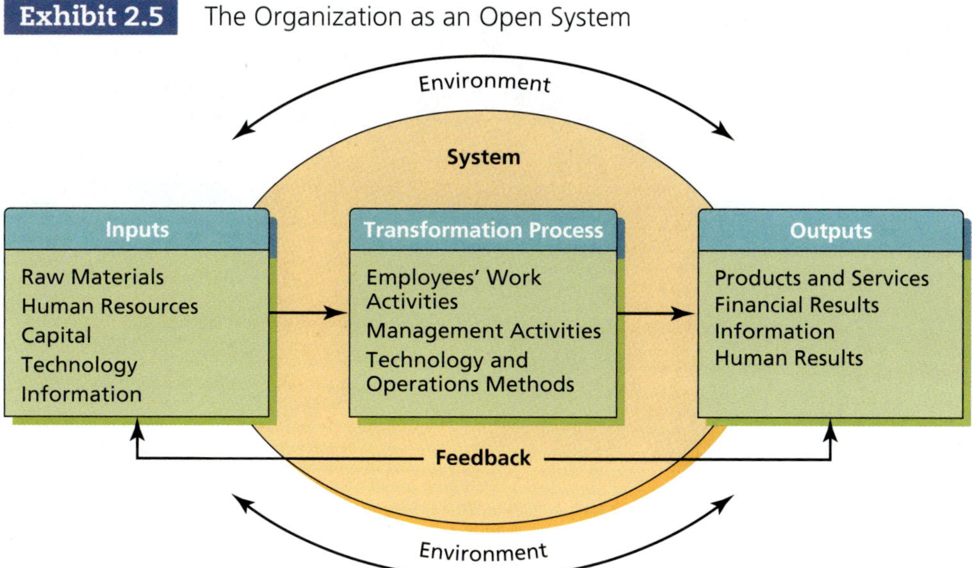

Source: Robbins, S., Coulter, M., & Langton, N. *Fundamentals of Management,* Sixth Canadian Edition. Toronto: Pearson (2011) p. 29. Reprinted with permission by Pearson Education Canada Inc.

theories (OK, most of them), students and workers often wrongly assume that a company's problems would be quickly and easily solved if management would take just a few simple steps. If this were true, few companies would have problems.

A second implication of the contingency approach is that managers need to look for key contingencies that differentiate today's situation or problems from yesterday's situation or problems. Moreover, it means that managers need to spend more time analyzing problems, situations, and employees before taking action to fix them. Finally, it means that as you read this text and learn about management ideas and practices, you need to pay particular attention to qualifying phrases such as "usually," "in these situations," "for this to work," and "under these circumstances." Doing so will help you identify the key contingencies that will help you become a better manager.

Go online at
www.nelson.com/4ltrpress/icanmgmt2
And access the essential Study Tools online for this chapter:

- **Flashcards**, to help you study
- **Interactive Quizzes**, to test your knowledge
- **Audio Chapter Summaries**, for chapter review
- **Crossword Puzzles and Beat the Clock**, to review key terms
- **What Would You Do? Cases**, for applying your knowledge to real-life situations
- **Self Assessments**, to learn about what kind of manager you are
- **Videos and Media Quizzing**, where you can watch a video about a real-life company and test yourself on what you've learned

Be sure to consult the Chapter Review Card at the back of the textbook.

3

Organizational Environments and Cultures

LEARNING OUTCOMES

LO1 Discuss how changing environments affect organizations.

LO2 Describe the four components of the general environment.

LO3 Explain the five components of the specific environment.

LO4 Describe the process that companies use to make sense of their changing environments.

LO5 Explain how organizational cultures are created and how they can help companies succeed.

This chapter examines the internal and external forces that affect business. First we'll examine the two types of external organizational environments: the general environment that affects all organizations, and the specific environment that is unique to each company. Then we'll learn how managers make sense of their changing general and specific environments. The chapter finishes with a discussion of internal organizational environments by focusing on organizational culture. But first, let's see how changes in external organizational environments affect the decisions and performance of a company.

Sony was for many decades one of the world's top electronics companies because of its ability to innovate, from the first commercially successful transistor radio to the Walkman, the first portable music player. The company then experienced a downturn, due to changes in its external environment, including heavy price competition in consumer electronics and the development of innovative products by other companies, such as (nowadays) the Apple iPad and personal video recorders. Executives at Sony have responded by generating a shift in the company's internal culture. Engineers from what were once separate divisions of the company are now sharing ideas and working together to develop new products that respond to consumer demand. In particular, customers want their various electronic devices to connect easily to one another and to the Internet. As a result, Sony has incorporated built-in Wi-Fi in almost all their television models and integrated NFC chips in their remote controls to allow for easy connection with consumer mobile devices. In the highly competitive television category, Sony's Bravia LED TV lineup includes 17 models that range from a 32-inch value-priced option all the way up to their powerhouse 84-inch Ultra HD model, which retails for $25,000.[1]

External Environments

External environments are the forces and events outside a company that have the potential to influence or affect it.

LO1 Changing Environments

Let's examine the three basic characteristics of changing external environments: ***1.1 environmental change, 1.2 environmental complexity, 1.3 resource scarcity,*** *and* ***1.4 the uncertainty that environmental change, complexity, and resource scarcity can create for organizational managers.***

1.1 Environmental Change

Environmental change is the rate at which a company's general and specific environments change. In **stable environments**, the rate of environmental change is slow. For instance, apart from the fact that ovens are more efficient, bread is baked, wrapped, and delivered fresh to stores each day much as it was decades ago. Although some new breads have become popular, the white and wheat breads that customers bought 20 years ago are still today's top sellers.

While baking companies have stable environments, Research In Motion (RIM), best known for bringing the BlackBerry smartphone to market, competes in an extremely dynamic external environment. In **dynamic environments**, the rate of environmental change is fast. Canada's RIM competes in an ever-changing wireless technology sector heavily influenced by technological innovations, changes in consumer demand, and the actions of ferocious competitors. From the company's introduction of the first wireless pager in 1996, to the launch of the BlackBerry phone in 1988, to its entry into the computer tablet category in 2011 and most recently, the launch of the Blackberry Z10 to compete with the iPhone and other smartphones, RIM has had to deal with sweeping changes in its organizational environment. Although RIM experienced astonishing growth and success early on the industry, it currently faces an uncertain future as it struggles to keep up with the frantic pace of technology, competitive offerings, and demanding customer markets.

You might expect a company's external environment to be *either* stable *or* dynamic. Research, though, suggests that companies often experience both. According to **punctuated equilibrium theory**, companies go through long periods of stability (equilibrium) during which incremental changes occur, followed by short periods of dynamic, fundamental change (revolutionary periods), which end with a return to stability (new equilibrium).[2]

One example of punctuated equilibrium is the Canadian airline industry. Twice in the past 30 years, that industry has experienced revolutionary periods. The first occurred with the advent of airline deregulation, which began in 1978 in response to US deregulation. Prior to deregulation, the industry was dominated by the "friendly duopoly" of CP Air and Air Canada, which shared over 95 percent of the market; however, the federal government controlled where airlines could fly, when they could fly, the prices they could charge,

Ilja Mašík/Dreamstime.com

Tom Wang/Shutterstock.com

External environments all events outside a company that have the potential to influence or affect it

Environmental change the rate at which a company's general and specific environments change

Stable environment an environment in which the rate of change is slow

Dynamic environment an environment in which the rate of change is fast

Punctuated equilibrium theory a theory according to which companies go through long, simple periods of stability (equilibrium), followed by short periods of dynamic, fundamental change (revolution), and ending with a return to stability (new equilibrium)

Environmental complexity the number of external factors in the environment that affect organizations

Simple environment an environment with few environmental factors

Complex environment an environment with many environmental factors

and the number of flights they could have on a particular route. Full deregulation was not seen in Canada until 1988, and by the time it did, airlines had more choices to make. Many competitors—such as Wardair, which was primarily a charter airline, and Pacific Western Airlines, a regional carrier—expanded, and new air carriers were started. Competition among the airlines was fierce, and Pacific Western purchased several smaller airlines, including Wardair. In 1987 it purchased the much larger CP Air to form Canadian Airlines. Canadian Airlines was a truly national carrier; although somewhat smaller than Air Canada, it was in a position to compete with Air Canada on an even basis. After substantially increased competition, two companies again dominated the skies, Canadian Airlines and Air Canada, and a period of relative stability developed. The dominance of these two carriers was first seriously challenged in 1996 with the emergence of WestJet Airlines, which started as a Western-based airline. Canadian, too, was a Western-based airline. Competition once again increased, and a faltering Canadian Airlines was purchased by Air Canada in 2000, leaving only two national carriers, Air Canada and WestJet. Several smaller carriers tried to exploit the failure of Canadian Airlines; some of them have since gone bankrupt, while others, such as Porter, a regional airline that operates from Billy Bishop Airport on Toronto Island, have met with success by operating smaller aircraft and appealing to business travellers. Air Canada and WestJet still dominate the Canadian skies, and no serious national challengers are on the horizon. These two periods of stability followed by revolution and regained stability illustrate punctuated equilibrium theory well.[3]

1.2 Environmental Complexity

Environmental complexity refers to the number and intensity of external factors in the environment that affect organizations. **Simple environments** have few environmental factors, whereas **complex environments** have many environmental factors. The dairy industry is an excellent example of a relatively simple external environment. Even accounting for decades-old advances in processing and automatic milking machines, milk is produced the same way today as it was 100 years ago. And while food manufacturers introduce dozens of new dairy-based products each year, Canadian milk production has grown only 1.7 percent per year over the last decade. In short, producing milk is a simple but highly competitive business that has experienced few changes.[4]

At the other end of the spectrum, few industries today face a more complex environment than the newspaper industry. For a century, making money selling newspapers was relatively simple: sell subscriptions for daily home delivery, and then sell classified ads and retail ads to reach those subscribers. In today's digital age, however, that business model doesn't work. First, revenues from classified ads—which had been extremely profitable for local newspapers—have dropped because of popular sites like craigslist.com, kijiji.ca, and ebayclassified.com, which allow free posting of classified ads.[5] Second, digital ads bring in substantially less revenue compared to print ads. Recent studies report that publishers only earn $1 in digital revenue for every $7 lost from print advertising, and these earnings don't generate enough revenue to cover the cost of "free" online versions of newspapers. Finally, because digital content is very inexpensive to distribute relative to print, most consumers expect Internet-based news to be free. As a result, many online newspapers, such as the *National Post,* the *New York Times,* and the *Wall Street Journal,* now charge for online access, but other newspapers may find it more difficult to do so. Says *Adweek* senior editor Mike Shields: "The *Journal* is not free. They never wavered or changed that. That is as key to the success as the content they deliver. That precedent is enviable and hard for someone [else] to copy, particularly if you've been giving away your content for ten years."[6]

Tetra Images/Getty Images/Donald Nausbaum/Photographer's Choice/Getty images

1.3 Resource Scarcity

The third characteristic of external environments is resource scarcity. **Resource scarcity** refers to the abundance or shortage of critical resources in the organization's external environment. For example, flat-screen LCD TVs were initially six times more expensive per inch than cathode TVs, and twice as expensive as rear-projection TVs, largely because there weren't enough LCD screen factories to meet demand; in other words, LCD factories were a scarce resource in this industry. Furthermore, those factories were expensive to build ($2 to $4 billion each) and the manufacturing process was complex and difficult to manage. As a result of this resource shortage, consumer electronics companies found themselves susceptible to price volatility; thus, they charged higher prices to consumers. But as sales of LCD TVs soared, more LCD factories were built to meet demand, which solved the problem of low manufacturing capacity. This, combined with an increase in competition, drove down consumer prices. In this industry, resource scarcity has undoubtedly played an important role in the changing external environment.[7]

1.4 Uncertainty

As Exhibit 3.1 shows, environmental change, environmental complexity, and resource scarcity affect environmental **uncertainty**, which refers to how well managers can understand or predict the external changes and trends affecting their businesses. Starting at the left side of the figure, environmental uncertainty is lowest when environmental change and environmental complexity are low and resources are plentiful. In these environments, managers feel confident that they can understand, predict, and react to the external forces that affect their businesses. By contrast, the right side of the figure shows that environmental uncertainty is highest when environmental change and complexity are high and resource scarcity is a problem. In these environments, managers may not be confident that they can understand, predict, and handle the external forces affecting their businesses.

Resource scarcity the abundance or shortage of critical organizational resources in an organization's external environment

Uncertainty extent to which managers can understand or predict which environmental changes and trends will affect their businesses

General environment the economic, technological, sociocultural, and political trends that indirectly affect all organizations

Specific environment the customers, competitors, suppliers, industry regulations, and advocacy groups that are unique to an industry and directly affect how a company does business

LO2 General Environment

As Exhibit 3.2 shows (see page 38), two kinds of external environments influence organizations: the general environment and the specific environment. The **general environment** consists of the economy and the technological, sociocultural, and political/legal trends that indirectly affect all organizations. Changes in any part of the general environment eventually affect most organizations. For example, when the Bank of Canada lowers its prime lending rate, most businesses benefit because banks and credit card companies often reduce the interest rates they charge for loans. Consumers can then borrow money more cheaply to buy homes, cars, refrigerators, and flat-screen TVs. But each organization also has a **specific environment** that is unique to its industry and that directly affects how it conducts day-to-day business. For example, when the cost of coffee beans increased dramatically, Starbucks increased its prices, and so did Kraft Foods, the maker of Maxwell House coffee.[8] But only coffee-related businesses were affected. The specific environment, which will be discussed in detail in Section 3 of this chapter, includes customers, competitors, suppliers, industry regulators, and advocacy groups.

*Let's take a closer look at the four components of the general environment: **2.1 the economy, 2.2 the technological, 2.3 sociocultural,** and **2.4 political/legal trends that indirectly affect all organizations.***

Exhibit 3.1 Environmental Change, Environmental Complexity, and Resource Scarcity

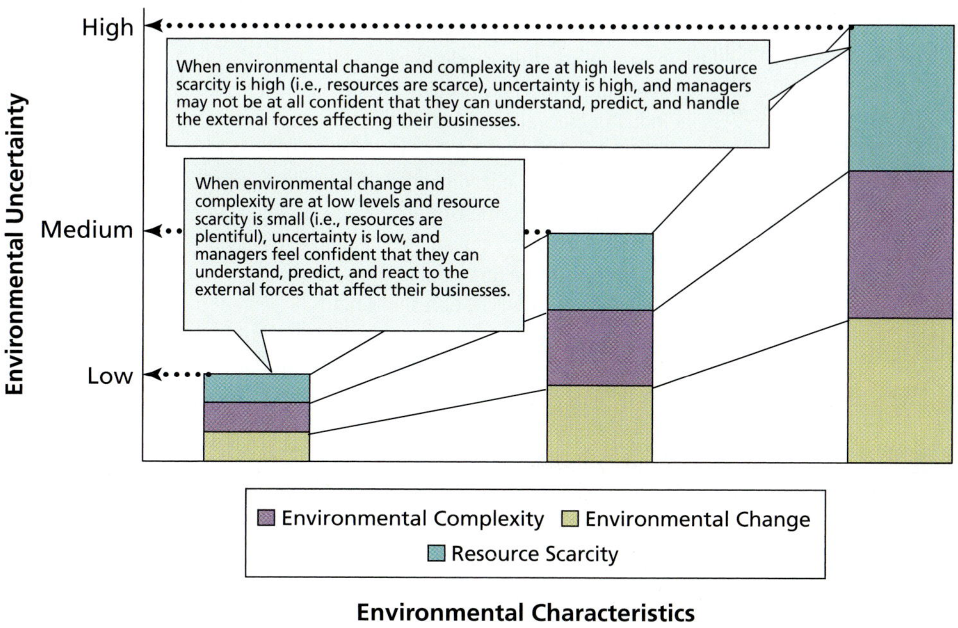

Exhibit 3.2 General and Specific Environments

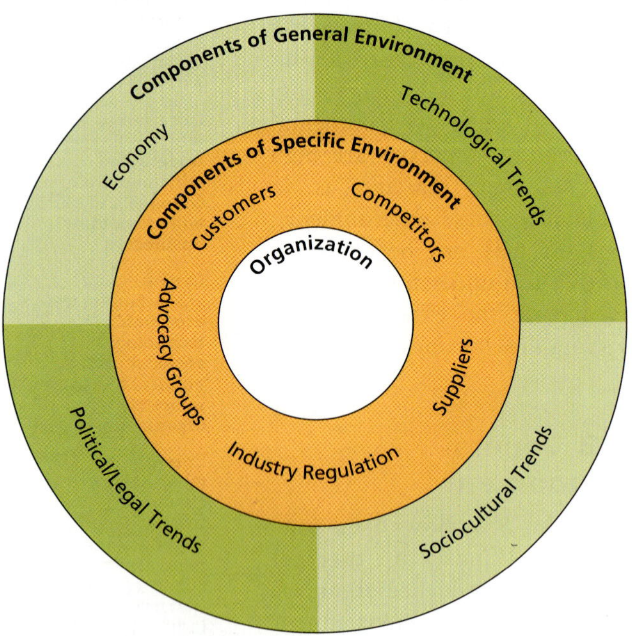

Source: From WILLIAMS/KONDRA/VIBERT, *Management, Second Edition.* © 2008 Nelson Education Ltd. Reproduced by permission. www.cengage.com/permissions

Business confidence indices that show managers' level of confidence about future business growth

2.1 Economy

The current state of a country's economy affects virtually every organization doing business there. In a growing economy, more people are working and wages are increasing, and as a result, consumers have more money to spend. More products are bought and sold in a growing economy than in a static or shrinking economy. Although an individual firm's sales will not necessarily increase, a growing economy does provide an environment favourable to business growth. In a shrinking economy, on the other hand, consumers have less money to spend and relatively fewer products are bought and sold. A shrinking economy thus makes growth for individual businesses more difficult. Because the economy influences basic business decisions such as whether to hire more employees, expand production, or take out loans to purchase equipment, managers scan their economic environments for signs of significant change.

Some managers try to predict future economic activity by tracking business confidence. **Business confidence indices** show how confident actual managers are about future business growth. The Conference Board of Canada surveys more than 1,500 business executives in Canada each quarter to compile the Index of Business Confidence (IBC), a measure of the business community's perceptions of the current economic situation and an indication of future plans relating to business growth. The same board surveys Canadian consumers to gauge consumer confidence by asking how they feel about the economy and their employment situation and whether they plan to purchase any big-ticket items. In addition, the Small Business Research Board surveys Canadian small business owners for their opinions on significant business issues and topics in order to gain valuable insights into the small business environment in Canada.[9] Managers often prefer business confidence indices to economic statistics because they know that other managers make business decisions that are in line with their expectations concerning the economy's future. So when business

The Economic Ripple Effect

A sudden change in a country's economy can send a ripple effect through the entire country or even the world. Difficulties in the US housing market began in 2008 when a large number of Americans, many of whom had poor credit histories, took advantage of low interest rates and forgiving credit standards in the form of subprime mortgages. As home prices fell and interest rates began to rise, many of these borrowers found themselves unable to meet their mortgage payments; the result was a record number of loan defaults and foreclosures, which forced a number of financial institutions into bankruptcy. As a result, consumer confidence began to slide, stock prices fell, and the credit market stalled. This led to reduced retail spending, especially on big-ticket items such as automobiles, an industry that relies on a stable credit market. The faltering of the US economy ignited a global financial crisis that had an impact on other industrialized countries, including Canada. The economic challenges facing the United States, Canada's largest trading partner, led to a decrease in Canadian exports and resulting slowdowns in the manufacturing sector. Canadian exports to the United States (which represent about 78 percent of the total value of Canadian exports) decreased by 31 percent from 2008 to 2009. The business and economic community kept a close eye on these economic developments and was relieved to see that by 2010, as global market conditions improved so did Canada's trading results, with both exports and imports increasing.

Used with the permission of the Bank of Canada.

Sources: P. Bergevin, "The global financial crisis and its impact on Canada", Library of Parliament, December 2008; J. Lorio, "October Auto Sales Screech to a Halt", *Automobile*; R. Ray, "Canada to feel impact from slowing US growth, economists say good news is the worst is already behind us," *Investment Executive*, 25 February 2008; http://www.conferenceboard.ca/HCP/Details/Economy/forecast-2010.aspx [accessed 6 May 2010].

confidence indices are dropping, a manager may decide against hiring new employees, increasing production, or taking out additional loans to expand the business.

2.2 Technological Component

Technology is an umbrella term for the knowledge, tools, and techniques used to transform inputs (raw materials, information, and so on) into outputs (products and services). For example, the inputs of authors, editors, and artists (knowledge and skills) and the use of equipment such as computers and printing presses (technology) transformed paper, ink, and glue (raw material) into this book (the finished product). In the case of a service company such as an airline, the technology consists of equipment, including airplanes, repair tools, and computers, as well as the knowledge of mechanics, ticketers, and flight crews. The output is the service of transporting people from one place to another.

Technology the knowledge, tools, and techniques used to transform input into output

Changes in technology can help companies provide better products or produce their products more efficiently. For example, advances in surgical techniques and imaging equipment have made open-heart surgery much faster and safer in recent years. While technological changes can benefit a business, they can also threaten it. Companies must embrace new technology and find effective ways to use it to improve their products and services or decrease costs. If they don't, they will lose out to those companies that do.

2.3 Sociocultural Component

The sociocultural component of the general environment refers to the demographic characteristics, general behaviour, attitudes, and beliefs of people in a particular society. Sociocultural changes and trends influence organizations in two important ways.

First, changes in demographic characteristics, such as the number of people with particular skills, the growth or decline in particular population segments, and evolving cultural norms (for example, changes in gender roles) affect how companies staff their businesses. Married women with children are much more likely to be working today than they were four decades ago (see Exhibit 3.3). In 1976, only 31.4 percent of women with children under six years old and 39.1 percent of women with children under 16 living at home worked. By 2009, those percentages had risen to 66.5 percent and 72.9 percent, respectively.

Second, changes in behaviour, attitudes, and beliefs affect the demand for a business's products and services. With traffic congestion creating longer commutes and both parents working longer hours, employees today are much more likely to value products and services that allow them to recapture free time with their families. Balancing work with family is a major concern for many Canadians and is a factor in determining commitment to an employer. Edmonton-based VIP Concierge & Errand was launched to meet the needs of busy working Canadians who want to spend more time with family and leisure activities and less time running errands. The services it provides include these: shopping (personal and grocery), meal delivery, pet sitting and dog walking, travel planning, car cleaning, and a wait service for cable, phone, or other home services. A recent study

Ernst Grasser/Stone/Getty Images

Exhibit 3.3 Demographics: Percentage of Married Women (with Children) Who Work

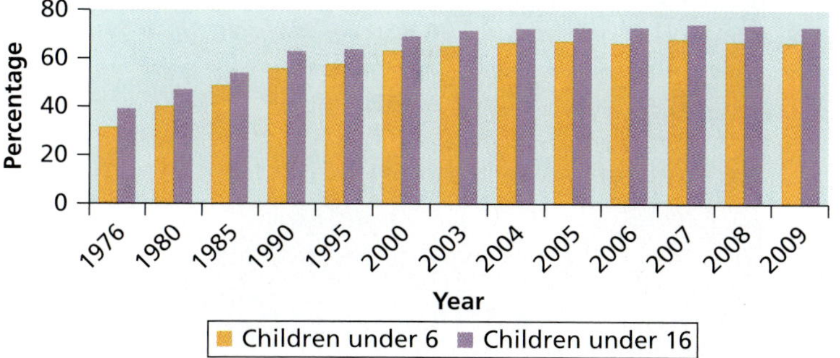

Source: Statistics Canada, *Women in Canada Sixth Edition: A Gender Based Statistical Report, 2010*, Catalogue No. 89-503-X, available at: http://www.statcan.gc.ca/pub/89-503-x/2010001/article/11387-eng.pdf

found that employees with greater work–life support are more balanced and committed to their employers and are more likely to achieve greater work outcomes.[10]

Organizations pursuing international growth would be wise to do their research prior to entering a foreign market, for widely different social and cultural norms may exist there. Foreign investment carries a much higher risk for organizations that do not take this precaution.

2.4 Political/Legal Component

The political/legal component of the general environment includes the laws, regulations, and court decisions that govern and regulate business behaviour. New laws and regulations continue to impose additional responsibilities on companies. For example, in Canada, the Personal Information Protection and Electronic Documents Act (PIPEDA) came into full effect in 2004. It applies to all personal information collected, used, or disclosed by private-sector organizations in the course of commercial activities. This federal legislation was introduced in response to growing consumer concerns about privacy and the handling of personal information in the digital age. Canadian businesses are now required to put systems in place to ensure that personal information such as names, addresses, phone numbers, and e-mails is not disclosed and is protected from theft. Also in 2004, Bill C-45, an amendment to the Canadian Criminal Code, was passed, establishing criminal liability for organizations' actions in terms of workplace health and safety, including penalties for violations resulting in injury or death.

Even though legal systems differ between Canada and the United States, there is sometimes a trickle-down effect whereby a law introduced in the US may result in similar legislation being passed in Canada. The increasing number of climate change lawsuits levelled against US oil companies, automakers, and electrical utilities has signalled to many Canadian companies and legal advisers that it would be wise to prepare for similar developments in Canada.[11]

Canadian companies looking to pursue international opportunities should carefully consider the political and legal practices in foreign markets, with a mind to navigating with any differences that exist with respect to political systems, government regulations, and laws about intellectual property, the labour force, and financial matters.

From a managerial perspective, the best medicine against legal risk is prevention. As a manager, it is your responsibility to educate yourself about the laws and regulations that could affect your business. Failure to do so may put you and your company at risk of sizable penalties and fines.

Helping Companies Enter New Markets

The Canadian government would like to see more Canadian companies follow in the footsteps of Valiant Machine and Tool Inc., a Canadian engineering design and manufacturing company headquartered in Windsor, Ontario, that invested in a high-tech manufacturing facility in Pune, India, and now employs 550 workers in Canada and India. To help other small and medium-sized enterprises navigate the challenging and often frustrating waters associated with foreign markets, the Canadian government promotes foreign investment promotional, and protection agreements with countries like India. "Small and medium-sized businesses like Valiant are the backbone of the Canadian economy and the engine of growth," said Minister of International Trade Ed Fast. "A foreign investment promotion and protection agreement with India will increase job-creating, two-way investment between our countries by giving both Canadian and Indian companies the predictability, stability and protection they need to expand their operations." For many Canadian companies, the uncertainty and unfamiliarity of the sociocultural, political, and legal environment of foreign markets is a major stumbling block in terms of pursing international opportunities. However, the strength of Canada's economy, labour market, and quality of life increasingly depends on the ability of Canadian businesses to capitalize on opportunities in the wider global community. Initiatives like foreign investment promotion and protection agreements help provide Canadian companies with a greater level of confidence in their global efforts. To date, Canada has agreements in force with 24 countries.

Sources: Foreign Affairs and International Trade Canada, "International Trade Minister Ed Fast Applauds Canadian Companies Expanding into High-Growth India," November 7, 2011, available at http://www.international.gc.ca/media_commerce/comm/news-communiques/2011/334.aspx?view=d; Export Development Canada, "Prospecting Growth in India and other markets can pay long-term," October 2, 2012 available at: http://www.theglobeandmail.com/partners/advedc1111/prospecting-growth-in-india-and-other-markets-can-pay-long-term/article4582725/; Carol Stephenson, *Ivey Business Journal*, "Mitigating the risk: Practical steps for expanding your business abroad," March/April 2010 available at http://www.iveybusinessjournal.com/departments/from-the-dean/mitigating-the-risk-practical-steps-for-expanding-your-business-abroad#.UO4–GdTwfw

Christopher Pillitz/Photonica World/Getty Images

LO3 Specific Environment

As you just learned, changes in any sector of the general environment (economic, technological, sociocultural, political/legal) eventually affect most organizations. Each organization also has a specific environment that is unique to its industry and that directly affects the way it conducts day-to-day business. For instance, if your customers decide to use another product, your main competitor cuts prices 10 percent, your best supplier can't deliver raw materials, federal regulators mandate reductions in pollutants in your industry, or environmental groups accuse your company of selling unsafe products, the impact from the specific environment on your business is immediate.

Let's examine how the ***3.1 customer, 3.2 competitor, 3.3 supplier, 3.4 industry regulation,*** *and* ***3.5 advocacy group components of the specific environment affect*** *businesses.*

3.1 Customer Component

Customers purchase products and services. Companies cannot exist without customer support. Monitoring customers' changing wants and needs is therefore critical to business success. There are two basic strategies for monitoring customers: reactive and proactive.

Reactive customer monitoring involves identifying and addressing customer trends and problems after they occur. One reactive strategy is to listen closely to customer complaints and respond to customer concerns. Companies that respond quickly to customer letters of complaint are viewed much more favourably than companies that are slow to respond or never respond.[12] In particular, studies have shown that when a company's follow-up letter thanks the customer for writing, offers a sincere, specific response to the complaint (not a form letter, but an explanation of how the problem will be handled), and contains a small gift, coupons, or a refund to make up for the problem, customers are much more likely to purchase products or services again from that company.[13]

Proactive monitoring of customers, on the other hand, means identifying and addressing customer needs, trends, and issues before they occur. In the gaming industry, many casinos focus on attracting high rollers who bet huge amounts of money, on the assumption that these customers are the key to profitability. However, Caesars Entertainment Corporation, which operates casino resorts on four continents under the Harrah's, Caesars, and Horseshoe brand names, has a different perspective. Harrah's casinos determined that 80 percent of its revenues and 100 percent of its profits come from "low rollers," the 30 percent of its customers who spend only $100 to $500 per visit. Harrah's calls them "avid experience players" because of the regularity with which they gamble. The trick to attracting and keeping these customers is to identify and address their needs, which Harrah's does through its electronic "Total Rewards" program cards that these frequent gamblers insert into slot machines or hand to blackjack table attendants whenever they place a bet. Thanks to the data obtained from those cards, Harrah's can identify what different customers need to keep them coming back to Harrah's—cash rewards for a local customer who plays the slot machines a lot or perhaps a free or "comped" hotel room for those travelling a distance. Having identified and met customers' needs, Harrah's now gets 43 percent of its customers' gambling business, compared to 36 percent before its Total Rewards program.[14]

Competitors companies in the same industry that sell similar products or services to customers

Competitive analysis a process for monitoring the competition that involves identifying competition, anticipating their moves, and determining their strengths and weaknesses

3.2 Competitor Component

Competitors are companies in the same industry that sell similar products or services to customers. For example, General Motors, Ford, Toyota, Honda, Nissan, Hyundai, Kia, and DaimlerChrysler are some of the companies that compete for automobile customers. In Canada, CBC, Bell Media, and Shaw Media (along with hundreds of regional cable channels) compete for TV viewers' attention. Often the difference between business success and failure comes down to whether your company is doing a better job of satisfying customer wants and needs than the competition. Consequently, companies need to keep close track of what their competitors are doing. To do this, managers perform **competitive analysis**, which involves deciding who your competitors are, anticipating their moves, and determining their strengths and weaknesses.

Managers often do a poor job of identifying potential competitors because they tend to focus on only two or three well-known competitors with similar goals and resources.[15] For example, Hoover, Dirt Devil, and (more recently) Oreck were competing fiercely in the market for vacuum cleaners. Because these companies produced relatively similar vacuum cleaners, they paid attention to one another and competed mostly on price. When Dyson entered the market with its radically different vacuum cleaner, which developed and maintained significantly more suction power, the company garnered 20 percent market share within its first twelve months on the shelves.[16] Only then did Hoover and Dirt Devil design their own bagless vacuums.

Pavel L Photo and Video/Shutterstock.com

Suppliers companies that provide material, human, financial, and informational resources to other companies

Supplier dependence the degree to which a company relies on a supplier because of the importance of the supplier's product to the company and the difficulty of finding other sources for that product

Buyer dependence the degree to which a supplier relies on a buyer because of the importance of that buyer to the supplier and the difficulty of finding other buyers for its products

Opportunistic behaviour a transaction in which one party in the relationship benefits at the expense of the other

Relationship behaviour mutually beneficial, long-term exchanges between buyers and suppliers

Industry regulation regulations and rules that govern the business practices and procedures of specific industries, businesses, and professions

Advocacy groups groups of concerned citizens who band together to try to influence the business practices of specific industries, businesses, and professions

Another mistake managers make is to underestimate potential competitors' capabilities. In the retail industry in particular, competition has intensified as retailers compete for many of the same consumers, and that means managers must keep a close eye on new competitors at all times. The expansion of US powerhouse retailer Target into the Canadian marketplace was undoubtedly an important topic of discussion for many Canadian retailers, influencing their plans and strategies. Anticipating Target's entry, Wal-Mart Canada invested $750 million in updates to existing stores and the conversion of 39 former Zellers locations. In addition, Wal-Mart continued to move full speed ahead with its strategy of increasing the grocery sections of its superstores, a defensive strategy that made sense in terms of competing with Target, which was known to be stronger in other areas, such as apparel and housewares. Sears Canada, meanwhile, began bracing itself for Target's arrival, installing a new CEO in 2011 and embarking on a strategy to reposition itself as a more "contemporary" retailer. When Hudson's Bay Co., Shoppers Drug Mart, and Loblaw Companies Ltd. announced major job cuts in 2012, retail analysts pointed to the imminent Target store openings as a contributing factor in these decisions.[17]

3.3 Supplier Component

Suppliers are companies that provide material, human, financial, and informational resources to other companies. A key factor influencing the impact and quality of the relationship between companies and their suppliers is how interdependent they are.[18] **Supplier dependence** refers to the degree to which a company relies on a given supplier because of the importance of its product to the company and the difficulty of finding other sources for that product. Supplier dependence is very strong in the diamond business, given that De Beers Consolidated Mines provides 66 percent of the world's wholesale diamonds and controls the supply, price, and quality of the best diamonds on the market. The company's 125 customers—or "sightholders," as they're known in the industry—are summoned to De Beers's London office 10 times a year and handed a shoebox of diamonds, which they are required to buy. If they refuse, they lose the opportunity to purchase any more diamonds.[19]

FreshPaint/Shutterstock.com

Buyer dependence is the degree to which a supplier relies on a buyer because of the importance of that buyer to the supplier's sales and the difficulty of finding other buyers for its products. Superior Industries, which makes car wheels, gets 85 percent of its $840 million in annual sales from Ford and GM. When the two automakers demanded that Superior match the low prices that Chinese wheel suppliers were offering, it had little choice. Superior's president, Steve Borick, says that the ultimatum was presented very simply: "They said, 'This is the price we are getting [from Chinese suppliers], for this product. You either match that, or we'll take our business to them.'" He adds, "It's that black and white. Close the [cost] gap [of 20 to 40 percent] no matter how" you do it.[20]

As the De Beers and Superior Industries examples show, a high degree of buyer or seller dependence can lead to **opportunistic behaviour**, in which one party benefits at the expense of the other. Suppliers are beginning to hit back at automakers that expect them to supply parts at prices that are attractive for the automaker and crippling for the supplier, pushing many of the latter into bankruptcy or out of business. When Michael Lord, the CEO of Bluewater Plastics, refused to sell parts at a too-low price, the purchasing manager of a Detroit automaker told him, "Obviously, you don't want to be strategic with us." Lord, however, was unfazed and confident that the purchasing manager would call back. "I know we aren't the only ones pushing back—the supplier world is changing."[21] Although opportunistic behaviour between buyers and suppliers will never be completely eliminated, many companies believe that both buyers and suppliers can benefit by improving the buyer–supplier relationship.[22]

In contrast to opportunistic behaviour, **relationship behaviour** focuses on establishing mutually beneficial, long-term relations between buyers and suppliers.[23] Toyota is well known for developing positive long-term relationships with its key suppliers. Donald Esmond, who runs Toyota's US division, says of suppliers, "I think what they appreciate ... is we don't go in and say, 'Reduce the costs by 6 percent; if you don't, somebody else is going to get the business.' We go in and say we want to come in and help you [figure out] where you can save costs so we can reduce our overall price. So it's a different approach."[24]

3.4 Industry Regulation Component

The political/legal component of the general environment affects *all* businesses, whereas the **industry regulation** component consists of regulations and rules that govern the practices and procedures of *specific* industries, businesses, and professions. Regulatory agencies affect businesses by creating and enforcing rules and regulations to protect consumers, workers, and/or society as a whole. For example, the responsibility for toy safety is shared among governments, the toy industry, and safety associations as well as consumers. The Canadian Toy Association's mission is to work at a national and international level to protect and improve industry practices through various committees such as the Safety and Government Relations Committee, which helps develop toy safety standards. All toys sold in Canada must meet safety requirements defined in the Hazardous Products Act and the Hazardous Products (Toys) Regulations. The toy industry recognizes that liaison among the various stakeholders is needed especially in terms of packaging, labelling, advertising, and the environment.[25]

3.5 Advocacy Groups

Advocacy groups are groups of concerned citizens who band together to influence the business practices of specific industries, businesses, and professions. The members of a group generally share the same point of view on a particular issue. For example, environmental advocacy groups might try to get manufacturers to reduce smokestack pollution emissions. Unlike the industry regulators, advocacy groups cannot force organizations to change their practices. They can, though, use a number of techniques to influence companies, including public communications, media advocacy, websites, and blogs, as well as product boycott campaigns.

The **public communications** approach relies on voluntary participation by the news media and the advertising industry to send out an advocacy group's message. Media advocacy is much more aggressive than the public communications approach. A **media advocacy** approach typically involves framing the group's concerns as public issues (affecting everyone); exposing questionable, exploitative, or unethical practices; and forcing media coverage by buying media time or creating controversy that is likely to receive extensive news coverage.

For example, the Liquor Control Board of Ontario's (LCBO) $1.6 million "Deflate the Elephant" campaign aimed at helping people open what is often an uncomfortable conversation (the elephant in the room) to prevent their friends and guests from drinking and driving. This campaign featured television commercials, online and print ads, and a special website; its purpose was to engage those people who are in a position to intervene when family or friends are at risk of getting behind the wheel when they have had too much to drink.[26]

Public communications an advocacy group tactic that relies on voluntary participation by the news media and the advertising industry to get the advocacy group's message out

Media advocacy an advocacy group tactic that involves framing issues as public issues; exposing questionable, exploitative, or unethical practices; and forcing media coverage by buying media time or creating controversy that is likely to receive extensive news coverage

Bunny Butchers

PETA (People for the Ethical Treatment of Animals), which has offices in the United States, England, Italy, and Germany, uses controversial publicity stunts and advertisements to try to change the behaviour of large organizations, fashion designers, medical researchers, and anyone else it believes is hurting or mistreating animals. In one of its more recent protests, PETA released a series of attention-getting advertisements featuring nude celebrities who would "rather go naked than wear fur" and "rather bare skin than wear skin." A number of designers have pledged to go animal-free. PETA is active against those that have not, engaging in activities such as smearing the windows of Jean-Paul Gaultier's Paris boutique with red "blood."

The Canadian Press (David Fisher/Rex Features)

MGMT FACT

Federal Regulatory Agencies and Responsibilities

Environmental Assessment Agency

Reduces and controls pollution through research, monitoring, standard setting, and enforcement activities

www.ceaa-acee.gc.ca

Candian Human Rights Commission

Promotes fair hiring and promotion practices

www.chrc-ccdp.ca

Canadian Radio-Television and Telecommunications Commission (CRTC)

Regulates communications by radio, television, wire, satellite, and cable

www.crtc.gc.ca

Bank of Canada

As the nation's central bank, controls interest rates and money supply and monitors the Canadian banking system to produce a growing economy with stable prices

www.bank-banque-canada.ca

Competition Tribunal

Restricts unfair methods of business competition and misleading advertising

www.hc-sc.gc.ca

Health Canada

Protects nation's health by making sure food, drugs, and cosmetics are safe

www.hc-sc.gc.ca

Canadian Industrial Relations Board

Monitors union elections and stops companies from engaging in unfair labour practices

www.cirb-ccri.gc.ca

Canadian Centre for Occupational Health and Safety

Saves lives, prevents injuries, and protects the health of workers

www.ccohs.ca

Product boycott an advocacy group tactic that involves protesting a company's actions by convincing consumers not to purchase its product or service

Environmental scanning searching the environment for important events or issues that might affect an organization

In a **product boycott**, an advocacy group tries to persuade consumers not to purchase a company's products or services. Members of the Rainforest Action Network (RAN) have chained themselves to woodpiles at select Home Depot stores to get the company to stop selling old-growth lumber. RAN has also partnered with Greenpeace Canada as part of a Canada/US coalition that promotes a boycott of products from Canada's boreal forest, one of the last intact forests in North America, which starts in Alaska and extends all the way to the Atlantic. In question are the logging practices used by the forest companies that supply many large US corporations with boreal wood. The coalition has sent correspondence to 500 major corporations, urging them to stop buying from logging companies that haven't shifted to sustainable logging and to decrease the number of flyers, catalogues, and magazines they produce.[27]

LO4 Making Sense of Changing Environments

In Chapter 1, you learned that managers are responsible for making sense of their business environment. As our discussions of the general and specific environments have indicated, however, doing so is not an easy task. Because external environments can be dynamic, confusing, and complex, managers use a three-step process to make sense of changes in the external environment: ***4.1 environmental scanning, 4.2 interpreting environmental factors,*** *and* ***4.3 acting on threats and opportunities.***

4.1 Environmental Scanning

Environmental scanning involves searching the environment for important events or issues that might affect an organization. Managers scan the environment to stay up to date on important factors in their industry. For example, when one-quarter of all new car buyers were purchasing sports utility vehicles (SUVs) (a highly profitable category for the industry), auto executives didn't paid much attention to environmental groups' complaints about SUVs' extremely poor gas mileage. Now, however, market research is showing that current SUV owners are unhappy with their vehicles' poor gas mileage. In addition, the rapid rise in retail gas prices and increasingly strong disapproval of SUVs by younger car buyers have resulted in large unsold inventories of SUVs.[28]

Managers also scan their environment to reduce uncertainty. Faced with the task of developing marketing campaigns to sell their companies' most important products, the chief marketing officers (CMOs) of the world's best organizations willingly pay $50,000 a year to join the "Marketing 50," an exclusive group of CMOs who meet several times a year to exchange ideas and pick one another's brains. Michael Linton, Best Buy's CMO, believes that the "Marketing 50" is fantastic for finding out what other companies and CMOs are doing, thereby reducing uncertainty: "It's impossible for any one company to know about every new tool, so hearing what is working for others helps."[29]

Organizational strategies also affect environmental scanning. In other words, managers pay close attention to trends and events that are directly related to their company's ability to compete in the marketplace.[30] Microsoft used to take software hackers to court to prosecute them for the damage they were doing. But now that Bill Gates has declared that security is Microsoft's top priority, the company is trying to hire friendly hackers, whose knowledge and skills can be used to help the company develop more secure products. According to Steven Toulouse, Microsoft's manager for security programs, "we have discovered things during the development of these products that we might not have discovered otherwise."[31]

Finally, environmental scanning contributes to organizational performance. Environmental scanning helps managers detect environmental changes and problems before they can become crises.[32] Companies whose CEOs do more environmental scanning have higher profits.[33] CEOs in better performing firms scan their firm's environment more often and more thoroughly than do CEOs in poorer performing firms.[34] Managers pay close attention to trends and events that are directly related to their company's ability to compete.

4.2 Interpreting Environmental Factors

After scanning, managers determine what environmental events and issues *mean* to the organization. Typically, managers view environmental events and issues as either threats or opportunities. When managers interpret environmental events as threats, they take steps to protect the company from further harm. For example, now that Internet phone service (VoIP) has emerged as a threat, traditional phone companies have been announcing billion-dollar plans to expand their fibre-optic networks so that they can offer phone (using VoIP), Internet service, and TV packages just like those the cable and satellite companies offer.[35]

By contrast, when managers interpret environmental events as opportunities, they consider strategic alternatives for exploiting those events to improve company performance. Apple developed the iPhone to meet consumer demand for a device that combined consumer electronics with telecommunications and computer functions, thus allowing users to send and receive e-mail, take pictures, surf the Web, update and browse social networking sites, use Bluetooth devices and faster WiFi networks, and (of course) download and play iTunes music, all with one device. The popularity of the iPhone spurred the introduction of more new phones on the market, along with specialized applications tailored to individual users' needs. Smartphones are more expensive than basic cellphones and were introduced during a recession, yet consumers have embraced them as having better value for money because of their multifunctionality.[36] The global market for high-end "smartphones"—full-featured mobile phones that also function as handheld personal computers—continues to grow, with smartphones representing 39.6 percent of all mobile handsets sold.[37]

© Hocus Focus Studio/iStockphoto.com

Cognitive maps graphic depictions of how managers believe environmental factors relate to possible organizational actions

4.3 Acting on Threats and Opportunities

After scanning for information on environmental events and issues and interpreting them as threats or opportunities, managers have to decide how to respond to these environmental factors. Deciding what to do during times of uncertainty is always difficult. Managers can never be completely confident that they have all the information they need or that they correctly understand the information they have.

Because it is impossible to comprehend all of the factors and changes, managers often rely on simplified models of external environments called cognitive maps. **Cognitive maps** summarize the perceived relationships among environmental factors and possible organizational actions. For example, the cognitive map shown in Exhibit 3.4 represents a clothing boutique owner's interpretation of her business environment. The map shows three kinds of variables. The first set of variables, shown as blue rectangles, are environmental factors, such as a Wal-Mart or a large mall 20 minutes away. The second set of variables, shown in green ovals, are potential actions that the boutique owner might take, such as a low-cost strategy; a good-value, good-service strategy; or a large selection of the latest fashions strategy. The third set of variables, shown as gold trapezoids, are company strengths, such as low employee turnover, as well as weaknesses, such as small size.

Exhibit 3.4 Cognitive Maps

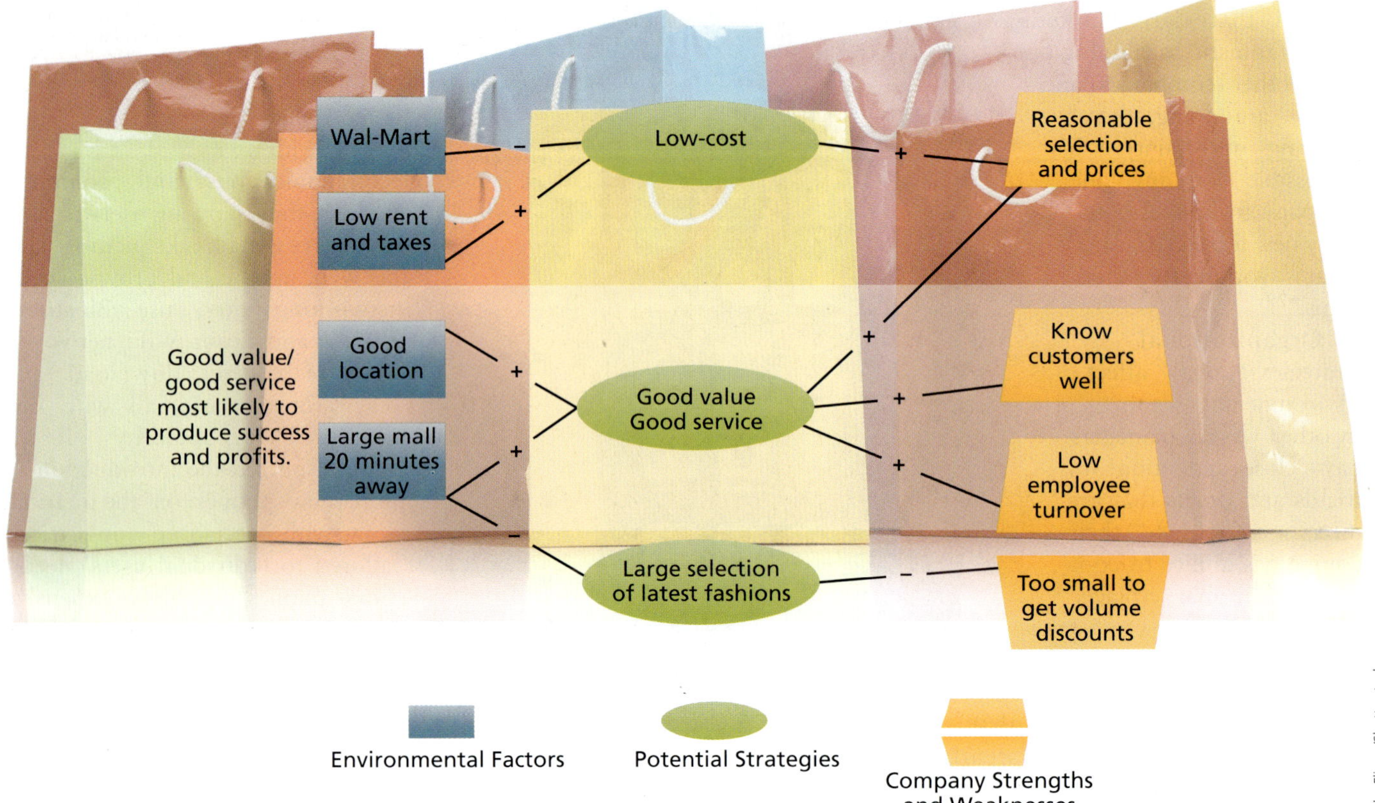

Internal environment the events and trends inside an organization that affect management, employees, and organizational culture

Organizational culture the values, beliefs, and attitudes shared by members of the organization

The plus and minus signs on the map indicate whether the manager believes there is a positive or a negative relationship between variables. For example, the manager believes that a low-cost strategy won't work because Wal-Mart is nearby. Offering a large selection of the latest fashions would not work either—not with the small size of the store and that large nearby mall. However, the manager believes that a good-value, good-service strategy would lead to success and profits because of the store's low employee turnover, good knowledge of customers, reasonable selection of clothes at reasonable prices, and good location.

Internal Environments

We have been looking at trends and events outside of companies that have the potential to affect them. By contrast, the **internal environment** consists of the trends and events *within* an organization that affect the management, employees, and organizational culture. Internal environments are important because they affect what people think, feel, and do at work. The internal environment at SAS, the leading provider of statistical software, is unlike that of most software companies. Instead of expecting employees to work 12- to 14-hour days, SAS has a seven-hour workday and closes its offices at 6 p.m. every evening. Employees receive unlimited sick days each year. To encourage employees to spend time with their families, there's an on-site day care facility, and the company cafeteria has plenty of highchairs and baby seats. Given SAS's internal environment, it shouldn't surprise you that almost no one quits. In a typical software company, 25 percent of the workforce quits each year to take another job. At SAS, only 4 percent leave.[38]

The key component in internal environments is **organizational culture**—that is, the key values, beliefs, and attitudes shared by members of the organization.

LO5 Organizational Cultures: Creation, Success, and Change

*Let's take a closer look at **5.1 how organizational cultures are created and maintained, 5.2 the characteristics of successful organizational cultures,** and **5.3 how companies can accomplish the difficult task of changing organizational cultures.***

5.1 Creating and Maintaining Organizational Cultures

A key source of organizational culture is the company founder. Founders like Bill Gates (Microsoft) create organizations in their own image and imprint them with their beliefs, attitudes, and values. Microsoft employees share founder Bill Gates's determination to stay ahead of software competitors. Says a Microsoft vice president:

"No matter how good your product, you are only 18 months away from failure."[39] Although the founder is instrumental in the creation of the organization's culture, eventually that person retires, dies, or leaves the company. When the founder is gone, how are that person's values, attitudes, and beliefs sustained in the organization? Answer: through stories and heroes.

Members tell **organizational stories** to make sense of events and changes in an organization and to emphasize culturally consistent assumptions, decisions, and actions.[40] At Wal-Mart, stories abound about founder Sam Walton's thriftiness as he strove to make Wal-Mart the low-cost retailer that it is today. Gary Reinboth, one of Wal-Mart's first store managers, tells the following story:

> *In those days, we would go on buying trips with Sam, and we'd all stay, as much as we could, in one room or two. I remember one time in Chicago when we stayed eight of us to a room. And the room wasn't very big to begin with. You might say we were on a pretty restricted budget.*[41]

Sam Walton's thriftiness permeates Wal-Mart to this day. Everyone flies coach rather than business or first class—and that includes top executives and the CEO. When employees travel on business, it's still the norm for them to share rooms (although two to a room, not eight!) at relatively inexpensive motels. Likewise, Wal-Mart will reimburse only up to $15 per meal on business travel, which is half to one-third the reimbursement rate at companies of similar size. (Remember, Wal-Mart is one of the largest companies in the world.)

A second way in which organizational culture is sustained is by recognizing and celebrating heroes. **Organizational heroes** are admired for their qualities and achievements within the organization. Clive Beddoe, founding shareholder, past president, and now chairman of the board of WestJet, earned his reputation for being a hands-on leader partly owing to his practice of spending time at airports across the country during the busy Christmas travel season, doing whatever was needed to help out, checking and loading bags, and even changing an airplane tire on one occasion. Besides not shying away from the front lines, Beddoe was known to celebrate the company's success randomly with employees, once renting out a sports bar in Calgary to throw a staff party for 700 employees *just because*—no official reason or milestone was being celebrated. The company continues to grow and prosper in a difficult industry, and earned the title of Canada's Most Admired Corporate Culture in 2005, 2006, 2007, 2008, and 2011.[42]

5.2 Successful Organizational Cultures

Preliminary research shows that organizational culture is related to business success. As shown in Exhibit 3.5, cultures based on adaptability, involvement, a clear vision, and consistency can help companies achieve higher profits, quality, sales growth, return on assets, and employee satisfaction.[43]

Adaptability is the ability to notice and respond to changes in the organization's environment. Cultures need to reinforce important values and behaviours; but at the same time, a culture becomes dysfunctional if it prevents change.

Organizational stories stories told by members to make sense of events and changes in an organization and to emphasize culturally consistent assumptions, decisions, and actions

Organizational heroes people celebrated for their qualities and achievements within an organization

Company vision a business's purpose or reason for existing

In cultures that promote higher levels of *employee involvement* in decision making, employees feel a greater sense of ownership and responsibility. Employee involvement has been part of the WestJet corporate culture since the Calgary-based airline was founded in 1996. Employees are empowered to rely on their own integrity and decision making to solve WestJet guest problems personally. They can issue flight credits to customers when situations arise such as overbookings or late plane arrivals; they can even order in refreshments for tired passengers who are stranded at the airport. In addition, the Employee Share Purchase Plan means that employees are also "owners" and are integral to the company's success. Recently, the employee-owners were asked to weigh in and provide their opinions during meetings with WestJet executives to discuss possible strategies to help guide the company in the future, in light of the economic challenges facing the airline industry. Company founder Clive Beddoe sums up the role of employees: "If there is one defining lesson to be drawn from WestJet, it's this: Put your employees first."[44]

Company vision is the business's purpose or reason for existing. In organizational cultures with a clear company vision, the organization's strategic purpose and direction are apparent to everyone in the company. At the Four Seasons luxury hotel chain, "treating all others as we would wish to be treated" is the company's Golden

Exhibit 3.5 Keys to Successful Organizational Culture

matis/Shutterstock.com

Consistent organizational culture when a company actively defines and teaches organizational values, beliefs, and attitudes

Rule. It was established by the company's founder, Isadore Sharp, and is the guiding principle that applies to all interactions with guests, business partners, and employees. Besides the Golden Rule, the company's goals, beliefs, and principles are formally communicated to help guide employees in their day-to-day activities and interactions with one another and with guests. As part of annual performance reviews, employees are evaluated on how well they embody the company's values as well as on their achievements in terms of development, mentorship, and interactions with people. President and COO Kathleen Taylor sums up the company's vision when she says: "Our founder had a theory that you couldn't have a guest focus in a luxury hotel business without an employee focus."[45]

Finally, in **consistent organizational cultures**, the company actively defines and teaches organizational values, beliefs, and attitudes. Consistent organizational cultures are also called *strong cultures* because the core beliefs are widely shared and strongly held. Everyone who has ever worked at McDonald's has been taught its four core values: quality, service, cleanliness, and value. Studies show that companies with consistent or strong corporate cultures generally outperform those with inconsistent or weak cultures.[46] Why? Because when core beliefs are widely shared and strongly held, it is easy for everyone to figure out what to do and what *not* to do in their efforts to achieve organizational goals.

Having a consistent or strong organizational culture doesn't guarantee good company performance. When core beliefs are widely shared and strongly held, it is very difficult to bring about needed change. Consequently, a company with a strong culture tends to perform poorly when it needs to adapt to dramatic changes in its external environment. Its consistency sometimes prevents it from adapting to those changes.[47] For example, McDonald's saw its sales and profits decline for a decade after customer eating patterns began to change. To turn around performance, the company developed hospitality and multilingual computer training programs and expanded its menu to include more healthful and snack-oriented selections. More than 5,000 McDonald's restaurants were remodelled over a three-year period; these now feature warmer lighting, upbeat music, flat screen TVs, and WiFi networks. The company's promotional message "I'm lovin' it" has gone from being derided by advertising executives to one of the most recognizable jingles in any market.[48]

5.3 Changing Organizational Cultures

As shown in Exhibit 3.6, organizational cultures exist on three levels.[49] On the first, or surface, level are the elements that can be seen and observed, such as symbolic artifacts (e.g., dress codes and office layouts) and workers' and managers' behaviours. Next, just below the surface, are the values and beliefs expressed by people in the company. You can't see these values and beliefs, but they become clear if you listen carefully to what people say and to how decisions are made or explained. Finally, there are unconsciously held assumptions and beliefs about the company, which are buried deep below the surface. These are the unwritten views and rules that are so strongly held and so widely shared that they are rarely discussed or even thought about unless someone attempts to change them or unknowingly violates them. Changing such assumptions and beliefs can be very difficult. Instead, managers should focus on the parts of the organizational culture they can control. These include observable surface-level items, such as workers' behaviours and symbolic artifacts, and expressed values and beliefs, which can be influenced through employee selection.

In 2002, a major ownership change occurred at Yellow Media (famous for its telephone directories and formerly known as Yellow Pages Group) when the company became independent. The resulting reorganization saw the exit of many senior managers at a time when competition in the industry was beginning to heat up and when the need to adapt to new technologies was apparent. According to Marc Tellier, president at the time, these changes created an opportunity for the company to change its corporate attitude from one of entitlement to one that would promote excellence.

Managers adopted a back-to-basics approach, examining the type of corporate culture they wanted and then giving

Exhibit 3.6 Three Levels of Organizational Culture

SEEN (Surface level)
- Symbolic artifacts such as dress codes
- Workers' and managers' behaviours

HEARD (Expressed values & beliefs)
- What people say
- How decisions are made and explained

BELIEVED (Unconscious assumptions & beliefs)
- Widely shared assumptions and beliefs
- Buried deep below surface
- Rarely discussed or thought about

© Thinkstock/Jupiterimages

thought to what values and behaviours were needed to achieve that vision. The desire for a customer-focused and performance-based culture emerged. With that, six values or "ground rules" were developed to help guide employee behaviour: customer focus, compete to win, teamwork, passion, respect, and open communication.[50] To communicate the new values and ultimately achieve the desired corporate philosophy, management used traditional communication channels with a twist, printing the six values on employee security passes and running town-hall-style meetings to spread the vision of the "new" Yellow Pages.[51] In addition, the company refocused its selection process for new hires, looking for individuals with values and beliefs consistent with the company's desired culture.

To facilitate the new organizational direction in a tangible way, the company brought its Montreal and Laval offices together in a new centralized head office complete with on-site fitness facility (with free memberships, organized walking groups, and instructor-led fitness classes); a healthy eating cafeteria; self-serve kitchen areas on every floor; outdoor eating areas to take advantage of the beautiful view of the St. Lawrence River; transit subsidies for employees; and a car pool sign-up system. Employees can listen to music while working and can participate in the many employee sports teams and social events organized throughout the year. As well, skills development is encouraged through tuition subsidies for courses or professional accreditations, in-house and online training programs, and a formal mentoring program.[52] Besides the visible transformation, changes to management and employee behaviours have been made to facilitate the new corporate culture. For example, employee opinions were solicited in the development of the company's six ground rules; some internal processes were redesigned to encourage greater individual accountability; senior management spent a day a week working alongside the sales force; and focus groups were established to provide feedback on the new head office location.[53]

The experience at Yellow Media demonstrates that although it is a daunting task, changes to corporate culture can be accomplished. As Josée Dykun, VP of Human Resources, explains, "strong corporate culture translates into alignment, performance and then financial results."[54] According to the *2010 Corporate Culture Study by Waterstone Human Capital*, 71 percent of respondents say their organization's corporate culture drives sales and revenue. According to Marty Parker, managing director of Waterstone Human Capital, organizations with successful corporate cultures place a high priority on creating great workplaces for their employees; however, they also enjoy financial returns. "Organizations want to deliver to their stakeholders and shareholders, and those with strong corporate cultures, quite simply, outperform their peers." In 2011, the top 10 companies on Canada's 10 Most Admired Corporate Cultures list outpaced the S&P/TSX by an average of over 1,300 percent in terms of three-year average revenue growth, and by over 700 percent in compound annual growth. All in all, a strong corporate culture is associated with more productive employees, greater customer satisfaction, better innovation, stronger confidence to develop new strategies, and improved hiring and employee retention; all of these have a positive impact on company performance.[55] See Exhibit 3.7 for a list of the 10 most admired Canadian corporate cultures.

Exhibit 3.7 Canada's 10 Most Admired Corporate Cultures (2011)

1. Agrium Inc. (Calgary)
2. CIBC (Toronto)
3. Coast Capital Savings Credit Union (Surrey)
4. ING Direct Canada (Toronto)
5. Kinross Gold Corporation (Toronto)
6. Ledcor Group of Companies (Vancouver)
7. Loblaw Companies Limited (Brampton)
8. RBC (Toronto)
9. Shoppers Drug Mart (Toronto)
10. WestJet Airlines (Calgary)

Source: Waterstone Human Capital Ltd. Reprinted by permission.

It's obvious that many organizations believe that developing and maintaining the right corporate culture is integral to success. In Waterstone Capital's 2010 Corporate Culture Study, 77 per cent of respondents said they measured their organization's corporate culture (since the first study results in 2006, this number had more than doubled). For example, management at Starbucks Canada asks employees to complete a Partner View Survey (Starbucks employees are considered "partners") every 18 months; the purpose is to measure the corporate culture. Participants are asked questions relating to job satisfaction and commitment to the company to help gauge how the company is doing in terms of one of its key values, which is, creating a great work environment for all partners. Although the survey is voluntary, by encouraging partners to complete the survey online at their individual store (on company time), and using the feedback to implement company-wide changes and initiatives, the company has achieved a greater than 90 percent participation rate. Survey results are compared to Starbucks operations in other countries and to the entire Starbucks organization; they are also tracked over time to see whether improvements are being made. According to Starbucks Canada President Colin Moore, "the Partner View Survey is a quantitative way for us to continue to ensure we're doing things that are consistent with our guiding principles and what we say we're going to do." Graham Lowe, founding partner of the Great Place to Work Institute Canada, in Kelowna, B.C., believes that "it's only now being recognized that an organization's culture can be a strategic advantage."[56]

4 Ethics and Social Responsibility

LEARNING OUTCOMES

LO1 Identify common kinds of workplace deviance.

LO2 Describe ethics guidelines and legislation in North America.

LO3 Describe what influences ethical decision making.

LO4 Explain what practical steps managers can take to improve ethical decision making.

LO5 Explain to whom organizations are socially responsible.

LO6 Explain for what organizations are socially responsible.

LO7 Explain how organizations can choose to respond to societal demands for social responsibility.

LO8 Explain whether social responsibility hurts or helps an organization's economic performance.

Today, it's not enough for companies to make a profit. We also expect managers to make a profit by doing the right things. Unfortunately, no matter what managers decide to do, someone or some group will be unhappy with the outcome. Managers don't have the luxury of choosing theoretically optimal, win–win solutions that are obviously desirable to everyone involved. In practice, solutions to ethical and social responsibility problems aren't optimal. Often, managers must be satisfied with a solution that just makes do or does the least harm. Rights and wrongs are rarely crystal clear to managers charged with doing the right thing; the business world is much messier than that.

What Is Ethical and Unethical Workplace Behaviour?

Ethics is the set of moral principles or values that defines right and wrong for a person or group. In a work environment, individuals at every level of an organization make decisions on a daily basis with respect to how to behave and what course of action to take, often relying on their own personal ethical principles to guide them. The Ethics Resource Center (ERC) conducts a biennial survey on ethics in the business world, examining the trends in business ethics from the perspective of the employee. According to the latest survey (2011), 45 percent of employees reported having observed misconduct in the workplace, with 65 percent of those reporting the misconduct, and 13 percent of employees said they had felt pressured to compromise their standards in order to do their jobs.[1]

The study identified two key influences reflected in today's business environment: the state of the economy, and the increased use of technology at work. During a period of economic difficulty, "the decisions and behaviours of their leaders are perceived by employees as a heightened commitment to ethics. As a result, employees adopt a higher standard of conduct for themselves."[2] In addition, the increased use of the Internet in the workplace, including social networking, presents new challenges in terms of ethical behaviour. Active social networkers (defined as employees who spend at least 30 percent of their workday on social network sites) have a more tolerant attitude toward a number of workplace behaviours. Half of active social networkers believe it is acceptable to keep copies of confidential work documents for possible use in future jobs, compared to 15 percent of non-active social networkers. In addition, active social networkers are more likely to buy personal items with the company credit card, take home company software, and share less than flattering information about their workplace on personal social networking sites.[3]

A previous ERC survey explored the implications of online social networks and found that 74 percent of employees surveyed believed that it was possible to damage a company's reputation through social media; however, 53 percent believed that their social networking pages were none of their employers' business.[4]

Other studies contain more positive news, highlighting that ethics is a growing concern among employees. Ninety-four percent of respondents said it was either vital or important that the company they work for be ethical; and 82 percent of a group of employees surveyed said "they would work for less to be at a company that had ethical business practices, and more than a third left a job because they disagreed with the actions of fellow employees or managers."[5] A 2010 study reported that nearly half of employees seeking new employment cited a loss of trust in their employer resulting from how business decisions were made as a reason for leaving.[6]

According to Sharon Allen, Chairman of Deloitte LLP, "regardless of the economic environment, business leaders should be mindful of the significant impact that trust in the workplace and transparent communication can have on talent management and retention strategies. By establishing a values-based culture, organizations can cultivate the trust necessary to reduce turnover and mitigate unethical behavior."[7] In short, much needs to be done to make workplaces more ethical, but—and this is very important—most managers and employees want this to happen.

Ethics the set of moral principles or values that defines right and wrong for a person or group

Ethical behaviour behaviour that conforms to a society's accepted principles of right and wrong

Workplace deviance unethical behaviour that violates organizational norms about right and wrong

Production deviance unethical behaviour that hurts the quality and quantity of work produced

LO1 Workplace Deviance

Ethical behaviour follows accepted principles of right and wrong. Depending on which study you look at, however, one-third to three-quarters of all employees admit that they have stolen from their employer, committed computer fraud, embezzled funds, vandalized company property, sabotaged company projects, faked injuries to receive workers' compensation benefits or insurance, or been "sick" from work when they weren't really sick. Experts estimate that unethical behaviours like these, which researchers call *workplace deviance*, may cost companies nearly $3.5 trillion a year, or roughly 5 percent of their revenues.[8]

Workplace deviance is unethical behaviour that violates organizational norms about right and wrong. As Exhibit 4.1 shows (see page 52), workplace deviance can be categorized by how deviant the behaviour is, from minor to serious, and by the target of the deviant behaviour—whether it is the organization or particular people in the workplace.[9]

Company-related deviance can affect both tangible and intangible assets. One kind of workplace deviance, **production deviance**, hurts the quality and quantity of

Property deviance unethical behaviour aimed at the organization's property or products

Employee shrinkage employee theft of company merchandise

Political deviance using one's influence to harm others in the company

Personal aggression hostile or aggressive behaviour toward others

work produced. Examples include leaving early, taking excessively long work breaks, intentionally working more slowly, or wasting resources. **Property deviance** is unethical behaviour aimed at company property or products. Examples include sabotaging, stealing, damaging equipment or products, and overcharging for services and then pocketing the difference. Fifty-eight percent of office workers acknowledge taking company property for personal use, according to a survey conducted for *Lawyers.com*.[10] Property deviance also includes the sabotage of company property, such as using "software bombs" to destroy company programs and data.[11]

The theft of company merchandise by employees, called **employee shrinkage**, is another common form of property deviance. Retail shrinkage costs Canadian retailers on average over $10.8 million per shopping day, over $4 billion annually, and approximately 1.04 percent of sales.[12] Small and independent businesses feel the negative impact of shrinkage even more since they often have fewer resources and less effective theft controls in place. This means that losses experienced by smaller businesses have a greater impact than they would in larger organizations.[13]

Retail employees use a variety of methods to commit crimes against their employers: leaving the store with merchandise; stashing unloaded merchandise in dumpsters and then returning after their shift to retrieve it (referred to as "dumpster diving"); acting as "sweethearts" for friends and family by discounting purchases; not charging for items at the checkout counter; allowing refunds with no receipts; or passing on credit card numbers to process gift cards.[14]

Whereas production and property deviance harm companies, political deviance and personal aggression are unethical behaviours that hurt particular people within companies. **Political deviance** involves using one's influence to harm others in the company. Examples include making decisions based on favouritism rather than performance, spreading rumours about coworkers, or blaming others for mistakes they didn't make. **Personal aggression** is hostile or aggressive behaviour toward others. Examples include sexual harassment, verbal abuse, stealing from coworkers, or personally threatening coworkers. One of the fastest-growing kinds of personal aggression is workplace violence. Almost one in five violent incidents in Canada occurs in the workplace of the victim, and 71 percent of all incidents of workplace violence are physical assaults.[15]

Exhibit 4.1 Types of Workplace Deviance

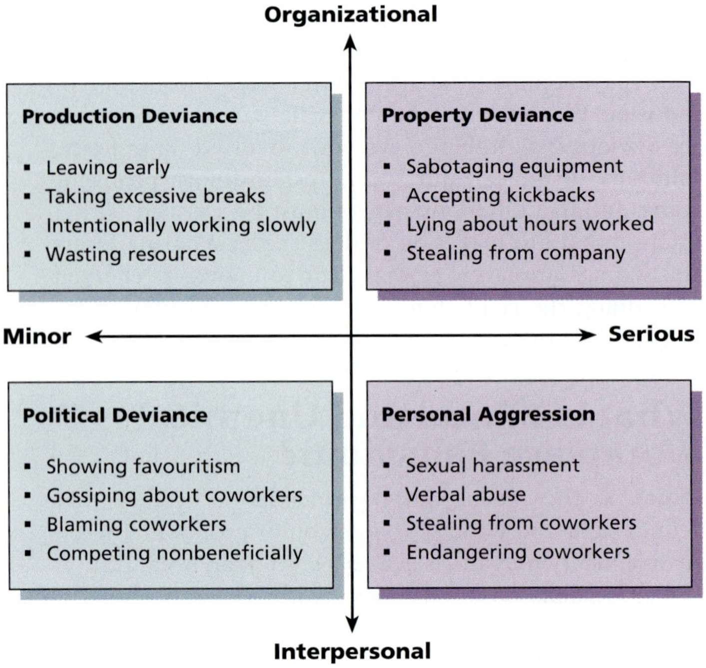

Organizational (top) — Interpersonal (bottom); Minor (left) — Serious (right)

	Minor	Serious
Organizational	**Production Deviance** ▪ Leaving early ▪ Taking excessive breaks ▪ Intentionally working slowly ▪ Wasting resources	**Property Deviance** ▪ Sabotaging equipment ▪ Accepting kickbacks ▪ Lying about hours worked ▪ Stealing from company
Interpersonal	**Political Deviance** ▪ Showing favouritism ▪ Gossiping about coworkers ▪ Blaming coworkers ▪ Competing nonbeneficially	**Personal Aggression** ▪ Sexual harassment ▪ Verbal abuse ▪ Stealing from coworkers ▪ Endangering coworkers

Source: S. L. Robinson & R. J. Bennett, "A Typology of Deviant Workplace Behaviors," (Figure), *Academy Management Journal*, 1995, Vol 38.

LO2 Ethics Guidelines and Legislation in North America

At present there is no national ethics legislation in Canada. However, in 1997 an International Code of Ethics was released by a group of Canadian companies to provide a general guideline for acceptable standards of conduct when doing business at home and in other countries. As illustrated in Exhibit 4.2, this voluntary code covers issues relating to community participation, environmental protection, human rights, business conduct, and employee rights. The code is intended to establish Canadian businesses as respected members of the global business community and is supported by the Department of Foreign Affairs and International Trade.[16]

Penalties for unethical behaviour can be substantial, with maximum fines approaching $300 million!

In the United States, the establishment of the US Sentencing Commission Guidelines for Organizations in 1991 signalled a change in the legal approach to handling unethical activities in business. Until that time, a company that was unaware of an employee's unethical activities could not be held responsible; however, since the new guidelines were established, companies can be prosecuted and punished *even if management doesn't know about the unethical behaviour*. Penalties can be substantial, with maximum fines approaching $300 million.[17] A 2004 amendment outlines much stricter ethics training requirements and emphasizes creating company cultures that value legal and ethical behaviour.[18]

Exhibit 4.2 International Code of Ethics for Canadian Business Principles

A. Concerning community participation and environmental protection, we will:
- strive within our sphere of influence to ensure a fair share of benefits to stakeholders impacted by our activities;
- ensure meaningful and transparent consultation with all stakeholders and attempt to integrate our corporate activities with local communities as good corporate citizens;
- ensure our activities are consistent with sound environmental management and conservation practices; and
- provide meaningful opportunities for technology cooperation, training and capacity building within the host nation.

B. Concerning human rights, we will:
- support and respect the protection of international human rights within our sphere of influence; and
- not be complicit in human rights abuses.

C. Concerning business conduct, we will:
- not make illegal and improper payments and bribes and will refrain from participating in any corrupt business practices;
- comply with all applicable laws and conduct business activities with integrity; and
- ensure contractors', suppliers', and agents' activities are consistent with these principles.

D. Concerning employee rights and health and safety, we will:
- ensure health and safety of workers is protected;
- strive for social justice and respect freedom of association and expression in the workplace; and
- ensure consistency with other universally accepted labour standards related to exploitation of child labour, forced labour and non-discrimination in employment.

Source: W. Cragg and K. McKague, "Compendium of Ethics Codes and Instruments of Corporate Responsibility," Toronto: Schulich School of Business York University, 2005.

How Do You Make Ethical Decisions?

On a cold morning in the midst of a winter storm, schools were closed, and most people had decided to stay home from work. Nevertheless, Richard Addessi had already showered, shaved, and dressed for the office. He kissed his wife Joan goodbye, but before he could get to his car, he fell dead on the garage floor of a sudden heart attack. Addessi was four months short of his 30-year anniversary with the company. Having begun work at IBM at the age of 18, he was just 48 years old.[19]

You're the vice president in charge of benefits at IBM. Given that he was only four months short of full retirement, do you award full retirement benefits to Richard Addessi's wife and daughters? If the answer is yes, they will receive his full retirement benefits of $1,800 a month and free lifetime medical coverage. If you say

Forget the Customers, Who's Watching Your Employees?

Employee theft can range from taking an extra plate of french fries without payment to being part of "a very sophisticated network of friends" facilitating theft and subsequent resale of items inside and outside of store operations. If you compare a dishonest retail employee to a typical shoplifter, the employee is far more harmful to the organization. Dishonest employees go to the same place every day, and the more they learn about the business, the more familiar they become with the tools that the loss prevention department employs. Ultimately they become more effective at stealing. Alcohol, apparel, and cosmetics are the most targeted categories and are highly resellable. Kaileen Millard-Ruff, director of retail at Toronto-based Match Marketing Group, said that technology now gives retail employees a greater opportunity than they would have had in the past to partner with external criminal networks, or resell goods anonymously online through sites such as eBay and Kijiji.

Source: H. Shaw, "Workers steal 33% of all goods that go missing at retailers: survey," *The Financial Post*, 31 October 2012, available at: http://business.financialpost.com/2012/10/31/workers-steal-33-of-all-goods-that-go-missing-at-retailers-survey/

Stockbyte/Getty Images

Ethical intensity the degree of concern people have about an ethical issue

Magnitude of consequences the total harm or benefit derived from an ethical decision

Social consensus agreement on whether behaviour is bad or good

Probability of effect the chance that something will happen and then harm others

Temporal immediacy the time between an act and the consequences the act produces

Proximity of effect the social, psychological, cultural, or physical distance between a decision maker and those affected by his or her decisions

no, his widow and two daughters will receive only $340 a month. They will also have to pay $473 a month just to continue their current medical coverage. As the VP in charge of benefits at IBM, what is the ethical thing for you to do?

LO3 Influences on Ethical Decision Making

Although some ethical issues are easily solved, many do not have clearly right or wrong answers. Although the answers are rarely clear, managers do need to have a clear sense of *how* to arrive at an answer in order to manage this ethical ambiguity well.

*The ethical answers that managers choose depend on **3.1 the ethical intensity of the decision, 3.2 the moral development of the manager, and 3.3 the ethical principles used to solve the problem.***

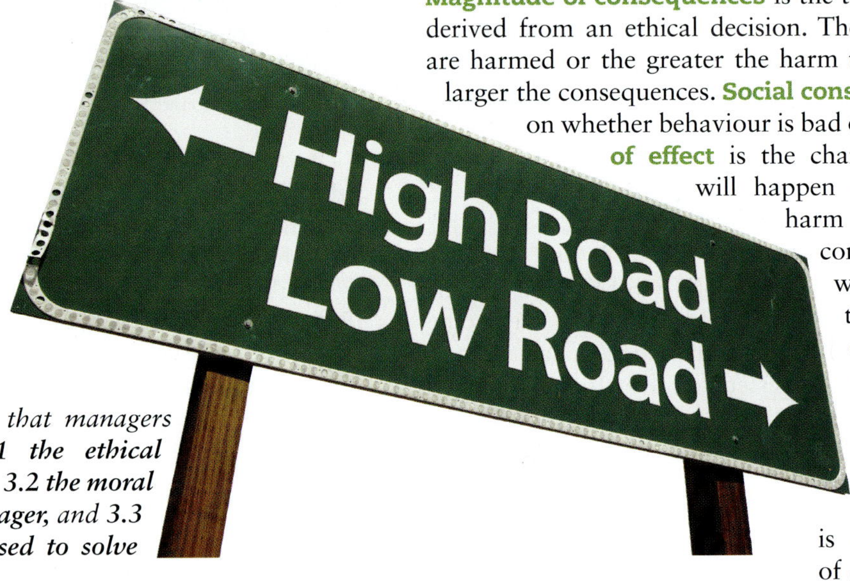

Andy Dean Photography/Shutterstock.com

3.1 Ethical Intensity of the Decision

Managers don't treat all ethical decisions the same. The manager who has to decide whether to deny or extend full benefits to Joan Addessi and her family is going to treat that decision much more seriously than the decision of how to deal with an assistant who has been taking computer paper home for personal use. These decisions differ in their **ethical intensity**, or the degree of concern people have about an ethical issue. When addressing an issue of high ethical intensity, managers are more aware of the impact their decision will have on others. They are more likely to view the decision as an ethical or moral decision rather than as an economic decision. They are also more likely to worry about doing the right thing.

Exhibit 4.3 Six Factors That Contribute to Ethical Intensity

Magnitude of consequences
Social consensus
Probability of effect
Temporal immediacy
Proximity of effect
Concentration of effect

Source: T.M. Jones, "Ethical Decision Making by Individuals in Organizations: An Issue Contingent Model," *Academy of Management Review* 16 (1991) 366–395.

Six factors must be taken into account when determining the ethical intensity of an action, as shown in Exhibit 4.3. **Magnitude of consequences** is the total harm or benefit derived from an ethical decision. The more people who are harmed or the greater the harm to those people, the larger the consequences. **Social consensus** is agreement on whether behaviour is bad or good. **Probability of effect** is the chance that something will happen and then result in harm to others. If we combine these factors, we can see the effect they can have on ethical intensity. For example, if there is *clear agreement* (social consensus) that a managerial decision or action is *certain* (probability of effect) to have *large negative consequences* (magnitude of consequences) in some way, then people will be highly concerned about that managerial decision or action, and ethical intensity will be high. Although Addessi's family will be profoundly affected by the decision, they are one family, and the magnitude of consequences and possibility of effect beyond them would be quite low if IBM decided to deny the benefits.

Although some ethical issues are easily solved, many do not have clearly right or wrong answers.

Temporal immediacy is the time between an act and the consequences the act produces. Temporal immediacy is stronger if a manager has to lay off workers next week as opposed to three months from now. **Proximity of effect** is the social, psychological, cultural, or physical distance of a decision maker from those affected by his or her decisions. Thus, proximity of effect is greater for the manager who works with employees who are to be laid off than it is for a manager who works where no layoffs will occur. If the person responsible for the decision were Addessi's direct supervisor, who had known him and his family throughout his tenure at the company, the ethical intensity would be higher than it would be for an executive who had never met him. Finally, whereas the magnitude of consequences is the total effect across all people, **concentration of effect** is how much an act affects the average person. Temporarily laying off 100 employees for 10 months without pay is a greater concentration of effect than temporarily laying off 1,000 employees for one month.

Which of these six factors has the most impact on ethical intensity? Studies indicate that managers are much more likely to view decisions as ethical when the magnitude of consequences (total harm) is high and there is a social consensus (agreement) that a behaviour or action is bad.[20]

3.2 Moral Development

A colleague at work has given you a pirated copy of the latest movie blockbuster. She left you a USB key in an envelope on your desk with a note saying that you should make a copy for yourself and get it back to her in a couple of days. You're tempted. No one would find out. Even if someone does, the movie studio isn't going to come after you. You don't plan on making copies of the movie to sell it, so does it really matter? What would you do?

In part, according to psychologist Lawrence Kohlberg, your decision will be based on your level of moral development. Kohlberg identified three phases of moral development with two stages in each phase (see Exhibit 4.4).[21] At the **preconventional level of moral development**, people decide based on selfish reasons. For example, if you are in Stage 1, the punishment and obedience stage, your primary concern will be to avoid trouble for yourself. So you won't copy the movie because you are afraid of being caught and punished. Yet in Stage 2, the instrumental exchange stage, you worry less about punishment and more about doing things that directly advance your wants and needs. So you copy the movie.

People at the **conventional level of moral development** make decisions that conform to societal expectations. In other words, they look to others for guidance on ethical issues. In Stage 3, the "good boy, nice girl" stage, you normally do what the other "good boys" and "nice girls" are doing. If everyone else is illegally copying movies, you will, too. But if they aren't, you won't either. In the law and order stage, Stage 4, you again look for external guidance, but do whatever the *law* permits, so you won't copy the software.

People at the **postconventional level of moral development** use internalized ethical principles to solve ethical dilemmas. In Stage 5, the social contract stage, you will refuse to copy the movie because, as a whole, society is better off when the rights of others—in this case, the rights of entertainment companies and movie studios—are not violated. In Stage 6, the universal principle stage, you might or might not copy the movie, depending on your principles of right and wrong. Moreover, you will stick to your principles even if your decision conflicts with the law (Stage 4) or what others believe is best for society (Stage 5). For example, those with socialist or communist beliefs might choose to copy the movie because they believe that goods and services should be owned by society rather than by individuals and corporations.

Kohlberg believed that people would progress sequentially from earlier to later stages as they became more educated and mature. But only 20 percent of adults ever reach the postconventional stage of moral development where internal principles guide their decisions. Most adults are in the conventional stage of moral development and look to others for guidance on ethical issues. This means that most people in the workplace look to and need leadership when it comes to ethical decision making.[22]

3.3 Principles of Ethical Decision Making

Beyond an issue's ethical intensity and a manager's level of moral maturity, the particular ethical principles that managers use will also affect how they solve ethical dilemmas. Unfortunately, there is no one ideal principle to use when making ethical business decisions. According to Professor LaRue Hosmer, a number of different ethical principles can be used to make business decisions: long-term self-interest, personal virtue, religious injunctions, government requirements, utilitarian benefits, individual rights, and distributive justice.[23] All of these ethical principles encourage managers and employees to take others' interests into account when making ethical decisions. At the same time, however, these principles can lead to very different ethical actions, as we can see by using these principles

Concentration of effect the total harm or benefit that an act produces on the average person

Preconventional level of moral development the first level of moral development, in which people make decisions based on selfish reasons

Conventional level of moral development the second level of moral development, in which people make decisions that conform to societal expectations

Postconventional level of moral development the third level of moral development, in which people make decisions based on internalized principles

Exhibit 4.4 Kohlberg's Stages of Moral Development

Stage 1	Stage 2	Stage 3	Stage 4	Stage 5	Stage 6
Punishment and Obedience	Instrumental Exchange	Good Boy, Nice Girl	Law and Order	Social Contract	Universal Principle
Preconventional		Conventional		Postconventional	
Self-Interest		Societal Expectations		Internalized Principles	

Source: W. Davidson III & D. Worrell, "Influencing Managers to Change Unpopular Corporate Behavior through Boycotts and Divestitures," *Business & Society* 34 (1995): 171–196.

Brian A Jackson/Shutterstock.com

Principle of long-term self-interest an ethical principle that holds that you should never take any action that is not in your or your organization's long-term self-interest

Principle of personal virtue an ethical principle that holds that you should never do anything that is not honest, open, and truthful and that you would not be glad to see reported in the newspapers or on TV

Principle of religious injunctions an ethical principle that holds that you should never take any action that is not kind and that does not build a sense of community

Principle of government requirements an ethical principle that holds that you should never take any action that violates the law, for the law represents the minimal moral standard

Principle of utilitarian benefits an ethical principle that holds that you should never take any action that does not result in greater good for society

Principle of individual rights an ethical principle that holds that you should never take any action that infringes on others' agreed-upon rights

Principle of distributive justice an ethical principle that holds that you should never take any action that harms the least fortunate among us: the poor, the uneducated, the unemployed

to decide whether to award full benefits to Joan Addessi and her children.

According to the **principle of long-term self-interest**, you should never take any action that is not in your or your organization's long-term self-interest. Although this sounds as if the principle promotes selfishness, it doesn't. What we do to maximize our long-term interests (save more, spend less, exercise every day, watch what we eat) is often very different from what we do to maximize short-term interests (max out our credit cards, be couch potatoes, eat whatever we want). At any given time, IBM has nearly 1,000 employees who are just months away from retirement. Because of the costs involved, it serves IBM's long-term interest to pay full benefits only after employees have put in their 30 years.

The **principle of personal virtue** holds that you should never do anything that is not honest, open, and truthful and that you would not be glad to see reported in the newspapers or on TV. Using the principle of personal virtue, IBM should quietly award Joan Addessi her husband's full benefits, avoiding the potential for negative media coverage.

The **principle of religious injunctions** holds that you should never take an action that is unkind or that harms a sense of community, such as the positive feelings that come from working together to accomplish a commonly accepted goal. Using this principle, IBM would be concerned foremost with compassion and kindness and award full benefits to Joan Addessi.

According to the **principle of government requirements**, the law represents the minimal moral standards of society, so you should never take any action that violates the law. Using this principle, IBM would deny full benefits to Joan Addessi because her husband did not work for the company for 30 years.

The **principle of utilitarian benefits** states that you should never take an action that does not result in greater good for society. In short, you should do whatever creates the greatest good for the greatest number. At first, this principle seems to suggest that IBM should award full benefits to Joan Addessi. If IBM did this with any regularity, however, the costs would be enormous, profits would shrink, and IBM would have to cut its stock dividend, harming countless shareholders, many of whom rely on IBM dividends for their retirement income. In this case, the principle does not lead to a clear choice.

The **principle of individual rights** holds that you should never take an action that infringes on others' agreed-upon rights. Using this principle, IBM would deny Joan Addessi full benefits. If it carefully followed the rules specified in its pension plan and granted Mrs. Addessi due process, meaning the right to appeal the decision, then IBM would not be violating her rights. In fact, it could be argued that providing full benefits to Mrs. Addessi would violate the rights of employees who had to wait 30 years to receive full benefits.

Finally, under the **principle of distributive justice**, you should never take any action that harms the least fortunate among us in some way. This principle is designed to protect the poor, the uneducated, and the unemployed. Although Joan Addessi could probably find a job, it's unlikely that she could easily find one that would support her and her daughters in the manner to which they were accustomed after she had spent 20 years as a stay-at-home mom. Using the principle of distributive justice, IBM would award her full benefits.

As mentioned at the beginning of this chapter, one of the practical aspects of ethical decisions is that no matter *what* you decide, someone or some group will be unhappy. This corollary is also true: No matter *how* you decide, someone or some group will be unhappy. Some will argue that you should have used a different principle or weighed concerns differently. Consequently, although all of these ethical principles encourage managers to balance others' needs against their own, they can also lead to very different ethical actions. So even when managers strive to be ethical, there are often no clear answers when it comes to doing the right thing. So, what did IBM decide to do? Since Richard Addessi had not completed 30 full years with the company, IBM officials felt they had no choice but to give Joan Addessi and her two daughters the smaller, partial retirement benefits. Do you think IBM's decision was ethical? It's likely many of you don't. You may wonder how the company could be so heartless

Nortel Falls from Grace

corgarashu/Shutterstock.com

It took over 10 years of litigation and court proceedings for the senior Nortel executives to finally hear the judge's verdict. It finally came in January 2013, as one the largest criminal trials in Canada's corporate history finally came to an end. Three ex-Nortel senior executives had been accused of manipulating accounting statements that shrouded the company's financial performance and led to the payout of more than $12 million in bonuses and share payments to themselves. Nortel was once considered a corporate Canadian success story, benefiting from the technology boom in 1999–2000 that helped propel the company's share price to a high of $124.50. In its heyday, this multinational telecommunications company had a roster of more than 90,000 employees and a corporate value of over $300 billion. Nortel's fall from grace began following the technology crash of 2000–01, when the company found itself in a fragile financial state, which would be further weakened by allegations that the company's CEO, CFO, and controller had doctored the books in 2002–03 to present a stronger financial position to their shareholders and the public. It wasn't long before the company's shares began to plummet, falling to penny-stock status. Then in 2009, the company filed for bankruptcy with large debts and even larger legal issues facing them. Many speculated whether the case would result in a harsh ruling for Nortel's owners, similar to the Enron case in the United States. However, the judge in his final ruling concluded that although Nortel had a history of setting up inflated accounting reserves, "the burden [of proof] in my view was not met" in terms of the accounting decisions that formed the basis of the case.

Sources: L. Nguyen, "Former Nortel execs to learn fate today," *Calgary Herald,* 13 January, 2013, available at: http://thechronicleherald.ca/business/425155-former-nortel-execs-to-learn-fate-today; J. McFarland and J. Blackwell, "Three former Nortel executives found not guilty of fraud," *The Globe and Mail,* 14 January 2013, available at: http://www.theglobeandmail.com/globe-investor/former-nortel-executives-claim-vindication-after-fraud-acquittal/article7319241/; L. Taylor, "Nortel verdict: pensioners not surprised by verdict but observers consider it a black mark," *The Toronto Star,* 14 January 2013, available at: http://www.thestar.com/business/companies/nortel/article/1314742--nortel-verdict-pensioners-not-surprised-now-await-outcome-of-mediation

as to deny Richard Addessi's family the full benefits to which you believe they were entitled. Yet others might argue that IBM did the ethical thing by strictly following the rules laid out in its pension benefit plan. Indeed, an IBM spokesperson stated that making exceptions would violate the country's federal Employee Retirement Income Security Act of 1974. After all, being fair means applying the rules to everyone.

LO4 Practical Steps to Ethical Decision Making

Managers can encourage more ethical decision making in their organizations by ***4.1 carefully selecting and hiring ethical employees, 4.2 establishing a specific code of ethics, 4.3 training employees to make ethical decisions,*** *and* ***4.4 creating an ethical climate.***

4.1 Selecting and Hiring Ethical Employees

As an employer, you can increase your chances of hiring honest people by giving job applicants integrity tests. **Overt integrity tests** estimate job applicants' honesty by directly asking them what they think or feel about theft or about punishment of unethical behaviours.[24] For example, an employer might ask an applicant, "Don't most people steal from their companies?" Surprisingly, unethical people will usually answer "yes" to such questions, because they believe that the world is basically dishonest and that dishonest behaviour is normal.[25]

Personality-based integrity tests indirectly estimate job applicants' honesty by measuring psychological traits such as dependability and conscientiousness. For example, prison inmates serving time for white-collar crimes (counterfeiting, embezzlement, and fraud) scored much lower than a comparison group of middle-level managers on scales measuring reliability, dependability, honesty, conscientiousness, and abiding by rules.[26] These results show that companies can selectively hire and promote people who will be more ethical.[27]

Overt integrity test a written test that estimates job applicants' honesty by directly asking them what they think or feel about theft or about punishment of unethical behaviours

Personality-based integrity test a written test that indirectly estimates job applicants' honesty by measuring psychological traits, such as dependability and conscientiousness

4.2 Codes of Ethics

Today, almost all large corporations have similar ethics codes in place. Still, two things must happen if those codes are to encourage ethical decision making and behaviour.[28] First, a company must communicate its code inside and outside the company. Johnson & Johnson's credo is an example of a well-communicated code of ethics. With the click of a computer mouse, anyone inside or outside the company can obtain detailed information about the company's specific ethical business practices.

Second, besides having an ethics code with general guidelines like "do unto others as you would have others do unto you," management must develop practical ethical standards and procedures specific to the company's line of business. Canadian Tire has established a set of ethical standards known as its Code of Business Conduct to help direct the actions of employees and individuals who act on behalf of the company. For example, a Canadian Tire employee who is unsure whether to accept an invitation to a business function can refer to the code and find that the expected procedure is to seek approval prior to accepting any invitation and to consider whether the event is relevant to his or her role in the company, whether the event is a networking opportunity, and whether acceptance would reduce his or her ability to be objective in making decisions regarding this business partner. The code is available on the company's website, so it is easily accessible to employees, suppliers, and customers alike. Complaints or concerns regarding potential violations of the code can be submitted to the company using the Business Conduct Hotline, or they can be reported through the company's website as part of the company's Business Conduct Compliance Program.[29]

4.3 Ethics Training

The first objective of ethics training is to develop employees' awareness of ethics.[30] This means helping employees recognize which issues are ethical issues and then avoid rationalizing unethical behaviour by thinking, "This isn't really illegal or immoral" or "No one will ever find out." To ensure that employees of the Royal Bank of Canada understand the company's code of conduct, at least once every two years, employees participate in a Web-based ethics training program that incorporates role plays as well as a testing feature designed to evaluate awareness of company principles and how an employee would respond to an ethical dilemma.[31] Several companies have even created board games to improve awareness of ethical issues.[32] Defence contractor Martin's ethics training program is aimed at creating "A Culture of Trust." Employees form small groups and engage in role playing and dialogue with one another about real-life scenarios such as managing relationships with coworkers, ethical use of company credit cards while on business travel, and managing conflicts of interest. The groups then develop outcomes to the scenarios. Because it is collective, this program not only conveys information about ethical behaviour but also builds accountability and a sense of "we're all in this together."[33]

The second objective for ethics training programs is to achieve credibility with employees. Some companies have hurt the credibility of their ethics programs by having outside instructors and consultants conduct the classes.[34] Employees often complain that outside instructors and consultants are teaching theory that has nothing to do with their work and the practical dilemmas they actually face on a daily basis. Boeing has established a number of ways to educate employees about ethical issues and to help them manage those issues in-house. These include providing ethics advisers who serve as mentors, as well as a disseminating a handbook that outlines how to make ethical decisions and that presents information in response to FAQs. Answers to "What do I do if …?" questions are easily accessible in the handbook and through the company's Ethics Line, which is available to employees throughout the company as well as to concerned stakeholders.[35] Ethics training becomes even more credible when top managers teach the initial ethics classes to their subordinates, who in turn teach their subordinates.[36]

The third objective of ethics training is to teach employees a practical model of ethical decision making. A basic model should help them think about the consequences their choices will have on others

Don't Be Evil

These three words form the basis for the Google Code of Conduct. The "Don't Be Evil" principle helps guide Googlers (Google employees) in how to approach and serve customers in order to provide customers with the best products and services possible, but also extends to how to treat fellow Googlers with respect. According to Google, the code recognizes that "everything we do in connection with our work at Google will be, and should be, measured against the highest possible standards of ethical business conduct. Trust and mutual respect among employees and users are the foundation of our success, and they are something we need to earn every day." Google has a reputation for quirkiness and an unconventional work environment (rooftop miniature golf, relaxation rooms complete with aquariums and massage chairs, music and DJ rooms); even so, they are very serious about their ethics code. It covers topics such as serving users with integrity, treating one another with integrity and respect, addressing conflicts of interest, preserving confidentiality, and protecting Google assets. Googlers are expected to adhere to the code and to bring concerns forward if they feel that fellow Googlers are falling short on their interpretation of the code. For Googlers, failure to follow the code can result in disciplinary action, including termination of employment, but the code also extends to any outside individuals, contractors, or consultants that do business with the company. If you want to read more about the code, google it!

Source: http://investor.google.com/corporate/code-of-conduct.html

Andresr/Shutterstock.com

and consider how they will choose between different solutions. Exhibit 4.5 presents a basic model of ethical decision making.

4.4 Ethical Climate

Organizational culture is key to fostering ethical decision making. Management consultant Andrea Plotnick observes about an ethics code: "You want it to be about embedding the right behaviours and the right decision-making process within everybody in the organization, so that it becomes part of the culture. That is how you will have success."[37] As mentioned previously, economic conditions can also play a role in the ethical climate within organizations. During tough economic times, when a company's future is in jeopardy, management may emphasize the importance of high standards and project a heightened commitment to ethics. As a result, employees may be less inclined to participate in unethical behaviours, adopting a higher standard of conduct for themselves.[38]

The Ethics Research Center cautions that when the economic business environment improves, misconduct may rise unless a strong ethical culture is in place.[39] To achieve such a culture, management must set the tone. Studies have found that the two major drivers of ethics culture are senior executives and supervisors. When researchers ask, "What is the most important influence on your ethical behaviour at work?", the answer comes back, "My manager." The first step in establishing an ethical climate is for managers, especially top managers, to act ethically themselves.[40]

A second step in establishing an ethical climate is for top management to be active in and committed to the company ethics program.[41] Business writer Dayton Fandray says: "You can have ethics offices and officers and training programs and reporting systems, but if the CEO doesn't seem to care, it's all just a sham. It's not surprising to find that the companies that really do care about ethics make a point of including senior management in all of their ethics and compliance programs."[42]

A third step is to put in place a reporting system that encourages managers and employees to report potential ethics violations. **Whistle-blowing**, that is, reporting others' ethics violations, is a difficult step for most people to take. Potential whistle blowers often feel that their reporting won't make an impact and fear that they, and not the ethics violators, will be punished. According to the 2011 National Business Ethics Survey, whistle-blowing is on the rise: 65 percent of employees surveyed said they had reported workplace misconduct when they observed it, compared to 63 percent in 2009 and 58 percent in 2007. However, 22 percent of employees reporting misconduct said they had experienced some form of retaliation as a result of their actions—an increase from 15 percent in 2009 and from 12 percent in 2007. According to the survey, retaliation mainly included being excluded from decisions and work activities by supervisors or management, along with responses from coworkers and supervisors such as verbal abuse or being given the cold shoulder (see Exhibit 4.6 on page 60). Retaliation may cause some employees to leave an organization, which negatively affects employee retention and workplace stability. In the same study, 70 percent of employees who experienced retaliation indicated they planned to leave their current employer within five years, compared to about 40 percent of employees who were not victims of retaliation.[43]

Whistle-blowing reporting others' ethics violations to management or legal authorities

What does the most to discourage whistle blowers, however, is lack of company action on their complaints.[44] Thus, the final step in developing an ethical climate is for management to fairly and consistently punish those who violate the company's code of ethics. Amazingly, not all companies fire ethics violators. In fact, 8 percent of the companies surveyed admitted that they would promote top performers even if they had violated ethical standards.[45]

Exhibit 4.5 A Basic Model of Ethical Decision Making

1. Identify the problem. What makes it an ethical problem? Think in terms of rights, obligations, fairness, relationships, and integrity. How would you define the problem if you stood on the other side of the fence?
2. Identify the constituents. Who has been hurt? Who could be hurt? Who could be helped? Are they willing players, or are they victims? Can you negotiate with them?
3. Diagnose the situation. How did it happen in the first place? What could have prevented it? Is it going to get worse or better? Can the damage now be undone?
4. Analyze your options. Imagine the range of possibilities. Limit yourself to the two or three most manageable. What are the likely outcomes of each? What are the likely costs? Look to the company mission statement or code of ethics for guidance.
5. Make your choice. What is your intention in making this decision? How does it compare with the probable results? Can you discuss the problem with the affected parties before you act? Could you disclose without qualm your decision to your boss, the CEO, the board of directors, your family, or society as a whole?
6. Act. Do what you have to do. Don't be afraid to admit errors. Be as bold in confronting a problem as you were in causing it.

Source: L.A. Berger, "Train All Employees to Solve Ethical Dilemmas," *Best's Review - Life Health Insurance Edition* 95 (1995): 70–80. © A.M. Best Company - used with permission.

Exhibit 4.6 Types of Retaliation Experienced as a Result of Reported Misconduct (2011)

Source: *2011 National Business Ethics Survey.* "Workplace Ethics in Transition" Ethics Resource Center, available online at http://www.ethics.org/nbes/files/FinalNBES-web.pdf. Reprinted by permission of the Ethics Resource Center.

Social responsibility a business's obligation to pursue policies, make decisions, and take actions that benefit society

Shareholder model a view of social responsibility that holds that an organization's overriding goal should be to maximize profit for the benefit of shareholders

What Is Social Responsibility?

Social responsibility is a business's obligation to pursue policies, make decisions, and take actions that benefit society.[46] Unfortunately, because there are strong disagreements over to whom and for what organizations are responsible, it can be difficult for managers to know what socially responsible corporate behaviour is, or what will be perceived as such. A recent McKinsey & Co. study of 1,144 top global executives found that 79 percent predicted that at least some responsibility for dealing with future social and political issues would fall on corporations; only 3 percent, however, said they were doing a good job of dealing with these issues.[47]

LO5 To Whom Are Organizations Socially Responsible?

There are two perspectives regarding to whom organizations are socially responsible: the shareholder model, and the stakeholder model. According to the late Nobel Prize–winning economist Milton Friedman, the only social responsibility that organizations have is to satisfy their owners, that is, company shareholders. This view—the **shareholder model**—holds that the only social responsibility businesses have is to maximize profits. By maximizing profits, the firm maximizes shareholder wealth and satisfaction. More specifically, as profits rise, the company shares owned by shareholders generally increase in value.

Friedman argued that it is socially irresponsible for companies to divert time, money, and attention away from maximizing profits toward social causes and charitable organizations. The first problem, he believed, is that organizations cannot act effectively as moral agents for all company shareholders. Although shareholders are likely to agree on investment issues concerning a company, it's highly unlikely they have common views on what social causes a company should or should not support. Instead of acting as moral agents, Friedman argued, companies should maximize profits for shareholders. Shareholders can then use their time and increased wealth to contribute to the charities, institutions, or social causes they want rather than to those that the company wants.

The second major problem, Friedman said, is that when time, money, and attention are diverted to social causes, market efficiency is undermined.[48] In competitive markets, companies compete for raw materials, talented workers, customers, and investment funds. A company that spends money on social causes will have less money to purchase quality materials or to hire talented workers who can produce valuable products at good prices. If customers find the company's products less desirable, its sales and profits will fall. If profits fall, the company's stock price will decline, and the company will have difficulty attracting investment funds that will allow it to grow.In the end, Friedman argues, diverting the firm's money, time, and resources to social causes hurts customers, suppliers, employees, and shareholders. Russell Roberts, an economist at George

Whistle-Blowing

In Canada, several high-profile cases of whistle-blowing by federal and provincial employees signalled a need for whistle-blowing legislation dealing specifically with public service employees. Former Olympic athlete Myriam Bedard claimed that she had been fired from her marketing job at VIA Rail after questioning invoices from advertising agencies—invoices indicating that public funds intended for government advertising in Quebec had been misused. This cracked open what would later be referred to as the Sponsorship Scandal. In 2004, Dr. Shiv Chopra and two other scientists were fired from their jobs at Health Canada after criticizing the department's drug approval processes and expressing concern over public health and safety in relation to the bovine growth hormone used in meat and milk production. As a result, Ontario's Public Service Act of 1993 was passed; later, in 2005, the Public Servants Disclosure Protection Act signalled "the federal government's broader commitment to ensure transparency, accountability, financial responsibility and ethical conduct in the public sector."

Sources: Whistleblower legislation Bill C-25, Disclosure Protection. *CBC News Online*, 28 April 2004. Accessed from: http://www.cbc.ca/news/background/whistleblower; A. Nikiforuk, "Bum Steer," *Globe and Mail*, 29 September 2006; D. Johansen and S. Spano, Bill C-11 The Public Servants Disclosure Protection Act, 18 October 2004, Revised 2 November 2005. Law and Government Division, Library of Parliament. Accessed from: http://www2.parl.gc.ca/Sites/LOP/LegislativeSummaries/Bills_ls.asp?Parl=38&Ses=1&1s=C11

Mason University, agrees: "Doesn't it make more sense to have companies do what they do best, make good products at fair prices, and then let consumers use the savings for the charity of their choice?"[49]

By contrast, under the **stakeholder model**, management's most important responsibility is not just maximizing profits, but the firm's long-term survival, which is achieved by satisfying not just shareholders, but the interests of multiple corporate stakeholders.[50] **Stakeholders** are persons or groups that are interested in and affected by the organization's actions.[51] They are called stakeholders because they have a stake in what those actions are. Consequently, stakeholder groups may try to influence the firm to act in their own interests.

Being responsible to multiple stakeholders raises two basic questions. First, how does a company identify its stakeholders? Second, how does a company balance the needs of different stakeholders? Distinguishing between primary and secondary stakeholders can help answer these questions.[52]

Some stakeholders are more important to the firm's survival than others. **Primary stakeholders** are groups on which the organization depends for its long-term survival. They include shareholders, employees, customers, suppliers, governments, and local communities. When managers are struggling to balance the needs of different stakeholders, the stakeholder model suggests that the needs of primary stakeholders take precedence over the needs of secondary stakeholders. But among primary stakeholders, are some more important than others? In practice, yes, as CEOs typically give somewhat higher priority to shareholders, employees, and customers than to suppliers, governments, and local communities.[53] Addressing the concerns of primary stakeholders is important because if a stakeholder group becomes dissatisfied and terminates its relationship with the company, the company could be seriously harmed or go out of business.

Secondary stakeholders, such as the media and special interest groups, can influence or be influenced by the company. Unlike the primary stakeholders, however, they do not engage in regular transactions with the company and are not critical to its long-term survival. Nevertheless, secondary stakeholders are still important because they can affect public perceptions and opinions about socially responsible behaviour. In 2008, for example, after five years of battling with People for the Ethical Treatment of Animals (PETA), KFC Canada signed an agreement promising to buy from suppliers who use "animal-welfare friendly" practices and announced it would begin to offer vegan options in its restaurants. The agreement effectively ended the boycott imposed by PETA on the Canadian division of KFC, although the campaign against KFC continued in the United States and worldwide. PETA's "Kentucky Fried Cruelty" campaign gained international exposure and included more than 12,000 protests at KFC restaurants as well as outside the homes of KFC executives.[54]

So, to whom are organizations socially responsible? Many commentators, especially economists and financial analysts, continue to argue that organizations are responsible only to shareholders. Increasingly, however, top managers have come to believe that they and their companies must be socially responsible to their stakeholders. Surveys

Stakeholder model a theory of corporate responsibility that holds that management's most important responsibility, long-term survival, is achieved by satisfying the interests of multiple corporate stakeholders

Stakeholders persons or groups with a "stake" or legitimate interest in a company's actions

Primary stakeholder any group on which an organization relies for its long-term survival

Secondary stakeholder any group that can influence or be influenced by a company and can affect public perceptions about its socially responsible behaviour

John Rensten/Digital Vision/Getty Images

Economic responsibility the expectation that a company will make a profit by producing a valued product or service

Legal responsibility a company's social responsibility to obey society's laws and regulations

Ethical responsibility a company's social responsibility not to violate accepted principles of right and wrong when conducting its business

Discretionary responsibility the expectation that a company will voluntarily serve a social role beyond its economic, legal, and ethical responsibilities

show that as many as 80 percent of top-level managers believe it is unethical to focus just on shareholders. Although there is not complete agreement, a majority of opinion makers would argue that companies must be socially responsible to their stakeholders.

LO6 For What Are Organizations Socially Responsible?

If organizations are to be socially responsible to stakeholders, what are they to be socially responsible *for*? Well, companies can best benefit their stakeholders by fulfilling their economic, legal, ethical, and discretionary responsibilities. Economic and legal responsibilities play a larger part in a company's social responsibility than do ethical and discretionary responsibilities. However, the relative importance of these various responsibilities depends on society's expectations of corporate social responsibility at a particular point in time.[55] A century ago, society expected businesses to meet their economic and legal responsibilities and little else. Today, when society judges whether businesses are socially responsible, ethical and discretionary responsibilities are considerably more important than they used to be.

Historically, **economic responsibility**—making a profit by producing a product or service valued by society—has been a business's most basic social responsibility. Organizations that don't meet their financial and economic expectations come under tremendous pressure. For example, company boards are very, very quick these days to fire CEOs. CEOs are three times more likely to be fired today than two decades ago. Typically, all it takes is two or three bad quarters in a row. William Rollnick, who became acting chairman of Mattel after the company fired its previous CEO, says: "There's zero forgiveness. You screw up and you're dead."[56] Indeed, in both Europe and the United States, nearly one-third of CEOs are fired because of their inability to successfully change their companies.[57]

Legal responsibility is a company's social responsibility to obey society's laws and regulations as it tries to meet its economic responsibilities. For example, various municipalities across Ontario have adopted anti-drive-through ordinances in response to environmental concerns about emissions generated by vehicles using drive-throughs. These bans pose a challenge for businesses with drive-throughs. One of these is TDL, the parent company of Tim Hortons, which has responded by commissioning a study that concludes that drive-throughs actually generate fewer vehicle emissions than parking lots. Tim Hortons cannot afford to walk away from this legal issue, considering that drive-throughs generate 50 percent of its revenue. TDL has succeeded in fighting restrictions in several Ontario cities. In Kingston, Ontario, however, the city planning committee has prohibited new drive-throughs in the city's historic downtown core.[58]

Ethical responsibility is a company's social responsibility not to violate accepted principles of right and wrong when conducting its business. For example, most people believe that KFC was wrong to run ads implying that its fried chicken was good for you and could help you lose weight. In one ad, one friend said to another, "Is that you? Man you look fantastic! What the heck you been doin'?" With his mouth full, the friend says, "Eatin' chicken." A voice-over then says, "So if you're watching carbs and going high protein, go KFC!" Two of KFC's fried chicken breasts, however, contain 780 calories and 38 grams of fat. Michael Jacobsen, executive director of the Center for Science in the Public Interest, says: "These ads take the truth, dip it in batter and deep-fry it. Colonel Sanders himself would have a hard time swallowing this ad campaign."[59] After running the ads for a brief time, KFC quietly pulled them.

Discretionary responsibilities pertain to the social roles that businesses play in society beyond their economic, legal, and ethical responsibilities. Discretionary responsibilities are voluntary and can be undertaken by large, multinational corporations as well as by small

© Shane Link/iStockphoto.com

Triple Bottom Line

The phrase "the triple bottom line" was coined by John Elkington, cofounder of the consulting organization SustainAbility. According to Elkington, companies should be preparing three distinct bottom lines. One is the traditional measure of profit—the "bottom line" of the profit-and-loss account. The second is the bottom line of a company's "people account"—a measure of how socially responsible a company has been throughout its operations. The third is the bottom line of the company's "planet" account—a measure of how environmentally responsible it has been. The triple bottom line (TBL) thus consists of three P's: profit, people, and planet. The intent is to measure the financial, social, and environmental performance of the company over a period of time. Only a company that produces a TBL is taking account of the full cost involved in doing business. The "bottom line" is that what you measure is what you get, because what you measure is what you are likely to pay attention to. Only when companies measure their social and environmental impact will we have socially and environmentally responsible organizations.

Source: *The Economist*, "Triple Bottom Line," http://www.economist.com/node/14301663. © The Economist Newspaper Limited, London (November 17, 2009).

Used with the permission of the Bank of Canada.
kurhan/Shutterstock.com
leonello calvetti/Shutterstock.com

businesses. For example, Sears Canada teamed up with Scouts Canada with a unique program that promotes environmental stewardship through tree-planting projects. Using in-store fundraising events like Round up Your Bill, Sears Canada is able to provide support and increased community awareness of this long-standing organization.[60]

At the opposite end of the spectrum, Bargains Group, a small, Toronto-based company that sources discounted clothing for resale to retailers, uses industry contacts and suppliers to donate sleeping bags and survival kits for street people, toys for the Salvation Army, and emergency supplies for victims of natural disasters.[61] Discretionary responsibilities such as these are voluntary. Companies are not considered unethical if they don't perform them. Today, however, corporate stakeholders expect companies to do much more than in the past to meet their discretionary responsibilities.

LO7 Responses to Demands for Social Responsibility

Social responsiveness refers to a company's strategy for responding to stakeholders' economic, legal, ethical, and discretionary expectations. A social responsibility problem exists whenever company actions do not meet stakeholder expectations. One model of social responsiveness identifies four strategies for responding to social responsibility problems: reactive, defensive, accommodative, and proactive. These strategies differ in the extent to which the company is willing to act to meet or exceed society's expectations.

A company using a **reactive strategy** will do less than society expects. It may deny responsibility for a problem or fight any suggestion that it should solve the problem. By contrast, a company using a **defensive strategy** will admit responsibility for a problem but do the least required to meet societal expectations. Second Chance Body Armor makes bulletproof vests for police officers. According to company founder Richard Davis, tests indicated that the protective material in its vests deteriorated quickly under high temperatures and humidity, which are the conditions under which they're typically used. Davis concluded that even vests that were only two years old were potentially unsafe. Yet he couldn't convince the company's executive committee to recall the vests (an accommodative strategy). Davis says he told the committee it had three choices: recall the vests

Social responsiveness refers to a company's strategy for responding to stakeholders' economic, legal, ethical, or discretionary expectations concerning social responsibility

Reactive strategy a social responsiveness strategy in which a company does less than society expects

Defensive strategy a social responsiveness strategy in which a company admits responsibility for a problem but does the least required to meet societal expectations

To Give or Not to Give?

Following the devastating earthquake in Haiti in 2010, many Canadian companies and organizations were quick to donate supplies, services, and funds to help with what was a staggering loss to a country ill-equipped to deal with such a monumental natural disaster. However, a recent poll of Canadian executives by Compas Inc. suggests that there are varying views regarding what a company's role should be in terms of charitable donations. Of those polled, 45 percent expressed their belief that charitable donations should be at the discretion of the individual shareholder. "Public corporations should leave it to the shareholders to give to charities," one CEO argued. Also, 35 percent of those polled believed that corporations should indeed support charitable causes. "Being a good corporate citizen means assisting those less fortunate—as long as it is done in the context of the entities' aims, objectives, and employees' desires," said another executive. When selecting a charity to support, executives valued efficiency and honesty, wanting to be assured that the donation would actually reach the intended recipients. In addition, local charities that benefit the surrounding community were preferred over those that were geographically far away. When asked whether they were in favour of encouraging employees to contribute to charities, the executives were split: 45 percent were in favour, 34 percent opposed.

Source: Adapted from J. Nelson, "A Corporate Responsibility?" *Canadian Business*, 1 March 2010, page 19. Reprinted by permission of Canadian Business.

KidStock/Blend Images/Getty Images

Accommodative strategy a social responsiveness strategy in which a company accepts responsibility for a problem and does all that society expects to solve that problem

Proactive strategy a social responsiveness strategy in which a company anticipates responsibility for a problem before it occurs and does more than society expects to address the problem

and stop selling them, do nothing and wait "until a customer is injured or killed," or wait until the problem became public and "be forced to make excuses as to why we didn't recognize and correct the problem."[62] After two vests were pierced by bullets, killing one police officer and wounding another, Second Chance announced that it would fix or replace 130,000 potentially defective vests. Although the company finally admitted responsibility for the problem, management decided to do only the minimum that society expected (fix a defective product). Second Chance, then, used a defensive strategy.

A company using an **accommodative strategy** will accept responsibility for a problem and take a progressive approach by doing all that can be expected to solve the problem. After a recall of millions of toys by Mattel Inc. in 2007, the Walt Disney Company announced it would begin independently testing toys featuring its characters. Disney hired companies to make random purchases of Disney-branded toys at retailers across the country to test for safety issues relating to small parts and the use of lead paint. Disney also started requiring licensees to submit their own test results, and it increased staffing in its Product Integrity Office.[63]

Finally, a company using a **proactive strategy** will anticipate responsibility for a problem before it occurs, do more than expected to address the problem, and lead the industry in its approach. Honda Motors announced that it would include side-curtain air bags (which drop from the roof and protect passengers' heads) and front-side air bags (which come out of the door to protect against side-impact collisions) as standard equipment on all of its cars. Although more expensive car brands, such as Lexus and Volvo, already included these safety features, Honda was the first to make them standard on all models. Exhibit 4.7 summarizes the discussion of social responsiveness.

LO8 Social Responsibility and Economic Performance

One question that managers often ask is, "Does it pay to be socially responsible?"

Early research on this question indicated there was no inherent relationship between social responsibility and economic performance.[64] Recent research, however, has led to different conclusions. There is a tradeoff between being socially responsible and economic performance.[65] And there is a small, positive relationship between being

Exhibit 4.7 Social Responsiveness

Reactive	Defensive	Accommodative	Proactive
Fight all the way	Do only what is required	Be progressive	Lead the industry

Withdrawal — Public Relations Approach — Legal Approach — Bargaining — Problem Solving

DO NOTHING ⟷ DO MUCH

Source: A.B.Carroll, "A Three-Dimensional Conceptual Model of Corporate Performance," *Academy of Management Review*, 1979, Vol 4 497–505.

socially responsible and economic performance that strengthens with corporate reputation.[66] Let's explore what each of these results means.

First, there is no tradeoff between being socially responsible and economic performance.[67] Being socially responsible usually won't make a business less profitable. What this suggests is that the costs of being socially responsible—and those costs can be high, especially early on—can be offset by a better product or corporate reputation, which results in stronger sales or higher profit margins. For example, Honda, which introduced the first hybrid car in North America, has long been an industry leader in fuel efficiency and environmentally friendly technology. So when it decided to enter the private plane market with the new HondaJet, it took the same approach, using lightweight composite materials instead of metal alloys in the plane's body, and working closely with General Electric to design an efficient, lightweight, powerful engine that when mounted above the wings (a unique design), further reduced fuel consumption. These features not only help the HondaJet use less fuel but also make the HondaJet lighter and faster than its competitors. The unique engine and wing design gives it more interior space, reduces cabin noise, and makes it cheaper to operate. And while it seats a pilot and just four passengers, the cost of flying the HondaJet will be no more expensive on a per-kilometre basis than the common Canadair CRJ-200 regional jet, which transports forty to fifty passengers. Honda believes that its socially responsible design will be the key to making the HondaJet profitable.[68]

Second, it usually *does* pay to be socially responsible, and that relationship becomes stronger particularly when a company or its products have a strong reputation for social responsibility.[69] For example, GE, long one of the most admired and profitable corporations in the world, was one of the first and largest *Fortune* 500 companies to make a strategic commitment to providing environmentally friendly products and services. CEO Jeffrey Immelt wants GE to "develop and drive the technologies of the future that will protect and clean our environment."[70] Is Immelt doing this because of personal beliefs? He says no. "It's no great thrill for me to do this stuff ... I never put it in right versus wrong terms." GE calls its strategy "ecoimagination," which it says is "helping to solve the world's biggest environmental challenges while driving profitable growth for GE." Says Immelt: "We invest in the basic strategies that we think are going to fit into [ecoimagination], but make money for our investors at the same time."[71] In just five years, GE has increased the number of its ecoimagination products from seventeen to eighty. As a result, it now sells more than $17 billion of such products and services each year, with annual revenue growth increasing by double digits.[72]

© Paul Chauncey/Alamy

Finally, even if there is generally a small positive relationship between social responsibility and economic performance that becomes stronger when a company has a positive reputation for social responsibility, and even if there is no tradeoff between being socially responsible and economic performance, social responsibility can have significant costs, and there is no guarantee that socially responsible companies will be profitable.

Socially responsible companies experience the same ups and downs in economic performance as traditional businesses. Ben & Jerry's, the ice cream company, became well known for its commitment to social responsibility, donating 7.5 percent of its pretax profits to support AIDS patients, homeless people, and the environment, However, despite its outstanding reputation as a socially responsible company, Ben & Jerry's consistently had financial troubles after going public (selling shares of stock to the public). In fact, its financial problems became so severe that the company was eventually sold to British-based Unilever.[73] Being socially responsible may be the right thing to do, and it is usually associated with increased profits, but it doesn't guarantee business success.

© Franck Boston/iStockphoto.com

Go online at
www.nelson.com/4ltrpress/icanmgmt2
And access the essential Study Tools online for this chapter:

- **Flashcards**, to help you study
- **Interactive Quizzes**, to test your knowledge
- **Audio Chapter Summaries**, for chapter review
- **Crossword Puzzles and Beat the Clock**, to review key terms
- **What Would You Do? Cases**, for applying your knowledge to real-life situations
- **Self Assessments**, to learn about what kind of manager you are
- **Videos and Media Quizzing for Part 1**
  - Chapter 1: Camp Bow Wow: Innovative Management for a Changing World
  - Chapter 2: Barcelona Restaurant Group: The Evolution of Management Thinking
  - Chapter 3: Camp Bow Wow: The Environment and Corporate Culture
  - Chapter 4: Theo Chocolate: Managing Social Ethics and Social Responsibility

Be sure to consult the Chapter Review Card at the back of the textbook.

5 Planning and Decision Making

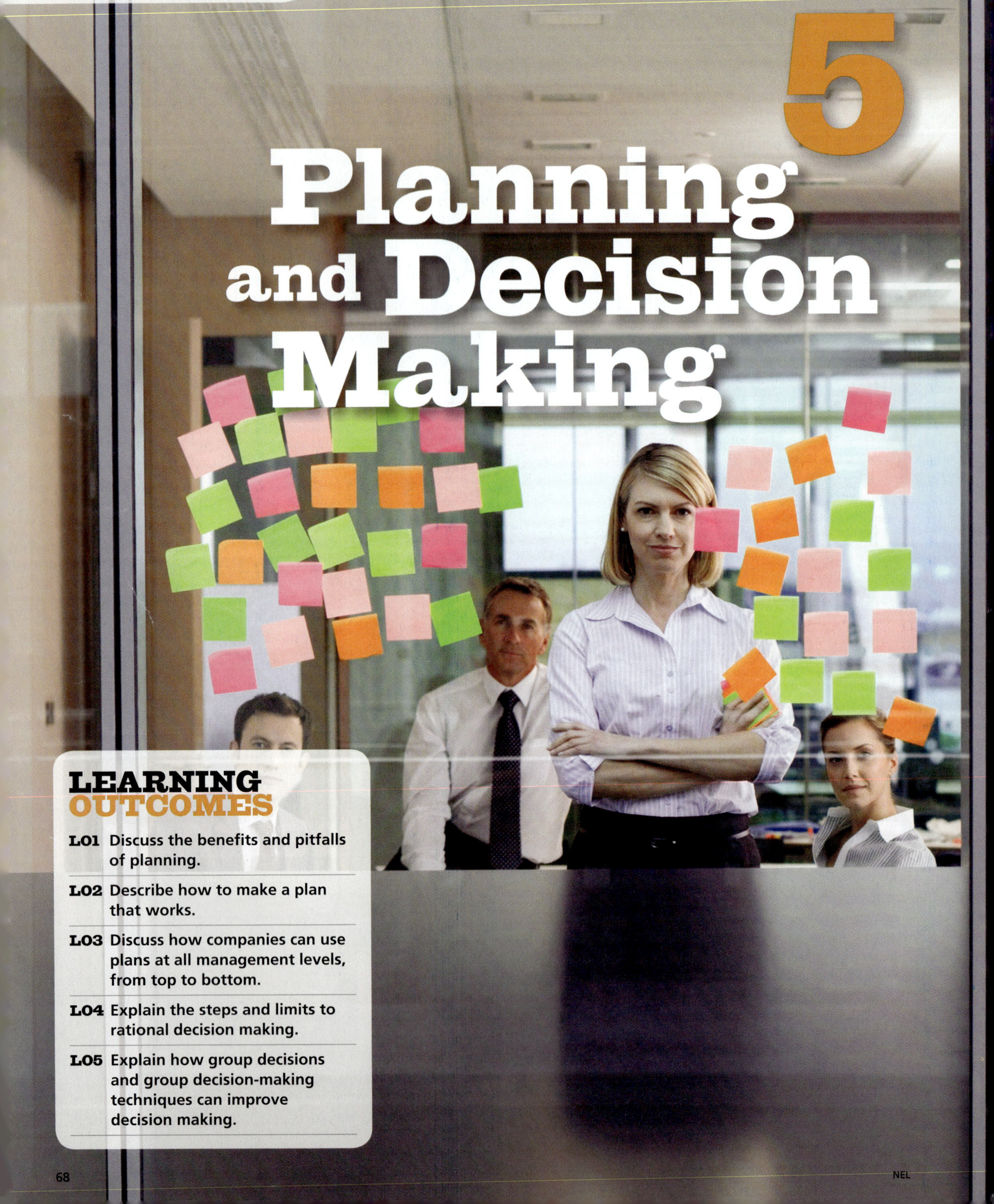

LEARNING OUTCOMES

LO1 Discuss the benefits and pitfalls of planning.

LO2 Describe how to make a plan that works.

LO3 Discuss how companies can use plans at all management levels, from top to bottom.

LO4 Explain the steps and limits to rational decision making.

LO5 Explain how group decisions and group decision-making techniques can improve decision making.

Even inexperienced managers know that planning and decision making are an important part of a manager's job. Figure out what the problem is. Generate potential solutions or plans. Pick the best one. Make it work. Experienced managers, however, know how hard it really is to make good plans and decisions. One seasoned manager says: "I think the biggest surprises are the problems. Maybe I had never seen it before. Maybe I was protected by my management when I was in sales. Maybe I had delusions of grandeur, I don't know. I just know how disillusioning and frustrating it is to be hit with problems and conflicts all day and not be able to solve them very cleanly."[1]

Planning

Planning is choosing a goal and developing a method or strategy to achieve that goal. In 2005, facing tougher regulations and an industry-wide reputation for purveying junk food, General Mills, one of the largest food companies in the world, began a corporate-wide initiative to improve the health profile of its products by setting specific nutritional standards goals for many of its product categories. Managers had to adapt old products and develop new ones that were higher in whole grains and lower in sugar and salt and that would encourage people to eat their vegetables. Setting clear standards for nutritional value and tying annual executive bonuses to achievement of these goals helped General Mills meet a number of its goals including these: reducing the sodium content in its top 10 product categories by 20 percent on average; lowering the sugar levels in cereals advertised to children to single-digit levels per serving; and removing trans fats from a significant portion of its products. By the end of fiscal year 2011, General Mills was able to report that nutritionally improved products accounted for 64 percent of its retail sales volume.[2]

LO1 Benefits and Pitfalls of Planning

Are you one of those naturally organized people who always make a daily to-do list and never miss a deadline? Or are you one of those flexible, creative, go-with-the-flow people who dislike planning because it restricts their freedom? Some people are natural planners. They love it and can see only its benefits. Others dislike planning and can see only its disadvantages. It turns out that *both* views have real value.

*Planning has advantages and disadvantages. Let's learn about **1.1 the benefits** and **1.2 the pitfalls of planning.***

1.1 Benefits of Planning

Planning offers four important benefits: intensified effort, persistence, direction, and the creation of task strategies.[3] First, managers and employees put forth greater effort when following a plan. Take two workers. Instruct one to "do your best" to increase production. Instruct the other to achieve a 2 percent increase in production each month. Research shows that the one with the specific plan will work harder.[4]

Planning choosing a goal and developing a strategy to achieve that goal

Second, planning leads to persistence, that is, to working hard for long periods. In fact, planning encourages persistence even when there may be little chance of short-term success.[5] Canadian soccer player Christine Sinclair knows how important hard work and persistence are to achieving success. Christine began playing soccer at a young age, and never shied away from practices or games. According to her family, she was so passionate about the game that she would do anything to stay on the field—even working out with her brother's teams whenever she could. Christine's brother Michael explains, "You couldn't get her off the field. She always had something special, but she always put in more time than anybody I know." Christine's natural talent, in addition to the time and persistence in training through the years translated into a lengthy list of impressive accomplishments—Canada's female player of the year nine times in a row (10 wins in total), nominated for FIFA world player of the year six times, 13 years with the Canadian national team, third all-time scoring female player (143 goals in 190 international matches), the first soccer player to ever receive the Lou Marsh Award as Canada's Top Athlete, and, of course an Olympic bronze medal in 2012.[6]

The third benefit of planning is direction. Plans encourage managers and employees to direct their persistent efforts *toward* activities that help accomplish their goals and *away* from activities that don't.[7] The fourth benefit of planning is that it encourages the development of task strategies. In other words, planning not only encourages people to work hard for extended periods and to engage in behaviours directly related to goal accomplishment, but also encourages them to think of better ways to do their jobs. Finally, perhaps the most compelling benefit of planning is that it has been proven to work for both companies and individuals. On average, companies with plans have larger profits and grow much faster than companies that don't.[8] The same holds true for individual managers and employees: there is no better way to improve the performance of the people who work in a company than to have them set goals and develop strategies for achieving those goals.

Despite the significant benefits associated with planning, planning is not a cure-all.

1.2 Planning Pitfalls

Despite the significant benefits associated with planning, it is not a cure-all. Plans won't fix all organizational

Echo/Cultura/Getty Images

Planning ...

Working for you by:	Working against you by:
• intensifying effort • increasing persistence • providing direction • creating task strategies	• impeding change • creating a false sense of certainty • allowing planners to plan things they don't understand how to accomplish

problems. In fact, many management authors and consultants believe that planning can harm companies in several ways.[9]

The first pitfall of planning is that it can impede change and prevent or slow needed adaptation. Sometimes companies become so committed to achieving the goals set forth in their plans or following the strategies and tactics spelled out in them that they fail to notice when their plans aren't working or their goals need to change. When it comes to environmentally sound cars, General Motors may have initially missed the boat because of its "culture wedded to big cars and horsepower." In the mid-1990s, when Toyota formed its "green group"—which led to the development of the company's first electric hybrid, the Prius—GM decided to kill its electric car program to focus on profitable SUVs (sports utility vehicles). However, as oil prices began to rise drastically and interest in electric vehicles continued to surge, GM was forced to play "catch up"; it restarted its work on hybrid vehicles in 2006. By 2010, GM had succeeded in launching the Chevy Volt, a battery-powered car that combines the use of off-peak electricity for overnight recharging of the batteries with daytime recharging by a small gas engine. However, the competitive arena for electric cars had changed quite a bit by then. The Volt now faces competition from a number of other manufacturers' models, including the Nissan Leaf, the Mini-E from Mini Cooper, the Toyota RAV4 EV, and the Ford Focus, as well as new entries from Tesla Motors and Fisker Automotive. Some still question GM's decision to abandon the electric car; a documentary titled *Who Killed the Electric Car?* speculated that other forces may have been at play that contributed to this costly decision, including pressure from large oil companies and other stakeholders in the automotive industry.[10]

Slavoljub Pantelic/Shutterstock.com

Exhibit 5.1 How to Make a Plan That Works

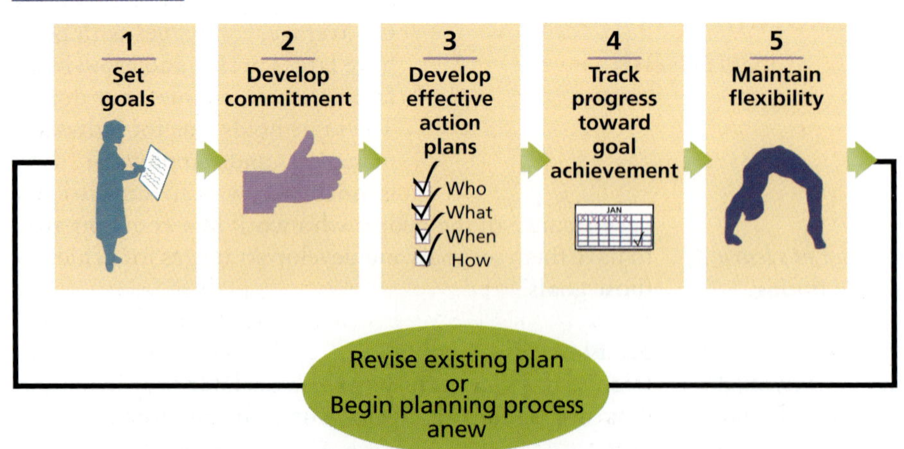

The second pitfall is that planning can create a false sense of certainty. Planners sometimes feel that they know exactly what the future holds for their competitors, their suppliers, and their companies. However, all plans are based on assumptions. "The price of gasoline will increase by 4 percent per year." "Exports will continue to rise." For plans to work, the assumptions on which they are based must hold true. If the assumptions turn out to be false, then the plans based on them are likely to fail.

The third potential pitfall of planning is the detachment of planners. In theory, strategic planners and top-level managers are supposed to focus on the big picture and not concern themselves with the details of implementation (i.e., carrying out the plan). According to management professor Henry Mintzberg, detachment leads planners to plan for things they don't understand.[11] Plans are meant to be guidelines for action, not abstract theories. Consequently, planners need to be familiar with the daily details of their businesses if they are to produce plans that can work.

LO2 How to Make a Plan That Works

Planning is a double-edged sword. If done right, it brings about tremendous increases in individual and organizational performance. If done wrong, it can have just the opposite effect and harm individual and organizational performance.

*In this section, you will learn how to make a plan that works. As depicted in Exhibit 5.1, planning consists of **2.1 setting goals, 2.2 developing commitment to the goals, 2.3 developing effective action plans, 2.4 tracking progress toward goal achievement,** and **2.5 maintaining flexibility**.*

2.1 Setting Goals

The first step in planning is to set goals. To direct behaviour and increase effort, goals need to be specific and challenging.[12] For example, deciding to "increase sales this year" won't direct and energize workers as much as deciding to "increase North American sales by 4 percent in the next six months." Specific, challenging goals provide a target for which to aim and a standard against which to measure success.

One way of writing effective goals for yourself, your job, or your company is to use the S.M.A.R.T. guidelines. **S.M.A.R.T. goals** are Specific, Measurable, Attainable, Realistic, and Timely.[13] Let's take a look at Nissan's zero-emissions program, which led to the development of the Leaf, an all-electric car, to see how it measures up to the S.M.A.R.T. guidelines for goals.

First, is the goal *Specific*? Yes, because "zero emissions" tells us that Nissan isn't just looking to *reduce* emissions but to eliminate them. And "all electric" rules out gas/electric hybrids like those produced by competitors. Besides being specific, the goal is *Measurable*, since Nissan has put a number on the emissions—namely, zero. Whether the goal is *Attainable* or not depends on whether the all-electric car performs as expected. Nissan has been researching lithium-ion battery technology for almost 20 years and claims to have developed a battery that can power a car up to 100 miles and recharge in just eight hours. Current trends in government regulation, consumer preferences for more environmentally friendly vehicles, and increasing gasoline prices suggest that an all-electric car is *Realistic* from a business standpoint, but that can't be determined until the Leaf is available to consumers. Finally, the goal is *Timely*—Nissan's goal was to roll out the Leaf in Japan and the United States in 2010, and it has achieved this. By 2012, it wanted to enter the European market and they did.

2.2 Developing Commitment to Goals

Just because a company sets a goal doesn't mean that people will try to accomplish it. If workers don't care about a goal, that goal won't encourage them to work harder or smarter. Thus, the second step in planning is to develop commitment to goals.[14]

Goal commitment is the determination to achieve a goal. Commitment to achieve a goal is not automatic. Managers and workers must choose to commit themselves to a goal. Facing a company-wide slowdown in revenue, the management at 1-800-GOT-JUNK, North America's largest junk removal franchise network, came up with a new business strategy for combating the recession, one that would allow the company to grow and become more sustainable in the future. The "100-Day Plan" was introduced with the clear expectation that the new strategy would be executed throughout the organization in 100 days. Brian Scudamore, founder and CEO of the company, explains that "having everyone moving with the same purpose in the same direction, we figured, would allow us to gain maximum momentum." "With only 100 days to execute," he added, "we had to be driving hard every single day."[15] Put another way, goal commitment is about really wanting to achieve a goal.

So how can managers bring about goal commitment? The most popular approach is to set goals collectively, as a team. At 1-800-GOT-JUNK, each franchisee was asked to set a revenue goal for the 100 Day Plan and to sign a commitment to that goal. Goals are more likely to be realistic and attainable when individuals participate in setting them. Another technique for gaining commitment to a goal is to make that goal public, as was the case at 1-800-GOT-JUNK. It held a company-wide conference call and Web presentation to introduce the plan, following that up with regular 100 Day Updates and a 100 Day Plan blog. Support from top management was also important; it included providing funds, speaking publicly about the plan, and participating in the plan itself. At 1-800-GOT-JUNK, frequent communication from top management ensured that the plan was being adopted throughout the organization.[16]

S.M.A.R.T. goals goals that are specific, measurable, attainable, realistic, and timely

Goal commitment the determination to achieve a goal

Action plan the specific steps, people, and resources needed to accomplish a goal

The Canadian Press/Jeremy Hainsworth

2.3 Developing Effective Action Plans

The third step in planning is to develop effective action plans. An **action plan** lists the specific steps (how), people (who), resources (what), and time period (when) for accomplishing a goal. Coming out of bankruptcy, corporate reorganization, and a government bailout, automotive manufacturer Chrysler presented a detailed plan for returning to profitability. First, it established a time period (*when*) by presenting an outline of what the company would do over the next five years. Second, it clearly identified *who* was behind the company's new strategic plan. CEO Sergio Machionne spearheaded a "painful and difficult" process of assessing Chrysler's strengths and weakness, during which "no stone [was] unturned." Third, Chrysler's plan explained *how* it would return to profitability by detailing a thorough makeover of its core brands Jeep, Chrysler, and Dodge. Under this plan, some older models would be redesigned and repackaged, while other models would be eliminated (such as the Jeep Commander and Chrysler Sebring). As for the

Proximal goals short-term goals or subgoals

Distal goals long-term or primary goals

resources (*what*), Chrysler's plan called for extensive collaboration with Italian automaker Fiat (which has a 20 percent stake in Chrysler), including borrowing technological and design innovations so that it could offer fuel-efficient, stylish vehicles to attract a new segment of North American consumers.[17]

2.4 Tracking Progress

The fourth step in planning is to track progress toward goal achievement. There are two accepted methods of tracking progress. The first is to set proximal goals and distal goals. **Proximal goals** are short-term goals or subgoals, whereas **distal goals** are long-term or primary.[18] The idea behind setting proximal goals is that achieving them may be more motivating and rewarding than waiting to reach far-off distal goals. Proximal goals are less intimidating and more attainable than distal goals, which often feel like biting off more than you can chew. Proximal goals enable you to achieve a distal goal one little piece at a time.

The second method of tracking progress is to gather and provide performance feedback. Regular, frequent performance feedback allows workers and managers to track their progress toward goal achievement and make adjustments in effort, direction, and strategies.[19] Proper action on performance feedback can keep you from failing to adapt, one of the pitfalls of planning. Exhibit 5.2 shows the impact of feedback on safety

picturegarden/Taxi/Getty Images

Exhibit 5.2 Effects of Goal Setting, Training, and Feedback on Safe Behaviour in a Bread Factory

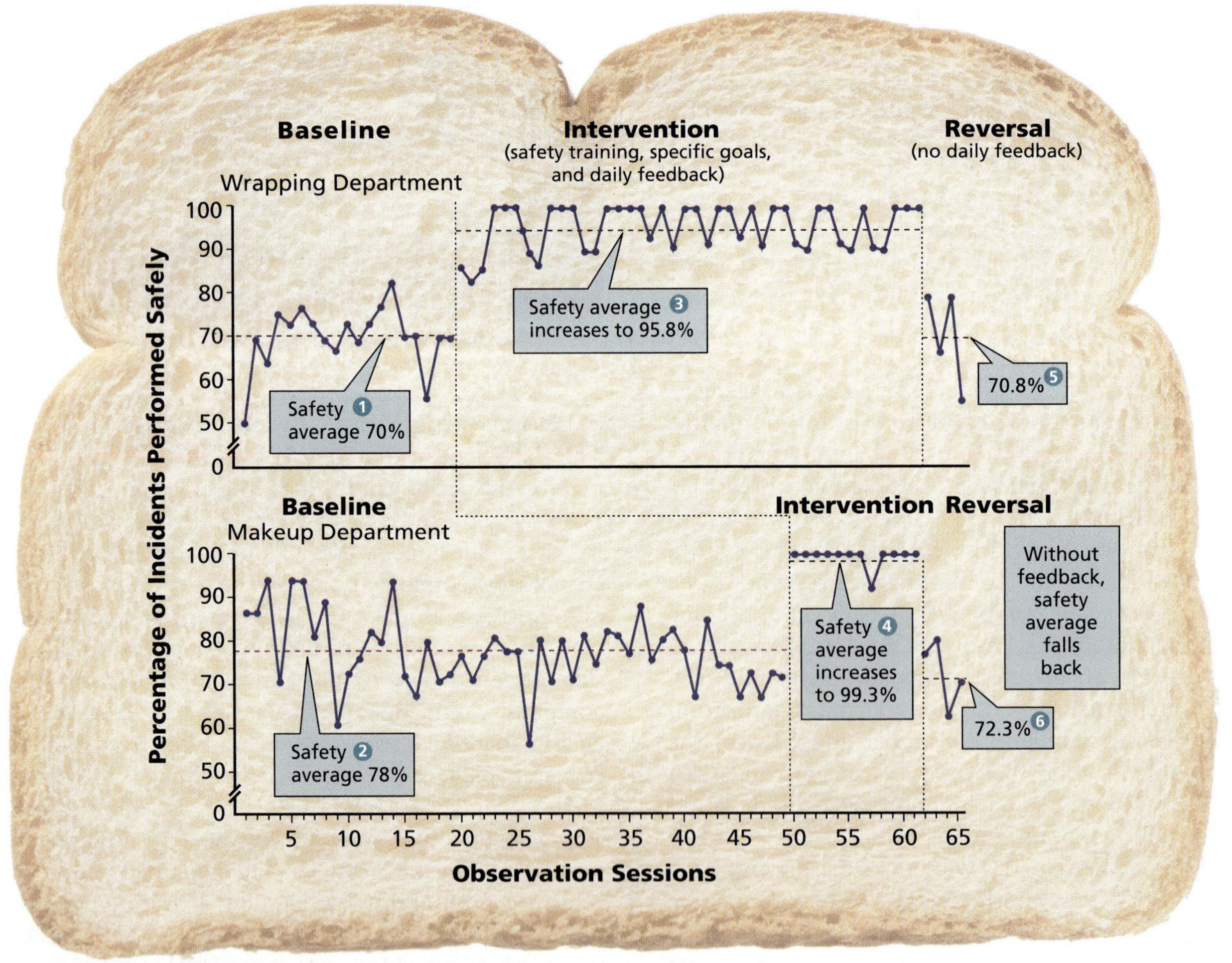

Baseline
Wrapping Department
Intervention
(safety training, specific goals, and daily feedback)
Reversal
(no daily feedback)
Safety average ❶ average 70%
Safety average ❸ increases to 95.8%
70.8% ❺
Baseline
Makeup Department
Intervention
Reversal
Safety ❷ average 78%
Safety ❹ average increases to 99.3%
72.3% ❻
Without feedback, safety average falls back
Percentage of Incidents Performed Safely
Observation Sessions

© Digital Vision/Photodisc/Jupiterimages

Source: Komaki, J. Barwick K. D., & Scott, L. R. "A Behavioral Approach to Occupational Safety: Pinpointing and Reinforcing Safe Performance in a Food Manufacturing Plant." *Journal of Applied Psychology* 63, (1978).

behaviour at a large bakery. During the baseline period, workers in the wrapping department, who measure and mix ingredients, roll the bread dough, and put it into baking pans, performed their jobs safely about 70 percent of the time (see dialogue box 1 in Exhibit 5.2). The baseline safety record for workers in the makeup department, who bag and seal baked bread and assemble, pack, and tape cardboard cartons for shipping, was somewhat better at 78 percent (see dialogue box 2). The company gave workers 30 minutes of safety training, set a goal of 90 percent safe behaviour, and then provided daily feedback (such as a chart similar to Exhibit 5.2). Performance improved dramatically. During the intervention period, safely performed behaviours rose to an average of 95.8 percent for wrapping workers (see dialogue box 3) and 99.3 percent for workers in the makeup department (see dialogue box 4), and never fell below 83 percent. In this instance, the combination of training, a challenging goal, and feedback led to a dramatic increase in performance.

The importance of feedback can be seen in the reversal stage, when the company quit posting daily feedback on safe behaviour. Without daily feedback, the percentage of safely performed behaviour returned to baseline levels, 70.8 percent for the wrapping department (see dialogue box 5) and 72.3 percent for the makeup department (see dialogue box 6). For planning to be effective, workers need both a specific, challenging goal and regular feedback so that they can track their progress. Indeed, further research indicates that the effectiveness of goal setting can be doubled by the addition of feedback.[20]

2.5 Maintaining Flexibility

Because action plans are sometimes poorly conceived and goals sometimes turn out not to be achievable, the last step in developing an effective plan is to maintain flexibility. One method of maintaining flexibility while planning is to adopt an options-based approach.[21] The goal of **options-based planning** is to keep options open by making small, simultaneous investments in many alternative plans. Then, when one or a few of these plans emerge as likely winners, you invest even more in these plans while discontinuing or reducing investment in the others. In part, options-based planning is the opposite of traditional planning. Whereas the purpose of an action plan is to commit people and resources to a particular course of action, the purpose of options-based planning is to leave those commitments open by maintaining **slack resources**, that is, a cushion of resources such as extra time, people, money, or production capacity, that can be used to address and adapt to unanticipated changes, problems, or opportunities.[22] Holding options open gives you choices. And choices, combined with slack resources, give you flexibility.

Options-based planning maintaining flexibility by making small, simultaneous investments in many alternative plans

Slack resources a cushion of extra resources that can be used with options-based planning to adapt to unanticipated change, problems, or opportunities

LO3 Planning from Top to Bottom

Planning works best when the goals and action plans at the bottom and middle of the organization support the goals and action plans at the top of the organization. In other words, planning works best when everybody pulls in the same direction. Exhibit 5.3 illustrates this planning continuity, beginning at the top with a clear definition of the company vision and ending at the bottom with the execution of operational plans.

*Let's see how **3.1 top managers create the organizational vision and mission, 3.2 middle managers develop tactical plans and use management by objectives to motivate employee efforts toward the overall vision and mission,** and **3.3 first-level managers use operational, single-use, and standing plans to implement the tactical plans.***

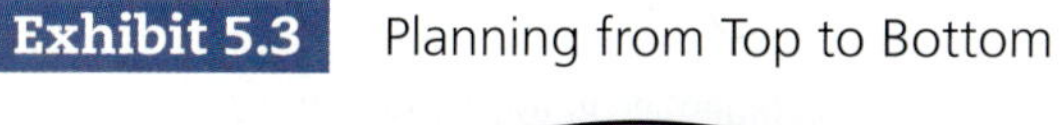
Exhibit 5.3 Planning from Top to Bottom

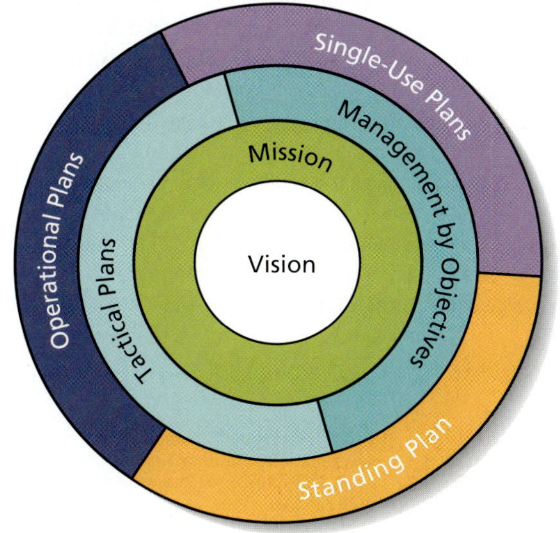

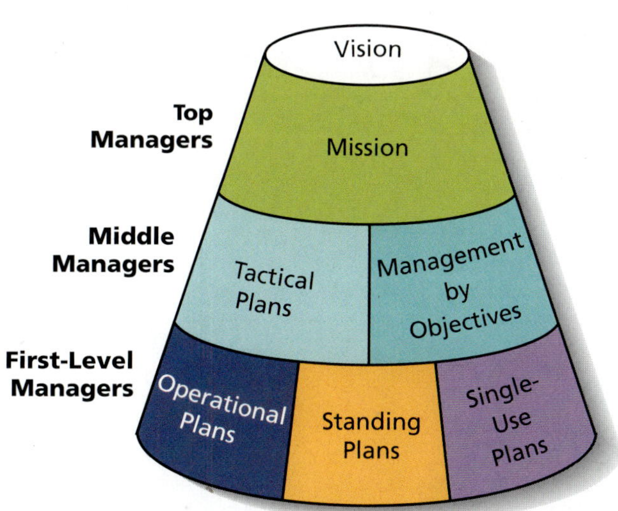

Strategic plans overall company plans that clarify how the company will serve customers and position itself against competitors over the next two to five years

Vision statement a statement of a company's purpose and the ultimate destination it hopes to reach, acting as a guide to individuals in an organization

Mission statement a broad statement of an organization's purpose that distinguishes the organization from others of a similar type

Tactical plans plans created and implemented by middle managers that specify how the company will use resources, budgets, and people over the next six months to two years to accomplish specific goals within its mission

3.1 Starting at the Top

Top management is responsible for developing long-term **strategic plans** that make clear how the company will serve customers and position itself against competitors in the next two to five years. Strategic planning begins with the creation of an organizational vision or mission.

A **vision statement** is a statement of a company's purpose and the destination it hopes to reach. It serves as a guide to individuals in an organization. A vision statement should be brief—no more than two sentences—and should also be enduring, inspirational, clear, and consistent with widely shared company beliefs and values. An example: "To be the No. 1 executive recruiter in B.C." Another, in this case Google's: "To organize the world's information and make it universally accessible and useful."[23]

An organization's mission, which should flow from its vision, is about how the organization plans to get there—in other words, how it plans to achieve its vision. To define the mission, a formal **mission statement** can be developed to provide a broad statement of an organization's purpose that distinguishes it from others of a similar type.[24] A mission statement can be an effective way to inspire employees and create shared values. For example, here is the mission statement for Starbucks: "To inspire and nurture the human spirit—one person, one cup and one neighbourhood at a time." That statement guides everyone in the organization and provides a focal point for the delivery of the company's products to its customers around the world. Even though regional differences are integrated into the company's strategy around the globe, the vision is the same whether Starbucks is selling its Assam black tea latte in Tokyo, its lemon poppy muffin in Moscow, or its iced caffe latte in Edmonton. The Starbucks vision is clear, inspirational, and consistent with the company's values and principles, which are meant to guide the organization on a day-to-day basis.[25] Other examples of organizational visions include these: yoga-inspired athletic apparel company lululemon's "creating components for people to live a longer, healthier, more fun life," and the Royal Canadian Legion's "to serve veterans and their dependants, promote remembrance and act in the service of Canada and its communities."[26]

3.2 Bending in the Middle

Middle management is responsible for developing and carrying out tactical plans to accomplish the organization's mission. **Tactical plans** specify how a company will use resources, budgets, and people to accomplish specific goals within its mission. Whereas strategic plans and objectives are used to focus company efforts over the next two to five years, tactical plans and objectives are used to direct behaviour, efforts, and attention over the next six months

Dreams on the Back of a Napkin

Company mission statements are often a source of frustration for members of a committee charged with writing one. Employees often read a cliché mission statement such as "We continually revolutionize business data to allow us to quickly integrate unique solutions to stay competitive in tomorrow's world" with glazed eyes. Such documents often get shoved in a drawer and make little impact on how people work. The process of plugging nouns and verbs into a formula, combined with a desire for it to be all-encompassing, can make a mission statement uninspiring and meaningless. According to Carmine Gallo, what makes a real difference in the work of an organization is not a bulky mission statement, but a concise and inspiring vision that can fit on the back of a napkin. It will stick. It will inspire members of the organization to be creative, and it'll motivate them to invest their energies into a shared dream.

Source: Gallo, C., "The Napkin Test; Why it's time to replace your company's bulky mission statement with a vision concise enough to fit on the back of a napkin." *BusinessWeek Online*, 10 December 2007, available online at http://www.businessweek. com/smallbiz/content/dec2007/sb2007127_010305.htm?chan=search [accessed 28 July 2008].

to two years. For example, two weeks before the official launch of Magnotta Wines, the company learned that the Liquor Control Board of Ontario (LCBO), the only retail distribution outlet for wine in Ontario, did not have any shelf space available for the fledgling winery. To continue with the company's mission, the company put an emergency plan in place that included selling its wines on-site at its winery for $3.95 a bottle—a considerably lower price than comparable wines sold at the LCBO. The company's tactical plans succeeded, garnering the winery valuable media and consumer attention—key elements needed to succeed in this competitive industry. As a result, Magnotta Wines was able to grow and expand its market, eventually establishing distributorships across Canada and international exports to the United States, Taiwan, and China.[27]

Management by objectives is a management technique often used to develop and carry out tactical plans. **Management by objectives**, or MBO, is a four-step process in which managers and their employees (1) discuss possible goals; (2) collectively select goals that are challenging, attainable, and consistent with the company's overall goals; (3) jointly develop tactical plans that lead to the accomplishment of tactical goals and objectives; and (4) meet regularly to review progress toward accomplishment of those goals.

3.3 Finishing at the Bottom

Lower level managers are responsible for developing and carrying out **operational plans**, which are the day-to-day plans for producing or delivering the organization's products and services. Operational plans direct the behaviour, efforts, and priorities of operative employees for periods ranging from 30 days to six months. There are three kinds of operational plans: single-use plans, standing plans, and budgets.

Single-use plans deal with unique, one-time-only events. For example, when the new owners of Alberta-based Blue Falls Manufacturing, a maker of portable hot tubs and spas, took over the company they quickly found out there was no inventory control system to identify component parts needed to service older hot tub models that had been sold to customers and dealers. There were over 1,100 components that didn't have part numbers, and searching for parts became a frustrating exercise; it sometimes took hours to find which part was needed for a particular model. So the company came up with a plan for an inventory system that would allow it to catalogue each piece of equipment for almost every model built since the company began in the late 1980s. Although time consuming, this plan allowed it to continue servicing its network of existing customers and dealers; it also established a process by which subsequent hot tub models and components could be tracked.[28]

Unlike single-use plans, which are created, carried out, and then never used again, **standing plans** can be used repeatedly to handle frequently recurring events. If you encounter a problem that you've seen before, someone in your company has probably written a standing plan that explains how to address it. Using this plan rather than reinventing the wheel will save you time. There are three kinds of standing plans: policies, procedures, and rules and regulations.

Policies indicate the general course of action that company managers should take in response to a particular event or situation. A well-written policy will also specify why the policy exists and what outcome the policy is intended to produce. Concerns surrounding the amount of time employees spend surfing the Internet while at work, as well as fears about computer virus attacks, have prompted many organizations to monitor Web surfing and develop policies for managing Internet use, including defining acceptable Web browsing and blocking access to non-work-related sites.[29] Social networking sites have permeated the workplace; a recent survey found that 77 percent of employees who have a Facebook account use it during work hours. From a manager's perspective, social networking sites can divert employees' attention away from work priorities; recent studies estimate that they have caused a decline in productivity of 1.5 percent at companies that allow full access to social media sites. It is not surprising, then, to hear that a 2012 study found that 54 percent of US companies now ban employees from using social networking sites like Twitter, Facebook, and LinkedIn while on the job.[30]

Procedures are more specific than policies because they indicate the series of steps that should be taken in response to a particular event. A manufacturer's procedure for handling defective products might include the following steps. Step 1: Rejected material is locked in a secure area, with "reject" documentation attached. Step 2: Material Review Board (MRB) identifies the defect and how far outside the standard the rejected products are. Step 3: MRB determines the disposition of the defective product as either

Management by objectives (MBO) a four-step process in which managers and employees discuss and select goals, develop tactical plans, and meet regularly to review progress toward goal accomplishment

Operational plans day-to-day plans, developed and implemented by lower-level managers, for producing or delivering the organization's products and services over a 30-day to six-month period

Single-use plans plans that cover unique, one-time-only events

Standing plans plans used repeatedly to handle frequently recurring events

Policy a standing plan that indicates the general course of action that should be taken in response to a particular event or situation

Procedure a standing plan that indicates the specific steps that should be taken in response to a particular event

Jetta Productions/Blend Images/Getty Images

Rules and regulations standing plans that describe how a particular action should be performed or what must happen or not happen in response to a particular event

Budgeting quantitative planning through which managers decide how to allocate available money to best accomplish company goals

Decision making the process of choosing a solution from available alternatives

Rational decision making a systematic process of defining problems, evaluating alternatives, and choosing optimal solutions

Problem a gap between a desired state and an existing state

Decision criteria the standards used to guide judgments and decisions

scrap or as rework. Step 4: Scrap is either discarded or recycled, and rework is sent back through the production line to be fixed. Step 5: If delays in delivery will result, MRB member notifies customer.[31]

Rules and regulations are even more specific than procedures because they specify what must or must not happen. They describe precisely how a particular action should be performed. For instance, many companies have rules and regulations forbidding managers from writing job reference letters for employees who have worked at their firms because a negative reference may prompt a former employee to sue for defamation of character.[32]

After single-use plans and standing plans, budgets are the third kind of operational plan. **Budgeting** is quantitative planning because it forces managers to decide how to allocate available money to best accomplish company goals. According to Jan King, author of *Business Plans to Game Plans,* "Money sends a clear message about your priorities. Budgets act as a language for communicating your goals to others."

What Is Rational Decision Making?

Decision making is the process of choosing a solution from available alternatives.[33] **Rational decision making** is a systematic process in which managers define problems, evaluate alternatives, and choose optimal solutions that provide maximum benefits to their organizations.

LO4 Steps and Limits to Rational Decision Making

*There are six steps in the rational decision-making process: **4.1 define the problem, 4.2 identify decision criteria, 4.3 weight the criteria, 4.4 generate alternative courses of action, 4.5 evaluate each alternative,** and **4.6 compute the optimal decision.** Then we'll consider **4.7 limits to rational decision making.***

Steps of the Rational Decision-Making Process

1. Define the Problem
2. Identify Decision Criteria
3. Weight the Criteria
4. Generate Alternative Courses of Action
5. Evaluate Each Alternative
6. Compute the Optimal Decision

4.1 Define the Problem

The first step in decision making is to identify and define the problem. A **problem** exists when there is a gap between a desired state (what is wanted) and an existing state (the situation you are actually facing). For many companies, a discrepancy between forecasted and actual financial results is often a red flag that a problem exists. During the last recession, international coffee giant Starbucks reported a decline in revenues and net income, likely related to the economic climate as well as to increased competition from companies like McDonald's that were attempting to steal market share.[34]

The presence of a gap between an existing state and a desired state is no guarantee that managers will make decisions to solve problems. Two things must occur for this to happen. First, managers have to be aware of the gap. But that isn't enough. Managers also have to be motivated to reduce the gap. In other words, managers have to know there is a problem and *want* to solve it. Finally, it's not enough to be aware of a problem and be motivated to solve it. Managers must also have the knowledge, skills, abilities, and resources to fix the problem. In the case of Starbucks, the company responded to its performance gap by closing nearly 1,000 stores and laying off employees in order to trim expenses by $100 million and to help restore profits. But it wasn't until McDonald's rolled out a national advertising campaign for its lower-priced McCafé mochas, lattes, and cappuccinos that Starbucks was finally motivated to cut product prices. CEO Howard Schultz said: "We know customers are looking for meaningful value, not just a lower price. In the coming days we're going to arm our consumers and partners with the facts about Starbucks coffee." Those facts included lowering the price of basic drinks, such as a "grande" iced coffee, by 45 cents to less than $2. With profits down 77 percent and same-store sales down 8 percent, and with McDonald's now selling specialty coffee drinks for $3 or less, Starbucks was motivated to take steps to keep customers who might be tempted by McDonald's lower prices.[35]

4.2 Identify Decision Criteria

Decision criteria are the standards used to guide judgments and decisions. Typically, the more criteria a potential solution meets, the better that solution will be.

Imagine that your regional sales manager asks for a recommendation on outfitting the sales force, many of whom travel regularly, with new laptops. What general factors will be most important? Reliability, price, warranty, service, and compatibility with existing software and hardware will all be important, but you must also consider the technical details. With technology changing so quickly, you'll probably want to buy laptops with as much capability and flexibility as you can afford.[36] But what will the sales force really need? How much memory storage will the users need? What kinds of programs will they use the most? How important is it that the laptop be compatible with other devices? Answering questions like these will help you identify the criteria that will guide the purchase of the new equipment.

4.3 Weight the Criteria

After identifying decision criteria, the next step is deciding which criteria are more or less important. Although there are numerous mathematical models for weighting decision criteria, all require the decision maker to provide an initial ranking of the criteria. Some use **absolute comparisons**, in which each criterion is compared to a standard or ranked on its own merits. Someone who wants to purchase a new car may consider the following criteria: predicted reliability, previous owners' satisfaction, predicted depreciation (the price you can expect when you sell the car), ability to avoid an accident, fuel economy, crash protection, acceleration, ride, and front seat comfort.

Different individuals will rank these criteria differently, depending on what they value or require in a car. Exhibit 5.4 shows the absolute weights that someone buying a car might use. Because these weights are absolute, each criterion is judged on its own importance, using a five-point scale, with "5" representing "critically important" and "1" representing "completely unimportant." In this instance, predicted reliability, fuel economy, and front seat comfort are rated most important, and acceleration and predicted depreciation are rated least important.

Another method uses **relative comparisons**, in which each criterion is compared directly to every other criterion.[37] Exhibit 5.5 shows six criteria that someone may use when buying a house. Moving across the first row, we see that the time of the daily commute has been rated more important (+1) than proximity to schools; less important (–1) than having an in-ground pool, recreation room, or a quiet street, and just as important as the house being brand new (0). Total weights, which are obtained by summing the scores in each column, indicate that the daily commute and proximity to schools are the most important factors for this home buyer, whereas an in-ground pool, a recreation room, and a quiet street are the least important.

Exhibit 5.4 Absolute Weighting of Decision Criteria for a Car Purchase

5 critically important
4 important
3 somewhat important
2 not very important
1 completely unimportant

1. Predicted reliability	1	2	3	4	(5)
2. Owner satisfaction	1	(2)	3	4	5
3. Predicted depreciation	(1)	2	3	4	5
4. Avoiding accidents	1	2	3	(4)	5
5. Fuel economy	1	2	3	4	(5)
6. Crash protection	1	2	3	(4)	5
7. Acceleration	(1)	2	3	4	5
8. Ride	1	2	(3)	4	5
9. Front seat comfort	1	2	3	4	(5)

4.4 Generate Alternative Courses of Action

After identifying and weighting the criteria that will guide the decision-making process, the next step is to identify possible courses of action that could solve the problem. The idea is to generate as many alternatives as possible. Let's assume that you're trying to select a city in Europe to be the location of a major office. After meeting with your staff, you generate a list of possible alternatives: Amsterdam, the Netherlands; Barcelona or Madrid, Spain; Berlin or Frankfurt, Germany; Brussels, Belgium; London, England; Milan, Italy; Paris, France; and Zurich, Switzerland.

Absolute comparisons a process in which each criterion is compared to a standard or ranked on its own merits

Relative comparisons a process in which each criterion is compared directly to every other

Exhibit 5.5 Relative Comparison of Home Characteristics

Home Characteristics	L	PS	IP	RR	QS	NBH
Daily commute (L)		+1	–1	–1	–1	0
Proximity to schools (PS)	–1		–1	–1	–1	–1
In-ground pool (IP)	+1	+1		0	0	+1
Recreation room (RR)	+1	+1	0		0	0
Quiet street (QS)	+1	+1	0	0		0
Newly built house (NBH)	0	+1	–1	0	0	
Total weight	+2	+5	–3	–2	–2	0

The Opposable Mind

When trying to solve a problem, creative thinking can help generate a variety of ideas, which are often then evaluated as separate options in an effort to come up with a solution. Roger Martin, dean of the Rotman School of Management, has a different view: he proposes that the ability to hold two opposing ideas in mind at the same time results in constructive tension that can lead to a "creative breakthrough." According to him, "a sure sign of a first-rate business intelligence is the ability to recognize two diametrically opposing ideas and meld them into a new model that is superior to either." In his book *The Opposable Mind: How Successful Leaders Win Through Integrative Thinking,* Martin uses Isadore Sharpe, the found of the luxury Four Seasons Hotel chain, as a prime example. As Martin tells it, "in the early 1970s, there were two dominant business models for would-be hoteliers: small hotels offering a few homey frills at modest prices and large, downtown hotels with expensive amenities that catered to business travelers. Rather than follow the lead of most business strategists, which is to look at a decision as a series of 'either-or' propositions and settle for the choice with the fewest downsides, Sharp held the two opposing models in his head, stared into the mystery of how to imagine a third way, and hit upon a design that would combine the best of the small hotel with the best of a large hotel." The concept proved to be a success for Sharpe; this Canadian-based company now has 90 hotels and resorts in 36 countries and continues to rely on the principles of friendliness and efficiency with high-quality service and luxury.

Sources: B. Breen, "Design Thursday: Roger Martin on "The Opposable Mind," *Fast Company,* 6 September 2007, available at: http://www.fastcompany.com/679333/design-thursday-roger-martin-opposable-mind, [accessed 1 March 2013], From Fast Company, September 6 www.fourseasons.com; http://rogerlmartin.com/library/books/the-opposable-mind/

Lightspring/Shutterstock.com

4.5 Evaluate Each Alternative

The next step is to systematically evaluate each alternative against each criterion. Because of the amount of information that must be collected, this step can take much longer and be much more expensive than other steps in the decision-making process. When selecting a European city for your office, you could contact economic development offices in each city, systematically interview businesspeople or executives who operate there, retrieve and use published government data on each location, or rely on published studies such as Cushman & Wakefield's *European Cities Monitor*, which conducts an annual survey of more than 500 senior European executives who rate European cities on 12 business-related criteria.[38]

No matter how you gather the information, the key is to use it to systematically evaluate each alternative against each criterion once you have it. Exhibit 5.6 shows how each of the 10 cities on your staff's list fared on each of the 12 criteria (higher scores are better), from qualified staff to freedom from pollution. London has the most qualified staff and the best access to markets and telecommunications, and is the easiest city to travel to and from, but it is also one of the most polluted cities on the list. Paris offers excellent access to markets and clients, but if your staff is multilingual, Amsterdam may be a better choice.

4.6 Compute the Optimal Decision

The final step in the decision-making process is to compute the optimal decision by determining the optimal value of each alternative. This is done by multiplying the rating for each criterion (Step 4.5) by the weight for that criterion (Step 4.3), and then summing those scores for each alternative course of action that you generated (Step 4.4). The 500 executives participating in Cushman & Wakefield's survey of the best European cities for business rated the 12 decision criteria in terms of importance, as shown in the first line of Exhibit 5.6. Access to quality staff, markets, and telecommunications was deemed most important. Freedom from pollution, on the other hand, while a concern, was not high on the list of priorities. To calculate the optimal value for Paris, its score in each category is multiplied by the weight for each category (.60 x .79 in the qualified staff category, for example). Then all of these scores are added together to produce the optimal value, as follows:

$$(.60 \times .79) + (.59 \times 1.11) + (.54 \times .79) + (.53 \times 1.39) + (.40 \times .21) + (.27 \times .26) + (.27 \times .57) + (.26 \times .31) + (.25 \times 1.10) + (.24 \times .45) + (.21 \times .61) + (.18 \times .16) = 3.22$$

Since London has a weighted average of 4.27 compared to 3.22 for Paris and 2.29 for Frankfurt, London clearly ranks as the best location for your company's new European office because of its large number of qualified staff; easy access to markets; outstanding ease of travel to, from, and within the city; excellent telecommunications; and top-notch business climate.

4.7 Limits to Rational Decision Making

In general, managers who diligently complete all six steps of the rational decision-making model will make better decisions than those who don't. So, when they can, managers should try to follow the steps in the rational decision-making model, especially for big decisions with long-range consequences.

To make perfect rational decisions, managers would have to operate in a perfect world with no real-world constraints. Of course, it never actually works like that in the real world. Managers face time and money constraints. They often don't have time to make extensive

Exhibit 5.6 Criteria Ratings Used to Determine the Best Locations for a New Office

	Qualified staff	Access to markets	Telecommunications	Travel to/from city	Cost of staff	Business climate	Languages spoken	Cost & value of office space	Travel within city	Available office space	Quality of life	Freedom from pollution	Weighted average	Ranking
Criteria Weights:	**60%**	**59%**	**54%**	**53%**	**40%**	**27%**	**27%**	**26%**	**25%**	**24%**	**21%**	**18%**		
Amsterdam	0.45	0.45	0.28	0.64	0.25	0.37	1.13	0.44	0.41	0.29	0.52	0.60	2.03	4
Barcelona	0.31	0.32	0.22	0.21	0.60	0.45	0.30	0.41	0.51	0.42	1.14	0.49	1.71	8
Berlin	0.38	0.29	0.42	0.27	0.46	0.29	0.49	0.67	0.62	0.73	0.31	0.25	1.78	6
Brussels	0.44	0.55	0.31	0.50	0.18	0.44	1.02	0.35	0.34	0.33	0.39	0.30	1.88	5
Frankfurt	0.55	0.72	0.57	1.29	0.11	0.17	0.58	0.28	0.25	0.37	0.22	0.15	2.29	3
London	1.32	1.37	1.21	1.71	0.11	0.52	1.38	0.18	1.11	0.49	0.42	0.11	4.27	1
Madrid	0.39	0.40	0.34	0.48	0.48	0.48	0.22	0.37	0.51	0.47	0.50	0.19	1.76	7
Munich	0.51	0.39	0.39	0.41	0.15	0.11	0.29	0.18	0.54	0.36	0.81	0.56	1.67	9
Paris	0.79	1.11	0.79	1.39	0.21	0.26	0.57	0.31	1.10	0.45	0.61	0.16	3.22	2
Zurich	0.28	0.22	0.31	0.26	0.03	0.66	0.54	0.12	0.39	0.16	0.61	0.95	1.41	10

Source: *European Cities Monitor 2011*, Cushman & Wakefield. Reprinted by permission.

© Jason Walton/iStockphoto.com

And the winner is ... London. When all the weights are calculated and compared, London is the best city in Europe for business.

lists of decision criteria. And they often don't have the resources to test all possible solutions against all possible criteria.

In theory, fully rational decision makers **maximize** decisions by choosing the optimal solution. In practice, limited resources along with attention, memory, and expertise problems make it nearly impossible for managers to maximize decisions. Consequently, most managers don't maximize—they satisfice. Maximizing is choosing the best alternative; **satisficing** is choosing a "good enough" alternative. In reality, however, the manager's limited time, money, and expertise mean that only a few alternatives will be assessed against a few decision criteria. In practice, the manager may visit two or three online computer or electronic retail sites, read a few recent computer reviews, and get bids from computer companies like Apple, Dell, Lenovo, Gateway, and Hewlett-Packard. The decision will be complete when the manager finds a good enough laptop computer that meets a few decision criteria.

Maximizing choosing the best alternative

Satisficing choosing a "good enough" alternative

LO5 Using Groups to Improve Decision Making

According to Blanchard's annual survey on corporate issues, 84 percent of companies use teams to handle special projects (i.e., to make decisions).[39] Why so many? When done properly, group decision making can lead to much better decisions than those typically made by individuals. In fact, many studies have found that groups consistently outperform individuals on complex tasks.

Groupthink a barrier to good decision making caused by pressure within a group for members to agree with one another

*Let's explore the **5.1 advantages and pitfalls of group decision making** and the following group decision-making methods: **5.2 structured conflict, 5.3 the nominal group technique,** and **5.4 the Delphi technique.***

5.1 Advantages and Pitfalls of Group Decision Making

Groups can do a much better job than individuals in two important steps of the decision-making process: defining the problem and generating alternative solutions. Group members usually possess different skills, experience, and knowledge, so groups are able to view problems from multiple perspectives and to gain access to more information. So groups find it easier to generate more alternative solutions. Studies have found that generating more solutions is critical to improving the quality of decisions. This can help groups perform better on complex tasks. It can also strengthen the commitment to making chosen solutions work.[40]

Still, group decision making has some pitfalls that can quickly erase these gains. One possible pitfall is groupthink. **Groupthink** occurs in highly cohesive groups when group members feel intense pressure to agree with one another so that the group can approve a proposed solution.[41] Because groupthink leads to consideration of a limited number of solutions and restricts discussion, it usually results in poor decisions. Groupthink is most likely to occur under the following conditions:

- The group is insulated from others with different perspectives.
- The group leader begins by expressing a strong preference for a particular decision.
- The group has no established procedure for systematically defining problems and exploring alternatives.
- Group members have similar backgrounds and experiences.[42]

Groupthink is thought to have contributed to the destruction of the US space shuttle *Columbia* in 2003. The foam used to insulate space shuttles often caused damage to the wing during launch. When *Columbia* re-entered the atmosphere, wing damage allowed superhot gas to enter the wing, which caused the shuttle to explode. Previous shuttle missions had unearthed this problem, and damage on this particular mission was suspected. However, NASA's culture did not allow individuals to be wrong, and its dependence on public and political support influenced decisions in favour of keeping missions on schedule even when delay would have allowed such problems to be investigated. Managers were reluctant to be the first to point out the problem, and requests for satellite images of the damage to *Columbia* during flight were ignored. The result? Loss of lives and a negative reputation for NASA—consequences worse than those that would have resulted from a delay to investigate the problems.[43]

When done properly, group decision making can lead to much better decisions.

A second potential problem with group decision making is that it takes considerable time. Reconciling schedules so that group members can meet takes time. Furthermore, it's a rare group that consistently holds productive task-oriented meetings to work through the decision process effectively. Some of the most common complaints about meetings (and thus decision making) are that the meeting's purpose is unclear, participants are unprepared, critical people are absent or late, conversation doesn't stay focused on the problem, and no one follows up on the decisions that were made. Marissa Mayer, CEO of Yahoo!, has strong opinions about group meetings, first demonstrated in her previous position as vice president of search products and user experience at Google. At Google she routinely held more than 70 meetings a week and was the last executive to hear a pitch before it was made to the cofounders. To keep meetings on track, Mayer set down six guidelines. Meetings must (1) have a firm agenda and (2) an assigned note taker. Meetings must occur (3) during established office hours, and (4) preferably in short, ten-minute micro-meetings. Those running the meeting should (5) discourage office politics and rely on data, and above all, they should (6) stick to the clock. Mayer's guidelines at Google helped meetings stay focused and productive. As the head of Yahoo!, Mayer continued to demonstrate her belief that when handled effectively, groups can improve the quality of decisions and business ideas. Her controversial decision to discontinue Yahoo!'s work-at-home policy for employees was based on her belief that in-person meetings provide greater insight and generate more business ideas.[44]

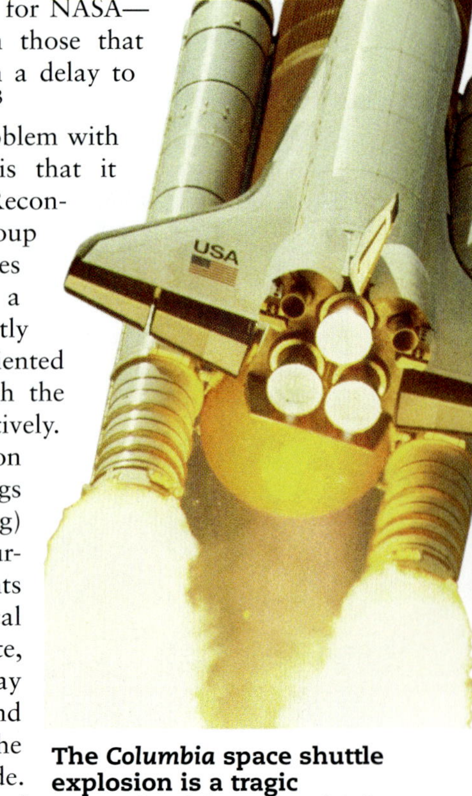

The *Columbia* space shuttle explosion is a tragic example of the groupthink gone wrong.

Strong-willed group members are a third possible pitfall to group decision making. Such an individual, whether the boss or a vocal group member, dominates group discussion and puts limits on how the problem is defined and what the solutions can be. Another potential problem is that the group members may not feel accountable for the decisions made and actions taken by the group unless they are personally responsible for some aspect of carrying out those decisions.

These pitfalls can lead to poor decision making, but this doesn't mean that managers should avoid using groups to make decisions. When facilitated well, group decision making can lead to much better decisions. The pitfalls of group decision making are not inevitable. Managers can overcome most of them by using the various techniques described next.

5.2 Structured Conflict

Most people view conflict negatively. Yet the right kind of conflict can lead to much better group decision making. **C-type conflict**, or "cognitive conflict," focuses on problem- and issue-related differences of opinion.[45] In c-type conflict, group members disagree because their different experiences and expertise lead them to view the problem and its potential solutions differently. C-type conflict is also characterized by a willingness to examine, compare, and reconcile those differences to produce the best possible solution.

By contrast, **a-type conflict**, meaning "aff-ective conflict," refers to the emotional reactions that can occur when disagreements become personal rather than professional. A-type conflict often results in hostility, anger, resentment, distrust, cynicism, and apathy. Unlike c-type conflict, a-type conflict undermines team effectiveness by preventing teams from engaging in the activities characteristic of c-type conflict that are critical to team effectiveness. Examples of a-type conflict statements are "your idea," "our idea," "my department," "you don't know what you are talking about," and "you don't understand our situation." Rather than focusing on issues and ideas, these statements focus on individuals.[46]

C-type conflict (cognitive conflict) disagreement that focuses on problem- and issue-related differences of opinion

A-type conflict (affective conflict) disagreement that focuses on individual or personal issues

Devil's advocacy a decision-making method in which an individual or a subgroup is assigned the role of a critic

Nominal group technique a decision-making method that begins and ends by having group members quietly write down and evaluate ideas to be shared with the group

Glow Images/Getty Images

Experienced managers likely find it easier to accept the idea that conflict in teams is inevitable (more important) is sometimes necessary for a team to succeed. To harness the positive effect of c-type conflict, and to minimize the negative impact of a-type conflict, managers would be wise to help team members realize that "winning" the argument doesn't necessarily lead to the best course of action. The best solutions are often those that involve some form of integration and a synthesis of differences.[47]

The **devil's advocacy** approach can be used to create c-type conflict by assigning an individual or a subgroup the role of critic. The following five steps establish a devil's advocacy program:

1. Generate a potential solution.
2. Assign a devil's advocate to criticize and question the solution.
3. Present the critique of the potential solution to key decision makers.
4. Gather additional relevant information.
5. Decide whether to use, change, or not use the originally proposed solution.[48]

When properly used, the devil's advocacy approach introduces c-type conflict into the decision-making process. Contrary to the common belief that conflict is bad, studies show that structured conflict leads to less a-type conflict, improved decision quality, and greater acceptance of decisions once they have been made.[49]

5.3 Nominal Group Technique

Nominal means "in name only." Accordingly, the **nominal group technique** received its name because it begins with a quiet time in which group members independently write down as many problem definitions and alternative solutions as possible. In other words, the nominal group technique begins by having group members act as individuals. After the quiet time the group leader asks each group member to share one idea at a time with the group. As they are read aloud, ideas are posted on flipcharts or

Delphi technique a decision-making method in which members of a panel of experts respond to questions and to one another until reaching agreement on an issue

Brainstorming a decision-making method in which group members build on one another's ideas to generate as many alternative solutions as possible

Electronic brainstorming a decision-making method in which group members use computers to build on one another's ideas and generate many alternative solutions

Production blocking a disadvantage of face-to-face brainstorming in which a group member must wait to share an idea because another member is presenting an idea

Evaluation apprehension fear of what others will think of your ideas

wallboards for all to see. This step continues until all ideas have been shared. In the next step, the group discusses the advantages and disadvantages of the ideas. The nominal group technique closes with a second quiet time in which group members independently rank the ideas presented. Group members then read their rankings aloud, and the idea with the highest average rank is selected.[50]

The nominal group technique improves group decision making by decreasing a-type conflict. But it also restricts c-type conflict. Consequently, the nominal group technique typically produces poorer decisions than does the devil's advocacy approach. Nonetheless, more than 80 studies have found that nominal groups produce better ideas than those produced by traditional groups.[51]

5.4 Delphi Technique

In the **Delphi technique**, the members of a panel of experts respond to questions and to one another until reaching agreement on an issue. The first step is to assemble a panel of experts. Unlike other approaches to group decision making, however, it isn't necessary to bring the panel members together in one place. Because the Delphi technique does not require the experts to leave their offices or disrupt their schedules, they are more likely to participate.

The second step is to create a questionnaire consisting of a series of open-ended questions for the experts. In the third step, the panel members' responses are analyzed, summarized, and fed back to the panel for reactions until the members reach agreement. Asking the members why they agree or disagree is important because it helps uncover their unstated assumptions and beliefs. Again, this process of summarizing panel feedback and obtaining reactions to that feedback continues until the panel members reach agreement.

5.5 Electronic Brainstorming

Brainstorming, in which group members build on others' ideas, is a technique for generating a large number of alternative solutions. Brainstorming has four rules:

1. The more ideas, the better.
2. All ideas are acceptable, no matter how wild or crazy they might seem.
3. Other group members' ideas should be used to come up with even more ideas.
4. Criticism or evaluation of ideas is not allowed.

In terms of decision making, brainstorming can generate a large number of ideas and possible solutions, although there are some disadvantages associated with this process. Fortunately, technology has been able to address some of these challenges through **electronic brainstorming** (EBS), where team members share information online, using computers to communicate possible solutions. These systems have helped remove some of the drawbacks of traditional face-to-face brainstorming, which can inhibit effective group decision making.

The first disadvantage that electronic brainstorming overcomes is **production blocking**, which occurs when you have an idea but have to wait to share it because someone else is already presenting an idea to the group. During this short delay, you may forget your idea or decide that it really wasn't worth sharing. Production blocking doesn't happen with EBS since group members can input ideas as they occur. In this way, there's no waiting your turn and the group can be exposed to a flow of ideas with very little effort.

The second disadvantage that EBS overcomes is **evaluation apprehension**, that is, being afraid of what others will think of your ideas. With EBS, there is less worry about being evaluated as ideas can be anonymous; this helps increase participation and creativity.

In the typical layout for EBS, all participants sit in front of computers around a U-shaped table. This configuration allows them to see their computer screens, the other participants, a large main screen, and a meeting leader or facilitator. Step 1 in electronic brainstorming is to anonymously generate as many ideas as possible. Groups commonly generate 100 ideas in a half-hour period. Step 2 is to edit the generated ideas, categorize them, and eliminate redundancies. Step 3 involves ranking the categorized ideas in terms of quality. Step 4, the last step, has three parts: generate a series of action steps, decide the best order for accomplishing these steps, and identify who is responsible for each step. All four steps are accomplished with computers and EBS software.[52]

Studies show that EBS is much more productive than face-to-face brainstorming. Four-person EBS groups produce 25 to 50 percent more ideas than four-person regular brainstorming groups, and 12-person EBS groups produce 200 percent more ideas than regular groups of the same size! In fact, because production blocking (i.e., waiting your turn) is not a problem with EBS, the number and quality of ideas generally increase with group size.[53]

Though it works much better than traditional brainstorming, EBS also has disadvantages. An obvious problem is the expense of computers, networks, software, and other equipment. As these costs continue to drop, however, EBS will become a viable option for more groups.

Another problem is that the anonymity of ideas may bother people who are used to having their ideas accepted by virtue of their position (i.e., the boss). On the other hand, one CEO said: "Because the process is anonymous, the sky's the limit in terms of what you can say, and as a result it is more thought-provoking. As a CEO, you'll probably discover things you might not want to hear but need to be aware of."[54]

A third disadvantage is that outgoing individuals who are more comfortable expressing themselves verbally may find it difficult to express themselves in writing. Finally, the most obvious problem is that participants have to be able to type. Those who can't type, or who type slowly, may be easily frustrated and find themselves at a disadvantage to experienced typists.

Brainwriting Techniques

Another take on traditional brainstorming is known as brainwriting, where group members sit together around a table; however, instead of expressing ideas through verbal communication, each participant writes down his or her ideas anonymously on sheets of papers or cards and then the ideas are distributed using a variety of formats to help spark more ideas. Some of the brainwriting approaches include the following:

- The 6-3-5 technique, where 6 group members each write down 3 ideas and then hand in their paper. This is repeated 5 times so that in the end, 108 ideas can be collected in a short amount of time.
- Brainpooling has participants record their ideas on a sheet of paper, then place their paper in the middle of the table and pick up someone else's paper, adding or modifying the ideas on that paper and then handing that paper in. The process continues until no one has any other ideas left.
- Idea card brainwriting attempts to generate extreme creativity, as participants each write down an absurd, off-the-wall idea or solution on an index card. The card is then passed to the person on the right, who then writes down the first thing that comes to mind after reading that card. The process continues for a few rounds and then the ideas are shared with the group.

Sources: L. Thompson, "How to neutralize a meeting tyrant," *CNN Money*, 11 February 2013, available at http://management.fortune.cnn.com/2013/02/11/meetings-conversation-dominator-work/, [accessed 1 March 2013]; N. Michinov, "Is Electronic Brainstorming or Brainwriting the Best Way to Improve Creative Performance in Groups?" *Journal of Applied Social Psychology*, 2012, 42, S1, pp.E222-E243; The Brainstorming Tweak: How to Boost Creativity in Groups, available at: http://www.spring.org.uk/2013/02/the-brainstorming-tweak-how-to-boost-creativity-in-groups.php

Monashee Frantz/OJO Images/Getty Images

Go online at
www.nelson.com/4ltrpress/icanmgmt2

And access the essential Study Tools online for this chapter:

- **Flashcards**, to help you study
- **Interactive Quizzes**, to test your knowledge
- **Audio Chapter Summaries**, for chapter review
- **Crossword Puzzles and Beat the Clock**, to review key terms
- **What Would You Do? Cases**, for applying your knowledge to real-life situations
- **Self Assessments**, to learn about what kind of manager you are
- **Videos and Media Quizzing**, where you can watch a video about a real-life company and test yourself on what you've learned

Be sure to consult the Chapter Review Card at the back of the textbook.

6

Organizational Strategy

LEARNING OUTCOMES

LO1 Specify the components of sustainable competitive advantage and explain why it is important.

LO2 Describe the steps involved in the strategy-making process.

LO3 Explain the different kinds of corporate-level strategies.

LO4 Describe the different kinds of industry-level strategies.

LO5 Explain the components and kinds of firm-level strategies.

Basics of Organizational Strategy

Fourteen years ago, Apple Computer was not in the music business. Then it released the iPod, which quickly set the standard for all other digital music devices. As the market matured, competitors tried to minimize Apple's competitive advantage by adding unique features to their own MP3 players. Sony entered the market, and so did SanDisk, Microsoft, and a host of other large players. Apple's continual improvements, however, allowed the iPod emerge on top with 83 percent of the market. But for how long?[1]

Apple dominates the recording industry, yet it is a computer company; witness its release of the iPad in 2010, the iPad2 in 2012, and the iPad Mini in 2013; all three have shaken up the computer industry.[2] Canada's BlackBerry did not exist until fairly recently, yet its BlackBerry at first took the smartphone industry by storm. Before falling from grace in 2012 (and losing more than 33 percent of its market share), the BlackBerry was a strategic darling.[3] With the new Z10 and Q10 in early 2013, Blackberry may have found the right strategy to be a winner again.

Apple has also had a huge impact on the smartphone industry with its various new iPhone entries, but again, it is a computer company—or is it? Google is a computer company, yet it has entered the smartphone industry with its Android phone, with Microsoft and Motorola fast on its heels. Even so, Samsung (with its Galaxy line) and Nokia still dominate the smartphone market.[4] How does a company decide which industries to enter, in which markets, and with which products?

How can dominant companies like Apple, Microsoft, Google, and Blackberry maintain their competitive advantage once strong, well-financed competitors enter the market? What can a company do to formulate better strategy? How does strategy relate to sustainable competitive advantage?

Resources the assets, capabilities, processes, information, and knowledge that an organization uses to improve its effectiveness and efficiency, create and sustain competitive advantage, and fulfill a need or solve a problem

Competitive advantage providing greater value for customers than competitors can

LO1 Sustainable Competitive Advantage

Resources are the assets, capabilities, processes, employees, information, and knowledge that an organization controls. Firms use their resources to improve organizational effectiveness and efficiency. Resources are vital to an organization's strategy because they can help companies create and sustain an advantage over competitors.[5]

Organizations can achieve a **competitive advantage** by using their resources to provide greater value for customers than competitors can. For example, the iPod's competitive advantage came from its simple, attractive design relative to its price. But Apple's most important advantage was being the first company to make it easy to legally purchase music online. Remember that prior to the iTunes store at iTunes.com, the only way to acquire digital music was by illegal file swapping. Apple negotiated agreements with nearly all of the major record labels to sell their music, and iTunes.com quickly became the premier

New Technology: An International Story

Apple developed its iPod out of existing technology. But CJ-Global Logistics Service (CJ-GLS), a Korean third-party logistics company, created new technology to solve old problems and, in the process, created a whole new business. Getting products to consumers efficiently involves managing not just boxes, but a lot of information as well. Invoices must be tracked. Boxes must be stored and inventory managed. Customers need to know when to expect delivery. CJ-GLS used a number of innovative methods to do this, including Internet-based delivery routing, sending delivery schedules to customers' PDAs, and tracking shipments with GPS. One of the most inefficient parts of the old process was managing inventory with bar codes. CJ-GLS replaced bar codes with an attachable chip containing inventory, storage, and delivery data that can be managed remotely through radio frequency identification (RFID). This approach to inventory yields no scanning errors and takes less time to manage. In addition, the chips have the capacity to store more information than a bar code and can easily be updated. RFID didn't just strengthen CJ-GLS's competitive advantage; it turned out to be a whole new way to manage logistics information.

Source: C. Kim, K. Yang, and J. Kim "A Strategy for Third-Party Logistics Systems: A Case Analysis Using the Blue Ocean Strategy," *Omega* 36 (August 2008) 522–534.

© Ryan McVay/Photodisc/Jupiterimages

Photo By RJ Sangosti/The Denver Post via Getty Images

Sustainable competitive advantage a competitive advantage that other companies have tried unsuccessfully to duplicate and have, for the moment, stopped trying to duplicate

Valuable resource a resource that allows companies to improve efficiency and effectiveness

Rare resources resources that are not controlled or possessed by many competing firms

Imperfectly imitable resources resources that are impossible or extremely costly or difficult for other firms to duplicate

platform for music downloading. Apple was a computer company, not a music company. Even so, it was able to use its resources to create a competitive advantage with an easy-to-understand site that provided free downloadable software for customers to use when organizing and managing their digital music libraries.[6]

The goal of most organizational strategies is to create and sustain a competitive advantage. A competitive advantage becomes a **sustainable competitive advantage** when other companies cannot match the value a firm is providing to customers. Sustainable competitive advantage is not the same as a *long-lasting* competitive advantage, although companies obviously want a competitive advantage to last a long time. Rather, a competitive advantage is *sustained* if competitors have tried and failed to duplicate the advantage and have, for the moment, stopped trying to do so. It's the corporate equivalent of your competitors saying, "We give up. You win. We can't do what you do, and we're not even going to try to do it any more." Four conditions must be met for a firm to achieve a sustainable competitive advantage. Its resources must be *valuable*, *rare*, *imperfectly imitable*, and *nonsubstitutable*.

Valuable resources allow companies to improve their efficiency and effectiveness. Unfortunately, changes in customer demand and preferences, competitors' actions, and technology can make once-valuable resources much less valuable.

Also, for competitive advantage to be sustainable, the valuable resources must also be rare. Think about it: How can a company sustain a competitive advantage if all of its competitors have similar resources and capabilities? Consequently, **rare resources**—resources that are not controlled or possessed by many competing firms—are necessary in order to sustain a competitive advantage. When Apple introduced the iPod, it was the only portable music player on the market that used hard drive technology. The iPod had an immediate advantage over its competitors because it satisfied consumers' desire to carry large numbers of songs on a portable device—something other MP3 systems and individual CD players could not do. But the technology that powered the iPod was readily available, so competitors were able to quickly imitate iPod's basic storage capacity. As competitors began introducing iPod look-alikes, Apple released new models called the iPod Touch (or iTouch), now on the fifth generation, the iPad, and the iPad Mini. With Wi-Fi and two cameras, these latest devices have the ability to make phone calls or open Skype as long as you have an Internet connection.

Clearly, valuable and rare resources can create temporary competitive advantage. For sustained competitive advantage, however, other firms must be unable to imitate or find substitutes for those valuable, rare resources. **Imperfectly imitable resources** are impossible or extremely costly or difficult to duplicate. For example, despite many attempts by competitors to imitate it, iTunes has retained its competitive lock on the music download business. Because it capitalized on Apple's reputation for developing customer-friendly software, the library of music, movies, and podcasts on iTunes is still two to three times larger than those of other music download sites. Because the company has developed a closed system for its iTunes and iPod, iPod owners can only download music from Apple's iTunes store. But consumers don't seem to mind. Kelly Moore, a sales representative for a Texas software company, takes her iPod everywhere she goes and keeps it synchronized with her iPad and iPhone. She says, "Once I find something I like, I don't switch brands."[7] She's not alone: it is projected that by 2015, people with iPads, iPods, and iPhones will be using iTunes to download more than 45 billion songs and 70 billion apps.[8] No other competitor will come close to those numbers.

Valuable, rare, imperfectly imitable resources can produce sustainable competitive advantage only if they are also

nonsubstitutable resources, meaning that no other resources can replace them and produce similar value or competitive advantage. The industry has produced equivalent substitutes for iTunes, but competitors have had to experiment with different business models in order to get customers to accept them.

For example, eMusic is a club retailer (like Costco or Sam's Club) that sells music downloads to club members for 25 to 50 percent less than iTunes and Amazon.com. At Microsoft's Zune Marketplace, customers can purchase songs, albums, and videos just like on iTunes, but the Zune Pass subscription allows you to download and stream every bit of music on the Zune Marketplace onto multiple devices, such as your PC, phone, and Xbox 360. Besides offering straight subscription models, some companies have experimented with price. iTunes charges 69 cents, 99 cents, or $1.29 per song; Amazon's online store typically charges 99 cents per song but also offers more than 25,000 songs at only 69 cents. Amazon is also aggressive with album prices, offering 100 albums a day for $5 and best-selling albums for $7.99. In response, Apple has removed digital rights management, which restricted the extent to which users can copy their music from one device to another.[9] It will take years to find out whether other music download sites will be an effective competitors against iTunes.

In summary, Apple has reaped the rewards of first-mover advantage from its interdependent iPod and iTunes. Apple's customer-friendly software, the capabilities of its iPod, the simple 99-cent-pay-as-you-go sales model of iTunes, and the unmatched list of music and movies that Apple makes available for download provide customers with a service that is valuable, rare, relatively nonsubstitutable, and, until recently, imperfectly imitable. Past success is, however, no guarantee of future success: Apple will have to continuously change and develop its offerings or risk being unseated by a more nimble competitor whose products are more relevant and have higher perceived value for consumers.

LO2 Strategy-Making Process

In order to produce sustainable competitive advantage, a company must have a strategy.[10] Exhibit 6.1 (on page 88) displays the three steps of the strategy-making process: ***2.1 assess the need for strategic change, 2.2 conduct a situational analysis,*** *and then* ***2.3 choose strategic alternatives.*** *Let's examine each of these steps in more detail.*

2.1 Assessing the Need for Strategic Change

The external business environment is much more turbulent than it used to be. With customers' needs constantly growing and changing, and with competitors working harder, faster, and smarter to meet those needs, the first step in creating a strategy is determining the need for strategic change. In other words, the company should determine whether it needs to change its strategy to sustain a competitive advantage.[11]

Determining the need for strategic change might seem easy to do, but really it's not. There's a great deal of uncertainty in strategic business environments. Furthermore, top-level managers are often slow to recognize the need for strategic change, especially at successful companies that have created and sustained competitive advantages. Because they are acutely aware of the strategies that made their companies successful, they continue to rely on those strategies even as the competition changes. In other words, success often leads to **competitive inertia**—a reluctance to change strategies or competitive practices that have succeeded in the past.

Besides being aware of the dangers of competitive inertia, what can managers do to improve the speed and accuracy with which they determine the need for strategic change? One method is to actively look for signs of strategic dissonance. **Strategic dissonance** is a discrepancy between a company's intended strategy and the strategic actions managers take when actually implementing that strategy.[12]

For example, when prominent Canadian businessman Edgar Bronfman, Jr., bought the struggling Warner Music Group, his strategy was to cut costs and change a company culture where excessive spending—not uncommon in the entertainment industry—was the norm. Accordingly, he laid off 1,200 employees to save $250 million and cut remaining salaries by as much as 50 percent. Yet a few weeks later, he contradicted his new cost-cutting strategy. First, he signed off on a $13,000 bill to charter a private jet to fly top company managers and the agents of the company's best-selling artists to the Grammy awards in Los Angeles. Then, despite his insistence that music industry professionals shouldn't be paid more than their counterparts in other industries, Bronfman quietly restored the salary cuts he had made after top executives complained.[13]

Strategic dissonance can indicate that managers are not doing what they should to carry out company strategy; but it can also mean that the intended strategy is out of date and needs to be changed.

2.2 Situational Analysis

A situational analysis can help managers determine the need for strategic change. A **situational analysis**, also called a **SWOT analysis** (*strengths, weaknesses, opportunities, threats*), is an assessment of the strengths and weaknesses in an organization's internal environment and the opportunities and threats in its external environment.[14]

Nonsubstitutable resource a resource that produces value or competitive advantage and has no equivalent substitutes or replacements

Competitive inertia a reluctance to change strategies or competitive practices that have been successful in the past

Strategic dissonance a discrepancy between a company's intended strategy and the strategic actions managers take when implementing that strategy

Situational (SWOT) analysis an assessment of the strengths and weaknesses in an organization's internal environment and the opportunities and threats in its external environment

Distinctive competence what a company can make, do, or perform better than its competitors

Core capabilities the internal decision-making routines, problem-solving processes, and organizational cultures that determine how efficiently inputs can be turned into outputs

Ideally, as shown in Step 2 of Exhibit 6.1, a SWOT analysis helps a company determine how to increase internal strengths and minimize internal weaknesses while maximizing external opportunities and minimizing external threats.

An analysis of strengths and weaknesses may be useful; but more vital to determining a strategic direction is an examination of the external forces acting the company. These external issues are called opportunities (if the forces are positive) or threats (if the forces may negatively affect the company).

Courtesy of T & T Supermarket, Inc.

However, let's start with an organization's internal environment—that is, its strengths and weaknesses. The internal assessment often begins with an assessment of its distinctive competencies and core capabilities. A **distinctive competence** is something that a company can make, do, or perform better than its competitors. For example, *Consumer Reports* magazine consistently ranks Toyota cars number one in quality and reliability.[15] Similarly, *PC Magazine* readers ranked Apple's desktop and laptop computers best in terms of service and reliability.[16]

Whereas distinctive competencies are tangible—for example, a product or service is faster, cheaper, or better—the core capabilities that produce distinctive competencies are not. **Core capabilities** are the less visible, internal decision-making routines, problem-solving processes, and organizational cultures that determine how efficiently inputs can be turned into outputs.[17] Distinctive competencies cannot be sustained for long without superior core capabilities. Offering Asian food products is a distinctive competence at T & T Supermarkets. At these stores, one can find every kind of Asian food imaginable. Most of the products T & T sells are exotic and unique. This company's goal is to enrich the lives of Asian families in Canada by offering them choice foods and household items in a comfortable shopping environment. It also hopes to introduce the colourful Asian food culture to Canada's multicultural society. "Freshness" is its most important operating value, one that it practises along with "customer satisfaction" to enhance its one-stop shopping convenience and personable service standards. This is an example of a focused differentiated approach. Loblaw's has recently purchased T & T Supermarkets to enhance Weston's corporate strategy.[18]

Exhibit 6.1 Three Steps of the Strategy-Making Process

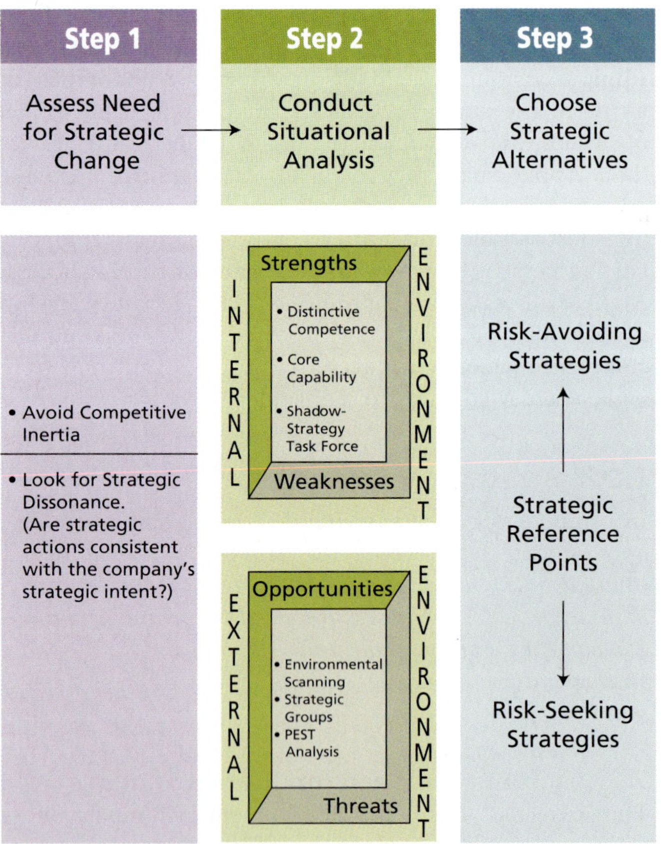

The second part of a situational analysis, after examining internal strengths and weaknesses, is to assess the opportunities and threats in the external environment. In Chapter 3, you learned that *environmental scanning* involves searching the environment for important events or issues that might affect the organization, such as pricing trends, new products, and advances in technology. In a situational analysis, managers use environmental

Shadow-Strategy Task Force

When looking for competitive issues, many managers look to competitors in the external environment. Others, however, prefer to examine the internal environment through a *shadow-strategy task force*. This strategy involves a company actively seeking out its own weaknesses and then thinking like its competitors, trying to determine how they can be exploited for competitive advantage. To make sure that the task force challenges conventional thinking, its members should be independent-minded, come from a variety of company functions and levels, and have the access and authority to question the company's current strategic actions and intent.

Source: W.B. Werther, Jr. and J.L. Kerr, "The Shifting Sands of Competitive Advantage," *Business Horizons* (May-June 1995): 11–17

scanning to identify specific opportunities and threats that can either improve or harm the company's ability to sustain its competitive advantage. They can do this by identifying strategic groups and forming shadow-strategy task forces.

The easiest way to examine factors in the external environment is to go through a **PEST analysis**. *Political* forces include government trade agreements, taxation, government ownership, and laws and regulations that may affect businesses. *Economic* forces include interest rates, exchange rates, GDP and other general economic indicators, unemployment, and other factors over which a company has no control. *Social* and Demographic factors include age, ethnicity, housing, purchasing psychometrics, and other changes or trends that affect consumer behaviours. *Technological* factors include new processes, new methods, new discoveries, and new ways of communicating, none of which, again, a company can control.[19] A company's strategy must take into account external (positive) opportunities and leverage them in a beneficial manner, while trying to overcome with external (negative) threats.[20]

A **strategic group** is a group of other companies within an industry that top managers choose and follow closely in order to compare, evaluate, and benchmark their own company's strategic threats and opportunities.[21] (*Benchmarking* involves identifying outstanding practices, processes, and standards at other companies and adapting them to your own.) Typically, managers include a company as part of their strategic group if they compete directly with it for customers or if it uses strategies similar to theirs. It's likely that the managers at Home Depot, a large Canadian home improvement and hardware retailer, assess strategic threats and opportunities by comparing their company to a strategic group consisting of the other home improvement and hardware retailers, as illustrated in Exhibit 6.2 on page 90.

When scanning the environment for strategic threats and opportunities, managers tend to categorize the different companies in their industry as core or secondary firms.[22] **Core firms** are the central companies in a strategic group. Home Depot operates 180 stores in all 10 Canadian provinces. The company has more than 35,000 employees in Canada and annual revenues over $8 billion. By comparison, Rona has 680 stores in 10 provinces and 27,000 Canadian employees. Clearly, Rona is the closest competitor to Home Depot and would probably be classified as a core firm in Home Depot's strategic group. Lowe's, a recent entry on the Canadian market, currently has only 16 stores (mostly in Ontario). It stocks 40,000 products in each store and has total annual revenues of more than $2 billion. Lowe's is in Home Depot's strategic group and must be one of the competitors they watch.[23]

Secondary firms use strategies related to but somewhat different from those of core firms. TIM-BR MART has more stores than Home Depot: 700 in Canada. But TIM-BR MART's franchise structure and small, individualized stores keep it from being a core firm in Home Depot's strategic group.[24] Likewise, Home

PEST an acronym that stands for the Political, Economic, Social/Demographic and Technological factors that affect a company and shape the company's strategy

Strategic group a group of companies within an industry that top managers choose to compare, evaluate, and benchmark strategic threats and opportunities

Core firms the central companies in a strategic group

Secondary firms the firms in a strategic group that follow strategies related to but somewhat different from those of the core firms

Exhibit 6.2 Core and Secondary Firms in the Home Improvement Industry

Strategic reference points the strategic targets managers use to measure whether a firm has developed the core competencies it needs to achieve a sustainable competitive advantage

Depot's management probably doesn't concern itself much with Canac-Marquis-Grenier, which has only two dozen stores in Quebec.[25] Managers need to be aware of the potential threats and opportunities posed by secondary firms, but they usually spend more time assessing the threats and opportunities associated with core firms.

2.3 Choosing Strategic Alternatives

After determining the need for strategic change and conducting a situational analysis, the last step in strategy making is to choose strategic alternatives that will help the company create or maintain a sustainable competitive advantage. According to strategic reference point theory, managers choose between two basic alternative strategies. They can choose a conservative, *risk-avoiding strategy* that aims to protect an existing competitive advantage. Or they can choose an aggressive, *risk-seeking strategy* that aims to extend or create a sustainable competitive advantage.

The choice to seek or avoid risk typically depends on whether top management views the company as falling above or below strategic reference points. **Strategic reference points** are the targets that managers use to measure whether their firm has developed the core competencies it needs to achieve a sustainable competitive advantage. If a hotel chain decides to compete by providing superior quality and service, then top management will track the success of this strategy through customer surveys or published hotel ratings such as those provided by vacationcanada.com. By contrast, if a hotel chain decides to compete on price, it will regularly conduct market surveys to check the prices of other hotels. The competitors' prices are the hotel managers' strategic reference points against which to compare their own pricing strategy. If competitors can consistently underprice them, then the managers need to determine whether their staff and resources have the core competencies to compete on price.

As shown in Exhibit 6.3, when a company is performing above or better than its strategic reference points, top management will typically be satisfied with

Exhibit 6.3 Strategic Reference Points

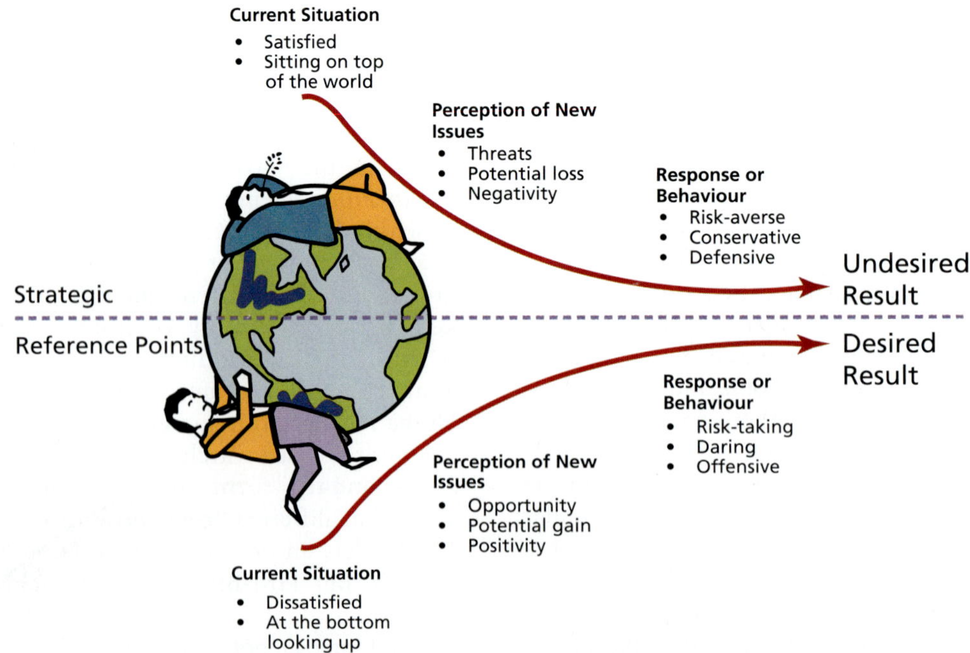

Source: A. Fiegenbaum, S. Hart, & D. Schendel, "Strategic Reference Point Theory," *Strategic Management Journal* 17 (1996): 219-235.

the company's strategy. Ironically, this satisfaction tends to make top management conservative and risk-averse. Since the company already has a sustainable competitive advantage, the worst thing that could happen would be to lose it, so new issues are viewed as threats, as are changes in the company's external environment. By contrast, when a company is performing below or worse than its strategic reference points, top managers tend to be dissatisfied with its strategy. In this case, managers are much more likely to choose a daring, risk-taking strategy. If the current strategy is producing substandard results, the company has nothing to lose by switching to risky new strategies in the hope that it can thereby create a sustainable competitive advantage. Managers of companies in this situation view new issues or changes in the external environment as opportunities for gain.

Strategic reference point theory is not deterministic, however. Managers are not predestined to choose risk-averse or risk-seeking strategies for their companies depending solely on their current situation. Indeed, one of the most important elements of the theory is that managers can influence the strategies chosen by their company by *actively changing and adjusting* the strategic reference points they use to judge strategic performance. A company that has become complacent after consistently surpassing its strategic reference points can change from a risk-averse to a risk-taking orientation by raising its performance standards (i.e., strategic reference points).

Canadian Tire is one of Canada's 35 largest publicly traded companies. It operates an interrelated network of businesses engaged in retailing (hard goods, apparel, petroleum) and services (financial, automotive). Well known for its Canadian Tire money, the company has over 475 stores. Each Canadian Tire store is operated by a franchisee. The buildings and lands are owned or leased by the company; everything inside the building, from fixtures to merchandise, is owned by the franchisee. Canadian Tire Corporation has tried twice to expand into the US market. In the 1980s it acquired the White Auto Store chain, concentrated in Texas; that attempt cost Canadian Tire $200 million in winding-up costs. In 1991 it made a second attempt by acquiring the Auto Source chain, with grand plans for 100 to 120 outlets in the US Midwest. It later sold the Auto Source chain. That attempt reportedly cost it $80.6 million. Both attempts were examples of a firm using an offensive-minded strategy that ultimately failed.[26] A daring strategy like this is emblematic of a red ocean (see box on page 101). Canada Tire has learned from these forays into the United States.

Meanwhile in Canada, the entry of new and more aggressive retailers such as Wal-Mart have caused Canadian Tire to sit up and take notice. It has revamped many of its stores, opened new stores in downtown locations, refurbished older stores, and overhauled many aspects of its strategy.[27] It is also now using new and highly innovative approaches to retail; one of these involves a business sustainability strategy that includes convenience kiosks, gas bar canopies, car washes, and other non-traditional "big box" offerings.[28] The US discount retailer Target, now picking up speed after opening stores in Canada recently, is a market leader in housewares, using pitch-perfect design, competitive pricing, and clever promotion to drive sales. Many existing retailers already compete in housewares, including Sears, the Bay, Stokes, Home Outfitters, and Wal-Mart, and even home improvement stores like Lowe's. How can Canadian Tire hope to win? "I think Canadian Tire can't just be tires or automotive. It has to be more than that," said Maureen Atkinson, a retail consultant at J.C. Williams Group. "They can't play everywhere so they are going to have to look for places they think they can play. I'm not sure housewares is the right place, but I think they do have to put a line in the sand and decide that this is going to be it."[29] Canadian Tire is certainly not going to be counted out in this round.

So even when (perhaps *especially* when) companies have achieved a sustainable competitive advantage, top managers must adjust or change strategic reference points

Werewolves or Widgets?

New opportunities make you re-evaluate your strategy, but change is not always good. ChipIn makes widgets, small programs that place an interactive icon on your website that can allow you to shop at other websites, check the weather, or conduct online transactions. To promote a new widget for Facebook pages, the company created an application that allows users to become a werewolf or a vampire and "bite" or "infect" other users. The application became one of the top 100 most downloaded widgets on Facebook, and other companies began to show interest in ChipIn's werewolves and vampires as tools for advertising their own products (which meant cash for ChipIn). The popularity of werewolves and vampires presented ChipIn with a potential strategy shift: Should the company start making Facebook applications? Carnet Williams remembered the Internet bubble days and decided to stick with what his company knew best: he sold off the werewolves and vampires in the interest of long-term growth.

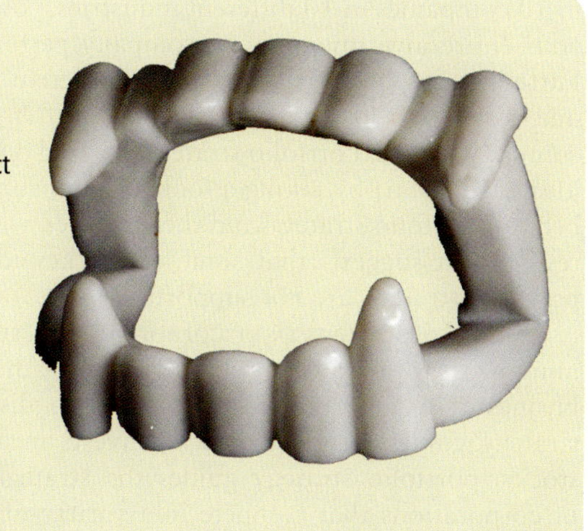

Source: A. Salkever, "To Embrace or Flee Facebook?" *Inc.* (January 2008) 56–58.

Diversification a strategy for reducing risk by owning a variety of items (stocks or, in the case of a corporation, types of businesses) so that the failure of one stock or one business does not doom the entire portfolio

Portfolio strategy a corporate-level strategy that minimizes risk by diversifying investment among various businesses or product lines

Acquisition the purchase of a company by another company

Unrelated diversification creating or acquiring companies in completely unrelated businesses

in order to challenge themselves and their employees to develop new core competencies for the future. Effective organizations often revise their strategic reference points to better focus managers' attention on new challenges and opportunities in their ever-changing business environment.

Corporate-, Industry-, and Firm-Level Strategies

To formulate effective strategies, companies must be able to answer these three basic questions:

- What business are we in?
- How should we compete in this industry?
- Who are our competitors, and how should we respond to them?

These simple but powerful questions are at the heart of corporate-, industry-, and firm-level strategies.

LO3 Corporate-Level Strategies

Corporate-level strategy is the overall organizational strategy that addresses the question "What business or businesses are we in or should we be in?" *There are two main approaches to corporate-level strategy that companies use to decide which businesses they should be in: **3.1 portfolio strategy** and **3.2 grand strategies.***

3.1 Portfolio Strategy

A standard strategy for stock market investors is **diversification**, or owning stocks in a variety of companies in different industries. The purpose of this strategy is to reduce the risk in one's stock portfolio (collection of stocks). The basic idea is simple. If you invest in 10 companies in 10 different industries, you won't lose your entire investment if one company performs poorly. Furthermore, because they're in different industries, one company's losses are likely to be offset by another company's gains. Portfolio strategy is based on these same ideas. We'll start by taking a look at the theory and ideas behind portfolio strategy and then proceed with a critical review that suggests that some of the key ideas behind portfolio strategy are *not* supported.

Portfolio strategy is a corporate-level strategy that minimizes risk by diversifying investment among various businesses or product lines.[30] Just as a diversification strategy guides an investor who invests in a variety of stocks, portfolio strategy guides the strategic decisions of corporations that compete in a variety of businesses. For example, portfolio strategy could be used to guide the strategy of a company like 3M, which has many locations in Canada and which makes 55,000 products for seven different business sectors: consumers and offices (Post-its, Scotch tape, etc.); display and graphics (for computers, smartphones, TVs); electronics and communications (flexible circuits used in printers and electronic displays); health care (medical, surgical, dental, and personal care products); industrial (tapes, adhesives, supply chain software); safety, security, and protection services (glass safety, fire protection, respiratory products); and transportation (products and components for the manufacture, repair, and maintenance of autos, aircraft, boats, and other vehicles).[31] Furthermore, just as investors consider the mix of stocks in their stock portfolio when deciding which ones to buy or sell, managers following portfolio strategy try to acquire companies that fit well with the rest of their corporate portfolio and to sell those that don't. Portfolio strategy provides the following guidelines to help companies make these difficult decisions.

First, according to portfolio strategy, the more businesses in which a corporation competes, the smaller its overall chances of failing. Think of a corporation as a stool and its businesses as the legs of the stool. The more legs or businesses added to the stool, the less likely it is to tip over. Using this analogy, portfolio strategy reduces 3M's risk of failing because the corporation's survival depends on essentially seven different business sectors. Managers employing portfolio strategy can either develop new businesses internally or look for potential new **acquisitions**, that is, other companies to buy.

Corporate-Level Strategies

PORTFOLIO STRATEGY (Section 3.1)	GRAND STRATEGIES (Section 3.2)
• Acquisitions, unrelated diversification, related diversification, single businesses to acquire • Boston Consulting Group matrix • Stars • Question marks • Cash cows • Dogs	• Growth • Stability • Retrenchment/recovery

Second, beyond adding new businesses to the corporate portfolio, portfolio strategy predicts that companies can reduce risk even more through **unrelated diversification**—creating or acquiring companies in completely unrelated businesses (more on the accuracy of this prediction later). According to portfolio strategy, when businesses are unrelated, losses in one business or industry should have a minimal impact on the performance of other companies in the corporate portfolio. One of the best examples of unrelated diversification is the international company Samsung of Korea. Samsung has businesses in electronics, machinery and heavy industries, chemicals, financial services, and other areas ranging from automobiles to hotels and entertainment.[32] Because most internally grown businesses tend to be related to existing products or services, portfolio strategy suggests that acquiring new businesses is the preferred method of unrelated diversification.

Third, investing the profits and cash flows from mature, slow-growth businesses into newer, faster growing businesses can reduce long-term risk. The best-known portfolio strategy for guiding investment in a corporation's businesses is the Boston Consulting Group (BCG) matrix. The **BCG matrix** is a portfolio strategy that managers use to categorize their corporation's businesses by growth rate and relative market share; this helps them decide how to invest corporate funds. BCG, which began as a consulting business in 1963, also introduced the now-ubiquitous concept of the experience curve (costs go down as experience increases), followed by the growth share matrix, shown in Exhibit 6.4.

The BGC matrix separates businesses into four categories based on how fast the market is growing (high-growth or low-growth) and the size of the business's share of that market (small or large). **Stars** are companies that have a large share of a fast-growing market. To take advantage of a star's fast-growing market and its strength in that market (large share), the corporation must invest substantially in it. The investment is usually worthwhile, however, because many stars produce sizable future profits. **Question marks** are companies that have a small share of a fast-growing market. If the corporation invests in these companies, they may eventually become stars, but their relative weakness in the market (small share) makes investing in question marks more risky than investing in stars. **Cash cows** are companies that have a large share of a slow-growing market. Companies in this situation are often highly profitable, hence the name "cash cow." Finally, **dogs** are companies that have a small share of a slow-growing market. As the name suggests, having a small share of a slow-growth market is often not profitable.

Since the idea is to redirect investment from slow-growing to fast-growing companies, the BCG matrix starts by recommending that the substantial cash flows from cash cows be reinvested in stars while the cash lasts (see arrow 1 in Exhibit 6.4) to help them grow even faster and obtain even more market share. Under this strategy, current profits help produce future profits. As market growth slows over time, some stars may turn into cash cows (see arrow 2).

Cash flows should also be directed to some question marks (see arrow 3). Although riskier than stars, question marks have great potential because of their fast-growing markets. Managers must decide which question marks are most likely to turn into stars (and therefore warrant further investment) and which ones are too risky and should be sold. It is hoped that over time, some question marks will become stars as their small markets become large ones (see arrow 4). Finally, because dogs lose money, the corporation should "find them new owners" or "take them to the pound." In other words, dogs should either be sold to other companies or be closed down and liquidated for their assets (see arrow 5).

Although the BCG matrix and other forms of portfolio strategy are relatively popular among managers, portfolio strategy has some drawbacks. The most significant: contrary to the predictions of portfolio strategy, evidence suggests that acquiring unrelated businesses is *not* useful. As shown in Exhibit 6.5 on page 94, there is a U-shaped relationship between diversification and risk. The left side of the curve shows that single businesses with

BCG matrix a portfolio strategy, developed by the Boston Consulting Group, that categorizes a corporation's businesses by growth rate and relative market share and helps managers decide how to invest corporate funds

Star a company with a large share of a fast-growing market

Question mark a company with a small share of a fast-growing market

Cash cow a company with a large share of a slow-growing market

Dog a company with a small share of a slow-growing market

Exhibit 6.4 Boston Consulting Group Matrix

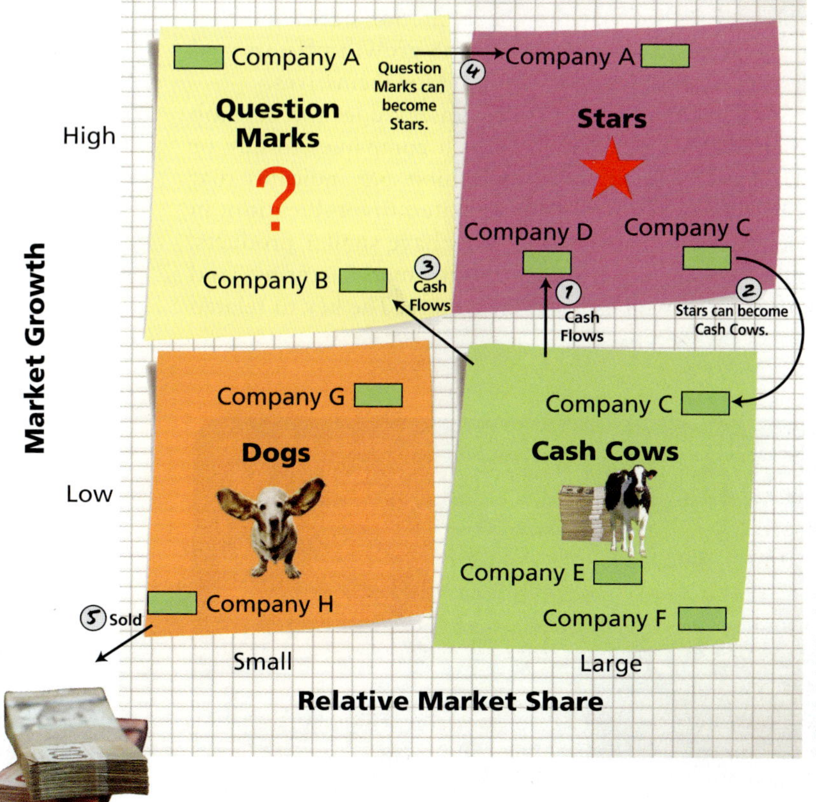

© Claudio Baldini/iStockphoto.com (graph paper); © Marie-france Belanger/iStockphoto.com (coloured notes); © Jason Lugo/iStockphoto.com (cow); © stevecoleimages/iStockphoto.com (dog); Photos.com / Used with permission of The Bank of Canada (money)

Related diversification creating or acquiring companies that share similar products, manufacturing, marketing, technology, or cultures

Grand strategy a broad corporate-level strategic plan used to achieve strategic goals and guide the strategic alternatives that managers of individual businesses or subunits may use

Growth strategy a strategy that focuses on increasing profits, revenues, market share, or the number of places in which the company does business

no diversification are extremely risky (if the single business fails, the entire business fails). So, in part, the portfolio strategy of diversifying is correct—competing in a variety of different businesses can lower risk. However, portfolio strategy is partly wrong, too—the right side of the curve shows that conglomerates composed of completely unrelated businesses are even riskier than single, undiversified businesses.

A second set of problems with portfolio strategy has to do with the dysfunctional consequences that occur when companies are categorized as stars, cash cows, question marks, or dogs. The BCG matrix often yields incorrect judgments about a company's potential. This is because it relies on past performance (i.e., previous market share and previous market growth), which is a notoriously poor predictor of future company performance.

Furthermore, using the BCG matrix can weaken the strongest performer in the corporate portfolio, the cash cow. As funds are redirected from cash cows to stars, corporate managers essentially take away the resources needed to exploit the cash cow's new business opportunities. As a result, the cash cow becomes less aggressive in seeking new business and in defending its present business. Finally, labelling a top performer as a cash cow can harm employee morale. Cash cow employees realize that they have inferior status and that they are now working to fund the growth of stars and question marks instead of working for themselves.

So, what kind of portfolio strategy does the best job of helping managers decide which companies to buy or sell? The U-shaped curve in Exhibit 6.5 indicates that the best approach is probably **related diversification**, in which the different business units have similar products, technologies, and approaches to manufacturing and marketing, as well as a similar culture. The key to related diversification is to acquire or create new companies with core capabilities that complement the core capabilities of businesses already in the corporate portfolio. Hormel Foods is an example of related diversification in the food business. The company both manufactures and markets a variety of foods from deli meats to salsa to the infamous SPAM® (which, by the way, stands for "spiced ham").

Exhibit 6.5 U-Shaped Relationship Between Diversification and Risk

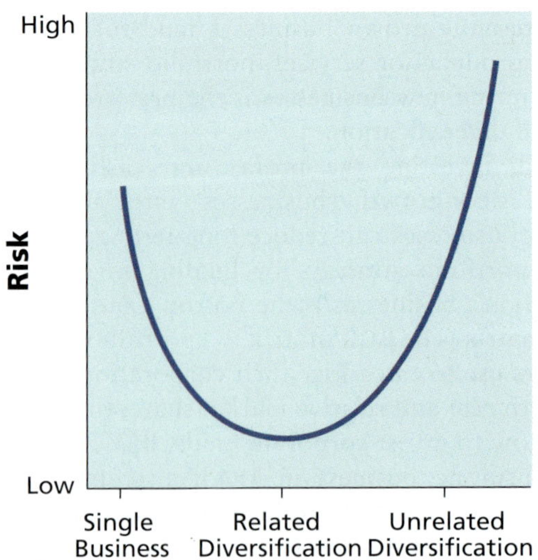

Source: Reprinted with permission of Academy of Management, P O Box 3020, Briar Cliff Manor, NY, 10510-8020. M. Lubatkin & P.J. Lane, "Psst - The Merger Mavins Still Have It Wrong" *Academy of Mangement Executive* 10 (1996) 21–39.

© AP Images

We began this section with the example of 3M and its 55,000 products, which it sells to seven different business sectors. While seemingly different, most of 3M's product divisions are based in some manner on its distinctive competencies in adhesives and tape (e.g., wet or dry sandpaper, Post-it notes, Scotchgard fabric protector, transdermal skin patches, reflective materials used in traffic signs, etc.). Furthermore, all of 3M's divisions share its strong corporate culture, which promotes and encourages risk taking and innovation. In sum, in contrast to a single, undiversified business or unrelated diversification, related diversification reduces risk because the different businesses can work as a team, relying on one another for needed experience, expertise, and support.

3.2 Grand Strategies

A **grand strategy** is a broad strategic plan to help an organization achieve its strategic goals.[33] Grand strategies guide the strategic alternatives that managers of individual businesses or subunits may use in deciding what businesses they should be in. There are three kinds of grand strategies: growth, stability, and retrenchment/recovery.

The purpose of a **growth strategy** is to increase profits, revenues, market share, or the number of places (stores, offices, locations) in which the company does business. Companies can grow in several ways. For example, they can grow externally by merging with or acquiring other companies in the same or different businesses.

Another way to grow is internally, directly expanding the company's existing business or creating and growing new businesses. In Canada, Staples sells office supplies in retail stores, online, and through catalogues to individuals as well as small and large businesses. The company wants to strengthen its ability to deliver supplies directly to consumers. In order to accomplish this, the company is seeking to grow externally by acquiring other companies that specialize in delivery.[34]

With a **stability strategy**, the company keeps doing what it has been doing, just doing it better. Companies following a stability strategy try to improve how they sell the same products or services to the same customers. For example, Subaru has been making four-wheel-drive station wagons for 30 years. Over the past decade, it has strengthened this focus by manufacturing only all-wheel-drive vehicles, such as the Subaru Legacy and Outback; both are popular in snowy and mountainous regions.[35] Companies often choose a stability strategy when their external environment doesn't change much or after they have struggled with periods of explosive growth.

The purpose of a **retrenchment strategy** is to turn around very poor company performance by shrinking the size or scope of the business or, if a company is in multiple businesses, by shutting down different lines of the business. The initial steps in a retrenchment strategy often include making significant cost reductions; laying off employees; closing poorly performing stores, offices, or manufacturing plants; and/or closing or selling entire lines of products or services.[36] BlackBerry had to go through a retrenchment in 2012, after its sales and market share plummeted. Its stock lost more than two-thirds of its value in 2012 after its BlackBerry was overtaken by more powerful devices from Apple and from manufacturers running the Android operating software. The company swung from a profit of US$934 million to a loss of $125 million. The Waterloo device maker says it will refocus on its core enterprise market. It will also consider options for turning the company around that could include partnerships with rivals. We will see if the retrenchment strategy succeeds so that the company passes into the recovery stage.

After cutting costs and reducing a business's size or scope, the second step in a retrenchment strategy is recovery. **Recovery** involves taking strategic actions return the company to a growth strategy. This two-step process of cutting and recovery is analogous to pruning roses. Before each growing season, roses should be cut back to two-thirds their normal size. Pruning doesn't damage the roses; it makes them stronger and more likely to produce beautiful, fragrant flowers. The retrenchment-and-recovery process is similar. Cost reductions, layoffs, and plant closings are sometimes necessary to restore companies to good health. Like pruning, those cuts are intended to allow companies to eventually return to growth (i.e., recovery). When company performance drops significantly, a strategy of retrenchment and recovery may help the company return to a successful growth strategy. Daimler experienced just this after it split from Chrysler. The company's ability to focus on its strengths in the luxury car industry (Daimler makes Mercedes-Benz) took it from a loss of €12 million to a profit of €1.69 billion.[37]

LO4 Industry-Level Strategies

Industry-level strategy addresses the question "How should we compete in this industry?"

*Let's find out more about industry-level strategies by discussing **4.1 the five industry forces that determine overall levels of competition in an industry** and **4.2 the positioning strategies** and **4.3 adaptive strategies** that companies can use to achieve sustained competitive advantage and above-average profits.*

4.1 Five Industry Forces

According to Harvard professor Michael Porter, five industry forces determine an industry's overall attractiveness and potential for long-term profitability. These forces are as follows: the character of the rivalry, the threat of new entrants, the threat of substitute products or services, the bargaining power of suppliers, and the bargaining power of buyers (see Exhibit 6.6 on page 100). The stronger these forces, the less attractive the industry becomes to corporate investors because it is more difficult for companies to make profits. Let's examine how these industry forces are bringing changes to several kinds of industries.

Character of the rivalry is a measure of the intensity of competitive behaviour between companies in an industry. Is the competition among firms aggressive and cutthroat, or do competitors focus more on serving customers than on attacking one another? Industry attractiveness and profitability both decrease when rivalry is cutthroat. One does not have to look hard to notice the intensity of the rivalry between Molson Canadian and Labatt's Blue.[38] The beverage industry is highly competitive in the soft drink sector as well, as illustrated by the intense rivalry between Coke® and Pepsi®. Does your school offer both, or has a deal been made that just offers the one product at your school? On the Internet, or in any Saturday paper across Canada, you will see pages and pages of car advertisements

{ The stronger the forces, the less attractive the industry. }

Stability strategy a strategy that focuses on improving the way in which the company sells the same products or services to the same customers

Retrenchment strategy a strategy that focuses on turning around very poor company performance by shrinking the size or scope of the business

Recovery the strategic actions taken after retrenchment to return to a growth strategy

Industry-level strategy a corporate strategy that addresses the question "How should we compete in this industry?"

Character of the rivalry a measure of the intensity of competitive behaviour between companies in an industry

Threat of new entrants a measure of the degree to which barriers to entry make it easy or difficult for new companies to get started in an industry

Threat of substitute products or services a measure of the ease with which customers can find substitutes for an industry's products or services

Bargaining power of suppliers a measure of the influence that suppliers of parts, materials, and services to firms in an industry have on the prices of these inputs

Bargaining power of buyers a measure of the influence that customers have on a firm's prices

Cost leadership the positioning strategy of producing a product or service of acceptable quality at consistently lower production costs than competitors can, so that the firm can offer the product or service at the lowest price in the industry

announcing "Year End Clearance," "Everything Must Go," and "New Models Now Available."[39] The current competition for selling you automobiles is as hot and vicious as it always was.

The **threat of new entrants** is a measure of the degree to which barriers to entry make it easy or difficult for new companies to get started in an industry. If new companies can easily enter the industry, then competition will increase and prices and profits will fall. On the other hand, if there are sufficient barriers to entry, such as large capital requirements to buy expensive equipment or plant facilities or the need for specialized knowledge, then competition will be weaker and prices and profits will generally be higher. For instance, high costs and intense competition make it very difficult to enter the video game business. With today's average video game taking 12 to 36 months to create, and millions to develop, and teams of highly paid creative workers to develop realistic graphics, captivating story lines, and innovative game capabilities, the barriers to entry for this business are obviously extremely high. The provinces of Quebec and British Columbia even compete with various tax incentives and tax breaks that help to raise the entry barriers.[40]

The **threat of substitute products or services** is a measure of the ease with which customers can find substitutes for an industry's products or services. If customers can easily find substitute products or services, the competition will be greater and profits will be lower. If there are few or no substitutes, competition will be weaker and profits will be higher. Generic medicines are some of the best-known examples of substitute products. Under Canadian patent law, a company that develops a drug has exclusive rights to produce and market that drug for 17 years. Prices and profits are generally high during this period if the drug sells well. After 17 years, however, the patent will expire, and any pharmaceutical company can manufacture and sell the same drug. When this happens, individual drug prices drop substantially, and the company that developed that patented drug typically sees its revenues drop sharply.

Exhibit 6.6 Porter's Five Industry Forces

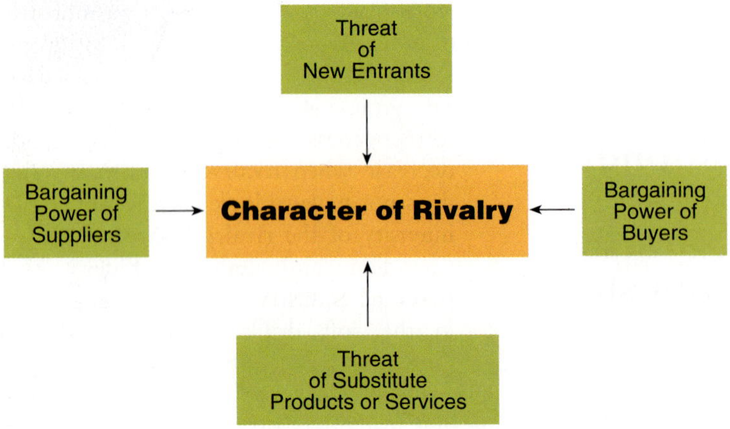

Threat of New Entrants → Character of Rivalry
Bargaining Power of Suppliers → Character of Rivalry
Bargaining Power of Buyers → Character of Rivalry
Threat of Substitute Products or Services → Character of Rivalry

Source: Reprinted with permission of Simon & Schuster Publishing Group from the Free Press edition of *COMPETITIVE STRATEGY: Techniques for Analyzing Industries and Competitors*, by Michael E. Porter.

Bargaining power of suppliers is a measure of the influence that suppliers of parts, materials, and services to firms in an industry have on the prices of these inputs. When companies can buy parts, materials, and services from numerous suppliers, the companies will be able to bargain with the suppliers to keep prices low. Today, there are so many suppliers of inexpensive, standardized parts, computer chips, and video screens that dozens of new companies are beginning to manufacture flat-screen TVs. In other words, the weak bargaining power of suppliers has made it easier for new firms to enter the HDTV business. On the other hand, if there are few suppliers, or if a company is dependent on a supplier with specialized skills and knowledge, then the suppliers will have the bargaining power to dictate price levels.

Bargaining power of buyers is a measure of the influence that customers have on the firm's prices. If a company sells a popular product or service to multiple buyers, then the company has more power to set prices. By contrast, if a company is dependent on just a few high-volume buyers, those buyers will typically have enough bargaining power to dictate prices. Remember that most "buyers" are other companies (B2B sales are far higher than direct retail sales for manufacturers in Canada). Wal-Mart is the largest single buyer in the history of retailing in Canada. The company buys 30 percent of all toothpaste, shampoo, and paper towels made by retail suppliers; 15 to 20 percent of all CDs, videos, and DVDs; 15 percent of all magazines; 14 percent of all groceries; and 20 percent of all toys. And, of course, Wal-Mart uses its purchasing power as a buyer to push down prices.[41] Very few individual consumers have that kind of buyer power.

4.2 Positioning Strategies

After analyzing industry forces, the next step in industry-level strategy is to protect your company from the negative effects of industry-wide competition and to create a sustainable competitive advantage. According to Michael Porter, there are three positioning strategies: cost leadership, differentiation, and focus.

Cost leadership means producing a product or service of comparable quality at consistently lower cost than competitors (because of production ability, sourcing ability, distribution ability, special processes, etc.) so that the firm can offer the product or service at the lowest price in the industry. Cost leadership protects companies from industry forces by deterring new entrants, who will have to match low costs and prices. Cost leadership also forces down the prices of substitute products and services, attracts bargain-seeking buyers, and increases bargaining power with suppliers, who have to keep their prices low if they want to do business with the cost leader.[42]

Differentiation means making your product or service sufficiently different from competitors' offerings that customers are willing to pay a premium price for the extra value or performance it provides. Differentiation protects companies from industry forces by reducing the threat of substitute products. It also protects companies by making it easier to retain customers and more difficult for new entrants trying to attract new customers. For example, why would anyone pay $2,300 for Whirlpool's Duet, a deluxe washer-dryer combination, when they could purchase a regular washer-dryer combination for $700 or less? The answer is that the Duet washer does huge loads, almost twice what normal washers hold, with less than half the water—just 16 gallons compared to 40 for conventional washers. So it's incredibly efficient in terms of water and energy and saves consumers time because they can wash and dry twice as many clothes at the same time.[43]

With a **focus strategy**, a company uses either cost leadership or differentiation to produce a specialized product or service for a limited, specially targeted group of customers in a particular geographic region or market segment. Focus strategies typically work in market niches that competitors have overlooked or have difficulty serving. Containerstore.com sells products in Canada to reorganize and rebuild your closets, sort out your kitchen drawers and cabinets, or add shelves, hooks, and storage anywhere in your home, office, or dorm room. But, unlike Wal-Mart, IKEA, or Canadian Tire, that's all it does.

4.3 Adaptive Strategies

Adaptive strategies are another set of industry-level strategies. Whereas the aim of positioning strategies is to minimize the effects of industry competition and build a sustainable competitive advantage, the purpose of adaptive strategies is to choose an industry-level strategy that is best suited to changes in the organization's external environment. There are four kinds of adaptive strategies: defending, prospecting, analyzing, and reacting.[44]

Defenders seek moderate, steady growth by offering a limited range of products and services to a well-defined set of customers. In other words, defenders aggressively "defend" their current strategic position by doing the best job they can to hold on to customers in a particular market segment.

Prospectors seek fast growth by searching for new market opportunities, encouraging risk taking, and being the first to bring innovative new products to market. Prospectors are analogous to gold miners who "prospect" for gold nuggets (i.e., new products) in hopes that the nuggets will lead them to a rich deposit of gold (i.e., fast growth).

Analyzers blend the defending and prospecting strategies. Analyzers seek moderate, steady growth *and* limited opportunities for fast growth. Analyzers are rarely first to market with new products or services. Instead, they try to simultaneously minimize risk and maximize profits by following or imitating the proven

Differentiation the positioning strategy of providing a product or service that is sufficiently different from competitors' offerings that customers are willing to pay a premium price for it

Focus strategy the positioning strategy of using cost leadership or differentiation to produce a specialized product or service for a limited, specially targeted group of customers in a particular geographic region or market segment

Defenders those who adopt an adaptive strategy aimed at defending strategic positions by seeking moderate, steady growth and by offering a limited range of high-quality products and services to a well-defined set of customers

Prospectors those who adopt an adaptive strategy that seeks fast growth by searching for new market opportunities, encouraging risk taking, and being the first to bring innovative new products to market

Analyzers those who adopt an adaptive strategy that seeks to minimize risk and maximize profits by following or imitating the proven successes of prospectors

Differentiation is what makes Whirlpool's $2,300 washer-dryer combination a hot product.

Fashion for the Rest of Us

Demand for products is changing strategies in the fashion world. Runway shows traditionally are held twice each year, exhibiting clothes for the next season six months out. But broader interest in Fashion Week among "real consumers" is creating demand for cheaper merchandise much sooner. This may change how the fashion industry works. Natalie Massenet, founder of the ready-to-wear website Net-a-Porter.com, suggests an adaptive strategy: four shows each year plus faster designing and manufacture.

Source: C. Binkley, R. Dodes, & R. Smith, "Notes From Fashion Week: Styles That Are Really Ready-to-Wear; New Economic Realities," *The Wall Street Journal* (7 February 2008) D10.

© Jim Arbogast/Digital Vision/Jupiterimages (model); © U.P.images/iStockphoto.com (background)

Reactors those who take an adaptive strategy of not following a consistent strategy, but instead reacting to changes in the external environment after they occur

Firm-level strategy a corporate strategy that addresses the question "How should we compete against a particular firm?"

Direct competition the rivalry between two companies that offer similar products and services, acknowledge each other as rivals, and react to each other's strategic actions

successes of prospectors. Tempur-Pedic, which is sold by Sleep Country Canada, is the fastest-growing bed company in part because it has replaced bed springs with visco foam. Traditional bed makers Sealy and Simmons (also major brands carried by Sleep Country Canada) sat back, analyzed, and came up with their own answers to visco foam. Simmons came out with its own visco bed, while Sealy moved to natural latex, which has many of the same qualities but which Sealy claims is better. Analyzing the market after Tempur-Pedic's release of visco helped Sealy and Simmons determine their strategies.[45]

Finally, unlike defenders, prospectors, or analyzers, **reactors** do not follow a consistent strategy. Rather than anticipating and preparing for external opportunities and threats, reactors tend to react to changes in their external environment after they occur. Not surprisingly, reactors tend to be poorer performers than defenders, prospectors, or analyzers. A reactor approach is inherently unstable, and firms that fall into this mode of operation must change their approach or face almost certain failure.

CP Photo by Boris SPREMO

LO5 Firm-Level Strategies

Microsoft brings out its Xbox 360 video game console; Sony counters with its PlayStation 3. Telus drops prices and increases monthly cellphone minutes; Bell Mobility strikes back with better reception and even lower prices and more data streaming. Attack and respond, respond and attack. **Firm-level strategy** addresses this question: "How should we compete against a particular firm?"

*Let's find out more about the firm-level strategies (i.e., direct competition between companies) by reading about **5.1 the basics of direct competition, and 5.2 the strategic moves involved in direct competition between companies.***

5.1 Direct Competition

Although Porter's five industry forces indicate the overall level of competition in an industry, most companies do not compete directly with all the firms in their industry. For example, McDonald's and Red Lobster are both in the restaurant business, but no one would characterize them as competitors. McDonald's offers low-cost, convenient fast food in a seat-yourself restaurant, while Red Lobster offers mid-priced, sitdown seafood dinners complete with servers and a bar.

Instead of competing with every other firm in an industry, most firms compete directly with just a few companies within the industry. **Direct competition** is the rivalry between two companies offering similar products and services that acknowledge each other as rivals and take offensive and defensive positions as they act and react to each other's strategic actions.[46] Two factors determine the extent to which firms will be in direct competition with each other: market commonality and resource similarity. **Market commonality** is the degree to which two companies have overlapping products, services, or customers in multiple markets. The more markets in which there is product, service, or customer overlap, the more intense the direct competition will be between the two companies. **Resource similarity** is the extent to which a competitor has similar amounts and kinds of resources—that is, similar assets, capabilities, processes, information, and knowledge for creating and sustaining an advantage over competitors. From a competitive standpoint, resource similarity means that your direct competitors can probably match the strategic actions that your company takes.

Exhibit 6.7 shows how market commonality and resource similarity interact to determine when and where companies are in direct competition.[47] The overlapping area in each quadrant (between the triangle and the rectangle, or between the different-coloured rectangles) depicts market commonality (overlapping products and services). The larger the overlap, the greater the market commonality. Shapes depict resource similarity (similar products and services), with rectangles representing one set of competitive resources and triangles representing another.

Quadrant I shows two companies in direct competition because they have similar resources at their disposal and a high degree of market commonality. These companies try to sell similar products and services to similar customers. McDonald's and Burger King would clearly fit here as direct competitors.

In Quadrant II, the overlapping parts of the triangle and rectangle show two companies going after similar customers with some similar products or services, but doing so with different competitive resources. McDonald's and Wendy's restaurants would fit here. Wendy's is after the same lunchtime and dinner crowds that McDonald's is. Nevertheless, with its more expensive hamburgers, fries, shakes, and salads, Wendy's is less of a direct competitor to McDonald's than Burger King is. For example, Wendy's Garden Sensation salads (using fancy lettuce varieties, grape tomatoes, and mandarin oranges) bring in customers who would have eaten at more expensive casual dining restaurants like Applebee's.[48] A representative from Wendy's says, "We believe you win customers by consistently offering a better product at a strong, everyday value."[49]

Market commonality the degree to which two companies have overlapping products, services, or customers in multiple markets

Resource similarity the extent to which a competitor has similar amounts and kinds of resources

In Quadrant III, the very small overlap shows two companies with different competitive resources and little market commonality. McDonald's and Denny's, with restaurants in most major Canadian cities, fit here. Although both are in the fast food business, there's almost no overlap in terms of products and customers. Furthermore, Denny's customers aren't likely to eat at McDonald's. In fact, Denny's is not really competing with other fast food restaurants, but with eating at home. Denny's sells full omelettes, pork chops, steaks, and full-fare dinners.[50]

Instead of "competing" with the entire industry, most firms compete directly with just a few companies.

Finally, in Quadrant IV, the small overlap between the two rectangles shows that McDonald's and Subway compete with similar resources but with little market commonality. In terms of resources, McDonald's sales are much larger, but Subway, with its 33,749 stores worldwide, has much faster growth, compared to McDonald's.[51] Although Subway and McDonald's compete, they aren't direct competitors in terms of market commonality in the way that McDonald's and Burger King are, because Subway, unlike McDonald's, sells itself as a provider of healthy fast food. Thus, the overlap is much smaller in Quadrant IV than in Quadrant I. With advertising featuring "Jared," who lost 245 pounds eating "healthier" food at Subway, the detailed nutritional information available in its stores, and its close relationship with various Heart Associations, Subway's goal "is to emphasize that the Subway brand represents all that is good about health and well-being."[52] Fast food customers eat at both restaurants, yet Subway's customers have been found to be twice as loyal as McDonald's customers, probably because of Subway's strategy of offering healthier foods.[53]

Exhibit 6.7 A Framework of Direct Competition

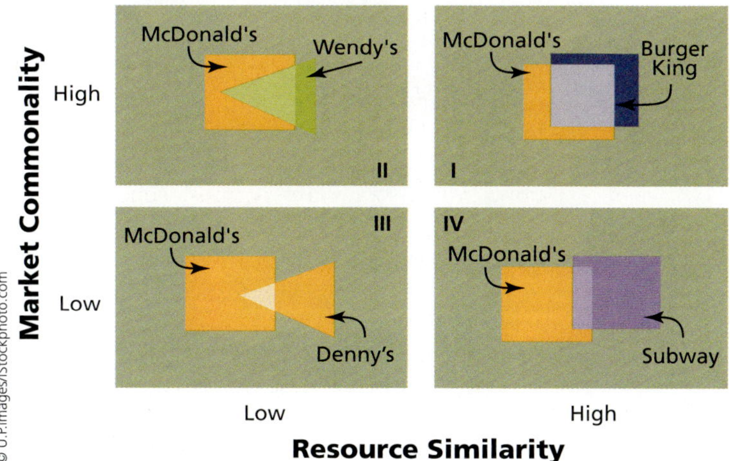

Source: Reprinted with permission of Academy of Management, P O Box 3020, Briar Cliff Manor, NY, 10510-8020. M. Chen, "Competitor Analysis and InterFirm Rivalry: Toward a Theoretical Integration," *Academy of Management Review* 21 (1996): 100–134. 21–39.

5.2 Strategic Moves of Direct Competition

Corporate-level strategies help managers decide what business to be in; industry-level strategies help them determine how to compete within an industry; firm-level strategies help managers determine when, where, and what strategic actions to take against a direct competitor. Firms in direct competition can make two

Dukin' Donuts

As of 2012, Tim Hortons had 4,071 restaurants, including 3,355 in Canada, 745 in the United States, 19 in the United Arab Emirates, and one in Oman. It plans to open up to 120 stores over the next five years in the Persian Gulf area, with a focus on Qatar, Bahrain, Kuwait, Oman, and the United Arab Emirates. In Canada, the iconic Tim Hortons has more than a 75 percent market share in coffee and baked goods, as well as an entry in the *Canadian Oxford Dictionary* for one of the chain's shorthand orders, a "double-double" (coffee with two creams and two sugars). Such entrenched success should indicate that Tim Hortons follows a risk-avoiding strategy. Not so! Tim Hortons' first foray into the US market was in New England, home turf for Dunkin' Donuts and thousands of small independents. Boston had five times the national average of donut shops per capita, at one shop per 5,143 residents. Providence had one shop per 4,226 people. Implementing such a risky strategy was brutal. But "Timmy's" is not a quitter; Hortons' CEO Paul House told investors, "We got our a** kicked in New England," but the company is still committed to a "good old street fight." In late 2010 Tim Hortons closed all 36 money-losing restaurants in the US Northeast, but it continues to open them in other parts of the US. One of the partners in the original Tim Hortons was optimistic: "America is a big country."

Sources: Yew, M. A.-T. "Tim Hortons opens in Oman" (2012). *The Toronto Star.* Available online at http://www.thestar.com/business/2012/11/12/tim_hortons_opens_in_oman.html; Tim Hortons Corporate Profile, available online at http://www.timhortons.com/ca/en/about/profile.html; D. Belkin, "A Canadian Icon Turns Its Glaze Southward," *Wall Street Journal,* 14 May 2007, B1.; "Tim Hortons to Close 36 Restaurants in New England," November 11, 2010, http://abcnews.go.com/Business/wireStory?id=12119540.

© Yong Hian Lim/iStockphoto.com

Attack a competitive move designed to reduce a rival's market share or profits

Response a competitive countermove, prompted by a rival's attack, to defend or improve a company's market share or profit

basic strategic moves: attacks and responses. These moves are made all the time in virtually every industry, but they are most noticeable in industries where multiple large competitors are pursuing customers in the same market space.

An **attack** is a competitive move designed to reduce a rival's market share or profits. Barnes & Noble and Amazon originally had pretty much the same price points for their e-readers. Hoping to increase its market share, Amazon decreased its price for a Kindle from $259 to $199. Barnes & Noble attacked by aggressively cutting the price on its Nook to $179.

A **response** is a countermove, prompted by a rival's attack, that is designed to defend or improve a company's market share or profit. There are two kinds of responses.[54] The first is to match or mirror your

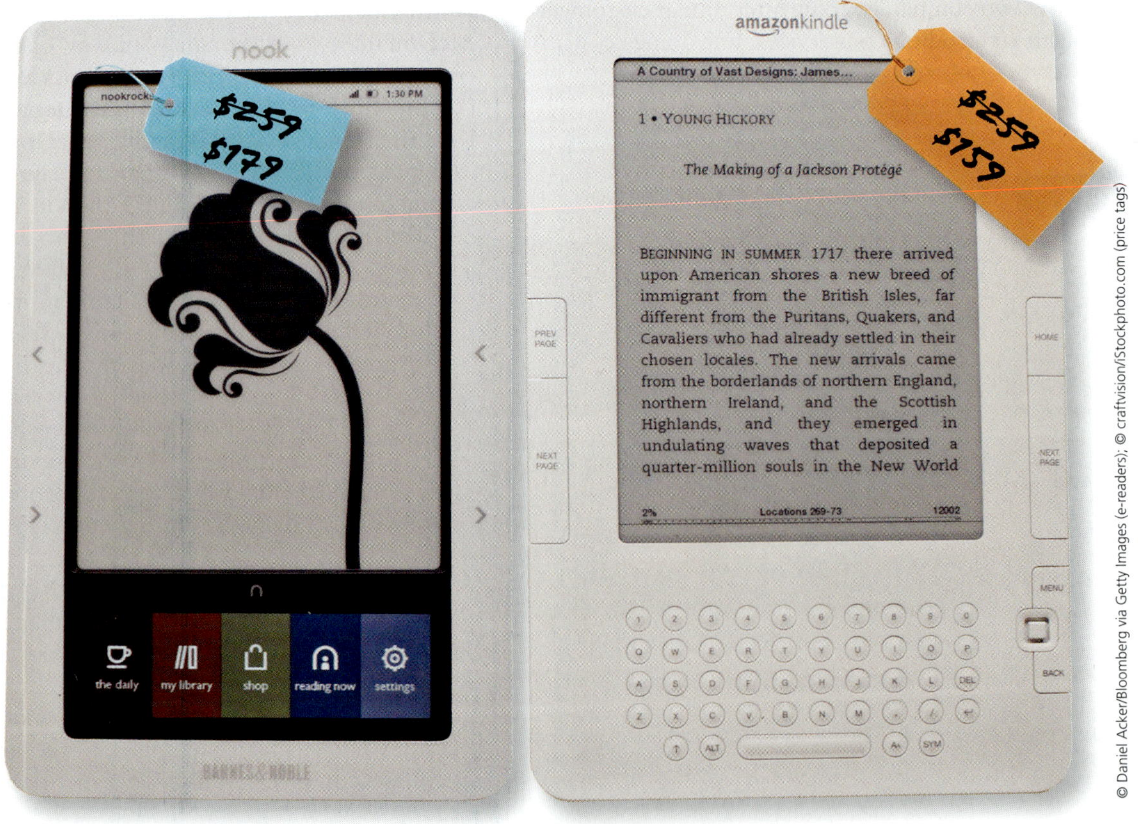

© Daniel Acker/Bloomberg via Getty Images (e-readers); © craftvision/iStockphoto.com (price tags)

competitor's move. This is what Amazon then did when it cut the price even further on its Kindle e-reader to $159. The battle still wages; both the Kindle and the Nook Simple Touch now cost $79.[55] The second kind of response is to respond along a different dimension from your competitor's move or attack. For example, instead of cutting prices, Borders responded to its two competitors' price cuts by offering a $20 Borders gift card with the purchase of each Kobo.[56]

Market commonality and resource similarity determine the likelihood of an attack or response—that is, whether a company is likely to attack a direct competitor or to strike back with a strong response when attacked. When market commonality is strong and companies have overlapping products, services, or customers in multiple markets, there is less motivation to attack and more motivation to respond to an attack. The reason for this is straightforward: when firms are direct competitors in a large number of markets, they have a great deal at stake. So when Amazon launched an aggressive price war with its e-reader, Barnes and Noble had no choice but to respond by cutting its own prices.

Whereas market commonality affects the likelihood of an attack or a response to an attack, resource similarity largely affects response capability—that is, how quickly and forcefully a company can respond to an attack. When resource similarity is strong, the responding firm will generally be able to match the strategic moves of the attacking firm. Consequently, a firm is less likely to attack firms with similar levels of resources because it is unlikely to gain any sustained advantage when the responding firms strike back. On the other hand, if one firm is substantially stronger than another (i.e., low resource similarity), then a competitive attack is more likely to produce sustained competitive advantage. The Kindle HD taps into the Amazon Appstore and its approximately 50,000 apps. The Nook provides access to Nook Apps, which has about 6,000 apps. The Kindle can also access Amazon's video services; Barnes & Noble has announced that it will soon launch Nook Video, which will serve up similar content. Amazon has a much larger online presence, and it hopes its price war will inflict serious financial damage on B&N, with minimal damage to itself.

In general, the more moves (i.e., attacks) a company initiates against direct competitors and the greater a company's tendency to respond when attacked, the better its performance. More specifically, attackers and early responders (companies that are quick to launch a retaliatory attack) tend to gain market share and profits at the expense of late responders. This is not to suggest that a "full-attack" strategy always works best. In fact, attacks can provoke harsh retaliatory responses. Consequently, when deciding when, where, and what strategic actions to take against a direct competitor, managers should always consider the possibility of retaliation.

Red Ocean, Blue Ocean

Using the ocean as a metaphor, Professors Renée Mauborgne and W. Chan Kim describe highly competitive markets as shark-infested waters. The water is red with blood from continual attacks and responses, and any gains made by one company are incremental at best and bound to be ceded in the next shark fight. The only hope for survival is to pursue innovations that take you out of the red ocean and into the deep blue ocean, where there are no competitors. If it sounds hard, and it is; but it's not impossible.

The war between the Nook and the Kindle is an example of a red ocean. Canadian Tire's original forays into the United States are another example; its new strategy of kiosks and new, smaller, more nimble stores could be seen as entering a blue ocean. Canada's own Cirque du Soleil is another clear example of a blue ocean. Cirque du Soleil created a whole new category of entertainment. Two other examples: Gmail lets you store unlimited e-mail for free; and Nintendo's Wii has redefined videogaming with simple games that combine elements of virtual reality.

© iLexx/iStockphoto.com (shark); © Ethan Miller/Reuters/Landov (performers)

Source: Renée Mauborgne, W. Chan Kem, *Blue Ocean Strategy* (Harvard University Press, 2005).

7

Innovation and Change

LEARNING OUTCOMES

LO1 Explain why innovation matters to companies.

LO2 Discuss the different methods that managers can use to effectively manage innovation in their organizations.

LO3 Discuss why not changing can lead to organizational decline.

LO4 Discuss the different methods that managers can use to better manage change as it occurs.

Organizational Innovation

Sometimes the solution to a problem causes another problem. Jernhusen AB, a Swedish property administration firm, is building a new office and retail building near Stockholm's Central Station. Problem number one: How should they heat it? Problem number two: How should they get rid of excess heat in the train station, generated by the 250,000 people who pass through it every day? As Karl Sundholm, representative of Jernhusen, puts it, "All people produce heat, and that heat is in fact fairly difficult to get rid of. Instead of opening windows and letting all that heat go to waste we want to harness it through the ventilation system." The innovative solution to both problems? Convert the heat in the station to hot water and pump it through the heating system of the new building using pipes that connect the building to the station. Sundholm estimates that the system will cost about 300,000 kronor (€32,000; C$52,000) to install, and it is likely to reduce energy consumption by 15 percent. Notes Per Berggren, Jernhusen's managing director: "It's more like thinking out of the box, being environmentally smart."[1]

Organizational innovation is the successful implementation of creative ideas in an organization.[2] **Creativity**, which is a form of organizational innovation, is the production of novel and useful ideas.[3] In the first part of this chapter, you will learn why innovation matters and how to manage innovation to create and sustain a competitive advantage. In the second part, you will learn about **organizational change**, which is a difference in the form, quality, or condition of an organization over time.[4] You will also learn about the risk of not changing and the ways in that companies can manage change. But first, let's deal with organizational innovations, like using body heat to warm buildings.[5]

LO1 Why Innovation Matters

We can only guess what changes technological innovations will bring in the next 20 years. It is likely that many of us will be carrying very powerful smartphone tablets. But will our devices send a message to the server at home to digitize the latest video release? Will the Internet make movie theatres and televisions obsolete? Will we edit our own i-news?[6] Who knows? The only thing we do know for sure about the next 20 years is that innovation will continue to change our lives drastically.

*Let's begin our discussion of innovation by learning about **1.1 technology cycles** and **1.2 innovation streams.***

1.1 Technology Cycles

In Chapter 3, you learned that *technology* consists of the knowledge, tools, and techniques used to transform inputs (raw materials, information, etc.) into outputs (products and services). Services in Canada make up more than 70 percent of our gross domestic product (GDP).[7] A **technology cycle** begins with the birth of a new technology; it ends when that technology reaches its limits and is replaced by a newer, substantially better technology.[8] Technology cycles occurred when air-conditioning supplanted fans, when Henry Ford's Model T replaced horse-drawn carriages, and when airplanes replaced trains as a means of cross-country travel.

From Gutenberg's invention of the printing press in the 1400s to the rapid advance of the Internet, studies of hundreds of technological innovations have shown that nearly all technology cycles follow an **S-curve pattern of innovation** (see Exhibit 7.1).[9] Early in a technology cycle, there is still much to learn, so progress is slow, as depicted by point A on the S-curve. The flat slope indicates that increased effort (i.e., money, research and development) brings only small improvements in technological performance. Fortunately, as the new technology matures, researchers figure out how to get better performance from it. This is represented by point B of the S-curve in Exhibit 7.1. The steeper slope indicates that small amounts of effort will result in significant increases in performance. At point C, the flat slope again indicates that further efforts to develop this particular technology will result in only small increases in performance. More important, however, point C indicates that the performance limits of that particular technology are being reached. In other words, additional significant improvements in performance are highly unlikely.

Intel's technology cycles have followed this pattern. Intel spends billions developing new computer chips as well as new production facilities to produce them. Intel has found that the technology cycle for its integrated circuits is about three years. In each three-year cycle, Intel spends billions to introduce a new chip, then improves the

Organizational innovation the successful implementation of creative ideas in organizations

Creativity the production of novel and useful ideas

Organizational change a difference in the form, quality, or condition of an organization over time

Technology cycle a cycle that begins with the birth of a new technology and ends when that technology reaches its limits and is replaced by a newer, substantially better technology

S-curve pattern of innovation a pattern of technological innovation characterized by slow initial progress, then rapid progress, and then slow progress again as a technology matures and reaches its limits

Exhibit 7.1 S-Curves and Technological Innovation

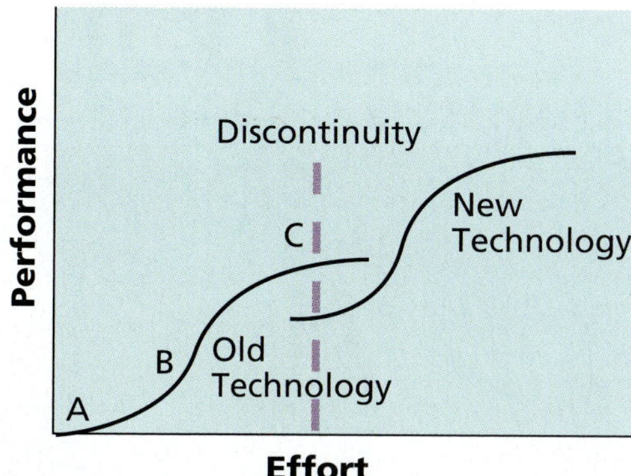

Source: R.N. Foster, *Innovation: The Attacker's Advantage* (New York: Summit, 1986).

ssuaphotos/Shutterstock.com

chip by making it a little bit faster each year, and, finally, replaces that chip at the end of the cycle with a brand-new chip that is substantially faster than the old chip. At first (point A), the billions Intel spends typically produce only small improvements in performance. But after six months to a year with a new chip design, Intel's engineering and production people typically figure out how to make the new chips much faster than they were initially (point B). Despite impressive gains in performance, Intel is unable to make a particular computer chip run any faster once the chip reaches its design limits.

After a technology has reached its limits at the top of the S-curve, significant improvements in performance usually come from radical new designs or new performance-enhancing materials (point C). In Exhibit 7.1, that new technology is represented by the second S-curve. The changeover or discontinuity between the old and new technologies is represented by the dotted line. At first, the old and new technologies will likely coexist. Eventually, however, the new technology will replace the old technology. When that happens, the old technology cycle will be complete, and a new one will have started. The changeover between Intel's newer and older computer chip designs typically takes about one year. Over time, improvements in existing technology (tweaking the performance of the current technology cycle), combined with the replacement of old technology with new (i.e., new, faster computer chip designs replace older ones), has increased the speed of Intel's computer processors by a factor of 70 in just 19 years.

The evolution of Intel's Pentium chips has been used here to illustrate S-curves and technology cycles. But it's important to note that technology cycles and technological innovation don't necessarily involve faster computer chips or cleaner automobile engines. Remember that *technology* is simply the knowledge, tools, and techniques used to transform inputs into outputs. So a technology cycle occurs whenever there are major advances or changes in the *knowledge*, *tools*, and *techniques* of a field or discipline, whatever they may be. For example, one of the most important technology cycles in the history of civilization occurred in 1859, when 1,300 miles of central sewer line were constructed throughout London to carry human waste to the sea more than 11 miles away. This sewer system replaced the practice of dumping raw sewage into streets, where it drained into public wells that supplied drinking water. Preventing waste runoff from contaminating water supplies stopped the spread of cholera that had killed millions of people for centuries in cities throughout the world.[10] Indeed, the water you drink today is safe thanks to this technological breakthrough. So when you think about technology cycles, don't automatically think "high technology." Instead, broaden your perspective by considering advances or changes in *any* kind of knowledge, tool, or technique.

1.2 Innovation Streams

In Chapter 6, you learned that organizations can create *competitive advantage* for themselves if they have a *distinctive competence* that allows them to make, do, or perform something better than their competitors. A competitive advantage becomes sustainable if other companies cannot duplicate the benefits obtained from that distinctive competence. Technological innovation can enable competitors to duplicate the benefits obtained from a company's distinctive advantage. It can also quickly turn a company's competitive advantage into a competitive disadvantage. For more than 110 years, Eastman Kodak was the dominant producer of photographic film worldwide. That is, until Kodak invented the digital camera (patent 4,131,919). But Kodak itself was unprepared for the rapid acceptance of its new technology, and its managers watched film quickly become obsolete for most camera users. Technological innovation turned Kodak's competitive advantage into a competitive disadvantage.[11] As a matter of fact, even digital camera sales have been declining for several years now, and by 2016 they are expected to be worth about one-third what they were.[12]

Joseph Balgazette designed the first interceptor sewers to carry London's sewage down the banks of the Thames to be dumped into the estuary.

Warren Goldswain/Shutterstock.com

As the Kodak example shows, companies that want to sustain a competitive advantage must understand and protect themselves from the strategic threats of innovation. In the long run, the best way for a company to do that is by creating a stream of its own innovative ideas and products year after year. Consequently, we define **innovation streams** as patterns of innovation over time that can create sustainable competitive advantage.[13] Exhibit 7.2 shows a typical innovation consisting of a series of technology cycles. Recall that a technology cycle begins with a new technology and ends when that technology is replaced by a newer, substantially better technology. The innovation stream in Exhibit 7.2 shows three such technology cycles.

Exhibit 7.2 Innovation Streams: Technology Cycles over Time

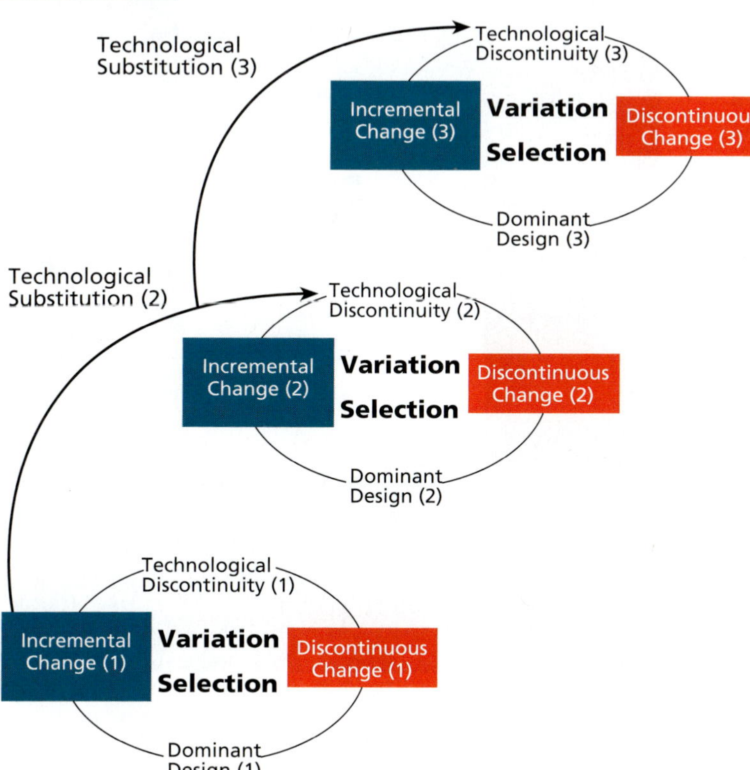

Source: *MANAGING STRATEGIC INNOVATION* by Tushman, Anderson, O'Reilly (1997) Fig. 1-1 - Originally from *Evolutionary Dynamics of Organisation* by Rosenkopf and Tushman (1994) published by Oxford University Press © 1997 by Oxford University Press, Inc. By permission of Oxford University Press, USA.

An innovation stream begins with a **technological discontinuity**, in which a scientific advance or a unique combination of existing technologies creates a significant breakthrough in performance or function. Technological discontinuities are followed by **discontinuous change**, which is characterized by technological substitution and design competition. **Technological substitution** occurs when customers then purchase new technologies to replace older technologies.

Discontinuous change is also characterized by **design competition**, in which the old technology and several different new technologies compete to establish a new technological standard or dominant design. For example, Toshiba and Sony competed for dominance in a new standard format for home video, Toshiba with its HD DVD technology and Sony with Blu-ray. Because of large investments in old technology, and because new and old technologies are often incompatible with each other, companies and consumers are reluctant to switch to a different technology during a design competition. Toshiba lost the design competition because Warner Bros., which had been using both technologies, decided to go exclusively with Blu-ray. Retailers followed suit, announcing their intention to focus on Blu-ray equipment and videos. Some "early adopters" of HD DVD will continue to use the technology for their collections, but most people will eventually use Blu-ray because it will dominate the market.[14] In addition, during design competition, the old technology usually improves significantly in response to the competitive threat from the new; this response slows the changeover from old to new.

Discontinuous change is followed by the emergence of a **dominant design**, which becomes the new accepted market standard for technology.[15] Dominant designs emerge in several ways. The best technology doesn't always become the dominant design, because a number of other factors come into play. One is critical mass—that is, a particular technology can become the dominant design simply because most people use it. Toshiba dropped HD DVD in part because, with a critical mass of Blu-ray adopters, Blu-ray had become the dominant design. Even more change is on the way; most people in the future will be purchasing multifunction devices.[16]

Innovation streams patterns of innovation over time that can create sustainable competitive advantage

Technological discontinuity a scientific advance or a unique combination of existing technologies creates a significant breakthrough in performance or function

Discontinuous change the phase of a technology cycle characterized by technological substitution and design competition

Technological substitution the purchase of new technologies to replace older ones

Design competition competition between old and new technologies to establish a new technological standard or dominant design

Dominant design a new technological design or process that becomes the accepted market standard

A design can also become dominant if it solves a practical problem. The QWERTY keyboard (named for the top left line of letters) became the dominant design for typewriters because it slowed down typists who caused mechanical typewriter keys to jam because they typed too fast. Computers can easily be switched to the DVORAK keyboard layout, which doubles typing speed and cuts typing errors by half, yet QWERTY lives on as the standard keyboard. The QWERTY keyboard solved a problem; with the advent of computers, that problem is no longer relevant; yet QWERTY remains the dominant technology because most people learned to type that way and continue to do so (see the text box "Protecting Innovation"). If you have ever hurriedly written "hgello" instead of "hello" or "fdear" instead of "dear," don't worry—help is available. Dominant designs can also emerge through independent standards bodies. The International Telecommunications Union (http://www.itu.ch), now an agency of the United Nations, establishes standards for the communications industry. The ITU was founded in Paris in 1865 because European countries all had different telegraph systems that could not communicate with one another. After three months of negotiations, 20 countries signed the International Telegraph Convention, which standardized equipment and instructions, enabling telegraph messages to flow seamlessly from country to country. Today, as in 1865, various standards are proposed, discussed, negotiated, and changed until agreement is reached on a final set of standards that communication industries (i.e., Internet, telephone, satellites, radio, etc.) will follow worldwide.

Canada and the United States have the weakest standards with respect to automobile fuel consumption, but they also have the toughest emission requirements. Researchers at Canada's National Research Council have created a technology that is helping enforce some of the world's toughest vehicle emission standards. "These levels are so low and detailed they can't be measured with previously used technologies," says Greg Smallwood, who leads the NRC's Ottawa-based combustion research team. "This is why they're so excited about our technology."[17]

Automakers are pursuing alternative fuel technologies such as ethanol and diesel in an effort to increase fuel economy and meet these legal standards. Although research into alternative fuel technologies tends to be adopted in a climate of high oil prices and abandoned when they fall, it is not impossible to envision a future in which gasoline-burning engines

Protecting Innovation

One of the risks in coming up with great new ideas is that someone might steal them. Published works, such as books and magazine articles, are protected by copyright, while designs for new devices such as the iPhone are protected by patents. BlackBerry® (formerly known as RIM®), the Canadian designer and manufacturer of the BlackBerry® smartphone, is headquartered in Waterloo, Ontario. Its legal department deals with patents, trademarks(™), industrial designs, integrated circuit topography, and copyrights (©). It has patented the keyboard design for people with chubby fingers. The trapezoid-shaped keys on the keyboard make it less likely that the wrong letter or number will be struck, according to the patent (U.S. Patent No. 8,175,664, "Angular keyboard for a handheld mobile communication device") granted by the US Patent and Trademark Office. BlackBerry has also had issues with patent law. The Government of Canada does not help companies such as BlackBerry, which has paid more than $600 million in settlements to fight off various companies, including Prism Technologies LLC and NTP. One of the current legal issues deals with Nokia and an alleged breach of the wireless local area networks (WLAN) patent held by the Finnish handset maker. Patent battles are very difficult and expensive to defend. The international law that deals with all of these issues is very complex, and legal actions usually take many years to settle.

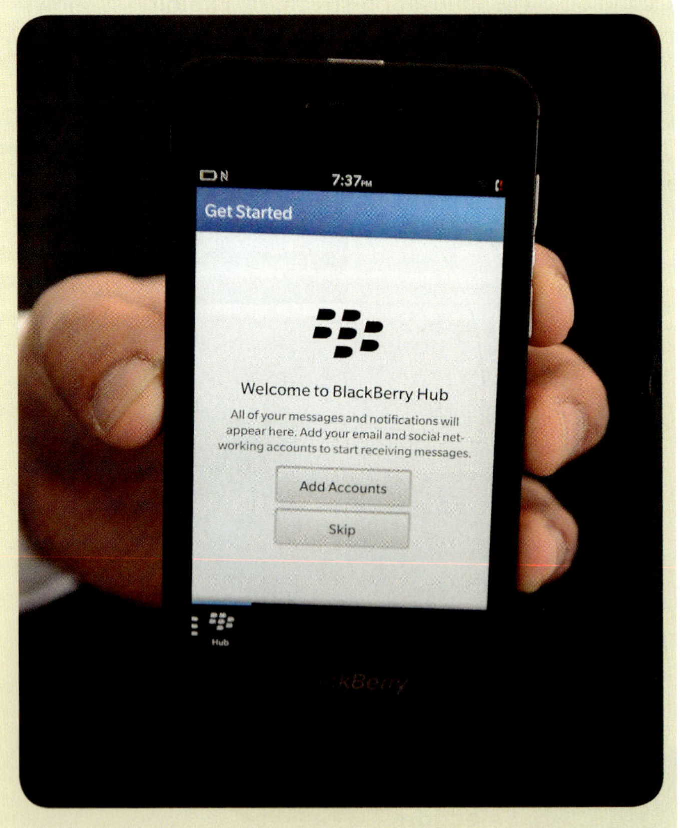

Photo Illustration by Kevork Djansezian/Getty Images

Sources: "RIM settles BlackBerry patent dispute with Prism (Update 2)," *Bloomberg Businessweek*, May 18, 2010, online at http://www.businessweek.com/news/2010-05-18/rim-settles-blackberry-patent-dispute-with-prism-update2-.html; "RIM shares jump on settlement of BlackBerry patent lawsuit," CBC News, March 16, 2005, online at http://www.cbc.ca/money/story/2005/03/16/rimsettle-050316.html; Tom Krazit, "Patent Office weakens NTP's BlackBerry patent case: Seven of eight patents thrown out in initial assessment," *Techworld*, 24 June 2005, online at http://news.techworld.com/mobile-wireless/3913/patent-office-weakens-ntps-blackberry-patent-case/

AP Photo/Damian Dovarganes

are no longer the dominant technology on the road.[18] Carmakers are going back to the drawing board in the hunt for fuel-saving technologies as hopes that electric vehicles will be the silver bullet for CO2 emissions look increasingly forlorn. "We can't get the necessary gains we need with traditional technology any more," Peugeot innovation chief Jean-Marc Finot said in a recent interview. "We're seeing a real break with the past."[19]

No matter how it happens, the emergence of a dominant design is a key event in an innovation stream. First, the emergence of such a design inevitably results in winners and losers. Technological innovation enhances competence but also destroys it. Companies that bet on the now-dominant design usually prosper. In contrast, when companies bet on the wrong design or the old technology, they may experience **technological lockout**, which occurs when a new dominant design (i.e., a significantly better technology) prevents a company from competitively selling its products or makes it difficult to do so.[20] Toshiba has now stopped producing HD DVD players. It will continue to make spare parts for existing machines, and it may apply the technology to downloading videos online. But it will shift its business strategy to other sectors, such as transparent flexible memory chips, which are replacing flash drives and hard drives in computers.[21] In fact, more companies are likely to go out of business in a time of discontinuous change and changing standards than in an economic recession or slowdown.

Second, the emergence of a dominant design signals a shift from design experimentation and competition to **incremental change**, a phase during which companies innovate by lowering costs and improving the performance of the dominant design. For example, manufacturing efficiencies enable Intel to cut the cost of its chips by one-half to two-thirds during a technology cycle, while doubling or tripling their speed. This focus on improving the dominant design continues until the next technological discontinuity occurs.

LO2 Managing Innovation

One consequence of technology cycles and innovation streams is that managers must be equally good at managing innovation in two very different circumstances. First, during discontinuous change, companies must find a way to anticipate and survive technological changes of the kind that can suddenly transform industry leaders into losers and industry unknowns into powerhouses. Companies that can't manage innovation following technological discontinuities risk quick organizational decline and dissolution. Second, after a new dominant design emerges following discontinuous change, companies must manage the very different process of incremental improvement and innovation. Companies that can't manage incremental innovation slowly deteriorate as they fall further behind industry leaders.

Unfortunately, what works well when managing innovation during discontinuous change doesn't work well when managing innovation during periods of incremental change (and vice versa). Consequently, to successfully manage innovation streams, companies

Technological lockout when a new dominant design (i.e., a significantly better technology) prevents a company from competitively selling its products or makes it difficult to do so

Incremental change the phase of a technology cycle in which companies innovate by lowering costs and improving the functioning and performance of the dominant technological design

Because they are both transparent and flexible, new memory chips could allow touchscreens to double as a memory location.

Courtesy of the James M Tour Group.

Creative work environments workplace cultures in which workers perceive that new ideas are welcomed, valued, and encouraged

Flow a psychological state of effortlessness, in which you become completely absorbed in what you're doing and time seems to pass quickly

need to be good at three things: *2.1 managing sources of innovation, 2.2 managing innovation during discontinuous change, and 2.3 managing innovation during incremental change.*

violetkaipa/Shutterstock.com

2.1 Managing Sources of Innovation

Innovation comes from great ideas. So a starting point for managing innovation is to manage the *sources* of innovation, that is, where new ideas come from. One source of new ideas is brilliant inventors. But only a few companies have the likes of an Edison, Marconi, or Canada's Alexander Graham Bell working for them. Given that great thinkers and inventors are in short supply, what might companies do to ensure a steady flow of good ideas?

Well, when we say that innovation begins with great ideas, we're really saying that innovation begins with creativity. As we defined it at the beginning of this chapter, creativity is the production of novel and useful ideas.[22] Although companies can't command employees to be creative ("You *will* be more creative!"), they can jump-start innovation by building **creative work environments** in which workers perceive that creative thoughts and ideas are welcomed and valued. As Exhibit 7.3 shows, creative work environments have six components that encourage creativity: challenging work, organizational encouragement, supervisory encouragement, work group encouragement, freedom, and a lack of organizational impediments.[23]

Work is *challenging* when it requires effort, demands attention and focus, and is perceived as important to others in the organization. According to researcher Mihaly Csikszentmihalyi (pronounced ME-high-ee CHICK-sent-me-high-ee), challenging work promotes creativity because it creates a rewarding psychological experience known as "flow." **Flow** is a psychological state of effortlessness in which you become completely absorbed in what you're doing and time seems to fly.[24] A key part of creating flow experiences, and thus creative work environments, is to achieve a balance between skills and task challenge. When workers can do more than is required of them, they become bored, and when their skills aren't sufficient to accomplish a task, they become anxious. When skills and task challenge are balanced, however, flow and creativity can occur.

Exhibit 7.3 Components of Creative Work Environments

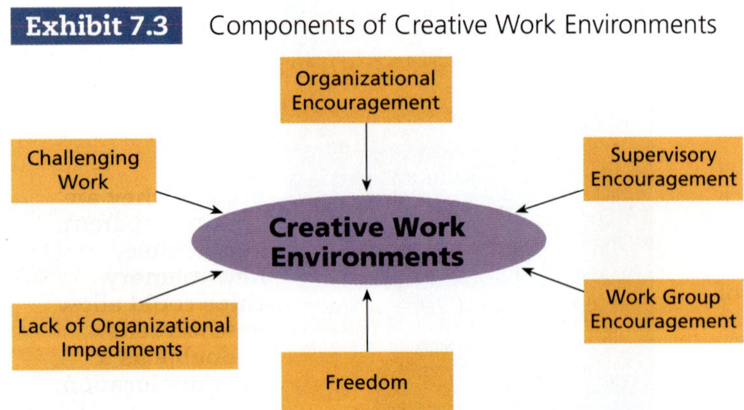

Source: T. M. Amabile, R. Conti, H. Coon, J. Lanzenby, and M. Herron, "Accessing the Work Environment for Creativity", *Academy of Management Journal* 39 (1996): 1154–1184.

A creative work environment requires three kinds of encouragement: organizational, supervisory, and work group encouragement. *Organizational encouragement* of creativity occurs when management encourages risk taking and new ideas, supports and fairly evaluates new ideas, rewards and recognizes creativity, and encourages the sharing of new ideas throughout the company. Many companies keep technology on a tight leash. But Douglas Merrill, CIO at Google, allows employees to use whatever hardware, operating systems, and software helps them be creative and get the job done efficiently, whether Google or another company designed them.[25] *Supervisory encouragement* of creativity occurs when supervisors provide clear goals, encourage open interaction with subordinates, and actively support development teams' work and ideas. *Work group encouragement* occurs when group members have diverse experience, education, and backgrounds and when the group fosters mutual openness to ideas; positive, constructive challenges to ideas; and shared commitment to ideas. CEO Marissa Mayer's decision in early 2013 to order Yahoo! Inc. staff to work in the company's offices was meant to enhance face time and increase creativity. This was a reversal of what the hyper-creative company had been doing since its inception. Only time will tell if she has got it right.[26]

An example of organizational and supervisory encouragement can be found at Adobe, which builds software for business and publishing. Every quarter, Adobe hosts the Idea Champion Showcase, a Canadian Idol-style "ideathon" during which six presenters get ten minutes each to pitch a new

Experiential approach to innovation an approach to innovation that assumes a highly uncertain environment and uses intuition, flexible options, and hands-on experience to reduce uncertainty and accelerate learning and understanding

Design iteration a cycle of repetition in which a company tests a prototype of a new product or service, improves on that design, and then builds and tests the improved prototype

Product prototype a full-scale, working model that is being tested for design, function, and reliability

Testing the systematic comparison of different product designs or design iterations

business idea involving product concept, packaging, technology, whatever. Top executives are not invited to the showcase because their tendency to be cautious makes them want to "hurl rocks" at nascent ideas before they have a chance to develop. Rick Bess is an idea mentor at Adobe. He developed the showcase after an internal study found that too many roadblocks were being thrown in front of new ideas, keeping them from penetrating the organizational hierarchy.[27]

Freedom means having autonomy over one's day-to-day work and a sense of ownership and control over one's ideas. Numerous studies have indicated that creative ideas thrive under conditions of freedom. At Royal Philips Electronics (Philips), all groups within the company have been given complete freedom to rethink every product with the goal of making it simpler for the end user to install and use.[28] 3M scientist Art Fry came up with a clever new item. He thought that if he could apply an adhesive (dreamed up by colleague Spencer Silver several years earlier) to the back of a piece of paper, he could create the perfect bookmark, (instead of loose paper, which is what he had been using in his church choir's hymn book). We now call his innovation the "Post-It." What is not as well known is that Fry came up with the now iconic product during his "15 percent time, a program at 3M that allows employees to use a portion of their paid time to chase rainbows and hatch their own ideas."[29]

To foster creativity, companies may also have to *remove impediments* to creativity from the work environment. Internal conflict, power struggles, rigid management structures, and a conservative bias toward the status quo can all discourage creativity. They can also create the perception that others in the organization will decide which ideas are acceptable and deserve support.

2.2 Experiential Approach: Managing Innovation During Discontinuous Change

A study of 72 product development projects in 36 computer companies across Canada, Europe, and Asia sheds light on how to manage innovation. Companies that succeeded during periods of discontinuous change (characterized by technological substitution and design competition, as described earlier) typically followed an experiential approach to innovation.[30] The **experiential approach to innovation** assumes that innovation is occurring within a highly uncertain environment and that the key to fast product innovation is to use intuition, flexible options, and hands-on experience to reduce uncertainty and accelerate learning and understanding. The experiential approach to innovation has five aspects: design iterations, testing, milestones, multifunctional teams, and powerful leaders.[31]

MGMT TREND

Facilitating Idea Flow

Doug Hall, who has a home in PEI, hosts "Brain Brew," a radio show that features new business ideas and answers questions from callers looking for advice on how to develop or market their own. Hall's newest innovation is Eureka!Ranch (http://www.eurekaranch.com), a website that aims to be an innovation marketplace, bringing together independent researchers and inventors, small businesses, and big businesses. The goal? Get new ideas into the marketplace by bringing people together. Big businesses can be slow at innovation but have the resources to produce and market the idea. Inventors have freedom to think and tend to be quick about innovation but often lack access to big business. Planet Eureka uses a job-hunt site model, where inventors can post their ideas and companies both large and small can search the site for the next "Eureka!"

Source: A. Cordeiro, "Online Market Lets Companies Buy and Sell Ideas," *The Wall Street Journal*, 22 April 2008, B7.

An "iteration" is a repetition. So a **design iteration** is a cycle of repetition in which a company tests a prototype of a new product or service, improves on the design, and then builds and tests the improved product or service prototype. A **product prototype** is a full-scale working model that is being tested for design, function, and reliability. **Testing** is a systematic comparison of different product designs or design iterations. Companies that want to create a new dominant design following a technological discontinuity quickly build, test, improve, and retest a series of different product prototypes. Rickster Powell has jumped from an airplane 20,000 times in order to test parachute designs. He and a partner strap cameras to their bodies to film the chute's deployment, which enables the manufacturers to look for problems. Only 9 out of 50 designs he's tested have actually been produced. Needless to say, he always wears a spare chute.[32]

By trying a number of very different designs or making successive improvements and changes in the same design, frequent design iterations reduce uncertainty and improve understanding. Simply put, the more prototypes you build, the more likely you are to learn what works and what doesn't. Also, when designers and engineers build a number of prototypes, they are less likely to fall in love with a particular prototype. Instead, they'll be more concerned about improving the product or technology as much as they can. Testing speeds up and improves the innovation process, too. When two very different design

Milestones formal project review points used to assess progress and performance

Multifunctional teams work teams composed of people from different departments

prototypes are tested against each other or the new design iteration is tested against the previous iteration, product design strengths and weaknesses quickly become apparent. Likewise, testing uncovers errors early in the design process, when they are easiest to correct. Finally, testing accelerates learning and understanding by forcing engineers and product designers to examine hard data about product performance. When there's hard evidence that prototypes are testing well, the confidence of the design team grows. Also, personal conflict between design team members is less likely when testing focuses on hard measurements and facts rather than personal hunches and preferences.

Milestones are formal project review points used to assess progress and performance. For example, a company that has put itself on a 12-month schedule to complete a project might schedule milestones at the 3-, 6-, and 9-month points on the schedule. By making people regularly assess what they're doing, how well they're performing, and whether they need to take corrective action, milestones provide structure to the general chaos that follows technological discontinuities. Milestones also shorten the innovation process by creating a sense of urgency that keeps everyone on task.

Multifunctional teams are work teams composed of people from different departments. Multifunctional teams accelerate learning and understanding by mixing and integrating technical, marketing, and manufacturing activities. By involving all key departments in development from the start, multifunctional teams speed innovation through early identification of new ideas or problems that would typically not have been generated or addressed until much later.

Powerful leaders provide the vision, discipline, and motivation to keep the innovation process focused, on time, and on target. Powerful leaders are able to get resources when they are needed, are typically more experienced, have high status in the company, and are held directly responsible for the product's success or failure. On average, powerful leaders can get innovation-related projects done nine months faster than leaders with little power or influence. One such powerful leader was Phil Martens, the former head of Ford's product development. With a year to go before introduction and Ford's hybrid Escape months behind schedule, he told the team, "We are going to deliver on time ... Anything you need you'll get."[33] Despite daily inquiries "from above," he promised no interruptions or interference from anyone—even top management. And when the team members needed something, they got it without waiting.

2.3 Compression Approach: Managing Innovation During Incremental Change

The experiential approach is used to manage innovation in highly *uncertain* environments during periods of *discontinuous* change; the compression approach is used to manage innovation in more *certain* environments during periods of *incremental* change. The goals of the experiential approach are significant improvements in performance and the establishment of a *new* dominant design; the goals of the compression approach are lower costs and incremental improvements in the performance and function of the *existing* dominant design.

The general strategies in each approach are different. With the experiential approach, the general strategy is to build something new, different, and substantially better. Because there's so much uncertainty—no one knows which technology will become the market leader—companies adopt a winner-take-all approach by trying to create the market-leading, dominant design. With the compression approach, the general strategy is to compress the time and steps needed to bring about small, consistent improvements in performance and functionality. Because a dominant technology design already exists, the general strategy is to continue improving the existing technology as rapidly as possible.

© Susan Van Etten Lawson

Extreme Makeover

Standing in front of her mirror, Hana Zalal, the president of Cargo Cosmetics, was holding a tube of lipstick and wondering how to redesign it. Then came a packaging epiphany: make it completely biodegradable.

An alumna of the University of Toronto's civil engineering program, she went to the university for help. Professor Mohini Sain took up the project and worked with Cargo and a local injection-moulding company for two years to figure out how to form corn into a lipstick tube at a "fast and cheap commercial rate." They succeeded. The new PlantLove lipstick tube decomposes in 47 days with composting, and the box it comes in is embedded with wildflower seeds and can be planted instead of discarded. And as you would expect, the lipstick itself is environmentally friendly and uses no mineral or petroleum oils or derivatives.

Source: S. Bhattacharya, "Cosmetics Company Cargo Takes Green and Floral Path," *Toronto Star*, 16 January 2007; "Lipstick Maker Goes Green with Biodegradable Tube," *CBC Canada*, 20 April 2007.

In short, a **compression approach to innovation** assumes that innovation is a predictable process, that incremental innovation can be planned using a series of steps, and that compressing the time it takes to complete those steps can speed up innovation. The compression approach to innovation has five aspects: planning, supplier involvement, shortening the time of individual steps, overlapping steps, and multifunctional teams.[34]

In Chapter 5, *planning* was defined as choosing a goal and a method or strategy to achieve that goal. When *planning for incremental innovation*, the goal is to squeeze or compress development time as much as possible, and the general strategy is to create a series of planned steps to accomplish that goal. Planning for incremental innovation helps avoid unnecessary steps and enables developers to sequence steps in the right order to avoid wasted time and delays between steps. Planning also reduces misunderstandings and improves coordination.

Most planning for incremental innovation is based on the idea of generational change. **Generational change** occurs when incremental improvements are made to a dominant technological design such that the improved version of the technology is fully backward compatible with the older version.[35] Software is backward compatible if a new version of the software will work with files created by older versions. Likewise, an important feature of gaming machines, such as the Xbox 360 and the Nintendo Wii, is their ability to play games purchased for earlier machines. In fact, the latest Game Boy can play games purchased more than 20 years ago.

Because the compression approach assumes that innovation can follow a series of preplanned steps, one way to shorten development time is through *supplier involvement.* Delegating some of the preplanned steps in the innovation process to outside suppliers reduces the amount of work that internal development teams must do. Plus, suppliers provide an alternative source of ideas and expertise that can lead to better designs. Rowmark, an international firm, produces thin plastic sheets that can be engraved or shaped by a thermoforming process. In an effort to improve the performance of their product, lower the cost of raw materials, and avoid disruptions in supply, it recruits the companies that supply its resins and additives to participate in the product design and manufacturing processes. Suppliers have knowledge that can help Rowmark put out a better product at a lower cost. Loyalty and flexibility are important, as is a cultural fit between the supplier and the manufacturer, because they are effectively becoming a single team. Eric Hausserman, Rowmark's vice president for manufacturing and technology, points out: "We see our suppliers as partners in every sense of the term."[36] In general, the earlier suppliers are involved, the quicker they catch and prevent future problems, such as unrealistic designs or mismatched product specifications.

Another way to shorten development time is simply to *shorten the time of individual steps* in the innovation process. A common way to do that is through computer-aided design (CAD). CAD speeds up the design process by allowing designers and engineers to make and test design changes using computer models rather than physically testing expensive prototypes. CAD also speeds innovation by making it easy to see how design changes affect engineering, purchasing, and production.

In a sequential design process, each step must be completed before the next step begins. But sometimes multiple development steps can be performed at the same time. *Overlapping steps* shorten the development process by reducing delays and waiting times between steps. Warner Bros. used overlapping steps to reduce the time it took to make the entire series of *Harry Potter* films—one for each of the first six books in J.K. Rowling's series and two for the last one. Because the actors were aging and would soon resemble adults more than high school students, Warner Bros. used new directors and new production teams for each of the movies in the *Harry Potter* series so that it could begin shooting the next film while the previous one was in post-production and the one prior to that was in the theatres.[37]

Compression approach to innovation an approach to innovation that assumes that incremental innovation can be planned using a series of steps and that compressing those steps can speed innovation

Generational change change based on incremental improvements to a dominant technological design such that the improved technology is fully backward compatible with the older technology

Organizational Change

The idea was simple. Build a series of electronics superstores and watch the customers and profits pour in. For a while, it seemed to work. Radio Shack created Incredible Universe and it grew to $72.5 million in less than four years as the company expanded to 17 stores, including several in Canada, each of which stocked an average of 85,000 products in a 17,000-square-metre building. That was more than four times the size of the now bankrupt Circuit City stores, a rival at the time. At the time, the largest big-box store in Canada was an Incredible Universe. Yet because of the size, inventory, and extras, the break-even point for each store was $70 million in sales per year. So despite rapid growth, the company was losing money at record rates. Managers were unable to change the store concept quickly enough to reverse the situation, so the parent company, Radio Shack, closed Incredible Universe just four years after its founding. Businesses operate in a constantly changing environment. Recognizing and adapting to internal and external changes can mean the difference between continued success and going out of business. Companies that fail to change run the risk of organizational decline.[38]

LO3 Organizational Decline: The Risk of Not Changing

Businesses operate in a constantly changing environment. Recognizing and adapting to internal and external changes can mean the difference between continued success and

Beating a Sluggish Economy

Starbucks, the ubiquitous coffee shop that popularized gourmet coffee, posted its first ever loss in July 2008. What got them down back then? Overexpansion, an increase in the price of commodities, competition from companies like McDonald's, which were making improved (and less expensive) coffee, and an overall slower economy. Starbucks closed 680 stores in 2008 (including 61 in Australia). Now all that is behind them. Thanks in part to the Target stores that are coming to Canada, Starbucks Canada will be undertaking the biggest expansion effort in its history in 2013, with plans to open more than 150 new locations across the country. "Starbucks will have more than 20,000 retail stores on six continents by 2014," says Starbucks CEO Howard Schultz, and they plan an accelerated growth strategy to open 3,000 new stores in the Americas by 2017 (that's 2 new stores per day!). Starbucks forecasts that China will become its second biggest market by 2015, with 1,500 stores in 70 cities. You won't have to walk far to get your next caffeine fix.

Source: L. Gunnison, "Black and Brew," Portfolio.com; Riley, J., (2009) "Starbucks closures - global economy or other factors to blame?" Tutor2u; Starbucks (2008). Starbucks Newsroom 31 July 2008.

© D. Hurst/GetStock.com

Organizational decline a large decrease in organizational performance that occurs when companies don't anticipate, recognize, neutralize, or adapt to the internal or external pressures that threaten their survival

going out of business. Companies that fail to change run the risk of organizational decline.[39]

Organizational decline occurs when companies don't anticipate, recognize, neutralize, or adapt to the internal or external pressures that threaten their survival.[40] In other words, decline occurs when organizations don't recognize the need for change. General Motors' loss of market share and eventual bankruptcy in late 2009 is an example of organizational decline. There are five stages of organizational decline: blinded, inaction, faulty action, crisis, and dissolution.[41]

In the *blinded stage*, decline begins because key managers fail to recognize the internal or external changes that will harm their organization. This "blindness" may be due to a simple lack of awareness about changes or an inability to understand their significance. It may also come from the overconfidence that can develop when a company has been successful.

In the *inaction stage*, as organizational performance problems become more visible, management may recognize the need to change but still take no action. The managers may be waiting to see if the problems will correct themselves. Or they may find it difficult to change the practices and policies that previously led to success. Possibly, too, they wrongly assume that they can easily correct the problems, so they don't feel the situation is urgent.

In the *faulty action stage*, faced with rising costs and decreasing profits and market share, management announces "belt tightening" plans designed to cut costs, increase efficiency, and restore profits. In other words, rather than recognizing the need for fundamental changes, managers assume that if they just run a tighter ship, company performance will return to previous levels.

In the *crisis stage*, bankruptcy or dissolution (i.e., breaking up the company and selling its parts) is likely to occur unless the company completely reorganizes the way it does business. At this point, however, companies typically lack the resources to fully change how they run themselves. Cutbacks and layoffs will have reduced the level of talent among employees. Furthermore, talented managers who were savvy enough to see the crisis coming will have found jobs with other companies, often with competitors.

FIVE STAGES OF ORGANIZATIONAL DECLINE

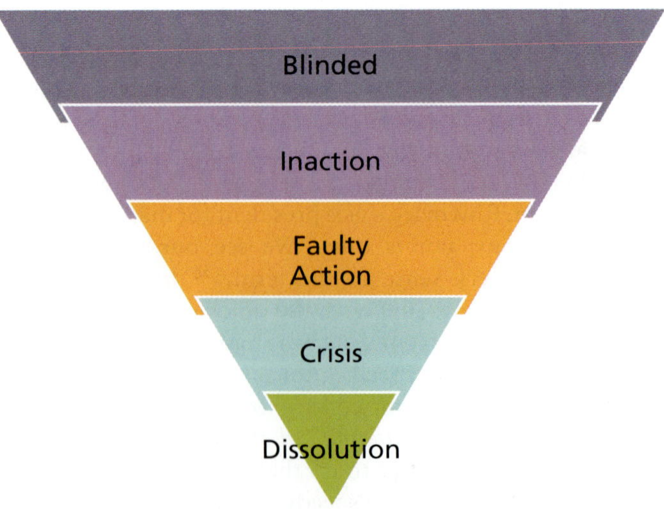

Arcady/Shutterstock.com

In the *dissolution stage*, after failing to make the changes needed to sustain the organization, the company is dissolved through bankruptcy proceedings or by selling assets in order to pay suppliers, banks, and creditors. At this point, a new CEO may be brought in to oversee the closing of stores, offices, and manufacturing facilities, the final layoffs of managers and employees, and the sale of assets.

Because decline is reversible at each of the first four stages, not all companies in decline reach final dissolution. GM aggressively cut costs, stabilized its shrinking market share, and used innovative production techniques in an effort to reverse a decline that had resulted in bankruptcy. GM in Canada made many changes to different plants, closed some assembly plants, discontinued several lines (Pontiac among them), and made new deals with unions and creditors.[42] General Motors had a highly successful initial public offering (IPO) after its bankruptcy and has made great leaps forward for a company that was once very much on the rails. Looking ahead, CNBC analyst Kevin Hall has stated that "the impending impact of 23 new product introductions by 2017 seem likely to boost GM's market share, which declined to 18 percent in 2012 from 19.6 percent in 2011."[43]

L04 Managing Change

According to social psychologist Kurt Lewin, change is a function of the forces that promote change and the opposing forces that slow or resist change.[44] **Change forces** include new strategic requirements (perhaps a new kind of differentiation), which are closely tied to competitor actions (remember the Porter analysis from Chapter 6); changes in government regulation (e.g., in trade policies, taxation, and environmental laws—remember the PEST from Chapter 6); and new technologies (including new manufacturing processes, new methods, and new machinery). These forces for change quite often cause disagreement and conflict, not necessarily over the *need* for change, but over *how* change is implemented, that is, over what we actually change in our organizations.

Change forces forces that produce differences in the form, quality, or condition of an organization over time

Resistance forces forces that support the existing state of conditions in organizations

Resistance to change opposition to change resulting from self-interest, misunderstanding and distrust, a low tolerance for change, and time and cost factors.

By contrast, **resistance forces** support the status quo, that is, the existing conditions in organizations. Change is difficult under any circumstances. In a study of heart bypass patients, doctors told participants straightforwardly to change their eating and health habits or they would die. Unbelievably, a full 90 percent of participants did *not* change their habits at all![45] This fierce resistance to change also applies to organizations.

Resistance to change is caused by self-interest, misunderstanding and distrust, and a general intolerance for change.[46] People resist change out of *self-interest* because they fear that change will cost or deprive them of something they value. For example, resistance might stem from a fear that the changes will result in a loss of pay, power, responsibility, or even perhaps one's job. People also resist change because of *misunderstanding and distrust*; they don't understand the change or the reasons for it, or they distrust the people—typically management—behind the change. Resistance isn't always visible at first, however. Some of the strongest resisters may initially support the changes in public, nodding and smiling their agreement, but then ignore the changes in private and do their jobs as they always have. Management consultant Michael Hammer calls this deadly form of resistance the "Kiss of Yes."[47]

EXAMPLE of LEWIN'S FORCE FIELD ANALYSIS

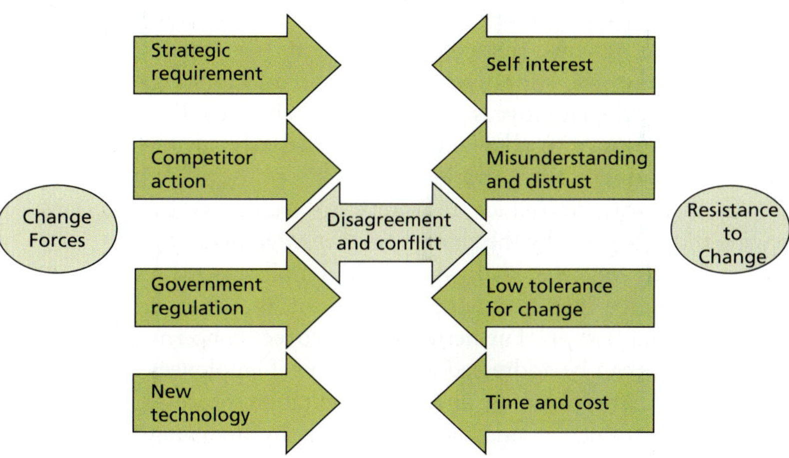

Source: Adapted from Lewin.

Unfreezing getting the people affected by change to believe that change is needed

Change intervention the process used to get workers and managers to change their behaviour and work practices

Refreezing supporting and reinforcing new changes so that they stick

Resistance may also come from a generally low tolerance for change. Some people are simply less capable of handling change than others. People with a *low tolerance for change* feel threatened by the uncertainty associated with change and worry that they won't be able to learn the new skills and behaviours they need in order to successfully negotiate change in their companies. The final factor usually falls into the *time and cost* area. People in an organization generally only accept that change is inevitable just at the point when they have the least amount of time and resources to effect the change—in other words, when it is too late!

Because resistance to change is inevitable, successful change efforts require careful management. In this section you will learn about ***4.1 managing resistance to change, 4.2 what not to do when leading organizational change,*** *and* ***4.3 different change tools and techniques.***

4.1 Managing Resistance to Change

According to Kurt Lewin, managing organizational change is a basic process of unfreezing, change intervention, and refreezing. **Unfreezing** is getting the people affected by change to believe that change is needed. During the **change intervention** itself, workers and managers change their behaviour and work practices. **Refreezing** involves supporting and reinforcing the new changes so that they stick.

Resistance to change is an example of frozen behaviour. Given the choice between changing and not changing, most people would rather not change. Because resistance to change is natural and inevitable, managers need to unfreeze resistance to change in order to create successful change programs. The following methods can be used to manage resistance to change: education and communication, participation, negotiation, top management support, and coercion.[48]

When resistance to change is based on insufficient, incorrect, or misleading information, managers should *educate* employees about the need for change and *communicate* change-related information to them. Managers must also supply the information and funding or other support employees need to make changes. For example, resistance to change can be particularly strong when one company buys another.

Another way to reduce resistance to change is by having those affected by the change *participate in planning and implementing the change process.* Employees who participate have a better understanding of the change and the need for it. Furthermore, employee concerns about change can be addressed as they occur if employees participate in the planning and implementation process. Procter & Gamble Canada did exactly this by involving the personnel from all levels when P&G needed to change to become more responsive to the market and more innovative. The original Swiffer duster was developed by a Japanese company; Procter & Gamble then teamed up with it to take the product global.[49] Innovation on a global scale is sometimes required. Tim Penner, CEO of P&G Canada, has indicated that P&G will become an innovator online and that he will be assigning as much as 20 percent of the advertising budget to digital media. Canada has often served as a testing ground for new products that P&G has eventually rolled out elsewhere in the world. Penner led the launch of Swiffer WetJet in Canada a year before its American rollout.[50] P&G Canada tries to blend the best R&D practices in the world with an understanding of local Canadian markets. "We truly think globally and act locally," he says. In doing so, P&G hopes to become the fastest growing consumer products company in Canada. It plans to achieve that leadership position "through innovation in everything we do," from innovative marketing programs that foster meaningful relationships with consumers, to productive partnerships with retailers and leading workplace practices for employees.[51]

Good Tip!

What to Do When Employees Resist Change

Unfreezing

- **Share reasons:** Share the reasons for change with employees.
- **Empathize:** Be empathetic to the difficulties that change will create for managers and employees.
- **Communicate:** Communicate the details simply, clearly, extensively, verbally, and in writing.

Change

- **Explain:** Explain the benefits, "what's in it for them."
- **Champion:** Identify a highly respected manager to manage the change effort.
- **Create opportunities for feedback:** Allow the people who will be affected by change to express their needs and offer their input.
- **Time it right:** Don't begin change at a bad time—for example, during the busiest part of the year or month.
- **Offer security:** If possible, maintain employees' job security to minimize fear of change.
- **Educate:** Offer training to ensure that employees are both confident and competent to handle new requirements.
- **Don't rush:** Change at a manageable pace.

Source: G.J. Iskat & J. Liebowitz, "What to Do When Employees Resist Change," *Supervision*, 1 August 1996.

Employees are also less likely to resist change if they are allowed to discuss and agree on who will do what after change occurs. Resistance to change also decreases when change efforts receive *significant managerial support.* But managers must do more than talk about the importance of change. They must provide the training, resources, and autonomy needed to make change happen. For example, with their distinguished 70-year history of hand-drawing Hollywood's most successful animated films (*Snow White*, *Bambi*, *The Little Mermaid*, *Beauty and the Beast*), the animators at the Walt Disney Company naturally resisted the move to computer-generated (CG) animation. So Disney supported the difficult change by putting all of its animators through a six-month "CG Boot Camp," where they learned how to draw animated characters with computers.[52]

Finally, resistance to change can be managed through **coercion**, or the use of formal power and authority to force others to change. Because of the intense negative reactions it can create (e.g., fear, stress, resentment, sabotage of company products), coercion should be used only during a crisis or when all other attempts to reduce resistance to change have failed.

Change efforts that lack vision tend to be confused, chaotic, and contradictory.

4.2 What Not to Do When Leading Change

So far, you've learned how to execute a basic change process (unfreezing, change, refreezing) and how to manage resistance to change. Harvard Business School professor John Kotter argues that when it comes to achieving successful organizational change, knowing what *not* to do is just as important as knowing what to do.[53]

Managers commonly make certain errors when they lead change. They make the first two errors during the unfreezing phase, when they try to get the people affected by change to believe that change is really needed. The first and potentially most serious error is *not establishing a great enough sense of urgency.* Indeed, Kotter estimates that more than half of all change efforts fail because the people affected are not convinced that change is necessary. People will feel a greater sense of urgency if a leader in the company makes a public, candid assessment of the company's problems and weaknesses. Celestica Inc., headquartered in Toronto, produces complex printed circuit assemblies, such as PC motherboards and networking cards, flat-screen TVs, and Xbox video game systems for Microsoft. When Craig Muhlhauser took over as president and CEO, Celestica was losing money and market share. Muhlhauser went to work right away. He informed employees that the company couldn't survive if it didn't change. Within his first 30 days as CEO, he reduced staff by 35 percent, moved new people into important positions, and had the attention of everyone in the company.[54]

Coercion using formal power and authority to force others to change

The second mistake that occurs in the unfreezing process is *not creating a powerful enough coalition.* Change often starts with one or two people, but it has to be supported by an expanding group if it is going to build enough momentum to impact an entire department, division, or company. Besides top management, Kotter recommends that key employees, managers, board members, customers, and even union leaders be members of a *core change coalition* that guides and supports organizational change. According to Muhlhauser, in a turnaround, there are three kinds of employees—those on your side, those on the fence, and those who will never buy in. The latter have to be let go, and those on the fence should be persuaded to contribute or leave. Says Muhlhauser: "Change is difficult, and as we make change, it is important to realize that there are people who are going to resist that change. In talking to those people, the objective is to move everybody into the column of supporters. But that is probably unachievable."[55] It's also important to strengthen this core change coalition's resolve by periodically bringing its members together for off-site retreats.

The next four errors that managers make occur during the change phase, when a change intervention is used to try to get workers and managers to change their behaviour and work practices. *Lacking a vision* for change is a significant error at this point. As you learned in Chapter 5, a *vision* is a statement of a company's purpose or reason for existing. A vision for change makes

Errors Managers Make When Leading Change

Unfreezing

1. Not establishing a great enough sense of urgency.
2. Not creating a powerful enough guiding coalition.

Change

3. Lacking a vision.
4. Undercommunicating the vision by a factor of ten.
5. Not removing obstacles to the new vision.
6. Not systematically planning for and creating short-term wins.

Refreezing

7. Declaring victory too soon.
8. Not anchoring changes in the corporation's culture.

Source: J. P. Kotter, "Leading Change: Why Transformation Efforts Fail," *Harvard Business Review* 73, no. 2 (March-April 1995):59.

clear where a company or department is headed and why the change is occurring. Change efforts that lack vision tend to be confused, chaotic, and contradictory. By contrast, change efforts guided by a vision are clear and easy to understand and can be effectively explained in five minutes or less. Procter & Gamble's beauty and grooming division accounts for one-third of its global sales. With beauty sales down 4 percent and grooming sales down 7 percent, division chief Ed Shirley has introduced a clear vision for changing the division. Said Shirley: "Our principal beauty focus has been winning with women, yet we're not broadly serving male consumers' needs outside of Gillette and fine fragrances."[56] The change, he said, "will require a cultural shift" as well as a change in the organizational structure based on gender, rather than products, "to better serve 'Him and Her.'"[57]

Undercommunicating the vision by a factor of ten is another mistake in the change phase. According to Kotter, companies mistakenly hold just one meeting to announce the vision. Or, if the new vision receives heavy emphasis in executive speeches or company newsletters, senior management then undercuts the vision by behaving in ways contrary to it. Successful communication of the vision requires that top managers link everything the company does to the new vision and that they "walk the talk" by behaving in ways consistent with the vision.

Even companies that begin change with a clear vision sometimes make the mistake of *not removing obstacles to the new vision.* They leave formidable barriers to change in place by failing to redesign jobs, pay plans, and technology to support the new way of doing things. One of Celestica's key obstacles was efficiently and effectively managing its supply chain; it worked with 4,000 suppliers around the world. The complexity of this supply chain network and the costs of uncoordinated transportation and shipping reduced the speed with which it could meet customer orders and made it difficult to keep costs low. CEO Craig Muhlhauser and his management team removed this obstacle by implementing Liveshare, an information system that gave it and its suppliers real-time data on sales, production, inventory, and shipping for all of its products. For example, if Best Buy wanted to buy more units of a top-selling video game, it used to have to contact Celestica via phone, e-mail, or fax to see how quickly the order could be delivered. Now, with Liveshare, it can see live, up-to-date numbers indicating how many of those video games are rolling off Celestica's production lines or are now on trucks en route to Best Buy trucking depots.[58]

Another error in the change phase is *not systematically planning for and creating short-term wins.* Most people don't have the discipline and patience to wait two years to see if the new change effort works. Change is threatening and uncomfortable, so people need to see an immediate payoff if they are to continue to support it. Kotter recommends that managers create short-term wins by choosing projects that are likely to work extremely well early in the change process. Celestica's Craig Muhlhauser understood the importance of short-term wins: "My approach was to look at the first thirty days, then at the first three months, then at the first twelve months and then I took a look at the three years. In a turnaround, you have to take hold very quickly. You have to show relatively quick hits [i.e., short-term wins] to show your turnaround strategy is working—and then you deal with a multitude of issues in a very focused way that will allow you to continue to show improvement."[59]

The last two errors that managers make occur during the refreezing phase, when attempts are made to support and reinforce changes so that they stick.

Beyond Chicken Noodle

Innovation and change is not just about computers and smartphones. We also have to innovate everyday things like soap and soup. Your grandmother's old standby may cure your cold and heal your soul, but it isn't good enough to revive Campbell Soup Company's downturn or achieve its goal of expanding into global markets without some really good applied "innovation." Campbell's must make sure the famous red label remains the leader in soup. But that will mean change and innovation. Chicken soup may be food for the soul in Canada …

… but not so much for the Chinese. The company has been relearning the ins and outs of soup in different cultures and establishing innovative strategies for breaking into those markets. Some tips for transformation and change: All things are possible. See the situation straight through thoroughly. Have high standards and look hard at consumer demands. Take the time to get it right. If we do not continually innovate, we die!

Source: J. Jargon, "Campbell's Chief Looks for Spash of Innovation," *The Wall Street Journal*, 30 May 2008, B8.

Photos.com (Jupiterimages)/ Andrew Harrer/Bloomberg via Getty Images

Declaring victory too soon is a tempting mistake during the refreezing phase. Managers typically declare victory right after the first large-scale success in the change process. Declaring success too early has the same effect as draining the gasoline out of a car: it stops change efforts dead in their tracks. With success declared, supporters of the change process stop pushing to make change happen. After all, why push when success has been achieved? Rather than declaring victory, managers should use the momentum from short-term wins to push for even bigger or faster changes. This maintains urgency and prevents change supporters from slacking off before the changes are frozen into the company's culture.

The last mistake that managers make is *not anchoring changes in the corporation's culture.* An *organization's culture* is the set of key values, beliefs, and attitudes shared by organizational members that determines the "accepted way of doing things" in a company. As you learned in Chapter 3, changing cultures is extremely difficult and slow. According to Kotter, two things help anchor changes in a corporation's culture. The first is showing people that the changes have actually improved performance. At Celestica, that proof was provided by the quick increase in quarterly profits, which led to a 60 percent increase in the company's stock price.[60] The second is to make sure that the people who get promoted fit the new culture. If they don't, it's a clear sign that the changes were only temporary. At Celestica, Muhlhauser created a culture of meritocracy that rewarded managers and employees for their contributions. The rewards came in the form of promotions, pay increases, and huge bonuses. Customer satisfaction improved. With the increasing demand for consumer products, such as smartphones, employees were excited about the prospects for Celestica. "We've got some new programs in the pipeline so we're optimistic about our ability to compete in and win in that market," said Muhlhauser.[61]

4.3 Change Tools and Techniques

Imagine your boss came to you and said, "All right, genius, you wanted it. You're in charge of turning around the division." How would you start? Where would you begin? How would you encourage change-resistant managers to change? What would you do to include others in the change process? How would you get the change process off to a quick start? Finally, what approach would you use to promote long-term effectiveness and performance? Results-driven change, the General Electric workout, and organizational development are three change tools and techniques that can be used to address these issues.

One reason why organizational change efforts fail is that they are activity-oriented rather than results-oriented. In other words, they focus primarily on changing company procedures, management philosophy, or employee behaviour. Typically, there is much buildup and preparation as consultants are brought in, presentations are made, books are read, and employees and managers are trained. There's a tremendous emphasis on "doing things the new way." But, with all the focus on "doing," almost no attention is paid to results, to seeing if all this activity has actually made a difference.

Results-driven change change created quickly by focusing on the measurement and improvement of results

General Electric workout a three-day meeting in which managers and employees from different levels and parts of an organization quickly generate and act on solutions to specific business problems

By contrast, **results-driven change** supplants the emphasis on activity with a laser-like focus on quickly measuring and improving results.[62] For example, top managers at Hyundai knew that if they were to compete successfully against the likes of Honda and Toyota, they would have to substantially improve the quality of their cars. So top managers guided the company's results-driven change process by increasing the number of quality teams from 100 to 865. After that, all employees were required to attend seminars on quality improvement and to use the results of industry quality studies (such as those published annually by J.D. Power and Associates) as their benchmark. Before the change, a new Hyundai averaged 23.4 initial quality problems; after the results-driven change efforts, that number dropped to 9.6.[63] Today, according to J.D. Power and Associates, Hyundai ranks seventh overall out of thirty-three automakers in initial car quality, behind Porsche, Acura, Mercedes-Benz, Lexus, Ford, and Honda.[64]

Another advantage of results-driven change is that managers introduce changes in procedures, philosophy, or behaviour only if they are likely to improve measured performance.[65] In other words, changes are tested to see whether they actually make a difference. Consistent with this approach, Hyundai invested $30 million in a test centre where cars were subjected to a sequence of extremely harsh conditions to allow engineers to pinpoint defects and fix problems.[66]

A third advantage of results-driven change is that quick, visible improvements motivate employees to continue to make additional changes to improve measured performance. A few years into Hyundai's change process, Chrysler and Mitsubishi Motors announced they would be using Hyundai-designed four-cylinder engines in their small and midsize cars, reinforcing the quality strides that Hyundai had made.[67] As a result of the superb quality of its cars, Hyundai's global sales actually rose 5 percent during the recession, when nearly every other auto manufacturer, including Toyota and Honda, saw their sales drop 25 to 35 percent.[68] Today, less than a decade after it took steps to address the quality of its cars, Hyundai is the fifth-largest automaker in the world.[69] As seen at Hyundai, the quick successes associated with results-driven change can be particularly effective at reducing resistance to change.[70] Exhibit 7.4 on page 118 describes the basic steps of results-driven change.

The **General Electric workout** is a special kind of results-driven change. The "workout" involves a three-day meeting that brings together managers and employees

Exhibit 7.4 How to Create a Results-Driven Change Program

1 Set measurable, short-term goals to improve performance.
2. Make sure your action steps are likely to improve measured performance.
3. Stress the importance of immediate improvements.
4. Solicit help from consultants and staffers to achieve quick improvements in performance.
5. Test action steps to see if they actually yield improvements. If they don't, discard them and establish new ones.
6. Use resources you have or that can be easily acquired. It doesn't take much.

Source: R. H. Schaffer & H. A. Thomson, J.D, "Successful Change Programs Begin With Results," *Harvard Business Review on Change* (Boston: Harvard Business School Press, 1998), 189–213.

Organizational development **a philosophy and collection of planned change interventions designed to improve an organization's long-term health and performance**

Change agent **the person formally in charge of guiding a change effort**

from different levels and parts of an organization to quickly generate and act on solutions to specific business problems.[71] On the first morning, the boss discusses the agenda and targets specific business problems that the group will solve. The boss then leaves, and an outside facilitator breaks the group (typically 30 to 40 people) into five or six teams and helps them spend the next day and a half discussing and debating solutions. On day three, in what GE calls a "town meeting," the teams present specific solutions to their boss, who has been gone since day one. As each team's spokesperson makes specific suggestions, the boss has only three options: agree on the spot, say no, or ask for more information so that a decision can be made by a specific, agreed-on date.[72]

GE boss Armand Lauzon sweated his way through a town meeting. To encourage him to say yes, his workers set up the meeting room to put pressure on him. He recalled: "I was wringing wet within half an hour. They had 108 proposals, I had about a minute to say yes or no to each one, and I couldn't make eye contact with my boss without turning around, which would show everyone in the room that I was chicken."[73] In the end, Lauzon agreed to all but eight suggestions. Furthermore, once those decisions were made, no one at GE was allowed to overrule them.

Organizational development is a philosophy and collection of planned change interventions designed to improve an organization's long-term health and performance. Organizational development takes a long-range approach to change; assumes that top management support is necessary for change to succeed; creates change by educating workers and managers to change ideas, beliefs, and behaviours so that problems can be solved in new ways; and emphasizes employee participation in diagnosing, solving, and evaluating problems.[74] As shown in Exhibit 7.5, organizational development interventions begin with the recognition of a problem. Then, the company designates a **change agent** to be formally in charge of guiding the change effort. This person can be someone from the company or a professional consultant. The change agent clarifies the problem, gathers information, works with decision makers to create and implement an action plan, helps evaluate the plan's effectiveness, implements the plan throughout the company, and then leaves (if from outside the company) after making sure the change intervention will continue to work.

Exhibit 7.5 General Steps for Organizational Development Interventions

1. **Entry**	A problem is discovered and the need for change becomes apparent. A search begins for someone to deal with the problem and facilitate change.
2. **Startup**	A change agent enters the picture and works to clarify the problem and gain commitment to a change effort.
3. **Assessment & feedback**	The change agent gathers information about the problem and provides feedback about it to decision makers and those affected by it.
4. **Action planning**	The change agent works with decision makers to develop an action plan.
5. **Intervention**	The action plan, or organizational development intervention, is carried out.
6. **Evaluation**	The change agent helps decision makers assess the effectiveness of the intervention.
7. **Adoption**	Organizational members accept ownership and responsibility for the change, which is then carried out through the entire organization.
8. **Separation**	The change agent leaves the organization after first ensuring that the change intervention will continue to work.

Source: W. J. Rothwell, R. Sullivan, and G. M. McLean, *Practicing Organizational Development: A Guide for Consultants* (San Diego: Pfeiffer & Co., 1995).

Exhibit 7.6 Different Kinds of Organizational Development Interventions

LARGE SYSTEM INTERVENTIONS	
Sociotechnical systems	An intervention designed to improve how well employees use and adjust to the work technology used in an organization.
Survey feedback	An intervention that uses surveys to collect information from the members, reports the results of that survey to the members, and then uses those results to develop action plans for improvement.
SMALL GROUP INTERVENTIONS	
Team building	An intervention designed to increase the cohesion and cooperation of work group members.
Unit goal setting	An intervention designed to help a work group establish short- and long-term goals.
PERSON-FOCUSED INTERVENTIONS	
Counselling/coaching	An intervention designed so that a formal helper or coach listens to managers or employees and advises them on how to deal with work or interpersonal problems.
Training	An intervention designed to provide individuals with the knowledge, skills, or attitudes they need to become more effective at their jobs.

Source: W. J. Rothwell, R. Sullivan, and G. M. McLean, *Practicing Organizational Development: A Guide for Consultants* (San Diego: Pfeiffer & Co., 1995).

Organizational development interventions are aimed at changing large systems, small groups, or people.[75] More specifically, the purpose of *large system interventions* is to change the character and performance of an organization, business unit, or department. *Small group intervention* focuses on assessing how a group functions and helping it work more effectively to accomplish its goals. *Person-focused intervention* is intended to increase interpersonal effectiveness by helping people become aware of their attitudes and behaviours and acquire new skills and knowledge. Exhibit 7.6 describes the most frequently used organizational development interventions for large systems, small groups, and people.

Go online at
www.nelson.com/4ltrpress/icanmgmt2
And access the essential Study Tools online for this chapter:

- **Flashcards**, to help you study
- **Interactive Quizzes**, to test your knowledge
- **Audio Chapter Summaries**, for chapter review
- **Crossword Puzzles and Beat the Clock**, to review key terms
- **What Would You Do? Cases**, for applying your knowledge to real-life situations
- **Self Assessments**, to learn about what kind of manager you are
- **Videos and Media Quizzing**, where you can watch a video about a real-life company and test yourself on what you've learned

Be sure to consult the Chapter Review Card at the back of the textbook.

8 Global Management

LEARNING OUTCOMES

LO1 Discuss the impact of global business and the trade rules and agreements that govern it.

LO2 Explain why companies choose to standardize or adapt their business procedures.

LO3 Explain the different ways that companies can organize and act ethically to do business globally.

LO4 Explain how to find a favourable business climate.

LO5 Discuss the importance of identifying and adapting to cultural differences.

LO6 Explain how to successfully prepare workers for international assignments.

What Is Global Business?

Global business is the buying and selling of goods and services by people from different countries. The Timex watch on my wrist as I write this chapter was purchased at a Wal-Mart in Manitoba. But since it was made in the Philippines, I participated in global business when I used my debit card at the Wal-Mart in Winnipeg, which is a wholly-owned subsidiary of Wal-Mart USA. Wal-Mart, for its part, had already paid Timex USA Group Inc., which in turn is owned by Timex Group B.V., a Dutch holding company (the corporate parent of several watchmaking companies around the globe, including Timex Group USA Inc.). Many of Timex Far East's wristwatches are manufactured by TMX Philippines Inc. in Lapu-Lapu, the Philippines, and they pay the company that employs the Filipino managers and workers who made my watch. Quite a story for a simple watch, but one that illustrates today's global environment.

Companies want to go global for a number of reasons: to grow into new markets while boosting their competitiveness, to cut manufacturing costs (by up to 45%!), and other similar drivers.[1]

Global business presents its own set of challenges for managers. How can you be sure that the way you run your business in one country is the right way to run that business in another? This chapter discusses how organizations answer that question. We will start by examining global business in two ways: first, by exploring its impact on Canadian businesses and then reviewing the basic rules and agreements that govern global trade. Next, we will examine how and when companies go global by examining the tradeoff between consistency and adaptation and discussing how to organize a global company. Finally, we will look at how companies decide where to expand globally, including finding the best business climate, adapting to cultural differences, and better preparing employees for international assignments.

LO1 Global Business, Trade Rules, and Trade Agreements

If you want a simple demonstration of the impact of global business, look at the tag on your shirt, the inside of your shoes, and the inside of your smartphone (which most of the world calls a "mobile"). Chances are that these three items were made in different places around the world. As I write this, my shirt, shoes, and mobile were made in Thailand, China, and Korea respectively. Where were yours made?

Let's learn more about ***1.1 the impact of global business, 1.2 how tariff and nontariff trade barriers have historically restricted global business, 1.3 how global and regional trade agreements today are reducing trade barriers worldwide,*** *and* ***1.4 how consumers are responding to changes in trade rules and agreements.***

1.1 The Impact of Global Business

Multinational corporations are corporations that own businesses in two or more countries. In 1970, more than half of the world's 7,000 multinationals were headquartered in just two countries: the United States and the United Kingdom. Today there are 77,175 multinationals—nearly 11.25 times as many as in 1970—and only 2,418 (3.1 percent) are based in the United States.[2] Today, 53,072 multinationals (68.8 percent of them) are based in other countries, such as Germany, Italy, Canada, and Japan, and 20,238 (26.2 percent) are based in developing countries (such as Colombia, South Africa, and Tunisia). Today, multinationals can be found by the thousands all over the world.

Global business the buying and selling of goods and services by people from different countries

Multinational corporation a corporation that owns businesses in two or more countries

Foreign direct investment a method of investment in which a company builds a new business or buys an existing business in a foreign country

Another way to appreciate the impact of global business is by examining investment from other countries. **Foreign direct investment** occurs when a company builds a new business or buys an existing business in a foreign country. US steelmaker Nucor made a direct foreign investment when it purchased Harris Steel of Canada Ltd.[3] Of course, companies from many other countries also own businesses in Canada. Companies from the United Kingdom, Japan, Germany, the Netherlands, the United States, France, Switzerland, and Luxembourg have the largest foreign direct investment in Canada. Overall, foreign companies invest more than $500 billion a year in Canada.

Foreign Direct Investment in Canada, 1998–2007
Cumulative at Year End

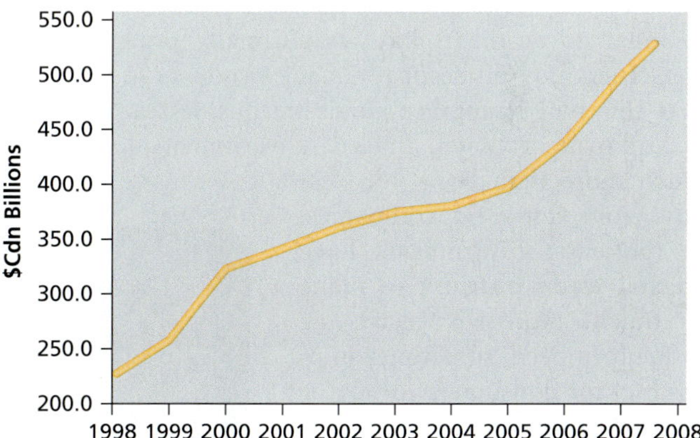

Sources: Statistics Canada: International Investment Position, May 2008 (http://www.investontario.com/siteselector/bcin_500.asp), accessed 19 May 2010); Government of Canada, 9 March 2010. Canada poised to Become "tariff-free zone" for manufacturers thanks to budget 2010. http://news.gc.ca/web/article=eng.co?m=index&nid=517440. Accessed 19 May 2010.

But foreign direct investment in Canada is only half the picture. Canadian companies themselves have made large foreign direct investments in countries around the world. For example, Molson, the brewer of Molson X, paid $700 million to acquire Brewery Group, the fourth-largest brewery in Mexico. Molson has since merged with Coors and is known as Molson Coors Brewing Company

Trade barriers government-imposed regulations that increase the cost and restrict the number of imported goods

Protectionism a government's use of trade barriers to shield domestic companies and their workers from foreign competition

Tariff a direct tax on imported goods

Nontariff barriers nontax methods of increasing the cost or reducing the volume of imported goods

Quota a limit on the number or volume of imported products

Voluntary export restraints voluntarily imposed limits on the number or volume of products exported to a particular country

Government import standard a standard ostensibly established to protect the health and safety of citizens but, in reality, often used to restrict imports

in Canada; meanwhile, SABMiller and Molson Coors Brewing Company have announced a joint venture known as MillerCoors for their US operations.[4]

Global management can be confusing. Consolidations are occurring in many industries worldwide. For example, Sapporo of Japan has acquired Canada's John Sleeman Breweries, mainly for the sake of its distribution network.[5]

Canadian companies have made their largest foreign direct investments in the United Kingdom, the United States, the Netherlands, and Australia. Note that there are many restrictions on foreign ownership in Canada. Broadcasting, aviation, liquor sales, mining, oil and gas, and pharmaceuticals are only some of the industries in which Canada restricts foreign ownership.

So whether it involves foreign companies investing in Canada or Canadian companies investing abroad, foreign direct investment is an increasingly important and common method of conducting global business.

1.2 Trade Barriers

Although today's consumers usually don't care where the products they buy come from (more on this in Section 1.4), national governments have traditionally preferred that consumers buy domestically made products in the hope that this will strengthen domestic businesses and keep unemployment down. Indeed, governments have done much more than hope you will buy from domestic companies. In the past, governments have erected **trade barriers** to make it much more expensive or difficult (indeed, sometimes impossible) for consumers to buy or consume imported goods. For example, the European Union places a 34 percent tax on frozen strawberries imported from China.[6]

The Canadian government imposes a tariff of 5 cents per litre on imported ethanol, which is blended with gasoline for use in automobiles.[7] By establishing these restrictions and taxes, the governments of the EU, China, and the United States are engaging in **protectionism**, which is the use of trade barriers to protect local companies and their workers from foreign competition.

Governments have used two general kinds of trade barriers: tariff and nontariff. A **tariff** is a direct tax on imported goods. Tariffs increase the prices of imported goods relative to domestic goods. **Nontariff barriers** are nontax methods of increasing the cost or reducing the volume of imported goods. There are five types of nontariff barriers: quotas, voluntary export restraints, government import standards, government subsidies, and customs valuation/classification. Because there are so many different kinds of nontariff barriers, they can be an even more potent approach to shielding domestic industries from foreign competition.

Quotas are specific limits on the number or volume of imported products. For example, because of strict quotas, yearly imports of raw sugar cane into Canada are limited.[8] Since this is well below the demand for sugar in Canada, domestic Canadian sugar prices are twice as high as sugar prices in the rest of the world.[9] Like quotas, **voluntary export restraints** limit the amount of a product that can be imported annually. The difference is that the exporting country rather than the importing country imposes restraints. Usually, however, the "voluntary" offer to limit exports occurs because the importing country has implicitly threatened to impose quotas. According to the World Trade Organization (see Section 1.3), however, voluntary export restraints are illegal and should not be used to restrict imports.[10]

In theory, **government import standards** are established to protect the health and safety of citizens. In reality, such standards are often used to restrict or ban imported goods. For example, the United States banned the importation of nearly all Canadian beef. Ostensibly, the ban was to prevent transmission of mad cow disease (BSE), but the US government was actually using this government import standard to protect its own beef

JIM YOUNG/Reuters /Landov

Who Pays Tariffs?

Tariffs on foreign imports are supposed to preserve Canadian jobs, but 74 percent of shoes worn by Canadians are made outside Canada, suggesting that there aren't many Canadian jobs in the shoe industry to save. Still, Canada imposes a tax on imported shoes that can skyrocket to 32 percent, and the tariff creates $2 billion of revenue, which is more than auto tariffs. Who pays? Since low-end footwear bears the brunt of the tariff, it's mostly lower income individuals who shop at retail outlets such as Wal-Mart Canada, where $5 of a $15 pair of tennis shoes may be duty.

Sources: Davison, J., "New duty-free limits will challenge Canadian retailers." *CBC News*, Posted: May 31, 2012, www.cbc.ca/news/business/story/2012/05/31/f-duty-free-limits.html; "Shot in the Foot," *The Wall Street Journal* (6 September 2008) A10.

Anthony Berenyi/Shutterstock.com

producers. Only after the WTO ruled that there was no scientific basis for the ban did the United States allow Canadian beef to be imported without restrictions.[11]

Many nations also use **subsidies**, such as long-term, low-interest loans, cash grants, and tax deferments, to develop and protect companies in specific industries. Not surprisingly, businesses complain about unfair trade practices when foreign companies receive government subsidies. For example, Embraer, the Brazilian jet airplane manufacturer, has long complained about the subsidies provided to Bombardier, a Canadian jet manufacturer. That particular dispute has been ongoing; the WTO has ruled on it many times. Meanwhile, the Canadian taxpayer picks up the subsidy costs.[12]

The last type of nontariff barrier is **customs classification**. When products are imported into a country, they are examined by customs agents, who must decide which of nearly 9,000 categories they fall under (see the Official Harmonized Tariff Schedule of Canada at **www.cbsa-asfc.gc.ca/trade-commerce/tariff-tarif** for more information). Classification is important because the category assigned by customs agents can greatly affect the size of the tariff and whether the item is subject to import quotas. For example, the Canadian Border Services Agency has several customs classifications for imported shoes. The tariff on imported leather or "nonrubber" shoes is about 10 percent, whereas the tariffs on imported rubber shoes, such as athletic footwear and waterproof shoes, range from 20 to 84 percent.[13] The difference is large enough that some importers try to make their rubber shoes look like leather, hoping to receive the nonrubber customs classification and, it follows, the lower tariff.

1.3 Trade Agreements

Because of trade barriers, imported goods were often much more expensive than domestic goods if they could be purchased at all. During the 1990s, however, the regulations governing global trade were transformed. The most significant change was that 124 countries agreed to adopt the **General Agreement on Tariffs and Trade (GATT)**. GATT, which was replaced in 1995 by the **World Trade Organization (WTO)**, brought about changes that continue to encourage international trade. The WTO, headquartered in Geneva, Switzerland, today has 150 member countries. It administers trade agreements, provides a forum for trade negotiations, handles trade disputes, monitors national trade policies, and offers technical assistance and training for developing countries.

In a number of ways, GATT made it much easier and cheaper for consumers in all countries to buy foreign products. First, it cut tariffs by an average of 40 percent worldwide by 2005. Second, it eliminated tariffs in 10 specific industries: beer, alcohol, construction equipment, farm machinery, furniture, medical equipment, paper, pharmaceuticals, steel, and toys. Third, it placed stricter limits on government subsidies. Fourth, GATT established protections for intellectual property, such as trademarks, patents, and copyrights. Protection of intellectual property has become an increasingly important issue in global trade because of widespread product piracy. For example, 90 percent of the computer software and 95 percent of the video games in China are illegal copies.[14] Finally, trade disputes between countries now are settled by WTO arbitration panels. Countries had once been able to use their veto power to cancel a panel's decision; today, WTO rulings are final.

The second major development that has reduced trade barriers has been the creation of **regional trading zones**. By treaty or agreement, the countries within these zones reduce or eliminate tariff and nontariff barriers

Subsidies government loans, grants, and tax deferments given to domestic companies to protect them from foreign competition

Customs classification a classification assigned to imported products by government officials that affects the size of the tariff and imposition of import quotas

General Agreement on Tariffs and Trade (GATT) a worldwide trade agreement that reduced and eliminated tariffs, limited government subsidies, and established protections for intellectual property

World Trade Organization (WTO) the successor to GATT, the only international organization dealing with the global rules of trade between nations. Its main function is to ensure that trade flows as smoothly, predictably, and freely as possible

Regional trading zones areas in which tariff and nontariff barriers on trade between countries are reduced or eliminated

World Trade Organization

FACT FILE

Location: Geneva, Switzerland
Established: 1 January 1995
Created by: Uruguay Round negotiations (1986–1994)
Membership: 159 countries (as of 2 March 2013)
Budget: 197,203,900 Swiss francs in 2013
Secretariat staff: 639 in 2013
Head: Roberto Carvalho de Azevêdo (Director-General)

Functions:
- Administering WTO trade agreements
- Forum for trade negotiations
- Handling trade disputes
- Monitoring national trade policies
- Technical assistance and training for developing countries
- Cooperation with other international organizations

Source: "What is the WTO?" available online at www.wto.org/english/thewto_e/whatis_e/ehatis_e.htm. Updated and used courtesy of the World Trade Organization.

Maastricht Treaty of Europe a regional trade agreement between most European countries

North American Free Trade Agreement (NAFTA) a regional trade agreement between the United States, Canada, and Mexico

Central America Free Trade Agreement (CAFTA-DR) a regional trade agreement between Costa Rica, the Dominican Republic, El Salvador, Guatemala, Honduras, Nicaragua, and the United States

Union of South American Nations (UNASUR) a regional trade agreement between Argentina, Brazil, Paraguay, Uruguay, Venezuela, Bolivia, Colombia, Ecuador, Peru, Guyana, Suriname, and Chile

among themselves. The largest and most important trading zones are in Europe (Maastricht Treaty), North America (North American Free Trade Agreement, or NAFTA), Central America (Central America Free Trade Agreement, or CAFTA-DR), South America (Union of South American Nations, or UNASUR), and Asia (Association of Southeast Asian Nations, or ASEAN, and Asia-Pacific Economic Cooperation, or APEC). The map in Exhibit 8.1 shows the extent to which free trade agreements govern global trade.

In 1992, Belgium, Denmark, France, Germany, Greece, Ireland, Italy, Luxembourg, the Netherlands, Portugal, Spain, and the United Kingdom implemented the **Maastricht Treaty of Europe**. The purpose of this treaty was to transform their 12 different economies and 12 currencies into one common economic market, called the European Union (EU), with one common currency, the euro. Austria, Finland, and Sweden joined the EU in 1995, followed by Cyprus, the Czech Republic, Estonia, Hungary, Latvia, Lithuania, Malta, Poland, Slovakia, and Slovenia in 2004, Bulgaria and Romania in 2007, and Croatia in July of 2013 bringing the total membership to 28 countries.[15] Macedonia and Turkey have applied and are still being considered for membership.[16] On January 1, 2002, a single common currency, the euro, went into circulation in 12 of the EU member countries (Austria, Belgium, Finland, France, Germany, Greece, Ireland, Italy, Luxembourg, the Netherlands, Portugal, and Spain).

Prior to the Maastricht Treaty, trucks carrying products were stopped and inspected by customs agents at each border. Furthermore, since the required paperwork, tariffs, and government product specifications could be radically different in each country, companies often had to file 12 different sets of paperwork, pay 12 different tariffs, produce 12 different versions of their basic products to meet various government specifications, and exchange money in 12 different currencies. Similarly, open business travel was complicated by inspections at each border crossing. If you lived in Germany but worked in Luxembourg, your car was stopped and your passport was inspected twice every day as you travelled to and from work. Also, every business transaction required a currency exchange, for example, from German marks to Italian lira, or from French francs to Dutch guilders. Imagine all of this happening to millions of trucks, cars, and businesspeople, and you can begin to appreciate the difficulty and cost of conducting business across Europe before the Maastricht Treaty.

NAFTA, the **North American Free Trade Agreement** between the United States, Canada, and Mexico, went into effect on January 1, 1994. More than any other regional trade agreement, NAFTA has liberalized trade between countries so that businesses can plan for one market (North America) rather than for three separate ones (the United States, Canada, Mexico). One of NAFTA's most important achievements was to eliminate most product tariffs *and* prevent Canada, the United States, and Mexico from increasing existing tariffs or introducing new ones. Mexican and Canadian exports to the United States have doubled since NAFTA went into effect. US exports to Mexico and Canada have doubled, too, which is twice as fast as US exports to any other part of the world.[17] Mexico and Canada now account for 36 percent of all US exports.[18]

CAFTA-DR, the new **Central America Free Trade Agreement** between the United States, the Dominican Republic, and the Central American countries of Costa Rica, El Salvador, Guatemala, Honduras, and Nicaragua, went into effect in August 2005. With a combined population of 347.6 million, the CAFTA-DR countries together are the tenth-largest US export market in the world and the second-largest US export market in Latin America after Mexico. US companies export more than $19 billion in goods each year to the CAFTA-DR countries. Furthermore, US exports to CAFTA-DR countries, which are increasing at 16 percent per year, are by far the fastest growing export market for US companies.[19]

On May 23, 2008, 12 South American countries signed the **Union of South American Nations (UNASUR)** Constitutive Treaty, uniting the former Mercosur

Exhibit 8.1 Global Map of Regional Trade Agreements

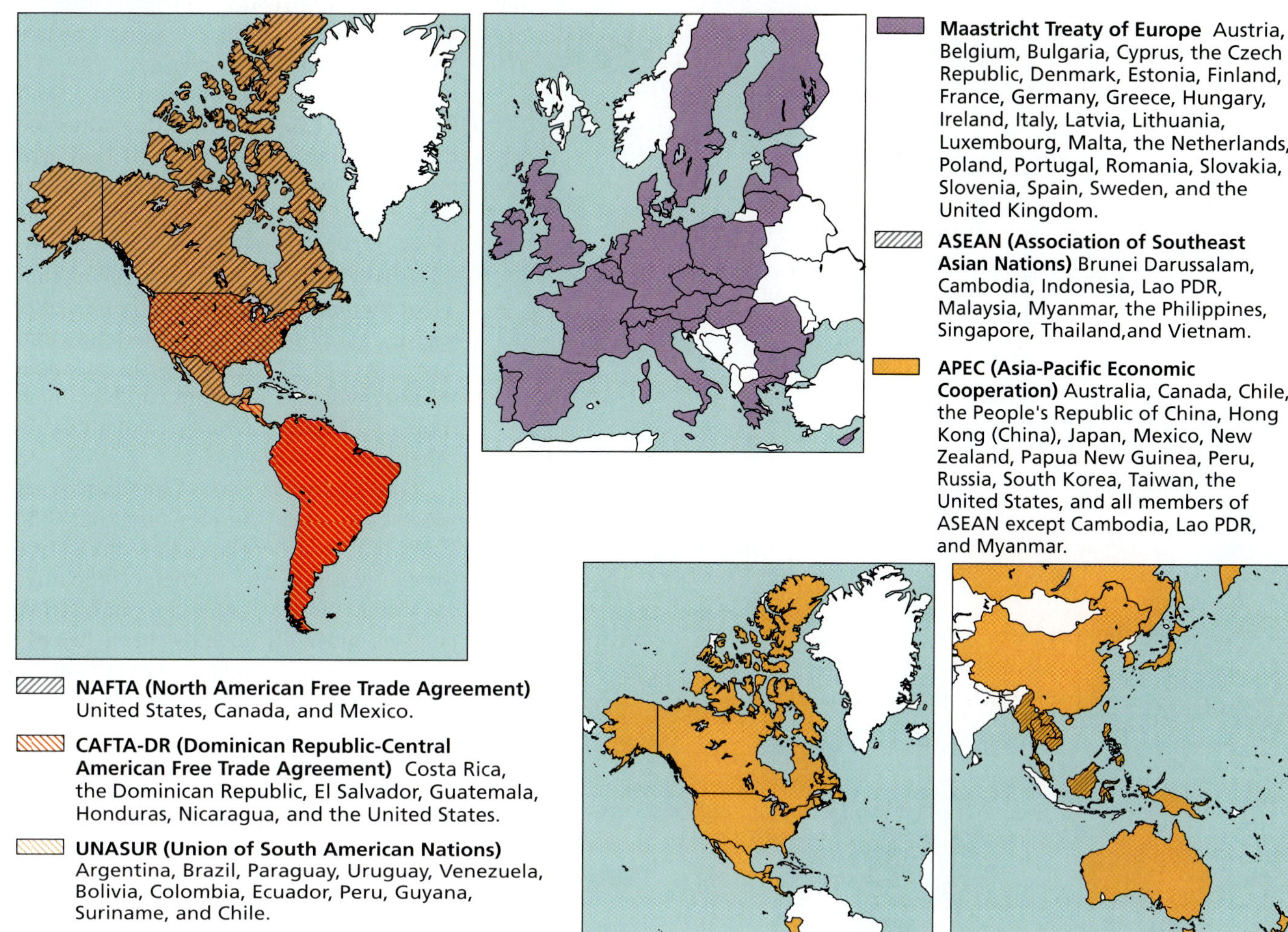

(Argentina, Brazil, Paraguay, Uruguay, Venezuela) and Andean Community (Bolivia, Colombia, Ecuador, Peru) alliances along with Guyana, Suriname, and Chile. UNASUR aims to create a unified South America by permitting free movement between nations, creating a common infrastructure (including an inter-oceanic highway), and establishing the region as a single market by eliminating tariffs by 2019. UNASUR is one of the largest trading zones in the world, encompassing 361 million people in South America with a combined GDP of nearly $1 trillion.[20]

ASEAN, the **Association of Southeast Asian Nations**, and APEC, **Asia-Pacific Economic Cooperation**, are the two largest and most important regional trading groups in Asia. ASEAN is a trade agreement between Brunei Darussalam, Cambodia, Indonesia, Lao PDR, Malaysia, Myanmar, the Philippines, Singapore, Thailand, and Vietnam. Together, these form a market of more than 558 million people. Canadian trade with ASEAN countries exceeds $78 billion a year. In fact, Canada is ASEAN's fifth-largest trading partner (Japan is its largest), and ASEAN's member nations constitute the eighth-largest trading partner of Canada. An ASEAN free trade area will begin in 2015 for the six original countries (Brunei Darussalam, Indonesia, Malaysia, the Philippines, Singapore, Thailand) and in 2018 for the newer member countries (Cambodia, Lao PDR, Myanmar, and Vietnam).[21]

APEC is a broader agreement that includes Australia, Canada, Chile, the People's Republic of China, Hong Kong (China),

Association of Southeast Asian Nations (ASEAN) a regional trade agreement between Brunei Darussalam, Cambodia, Indonesia, Lao PDR, Malaysia, Myanmar, the Philippines, Singapore, Thailand, and Vietnam

Asia-Pacific Economic Cooperation (APEC) a regional trade agreement between Australia, Canada, Chile, the People's Republic of China, Hong Kong, Japan, Mexico, New Zealand, Papua New Guinea, Peru, Russia, South Korea, Taiwan, the United States, and all members of ASEAN, except Cambodia, Lao PDR, and Myanmar

Japan, Mexico, New Zealand, Papua New Guinea, Peru, Russia, South Korea, Taiwan, the United States, and all the members of ASEAN except Cambodia, Lao PDR, and Myanmar. APEC's 21 member countries contain 2.6 billion people, account for 47 percent of all global trade, and have a combined GDP of over $19 trillion. APEC countries began reducing trade barriers in 2000; all the reductions will not be completely phased in until 2020.[22]

The Ambassador Bridge in Windsor is the busiest border crossing between Canada and the United States, carrying 25 percent of all trade between the two countries, or roughly $100 billion in annual trade going in both directions.

Photo by Jeffrey Sauger/Bloomberg via Getty Images

1.4 Consumers, Trade Barriers, and Trade Agreements

The average worker earns nearly $54,930 a year in Switzerland, $59,590 in Norway, $38,980 in Japan, and $42,640 in Canada. Yet after adjusting these incomes for how much they can buy, the Swiss income is equivalent to just $37,080, the Norwegian income to $40,420, and the Japanese income to $31,410![23] This is the same as saying that $1 of income can buy you only 68 cents' worth of goods in Switzerland and Norway, and 81 cents' worth in Japan. In other words, Canadians can buy much more with their incomes than those in other countries can.

One reason why Canadians get more for their money is that the Canadian marketplace has been one of the easiest for foreign companies to enter. Some Canadian industries, such as agriculture, have been heavily protected from foreign competition by trade barriers; but for the most part, Canadian consumers (and businesses) have had plentiful choices between Canadian-made and foreign-made products. More important, the high level of competition between foreign and domestic companies that has created these choices has helped keep prices low in Canada. Furthermore, it is precisely the lack of choice and the low level of competition that has kept prices higher in countries that have not been as open to foreign companies and products. For example, Japanese trade barriers are estimated to cost Japanese consumers more than $100 billion a year.[24]

Free trade agreements are important to consumers because they increase choices, competition, and purchasing power and thereby decrease what people pay for food, clothing, necessities, and luxuries. Accordingly, today's consumers rarely care where their products and services come from.

Free trade agreements matter to managers because, as you're about to read, while those agreements create new business opportunities, they also intensify competition, and addressing that competition is a manager's job.

How to Go Global?

Once a company has decided it will go global, it must decide *how* to go global. For example, if you decide to sell in Singapore, should you try to find a local business

Note that the penny was discontinued in May 2012 and soon we won't see this anymore!

partner who speaks the language, knows the laws, and understands the customs and norms of Singapore's culture, or should you simply export your products from your home country? What do you do if you are also entering Eastern Europe, perhaps starting in Hungary? Should you use the same approach in Hungary that you used in Singapore?

LO2 Consistency or Adaptation?

In this section, we return to a key issue: How can you be sure that the way you run your business in one country is the right way to run that business in another? In other words, how can you strike the right balance between global consistency and local adaptation?

Global consistency means that when a multinational company has offices, manufacturing plants, and distribution facilities in different countries, it will use the same rules, guidelines, policies, and procedures to run those offices, plants, and facilities. Managers at company headquarters value global consistency because it simplifies decisions. By contrast, a company with a **local adaptation** policy modifies its standard operating procedures to adapt to differences in foreign customers, governments, and regulatory agencies. Local adaptation is typically more important to the local managers who are charged with making the international business successful in their countries.

Companies that lean too much toward global consistency run the risk of following management procedures that are poorly suited to particular countries' markets, cultures, and employees (i.e., a lack of local adaptation). MTV made this mistake when going global. According to Divya Gupta, president of Media Edge, which helps companies buy advertising in India, "MTV, when it first entered the country, made the mistake of coming in as MTV. No changes." MTV quickly learned from this mistake and stopped showing Western videos in international locations. Instead, it started featuring local music and shows, like *Mochilão* in Brazil, a travel show hosted by a popular model who backpacks to famous sites.[25]

But companies that focus too much on local adaptation run the risk of losing the cost efficiencies and productivities that result from standardized rules and procedures. A decade into its development, MTV International was profitable, but not by much. It had access to huge markets—in fact, 80 percent of MTV viewers are outside North America—but access to those markets was slow to translate into large profits. Why? Because of the enormous cost of building new studios, acquiring new talent, and developing local content for so many different international markets.

Global consistency when a multinational company has offices, manufacturing plants, and distribution facilities in different countries and runs them all using the same rules, guidelines, policies, and procedures

Local adaptation when a multinational company modifies its rules, guidelines, policies, and procedures to adapt to differences in foreign customers, governments, and regulatory agencies

Exporting selling domestically produced products to customers in foreign countries

LO3 Forms of Global Business

In the past, companies have generally followed the *phase model of globalization.* That is, they have made the transition from a domestic company to a global one in the following sequence: ***3.1 exporter, 3.2 cooperative contracts, 3.3 strategic alliances, and 3.4 wholly owned affiliates.*** At each step, the company grows larger, uses the resulting resources to enter more global markets, depends less on home country sales, and becomes more committed to its global orientation. Some companies, however, do not follow the phase model of globalization.[26] Instead, they skip phases on their way to becoming more global and less domestic. Other companies don't follow the phase model at all. These are known as ***3.5 global new ventures.*** This section reviews these forms of global business.[27]

3.1 Exporting

When companies produce products in their home countries and sell them to customers in foreign countries, they are **exporting**. The city of Honghe, about 90 minutes from Shanghai, is one of China's largest sweater producers. Half of its 100,000 citizens work in more than 100 factories that produce about 200 million sweaters for export each year. The sweater export business generates $650 million per year in revenue.[28]

Exporting as a form of global business offers many advantages. It makes the company less dependent on sales in its home market and provides greater control over research, design, and production decisions. Although advantageous in a number of ways, exporting also has its disadvantages. The primary disadvantage is that many exported goods are subject to tariff and nontariff barriers that can substantially increase their final cost to consumers. A second disadvantage is that transportation costs can significantly increase the prices of exported products. Yet a third disadvantage: companies that export depend on foreign importers for product distribution. If, for example, the foreign importer makes a mistake on

Bubbly Imports

Although you can build a plant to manufacture cars, textiles, or toys virtually anywhere in the world, some products must be imported because they can only be produced in one place. Chardonnay grapes, commonly used to make sparkling wine, can be grown anywhere you can plant a vineyard, but champagne comes solely from one small region in France. Every wine has a unique characteristic called *terroir*, which comes from a combination of the grape variety and the soil and climate in which it is grown. The unique climate and chalky soil of the Champagne region makes champagne unique. It cannot be replicated anywhere else in the world. The name champagne, like burgundy, is legally protected in France, where it can be used only for wines from that region. Other sparkling wines from California, Spain (Cava), and the Italian Piedmont (Asti) each have their own unique *terroir*. Drink and enjoy, but don't call it champagne. Canada supports this approach to naming, mainly because it is hard to fight this logic, but also because Canada wants to claim the rights to Canadian maple syrup and rye whiskey (among others).

Sources: Zahn, L.A., (2102). "Australia Corked Its Champagne and So Should We: Enforcing Stricter Protections for Semi-Generic Wines in the United States," *Journal of Transnational Law & Contemporary Problems*, http://papers.ssrn.com/sol3/papers.cfm?abstract_id=2006612; Office of Champagne, USA, available online at http://www.champagne.us (accessed 6 August 2008).

Cooperative contract an agreement in which a foreign business owner pays a company a fee for the right to conduct that business in his or her country

Licensing an agreement in which a domestic company, the licensor, receives royalty payments for allowing another company, the licensee, to produce the licensor's product, sell its service, or use its brand name in a specified foreign market

Franchise a collection of networked firms in which the manufacturer or marketer of a product or service, the franchisor, licenses the entire business to another person or organization, the franchisee

the paperwork that accompanies a shipment of imported goods, those goods can be returned to the foreign manufacturer at the manufacturer's expense.

Canada used to be one of the most expensive places in the world to produce cars. But the fluctuating dollar and new contracts with workers are making production cheaper, prompting companies to rethink their strategies. Canadian automakers such as Chrysler are exporting Canadian-made cars to Europe, China, and Brazil. Chrysler is even moving some of its European production into Canada. Moreover, foreign companies like BMW AG are ramping up their foreign direct investment in Canada, manufacturing their cars here for export to Europe.[29]

3.2 Cooperative Contracts

When an organization wants to expand its business globally without making a large financial commitment to do so, it may sign a **cooperative contract** with a foreign business owner, who pays the company a fee for the right to conduct that business in his or her country. There are two kinds of cooperative contracts: licensing and franchising.

Under a **licensing** agreement, a domestic company, the *licensor*, receives royalty payments for allowing another company, the *licensee*, to produce its product, sell its service, or use its brand name in a particular foreign market. For example, brands like Coors Light, which consumers associate with an American company, are brewed in Canada by Molson under licence from the Coors Brewing Company in the United States. Licensing is favourable in this instance because of Canada's complex distribution system.

A key advantage of licensing is that it allows companies to earn additional profits without investing more money. As foreign sales increase, so do the royalties paid to the licensor by the foreign licensee. Moreover, it is the licensee, not the licensor, who invests in production equipment and facilities to produce the licensed product. Licensing also helps companies avoid tariff and nontariff barriers. Since the licensee manufactures the product within the foreign country, tariff and nontariff barriers don't apply.

The biggest disadvantage associated with licensing is that the licensor gives up control over the quality of the product or service sold by the foreign licensee. Unless the licensing agreement contains specific restrictions, the licensee controls the entire business from production to marketing to final sales. Many licensors include inspection clauses in their licence contracts, but closely monitoring product or service quality from thousands of miles away can be difficult. An additional disadvantage is that licensees can eventually become competitors, especially when a licensing agreement includes access to important technology or proprietary business knowledge.

A **franchise** is a collection of networked firms in which the manufacturer or marketer of a product or service, the *franchisor*, licenses the entire business to another person or organization, the *franchisee*. For the price of an initial franchise fee plus royalties, franchisors provide franchisees with training, assistance with marketing and advertising, and an exclusive right to conduct business in a particular location. More than 400 companies franchise their businesses to foreign franchise partners. Overall, franchising is a fast way to enter foreign markets. Over the past 20 years, franchisors have more than doubled their global franchises; there are now more

Double-Double in Afghanistan

When Canada was fighting in Afghanistan, Tim Hortons went forward with battlefield baristas. It hired civilians to provide support on the ground for our troops, in the heart of the conflict in Kandahar. Spokeswoman Birgitte Smiley said that staff were taught "customs of the country, as well as ... about Canadian Forces culture. As well, they go through drills in case of an emergency." The franchise was housed in a shipping container, with holes for windows and a coffee bar inside. "This is about serving you as you continue to do the outstanding job Canada asks of you," Major General Langton told his soldiers. The idea came about because the troops had passed on to the Canadian High Command that the one thing they would really like on the base would be a Tim Hortons. "We hope this little piece of home will make your lives in Afghanistan just a little bit easier," Langton told them.

Sources: "Tim Hortons brings a taste of home to troops in Kandahar," www.timhortons.com/ca/en/about/news_archive_2006h.html (accessed 17 June 2010); "Tim Hortons hiring for Afghanistan," www.canada.com/theprovince//news/story.html (accessed 17 June 2010).

The Canadian Press/Jake Wright

than 100,000 global franchise units. Remember that the KFC or McDonald's restaurant in Indonesia, or Vietnam, is owned by a local business person, much the same as it is here at home in Canada.

Franchising has many advantages. However, franchisors face a loss of control when they sell businesses to franchisees who are thousands of miles away. And while there are exceptions, franchising success may be somewhat culture-bound. In other words, because most global franchisors begin by franchising their businesses in similar countries or regions (Canada is by far the first choice for American companies taking their first step into global franchising), and because 65 percent of franchisors make absolutely no change in their business for overseas franchisees, that success may not generalize to cultures with different lifestyles, values, preferences, and technological infrastructures.

3.3 Strategic Alliances

Companies forming **strategic alliances** combine key resources, costs, risks, technology, and people. The most common strategic alliance is a **joint venture**, which occurs when two existing companies collaborate to form a third company. The two founding companies remain intact and unchanged except that together they now own the newly created joint venture. One of the oldest and most successful global joint ventures is Fuji-Xerox, a joint venture between Fuji Film of Japan and US-based Xerox Corporation, which makes copiers and automated office systems. More than 45 years after its creation, Fuji-Xerox employs over 42,000 people and has close to $9.1 billion in revenues.[30]

One advantage of global joint ventures is that, like licensing and franchising, they help companies avoid tariff and nontariff barriers to entry. Another advantage is that companies participating in a joint venture bear only part of the costs and risks of that business. Many companies find this attractive because it is expensive to enter foreign markets and develop new products. For example, Arrow Energy Ltd. is an oil and natural gas exploration and production company based in Calgary. It is partnering with Royal Dutch Shell PLC in a global joint venture that will mine natural gas from coal seams in Australia and export it for the global market. Global joint ventures can be especially advantageous to smaller local partners. They link up with larger, more experienced foreign firms that bring advanced management, resources, and business skills to the joint venture.[31]

Strategic alliance an agreement in which companies combine key resources, costs, risk, technology, and people

Joint venture a strategic alliance in which two existing companies collaborate to form a third, independent company

Global joint ventures are not without problems. Because companies share costs and risks with their joint venture partners, they must also share profits. Also, managing global joint ventures can be difficult because they represent a merging of four cultures: the country and organizational cultures of the first partner and the country and organizational cultures of the second partner. Often, to be fair to all involved, each partner in the global joint venture will have equal ownership and power. But this can result in power struggles and a lack of leadership. Because of these problems, companies forming global joint ventures should carefully develop detailed contracts that specify the obligations of each party. This care is important because the rate of failure for global joint ventures is as high as 70 percent.[32]

3.4 Wholly Owned Affiliates (Build or Buy)

Around one-third of multinational companies enter foreign markets through wholly-owned affiliates. Unlike licensing arrangements, franchises, or joint ventures,

Wholly owned affiliates foreign offices, facilities, and manufacturing plants that are 100 percent owned by the parent company

Global new ventures new companies that are founded with an active global strategy and have sales, employees, and financing in different countries

Purchasing power a comparison of the relative cost of a standard set of goods and services in different countries

wholly owned affiliates are 100 percent owned by the parent company. For example, Honda Motors of Canada in Cookstown, Ontario, is 100 percent owned by Honda Motors of Japan.

The primary advantage of wholly owned businesses is that the parent company receives all of the profits and has complete control over the foreign facilities. The biggest disadvantage is the expense of building new operations or buying existing businesses. The payoff can be enormous if a wholly-owned affiliate succeeds; but the losses can be immense if it fails because the parent company assumes all of the risk.

© Kazuhiro Nogi/AFP/Getty Images

3.5 Global New Ventures

Companies used to evolve slowly from small operations selling in their home markets to large businesses selling to foreign markets. Furthermore, as companies went global, they usually followed the phase model of globalization. Recently, however, three trends have combined to allow companies to skip the phase model when going global. First, quick and reliable air travel can transport people nearly anywhere in the world within a day. Second, low-cost communication technologies, such as international e-mail, teleconferencing, phone conferencing, and the Internet, are making it easier to communicate with global customers, suppliers, managers, and employees. Third, there is now a critical mass of businesspeople with extensive personal experience in all aspects of global business.[33] This combination of developments has made it possible to start companies that are global from inception. **Global new ventures** are companies that are founded with an active global strategy, with sales, employees, and financing in different countries.[34]

There are several different kinds of global new ventures; all of them, though, share two factors. First, the founders successfully develop and communicate their company's global vision from inception. Second, rather than going global one country at a time, new global ventures bring a product or service to market in several foreign markets at the same time. VistaPrint, a large printer in Canada, is actually headquartered in Lexington, Massachusetts. VistaPrint receives 15,000 orders a day from customers in 120 different countries, who design their business cards, brochures, and invitations online using 17 different VistaPrint websites, each representing a different language or location. Printing happens at two automated production facilities, one in the Netherlands and the other in Canada. Once printed, the products are cut and sized by robots and then packaged and delivered just three days after ordering. Regarding VistaPrint's commitment to worldwide customers, founder Robert Keane says: "It's often hard for startups to find their way out of their home nation. But you have to—it's not that type of world anymore."[35]

Where to Go Global?

Deciding *where* to go global is just as important as deciding *how* your company will go global. Other parts of this equation include *what* to go global with (your services and your goods) and *who* to go global with (in strategic alliances, mergers, or with licensing).

LO4 Finding the Best Business Climate

When deciding where to go global, companies look for countries or regions with a promising business climate, promising partners, and promising markets for their products and services.

An attractive global business ***climate 4.1 positions the company for easy access to growing markets, 4.2 is an effective but cost-efficient place to build an office or manufacturing facility,*** *and* ***4.3 minimizes the political risk to the company.***

4.1 Growing Markets

The most important factor in an attractive business climate is access to a growing market. Two factors help companies determine the growth potential of foreign markets: purchasing power and foreign competitors. **Purchasing power** is measured by comparing the relative cost of a standard set of goods and services in different countries. In Tokyo, a can of Coke costs the equivalent of CAD$1.27.[36] Because a can of Coke costs only about $1.00 in Canada, the average Canadian would have slightly more purchasing power than the average Japanese. Purchasing power is strong in countries like Mexico, India, and China, even though they have low average levels of income. This is because basic living expenses, such as

Exhibit 8.2 How Consumption of Coca-Cola Varies with Purchasing Power around the World

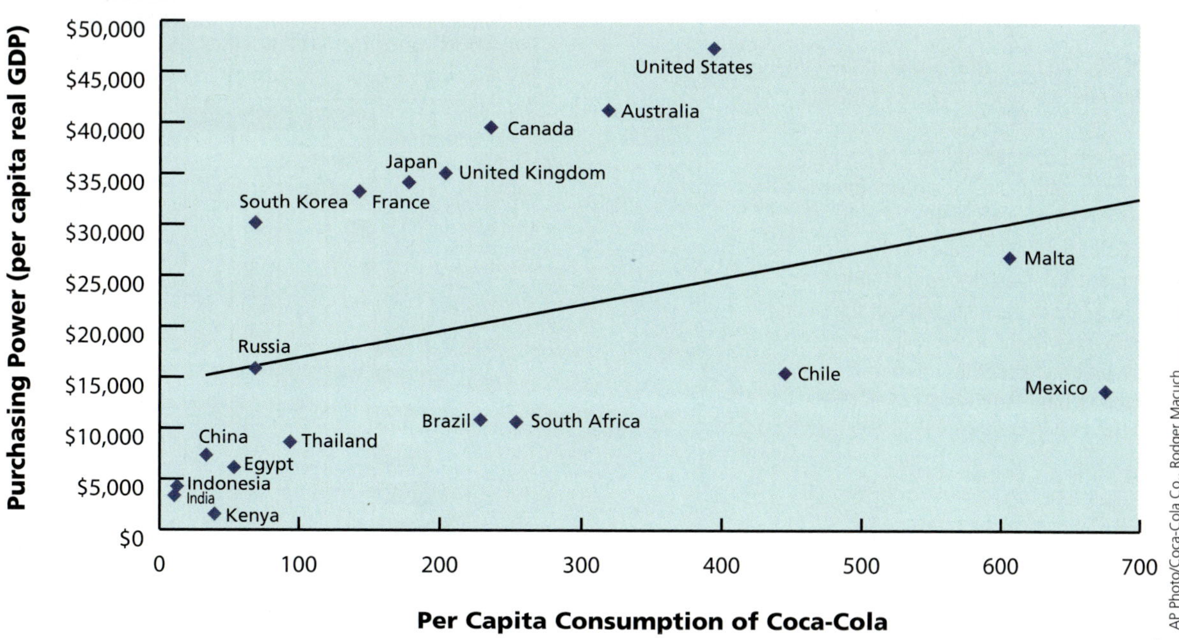

Sources: "Per Capita Consumption of Our Beverages," The Coca-Cola Company, accessed June 14, 2009, http://www.thecoca-colacompany.com/ourcompany/ar/percapitaconsumption.html; "Per Capita Consumption of Our Beverages, 1988, 1998, 2008," The Coca-Cola Company, accessed June 14, 2009, http://www.thecoca-colacompany.com/ourcompany/ar/pdf/perCapitaConsumption2008.pdf; "Rank Order—GDP—Per Capita (PPP)," *The World Factbook* (September 7, 2008), accessed June 14, 2009, http://www.cia.gov/cia/publications/factbook/rankorder/2004rank.

AP Photo/Coca-Cola Co., Rodger Macuch

Even Coca-Cola, which is available in over 200 countries, still has tremendous potential for further global growth. Currently, the Coca-Cola Company gets about 80 percent of its sales from its 16 largest markets.

food, shelter, and transportation, are very inexpensive in those countries, so consumers still have money to spend after paying for necessities. Because basic living expenses are so low in China, Mexico, and India, purchasing power is strong, and millions of Chinese, Mexican, and Indian consumers increasingly have extra money to spend on what they want in addition to what they need.[37]

Consequently, countries with high and growing levels of purchasing power are good choices for companies looking for attractive global markets. As Exhibit 8.2 shows, Coke has found that the per capita consumption of Coca-Cola, or the number of Cokes a person drinks per year, rises directly with purchasing power. The more purchasing power people have, the more likely they are to purchase soft drinks.

The second part of assessing the growth potential of global markets involves analyzing the degree of global competition, which is determined by the number and quality of companies that already compete in a foreign market. Intel has been in China for 20 years not only because of the size of the potential market but also because there was almost no competition. Now that China is the third-largest computer chip market in the world, Intel faces competition from AMD, Intel's primary competitor, which entered China four years ago, and Shanghai Semiconductor Manufacturing International, a five-year-old Chinese company that manufactures low-end chips.[38]

4.2 Choosing an Office/Manufacturing Location

Companies do not have to establish an office or manufacturing location in each country they enter. They can license, franchise, or export to foreign markets, or they can serve a larger region from one country. But there are many reasons why a company might choose to establish a location in a foreign country. Some foreign offices are established through global mergers and acquisitions; for example, IBM's ThinkPad brand was acquired by Beijing-based computer maker Lenovo. While Lenovo maintains offices in both places, top executives hold their monthly meetings at a different location each time—a strategy that Bill Amelio, CEO of Lenovo, calls "worldsourcing." Other companies are seeking a tax haven (although this is more difficult for Canadian companies due to legal concerns), or they want to reflect their customer base, or they are striving to create a global brand. Although a company must be legally incorporated in one place, some companies have anywhere from 9 to 23 global hubs and don't regard any one of them as more central than the others.[39]

Thus, the criteria for choosing an office/manufacturing location are different from the criteria for entering a foreign market. Instead of focusing on costs alone, companies should consider both qualitative and quantitative factors. Two key qualitative factors are workforce quality and company strategy. Workforce quality is important because it is often difficult to find workers with the specific skills, abilities, and experience that a company needs to run its business. Workforce quality is one reason why companies doing business in Europe often locate their customer call centres in the Netherlands. Workers in the Netherlands are the most linguistically gifted in Europe, with 73 percent speaking two languages, 44 percent speaking three, and 12 percent speaking more than three.[40]

The Big Mac Index

Every year since 1986, *The Economist* has published the Big Mac Index. The index compares the price for a Big Mac in dozens of countries around the world and uses its results to determine a country's purchasing power and value its exchange rate against the dollar (undervalued, overvalued, or right on the mark). Why the Big Mac? Well, like a Coke, the Big Mac is one of the few truly global consumer products. A McDonald's Big Mac costs an average of $3.82 in Canada, $4.16 in the United Kingdom, and $6.56 in Switzerland. Not all products are more expensive in other countries. In some, they are cheaper; for example, a Big Mac costs $2.45 in China and $2.70 in Mexico.

Source: "The Big Mac Index," *The Economist*, available online at http://www.economist.com/markets/indicators/displaystory.cfm?story_id=8649005.

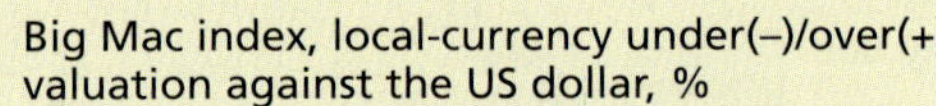

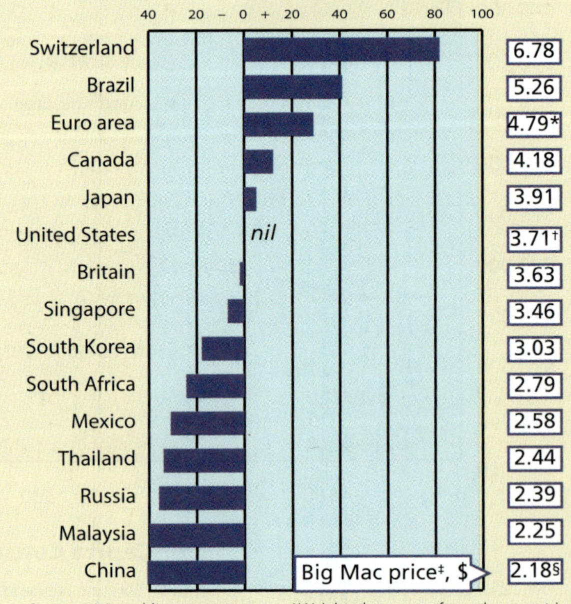

Source: McDonald's, *The Economist*

*Weighted average of member countries
†Average of four cities
‡At market exchange rate (October 13th)
§Average of two cities

A company's strategy is also important when it is choosing a location. For example, a company pursuing a low-cost strategy may need plentiful raw materials, low-cost transportation, and low-cost labour. A company pursuing a differentiation strategy (typically a higher priced, better product or service) may need access to high-quality materials and a highly skilled and educated workforce.

Quantitative factors such as the kind of facility being built, tariff and nontariff barriers, exchange rates, and transportation and labour costs should also be considered when choosing an office/manufacturing location. Each year, Cushman & Wakefield publishes its "European Cities Monitor" to help companies compare the pluses and minuses of the business climate in various cities. Similar information is available for other parts of the world. Exhibit 8.3 offers a quick overview of the best cities for business based on a variety of criteria. This information is a good starting point if your company is trying to decide where to put an international office or manufacturing plant.

4.3 Minimizing Political Risk

When managers think about political risk in global business, they envision burning factories and riots in the streets. Although political events such as these receive dramatic and extended coverage from the media, the political risks that most companies face usually are not covered as breaking stories on CTV and CBC. The negative consequences of *ordinary* political risk can be just as devastating to companies that fail to identify and minimize it.[41]

The political risks that most companies face usually are not covered as breaking stories on CTV and CBC.

When conducting global business, companies should attempt to identify two types of political risk: political uncertainty and policy uncertainty.[42] **Political uncertainty** is associated with the risk of sweeping regime change that can result from war, revolution, the death of a political leader, social unrest, or other influential events. **Policy uncertainty** refers to the risk associated with changes in laws and government policies that directly affect how foreign companies conduct business.

Political uncertainty the risk of major changes in political regimes that can result from war, revolution, death of political leaders, social unrest, or other influential events

Policy uncertainty the risk associated with changes in laws and government policies that directly affect the way foreign companies conduct business

Exhibit 8.3 World's Best Cities for Business

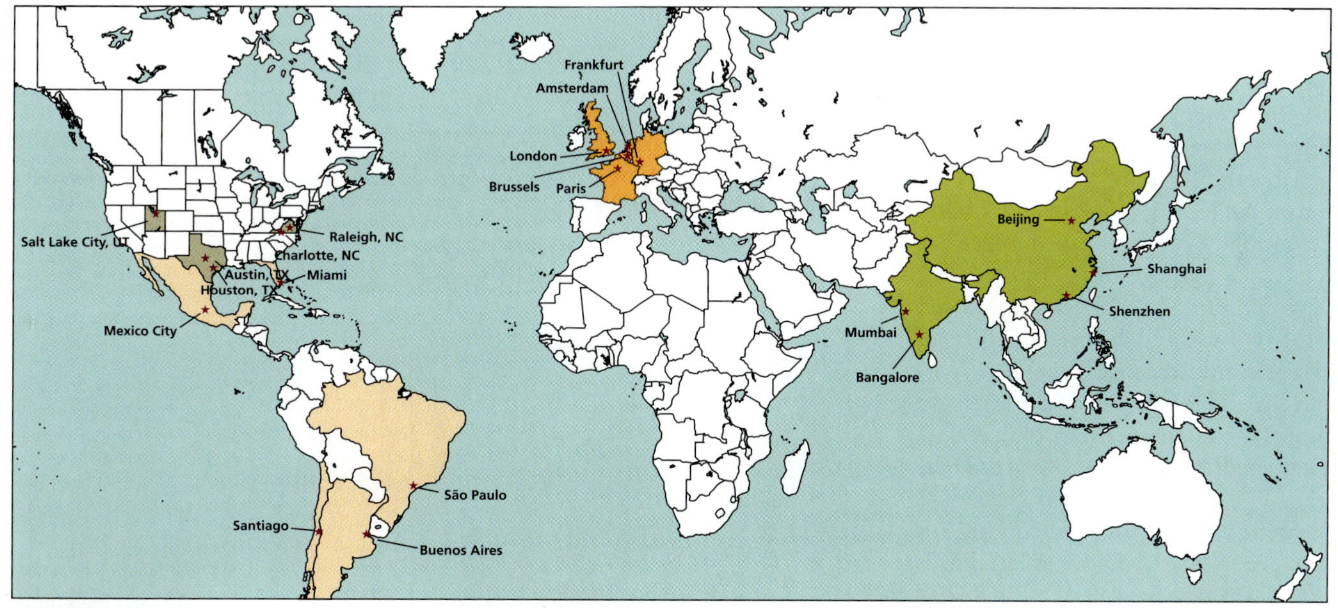

North America

1. Raleigh, NC
2. Austin, TX
3. Salt Lake City, UT
4. Houston, TX
5. Charlotte, NC

Latin America

1. São Paulo
2. Santiago
3. Miami
4. Mexico City
5. Buenos Aires

Europe

1. London
2. Paris
3. Frankfurt
4. Amsterdam
5. Brussels

Asia Pacific

1. Shanghai
2. Beijing
3. Shenzhen
4. Bangalore
5. Mumbai

Sources: European Cities Monitor 2007. Cushman & Wakefield [online] http://www.berlin-partner.de/fileadmin/chefredaktion/documents/pdf_Presse/European_Investment_Monitor_2007.pdf, accessed 18 September 2008; K. Badenhausen, Forbes.com, "Best Places for Business and Careers," http://www.forbes.com/lists/2005/05/05bestplaces.html, 17 February 2007; "Shanghai, Beijing, Shenzhen Top 3 in Best City Survey," *Fortune China*, http://www.fortunechina.com/pdf/Best%20Cities%Press%20Release%20(English)%202004.12.01.pdf, 13 February 2007; R. Sridharan, "BestCities, Really?" *Business Today*, 13 August 2006, 62; "Miami Is the Best City for Doing Business in Latin America, According to *AmericaEconomia* Magazine," *PR Newswire*, 24, April 2003.

Emerging Markets: India

In many ways, India appears to be a global business nightmare. People speak dozens of different languages throughout the country. Getting around is a challenge due to a terrible infrastructure. Foreign companies must deal with tight regulations on foreign investment, slow bureaucratic culture, and the politics of family-owned big business. UPS delivery people, for example, must often ask for directions because there are no street numbers. Day-to-day traffic is worse than on the busiest Canadian freeway: it can be hard to tell a parked car from a moving one. To top it all off, packages must be shrink-wrapped during monsoon season. That said, India—with 1.1 billion people, 9 percent annual economic growth, a growing middle class demanding imported goods, and cities full of entrepreneurs on the cutting edge of global business—is one of the hottest markets in the world. For example, India has 8 million new cell phone subscribers per month. Like many of his fellow Indian expats, Arun Sarin, CEO of Vodafone Group PLC, left India in the 1970s because of limited business opportunities, but is now going home. India is a place companies cannot afford to ignore.

Sources: B. Stanley, "UPS Battles Traffic Jams to Gain Ground in India," *The Wall Street Journal*, 25 January 2008, A1; C. Bryan-Low, "To Revive Vodafone, CEO Bets on India," *The Wall Street Journal*, 22 February 2008, A1.

Policy uncertainty is the most common—and perhaps most frustrating—form of political risk in global business. For example, the Kremlin has cleaned up Russia's once-inefficient auto industry, making it attractive to Western investors. Growth-starved auto companies like Renault have taken the bait. In fact, $80 million of private capital entered Russia in 2007. But such investment is a risk because 40 percent of the industry is owned by the Kremlin, making foreign investors subject to government policy. An example of what can happen as policy winds change: in February 2007, the Kremlin raided BP PLC and TNK-BP, its joint venture, and accused the foreign investor of industrial espionage.[43]

Several strategies can be used to minimize or adapt to the political risk inherent in global business. An *avoidance strategy* is used when the political risks associated with a foreign country or region are viewed as too great. Firms that are already invested in high-risk areas may divest or sell their businesses. If they have not yet invested, they will likely postpone their investment until the risk shrinks. Exhibit 8.4 shows the long-term political risk for various countries in the Middle East (higher scores indicate less political risk). The following factors, which were used to compile these ratings, indicate greater political risk: government instability, poor socioeconomic conditions, internal or external conflict, military involvement in politics, religious and ethnic tensions, high foreign debt as a percentage of GDP, exchange rate instability, and high inflation.[44] An avoidance strategy would likely be

Exhibit 8.4 Overview of Political Risk in the Middle East

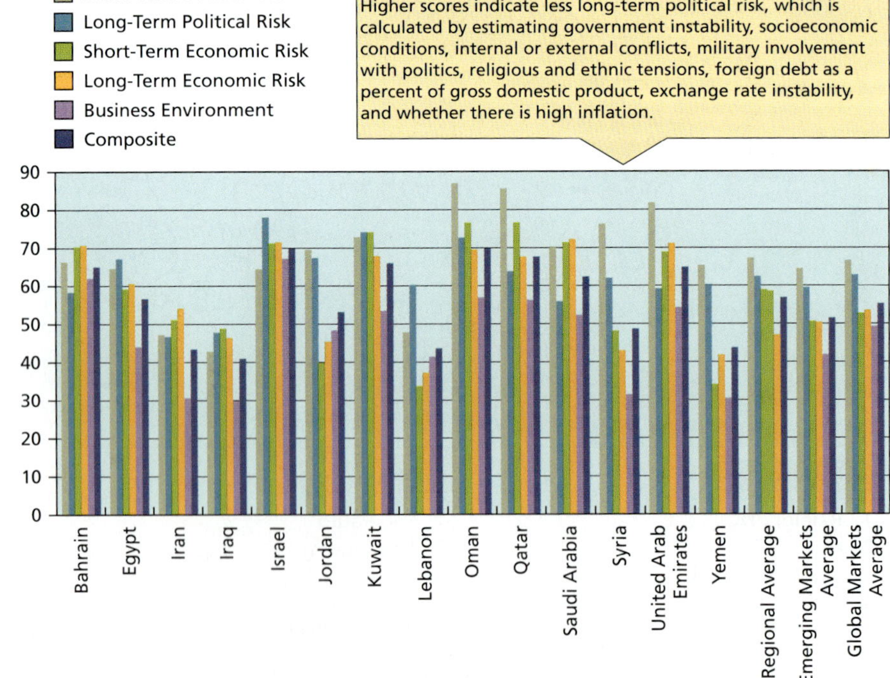

Source: Middle East Overview Chart, Business Monitor International Country Risk Ratings, *Business Monitor Online*. © 2010 Business Monitor International.

used for the riskiest countries shown in Exhibit 8.4, such as Iran and Lebanon, but would probably not be needed for the least risky countries, such as Israel, Jordan, and Oman. Risk conditions and factors change, so be sure to make risk decisions with the latest available information from resources such as the PRS Group (www.prsgroup.com), which supplies information about political risk to 80 percent of the *Fortune* 500 companies.

Control is an active strategy to prevent or reduce political risks. Firms using a control strategy lobby foreign governments or international trade agencies to change laws, regulations, or trade barriers that hurt their business in that country. Emerson Electric Co. had virtually no business for its InSinkErator garbage disposals in Europe during the 1990s. The company lobbied European governments to convince them of the environmentally friendly impact of a waste disposer over other methods of getting rid of food waste. Composting involves a lot of garbage trucks, and landfills emit poisonous methane. Garbage disposals are the cheapest method for disposing of food waste; they also enable water treatment plants to turn methane that comes through the sewer system into power, and they reduce the carbon footprint by reducing the amount of waste transported by trucks. Now Emerson sells more than 100,000 disposals each year in Europe.[45]

Another method for dealing with political risk is *cooperation,* which involves using joint ventures and collaborative contracts such as franchising and licensing. Although cooperation does not eliminate the political risk of doing business in a country, it can limit the risk associated with foreign ownership of a business. For example, a German company forming a joint venture with a Chinese company to do business in China may structure the joint venture contract so that the Chinese company owns 51 percent or more of the joint venture. Doing so qualifies the joint venture as a Chinese company and exempts it from Chinese laws that apply to foreign-owned businesses. However, as we saw with the BP-TNK joint venture in Russia, cooperation cannot always protect against *policy risk* if a foreign government changes its laws and policies to directly affect how foreign companies conduct business.

National culture the set of shared values and beliefs that affects the perceptions, decisions, and behaviour of the people from a particular country

Ethnocentrism generally judging and interpreting people and mannerisms of another culture solely by the values and standards of our own culture

Much has been made of most favoured nation (MFN) status as it is applied by Canada, the United States, and other countries. This designation is used to reduce tariffs, extend cooperative trading agreements, and prevent discriminatory treatment. Most WTO member countries grant MFN trading designations to one another, and this does increase trade.[46]

LO5 Becoming Aware of Cultural Differences

National culture refers to the shared values and beliefs that affect the perceptions, decisions, and behaviour of the people of a particular country. The first step in dealing with culture is to recognize that there are meaningful differences. Professor Geert Hofstede spent 20 years studying cultural differences in 53 countries. His research found that there are five consistent cultural dimensions across countries: power distance, individualism, masculinity, uncertainty avoidance, and short-term versus long-term orientation.[47] Hofstede's work is especially useful if we want to avoid charges of **ethnocentricity**, where everything is seen from the perception of an individual's home country. The most famous example, of course, is when the loud, rather large

Where in the World ...?

MoneySense, a Canadian financial website, publishes an interactive map with information on doing business around the world. The top 18 countries are rated for value and momentum. Slower growth countries usually have modest investment levels or requirements, which can make for terrific value. In May 2010, Apple passed Microsoft, Google, and all other companies in terms of market capitalization, and then doubled again in value to more than $600 billion. The volatility continues: Apple lost more than $35 billion in one day and fell below $500 billion in early 2013. That kind of money can buy a lot of businesses in many of the 18 countries listed on the interactive map. Additionally, the "momentum" of the various countries is a measure of how fast they are growing. Certainly, India and China are growing faster than many other countries, but as indicated during the economic and worldwide banking crisis of 2009, and then the continuing slowdown through 2013, some of these countries can have their momentum severely dented.

Sources: Rothery, N., Dec 2009. "Where in the World to Invest," http://www.moneysense.ca/2009/12/18/where-in-the-world-should-you-invest-2/ (accessed 16 June 2010); Guglielmo, C. & Bass, D., 2010. "Apple Overtakes MicroSoft," http//:www.businessweek.com/news/2010-05-26/apple-overtakes-microsoft-in-market-capitalization-update3-.html (accessed 16 June 2010).

kostasgr/Shutterstock.com

Culture shock the disorientation we might feel when experiencing an unfamiliar way of life due to a business trip to a new country, or to a move between social environments, if we get posted on an international assignment to a new, unfamiliar country

man dressed in an Hawaiian shirt yells out for more coffee and wonders why no one speaks English in central Paris. The other thing that Hofstede's work can help us deal with is **culture shock**—that is, with why some cultures feel it is rude to eat using your left hand, or why pointing your feet in someone's direction is considered deeply insulting. None of us want to get caught out and made to feel that we are insensitive. While Hofstede's work, like that of GLOBE (see later), might seem as if it "stereotypes" various countries or cultures, it is not meant to do so. It is meant to help us explore the cultural differences between North American companies and their suppliers and customers around the globe.

Power distance is the extent to which people in a country tolerate unequal distribution of power in society and organizations. In countries where power distance is weak, such as Denmark and Sweden, employees don't like their organization or their boss to have power over them or tell them what to do. They want to have a say in decisions that affect them. As Exhibit 8.5 shows, Russia and China, with scores of 95 and 80, respectively, are much stronger in power distance than Germany (35), the Netherlands (38), Canada (39), and the United States (40). Canada's power distance is relatively low, at 39, compared to the world average of 55. This may indicate a feeling of greater equality between societal levels, which include government, work organizations, and families. This orientation may reinforce cooperative interaction across power levels and may create a more stable cultural environment. The tensions between Quebec and other Canadian provinces should be noted. Quebeckers tend to be more private and reserved.

Individualism is the degree to which societies believe that individuals should be self-sufficient. In individualistic societies, employees put loyalty to themselves first and loyalty to their company and work group second. In Exhibit 8.5, the Netherlands (80), Canada (80), France (71), and Germany (67) are the strongest in individualism, while Indonesia (14), West Africa (20), and China (20) are the weakest. Most Canadians have "individualism" as their highest ranking dimension (80). It is probably not much of a surprise that the United States scores 91 on individualism, even higher than Canada (and higher than almost every other country in the world). Success tends to be measured by personal achievement; this is indicative of a society with a more individualistic attitude in which people have looser bonds with others. People are viewed as more self-reliant and as focusing on themselves and their close family members. Canadians may be self-confident and open to discussions on general topics, but they place their personal privacy off limits to all but the closest of friends.

Quantity/quality of life captures the difference between highly assertive and highly nurturing cultures. *Quantity*-of-life cultures emphasize assertiveness, competition, material success, and achievement, whereas *quality*-of-life cultures emphasize the importance of relationships, modesty, caring for the weak, and, generally, the quality of a person's life. In Exhibit 8.5, Japan (95), Germany (66), and Canada (49) have high quantity-of-life orientations (the United States beats Canada here too, with a score of 62), while the Netherlands (14) has the most quality-of-life orientation.

Exhibit 8.5 Hofstede's Five Cultural Dimensions

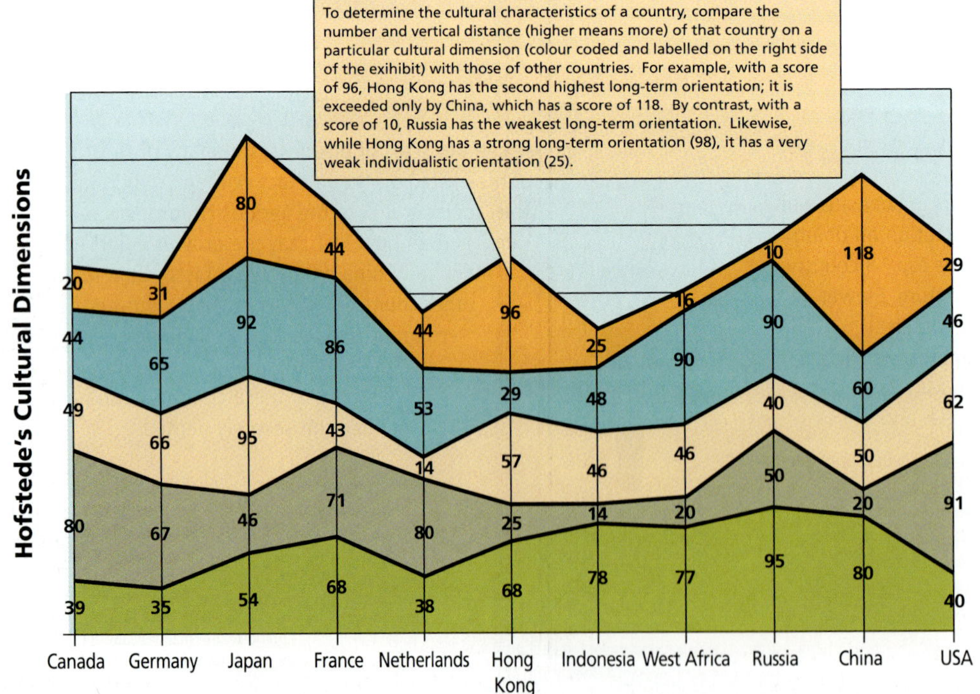

Source: G. H. Hofstede, "Cultural Contraints in Management Theories," *Academy of Management Executive* 7, no. 1 (1993): 81–94.

Uncertainty avoidance refers to the degree to which people in a country are uncomfortable with unstructured, ambiguous, unpredictable situations. In countries with strong uncertainty avoidance, such as Greece and Portugal, people tend to be aggressive and emotional and to seek security rather than uncertainty. In Exhibit 8.5, Japan (92), France (86), West Africa (90), and Russia (90) are strongest in uncertainty avoidance, while Hong Kong (29) is the weakest.

Short-term/long-term orientation addresses whether cultures are oriented to the present and seek immediate gratification or to the future and defer gratification. Not surprisingly, countries with short-term orientations are consumer driven, whereas countries with long-term orientations are savings driven. In Exhibit 8.5, China (118) and Hong Kong (96) have very strong long-term orientations, while Russia (10), West Africa (16), Indonesia (25), Canada (23), the USA (29), and Germany (31) have very strong short-term orientations. Canadians' lowest ranking dimension—"long-term orientation," at 23—compares to an average of 45 among the 23 countries surveyed. This low ranking may be indicative of Canadians' belief in meeting their obligations and tends to reflect an appreciation for cultural traditions, which may explain our acceptance of multiculturalism. To generate a graphical comparison of two different countries' cultures, go to **geert-hofstede.com/countries.html**. Select a "home culture." Then select a "host culture." A graph comparing the countries on each of Hofstede's five cultural differences will be generated automatically.

Interested students can further explore these issues in the GLOBE research program, which has expanded the Hofstede model of five dimensions of national cultures to 18. A reanalysis in 2013 based on GLOBE's 2004 summary produced five meta-factors. One, roughly corresponding to power distance, was significantly correlated with GNP per capita.[48]

Cultural differences affect perceptions, understanding, and behaviour. Recognizing cultural differences is vital to succeeding in global business. Nevertheless, as Hofstede has pointed out, descriptions of cultural differences are based on averages—the *average* level of uncertainty avoidance in Portugal, the *average* level of power distance in Argentina, and so forth. Accordingly, says Hofstede, "if you are going to spend time with a Japanese colleague, you shouldn't assume that overall cultural statements about Japanese society automatically apply to this person."[49] Similarly, cultural beliefs may differ significantly from one part of a country to another.[50]

After becoming aware of cultural differences, the second step is deciding how to adapt your company to those differences. Unfortunately, studies investigating the effects of cultural differences on management practice point more to difficulties than to easy solutions. One problem is that different cultures will probably perceive management policies and practices differently. For example, blue-collar workers in France and Argentina, all of whom performed the same factory jobs for the same multinational company, perceived its company-wide safety policy differently.[51] French workers perceived that safety wasn't very important to the company, but Argentine workers thought it was. The fact that something as simple as a safety policy can be perceived differently across cultures shows just how difficult it can be to standardize management practices across different countries and cultures.

Expatriate someone who lives and works outside his or her native country

LO6 Preparing for an International Assignment

An **expatriate** is someone who lives and works outside his or her native country. When expatriates fail in overseas assignments, primarily it is because they find it difficult to adjust to linguistic, cultural, and social differences. The United States is the biggest destination for Canadians, with upwards of 1.5 million expatriates living there. The United Kingdom is the next largest destination, with almost 750,000 expats, followed by China, with 250,000. Some research has found that large numbers of expatriates return home before they have completed their overseas assignments.[52] Of those who do complete them, about one-third are judged by

MGMT TREND

Wanted: International Experience

Working as an expat has always had an appeal to those who love experiencing other cultures. And expats have helped companies find a place in markets all over the world. Research has found, however, that overseas experience also makes for better managers. A research study at Northwestern's Kellogg School of Management found that 60 percent of students who lived abroad were able to solve a creative thinking problem, compared to just 42 percent of students who did not live abroad. In another study, conducted at the Sorbonne in Paris, researchers showed students three words and were asked to come up with another word that linked all of them. Those who studied abroad were able to give more correct answers than those who did not. So what's a great way to develop great managers? Send them overseas![53] Check out the information at the Canadian Bureau for International Education for additional information (www.cbie-bcei.ca).[54]

Source: William W. Maddux, Adam D. Galinsky, Carmit T. Tadmor, "Be a Better Manager: Live Abroad," *Harvard Business Review*, September 9, 2010, accessed November 20, 1010, http://hbr.org/2010/09/be-a-better-manager-live-abroad/ar/1.

their companies to have been no better than marginally effective.[55] As a student you might want to take advantage of opportunities to study abroad.[56]

Since the average cost of sending an employee on a three-year international assignment is $1 million, failure in those assignments can be extraordinarily expensive.[57] *The chances for a successful international assignment can be increased through* ***6.1 language and cross-cultural training*** *and* ***6.2 consideration of spouse, family, and dual-career issues.***

6.1 Language and Cross-Cultural Training

Pre-departure language and cross-cultural training can reduce the uncertainty that expatriates feel, the misunderstandings that arise between expatriates and natives, and the inappropriate ways that expatriates unknowingly behave when they travel to a foreign country. Indeed, simple things like using a phone, locating a public toilet, asking for directions, finding out how much things cost, exchanging greetings, or understanding what people want can become tremendously complex when expatriates don't know a foreign language or a country's customs and cultures.

Expatriates who receive pre-departure language and cross-cultural training make faster adjustments to foreign cultures and perform better on their international assignments.[58] Unfortunately, only one-third of the managers who go on international assignments are offered any kind of pre-departure training, and only half of those actually participate in the training![59] This is somewhat surprising given the failure rates for expatriates and the high cost of those failures. Furthermore, with the exception of some language courses, pre-departure training is not particularly expensive or difficult to provide. Three methods can be used to prepare workers for international assignments: documentary training, cultural simulations, and field experiences.

Documentary training focuses on identifying specific critical differences between cultures. For example, when 60 workers at Axcelis Technologies were preparing to do business in India, they learned that while North Americans make eye contact and shake hands firmly when greeting others, Indians, as a sign of respect, do just the opposite, avoiding eye contact and shaking hands limply.[60]

After learning specific critical differences through documentary training, trainees can then participate in *cultural simulations,* in which they practise adapting to cultural differences. After the workers at Axcelis Technologies learned about key differences between their culture and India, they practised adapting to those differences by role playing. Some Axcelis workers would take the roles of Indian workers, while other Axcelis workers would play themselves and try to behave in a way consistent with Indian culture. As they role played, Indian music played loudly in the background, and they were coached on what to do or not do. Axcelis human resources director Randy Longo says, "at first, I was skeptical and wondered what I'd get out of the class. But it was enlightening for me."

MGMT FACT

Bilingualism—A Growing Trend

There are over 5 million people in Canada who speak more than one language. At least 35 percent of Canadians speak more than one language. Moreover, fewer than 2 percent of Canadians cannot speak at least one of the two official languages. Around 5.8 million people in Canada are able to speak both official languages. Bilingual, in Canada, generally refers to being able to speak both French and English; only 17.5 percent of Canadians, by this definition, are bilingual. More than half of Vancouverites and Torontonians were born outside Canada. This has led to a greater use of English as a second language, and also to a great deal of linguistic and cultural diversity. In Europe even more value is placed on the ability to speak multiple languages; more Europeans are multilingual, speaking three or more languages, than are bilingual. Being able to communicate in multiple languages is an important asset in any business and can help give a company the edge it needs to succeed in a competitive market. Statistics Canada, focusing on about 200 languages that make up the linguistic portrait of Canada, indicates that most of those people (almost 6 million) speak English plus an immigrant language such as Punjabi or Mandarin. About 80 per cent of immigrant-language speakers lived in Toronto, Montreal, Vancouver, Calgary, Edmonton, and Ottawa-Gatineau.

Sources: City of Toronto, "Facts," http://www.toronto.ca/toronto_facts/diversity.htm; D. Todd, "Vancouver Teens Most Inter-Racial: Poll," *Vancouver Sun*, August 14, 2009.

Finally, *field simulation* training places trainees in an ethnic neighbourhood for three to four hours to talk to residents about cultural differences. For example, an electronics manufacturer prepared workers for assignments in South Korea by having trainees explore a nearby South Korean neighbourhood and talk to shopkeepers and people on the street about South Korean politics, family orientation, and day-to-day living practices.

FER737NG/Shutterstock

6.2 Spouse, Family, and Dual-Career Issues

Not all international assignments are difficult for expatriates and their families. That said, the evidence clearly shows that how well an expatriate's spouse and family adjust to the foreign culture is the most important factor in determining the success or failure of an international assignment.[61] Barry Kozloff of Selection Research International says that "the cost of sending a family on a foreign assignment is around $1 million and their failure to adjust is an enormous loss."[62] Unfortunately, despite its importance, there has been little systematic research on what does and does not help expatriates' families adapt. A number of companies, however, have found that adaptability screening and intercultural training for families can lead to more successful overseas adjustment.

Only one-third of the managers who go on international assignments are offered any kind of Pre-Departure training.

Adaptability screening is used to assess how well managers and their families are likely to adjust to foreign cultures. Prudential Relocation Management's international division has developed an "Overseas Assignment Inventory" to help the Canadian International Development Agency select people who will adapt well by assessing the open-mindedness of a spouse and family, respect for others' beliefs, sense of humour, and marital communication.[63]

Only 40 percent of expatriates' families receive language and cross-cultural training, yet such training is just as important for the families of expatriates as for the expatriates themselves.[64] In fact, it may be more important because, unlike expatriates, whose professional jobs often shield them from the full force of a country's culture, spouses and children are fully immersed in foreign neighbourhoods and schools. Households must be run, shopping must be done, and bills must be paid. Unfortunately, expatriate spouse Laurel Larsen, despite two hours of Chinese lessons a week, hasn't learned enough of the language to communicate with the family's baby sitter. She has to phone her husband, who became fluent in Chinese in his teens, to translate. Similarly, expatriates' children must deal with different cultural beliefs and practices. While the Larsens' three daughters love the private international school they attend, they still have had difficulty adapting to the incredible differences they perceive in inner China.[65]

Go online at
www.nelson.com/4ltrpress/icanmgmt2
And access the essential Study Tools online for this chapter:

- **Flashcards**, to help you study
- **Interactive Quizzes**, to test your knowledge
- **Audio Chapter Summaries**, for chapter review
- **Crossword Puzzles and Beat the Clock**, to review key terms
- **What Would You Do? Cases**, for applying your knowledge to real-life situations
- **Self Assessments**, to learn about what kind of manager you are
- **Videos and Media Quizzing for Part 2**
  - Chapter 5: Plant Fantasies: Managerial Decision Making
  - Chapter 6: Theo Chocolate: Strategy Formulation and Execution
  - Chapter 7: Holden Outerwear: Managing Change and Innovation
  - Chapter 8: Holden Outerwear: Managing in a Global Environment

Be sure to consult the Chapter Review Card at the back of the textbook.

9 Designing Adaptive Organizations

LEARNING OUTCOMES

LO1 Describe the departmentalization approach to organizational structure.

LO2 Explain organizational authority.

LO3 Discuss the different methods for job design.

LO4 Explain the methods that companies are using to redesign internal organizational processes (i.e., intra-organizational processes).

LO5 Describe the methods that companies are using to redesign external organizational processes (i.e., inter-organizational processes).

Structure and Process

Organizational structure is the vertical and horizontal configuration of departments, authority, and jobs within a company. Organizational structure is concerned with vertical questions such as "Who reports to whom?" as well as horizontal questions such as "Who does what?" and "Where is the work done?" For example, Sony Corporation is a global company with operations all over the world as well as a number of divisions to handle different sectors of the company's business, each headed by its own president or CEO. Sony's North American headquarters is in New York City, but its many affiliated companies and operations span the continent. PlayStation products are developed and managed in Foster City, California, by Sony Computer Entertainment. Sony cameras and camcorders, TV and home theatre equipment, computers, MP3 players, headphones, and mobile phones are handled in San Diego by Sony Electronics. The Spider-Man films and the long-running *Jeopardy*! game show are brought to you by Sony Pictures Entertainment, headquartered in Culver City, California; while the music of Beyoncé, Justin Timberlake, Pink, Shakira, and Carrie Underwood comes courtesy of Sony Music Entertainment in New York City.[1] Companies like Sony use organizational structure to set up departments and relationships among employees in order to make business happen. You can see Sony's organizational structure in Exhibit 9.1.

An **organizational process** is the collection of activities that transform inputs into outputs that customers value.[2] Organizational process asks: How do things get done? For example, Ubisoft, one of the world's largest independent developers of interactive entertainment products, uses basic internal and external processes to develop video games (see Exhibit 9.2 on page 142). The process starts when Ubisoft gets external feedback from customers through their own website, e-mail, social media sites, and retailers. This information helps Ubisoft understand customers' needs and problems and identify important gaming issues and needed changes and functions, as well as market trends in terms of content and format. Ubisoft then updates existing games, besides working on new games, testing these internally within the company and then externally through its beta-testing process. During this latter process, customers who volunteer or are selected by Ubisoft give the company extensive feedback, which is then used to make improvements. After final corrections are made to a game, the company distributes and sells it to customers. Those customers then start the process again by giving Ubisoft more feedback.

Organizational structure the vertical and horizontal configuration of departments, authority, and jobs within a company

Organizational process the collection of activities that transform inputs into outputs that customers value

Organizational process is just as important as organizational structure. You'll learn about both in this chapter.

Designing Organizational Structures

Procter & Gamble (P&G), the largest consumer packaged goods company in the world, owns some of the world's best-known brands, including Tide, Crest, Charmin, Pringles, and Pampers. P&G's product lines include 25 billion-dollar brands (i.e., brands that generate more than $1 billion in annual sales), 20 half-billion-dollar brands, and, just recently, the company's first 10-billion-dollar brand, Pampers diapers. Over the past decade, P&G has restructured its operations several times, most recently by grouping its Global Business Units into four industry-based sectors: Baby, Feminine, and Family Care; Beauty; Health and Grooming; and Fabric and Home Care. Each sector is comprised of businesses that focus on common consumer benefits, that share technologies, and that face common competitors. Under the leadership of a group president, each sector is responsible for all innovation, profitability, and shareholder returns for its own businesses,

Exhibit 9.1 Sony Corporation's Organizational Chart

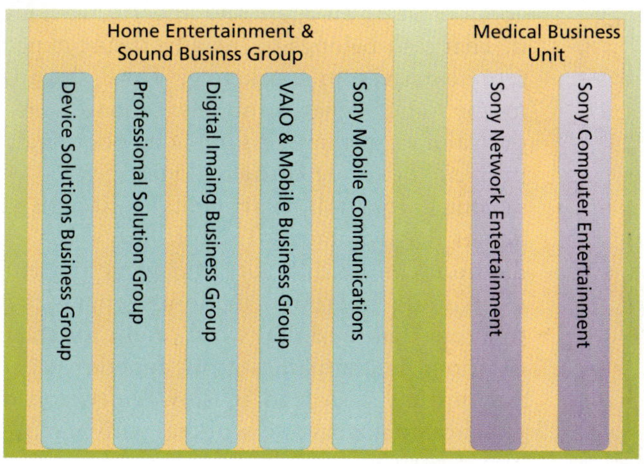

Source: "Sony Corp. Info: Organizational Data," 1 August 2012, accessed 29 May 2013, available at: http://www.sony.net/SonyInfo/CorporateInfo/Data/organization.html

Adriano Castelli/Shutterstock.com

Exhibit 9.2 Process View of Ubisoft's Organization

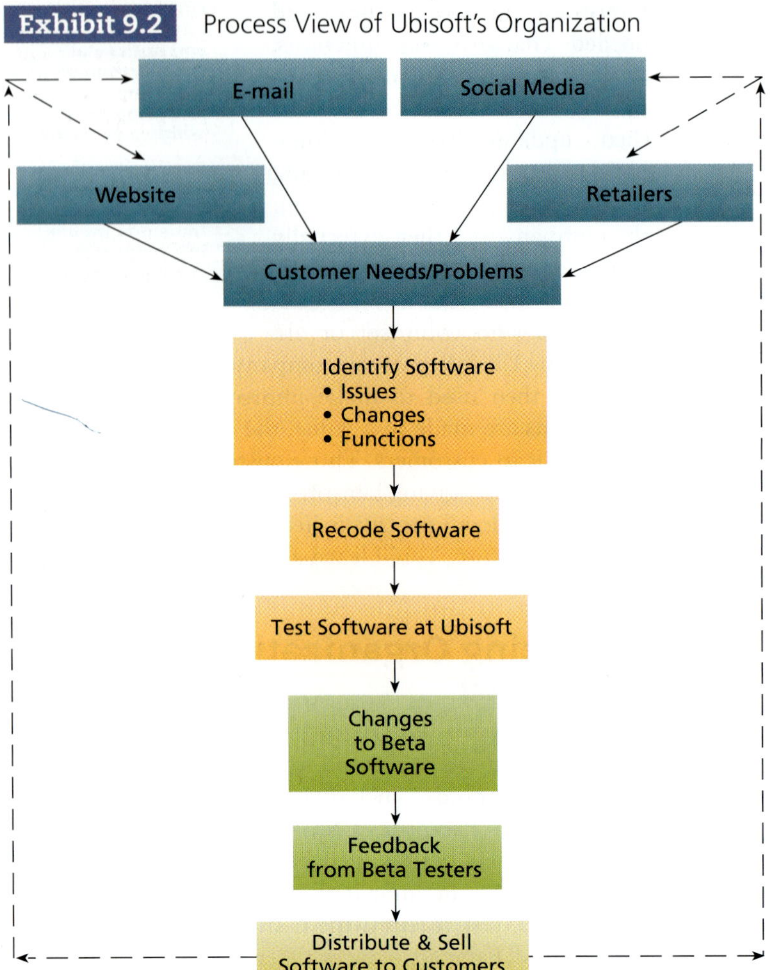

and focuses solely on the brands and consumers in its own category as well as on competitors around the world. P&G's organizational structure also includes market development and global business services to support each sector and assist with developing market plans at the local level. According to P&G, the organizational structure plays an integral role in the company's ability to grow and to reap the benefits of its global scale as well as maintain a local focus with consumers and retail customers around the globe.[3]

Departmentalization subdividing work and workers into separate organizational units responsible for completing particular tasks

Functional departmentalization organizing work and workers into separate units responsible for particular business functions or areas of expertise

LO1 Departmentalization

Traditionally, organizational structures have been based on some form of departmentalization. **Departmentalization** is a method of subdividing work and workers into separate units that take responsibility for completing particular tasks.[4]

studiomode/GetStock.com

*Traditionally, organizational structures have been created by departmentalizing work according to five methods: **1.1 functional, 1.2 product, 1.3 customer, 1.4 geographic,** and **1.5 matrix.***

1.1 Functional Departmentalization

The most common organizational structure is functional departmentalization. Companies tend to use this structure when they are small or just starting out. **Functional departmentalization** organizes work and workers into separate units responsible for particular business functions or areas of expertise. A common functional structure might have individuals organized into accounting, sales, marketing, production, and human resources departments.

Not all functionally departmentalized companies have the same functions. The insurance company and the advertising agency shown in Exhibit 9.3 both have sales, accounting, human resources, and information systems departments, as indicated by the orange boxes. The purple and green boxes indicate the functions that are different. As would be expected, the insurance company has separate departments for life, auto, home, and health insurance. The advertising agency has departments for artwork, creative work, print advertising, and radio advertising. So the functional departments in a company that uses functional structure depend in part on the business or industry the company is in.

Functional departmentalization has some advantages. First, it allows work to be done by highly qualified specialists. While the accountants in the accounting department take responsibility for producing accurate revenue and expense figures, the engineers in research and development can focus their efforts on designing a product that is reliable and simple to manufacture. Second, it lowers costs by reducing duplication. When the engineers in research and development come up with that fantastic new product, they don't have to worry about creating an aggressive advertising campaign to sell it. That task belongs to the advertising experts and sales representatives in marketing. Third, because everyone in the same department has similar work experience or training, communication and coordination are less problematic for departmental managers.

But functional departmentalization also has a number of disadvantages. To start, cross-department coordination can be difficult. Managers and employees are often more interested in doing what's right for their function than in doing what's right for the entire organization. As companies grow, functional departmentalization may also lead to slower decision making and produce managers and workers with narrow experience and expertise.

Exhibit 9.3 Functional Departmentalization

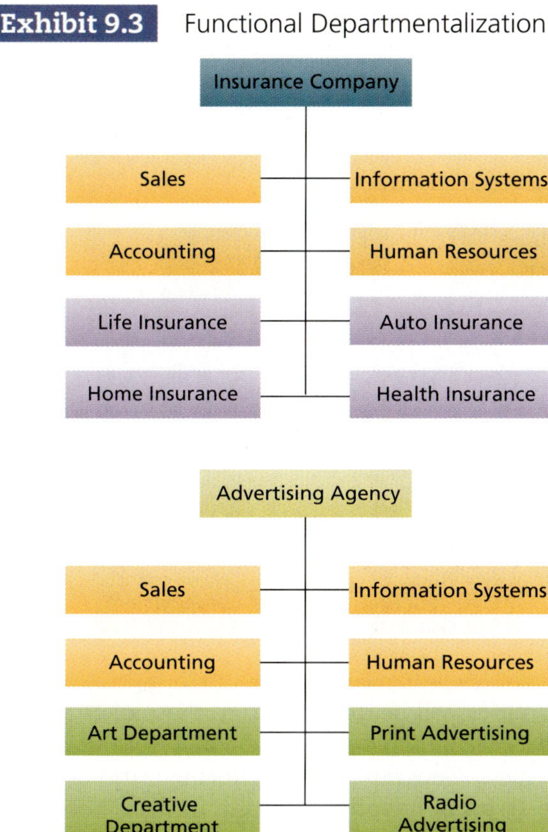

1.2 Product Departmentalization

Product departmentalization organizes work and workers into separate units responsible for producing particular products or services. Exhibit 9.4 shows the product departmentalization structure used by United Technologies (UTC), which is organized along five different product lines: Otis, Pratt & Whitney, Sikorsky, UTC Aerospace Systems, and UTC Climate, Controls, and Security.[5]

One of the advantages of product departmentalization is that, like functional departmentalization, it allows managers and workers to specialize in one area. Unlike in functional departmentalization, however, managers and workers develop a broader set of experiences and expertise related to an entire product line. Likewise, product departmentalization makes it easier for top managers to assess the performance of work units. For example, because of the clear separation of its six different product divisions, UTC's top managers can easily compare the performance of the Otis and Pratt & Whitney divisions. The divisions had similar revenues: $12.1 billion for Otis (elevators and escalators) and $14 billion for Pratt & Whitney (commercial and military engines); however, when you examine profitability, Otis's profits were $2.5 billion compared to $1.6 billion for Pratt & Whitney.[6] Finally, decision making should be faster because managers and workers are responsible for the entire product line rather than for separate functional departments; in other words, there are fewer conflicts than under functional departmentalization.

The main disadvantage of product departmentalization is duplication. For example, you can see in Exhibit 9.4 that UTC's Otis and Pratt & Whitney divisions both have customer service, engineering, human resources, legal, manufacturing, and procurement departments. If UTC were organized by function instead, one lawyer could handle matters related to both elevators and aircraft engines instead of working on only one or the other. Duplication like this often results in higher costs.

Product departmentalization organizing work and workers into separate units responsible for producing particular products or services

Customer departmentalization organizing work and workers into separate units responsible for particular kinds of customers

A second disadvantage involves the challenge of coordinating across the different product departments. UTC probably has difficulty standardizing its policies and procedures in product departments as different as Carrier (heating, ventilating, and air-conditioning) and Sikorsky (military and commercial helicopters).

1.3 Customer Departmentalization

Customer departmentalization organizes work and workers into separate units responsible for particular

Exhibit 9.4 Product Departmentalization: United Technologies

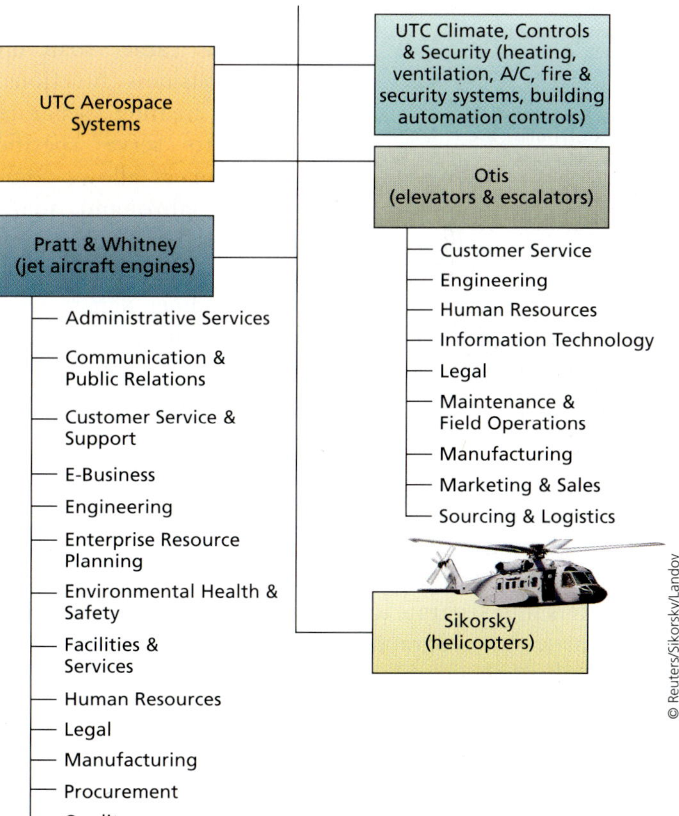

Source: *United Technologies Corportation 2009 Annual Report*, United Technologies, [Online] available at http://www.utc.com/About+UTC/Company+Reports/2009+Annual+Report+English [accessed June 7, 2010].

Exhibit 9.5 Customer Departmentalization: Distribution Company

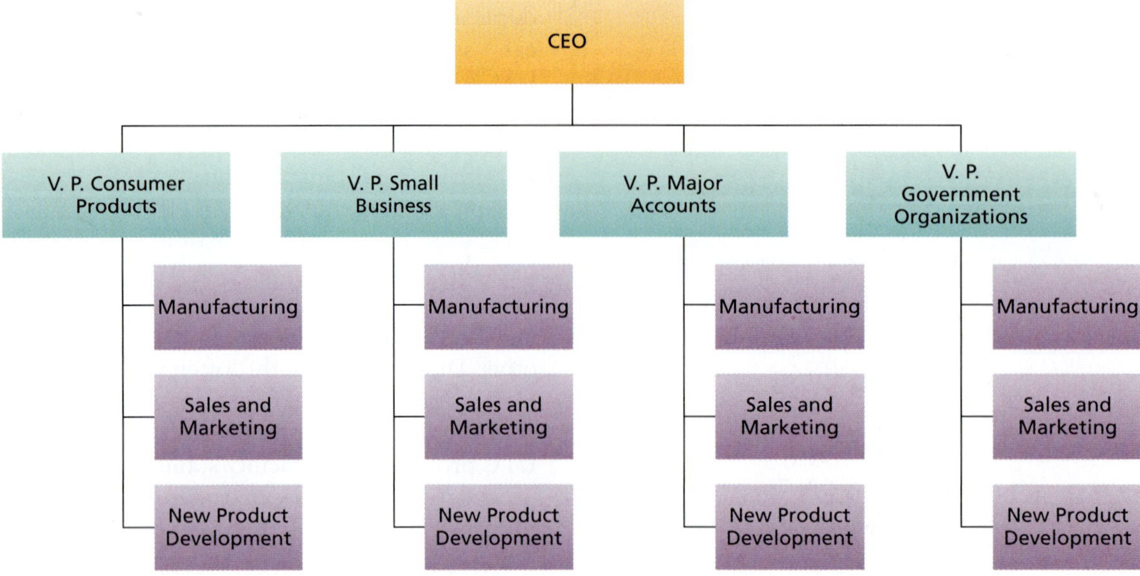

Geographic departmentalization organizing work and workers into separate units responsible for doing business in particular geographic areas

Matrix departmentalization a hybrid organizational structure in which two or more forms of departmentalization, most often product and functional, are used together

kinds of customers. For example, Exhibit 9.5 shows a distribution company that is organized into departments that cater to small and large businesses, consumers, and government customers. The primary advantage of customer departmentalization is that it focuses the organization on customer needs rather than on products or business functions. Furthermore, creating separate departments to serve specific kinds of customers allows companies to specialize and adapt their products and services to customer needs and problems.

The primary disadvantage of customer departmentalization is that, like product departmentalization, it leads to duplication of resources. Also, it can also be difficult to achieve coordination across different customer departments. Finally, the emphasis on meeting customers' needs may lead workers to make decisions that please customers but hurt the business.

1.4 Geographic Departmentalization

Geographic departmentalization organizes work and workers into separate units responsible for doing business in particular geographic areas. Exhibit 9.6 shows an example of geographic departmentalization.

The primary advantage of geographic departmentalization is that it helps companies respond to the demands of different markets. This can be especially important when the company sells in different parts of the country as well as in different countries, for cultural preferences can vary widely, and so can external business environments. For example, a dairy in Canada that sells to consumers in Western Canada will find that preferences for cheeses on the Prairies will be different from those of consumers in Quebec. Geographic segregation can help to address those issues. Geographic departmentalization is also useful in terms of adapting to the differences in business environments in different countries. For example, in the United States, there are extensive federal, state, and local government regulations relating to food production and the pricing of milk is based on public policy decisions. Overseas, the European Union has a multitude of food-related laws covering production, processing, and distribution; also, in Germany and the United Kingdom, standards for cheese are based on international standards overseen by the World Health Organization.[7] Another advantage is that geographic departmentalization can reduce costs by locating unique organizational resources closer to customers. For instance, it is much cheaper for a dairy to build cheese manufacturing plants in the United Kingdom than to manufacture cheese in Canada and then transport it overseas.

The primary disadvantage of geographic departmentalization is that it can lead to duplication of resources. For example, while it may be necessary to adapt products and marketing to different geographic locations, it's doubtful that a dairy needs significantly different inventory tracking systems from location to location. Also, even more than with the other forms of departmentalization, it can be difficult to coordinate departments that are literally thousands of miles from one another and whose managers have very limited contact with one another.

1.5 Matrix Departmentalization

Matrix departmentalization is a hybrid structure in which two or more forms of departmentalization are used together. The most common matrix combines the product and functional forms of departmentalization, as shown in Exhibit 9.7, but other forms are also possible. Product managers and functional managers have equal authority within the organization, and employees report to both of

Exhibit 9.6 Geographic Departmentalization for a Dairy Company

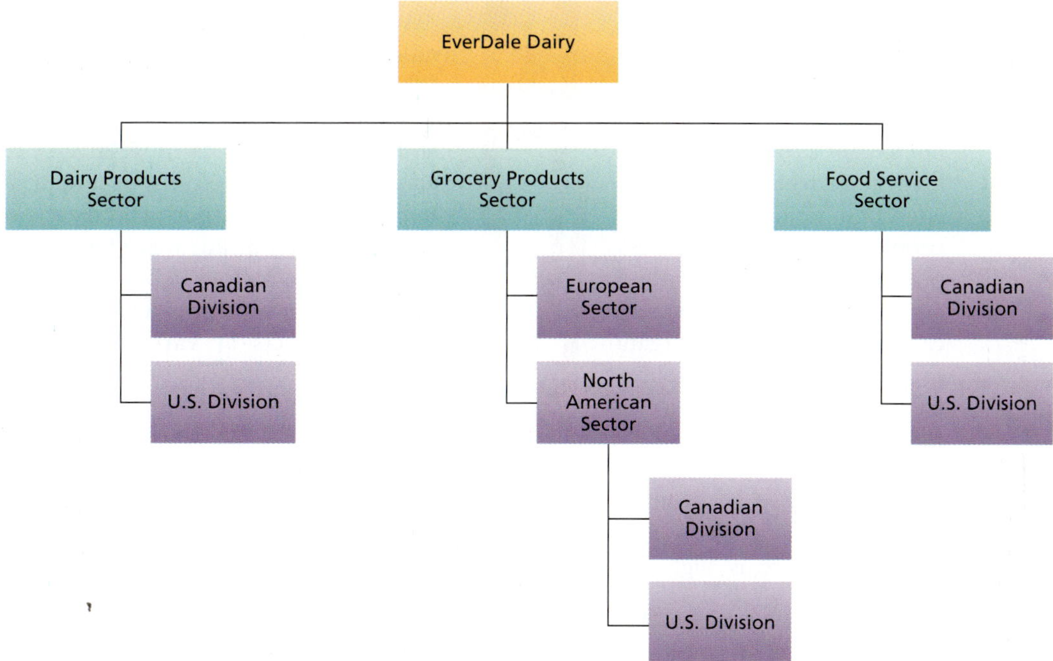

them. Referring again to Exhibit 9.7, which illustrates a matrix form for a medium-sized company, each product manager relies on employees from manufacturing, design, and marketing to work on the product lines they oversee in order to serve the various markets and customers where the company's products are sold. When the manufacturing, design, and marketing functions are kept intact, employees can develop the in-depth expertise to serve all product

Exhibit 9.7 Dual Authority Structure in a Matrix Organization

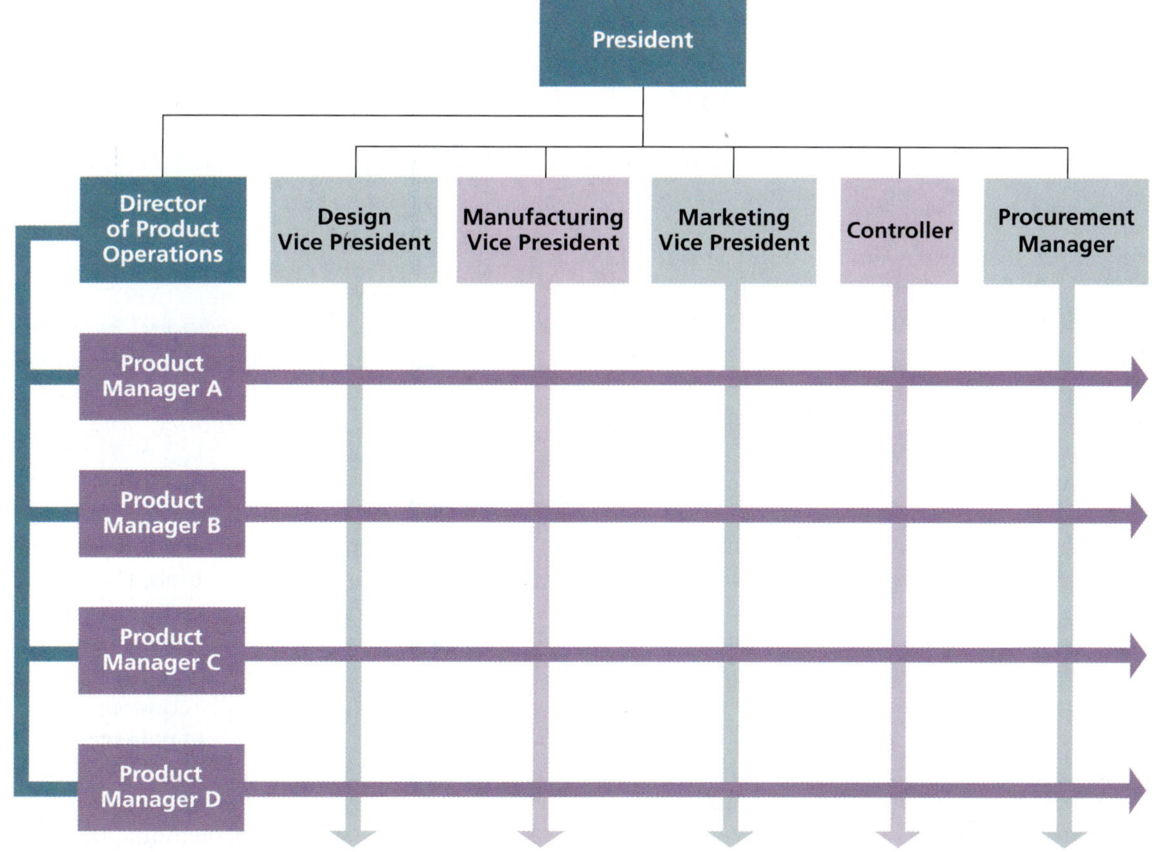

Source: From DAFT/ARMSTRONG. *Organization Theory and Design*, 2E. © 2012 Nelson Education Ltd. Reproduced by permission. www.cengage.com/permissions.

Simple matrix a form of matrix departmentalization in which managers in different parts of the matrix negotiate conflicts and resources

Complex matrix a form of matrix departmentalization in which managers in different parts of the matrix report to matrix managers, who help them sort out conflicts and problems

Authority the right to give commands, take action, and make decisions to achieve organizational objectives

Chain of command the vertical line of authority that clarifies who reports to whom throughout the organization

lines efficiently. The matrix structure works best when certain conditions are met. For example, a medium-sized organization with scarce resources and a moderate number of product lines will find a matrix organization efficient in terms of allocating people and equipment across products. As well, the dual authority structure of a matrix can be useful for an organization that needs to ensure a balance between product and functional managers. Lastly, when an organization operates in a complex and unstable environment with frequent external changes, and when there is high interdependence among departments, the vertical and horizontal channels in a matrix organization can be used to better process information and facilitate coordination, for which there is a greater need.

Several things distinguish matrix departmentalization from the other traditional forms of departmentalization.[8] First, most employees report to two bosses, one from each core part of the matrix. Second, by virtue of their hybrid design, matrix structures lead to much more cross-functional interaction than other forms of departmentalization. In fact, while matrix workers are typically members of only one functional department (based on their work experience and expertise), they are also commonly members of several ongoing project, product, or customer groups. Third, because of the high level of cross-functional interaction, matrix departmentalization requires significant coordination between managers in the different parts of the matrix. In particular, managers have the complex job of tracking and managing the multiple demands (project, product, customer, or functional) on employees' time.

The primary advantage of matrix departmentalization is that it allows companies to efficiently manage large, complex tasks such as researching, developing, and marketing, or carrying out complex global businesses. Efficiency comes from avoiding duplication. For example, rather than having an entire marketing function for each project, the company simply assigns and reassigns workers from the marketing department as they are needed at various stages of product completion. More specifically, an employee from a department may simultaneously be part of five different ongoing projects, but may be actively completing work on only a few projects at a time.

Another advantage is the pool of resources available to carry out large, complex tasks. Because of the ability to quickly pull in expert help from all the functional areas of the company, matrix project managers have a much more diverse set of expertise and experience at their disposal than do managers in the other forms of departmentalization.

The primary disadvantage of matrix departmentalization is the high level of coordination required to manage the complexities involved in running large, ongoing projects at various levels of completion. Matrix structures are notorious for confusion and conflict between project bosses in different parts of the matrix. Disagreements or misunderstandings about schedules, budgets, available resources, and the availability of employees with particular functional expertise are common. Another disadvantage is that matrix structures require much more management skill than the other forms of departmentalization.

Because of these problems, many matrix structures evolve from a **simple matrix**, in which managers in different parts of the matrix negotiate conflicts and resources directly, to a **complex matrix**, in which specialized matrix managers and departments are added to the organizational structure. In a complex matrix, managers from different parts of the matrix might report to the same matrix manager, who helps them sort out conflicts and problems.

LO2 Organizational Authority

The second part of traditional organizational structures is authority. **Authority** is the right to give commands, take action, and make decisions to achieve organizational objectives.[9]

*Traditionally, organizational authority has been characterized by the following dimensions: **2.1 chain of command, 2.2 line versus staff authority, 2.3 delegation of authority,** and **2.4 degree of centralization.***

2.1 Chain of Command

Turn back a few pages to Sony's organizational chart in Exhibit 9.1. If you place your finger on any position in the chart—say, the Sales and Marketing department of the Major Accounts division—you can trace a line upward to the company's CEO. This line, which vertically connects every job in the company to higher levels of management, represents the chain of command. The **chain of command** is the vertical line of authority that clarifies who reports to whom throughout the organization;

span of control refers to the number of individuals who report directly to a manager or supervisor. People higher in the chain of command have the right, *if they so choose*, to give commands, take action, and make decisions concerning activities occurring anywhere below them in the chain. In the following discussion about delegation and decentralization, you will learn that managers don't always choose to exercise their authority directly.[10]

A key assumption underlying the chain of command is **unity of command**, which means that workers should report to just one boss.[11] In practical terms, this means that only one person can be in charge at a time. Matrix organizations, in which employees have two bosses, automatically violate this principle. This is one of the primary reasons why matrix organizations are difficult to manage. Unity of command serves an important purpose: to prevent the confusion that may arise when an employee receives conflicting commands from two different bosses.

2.2 Line Versus Staff Authority

A second dimension of authority is the distinction between line and staff authority. **Line authority** is the right to command immediate subordinates in the chain of command. For example, Sony CEO Kazua Hirai has line authority over the head of Sony Entertainment Business Group, which contains Sony Pictures. Hirai can issue orders to that division president and expect them to be carried out. In turn, the head of Sony Entertainment Business Group can issue orders to his subordinates and expect them to be carried out.

Staff authority is the right to *advise* but not command others who are not subordinates in the chain of command. For example, a manager in human resources at Sony might advise the manager in charge of Sony's TV Business Group on a hiring decision but cannot order him or her to hire a certain applicant.

The terms *line* and *staff* are also used to describe different functions within the organization. A **line function** is an activity that contributes directly to creating or selling the company's products. So, for example, activities that take place within the manufacturing and marketing departments would be considered line functions. A **staff function**, such as accounting, human resources, or legal services, does not contribute directly to creating or selling the company's products; instead, it supports line activities. For example, marketing managers might consult with the legal staff to make sure the wording of a particular advertisement is legal.

2.3 Delegation of Authority

Managers can exercise their authority directly by completing tasks themselves, or they can choose to pass on some of their authority to subordinates. **Delegation of authority** is the assignment of direct authority and responsibility to a subordinate to complete tasks for which the manager is normally responsible.

When a manager delegates work, three transfers occur, as illustrated in Exhibit 9.8. First, the manager transfers full responsibility for the assignment to the subordinate. According to Murray Martin, former CEO of Pitney Bowes Worldwide, the higher up you rise in an organization, the more you must be willing to delegate. "I think that if you are looking at companies that have long-term, continuous success, it is with CEOs that have been able to disperse power, rather than centralize power."[12] The challenge of delegation does not apply just to large organizations; small businesses and start-up ventures can also find delegation useful to support growth. For many entrepreneurs, letting go of day-to-day operations and decision making is not easy; even so, it is often critical for them to do so if the business is past the start-up phase and transitioning to growth. That is when owners need to be able to focus on developing and executing strategies for growth instead of

Span of control the number of individuals who report directly to a manager

Unity of command a management principle that workers should report to just one boss

Line authority the right to command immediate subordinates in the chain of command

Staff authority the right to advise, but not command, others who are not subordinates in the chain of command

Line function an activity that contributes directly to creating or selling the company's products

Staff function an activity that does not contribute directly to creating or selling the company's products, but instead supports line activities

Delegation of authority the assignment of direct authority and responsibility to a subordinate to complete tasks for which the manager is normally responsible

Exhibit 9.8 Delegation: Responsibility, Authority, and Accountability

Source: Pringle, Charles D.; Jennings, Daniel F.; Source: C. D. Pringle, D. F. Jennings, and J. G. Longenecker, *Managing Organizations: Functions and Behaviors* © 1990 Pearson Education, Inc. Adapted by permission of the author.

Centralization of authority the location of most authority at the upper levels of the organization

Decentralization the location of a significant amount of authority in the lower levels of the organization

devoting all their time to daily operations or to activities that could be carried out by others. This means that having the right people in place is vital to effective delegating. Alex Krohn, owner of Gossamer Threads Inc., a software and Web-hosting company based in Vancouver, believes that recruitment and building a solid team are needed for effective delegation to occur. That in turn means finding "the right people and make sure you can trust them to deliver the same quality of service you were providing."[13] To summarize, many managers find it difficult to delegate, but "the job of the leader is to conduct the orchestra, not play all the instruments."[14]

One reason it is difficult for some managers to delegate is that they often fear the task won't be done as well as if they did it themselves. However, one CEO says, "if you can delegate a task to somebody who can do it 75 percent to 80 percent as well as you can today, you delegate it immediately." Why? Many tasks don't need to be done perfectly; they just need to be *done*. And delegating tasks that someone else can do frees managers to assume other important responsibilities.

Delegating authority can generate a related problem: micromanaging. Sometimes managers delegate only to later interfere with how the employee is performing the task. "Why are you doing it that way? That's not the way I do it." But delegating full responsibility means that the employee—not the manager—is now completely responsible for task completion. Good managers need to trust their subordinates to do the job.

The second transfer that occurs with delegation is that the manager gives the subordinate full authority over the budget, resources, and personnel needed to do the job. To do the job effectively, subordinates must have the same tools and information at their disposal that managers had when they were responsible for the same task. In other words, for delegation to work, delegated authority must be commensurate with delegated responsibility.

The third transfer that occurs with delegation is the transfer of accountability. The subordinate now has the authority and responsibility to do the job and in return is accountable for getting the job done. In other words, managers delegate their authority and responsibility to subordinates in exchange for results.

2.4 Degree of Centralization

If you've ever called a company's toll-free number with a complaint or a special request and been told by the customer service representative, "I'll have to ask my manager," or "I'm not authorized to do that," you know that centralization of authority exists in that company. **Centralization of authority** is the location of most authority at the upper levels of the organization. In a centralized organization, managers make most decisions, even the relatively small ones. That's why the customer service representative you called couldn't make a decision without first asking the manager.

If you are lucky, however, you may have talked to a customer service representative at another company who said, "I can take care of that for you right now." In other words, the person was able to handle your problem without any input from or consultation with company management. **Decentralization** is the location of a significant amount of authority in the lower levels of the organization. An organization is decentralized if it has a high degree of delegation at all levels. In a decentralized organization, workers closest to problems are authorized to make the decisions necessary to solve the problems on their own.

Decentralization has a number of advantages. It develops employee capabilities throughout the company and leads to faster decision making and more satisfied customers and employees. Bayshore Home Health is the largest provider of home and community health care services in Canada, with more than 50 locations across the country. The company has adopted a decentralized approach by encouraging employees to make decisions locally; management believes that "decision making is best when it is made as close to the client as possible."[15]

Another company in the health care industry, Trillium Health Centre (THC) in Ontario, has found much success with a decentralized organizational structure. THC is a merger of two hospitals, both of which had been operating under a traditional hierarchical structure, which is common in health care organizations. With the decentralized structure, each of the centre's 10 divisions has the ability to set its own vision, goals, and objectives and is supported by partnership councils led and chaired by staff and supported by management. The decision to employ a distributed leadership environment has been well received and has enhanced employee engagement on a collective level.[16] A study of 1,000 large companies found that those with a high degree of decentralization outperformed those with a low degree of decentralization in terms of return on assets (6.9 versus 4.7 percent), return on investment (14.6 versus 9.0 percent), return on equity (22.8 versus 16.6 percent), and return on sales (10.3 versus 6.3 percent). Surprisingly, the same study found that few large companies actually are decentralized. Specifically, only 31 percent of employees in these 1,000 companies were responsible for recommending improvements to management. Overall, just 10 percent of employees received the training and information they needed to support a truly decentralized approach to management.[17]

With results like these, the key question is no longer *whether* companies should decentralize, but *where* they should decentralize. One rule of thumb is to stay

iodrakon/Shutterstock.com

centralized where standardization is important and to decentralize where standardization is unimportant. **Standardization** is solving problems by consistently applying the same rules, procedures, and processes. Kwik Kopy Printing Canada, a franchise business with 70 locations across Canada, uses a standardized process when recruiting and selecting potential franchisees. The company believes that selecting the right franchisees is a critical decision that affects brand awareness, the success of locations, and the company's overall financial performance. When a poor selection is made, it causes a ripple effect throughout the company; that is why management has a standardized system for dealing with this vital task. The selection process includes a series of personal interviews to assess the franchisee's skills, as well as profile testing to uncover the franchisee's strengths and weaknesses. Meetings with head office personnel and existing franchises are also part of the selection process. In addition, potential franchisees must provide financial documentation to show they have sufficient equity to purchase the business. Kwik Kopy's president, Brett Harding, admits that to some the selection process may seem very long and structured. But, as he puts it, "no one gets married after the first date. Good franchising is about relationships."[18]

LO3 Job Design

1. "Welcome to McDonald's. May I have your order please?"
2. Listen to the order. Repeat it for accuracy. State the total cost. "Please drive to the second window."
3. Take the money. Make change.
4. Give customers drinks, straws, and napkins.
5. Give customers food.
6. "Thank you for coming to McDonald's."

Could you stand to do the same simple tasks an average of 50 times per hour, 400 times per day, 2,000 times per week, 8,000 times per month? Few can. Fast food workers rarely stay on the job more than six months.[19] According to the National Restaurant Association, fast food restaurants have an average turnover rate of 60 percent.[20]

The shape of a job is closely related to how happy and fulfilled an employee feels doing it. In this next section, you will learn about **job design**—the number, kinds, and variety of tasks that individual workers perform in doing their jobs.

*You will learn **3.1 why companies continue to use specialized jobs** and **3.2 how job rotation, job enlargement, job enrichment**, and **3.3 the job characteristics model** are being used to overcome the problems associated with job specialization.*

3.1 Job Specialization

Job specialization occurs when a job is composed of a small part of a larger task or process. Specialized jobs are characterized by simple, easy-to-learn steps, low variety, and high repetition, like the McDonald's drive-through window job just described. A clear disadvantage of specialized jobs is that, being so easy to learn, they quickly become boring. This in turn can lead to low job satisfaction and high absenteeism and employee turnover, all of which are very costly to organizations.

Why, then, do companies continue to create and use specialized jobs? As we learned from Taylor and the Gilbreths in Chapter 2, economy is a key reason why the pioneers of scientific management sought to standardize tasks. Once a job has been specialized, it takes little time to learn and master, which translates into enhanced productivity. For example, every Taco Bell has two food production lines, one for the drive-through and the other dedicated to the walk-up counter. Those lines are further broken down into distinct jobs—Steamers, Stuffers, and Expeditors—and three prep areas—hot and cold holding areas and wrapping. The Stuffer in the hot holding area follows the prescribed three-step process to stir, scoop, and tap to fill the tortillas with beef, using Taco Bell's own BPT, or beef portioning tool to make sure the same quantity of beef gets placed inside the tortillas every time.[21] At most fast food restaurants like Taco Bell, every task has been engineered to make the process as simple as possible. Because the work is designed to be simple, wages can remain low, since it isn't necessary to pay high salaries to attract highly experienced, educated, or trained workers.

Standardization solving problems by consistently applying the same rules, procedures, and processes

Job design the number, kind, and variety of tasks that individual workers perform in doing their jobs

Job specialization a job composed of a small part of a larger task or process

Job rotation periodically moving workers from one specialized job to another to give them more variety and the opportunity to use different skills

Job enlargement increasing the number of different tasks that a worker performs within one particular job

3.2 Job Rotation, Enlargement, and Enrichment

Because of the efficiency of specialized jobs, companies are often reluctant to eliminate them. Consequently, job redesign efforts have focused on modifying jobs to keep the benefits of specialized jobs while reducing their obvious costs and disadvantages. Three methods—job rotation, job enlargement, and job enrichment—have been used to try to improve specialized jobs.[22]

Job rotation attempts to overcome the disadvantages of job specialization by periodically moving workers from one specialized job to another to give them more variety and the opportunity to use different skills. For example, a "mirror attacher" in an automobile plant might attach mirrors in the first half of the day's work shift and then install bumpers during the second half. Because employees simply switch from one specialized job to another, job rotation allows companies to retain the economic benefits of specialized work. At the same time, the greater variety of tasks makes the work less boring and more satisfying for workers.

Another way to counter the disadvantages of specialization is to enlarge the job. **Job enlargement** increases the number of different tasks that a worker performs within one particular job. So instead of being

Job enrichment increasing the number of tasks in a particular job and giving workers the authority and control to make meaningful decisions about their work

Job characteristics model (JCM) an approach to job redesign that seeks to formulate jobs in ways that motivate workers and lead to positive work outcomes

Internal motivation motivation that comes from the job itself rather than from outside rewards

assigned just one task, workers with enlarged jobs are given several tasks to perform. For example, an enlarged "mirror attacher" job might include attaching the mirror, checking to see that the mirror's power adjustment controls work, and then cleaning the mirror's surface. Although job enlargement increases variety, many workers report feeling more stress when their jobs are enlarged. Consequently, many workers view enlarged jobs as simply more work, especially if they are not given additional time to complete the additional tasks. In comparison, **job enrichment** attempts to overcome the deficiencies in specialized work by increasing the number of tasks and by giving workers the authority and control to make meaningful decisions about their work.[23]

3.3 Job Characteristics Model

In contrast to job rotation, job enlargement, and job enrichment, which focus on providing variety in job tasks, the **job characteristics model (JCM)** is an approach to job redesign that seeks to formulate jobs in ways that motivate workers and lead to positive work outcomes.[24] As shown in the far right column of Exhibit 9.9, the primary goal of the model is to create jobs that result in positive personal and work outcomes such as internal work motivation, satisfaction with one's job, and work effectiveness. Of these, the central concern of the JCM is internal motivation. **Internal motivation** is motivation that comes from the job itself rather than from outside rewards, such as a raise or praise from the boss. If workers feel that performing the job well is itself rewarding, then the job has internal motivation. Statements such as "I get a nice sense of accomplishment" or "I feel good about myself and what I'm producing" are examples of internal motivation.

Moving to the left in Exhibit 9.9, you can see that the JCM specifies three critical psychological states that must occur for work to be internally motivating. First, workers must *experience the work as meaningful*; that is, they must view their job as being important. Second, they must *experience responsibility for work outcomes*—they must feel personally responsible for the work being done well. Third, workers must have *knowledge of results*; that is, they must know how well they are performing their jobs. All three critical psychological states must occur for work to be internally motivating.

Grocery store cashiers usually have knowledge of results. When you're slow, your checkout line grows long. If you make a mistake, customers point it out: "No, I think that's on sale for $2.99, not $3.99." Likewise, cashiers experience responsibility for work outcomes. At the end of the day, the register is totalled and the money is counted. Ideally, the money matches the total sales in the register. If the money in the till is less than what's recorded in the register, most stores make the cashier pay the difference. Consequently, most cashiers are very careful to avoid being caught short at the end of the day. Nonetheless, despite knowing the results and experiencing responsibility for work outcomes, most grocery store cashiers (at least where I shop) aren't internally motivated

Exhibit 9.9 Job Characteristics Model

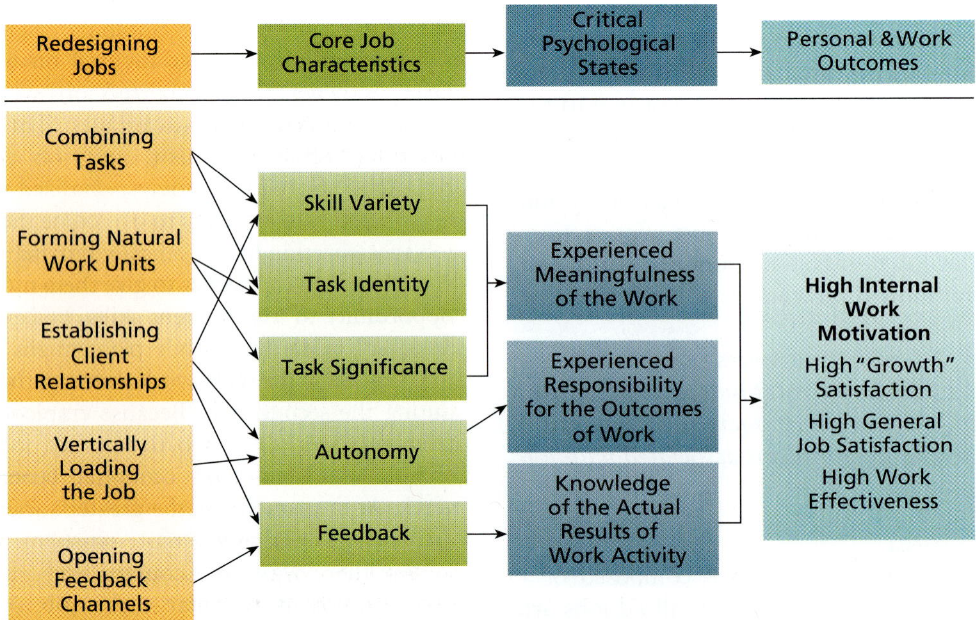

Source: J. RICHARD HACKMAN & GREG R. OLDHAM, *WORK REDESIGN, 1st Edition*, ©1980. Reprinted by permission of Pearson Education, Inc., Upper Saddle River, New Jersey.

because they don't experience the work as meaningful. With scanners, it takes little skill to learn or do the job. Anyone can do it. In addition, cashiers have few decisions to make, and the job is highly repetitive.

What kinds of jobs produce the three critical psychological states? Moving another step to the left in Exhibit 9.9, you can see that these psychological states arise from jobs that are strong on five core job characteristics: skill variety, task identity, task significance, autonomy, and feedback. **Skill variety** is the number of different activities performed in a job. **Task identity** is the degree to which a job, from beginning to end, requires completion of a whole and identifiable piece of work. **Task significance** is the degree to which a job is perceived to have a substantial impact on others inside or outside the organization. **Autonomy** is the degree to which a job gives workers the discretion, freedom, and independence to decide how and when to accomplish the work. Finally, **feedback** is the amount of information the job provides to workers about their work performance.

To illustrate how the core job characteristics work together, let's use them to more thoroughly assess why the McDonald's drive-through window job is not particularly satisfying or motivating. To start, skill variety is low. Except for the size of an order or special requests ("no onions"), the process is the same for each customer. At best, task identity is moderate. Although you take the order, handle the money, and deliver the food, others are responsible for a larger part of the process—preparing the food. Task identity will be even lower if the McDonald's has two drive-through windows because each drive-through window worker will have an even more specialized task. The first is limited to taking the order and making change, while the second just delivers the food. Task significance, the impact you have on others, is probably low. Autonomy is also very low: McDonald's has strict rules about dress, cleanliness, and procedures. But the job does provide immediate feedback, such as positive and negative customer comments, car horns honking, the amount of time it takes to process orders, and the number of cars in the drive-through. With the exception of feedback, the low levels of the core job characteristics show why the drive-through window job is not internally motivating for many workers.

Why isn't the drive-through job particularly satisfying or motivating?

What can managers do when jobs aren't internally motivating? The far left column of Exhibit 9.9 lists five job redesign techniques that managers can use to strengthen a job's core characteristics. *Combining tasks* increases skill variety and task identity by joining separate, specialized tasks into larger work modules. For example, some trucking firms are now requiring their drivers to load their rigs as well as drive them. The hope is that involving drivers in loading will ensure that trucks are properly loaded, thus reducing damage claims.

Work can be formed into *natural work units* by arranging tasks according to logical or meaningful groups. Although many trucking companies randomly assign drivers to trucks, some have begun assigning drivers to particular geographic locations (e.g., Western Canada or Quebec) or to truckloads that require special driving skill (oversized loads, chemicals, etc.). Forming natural work units increases task identity and task significance.

Establishing client relationships increases skill variety, autonomy, and feedback by giving employees direct contact with clients and customers. In some companies, truck drivers are expected to establish business relationships with their regular customers. When something goes wrong with a shipment, customers are told to call drivers directly.

Vertical loading means pushing some managerial authority down to workers. For truck drivers, this means they have the same authority as managers to resolve customer problems. In some companies, if a late shipment causes problems for a customer, the driver has the authority to fully refund the cost of that shipment (without first obtaining management's approval).

Skill variety the number of different activities performed in a job

Task identity the degree to which a job, from beginning to end, requires the completion of a whole and identifiable piece of work

Task significance the degree to which a job is perceived to have a substantial impact on others inside or outside the organization

Autonomy the degree to which a job gives workers the discretion, freedom, and independence to decide how and when to accomplish the job

Feedback the amount of information the job provides to workers about their work performance

Ruslan Kuzmenkow/Shutterstock.com

Mechanistic organization an organization characterized by specialized jobs and responsibilities; precisely defined, unchanging roles; and a rigid chain of command based on centralized authority and vertical communication

Organic organization an organization characterized by broadly defined jobs and responsibility; loosely defined, frequently changing roles; and decentralized authority and horizontal communication based on task knowledge

Intra-organizational process the collection of activities that take place within an organization to transform inputs into outputs that customers value

The last job redesign technique offered by the model, *opening feedback channels*, means finding additional ways to give employees direct, frequent feedback about their job performance.

Designing Organizational Processes

More than 40 years ago, Tom Burns and G. M. Stalker described how two kinds of organizational designs—mechanistic and organic—are appropriate for different kinds of organizational environments.[25] **Mechanistic organizations** are characterized by specialized jobs and responsibilities; precisely defined, unchanging roles; and a rigid chain of command based on centralized authority and vertical communication. This type of organization works best in stable, unchanging business environments. By contrast, **organic organizations** are characterized by broadly defined jobs and responsibilities; loosely defined, frequently changing roles; and decentralized authority and horizontal communication based on task knowledge. This type of organization works best in dynamic, changing business environments.

The organizational design techniques described in the first half of this chapter—departmentalization, authority, and job design—are better suited for mechanistic organizations and the stable business environments that were more prevalent before 1980. In contrast, the organizational design techniques discussed next are more appropriate for organic organizations and for the increasingly dynamic environments in which today's businesses compete.

The key difference between these approaches is that mechanistic ones focus on organizational structure while organic ones focus on organizational processes—that is, on collections of activities that transform inputs into outputs valued by customers.

LO4 Intra-Organizational Processes

An **intra-organizational process** is the collection of activities that take place within an organization to transform inputs into outputs that customers value.

*Let's take a look at how companies are using **4.1 re-engineering** and **4.2 empowerment** to redesign intra-organizational processes like these.*

4.1 Re-engineering

In their best-selling book *Reengineering the Corporation*, Michael Hammer and James Champy define **re-engineering** as "the *fundamental* rethinking and *radical* redesign of business *processes* to achieve *dramatic* improvements in critical, contemporary measures of performance, such as cost, quality, service and speed."[26] Hammer and Champy further explain the four key words shown in italics in this definition. The first key word is *fundamental*. When re-engineering organizational designs, managers must ask themselves, "Why do we do what we do?" and "Why do we do it the way we do?" The usual answer is, "Because that's the way we've always done it." Fundamental rethinking involves getting behind "that's the way we've always done it" and pursuing answers to these questions down to the foundations so that processes are actually achieving business goals. The second key word is *radical*. Re-engineering is about significant change, about starting over by throwing out the old ways of getting work done. The third key word is *processes*. Hammer and Champy note that "most business people are not process oriented; they are focused on tasks, on jobs, on people, on structures, but not on processes." The fourth key word is *dramatic*. Re-engineering is about achieving quantum improvements in company performance.

An example from IBM Credit's operation illustrates how work can be re-engineered.[27] IBM Credit lends businesses money to buy IBM computers. Previously, the loan process began when an IBM salesperson called the home office to obtain credit approval for a customer's purchase. The first department involved in the process took the credit information over the phone from the salesperson and recorded it on the credit form. The credit form was sent to the credit checking department, then to the pricing department (where the interest rate was determined), and on through a total of five departments. In all, it took the five departments six days to approve or deny the customer's loan. Of course, this delay cost IBM business. Some customers got their loans elsewhere. Others, frustrated by the wait, simply cancelled their orders.

Finally, two IBM managers decided to walk a loan straight through each of the departments involved in the process. At each step, they asked the workers to stop what they were doing and immediately process their loan application. They were shocked by what they found. From start to finish, the entire process took just 90 minutes! The six-day turnaround time was almost entirely due to delays in handing off the work from one department to another. The solution: IBM redesigned the process so that one person, not five people in five separate departments, now handles the entire loan approval process without any hand-offs. Approval time has dropped from six days to four hours, and this has allowed IBM Credit to increase the number of loans it handles by a factor of 100.

Re-engineering fundamental rethinking and radical redesign of business processes to achieve dramatic improvements in critical measures of performance, such as cost, quality, service, and speed

Task interdependence the extent to which collective action is required to complete an entire piece of work

Pooled interdependence work completed by having each job or department independently contribute to the whole

Re-engineering changes an organization's orientation from vertical to horizontal. Instead of taking orders from upper management, lower- and middle-level managers and workers take orders from a customer, who is at the beginning and end of each process. Instead of running independent functional departments, managers and workers in different departments take ownership of cross-functional processes. Instead of simplifying work so that it becomes increasingly specialized, re-engineering complicates work by giving workers increased autonomy and responsibility for complete processes.

In essence, re-engineering changes work by changing **task interdependence**, that is, the extent to which collective action is required to complete an entire piece of work. As shown in Exhibit 9.10 (page 154), there are three kinds of task interdependence.[28] In **pooled interdependence**, each job or department

In Plain English ...

The definition of intra-organizational process tells you exactly what it is, but here's a quick example to help you get to "Oh, that's it."

The steps involved in an automobile insurance claim are a good example of an intra-organizational process:

1. Document the loss (i.e., the accident).
2. Assign an appraiser to determine the dollar amount of damage.
3. Make an appointment to inspect the vehicle.
4. Inspect the vehicle.
5. Write an appraisal and get the repair shop to agree to the damage estimate.
6. Pay for the repair work.
7. Return the repaired car to the customer.

CandyBox Images/Shutterstock.com

Sequential interdependence work completed in succession, with one group's or job's outputs becoming the inputs for the next group or job

Reciprocal interdependence work completed by different jobs or groups working together in a back-and-forth manner

independently contributes to the whole. In **sequential interdependence**, work must be performed in succession, as one group's or job's outputs become the inputs for the next group or job. Finally, in **reciprocal interdependence**, different jobs or groups work together in a back-and-forth manner to complete the process. By reducing the hand-offs between different jobs or groups, re-engineering decreases sequential interdependence. Likewise, re-engineering decreases pooled interdependence by redesigning work so that formerly independent jobs or departments now work together to complete processes. Finally, re-engineering increases reciprocal interdependence by making groups or individuals responsible for larger, more complete processes in which several steps may be accomplished at the same time.

As an organizational design tool, re-engineering promises big rewards, but it has also come under severe criticism. The most serious complaint is that because it allows a few workers to do the work formerly done by many, re-engineering is simply a corporate code word for cost cutting and worker layoffs.[29] Likewise, for that reason, detractors claim that re-engineering hurts morale and performance. Today, even re-engineering gurus Hammer and Champy admit that roughly 70 percent of all re-engineering projects fail because of the effects on people in the workplace. Says Hammer, "I wasn't smart enough about that [the people issues]. I was reflecting my engineering background and was insufficiently appreciative of the human dimension. I've [now] learned that's critical."[30]

Exhibit 9.10 Re-engineering and Task Interdependence

Pooled Interdependence

Finished Product

Sequential Interdependence

Finished Product

Reciprocal Interdependence

Finished Product

Ubisoft's Gameplan

An important global player in the video game industry, Ubisoft employs more than 6,300 people worldwide, with 2,700 employees between their Montreal and Toronto offices. According to Ubisoft Montreal CEO Yannis Mallat, the company's strong performance is a direct result of investing in new technology and in employees, while still managing costs. The company's decision to embrace the concept of larger development teams and cross-studio collaboration has led to a marked increase in productivity. Although Ubisoft employs a lean management structure, with managers charged with leading larger teams, the company prides itself on its bottom-up approach, which stimulates employee creativity and empowerment. Skill development for employees is a primary focus; it includes extensive training opportunities for employees, a group training portal, and expanded communication channels such as open forums, instant messaging, Web conferencing, and the use of video to facilitate collaboration, organization, and the sharing of key information among teams and projects. As Mallat explains, "You gather as much talent as possible, and you give them three things: Trust, means, and insane challenges. Usually they come back with pretty good stuff. It's OK to invest more when you get more in return."

Sources: B. Sinclair, "No Room for B-Games" says Ubisoft Montreal Head, Games Industry International, 11 April 2013, available at: http://www.gamesindustry.biz/articles/2013-04-10-no-room-for-b-games-says-ubisoft-montreal-head; Ubisoft Financial Report 2011, available at: https://www.ubisoftgroup.com/comsite_common/en-US/images/2467tcm9927495.pdf Ubisoft Financial Report 2012, available at: https://www.ubisoftgroup.com/comsite_common/en-US/images/Annual_Report_2012tcm9956562.pdf

Genevieve Ross/AP Images for Ubisoft

4.2 Empowerment

Another way of redesigning intra-organizational processes is through empowerment. **Empowering workers** means permanently passing decision-making authority and responsibility from managers to workers. For workers to be fully empowered, companies must give them the information and resources they need to make and carry out good decisions and then reward them for taking individual initiative.[31] Unfortunately, this doesn't happen often enough. As Michael Schrage, author and MIT researcher, wrote:

> *A warehouse employee can see on the intranet that a shipment is late but has no authority to accelerate its delivery. A project manager knows—and can mathematically demonstrate—that a seemingly minor spec change will bust both her budget and her schedule. The spec must be changed anyway. An airline reservations agent tells the Executive Platinum Premier frequent flier that first class appears wide open for an upgrade. However, the airline's yield management software won't permit any upgrades until just four hours before the flight, frequent fliers (and reservations) be damned. In all these cases, the employee has access to valuable information. Each one possesses the "knowledge" to do the job better. But the knowledge and information are irrelevant and useless. Knowledge isn't power; the ability to act on knowledge is power.*[32]

When workers are given the proper information and resources and are allowed to make good decisions, they experience strong feelings of empowerment. **Empowerment** is a feeling of intrinsic motivation in which workers perceive their work to have meaning and perceive themselves to be competent, having an impact, and capable of self-determination.[33] Work has meaning when it is consistent with personal standards and beliefs. Workers feel competent when they believe they can perform an activity with skill. The belief that they are having an impact comes from a feeling that they can affect work outcomes. A feeling of self-determination arises from workers' belief that they have the autonomy to choose how best to do their work.

Empowerment can lead to changes in organizational processes because meaning, competence, impact, and self-determination produce empowered employees who take active, rather than passive, roles in their work.

LO5 Inter-Organizational Processes

An **inter-organizational process** is a collection of activities that occur *among companies* to transform inputs into outputs that customers value. In other words, many companies work together to create a product or service that keeps customers happy. For example, when you purchase a pair of jeans from a retail clothing chain like American Eagle, you're not just buying from American Eagle—you're also buying from a network of suppliers in other countries and from that company's sourcing team, which generates the correct fabrics and the entire line of clothing carried in American Eagle stores. That team then manufactures the first product prototypes and sends them to the company's design team for final inspection and possibly last-minute changes.

In this section, you'll explore inter-organizational processes by learning about ***5.1 modular organizations*** *and* ***5.2 virtual organizations.***[34]

Empowering workers permanently passing decision-making authority and responsibility from managers to workers by giving them the information and resources they need to make and carry out good decisions

Empowerment feelings of intrinsic motivation, in which workers perceive their work to have impact and meaning and perceive themselves to be competent and capable of self-determination

Inter-organizational process a collection of activities that take place among companies to transform inputs into outputs that customers value

Modular organization an organization that outsources noncore business activities to outside companies, suppliers, specialists, or consultants

5.1 Modular Organizations

Except for the core business activities that they can perform better, faster, and more cheaply than others, **modular organizations** outsource all remaining business activities to outside companies, suppliers, specialists, or consultants. The term *modular* is used because the business activities purchased from outside companies can be added or dropped as needed, much like adding pieces to a three-dimensional puzzle. Exhibit 9.11 depicts a modular organization in which the company has chosen to keep training, human resources, sales, product design, manufacturing, customer service, research and development, and information

Exhibit 9.11 Modular Organization

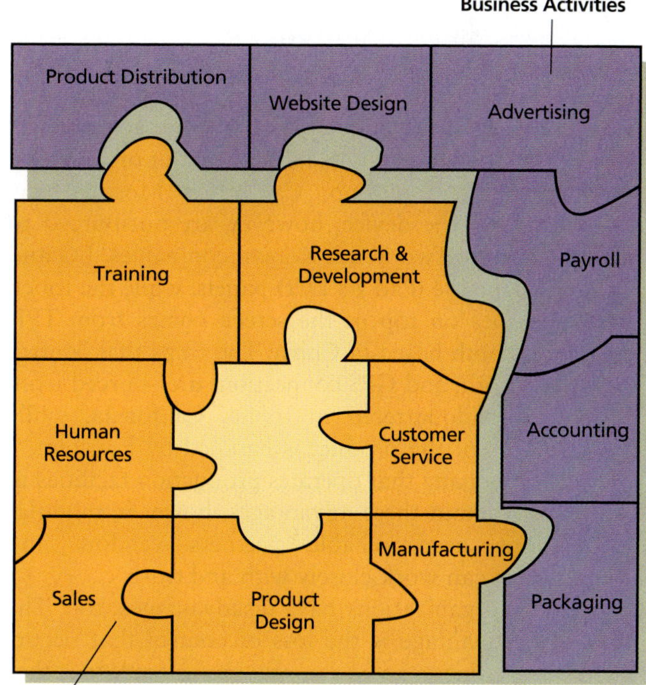

The Virtual Office

Is the virtual workplace the way of the future? Over the past decade, the number of people who participate in virtual work has increased dramatically. Indeed, it is estimated that at least 10 percent of today's workforce telecommutes from home—three times the level of 2000. The reasons for this trend? Internet technology has made it possible for many employees to perform virtual work; employees are embracing the flexibility and autonomy that telecommuting provides; and organizations are realizing higher productivity and savings in labour and real estate costs. IBM, for example, saves $100 million a year by allowing 42 percent of its employees to work remotely. There are challenges, however, including these: employees must be helped to find the right work–life balance (i.e., to avoid working on holidays or weekends); workplace isolation must be overcome (i.e., when empoyees want advice or simply miss social interaction); the lack of face-to-face communication must be compensated for (the volume of communication may be high but not necessarily efficient); and so must the lack of visibility (the feeling that efforts are not being noticed or that it is more difficult to be promoted).

Source: J. Mulki, F. Bardhi, F. Lassk, and J. Nanavaty-Dahl, "Set Up Remote Workers to Thrive," *MIT Sloan Management Review*, October 1, 2009, http://sloanreview.mit.edu/the-magazine/articles/2009/fall/51116/set-up-remote-workers-to-thrive.

Fuse/Jupiterimages

Virtual organization an organization that is part of a network in which many companies share skills, costs, capabilities, markets, and customers to collectively solve customer problems or provide specific products or services

technology as core business activities, but has outsourced the noncore activities of product distribution, Web page design, advertising, payroll, accounting, and packaging.

Modular organizations have several advantages. First, because they pay for outsourced labour, expertise, or manufacturing capabilities only when needed, they can cost significantly less to run than traditional organizations. For example, most of the design and marketing work for Apple's iPad 2 is run out of company headquarters in Cupertino, California. Most of the components for the device, however, are outsourced to other companies. Two South Korean companies, LG and Samsung, make the iPad 2's LCD panels, while the touch panel that goes on top of the screen comes from TPK and Wintek, both based in China. The chips that control Wi-Fi, Bluetooth, and GPS connections are sourced from Broadcom, headquartered in Irvine, California, while final assembly of the product is handled by Foxconn, a Taiwanese company that operates production facilities in China.[35] To obtain these advantages, however, modular organizations need reliable partners—vendors and suppliers they can work closely with and trust.

Modular organizations have disadvantages, too. The primary disadvantage is the loss of control that occurs when key business activities are outsourced to other companies. Also, companies may reduce their competitive advantage in two ways if they mistakenly outsource a core business activity. First, as a result of competitive and technological change, the noncore business activities a company has outsourced may suddenly become the basis for competitive advantage. Second, related to that point, suppliers to whom work is outsourced can sometimes become competitors.

5.2 Virtual Organizations

In contrast to modular organizations, in which the inter-organizational process revolves around a central company, a **virtual organization** is part of a network in which many companies share skills, costs, capabilities, markets, and customers with one another. Exhibit 9.12 shows a virtual organization in which, for "today," the parts of a virtual company consist of product design, purchasing, manufacturing, advertising, and information technology. Unlike modular organizations, in which the outside organizations are tightly linked to one central company, virtual organizations work with some companies in the network alliance but not with all. So, whereas a puzzle with various pieces is a fitting metaphor for a modular organization, a potluck dinner is an appropriate metaphor for a virtual organization. All participants bring their finest food dish but eat only what they want.

Another difference is that the working relationships between modular organizations and outside companies tend to be more stable and longer lasting than the shorter, often temporary relationships found among the virtual companies in a network alliance. The composition of a virtual organization is always changing. The combination

Exhibit 9.12 Virtual Organizations

© Mike Powell/Lifesize/Jupiterimages

of network partners that a virtual corporation has at any one time depends on the expertise needed to solve a particular problem or provide a specific product or service. This is why the businessperson in the network organization shown in the photo is saying, "Today, I'll have ..." Tomorrow, the business could want something completely different. In this sense, the term *virtual organization* means the organization that exists "at the moment." Virtual organizations have a number of advantages. They let companies share costs. And because members can quickly combine their efforts to meet customers' needs, they are fast and flexible.

As with modular organizations, a disadvantage of virtual organizations is that once work has been outsourced, it can be difficult to control the quality of work done by network partners. The greatest disadvantage, however, is that tremendous managerial skills are required to make a network of independent organizations work well together, especially since their relationships tend to be short and based on a single task or project. Virtual organizations are using two methods to solve this problem. The first is to use a *broker*. In traditional, hierarchical organizations, managers plan, organize, and control. But with the horizontal, inter-organizational processes that characterize virtual organizations, the job of a broker is to create and assemble the knowledge, skills, and resources from different companies for outside parties, such as customers.[36] The second way to make networks of virtual organizations more manageable is to use a *virtual organization agreement* that, somewhat like a contract, specifies the schedules, responsibilities, costs, payouts, and liabilities for participating organizations.

Go online at
www.nelson.com/4ltrpress/icanmgmt2
And access the essential Study Tools online for this chapter:

- **Flashcards**, to help you study
- **Interactive Quizzes**, to test your knowledge
- **Audio Chapter Summaries**, for chapter review
- **Crossword Puzzles and Beat the Clock**, to review key terms
- **What Would You Do? Cases**, for applying your knowledge to real-life situations
- **Self Assessments**, to learn about what kind of manager you are
- **Videos and Media Quizzing**, where you can watch a video about a real-life company and test yourself on what you've learned

Be sure to consult the Chapter Review Card at the back of the textbook.

10 Leading Teams

LEARNING OUTCOMES

LO1 Explain the good and bad of using teams.

LO2 Recognize and understand the different kinds of teams.

LO3 Understand the general characteristics of work teams.

LO4 Explain how to enhance work team effectiveness.

Why Use Work Teams?

Two-thirds of executives in Canada believe they significantly improve their effectiveness by establishing work teams.[1] But this has only been the case for the last 25 years. Procter & Gamble and Cummins Engine began using teams in 1962 and 1973 respectively, but many international companies—including Boeing, Caterpillar, Ford Motor Company, and General Electric—did not set up their first teams until the 1980s.[2] In other words, teams are a relatively new phenomenon, and there's still much for organizations to learn about managing them.

A **work team** consists of a small number of people with complementary skills who hold themselves mutually accountable for pursuing a common purpose, achieving performance goals, and improving interdependent work processes.[3] Although work teams are not the answer for every situation or organization, if the right teams are used properly and in the right settings, they can dramatically improve company performance and instill a sense of vitality in the workplace that is otherwise difficult to achieve.

LO1 The Good and Bad of Using Teams

Let's begin our discussion of teams by learning about ***1.1 the advantages of teams, 1.2 the disadvantages of teams,*** *and* ***1.3 when to use and not use teams.***

1.1 The Advantages of Teams

Companies are making greater use of teams because they have been shown to improve customer satisfaction, product and service quality, employee job satisfaction, and decision making.[4] Teams help businesses increase *customer satisfaction* in several ways. For example, work teams can be trained to meet the needs of specific customers. Hewitt Associates, a consulting firm with offices in Calgary, Montreal, Toronto, and Vancouver, manages benefits administration for hundreds of multinational client firms. To ensure customer satisfaction, Hewitt re-engineered its customer service centre and created specific teams to handle benefits-related questions posed by employees of specific client organizations.[5] Businesses also create problem-solving teams and employee involvement teams to study ways to improve overall customer satisfaction and make recommendations for improvements. Teams like these typically meet on a weekly or monthly basis.

Teams also help firms improve *product and service quality* in several ways.[6] In contrast to traditional organizational structures where management is responsible for organizational outcomes and performance, teams take direct responsibility for the *quality* of the products and services they produce. At Whole Foods, a supermarket chain with stores in Vancouver and Toronto that sells groceries and health foods, the 10 teams that manage each store are responsible for store quality and performance; they are also directly accountable in that the size of their team bonus depends on the store's performance. Productive teams get an extra $1.50 to $2.00 per hour in every other paycheque.[7]

Another reason for using teams is that teamwork often leads to increased *job satisfaction*.[8] Teamwork can be more satisfying than traditional work because it gives workers a chance to improve their skills. This is often accomplished through **cross-training**, in which team members are taught how to do all or most of the jobs performed by the other team members. The advantage for the organization is that cross-training allows a team to function normally when one member is absent, quits, or is transferred. The advantage for workers is that cross-training broadens their skills and increases their capabilities while also making their work more varied and interesting. A second reason why teamwork is satisfying is that work teams often receive proprietary business information that is available only to managers at most companies. For example, Whole Foods has an "open books, open door, open people" philosophy.[9] Team members are given full access to their store's financial information and everyone's salaries, including those of the store manager and the CEO.[10] Team members also gain job satisfaction from unique leadership responsibilities that are not typically available in traditional organizations. For example, rotating leadership among team members can lead to more participation and cooperation in team decision making and to improved team performance.[11]

Finally, teams share many of the advantages of group decision making discussed in Chapter 5. For instance, because team members possess different knowledge, skills, abilities, and experiences, a team is able to view problems from multiple perspectives. This diversity of viewpoints increases the likelihood that team decisions will solve the underlying causes of problems and not just address the symptoms. Carol Stephenson, Dean of the Richard Ivey School of Business, found that adding women to diversify senior teams and boards brought a different perspective to decision making. Here she quoted the poet Ezra Pound, who once said that "when two men in business always agree, one of them is unnecessary."[12]

Because increased knowledge and information are available to teams, it is easier for them to generate more alternative solutions, something that is vital to improving the quality of decisions. Also, because team members are involved in decision making, they are likely to be more committed to making those decisions work. In short, teams can do a much better job than individuals in two important steps of the decision-making process: defining the problem and generating alternative solutions.

Work team a small number of people with complementary skills who hold themselves mutually accountable for pursuing a common purpose, achieving performance goals, and improving interdependent work processes

Cross-training training team members to do all or most of the jobs performed by the other team members

Social loafing behaviour in which team members withhold their efforts and fail to perform their share of the work

Groupthink when members of highly cohesive groups feel intense pressure not to disagree with one another so that the group can approve a proposed solution

1.2 The Disadvantages of Teams

Teams can significantly improve customer satisfaction, product and service quality, speed and efficiency in product development, employee job satisfaction, and decision making. However, using teams does not guarantee these positive outcomes. In fact, if you have ever participated in an in-class team project, you are probably already aware of some of the disadvantages of work teams: initially high turnover, social loafing, and the problems associated with group decision making.

> **Using teams does not guarantee positive outcomes.**

The first disadvantage of work teams is *initially high turnover.* Teams aren't for everyone, and some workers balk at the responsibility, effort, and learning required in team settings.

Social loafing occurs when workers withhold their efforts and fail to perform their share of the work.[13] A 19th-century French engineer named Maximilian Ringlemann first documented social loafing when he found that one person pulling on a rope alone exerted an average of 63 kilograms of force on the rope. In groups of three, the average force dropped to 53 kilograms per person. In groups of eight, the average dropped to just 31 kilograms per person. Ringlemann concluded that the larger the team, the smaller the individual effort. In fact, social loafing is more likely to occur in larger groups, where identifying and monitoring the efforts of individual team members can be difficult.[14] In other words, social loafers count on being able to blend into the background, where their lack of effort isn't easily spotted. From team-based class projects, most students in Canadian universities and colleges already know about social loafers, or "slackers," who contribute poor, little, or no work whatsoever. Not surprisingly, a study of 250 student teams found that the most talented students are typically the least satisfied with teamwork because they have to carry slackers and do a disproportionate share of their team's work. Perceptions of fairness are negatively related to the extent of social loafing within teams.[15]

Finally, teams share many of the *disadvantages of group decision making* discussed in Chapter 5, such as **groupthink**. In *groupthink*, members of highly cohesive groups feel intense pressure not to disagree with one another so that the group can approve a proposed solution. Because groupthink restricts discussion and leads to consideration of a limited number of alternative solutions, it usually results in poor decisions. Also, team decision making takes considerable time, and team meetings can often be unproductive and inefficient. Another possible pitfall is *minority domination*, where just one or two people dominate team discussions, restricting consideration of different problem definitions and alternative solutions. Finally, team members may not feel accountable for the decisions and actions taken by the team.

1.3 When to Use Teams

As the two previous subsections made clear, teams have significant advantages *and* disadvantages. Therefore, the question is not *whether* to use teams, but *when* and *where* to use them for maximum benefit and minimum cost. As Doug Johnson, associate director at the Center for the Study of Work Teams, puts it: "Teams are a means to an end, not an end in themselves."[16] Exhibit 10.1 provides additional guidelines on when and when not to use teams.[17]

Is this your team at school?

Exhibit 10.1 When to Use and When Not to Use Teams

Use Teams When . . .	Don't Use Teams When . . .
✓ there is a clear, engaging reason or purpose.	✗ there isn't a clear, engaging reason or purpose.
✓ the job can't be done unless people work together.	✗ the job can be done by people working independently.
✓ rewards can be provided for teamwork and team performance.	✗ rewards are provided for individual effort and performance.
✓ ample resources are available.	✗ the necessary resources are not available.
✓ teams will have clear authority to manage and change how work gets done.	✗ management will continue to monitor and influence how work gets done.

Source: R. Wageman, "Critical Success Factors for Creating Superb Self-Managing Teams," *Organizational Dynamics* 26, no. 1 (1997): 49–61.

First, teams should be used when there is a clear and engaging reason or purpose for using them. Too many companies use teams because they're popular or because the companies assume that teams can fix all problems. Teams are much more likely to succeed if they know why they exist and what they are supposed to accomplish; teams are more likely to fail if they don't.

Second, teams should be used when the job can't be done unless people work together. This typically means that teams are needed when tasks are complex, require multiple perspectives, or require repeated interactions with others. If tasks are simple and don't require multiple perspectives or repeated interaction with others, teams should not be used.[18] For instance, production levels dropped by 23 percent when Levi Strauss introduced teams in its factories. Levi Strauss's mistake was assuming that teams were appropriate for garment work, where workers perform single, specialized tasks, such as sewing zippers or belt loops. Because this kind of work does not require interaction with others, Levi Strauss unwittingly pitted the faster workers against the slower workers on each team. Arguments, infighting, insults, and threats were common between faster workers and the slower workers who held back team performance. One seamstress had to physically restrain an angry coworker who was about to throw a chair at a faster worker who was constantly nagging her about her slow pace.[19]

Third, teams should be used when rewards can be provided for teamwork and team performance. Rewards that depend on team performance rather than individual performance are the key to rewarding team behaviours and efforts. You'll read more about team rewards later in the chapter, but for now it's enough to know that if the type of reward (individual versus team) is not matched to the type of performance (individual versus team), teams won't work. Research carried out at Queen's University in Kingston, Ontario, found that team rewards for virtual teams work very effectively and should become "best practices."[20]

LO2 Kinds of Teams

Let's continue our discussion of teams by learning about the different kinds of teams that companies use to make themselves more competitive. *We look first at*

Factors That Encourage People to Withhold Effort in Teams

1. **The presence of someone with expertise.** Team members will withhold effort when another team member is highly qualified to make a decision or comment on an issue.
2. **The presentation of a compelling argument.** Team members will withhold effort if the arguments for a course of action are very persuasive or similar to their own thinking.
3. **Lacking confidence in one's ability to contribute.** Team members will withhold effort if they are unsure about their ability to contribute to discussions, activities, or decisions. This is especially so for high-profile decisions.
4. **An unimportant or meaningless decision.** Team members will withhold effort by mentally withdrawing or adopting a "who cares" attitude if decisions don't affect them or their units, or if they don't see a connection between their efforts and their team's successes or failures.
5. **A dysfunctional decision-making climate.** Team members will withhold effort if other team members are frustrated or indifferent or if a team is floundering or disorganized.

Sources: P. W. Mulvey, J. F. Veiga, and P. M. Elsass, "When Teammates Raise a White Flag," *Academy of Management Executive* 10, no. 1 (1996): 40–49. See also: Powell, A., Galvin, J., & Piccoli, G. (2006). "Antecedents to team member commitment from near and far: A comparison between collocated and virtual teams," *Information Technology & People* Vol. 19 Iss: 4, pp. 299–322 for reasons that might have people withhold efforts using Google Docs or Drop Box for team projects in your school.

Traditional work group a group composed of two or more people who work together to achieve a shared goal

Employee involvement team team that provides advice or makes suggestions to management concerning specific issues

2.1 how teams differ in terms of autonomy, which is the key dimension that makes one team different from another, and then at 2.2 some special kinds of teams.

2.1 Autonomy, the Key Dimension

Teams can be classified in a number of ways, such as permanent or temporary, functional or cross-functional. However, studies indicate that the key differences among teams relate to the amount of autonomy they possess.[21] *Autonomy* is the degree to which workers have the discretion, freedom, and independence to decide how and when to do their work.

Exhibit 10.2 shows how five kinds of teams differ in terms of autonomy. Moving left to right across the autonomy continuum at the top of the exhibit, traditional work groups and employee involvement groups have the least autonomy, semiautonomous work groups have more autonomy, and, finally, self-managing teams and self-designing teams have the most autonomy. Moving from bottom to top along the left side of the exhibit, note that the number of responsibilities given to each kind of team increases directly with its autonomy. Let's review each of these kinds of teams and their autonomy and responsibilities in more detail.

The smallest amount of autonomy is found in **traditional work groups**, where two or more people work together to achieve a shared goal. In these groups, workers are responsible for doing the work or executing the task, but they do not have direct responsibility for or control over their work. Workers report to managers who are responsible for their performance and who have the authority to hire and fire them, make job assignments, and control resources.

Employee involvement teams, which have somewhat more autonomy, meet on company time on

Exhibit 10.2 Team Autonomy Continuum

Low Team Autonomy ⟷ High Team Autonomy

Responsibilities	Traditional Work Groups	Employee Involvement Groups	Semi-Autonomous Work Groups	Self-Managing Teams	Self-Designing Teams
Control Design of					
Team					✓
Tasks					✓
Membership					✓
Production/Service Tasks					
Make decisions				✓	✓
Solve problems				✓	✓
Major Production/Service Tasks					
Make decisions			✓	✓	✓
Solve problems			✓	✓	✓
Information			✓	✓	✓
Give Advice/Make Suggestions		✓	✓	✓	✓
Execute Task	✓	✓	✓	✓	✓

Sources: R.D. Banker, J.M. Field, R.G. Schroeder, & K.K. Sinha, "Impact of Work Teams on Manufacturing Performance: A Longitudinal Field Study," *Academy of Management Journal* 39 (1996): 867–890; J.R. Hackman, "The Psychology of Self-Management in Organizations," in *Psychology and Work: Productivity, Change, and Employment*, ed. M.S. Pallak & T. Perlof (Washington, DC: American Psychological Association), 85–136.

a weekly or monthly basis to provide advice or make suggestions to management concerning specific issues such as plant safety, customer relations, or product quality.[22] Although they offer advice and suggestions, they do not have the authority to make decisions. Membership on these teams is often voluntary, but members may be selected because of their expertise. The idea behind employee involvement teams is that the people closest to the problem or situation are best able to recommend solutions.

Semiautonomous work groups not only provide advice and suggestions to management but also have the authority to make decisions and solve problems related to the major tasks required to produce a product or service. Semiautonomous groups regularly receive information about budgets, work quality and performance, and competitors' products. Furthermore, members of semiautonomous work groups are typically cross-trained in a number of different skills and tasks. In short, semiautonomous work groups give employees the authority to make decisions that are typically made by supervisors and managers.

That authority is not complete, however. Managers still play a role—albeit a much reduced one—in supporting the work of semiautonomous work groups. In these groups, managers ask good questions, provide resources, and facilitate performance of group goals.

Self-managing teams differ from semiautonomous work groups in that team members manage and control *all* of the major tasks that are *directly related* to production of a product or service without first getting approval from management. This includes managing and controlling the acquisition of materials, making a product or providing a service, and ensuring timely delivery.

A **self-designing team** has all the characteristics of a self-managing team, but it also controls and changes the design of the team itself, the tasks it does, and how and when it does them, as well the membership of the team.

2.2 Special Kinds of Teams

Companies are increasingly using several other kinds of teams that can't easily be categorized in terms of autonomy: cross-functional teams, virtual teams, and project teams. Depending on how these teams are designed, they can be low or high in autonomy.

Cross-functional teams are composed of employees from different functional areas of the organization.[23] Because their members have different functional backgrounds, education, and experience, these teams usually tackle problems from multiple perspectives and generate more ideas and alternative solutions, all of which are especially important when trying to innovate or do creative problem solving.[24] Cross-functional teams can be used almost anywhere in an organization and are often used in conjunction with matrix and product organizational structures (see Chapter 9). They can entail part-time/temporary team assignments or full-time/long-term ones.

Cessna, which manufactures airplanes using engines from Pratt & Whitney Canada, created cross-functional teams for purchasing parts. With workers from purchasing, manufacturing engineering, quality engineering, product design engineering, reliability engineering, product support, and finance, each team addressed make-versus-buy decisions (i.e., make it themselves or buy from others), sourcing (who to buy from), internal plant and quality improvements, and the external training of suppliers to reduce costs and increase quality.[25]

Virtual teams are groups of geographically and/or organizationally dispersed coworkers who use a combination of telecommunications and information technologies to accomplish an organizational task.[26] Virtual teams rarely meet face-to-face; instead, the members use e-mail, videoconferencing, and group communication software. MySQL, an open source database software developer, has 320 workers in 25 countries, strewn from Montreal to Ukraine. They communicate with one another using

Semiautonomous work group a group that has the authority to make decisions and solve problems related to the major tasks of producing a product or service

Self-managing team a team that manages and controls all of the major tasks of producing a product or service. Students will also see this referred to as self-directed work teams (see the highlighted box below for an example).

Self-designing team a team that has the characteristics of self-managing teams but also controls team design, work tasks, and team membership

Cross-functional team a team composed of employees from different functional areas of the organization

Virtual team a team composed of geographically and/or organizationally dispersed coworkers who use telecommunication and information technologies to accomplish an organizational task

Self-Directed Teams

Pixland/Jupiterimages

Self-directed teams (also known as self-managing teams) can have a high failure rate. In a study carried out at a western Canadian university, on a team project that was worth 40 percent of the final grade, each student was required to contribute to the final self-directed team project. Each team was to design and re-engineer a workplace process. The study found that despite being told specifically that they all must contribute, several students did not perform their roles adequately, conflict was allowed to escalate to disruptive levels, and team efficiency was extremely low (does this sound like one of your student teams?).

On the other hand, research has shown that for Canadian companies such as Dofasco, Steel Case Equipment, LOF Glass, and Laurel Steel, results have been positive. These studies found increased flexibility, productivity gains, improved quality, increased commitment, and improved customer service. The key, says, Michael Piczak, is to train and support management for the implementation of the new self-directed work team process. Students at university may still be learning and acquiring these valuable skills.

Sources: Coetzer, G.H. & Trimble, R. T. (2010). "An Empirical examination of the relationship between adult attention deficit, cooperative conflict management and efficacy for working in teams," *American Journal of Business* (25) 1, 23–33; M.W. Piczak, "Self-Directed Work Teams: An Implementation Guide," http://www.spin.mohawkcollege.ca/courses/pizcakm/oh&s&sdwts.ppt.

a company chat room (or Skype when live voice conversations are necessary) and are accountable for completing tasks on a program called Worklog. Oleksandr Byelkin lives in Lugansk, Ukraine; not only does he have poor phone service, but he also doesn't speak English very well. Even MySQL's holiday party was online.[27]

Virtual teams can be employee involvement teams, self-managing teams, or nearly any kind of team discussed in this chapter. Virtual teams are often (but not necessarily) temporary teams that have been set up to accomplish a specific task.[28] Ike Hall, an adjunct professor at Athabasca University's online MBA program (the largest MBA program in Canada), indicates that team projects and interactions carried out in a virtual environment can produce excellent results. Experience working in this manner can be very useful, given that more and more Canadian businesses will require executives who can utilize virtual teams effectively.[29]

The principal advantage of virtual teams is their flexibility. Employees can work with one another regardless of physical location, time zone, or organizational affiliation.[30] Because the team members don't meet in a physical location, virtual teams also find it much easier to include other key stakeholders such as suppliers and customers. Virtual teams also have certain efficiency advantages over traditional teams. Because the teammates do not meet face-to-face, a virtual team typically requires a smaller time commitment than a traditional team does.[31]

A drawback to virtual teams is that the team members must learn to express themselves in new contexts.[32] The give-and-take that naturally occurs in face-to-face meetings is more difficult to achieve through videoconferencing or other methods of virtual teaming. Indeed, several studies

Good Tip!

Tips for Managing Successful Virtual Teams

1. Select people who are self-starters and strong communicators.
2. Keep the team focused by establishing clear, specific goals and by explaining the consequences and importance of meeting these goals.
3. Provide frequent feedback so that team members can measure their progress.
4. Keep team interactions upbeat and action-oriented by expressing appreciation for good work and completed tasks.
5. Personalize the virtual team by periodically bringing team members together and by encouraging team members to share information with one another about their personal lives. This is especially important when the virtual team first forms.
6. Improve communication through increased telephone calls, e-mails, and Internet messaging, and videoconference sessions.
7. Periodically ask team members how well the team is working and what can be done to improve performance.
8. Empower virtual teams so that they have the discretion, freedom, and independence to decide how and when to accomplish their jobs.

Sources: W. F. Cascio, "Managing a Virtual Workplace," *Academy of Management Executive* 14 (2000): 81–90; B. Kirkman, B. Rosen, P. Tesluk, and C. Gibson, "The Impact of Team Empowerment on Virtual Team Performance: The Moderating Role of Face-to-Face Interaction," *Academy of Management Journal* 47 (2004): 175–192; S. Furst, M. Reeves, B. Rosen, and R. Blackburn, "Managing the Life Cycle of Virtual Teams," *Academy of Management Executive* (May 2004): 6–20; C. Solomon, "Managing Virtual Teams," *Workforce* 80 (June 2001): 60; Gazor, H. "A Literature Review on Challenges of Virtual Team's Leadership" *Journal of Sociological Research* Vol 3, No 2, (2012): 69–73.

have shown that physical proximity enhances information processing in teams.[33] To minimize these problems, some companies bring virtual team members physically together on a regular basis.

Project teams are created to complete specific, one-time projects or tasks within a limited time.[34] They are often used to develop new products, significantly improve existing products, roll out new information systems, or build new factories or offices. The project team is typically led by a project manager who bears the overall responsibility for planning, staffing, and managing the team, which usually includes employees from different functional areas. Effective project teams demand both individual and collective responsibility.[35] One advantage of project teams is that drawing employees from different functional areas can reduce or eliminate communication barriers. As long as team members feel free to express their ideas, thoughts, and concerns, free-flowing communication encourages cooperation among separate departments and typically speeds up the design process.[36]

Another advantage of project teams is their flexibility. When projects are finished, project team members either move on to the next project or return to their functional units. At BCIT (which stands for "Being Crammed into Teams"), teamwork is a big deal and students take the lessons to heart. When your school project team breaks up, and you continue on other team tasks, you take good experiences of what *to do* and what *not to do* forward into other university or college student projects and, eventually, into the workplace. As another example, publication of this book required designers, editors, page compositors, and Web designers, among others. When the task was finished, these people applied their skills to other textbook projects. Because of this flexibility, project teams are often used with the matrix organizational designs discussed in Chapter 9.

Managing Work Teams

"Why did I ever let you talk me into teams? They're nothing but trouble."[37] Lots of managers have this reaction after making the move to teams. Many don't realize that this reaction is normal, both for them and for workers. In fact, such a reaction is characteristic of the *storming* stage of team development (see Section 3.5). Managers who are familiar with these stages, and with other important characteristics of teams, will be better prepared to manage the changes that are sure to occur when companies make the switch to team-based structures. A University of Edmonton study found that a mandatory team experience, one that was case-based and that involved all of the students registered in the university's Faculties of Health, produced highly useful skills. The students formed interprofessional student teams (nursing, physiotherapy, medicine, diagnostic technology), where they learned team skills and specific information about how to interact with the other professions. In this way they gained knowledge about the roles, knowledge, and contributions that could be made by professions other than their own.[38]

Project team a team created to complete specific, one-time projects or tasks within a limited time

Norms informally agreed-on standards that regulate team behaviour

LO3 Work Team Characteristics

Understanding the characteristics of work teams is essential for making teams an effective part of an organization. *Therefore, in this section you'll learn about* ***3.1 team norms, 3.2 team cohesiveness, 3.3 team size, 3.4 team conflict,*** *and* ***3.5 the stages of team development.***

3.1 Team Norms

Over time, teams develop **norms**, which are informally agreed-upon standards that regulate team behaviour.[39] Norms are valuable because they let team members know what is expected of them. At Nucor Steel (which purchased Harris Steel of Canada for $1.07 billion in 2007), work groups expect their members to get to work on time. To reinforce this norm, anyone who is late to work will not receive the team bonus for that day (assuming the team is productive). A worker who is more than 30 minutes late will not receive the team bonus for the entire week. Losing a bonus matters at Nucor because work group bonuses can easily double a worker's take-home pay.[40]

Studies indicate that norms are one of the most powerful influences on work behaviour because they regulate the everyday actions that allow teams to function effectively. Effective work teams develop norms relating to the quality and timeliness of job performance, absenteeism, safety, and expression of ideas. Team norms are often associated with positive outcomes, such as stronger organizational commitment, more trust in management, and stronger job and organizational satisfaction.[41] A recent study compared business students from Canada with business students from another country and found that the norms exhibited by Canadian students demonstrated different ethical attitudes toward questionable business practices at the individual level. Social norms in Canada, compared to those of other countries, were found to be a factor.[42]

NASA Goddard Space Flight Center

Cohesiveness the extent to which team members are attracted to a team and motivated to remain in it

Norms can also influence team behaviour in negative ways. For example, most people would agree that the following are negative behaviours: damaging organizational property; saying or doing something to hurt someone at work; intentionally doing one's work badly, incorrectly, or slowly; griping about coworkers; deliberately breaking rules; or doing something to harm the company. A study of workers from 34 teams in 20 different organizations found that teams with negative norms strongly influenced their team members to engage in these negative behaviours. In fact, the longer individuals were members of a team with negative norms and the more often they interacted with their teammates, the more likely they were to engage in negative behaviours. Since team norms typically develop early in the life of a team, these results indicate how important it is for teams to establish positive norms from the outset.[43] Results from a recent study of female MBA graduates suggest that while Canadian women have similar career profiles to men, women still lag behind their male counterparts after graduation. At the same time, women encounter intractable career barriers in the form of negative norms at both the individual level and the organizational level.[44] Negative norms are something we must continue to combat, starting in classrooms. As investment oracle Warren Buffett stated in a 2013 interview with Belinda Gates: "50% of the talent of the country we pushed off in a corner for almost 200 years ... We still have a way to go."[45] His words echo findings that were presented to the World Economic Forum in the 2012 Gender Gap Report.[46] Again, we owe it to Canada, and to the female students in our schools, to ensure that these negative norms do not continue here or in the rest of the world.

{ Studies indicate that norms are one of the most powerful influences on work behaviour. }

3.2 Team Cohesiveness

Cohesiveness is another important characteristic of work teams. **Cohesiveness** is the extent to which team members are attracted to a team and motivated to remain in it.[47] The level of cohesiveness in a group is important for several reasons. To start, cohesive groups have a better chance of retaining their members. As a result, cohesive groups typically experience lower turnover.[48] In addition, team cohesiveness promotes cooperative behaviour, generosity, and a willingness on the part of team members to assist one another.[49] When team cohesiveness is high, team members are more motivated to contribute to the team because they want to gain the approval of other team members. Studies have established clearly that for these reasons and others, cohesive teams consistently perform better.[50] Furthermore, cohesive teams quickly achieve high levels of performance. By contrast, teams low in cohesion take much longer to reach the same levels of performance.[51]

Watch out for situations where the team members' goals conflict with those of the organization. When this happens, team cohesiveness can lead to weak performance. Take, for instance, the recent NHL lockout that ended in 2013. The players were highly cohesive (as expected of a sports team), but their goals were very different from the owners'. The result, fully to be expected, was very low productivity—no teams played. Much the same happens with highly cohesive union groups, where productivity declines because the team's goals diverge from those of the organization.

To promote team cohesiveness, first, make sure that all team members are present at team meetings and activities. Team cohesiveness suffers when members are allowed to withdraw from the team and miss team meetings and events.[52] Second, create additional opportunities for teammates to work together by rearranging work schedules and creating common workspaces. When task interdependence is high and team members have plenty of chances to work together, team cohesiveness tends to increase.[53] Third, engaging in nonwork activities as a team can help build cohesion. At a company where teams put in extraordinarily long hours coding computer software, the software teams maintained cohesion by doing "fun stuff" together. Team leader Tammy Urban says: "We went on team outings at least once a week. We'd play darts, shoot pool. Teams work best when you get to know each other outside of work—what people's interests are, who they are. Personal connections go a long way when you're developing complex applications in our kind of time frames."[54] Finally, companies build team cohesiveness by making employees feel that they are part of a special organization. For example, all the new hires at Disney World are required to take a course titled "Traditions One," where they learn the traditions and history of the Walt Disney Company (including the names of the seven dwarfs!). The purpose of Traditions One is to instill team pride in working for Disney.

3.3 Team Size

The relationship between team size and performance appears to be curvilinear. Very small or very large teams may not perform as well as medium-sized teams. For most teams, the right size is six to nine members.[55] This size is conducive to high team cohesion, which has a positive effect on team performance. A team of this size is small enough for the team members to get to know one another and for each member to have an opportunity to contribute in a meaningful way to the team's success. But at the same time, the team is large enough to take advantage of team

Grant Halverson/Getty Images

members' diverse skills, knowledge, and perspectives. Finally, it is easier to instill a sense of responsibility and mutual accountability in teams of this size.[56]

By contrast, when teams get too large, team members find it difficult to get to know one another, and the team may splinter into smaller subgroups. When this occurs, subgroups sometimes argue and disagree, weakening overall team cohesion. As teams grow, there is also a greater chance of *minority domination,* where just a few team members dominate team discussions. Even if minority domination doesn't occur, larger groups may not have time for all team members to share their input. And when team members feel that their contributions are unimportant or not needed, the result is less involvement, effort, and accountability to the team.[57] Large teams also face logistical problems such as finding an appropriate time or place to meet. Finally, social loafing is much more common in large teams.

Team performance can also suffer when a team is too small. Teams with just a few people may lack the diversity of skills and knowledge found in larger teams. Also, teams that are too small are unlikely to gain the advantages of team decision making (i.e., multiple perspectives, generating more ideas and alternative solutions, stronger commitment) found in larger teams.

What signs indicate that a team's size needs to be changed? If decisions are taking too long, if the team is having difficulty making decisions or taking action, if a few members dominate the team, if team members lack commitment, or if their efforts are weak, chances are the team is too big. By contrast, if a team is having difficulty coming up with ideas or generating solutions, or if the team does not have the expertise to address a specific problem, chances are the team is too small.

Overall, team size is an important characteristic of successful teams. As much as we might not like teams, learning to work with (and within) teams is required for success in the business world.[58]

3.4 Team Conflict

Conflict and disagreement are inevitable in most teams. But this shouldn't surprise anyone. From time to time, people who work together are going to disagree about what and how things get done. What causes conflict in teams? Although almost anything can lead to conflict—casual remarks that unintentionally offend a team member, or fighting over scarce resources—the primary cause of team conflict is disagreement over team goals and priorities.[59] Other common causes of team conflict include disagreements over task-related issues, interpersonal incompatibilities, and simple fatigue.

The key to dealing with team conflict is not avoiding it, but rather making sure that the team experiences the right *kind* of conflict. In Chapter 5, you learned about *c-type conflict*, or *cognitive conflict*, which focuses on problem-related differences of opinion, and *a-type conflict*, or *affective conflict*, which refers to the emotional reactions that can arise when disagreements become personal rather than professional.[60] Cognitive conflict is strongly associated with improvements in team performance, whereas affective conflict is strongly associated with decreases in team performance.[61]

With cognitive conflict, team members disagree because their different experiences and expertise lead them to different views of the problem and its solutions. Professors often require that teams come up with three alternatives and then ask students to choose the best one. We deliberately introduce conflict with such requests. Indeed, managers who participated on teams that emphasized cognitive conflict described their teammates as "smart," "team players," and the "best in the business." They described their teams as "open," "fun," and "productive." One manager summed up the positive attitude that team members had about cognitive conflict

How to Have a Good Flight

1. Work with more information to make discussion productive rather than contentious.
2. Generate several alternative solutions. Two solutions will generate debate. More than two will generate productive discussion.
3. Establish common goals.
4. Use your sense of humour.
5. Create and maintain a balance of power.
6. Do not force consensus.

Source: K. M. Eisenhard, J. L. Kahwajy, & L. J. Bourgeois III, "How Management Teams Can Have a Good Fight," *Harvard Business Review* 75.4 (July–August 1997): 77–85.

by saying, "We scream a lot, then laugh, and then resolve the issue."[62] Thus, cognitive conflict is also characterized by a willingness to examine, compare, and reconcile differences to produce the best possible solution. We need to do this to come up with the best answer. But we also must learn to do it in a constructive, diplomatic, and tactful manner. Critique is not criticism.

By contrast, affective conflict often results in hostility, anger, resentment, distrust, cynicism, and apathy. Managers who participated on teams that emphasized affective conflict described their teammates as "manipulative," "secretive," "burned out," and "political."[63] Not surprisingly, affective conflict can make people uncomfortable and cause them to withdraw or decrease their commitment to a team.[64] Affective conflict also lowers the satisfaction of team members; it may also lead to personal hostility between coworkers and reduce team cohesiveness.[65] Cognitive conflict is beneficial; affective conflict undermines team performance by preventing teams from engaging in the kinds of activities that are vital to team effectiveness.

To handle team conflict, first, managers need to realize that emphasizing cognitive conflict alone won't be enough. Studies have found that cognitive and affective conflicts often occur together in a given team activity. Sincere attempts to reach agreement on a difficult issue can quickly deteriorate from cognitive to affective conflict if the discussion turns personal and tempers and emotions flare. While cognitive conflict is clearly the better approach to take, efforts to engage in cognitive conflict should be managed well and checked before they deteriorate and the team becomes unproductive.

Can teams disagree and still get along? Fortunately, they can. In an attempt to study this issue, researchers examined team conflict in 12 high-tech companies. In four of those companies, work teams used cognitive conflict to address problems but did so in a way that minimized the occurrence of affective conflict.

There are several ways that teams can have a good fight.[66] First, work with more information rather than less. If data are plentiful, objective, and up-to-date, teams will focus on issues, not personalities. Second, develop multiple alternatives to enrich debate. Focusing on multiple solutions diffuses conflict by getting the team to keep searching for a better solution. Positions and opinions are naturally more flexible when there are five alternatives rather than just two. Third, establish common goals. Remember, most team conflict arises from disagreements over team goals and priorities. Therefore, common goals encourage collaboration and minimize conflict over a team's purpose. Fourth, inject humour into the workplace. Humour relieves tension, builds cohesion, and just makes being in teams fun. Fifth, maintain a balance of power by involving as many people as possible in the decision process. And sixth, resolve issues without forcing a consensus. Consensus means that everyone must agree before decisions are finalized. Also ensure you never "vote." Voting is not consensus. Consensus is discussing and agreeing. Quite often a vote is just an easy (and ineffective) way out of a tough situation. Requiring consensus gives everyone on the team veto power. Nothing gets done until everyone agrees, which, of course, is nearly impossible. As a result, insisting on consensus usually promotes affective rather than cognitive conflict. If team members can't agree after constructively discussing their options, it's better to have the team leader make the final decision. Most team members can accept the team leader's choice if they've been thoroughly involved in the decision process.

Team goals lead to much higher team performance 93 percent of the time.

Forming the first stage of team development, in which team members meet one another, form initial impressions, and begin to establish team norms

Storming the second stage of development, characterized by conflict and disagreement, in which team members disagree over what the team should do and how it should do it

3.5 Stages of Team Development

As teams develop and grow, they pass through four stages of development. As shown in Exhibit 10.3 on page 170, those stages are forming, storming, norming, and performing.[67] Although not every team passes through each of these stages, teams that do tend to be better performers.[68] This holds true even for teams composed of seasoned executives. After a period of time, however, if a team is not managed well, its performance may start to deteriorate as the team begins a process of decline and progresses through the stages of de-norming, de-storming, and de-forming.[69]

Forming is the initial stage of team development. This is the getting-acquainted stage, during which team members first meet one another, form initial impressions, and try to get a sense of what it will be like to be part of the team. Some of the first team norms will be established during this stage, as team members begin to find out what behaviours will and won't be accepted by the team. During this stage, team leaders should allow time for team members to get to know one another, set early ground rules, and begin to establish a preliminary team structure.

Conflicts and disagreements often characterize the second stage of team development, **storming**. As team members begin working together, different personalities and work styles may clash. Team members become more assertive at this stage and more willing to state opinions. This is also the stage when team members jockey for position and try to establish a favourable role for themselves on the team. In addition, team members

Exhibit 10.3 Stages of Team Development

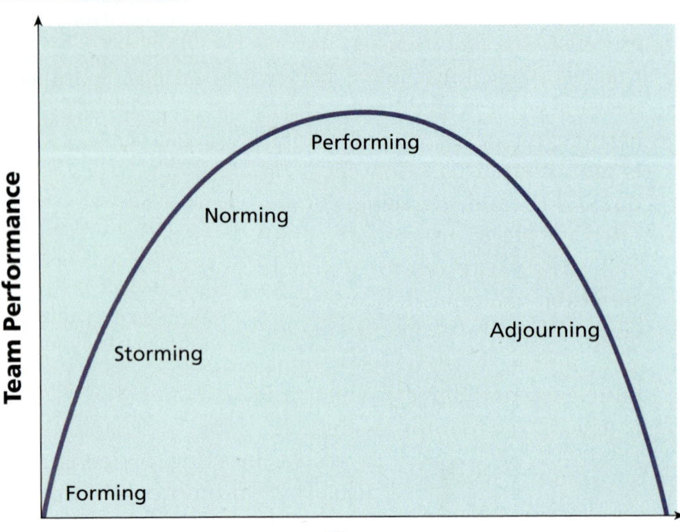

Sources: J. F. McGrew, J. G. Bilotta, and J. M. Deeney, "Software Team Formation and Decay: Extending the Standard Model for Small Groups," *Small Group Research* 30, no. 2 (1999): 209–234; B.W. Tuckman, "Development Sequence in Small Groups," *Psychological Bulletin* 63, no. 6 (1965): 384–399

Norming the third stage of team development, in which team members begin to settle into their roles, group cohesion grows, and positive team norms develop

Performing the fourth stage of team development, in which performance improves because the team has matured into an effective, fully functioning team

Adjourning the final stage of Bruce Tuckman's model of team development, in which a company wraps up the team and takes any lessons learned forward to other teams (with three important sub-stages; de-norming, de-storming, and de-forming)

are likely to disagree about what the group should do and how it should do it. Team performance is still relatively low, given that team cohesion is weak and team members are still reluctant to support one another. Since teams that get stuck in the storming stage are almost always ineffective, it is important for team leaders to focus the team on team goals and on improving team performance. Team members need to be particularly patient and tolerant with one another in this stage.

During **norming**, the third stage of team development, team members begin to settle into their roles as team members. Positive team norms will have developed by this stage, and teammates should know what to expect from one another. Petty differences should have been resolved, friendships will have developed, and group cohesion will be relatively strong. At this point, team members will have accepted team goals, be operating as a unit, and, as indicated by the increase in performance, be working together effectively. This stage can be very short and is often characterized by someone on the team saying, "I think things are finally coming together." Note, however, that teams may cycle back and forth between storming and norming several times before finally settling into norming.

In one of the last stages of team development, **performing**, performance improves because the team has finally matured into an effective, fully functioning team. At this point, members should be fully committed to the team and think of themselves as members of a team and not just as employees. Team members often become intensely loyal to one another at this stage and feel mutual accountability for team successes and failures. Trivial disagreements, which can take time and energy away from the work of the team, should be rare. At this stage, teams get a lot of work done, and it is fun to be a team member. But the team should not become complacent.

Without effective management, the team's performance may begin to decline as it passes through the stages of de-norming, de-storming, and de-forming (these three stages are also known as adjourning).[70]

Adjourning entails three important subactivities: de-norming, de-storming, and de-forming. *De-norming* provides team members with an opportunity to internalize what they have learned and to set out new objectives and new norms as they move on to other tasks and assignments (quite often with new teams). It enables them to adapt to new tasks. Also, team members need to celebrate their successes. In this regard, celebrations are a useful way to help them *de-storm* (this is important even in virtual teams).[71] Celebrations are not parties; rather, they are venues for recognizing the results that teams have achieved. *De-forming*, the final part of adjourning, allows team members to aim their sights forward and create new relationships, new communication approaches, and new interactions with other members of the organization.[72]

LO4 Enhancing Work Team Effectiveness

Making teams work is a difficult challenge. *Companies can increase the likelihood that teams will succeed by carefully managing* ***4.1 the setting of team goals and priorities*** and ***4.2 how work team members are selected, 4.3 trained, and 4.4 compensated.***[73]

4.1 Setting Team Goals and Priorities

In Chapter 5, you learned that setting specific, measurable, attainable, realistic, and timely *(i.e., S.M.A.R.T.)* goals is one of the most effective means for improving individual job performance. Fortunately, team goals also improve team performance, especially when they are *specific* and *challenging*. In fact, team goals lead to much higher team performance 93 percent of the time.[74] For example, Nucor Steel, with its Canadian affiliates, sets specific, challenging hourly goals for its production teams, each of which is comprised of first-line supervisors and production and maintenance workers. Nucor production teams have a goal of eight tons of steel per hour, and receive a 5 percent bonus for every ton over eight tons that they produce each hour. With no limit on the bonuses they can receive, Nucor's production teams produce an average of 35 to 40 tons of steel per hour![75]

Canada's RMC Teamwork Is Tops

A nine-member team from Canada's Royal Military College has beaten Sandhurst (Britain's Royal Military Academy) and West Point (US Military Academy) three years in a row. The competition includes equipment inspection, tactical boat manoeuvring, marksmanship, first aid, river crossing, wall obstacles, radio communications, and other tasks that challenge the teams to their physical and mental limits. The team trained six days a week, on top of already demanding engineering academic courses and other military duties. It competed against 38 other teams from the United States and the United Kingdom, and—for the first time—a team from the National Military Academy of Afghanistan. "I am particularly impressed with the dedication of the cadets on the team," states Captain Kevin Wright, coach of the team. "They make tremendous sacrifices for the team." Without clear teamwork, no one person can finish the course. The team is only as strong as its weakest link and only as fast as its slowest member. Teamwork is emphasized at the Royal Military College of Canada; it is ingrained in the cadets to utilize these teamwork skills in their lifelong careers in the military or in civilian life.

Source: Stefko, S. (2007). "RMC Wins at Sandhurst competition - again!" *The Maple Leaf*, 10(14). Accessed June 3, 2010, from www.forces.gc.ca/site/commun/m.-fe/article-ang.asp?id=3062

Mario Poirier/*The Maple Leaf magazine*, 23 September 2009, Vol. 12, No. 31, cover.

Setting *specific* team goals is vital to team success. One reason why is that increasing a team's performance is inherently more complex than just increasing one individual's job performance. Consider that any one team is likely to involve at least four different kinds of goals: each member's goal for the team, each member's goal for himself or herself on the team, the team's goal for each member, and the team's goal for itself.[76] Without a specific, challenging goal for the team itself (the last of the four goals listed), team members may head off in all directions while pursuing these other goals. Consequently, setting a specific, challenging goal *for the team* clarifies team priorities by providing a clear focus and purpose.

The setting of challenging team goals affects how hard team members work. In particular, challenging goals greatly reduce social loafing. When faced with reasonably difficult goals, team members necessarily expect everyone to contribute. Consequently, they are much more likely to notice and complain if a teammate isn't doing his or her share. When teammates know one another well, when team goals are specific, when team communication is good, and when teams are rewarded for team performance (discussed below), there is only a 1 in 16 chance that teammates will be social loafers.[77]

Companies and teams can take steps to ensure that team goals lead to superior team performance. One increasingly popular approach is to give teams stretch goals. *Stretch goals* are extremely ambitious goals that workers don't know how to reach.[78] The purpose of stretch goals is to achieve extraordinary improvements in performance by forcing managers and workers to throw away old, comfortable solutions and adopt radical solutions they have never used before.[79]

For stretch goals to motivate teams,[80] those teams must have a high degree of autonomy or control over how they achieve their goals. Also, they must be empowered with control over resources such as budgets, workspaces, computers, and whatever else they need to do their work. Nick Mutton, executive vice president of Four Seasons Hotels and Resorts, says that to meet tough goals, staff must be rewarded for appropriate behaviours and must feel as respected and as cared for as the guests.[81]

Structural accommodation the ability to change organizational structures, policies, and practices in order to meet stretch goals

Bureaucratic immunity the ability to make changes without first getting approval from managers or other parts of an organization

Individualism–collectivism the degree to which a person believes that people should be self-sufficient and that loyalty to one's self is more important than loyalty to team or company

Team level the average level of ability, experience, personality, or any other factor on a team

In addition, teams require structural accommodation. **Structural accommodation** entails providing teams with the ability to change organizational structures, policies, and practices if doing so will help them meet their stretch goals. Finally, successful teams have **bureaucratic immunity**. That is, they no longer have to go through the frustratingly slow process of multilevel reviews and sign-offs before making changes. Teams that have been granted bureaucratic immunity are immune from the influence of various organizational groups and are accountable only to top management. As a result, they can act quickly and even experiment with little fear of failure.

© Ryan Burke/iStockphoto.com

© AP Images/© U.P.images/iStockphoto.com

4.2 Selecting People for Teamwork

Professor Edward Lawler writes that "people are very naive about how easy it is to create a team. Teams are the Ferraris of work design. They're high performance but high maintenance and expensive."[82] He adds that teams make workplaces extremely *effective*, not just fast. They are a very good use of resources (time, people, and money). That said, it's almost impossible to have an effective work team without carefully selecting people who are suited for teamwork or for working on a particular team. A focus on teamwork (individualism/collectivism), team level, and team diversity can help companies choose the right team members.[83] We may think we can always simply choose the best players, but that is not necessarily the way to success. We are hired for those high-paying jobs once we graduate from university so that we can develop teams. We are hired to take low-performance teams and turn them into higher performance teams. How do we do that? To answer that question, let's look at what makes successful team players.

Are you more comfortable working alone than with others? If you are, you may not be well suited for teamwork. Studies have found that job satisfaction is higher in teams when team members prefer working with others.[84] An indirect way to measure someone's preference for teamwork is by assessing that person's degree of individualism or collectivism. **Individualism–collectivism** refers to the degree to which a person believes that people should be self-sufficient and that loyalty to oneself is more important than loyalty to one's team or company.[85] Review how Hofstede uses these definitions in Chapter 8. *Individualists*, who put their own welfare and interests first, generally prefer independent tasks in which they work alone; *collectivists*, who put group or team interests ahead of self-interests, generally prefer interdependent tasks in which they work with others. Also, collectivists would rather cooperate than compete and are fearful of disappointing team members or of being ostracized from teams. Given these differences, it makes sense to select team members who are collectivists rather than individualists. Many companies use individualism–collectivism as an initial screening device for team members. But if team diversity is desired, individualists may also be appropriate (see below). To determine your preference for teamwork, take the Team Player Inventory shown in Exhibit 10.4.

Team level refers to the average level of ability, experience, personality, or any other factor on a team. For example, a high level of team experience means that a team has especially experienced team members. This does not mean that every member of the team has considerable experience, but that enough team members do to significantly raise the average level of experience on the team. Team level is used to guide the selection of teammates when teams need a particular set of skills or capabilities to do their jobs well. For example, employees at Bombardier's Montreal plant are graduates of certified engineering schools in Quebec, or in other provinces, and the company's designers are registered professional engineers in the province.[86]

Exhibit 10.4 The Team Player Inventory

	Strongly Disagree				Strongly Agree
1. I enjoy working on team/group projects.	1	2	3	4	5
2. Team/group project work easily allows others to not pull their weight.	1	2	3	4	5
3. Work that is done as a team/group is better than work done individually.	1	2	3	4	5
4. I do my best work alone rather than in a team/group.	1	2	3	4	5
5. Team/group work is overrated in terms of the actual results produced.	1	2	3	4	5
6. Working in a team/group gets me to think more creatively.	1	2	3	4	5
7. Teams/groups are used too often when individual work would be more effective.	1	2	3	4	5
8. My own work is enhanced when I am in a team/group situation.	1	2	3	4	5
9. My experiences working in team/group situations have been primarily negative.	1	2	3	4	5
10. More solutions/ideas are generated when working in a team/group situation than when working alone.	1	2	3	4	5

Reverse score items 2, 4, 5, 7, and 9. Then add the scores for items 1 to 10. Higher scores indicate a preference for teamwork, whereas lower total scores indicate a preference for individual work.

Team diversity represents the variances in ability, experience, personality, or any other factor on a team.[87] From a practical perspective, team diversity is important. Professor John Hollenbeck explains: "Imagine if you put all the extroverts together. Everyone is talking, but nobody is listening. [By contrast,] with a team of [nothing but] introverts, you can hear the clock ticking on the wall."[88] Strong teams have talented members (i.e., team level), and in addition, those talented members vary in terms of abilities, experience, and personality. For example, teams with strong team diversity on job experience have a mix of team members ranging from seasoned veterans to people with three or four years of experience to rookies with little or no experience. Team diversity is used to guide the selection of team members when teams must complete a wide range of different tasks or when tasks are especially complex.

Once the right team has been put together in terms of individualism–collectivism, team level, and team diversity, it's important to keep the team together as long as practically possible. Interesting research by the National Transportation Safety Board found that 73 percent of the serious mistakes made by jet cockpit crews are made the very first day that a crew flies together as a team; also, of that 73 percent, 44 percent occur on their *very first flight* together that day (pilot teams fly two to three flights per day). Moreover, research has shown that fatigued pilot crews who have worked together before make significantly fewer errors than rested crews who have never worked together.[89] Their experience working together helps them overcome their fatigue and outperform new teams that have not worked together before. So, once you've created effective teams, keep them together as long as possible. Imagine the Emergency Room at St. Paul's Hospital in Vancouver. Wouldn't you feel much more confident with a team of physicians, surgeons, nurses, diagnostic technicians, and pharmacists who have worked together for a while?[90] Of course you would, which is why ER teams throughout Canada try to keep their teams together.

Team diversity the variances or differences in ability, experience, personality, or any other factor on a team

4.3 Team Training

After selecting the right people for teamwork, you need to train them. To succeed, teams need significant training in interpersonal skills, decision-making and problem-solving skills, and conflict resolution skills, in addition to technical training. Organizations that create work

Top 10 Problems Reported by Team Leaders

1. Confusion about their new roles and about what they should be doing differently.
2. Feeling they've lost control.
3. Not knowing what it means to coach or empower.
4. Having personal doubts about whether the team concept will really work.
5. Uncertainty about how to deal with employees' doubts about the team concept.
6. Confusion about when a team is ready for more responsibility.
7. Confusion about how to share responsibility and accountability with the team.
8. Concern about promotional opportunities, especially about whether the "team leader" title carries any prestige.
9. Uncertainty about the strategic aspects of the leader's role as the team matures.
10. Not knowing where to turn for help with team problems, as few, if any, of their organization's leaders have led teams.

Source: B. Filipczak, M. Hequet, C. Lee, M. Picard, and D. Stamps, "More Trouble with Teams," *Training*, October 1996: 21.

Interpersonal skills skills, such as listening, communicating, questioning, and providing feedback, that enable people to have effective working relationships with others

teams often underestimate the amount of training required to make teams effective. This mistake occurs often in successful organizations: managers assume that if employees can work effectively on their own, they can work effectively on teams. Actually, companies that use teams successfully provide thousands of hours of training to make sure their teams work. Stacy Myers, a consultant who helps companies implement teams, says: "When we help companies move to teams, we also require that employees take basic quality and business knowledge classes as well. Teams must know how their work affects the company, and how their success will be measured."[91] Quite often at business schools in Canada, we thrust people onto teams. The reason for this is to provide the training you will require once you go out into the workforce. Not every organization, however, can afford to send people to school. This is one reason why you will be valuable to your new employer: you have studied and practised team training.

Most commonly, members of work teams receive training in interpersonal skills. **Interpersonal skills** such as listening, communicating, questioning, and providing feedback enable people to develop effective working relationships with others. Because of teams' autonomy and responsibility, many companies also give team members training in decision-making and problem-solving skills to help them do a better job of cutting costs and improving quality and customer service. Many organizations also teach team conflict resolution skills. Delta Faucet Canada produces plumbing and mechanical devices:

> *Teams at Delta Faucet have specific protocols for addressing conflict. For example, if an employee's behaviour is creating a problem within a team, the team is expected to work it out without involving the team leader. Two team members will meet with the "problem" team member and work toward a resolution. If this is unsuccessful, the whole team meets and confronts the issue. If necessary, the team leader can be brought in to make a decision, but ... it is a rare occurrence for a team to reach that stage.*[92]

Firms must also provide team members with the *technical training* they need to do their jobs, particularly if they are being cross-trained to perform all of the different jobs on the team. Cross-training is less appropriate for teams of highly skilled workers. For instance, it is unlikely that a group of engineers, computer programmers, and systems analysts would be cross-trained for one another's jobs.

Team leaders need training, too, as they often feel unprepared for their new duties. New team leaders face myriad problems ranging from confusion about their new role to not knowing where to turn for help when their team has problems. The solution is extensive training.

4.4 Team Compensation and Recognition

Compensating teams correctly is very difficult. One survey found that only 37 percent of companies were satisfied with their team compensation plan and that even fewer—just

Pojoslaw/Shutterstock.com

10 percent—were "very positive."[93] According to Monty Mohrman of the Center for Effective Organizations, one problem is that "there is a very strong set of beliefs in most organizations that people should be paid for how well they do. So when people first get put into team-based organizations, they really balk at being paid for how well the team does. It sounds illogical to them. It sounds like their individuality and their sense of self-worth are being threatened."[94] Consequently, companies need to choose a team compensation plan with care, and having done so, they must explain thoroughly to their employees how teams will be rewarded. For team compensation to work, it is vital that the type of reward (individual versus team) match the type of performance (individual versus team). The more each team member knows about rewards, the better the whole team performs.

Employees can be compensated for team participation and accomplishments in three ways: skill-based pay, gainsharing, and nonfinancial rewards. **Skill-based pay** programs pay employees for learning additional skills or knowledge.[95] These programs encourage employees to acquire the additional skills they will need to perform multiple jobs within a team, and to share that knowledge with others within their work groups.[96]

In **gainsharing** programs, companies share the financial value of performance gains such as productivity increases, cost savings, or quality improvements with their workers.[97]

Nonfinancial rewards are another way to reward teams for their performance. These rewards, which can range from vacation trips to T-shirts, plaques, and coffee mugs, are especially effective when coupled with management recognition, such as awards, certificates, and praise.[98] Professor Berglas notes that an A+ player "will crave praise, but unless it is sincere and tailored to them, they will suspect that it is fabricated and dismiss it out of hand." Companies want to keep the A+ players on their business teams performing for them. "Just because they think they're great doesn't mean they're not!"[99]

Skill-based pay compensation system that pays employees for learning additional skills or knowledge

Gainsharing a compensation system in which companies share the financial value of performance gains, such as productivity, cost savings, or quality, with their workers

Nonfinancial awards tend to be most effective when teams or team-based interventions, such as total quality management (see Chapter 18), are first introduced.[100]

Which team compensation plan should your company use? In general, skill-based pay is most effective for self-managing and self-directing teams performing complex tasks. In these situations, the more each team member knows and can do, the better the whole team performs. By contrast, gainsharing works best in relatively stable environments where employees can focus on improving productivity, cost savings, or quality.

Go online at
www.nelson.com/4ltrpress/icanmgmt2
And access the essential Study Tools online for this chapter:

- **Flashcards**, to help you study
- **Interactive Quizzes**, to test your knowledge
- **Audio Chapter Summaries**, for chapter review
- **Crossword Puzzles and Beat the Clock**, to review key terms
- **What Would You Do? Cases**, for applying your knowledge to real-life situations
- **Self Assessments**, to learn about what kind of manager you are
- **Videos and Media Quizzing**, where you can watch a video about a real-life company and test yourself on what you've learned

Be sure to consult the Chapter Review Card at the back of the textbook.

11 Managing Human Resource Systems

LEARNING OUTCOMES

LO1 Explain how different employment laws affect human resource practice.

LO2 Explain how companies use HR planning and recruiting to find qualified job applicants.

LO3 Describe the selection techniques and procedures that companies use when deciding which applicants should receive job offers.

LO4 Describe how to determine training needs and select the appropriate training methods.

LO5 Discuss how to use performance appraisal to give meaningful performance feedback.

LO6 Describe basic compensation strategies and discuss the four kinds of employee separations.

What Is HRM?

Human resource management (HRM), or the process of finding, developing, and keeping the right people to form a qualified workforce, is one of the most difficult and important of all management tasks. This chapter is organized around the three parts of the human resource management process shown in Exhibit 11.1: attracting, developing, and keeping a qualified workforce.

This chapter will walk you through the steps of the HRM process. HRM starts with the strategy of the corporation as outlined in Chapter 6. The corporation's vision, mission, and strategy must be understood by the human resources manager so that the HRM plan can emulate, and help accomplish, the organization's strategic objectives. We explore how companies use recruiting and selection techniques to attract and hire qualified employees to fulfill those needs. Then we discuss how training and performance appraisal can develop the knowledge, skills, and abilities of the workforce. The chapter concludes with a review of compensation and employee separation—that is, how companies can keep their best workers through effective compensation practices and how they can manage the separation process when employees leave the organization.

Exhibit 11.1 The Human Resource Management Process

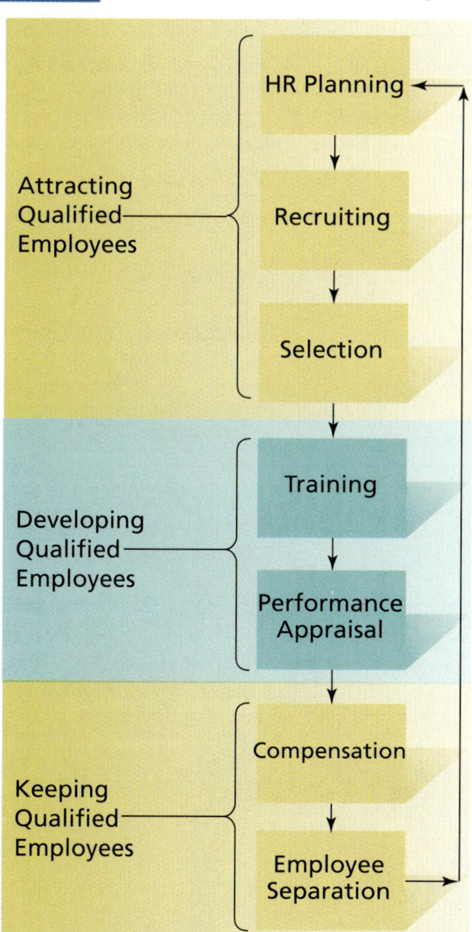

fotoscool/Shutterstock.com

The Legal Context

Before we explore how human resource systems work, you need to better understand the complex legal environment in which they exist. So we'll begin the chapter by reviewing the federal and provincial laws that govern human resource management decisions.

Human resource management (HRM) the process of finding, developing, and keeping the right people to form a qualified workforce

Bona fide occupational qualification (BFOQ) an exception in employment law that permits sex, age, religion, and the like to be used when making employment decisions, but only if they are "reasonably necessary to the normal operation of that particular business"

LO1 Employment Legislation

Canada's employment laws rest primarily with the provinces and territories. The federal government has laws that quite often mirror those of the provinces, but human rights, employment standards, labour relations, health and safety, employment equity, and other employment-related legislation belongs to the ten provinces and three territories. Canada's legal system is based on both British and French colonial law. The Constitution Act of 1867 (formerly known as the British North America Act) laid the foundation for our systems today. Part I of the Canadian Labour Code sets out industrial relations (bargaining rights, strikes, union certifications); Part II sets out occupational health and safety guidelines; Part III sets out standards for hours, wages, vacations, and holidays.[1]

To streamline the legal system somewhat, the governments in each jurisdiction have created special bodies, such as the B.C. Human Rights Tribunal, to enforce compliance and to assist in the interpretation of these complex laws. "Regulations" are also drafted, and they become part of the "act" or law in Canada. Regulations also help us interpret the law.

Most provinces have an employment (labour) standards act. These acts set out items that are defined in the Canadian Labour Code. Such items may be specific to a particular province (e.g., St-Jean-Baptiste Day is a paid holiday in Quebec, whereas Remembrance Day is a paid holiday in Newfoundland and Labrador). Pay equity (equal pay for equal work) is another area addressed by employment standards acts. An employer cannot pay women differently who are performing the same work as men. The difficulty arises when we try to compare work of equal value. Should a nurse (a female-dominated job) be paid the same as a firefighter (a male-dominated job)?

The Canadian Charter of Rights and Freedoms was enacted under the government of Pierre Trudeau in 1982. It is part of Canada's constitution, and it covers several fundamental freedoms that affect the workplace. Section 15a of the Charter prohibits discrimination along most of the lines we are familiar with (race, creed, colour, religion, gender, etc.); Section 15b of the Charter allows certain hiring practices for the "amelioration" of past injustices.[2] There are some additional areas where there are **bona fide occupational qualifications (BFOQs)**. For example, if Victoria's Secret hires models for its lingerie, it probably won't be taken to task for hiring women, as this would be seen as a BFOQ. In Burnaby and Richmond, B.C., there were ongoing investigations into gender discrimination against female firefighters for more than 12 years (note that we don't use the term fireman anymore); in 2012 Burnaby was still updating its firehalls to accommodate women firefighters.[3] The B.C. Supreme Court determined that an aerobic standard for firefighters was not a BFOQ because it was not related to an individual's performance on the job; the same court ruled that there had been systematic discrimination on a prohibited ground.[4]

Human Rights Commissions in each province and territory have been established under the Canadian Human Rights Act. They are responsible for enforcing the Canadian Human Rights Act. The Canadian Human Rights Commission provides guidelines and support to the various provincial agencies.[5] The provincial Human Rights Commissions investigate and hold hearings on issues relating to complaints under the various labour acts. *Let's explore employment legislation by reviewing* ***1.1 the major federal employment laws that affect human resource practice, 1.2 the concept of employment discrimination,*** *and* ***1.3 the laws regarding harassment in the workplace.***

1.1 Federal Employment Laws

Exhibit 11.2 lists some of the major federal and provincial employment laws and their websites, where you can find more detailed information. The general effect of these laws, which are still evolving through court decisions, is that employers may not discriminate in employment decisions on the basis of gender, sexual orientation, age, religion, colour, national origin, race, or disability. The intent is to make these factors irrelevant in employment decisions. Stated another way, employment decisions should be based on factors that are "job related," "reasonably necessary," or a "business necessity" for successful job performance. The only time that gender, age, religion, and the like can be used to make employment decisions is when they are considered bona fide occupational qualifications.

Note well that these laws apply to the entire HRM process and not just to selection decisions (i.e., hiring and promotion). Thus, these laws also cover all training and development activities, performance appraisals, terminations, and compensation decisions. Employers

Exhibit 11.2 Some Major Federal and Provincial Employment Laws

Constitution Act (BNA) of 1867	http://laws.justice.gc.ca/en/const/index.html	Sets out basic federal and provincial responsibilities
Canadian Charter of Rights and Freedoms	http://laws.justice.gc.ca/en/charter	Sets out the 15 basic areas of freedoms in Canada
Canadian Human Rights Act	http://laws.justice.gc.ca/en/H-6/index.html	Act prohibiting discrimination on a number of grounds
Canadian Labour Code	http://laws.justice.gc.ca/eng	Lays out responsibilities of each province and provides national guidelines
Employment Equity and Pay Equity Legislation	http://laws.justice.gc.ca/en/E-5.401/index.html	Requires equal pay for equal work
Workers Compensation Act (Manitoba)	http://web2.gov.mb.ca/laws/statutes/ccsm/w200e.php	Provincial act that lays out safety standards
Ontario Employment Standards Act 2000	http://www.e-laws.gov.on.ca/html/statutes/english/elaws	Ontario's employment requirements, including written notice of termination, termination pay, and mass termination
Quebec Labour Standards Act	http://www.cnt.gouv.qc.ca/fileadmin/pdf/publications/c_0149a.pdf	Quebec's labour standards sets out conditions of employment in the province

Pete Spiro/Shutterstock.com

who use gender, age, race, or religion to make employment-related decisions when those factors are unrelated to an applicant's or employee's ability to perform a job may face charges of discrimination before Human Rights Tribunals, as well as employee lawsuits.

Each province has its own act dealing with workplace safety. Requirements relating to safety equipment, accident investigation, workplace hazardous materials information sheets (WHMISs), and safe work procedures are detailed in these provincial acts, which are administered by boards appointed by the provincial and territorial governments. These boards set safety and health standards for employers and employees and conduct inspections to determine whether those standards are being met. Employers who do not meet standards may be fined.[6]

1.2 Employment Discrimination

Discrimination generally falls under one of the general headings in the Charter of Rights and Freedoms. Discrimination typically leads to an investigation by a provincial or territorial Human Rights Commission. Discrimination may be intentional or unintentional. Generally, discrimination based on race, religion, ethnic origin, and so forth is easy to see. Unintentional discrimination is harder to see. Minimum height and weight requirements, which used to be common for police forces, can screen out females or Canadians of Asian origin, who tend to be shorter. Also, some job evaluation systems may include culturally (non-job-related) biased questions; and some job situations may discriminate against some cultures.

1.3 Workplace Harassment

Workplace harassment is prohibited by several laws, both federal and provincial. Workplace harassment does not have to be sexual in nature, although it commonly is. Harassment can also mean that someone is bullying you about your work or tormenting you simply because you are a man or a woman. Expressing stereotypes about one gender or the other, for example, can be a form of harassment.[7]

In some provinces, these cases are handled by the Human Rights Commission; in other provinces, by a Human Rights Tribunal. Most of these cases involve infractions of the Labour Code and are dealt with under the Human Rights Act. In other cases, individuals—and employers—deal with these issues through the civil courts. *Alpaerts v. Obront* was one case that had limited success in challenging the exclusive remedial jurisdiction of the Labour Code. The plaintiff alleged sexual harassment in her workplace to the point of constructive dismissal (i.e., intolerable circumstances). She sued for wrongful dismissal, alleging in part human rights violations by the employer. The case was allowed to proceed, partly on the basis that the plaintiff had a cause of action separate from the code violation. The court was concerned that if a code complaint had been brought at the same time, the result could have been different and a stay might have been merited.[8] None of the provinces—or, for that matter, the Canadian Human Rights Commission—will investigate without the formal filing of a complaint.

Sexual harassment occurs when employment outcomes, such as hiring, promotion, or simply keeping one's job, depend on whether an individual submits to being sexually harassed. Note that harassment need not be sexual in nature. A **hostile work environment** occurs when unwelcome and demeaning behaviour creates an intimidating, hostile, and offensive work environment. There may be no economic injury—that is, requests for harassment aren't tied to economic outcomes. However, they can lead to psychological injury from a stressful work environment. Dora Cooke had known her eventual boss Patrice Comeau for most of her life. When Comeau and a partner opened a Sudbury, Ontario, office of HTS Engineering Ltd., they needed an assistant and Cooke was offered the job. The relationship soon soured. Dora Cooke was called an "idiot" and "pathetic." In this case, an Ontario judge ruled that when performance management is not meant to be corrective, but is designed to intimidate or insult an employee, it amounts to bullying.[9]

Sexual harassment a form of discrimination in which unwelcome sexual advances, requests for sexual favours, or other verbal or physical conduct of a sexual nature occur while performing one's job; another form of sexual harassment is when employment outcomes, such as hiring, promotion, or simply keeping one's job, depend on whether an individual submits to sexual harassment.

Hostile work environment a form of harassment in which unwelcome and demeaning behaviour creates an intimidating and offensive work environment

Not all bullies are managers. In one B.C. case a court sided with an employee when a coworker was consistently rude and hostile, screaming, swearing at, and belittling her, often in front of customers. Because the employer was aware of the abusive behaviour, and failed to take appropriate steps to stop it, it amounted to vicarious liability against the employer for harassment.[10]

One province defines harassment as "engaging in a course of vexatious comment or conduct against a worker in a workplace that is known or ought reasonably to be known as unwelcome." In Quebec, the first province to prohibit "psychological harassment" at work, the Labour Standards Tribunal listed some examples of bullying: "rude, degrading or offensive remarks, spreading rumours, ridicule, shouting abuse, belittling employees, ignoring them or making fun of their personal choices."[11] Harassment has been endemic in some Canadian organizations, such as the RCMP, and it will take concerted efforts of today's managers as well as future managers (the students reading this textbook) to make Canada an harassment-free place to work.[12]

What should companies do to make sure that harassment laws are not violated?[13] First, they should respond immediately when harassment is reported. A quick response encourages victims of harassment to report problems to management rather than to a lawyer or a Human Rights Tribunal. Furthermore, a quick and fair investigation may serve as a deterrent to future harassment. Next, take the time to write a clear, understandable harassment

Human resources planning an umbrella term that encompasses overarching philosophies, policies, and practices that are in line with the organization's strategy

Recruiting the process of developing a pool of qualified job applicants

Job analysis a purposeful, systematic process for collecting information on the important work-related aspects of a job in line with the organization's strategic direction

policy that is strongly worded, gives specific examples of what constitutes workplace harassment, and spells outs sanctions and punishments, and disseminate it throughout the company. This lets potential harassers and victims know what will not be tolerated and how the firm will deal with harassment should it occur.

Next, establish clear reporting procedures that indicate how, where, and to whom incidents of harassment can be reported. The best procedures ensure that a complaint will receive a quick response, that impartial parties will handle the complaint, and that the privacy of the accused and accuser will be protected. Students, who quite often have to deal with harassment, can get help. The students at Simon Fraser University can go to a nonthreatening Human Rights Office representative to get help and guidance. Students at UBC can receive help from their Equity Office in dealing with unwanted advances. BCIT has a Harassment and Discrimination Advisory Office to help students and staff deal with these kinds of issues.[14]

Finally, managers should be aware that most provinces and many municipalities have their own employment-related laws and enforcement agencies. So compliance with federal law is often not enough. In fact, organizations can be in full compliance with federal law and at the same time be in violation of provincial or municipal harassment laws. These laws are constantly being updated, through jurisprudence established in court cases as well as through legislative authority established by the provinces.

© Peter Finnie/iStockphoto.com

Finding Qualified Workers

Wade Miller, a founder of Manitoba's Pinnacle Staffing Solutions, says: "We thought we could do better and treat people differently." Recalls Mr. Miller, who left the Blue Bombers in April 2006 after an 11-year career: "Demographics are changing. As time goes by, there will be a need for businesses to find top talent. It's a good market segment to be in." He adds that the philosophy at Pinnacle can be summarized by this phrase: "Great people create great organizations."[15]

LO2 HR Planning

Human resources planning ensures that the organization has the appropriate human resources to implement its chosen strategy. If the organization has adopted a strategy of customer service, for example, then the HR department must ensure that its policies, processes, and actions will help the organization realize that chosen "customer service" strategy. HR planning ensures that all parts of the HR function embrace the chosen strategy and ensures that the other functional departments (finance, manufacturing, marketing, etc.) have the human resources they need to accomplish their own strategic "customer service" objectives.

Recruiting is the process of developing a pool of qualified job applicants. *Let's examine* ***2.1 what job analysis is and how it is used in recruiting, 2.2 how companies use internal recruiting,*** *and* ***2.3 external recruiting to find qualified job applicants.***

2.1 Job Analysis and Recruiting

Job analysis is a "purposeful, systematic process for collecting information on the important work-related aspects of a job."[16] The information derived from job analysis is absolutely vital to effective HR planning. Typically, a job analysis collects four kinds of information:

- work activities, such as what workers do and how, when, and why they do it;
- the tools and equipment used to do the job;
- the context in which the job is performed, such as the actual working conditions or schedule; and
- the personnel requirements for performing the job, meaning the knowledge, skills, and abilities needed to do a job well.[17]

Job analysis information can be collected by having job incumbents and/or supervisors complete questionnaires, by direct observation, by interviews, or by filming employees as they perform their jobs.

Job descriptions and job specifications are two of the most important results of a job analysis. A **job description** is a written description of the basic tasks, duties, and responsibilities required of an employee holding a particular job. **Job specifications**, which are often included in a separate section of a job description, summarize the qualifications needed to successfully perform the job. Exhibit 11.3 shows a job recruitment notice for a firefighter in Calgary, Alberta.

Job description a written description of the basic tasks, duties, and responsibilities required of an employee holding a particular job to help the organization realize its strategy

Job specifications a written summary of the qualifications needed to successfully perform a particular job to enable the organization to reach its organizational objectives

Because a job analysis specifies what a job entails as well as the knowledge, skills, and abilities that are needed to do the job well, companies must complete a job analysis *before* beginning to recruit job applicants. Job analysis, job descriptions, and job specifications comprise the foundation on which all critical human resource activities are built. They are used during recruiting and selection to match applicant qualifications with the requirements of the job. So it is critically important that job descriptions be accurate. Unfortunately, they aren't always so. Apartment Investment & Management Co. (Aimco) discovered that its high turnover rate was due in part to poorly written job descriptions. The descriptions focused on education and experience more than on actually explaining what an employee would do on the job and what the company culture was like. And those descriptions, when they did explain the job, were abstract and laden with jargon, making them unclear. Consequently, many new hires found themselves in an incompatible culture or in jobs they did not like or could not do.[18]

Job descriptions are also used throughout the staffing process to ensure that selection devices and the decisions based on these devices are job-related. The questions asked in an interview should be based on the most important work activities identified by a job analysis. Likewise, during performance appraisals (see Section 11.5, page 190), employees should be evaluated in areas that a job analysis has identified as the most important in a job.

Exhibit 11.3 Job Recruitment Notice for a Firefighter for the City of Calgary, Alberta

Looking for a challenging and exciting career? Firefighting may be for you ...
We're looking for physically fit men and women—motivated individuals known for integrity, professionalism, and drive. Join our team of more than 1,200 firefighters dedicated to fire education, prevention, and safety.

Professionalism

A professional firefighting career offers excellent benefits, opportunities and job security. We can offer you the opportunity to be part of a highly-skilled team whose members are admired and valued by the community they serve and protect. Recruits are trained in-house to the highest international standards. We provide numerous professional development opportunities for firefighters to enhance their knowledge and skills in the latest firefighting and rescue techniques. There are multiple support divisions—including aquatic and high-angle rescue teams, fire prevention, arson investigation, community safety, or training—where firefighters can diversify their experience and career.

The Place to Be

Calgary is a young, energetic and diverse city that offers world-class arts, entertainment and recreation opportunities. With a population of more than a million people, it is one of the fastest-growing cities in North America. Calgary provides an unsurpassed quality of life for families. Its close proximity to the Rocky Mountains guarantees year-round adventure.

Pride. Professionalism. Teamwork. Respect. These are our core values. If you share them, review the links on this website and consider joining our team.

Source: City of Calgary, Firefighter Recruitment, 2010. http://content.calgary.ca/CCA/City+Hall/Business+Units/Calgary+Fire+Department/Firefighter+Recruitment/Firefighter+Recruitment.htm (accessed 19 June 2010). Courtesy of the City of Calgary, 2010.

Monkey Business Images/Shutterstock.com

Internal recruiting the process of developing a pool of qualified job applicants from people who already work in the company

Succession planning deals with evaluating the needs that are required in future years in terms of staffing to replace people who retire, or who may leave, and to provide personnel for needed strategic growth requirements

External recruiting the process of developing a pool of qualified job applicants from outside the company

Realistic job previews a tool used to explain to potential new employees both the positive and negative aspects of a new job

Job analyses, job descriptions, and job specifications also help companies meet the legal requirement that their human resource decisions be job-related. To be judged *job-related*, recruitment, selection, training, performance appraisals, and employee separations must be valid and be directly related to the important aspects of the job as identified by a careful job analysis. Job requirements, if they have the potential to discriminate against members of protected groups, must then meet the standards set by the *Meiorin* decision (*BC Public Service Relations Commission vs. BCBSEU*).[19] In *Meiorin* the Supreme Court of Canada found that an organization's new job requirements were not based on job-related information and that its job analysis was seriously flawed. Canadian Human Rights Commissions and courts recognize the US *Uniform Guidelines for Employee Selection Procedures*. Additionally, the Canadian Society of Industrial Organizational Psychology has adapted those principles in the "Guidelines" for developing equitable selection systems in Canada.[20] In practice, if not in law, the starting point for defensible selection is an appropriate job analysis system.

2.2 Internal Recruiting

Internal recruiting, sometimes called "promotion from within," is the process of developing a pool of qualified job applicants from people who already work in the company. Internal recruiting improves employee commitment, morale, and motivation. It also reduces recruitment start-up time and costs, and because employees are already familiar with the company's culture and procedures, they are more likely to succeed in their new jobs. Job posting and career paths are two methods of internal recruiting.

Job posting involves advertising job openings within the company to existing employees. Typically, a job description and its requirements are posted on a bulletin board, in a company newsletter, or in a computerized job bank that only employees can access.

A *career path* is a planned sequence of jobs through which employees may advance within an organization. For example, a person who starts as a sales representative may move up to sales manager and then to district or regional sales manager. Career paths help employees focus on long-term goals and development; they also help companies retain employees. Career paths are useful in **succession planning**. Succession planning is critical as employees in an organization must develop the correct strategic attributes and skills if they are to move ahead in the organization. Any organization would be wise to help its employees become more promotable.[21]

2.3 External Recruiting

External recruiting involves developing a pool of qualified job applicants from outside the company. External recruitment methods include placing advertisements (in newspapers, magazines, direct mail, radio, or television), generating employee referrals (asking current employees to recommend possible job applicants), encouraging walk-ins (people who apply on their own), approaching outside organizations (universities, technical/trade schools, professional societies), using employment services (provincial, federal, or private employment agencies, temporary help agencies, professional search firms), holding special events (career conferences, job fairs), and developing Internet job sites. Studies have found that for office/clerical and production/service employees, the most commonly used methods are employee referrals, walk-ins, newspaper ads, and provincial employment agencies. For professional/technical employees, the most common tools are newspaper ads and college/university recruitment services.

Realistic job previews ensure that new applicants are provided with sufficient information to arrive at an informed decision. They provide information about pay and hours of work, but they also discuss aspects of the job such as promotion rates, job progression, amount of flexibility, self-autonomy, stress, interaction with customers, amount of travel, and the corporate culture. Generally, job previews set out the positive and negative aspects of both the job and the organization. One quantitative meta-analysis of realistic job previews found that they led to higher performance, lower attrition, more accurate expectations of the job, and more positive affective reactions to it.[22]

When recruiting managers, organizations tend to rely most heavily on newspaper ads, employee referrals, and search firms.[23] Most students will find themselves relying more and more on Web searches, utilizing sites such as monster.ca, workopolis.ca, facebook.ca, linkedin.ca, and vancouverjobshop.ca. In the coming decade, networking will become an increasing important tool for new graduates.[24]

Companies are now hiring nontraditional people in nontraditional ways. One of these nontraditional ways is the Langley-based website 55pluspros.ca, which has been launched to help match older workers with employers seeking experienced and qualified professionals. "There are two reasons for this," Website founder Sherry Baker said in an interview. "There are more and more people retiring who realize that if they want to maintain their lifestyle, they'll have to make more money than what they get with their pension." Also, many are retiring in their mid-50s, while they're still healthy and energetic. They realize that they want to do something else more meaningful with their lives. "Most of them want to work part time, but they want to utilize their skills and training in a meaningful way," says Baker.[25]

Baidu, a Beijing-based search engine company, seeks out the best Web engineers by hosting an annual programming competition.[26]

As noted earlier, some companies are now recruiting applicants through Internet job sites such as monster.ca, vancouverjobshop.ca, and BCJobs.ca. Companies can post job openings for 30 days on one of these sites for about half the cost of running an ad just once in a Sunday newspaper. Besides that, Internet job listings generate nine times as many résumés as one ad in the Sunday newspaper.[27] And because these sites attract so many applicants and offer so many services, companies can find qualified applicants without resorting to recruitment firms, which typically charge one-third or more of a new hire's salary.[28]

LO3 Selection

After the recruitment process has produced a pool of qualified applicants, a selection process determines which applicants have the best chance of performing well on the job. **Selection** is the process of gathering information about job applicants to decide who should be offered the job. **Validation** is the process of determining how well a selection test or procedure predicts future job performance. The more accurate the prediction of future job performance, the more valid the test.

Let's examine common selection procedures, such as ***3.1 application forms and résumés, 3.2 references and background checks,*** *3.3 selection tests, and* ***3.4 interviews.***

3.1 Application Forms and Résumés

Usually, the first selection devices that job applicants encounter are application forms and résumés. These contain similar information, such as the applicant's name, address, and job and educational history. Although an application form often asks for information already provided by the résumé, most organizations prefer to collect this information in their own format (i.e., the application form) for entry into a human resource information system.

Employment laws apply to application forms just as they do to all selection devices. Application forms are allowed to ask applicants only for valid, job-related information. Even so, they often ask applicants for non-job-related information such as marital status, maiden name, age, or date of high school graduation. (See various websites, such as the Alberta Human Rights Commission website, www.albertahumanrights.ab.ca, for information on pre-employment questions.[29]) There is quite a bit of information that companies are not permitted to request in application forms, during job interviews, or in any other part of the selection process. Courts will assume that you consider all of the information you request of applicants, even if you don't. So be sure to ask only those questions that directly relate to the candidate's ability and motivation to perform the job.

Résumés also pose problems for companies, but in a different way. Studies have found that as many as one-third of job applicants intentionally falsify some information on their résumés and that 80 percent of the information on résumés may be misleading.[30] Therefore, managers should verify the information collected via résumés and application forms by comparing it with additional information collected during interviews and other stages of the selection process, such as references and background checks (see below).

3.2 References and Background Checks

Nearly all companies ask the applicant to provide **employment references**, such as previous employers or coworkers, whom they can contact to learn more

Selection the process of gathering information about job applicants to decide who should be offered a job

Validation the process of determining how well a selection test or procedure predicts future job performance. The better or more accurate the prediction of future job performance, the more valid a test is said to be.

Employment references sources such as previous employers or coworkers who can provide job-related information about job candidates

Preventing Brain Drain

Recruiting and retaining the most skilled and knowledgeable workers is in every company's best interest. In a global economy that increasingly relies on information rather than natural resources, it's also in every country's best interest. Some areas of the world are downright dangerous for smart people. Between 2003 and 2006, 380 of Iraq's academics and doctors were assassinated. Other countries increasingly want to attract the best talent. Saudi Arabia's king, for example, spent $12.5 billion on a new research university to cultivate talent at home. Countries can also attract talent globally by easing "tariffs" on incoming workers and making it easier for them to get work permits. Geoff Colvin, senior editor at *Fortune* magazine, says, "This international fight for talent will get much more serious. With luck it will lead to something new: a free market in brainpower."

Sources: G. Colvin, "The Battle for Brainpower", *Fortune* (10 December 2007) 34–35; C. Caulcutt, "Iraq's Deadly Brain Drain," France 24, (11 May 2008) available online at http://www.france24.com/en/20080510-iraqs-deadly-brain-drain-iraq (accessed 14 August 2008).

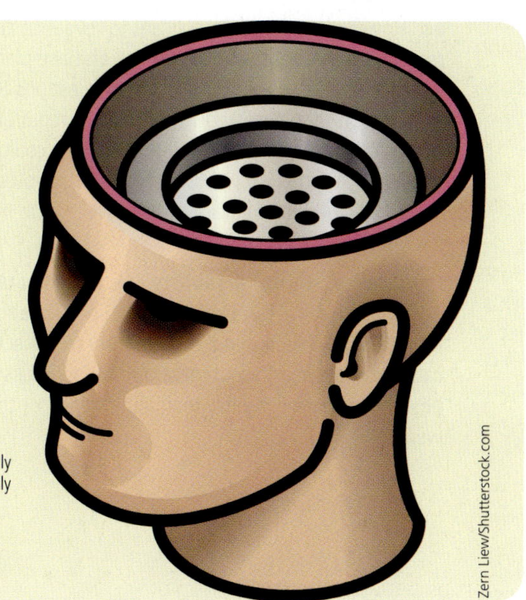
Zern Liew/Shutterstock.com

Don't Ask (Topics to Avoid in an Interview—They May Be Illegal!)

1. **Gender, marital status, or family status.** Do not ask the applicant to specify Mr., Mrs., Miss, or Ms. on an application form.
2. **Source of income.** Any inquiry concerning source of income must be job-related. You can request information about former employment. Avoid inquiries about other sources of income that may have a stigma attached to them, such as social assistance, disability pension, or child maintenance, unless you have a job-related reason for asking.
3. **Previous names.** Asking an applicant to provide previous names can cause the applicant to indirectly disclose marital status, gender, place of origin, or ancestry. Any inquiry that requires an applicant to disclose this information would be contrary to the Alberta Human Rights Act, unless there is a business reason for doing so that is acceptable under the act.
4. **Next of kin.** Asking for names of relatives or next of kin before hiring is not recommended. Such information can reveal the gender, marital status, place of origin, or ancestry of the applicant.
5. **Dependants and child care.** Avoid inquiries about an applicant's spouse, number of children or dependants, child care arrangements, or plans to have children. The answers to these questions are usually not related to the job and can reveal gender and marital or family status. Inquiries that focus on willingness to work the required schedule, to work rotating shifts, or to relocate are clearly business-related and are acceptable.
6. **Age and date of birth.** It is not advisable to ask for applicant's date of birth or age, unless the applicant is under 18. In employment situations where there is a legal minimum age requirement, you can verify that the applicant meets the legal age requirement.
7. **Previous address.** It is not acceptable to request a previous address, unless it is for a business-related purpose that is acceptable under the act.
8. **Citizenship.** Citizenship is not specifically dealt with in the act. However, asking the applicant to reveal citizenship could require a non-Canadian applicant to disclose place of origin, which is protected under the act. Ask questions to solicit information that is related to the specific requirements of the job to be performed. Appropriate questions could include: Are you legally entitled to work in Canada? Are you a Canadian citizen or landed immigrant? Yes __ No __ (Do not distinguish between the two.)
9. **Physical or mental disability.** It is not acceptable to ask questions that are not related to the specific job to be performed. With this in mind, it is contrary to the act to ask applicants to provide information about the general state of their physical or mental health, their appearance, or their height or weight.
10. **Sexual orientation.** Avoid inquiries about an applicant's sexual orientation. It is unacceptable to express a preference for an applicant to be heterosexual, homosexual, or bisexual unless you have a business-related reason for expressing a preference, and the reason is acceptable under the act.
11. **Workers' Compensation.** Asking if the applicant has received or is receiving Workers' Compensation indirectly requires an applicant to provide information about a physical injury or disability. This can be contrary to the act.
12. **Language ability.** It is appropriate to ask applicants if they have some proficiency in the languages that are specifically required for the job. The job description and employment advertisement should specify which languages are required. The level of language ability required should match the job requirements.
13. **Educational institutions.** You can request the names and addresses of academic, vocational, technical, and professional institutions attended and the nature and level of education received. Requiring information that reflects either the religious or racial affiliation of schools or other institutions attended is not advisable as it could reveal religious beliefs or race.
14. **Religious beliefs.** Avoid requesting information about applicants' religious beliefs, including which religious holidays and customs they observe, which church they attend, or whether their clothing is prescribed by their religion. It is permissible for an employer to specify the hours of work in a job advertisement. A job advertisement may indicate that the position will require shift, evening, or weekend work, or that it is functional 365 days per year. Courts and tribunals have said that the employer must make all efforts up to the point of undue hardship to accommodate the religious beliefs of an employee. In turn, the employee is expected to cooperate fully with the employer's efforts. Undue hardship may occur if accommodation would create the following conditions for an employer: an intolerable financial cost, serious disruption to a business or workplace, or other serious issues that cannot be overcome.

Source: Adapted from http://www.albertahumanrights.ab.ca/publications/bulletins_sheets_booklets/sheets/hr_and_employment/pre_employment_inquiries.asp with the permission of the Alberta Human Rights Commission.

about the candidate. **Background checks** are used to verify the truthfulness and accuracy of the information that applicants provide about themselves and to uncover negative, job-related background information not provided by applicants. Background checks are conducted by contacting "educational institutions, prior employers, court records, police and governmental agencies, and other informational sources either by telephone, mail, remote computer access, or through in-person investigations."[31]

Unfortunately, previous employers are increasingly reluctant to provide references or background check information. It is unlikely that Canadian employers will be sued for honestly providing unfavourable references. Yet at the same time, employers are quite vulnerable to being sued in cases where they knowingly hold back unfavourable information, especially if an employee is hired and subsequently causes harm to the new employer or its clients.[32] Many previous employers provide only dates of employment, positions held, and date of separation.

A former employer should not impede a former employee's job search. The Supreme Court of Canada ruled that employers have an obligation to act in good faith when an employee is terminated. In *Jack Wallace v. The United Grain Growers*, the plaintiff was awarded 24 months' salary when it was found that United Grain Growers neglected to provide a reference letter for him to secure a new job.[33]

With previous employers generally unwilling to give full and candid references, and with negligent hiring lawsuits awaiting companies that don't get such references and background information, what can companies do? To start with, they can conduct criminal record checks, especially if the job for which the person is applying involves money, drugs, control over valuable goods, or access to the elderly, children with disabilities, or people's homes.[34] According to the Society for Human Resource Management, 96 percent of companies conduct background checks and 80 percent conduct criminal record checks.[35]

Next, they can ask the applicant to sign a waiver that permits them to check references, run a background check, or contact anyone with knowledge of the applicant's work performance or history. Likewise, they can ask the applicant if there is anything he or she would like the company to know or if the company is likely to hear anything unusual when contacting references.[36] This is often enough to get the applicant to share information that might otherwise have been withheld. The company, once it has finished checking, should keep its findings confidential to minimize the chances of a defamation charge.

Finally, many companies are starting to perform social media background checks. Certainly, applicants should be careful about what they have posted on sites such as Facebook and Twitter. It may well make sense for a job applicant to delete anything that might be embarrassing.[37]

3.3 Selection Tests

Selection tests can tell decision makers who will likely do well in a job and who won't. Applicants take a test that measures something directly or indirectly related to doing well on the job. The selection tests discussed here are specific ability tests, cognitive ability tests, personality tests, and work sample tests. Also discussed here are assessment centres and biographical data.

Background checks procedures used to verify the truthfulness and accuracy of information that applicants provide about themselves and to uncover negative, job-related background information not provided by applicants

Specific ability tests (aptitude tests) tests that measure the extent to which an applicant possesses the particular kind of ability needed to do a job well

Specific ability tests measure the extent to which an applicant possesses the particular abilities needed to do a job well. Specific ability tests are also called **aptitude tests** because they measure aptitude for doing a particular task well. If you decide to go on for an MBA after you have completed your undergraduate degree (and after you have worked for a few years), you will most likely be required to take the GMAT (Graduate Management Admissions Test). If you apply to law school in Canada, you will likely need to write the LSAT (Law School Admissions Test). These tests are predictors of how well students will do in those graduate schools. Specific ability tests also exist for mechanical, clerical, sales, and physical work. For example, clerical workers have to be good at accurately reading and scanning numbers. Exhibit 11.4 shows items similar to those found on the Minnesota Clerical Test, in which applicants have only a short time to determine whether two columns of numbers and letters are identical. Applicants who are good at this are likely to do well as clerical or entry-level workers. About one-third of Canadian

Exhibit 11.4 Clerical Test Items Similar to Those Found on the Minnesota Clerical Test

NUMBERS/LETTERS		SAME	
1. 3468251	3467251	Yes O	No O
2. 4681371	4681371	Yes O	No O
3. 7218510	7218520	Yes O	No O
4. ZXYAZAB	ZXYAZAB	Yes O	No O
5. ALZYXMN	ALZYXNM	Yes O	No O
6. PRQZYMN	PRQZYMN	Yes O	No O

Source: N.W. Schmitt and R.J. Klimoski, *Research Methods in Human Resource Management*, (Mason, OH, South-Western, 1991). Used with permission from the authors.

Cognitive ability tests tests that measure the extent to which applicants have abilities in perceptual speed, verbal comprehension, numerical aptitude, general reasoning, and spatial aptitude

Biographical data (biodata) extensive surveys that ask applicants questions about their personal backgrounds and life experiences

Work sample tests tests that require applicants to perform tasks that are actually done on the job

Assessment centres a series of managerial simulations, graded by trained observers, that are used to determine applicants' capability for managerial work

companies currently use formal assessments during recruitment. David Towler, president of Creative Organizational Design in Kitchener, Ontario, says that he is "gob-smacked that some companies do no testing at all. It costs only $20–$150 to make sure you have not hired someone else's reject." It can cost thousands of dollars to replace a bad hire.[38]

Cognitive ability tests measure applicants' verbal comprehension, numerical aptitude, general reasoning, and spatial aptitude. In other words, they indicate how quickly and how well people understand words, numbers, logic, and spatial dimensions. Specific ability tests predict job performance in only particular types of jobs, whereas cognitive ability tests accurately predict job performance in almost all kinds of jobs.[39] This is because people with strong cognitive or mental abilities are usually good at learning new things, processing complex information, solving problems, and making decisions—abilities that are important in almost all jobs.[40] In fact, cognitive ability tests are almost always the best predictors of job performance. If you were allowed to use just one selection test, a cognitive ability test would be the one to use.[41] (In practice, though, companies use a battery of tests because doing so leads to much more accurate selection decisions.)

Biographical data, or **biodata**, are extensive surveys that ask applicants questions about their personal background and life experiences. The basic idea behind biodata is that past behaviour is the best predictor of future behaviour. Most biodata questionnaires have over 100 items that gather information about habits and attitudes, health, interpersonal relations, money, family life (parents, siblings, childhood years, teen years), personal habits, current home (spouse, children), hobbies, education and training, values, preferences, and work.[42] Biodata can be a very good predictor of future job performance, especially in an entry-level job.

You may have noticed that some of the information requested in biodata surveys is related to topics that employers should avoid in applications, interviews, or other parts of the selection process. This information can be requested in biodata questionnaires provided that the company can demonstrate that the information is job-related (i.e., valid) and does not have an adverse impact on protected groups of job applicants. Biodata surveys should be reviewed by HR professionals for legality, validated and tested for adverse impact, and thoroughly vetted by knowledgeable professionals before they are used to make selection decisions.[43] For example, studies have found that married Canadian military recruits have a much higher attrition rate than single recruits, yet it is illegal in Canada to discriminate against anyone on the basis of marital status.[44]

Work sample tests, also called *performance tests,* require applicants to perform tasks that are actually done on the job. Unlike specific ability, cognitive ability, biographical data, and personality tests, which are indirect predictors of job performance, work sample tests directly measure job applicants' capabilities for the job. So, for example, one computer-based work sample test in the real estate industry has applicants assume the role of a real estate agent who must decide how to interact with virtual clients in a game-like scenario. And, as in real life, the clients are variously frustrating, confused, demanding, or indecisive. In one situation, the wife loves the house but the husband hates it. The applicants, just like actual real estate agents, must demonstrate what they will do in these realistic situations.[45] This work sample simulation provides real estate companies with direct evidence of whether applicants will be able to do the job if they are hired. Work sample tests are generally very good at predicting future job performance; however, they can be expensive to administer and can be used for only one kind of job. For example, an auto dealership could not use a work sample test for mechanics as a selection test for sales representatives.

Coprid/Shutterstock.com

Assessment centres use a series of job-specific simulations, which are then graded by multiple trained observers to determine applicants' ability to perform managerial work. Unlike the previously described selection tests, which are commonly used for specific jobs or entry-level jobs, assessment centres are most often used to select applicants who have high potential to be good managers. Assessment centres often last two to five days and require participants to complete a number of tests and exercises that simulate managerial work.

Some of the more common assessment centre exercises are in-basket exercises, role plays, small-group presentations, and leaderless group discussions. An *in-basket exercise* is usually a computer-simulated test in which the applicant is given a manager's in-basket containing e-mails, memos, phone messages, VoIP messages, organizational policies, and other communications normally received by and available to managers. Applicants have a limited time to

Exhibit 11.5 In-Basket Item for an Assessment Centre for Police Supervisors

The Justice Institute of British Columbia provides a Supervisory or Manager Centre "In-Basket" exercise that stimulates an e-mail inbox in a role play exercise. Police agencies submit current operational information, which is then used to custom-design the electronic e-mail exercise. Candidates log on and assess and take action on documentation pertinent to their organization. All meetings and commitments can be entered into the electronic calendar contained in the program. Candidates are expected to answer all e-mail, "cc" the appropriate recipients, and send new e-mails in response to the problems posed. The In-Basket exercise can be accessed by a computer from anywhere in the world. Marking is a little easier (because there is less poor handwriting!), and both the administering organization and the candidate can monitor while the exercise is in progress.

Source: JIBC Police Academy, 2010. Welcome to te Assessment Centre electronic in-basket. http://www.jibc.ca/police/programs/assessment_centre/assessment_centre_inbasket.htm. Accessed 26 June 2010.

read through the in-basket, prioritize the items, and decide how to deal with each item. Experienced managers then score the applicants' decisions and recommendations. Exhibit 11.5 describes an in-basket exercise used by an assessment centre in B.C.

In a *leaderless group discussion*, another common assessment centre exercise, a group of six applicants is given approximately two hours to solve a problem, but no one is put in charge (hence "leaderless"). Trained observers watch and score each participant on the extent to which he or she facilitates discussion, listens, leads, persuades, and works well with others.

Tests are not perfect predictors of job performance. Some people who do well on selection tests will do poorly in their jobs. Likewise, some people who do poorly on selection tests (and therefore weren't hired) would have been very good performers. Nonetheless, valid tests minimize these selection errors (hiring people who should not have been hired and not hiring people who should have been hired) while maximizing correct selection decisions. In short, tests make it more likely that you'll hire the right person for the job. While tests aren't perfect, almost nothing predicts future job performance as well as the selection tests discussed here.[46] Again, before using them, make sure they are legal in your jurisdiction.[47]

Interviews a selection tool in which company representatives ask job applicants job-related questions to determine whether they are qualified for the job

Unstructured interviews interviews in which interviewers are free to ask the applicants anything they want

Structured interviews interviews in which all applicants are asked the same set of standardized questions, usually including situational, behavioural, background, and job knowledge questions

3.4 Interviews

In **interviews**, company representatives ask applicants job-related questions to determine whether they are qualified for the job. Interviews are probably the most frequently used and heavily relied upon tools for selecting among job candidates. There are several basic kinds of interviews: unstructured, structured, and semistructured.

In **unstructured interviews**, interviewers are free to ask applicants anything they want, and studies show that they do. Because interviewers often disagree about which questions should be asked during interviews, different interviewers tend to ask applicants very different questions.[48] Furthermore, individual interviewers seem to have a tough time asking the same questions from one interview to the next. This high level of inconsistency reduces the validity of unstructured interviews as a selection device because comparing applicant responses can be difficult. As a result, unstructured interviews are about half as accurate as structured interviews at predicting which job applicants should be hired.

By contrast, with **structured interviews**, standardized interview questions are prepared ahead of time so that all applicants are asked the same job-related questions.[49] Structuring interviews ensures that interviewers ask only for important, job-related information. This approach improves the accuracy, usefulness, and validity of the

Finding the Perfect Mate

While it may not be healthy to be married to your job, the process of finding one can often feel like dating. Sometimes it even looks like dating. An increasing number of retiring baby boomers and a shortage of skilled workers means that positions need to be filled more quickly, and some companies are turning to speed dating as a new interview strategy. As many as 200 candidates appear for a daylong interviewing event, where they spend five minutes each with various recruiters. Ill-fitting candidates can be eliminated early in the process, recruiters can easily remember candidates without searching through notes, and decisions are made more quickly.

Source: S. E. Needleman, "Speed Interviewing Grows as Skills Shortage Looms," *The Wall Street Journal*, 6 November 2007, B15.

AP Photo/Tim Johnson

interview; in addition, it is less likely that interviewers will ask questions that violate employment laws (see the "Don't Ask—It May Be Illegal!" box on page 184 for a list of these topics).

The primary advantage of structured interviews is that comparing applicants is much easier because they are all asked the same questions. Structured interviews typically contain four types of questions: situational, behavioural, background, and job knowledge. Situational questions ask applicants how they would respond in a hypothetical situation (e.g., "What would you do if …"). These questions are more appropriate for hiring new graduates, who are unlikely to have encountered real work situations because of their limited experience. Behavioural questions ask applicants what they did in previous jobs that is similar to what is required for the job for which they are applying (e.g., "In your previous jobs, tell me about …"). These questions are more appropriate for hiring experienced individuals. Background questions ask applicants about their work experience, education, and other qualifications (e.g., "Tell me about the training you received at …"). Finally, job knowledge questions ask applicants to demonstrate their job knowledge (e.g., for nurses, "Give me an example of a time when one of your patients had a severe reaction to a medication. How did you handle it?").[50]

Semistructured interviews are in between structured and unstructured interviews. A large part of the semistructured interview (perhaps as much as 80 percent) is based on structured questions, but some time is set aside for unstructured interviewing to allow the interviewer to probe into ambiguous or missing information uncovered during the structured portion of the interview.

Contrary to what you've probably heard, recent evidence indicates that even unstructured interviews do a fairly good job.[51] When conducted properly, however, structured interviews can lead to much more accurate hiring decisions than unstructured ones. The validity of structured interviews can sometimes rival that of cognitive ability tests. But even more important, because interviews are especially good at assessing applicants' interpersonal skills, they work particularly well with cognitive ability tests. The combination (i.e., smart people who work well in conjunction with others) leads to even better selection decisions than using either alone.[52] Exhibit 11.6 provides guidelines for conducting effective structured employment interviews.

Exhibit 11.6 Guidelines for Conducting Effective Structured Interviews

Interview Stage	What to Do
	• Identify and define the knowledge, skills, abilities, and other (KSAO) characteristics needed for successful job performance. • For each essential KSAO, develop key behavioural questions that will elicit examples of past accomplishments, activities, and performance. • For each KSAO, develop a list of things to look for in the applicant's responses to key questions.
	• Create a relaxed, nonstressful interview atmosphere. • Review the applicant's application form, résumé, and other information. • Allocate enough time to complete the interview without interruption. • Put the applicant at ease; don't jump right into heavy questioning. • Tell the applicant what to expect. Explain the interview process. • Obtain job-related information from the applicant by asking those questions prepared for each KSAO. • Describe the job and the organization to the applicant. Applicants need adequate information to make a selection decision about the organization.
	• Immediately after the interview, review your notes and make sure they are complete. • Evaluate the applicant on each essential KSAO. • Determine each applicant's probability of success and make a hiring decision.

Sources: B.M. Farrell, "The Art and Science of Employment Interviews," *Personnel Journal* 65 (1986): 91–94; Catano, V. et al. *Recruitment and Selection in Canada.* Toronto: Nelson Education, [2009], © 2010. p. 431.

Developing Qualified Workers

According to the Canadian Society for Training and Development, a typical investment in employee training increases productivity by an average of 17 percent, reduces employee turnover, and makes companies more profitable.[53] Giving employees the knowledge and skills they need to improve their performance is just the first step in developing employees, however. The second step—and not enough companies do this—is giving employees formal feedback about their actual job performance.

LO4 Training

Training means providing opportunities for employees to develop the job-specific skills, experience, and knowledge they need to do their jobs or improve their performance. Canadian companies spend more than $5 billion a year on training. *To make sure those training dollars are well spent, companies need to* ***4.1 determine specific training needs, 4.2 select appropriate training methods,*** *and* ***4.3 evaluate training.***

4.1 Determining Training Needs

Needs assessment is the process of identifying and prioritizing the learning needs of employees. Needs assessments can be conducted by identifying performance deficiencies, listening to customer complaints, surveying employees and managers, or formally testing employees' skills and knowledge.

Note that training should never be conducted without first performing a needs assessment. Sometimes training isn't needed at all or isn't needed for all employees. Unfortunately, many organizations simply require all employees to attend training whether they need it or not. As a result, employees who aren't interested or who don't need the training may react negatively during or after training. Likewise, employees who should be sent for training but aren't may also react negatively. Consequently, a needs assessment is an important tool for deciding who should or should not attend training.

© Imageegaml/iStockphoto.com

Training developing the skills, experience, and knowledge employees need to perform their jobs or improve their performance

Needs assessment the process of identifying and prioritizing the learning needs of employees

Employment law restricts employers from discriminating on the basis of age, gender, race, colour, religion, national origin, or disability when selecting training participants. Just as with hiring decisions, the selection of training participants should be based on job-related information.

Finally, if the company's technology infrastructure can support it, e-learning can be much faster than traditional training methods.

4.2 Training Methods

Assume that you're a training director for a major oil company and that you're in charge of making sure all employees know to respond effectively in case of an oil spill off the Labrador coast. Keep in mind the lessons learned from the BP oil spill in the Gulf of Mexico during the early summer of 2010.[54] Exhibit 11.7 (see page 190) lists a number of training methods you could use: films and videos, lectures, planned readings, case studies, coaching and mentoring, group discussions, on-the-job training, role playing, simulations and games, vestibule training, and computer-based learning. Which method would be best?

When choosing the best method, consider various factors such as the number of people to be trained, the cost of training, and the objectives of the training. For instance, if the training objective is to impart information or knowledge to trainees, then you should use films and videos, lectures, and planned readings. In our example, trainees might read a manual or attend a lecture about how to seal a shoreline to keep it from being affected by the spill.

If the objective is to develop analytical and problem-solving skills, then use case studies, coaching and mentoring, and group discussions. In our example, trainees might view a video documenting how a team handled exposure to hazardous substances, talk with first responders, and discuss what they would do in a similar situation.

If practising, learning, or changing job behaviours is the objective, then use on-the-job training, role playing, simulations and games, and vestibule training. In our example, trainees might participate in a mock shoreline cleanup to learn what do in the event oil comes to shore. This simulation could take place on an actual shoreline or on a video-game-like virtual shoreline.

If training is supposed to meet more than one of these objectives, then your best choice may be to combine one of the previous methods with computer-based training.

These days, many companies are adopting Internet training, or "e-learning." E-learning can offer several advantages. Because employees don't need to leave their jobs, travel costs are greatly reduced. Also, because employees can take

Exhibit 11.7 Five Myths of Training

Myth #1	"I can't measure the results of my training effort." Recent years have seen the proliferation of technology and methods to measure the impact of almost any program.
Myth #2	"I don't know what information to collect." Well-conceived needs assessments reveal quantifiable measures of performance and help determine what information to collect to ascertain if the program worked.
Myth #3	"If I can't calculate the return on investment, then the training is useless." A good HRM professional is required to do this, but there may be reasons other than economics to implement a training program, and a brief. Subjective appraisal may be more appropriate.
Myth #4	"Measurement of training is only effective in the production and financial arenas." All functional areas should be prepared to find ways to show their contribution.
Myth #5	"There are too many variables affecting the behaviour change for me to evaluate the impact of training." While it is true that many variables can affect performance after a training program (including the participant's self-motivation, work environment, peer pressure and on-going reinforcement), wishing for less-complex duties and responsibilities is like wishing that you didn't have to write that big term paper. Figure out how to do it and get it done!

Source: Phillips, J.J. (2010). *Handbook of Training Evaluation and Measurement Methods* (3rd Ed.). Taylor & Francis/Rutledge: New York.

Performance appraisal **the process of assessing how well employees are doing their jobs**

the training modules when it is convenient (in other words, they don't have to fall behind at their jobs to attend week-long training courses), workplace productivity should increase and employee stress should decrease.

There are, however, several disadvantages to e-learning. First, despite its increasing popularity, it's not always the appropriate training method. E-learning can be a good way to impart information, but it isn't always as effective for changing job behaviours or for developing problem-solving and analytical skills. Second, e-learning requires a significant investment in computers and high-speed Internet and network connections for all employees. Finally, although e-learning can be faster, many employees find it so boring and unengaging that they may choose to do their jobs rather than complete e-learning courses when sitting alone at their desks. E-learning may become more interesting, however, as more companies incorporate game-like features such as avatars and competition into their e-learning courses.

Dow Chemical Canada now has the ability to provide e-learning or e-training to all its employees through its Learn@dow.now Web-based training system.[55] Likewise, Cisco Systems offers 4,500 e-learning courses to its managers and employees.[56] And British Telecom used an avatar-based course to train 4,500 salespeople in just over a month. Traditional classroom training would have cost twice as much and taken twice as long to deliver.[57] These companies all determined that the advantages of e-learning far outnumbered the disadvantages.

Ivelin Radkov/Shutterstock.com

4.3 Evaluating Training

After selecting a training method and conducting the training, the last step is to evaluate the training. Training can be evaluated in four ways: on *reactions* (how satisfied trainees were with the program), on *learning* (how much employees improved their knowledge or skills), on *behaviour* (how much employees actually changed their on-the-job behaviour because of training), or on *results* (how much training improved job performance—for example, how much it increased sales or quality, or decreased costs).[58] In general, if done well, training provides meaningful benefits for most companies. A study by the Canadian Society for Training and Development found that even a small training budget can produce a 15 percent increase in sales, or a 22 percent reduction in rejected parts.[59]

LO5 Performance Appraisal

Performance appraisal is the process of assessing how well employees are doing their jobs. Most employees and managers intensely dislike performance appraisals. One manager says: "I hate annual performance reviews. I hated them when I used to get them, and I hate them now that I give them. If I had to choose between performance reviews and paper cuts, I'd take paper cuts every time. I'd even take razor burns and the sound of fingernails on a blackboard."[60] Unfortunately, attitudes like this are all too common. In fact, 70 percent of employees are dissatisfied with the performance appraisal process at their company. And according to the Society for Human Resource Management, 90 percent of human resource managers are dissatisfied with their company's performance appraisal system.[61]

Let's explore how companies can avoid some of these problems with performance appraisals ***by 5.1 accurately measuring job performance*** *and* ***5.2 effectively sharing performance feedback with employees.***

5.1 Accurately Measuring Job Performance

Workers often have strong doubts about the accuracy of their performance appraisals—and they may be right. For example, it's widely known that assessors are prone to errors when rating worker performance. One of the reasons managers make these errors is that they often don't spend enough time gathering or reviewing performance data. To minimize rating errors and improve the accuracy of job performance measures, two general approaches have been taken: improving performance appraisal measures themselves, and training performance raters to be more accurate.

One way for companies to improve performance appraisals is to use as many objective performance measures as possible. **Objective performance measures** are measures of performance that are easily counted or quantified. Common objective performance measures include output, scrap, waste, sales, customer complaints, and rejection rates.

Common Rating Errors

Central tendency error occurs when assessors rate all workers as average or in the middle of the scale.

Halo error occurs when assessors rate a particular worker as performing at the same level (good, bad, or average) in all parts of his or her job.

Leniency error occurs when assessors rate all workers as performing particularly well.

PeskeyMonkey/E+/Getty Images

But when objective measures aren't available—and frequently they aren't—subjective measures have to be used instead. Subjective performance measures require that someone judge or assess a worker's performance. The most common kind of subjective performance measure is the graphic rating scale (GRS; see Exhibit 11.8 on page 192). Graphic rating scales are most widely used because they are easy to construct, but they are very susceptible to rating errors.

Objective performance measures measures of job performance that are easily and directly counted or quantified

Behavioural observation scales (BOSs) rating scales that indicate the frequency with which workers perform specific behaviours that are representative of the job dimensions critical to successful job performance

Rater training training performance appraisal raters in how to avoid rating errors and increase rating accuracy

A popular alternative to graphic rating scales is the **behavioural observation scale (BOS)**. BOS requires raters to rate the frequency with which workers perform specific behaviours representative of the job dimensions that are critical to successful job performance. Exhibit 11.8 on page 192 shows a BOS for two important job dimensions for a retail salesperson: customer service, and money handling. Notice that each dimension lists several specific behaviours characteristic of a worker who excels in that dimension of job performance. (Normally, the scale would list 7 to 12 items per dimension, not 3 as in the exhibit.) Notice also that the behaviours are good behaviours, meaning they indicate good performance, and that the rater is being asked to judge how frequently an employee engaged in those good behaviours. The logic behind the BOS is that better performers engage in good behaviours more often.

BOSs work well for rating critical dimensions of performance. Also, studies have found that managers strongly prefer BOSs when giving performance feedback; when differentiating between poor, average, and good workers; when identifying training needs; and when measuring performance. In response to the statement, "If I were defending a company, this rating format would be an asset to my case," lawyers strongly preferred BOSs over other kinds of subjective performance appraisal scales.[62]

The second approach to improving the measurement of workers' job performance is **rater training**. Most effective in this regard is frame-of-reference training, in which a group of trainees learn how to conduct performance appraisals by watching a videotape of an employee at work. Next, they evaluate the performance of the person in the videotape. A trainer (i.e., subject matter expert) then shares his or her evaluations, and trainees' evaluations are compared with the expert's. The expert then explains his or her evaluations. This process is repeated until the differences in evaluations by trainees and evaluations by the expert are minimized. The logic behind frame-of-reference training is that by adopting the frame of reference used by an expert, trainees will be able to accurately observe, judge, and use the scale to evaluate performance of others.[63]

Exhibit 11.8 Subjective Performance Appraisal Scales

Graphic Rating Scale

	Very Poor	Poor	Average	Good	Very Good
Example 1: Quality of work performed is	1	2	3	4	5

	Very Poor (20% errors)	Poor (15% errors)	Average (10% errors)	Good (5% errors)	Very Good (less than 5% errors)
Example 2: Quality of work performed is	1	2	3	4	5

Behavioural Observation Scale

Dimension: Customer Service	Almost Never				Almost Always
1. Greets customers with a smile and a "hello."	1	2	3	4	5
2. Calls other stores to help customers find merchandise that is not in stock.	1	2	3	4	5
3. Promptly handles customer concerns and complaints.	1	2	3	4	5

Dimension: Money Handling	Almost Never				Almost Always
1. Accurately makes change from customer transactions.	1	2	3	4	5
2. Accounts balance at the end of the day, no shortages or surpluses.	1	2	3	4	5
3. Accurately records transactions in computer system.	1	2	3	4	5

360-degree feedback a performance appraisal process in which feedback is obtained from the boss, subordinates, peers and coworkers, and the employees themselves

5.2 Sharing Performance Feedback

After gathering accurate performance data, the next step is to share performance feedback with employees. Unfortunately, even when performance appraisal ratings are accurate, the appraisal process often breaks down at the feedback stage. Employees become defensive and dislike hearing any negative assessments of their work, no matter how small. Managers become defensive, too, and dislike giving appraisal feedback as much as employees dislike receiving it.

What can be done to overcome the inherent difficulties in performance appraisal feedback sessions? Since performance appraisal ratings have traditionally been the judgments of just one person, the boss, one possibility is to use **360-degree feedback**. In this approach, feedback comes from four sources: the boss, subordinates, peers and coworkers, and the employees themselves. The data, which are obtained anonymously (except for the feedback from the boss), are compiled into a feedback report that compares the employee's self-ratings with those of the boss, subordinates, peers, and coworkers. Usually, a consultant or human resource specialist discusses the results with the employee. The advantage of 360-degree programs is that feedback such as "You don't listen" is often more credible when it comes from several people.

Herbert Meyer, who has been studying performance appraisal feedback for more than 30 years, recommends a list of topics for discussion in performance appraisal feedback sessions (see Exhibit 11.9).[64]

How these topics are discussed in a review session is important for its success. Managers can do three things to make performance reviews as comfortable and productive as possible. First, they can separate developmental feedback, which is designed to improve future performance, from administrative feedback, which is used as a reward for past performance (e.g., raises). When managers give developmental feedback, they're acting as coaches, but when they give administrative feedback, they're acting as judges. These two roles, coaching and judging, are clearly incompatible. As coaches, managers are encouraging, pointing out opportunities for growth and improvement, and employees are typically open and receptive to feedback. But as judges, managers are evaluative, and employees are typically defensive and closed to feedback.

Second, Meyer suggests that performance appraisal feedback sessions be based on self-appraisals, in which employees carefully assess their own strengths, weaknesses, successes, and failures in writing. Because employees play an active role in the review of their performance, managers can be coaches rather than judges. Also, because the focus is on goals and development, both employees and managers are likely to be more satisfied with the process and more committed to plans and changes. And because the focus is on development and not administrative assessment, self-appraisals lead to more candid self-assessments than traditional supervisory

Exhibit 11.9 What to Discuss in a Performance Appraisal Feedback Session

- Overall progress—an analysis of accomplishments and shortcomings. There should be no surprises coming into the interview.
- Problems encountered in meeting job requirements. The discussion should also include any goals from the employee on the 360 feedback system.
- Opportunities to improve performance. Give employees praise and comments on their strong points. Telling them what they did wrong can be useful, but they won't necessarily know what to do right. Telling them what they did right helps them remember these behaviours.
- Long-range plans and opportunities—for the job and for the individual's career. This should be part of HR planning, HR training, and HR succession planning.
- General discussion of possible plans and goals for the coming year, again including the employee's 360 goals.

Sources: I.M. Jawahar, "Correlates of Satisfaction with Performance Appraisal Feedback," *Journal of Labor Research* 27, no. 2 (2006): 213–236; H.H. Meyer, "A Solution to the Performance Appraisal Feedback Enigma," *Academy of Management Executive* 5, no. 1 (1991): 68–76; and S.C. Payne, M.T. Horner, W.R. Boswell, A.N. Schroeder, & K.J. Stine-Cheyne, "Comparison of Online and Traditional Performance Appraisal Systems," *Journal of Managerial Psychology* 24, no. 6 (2009): 526–544.

Good Tip!

Next time you have to talk with someone about their performance, follow these four steps:

1. Be specific. Feedback needs to be actionable. Use concrete examples to back up your conclusions. Avoid generalized character attacks. Instead, describe the behaviour.
2. State the impact. Tell the person how his behaviour is affecting you, the team, or the organization.
3. Prescribe. Be specific about what needs to change. Often employees won't know what to change unless you tell them.
4. Do it often. Get in the habit of praising good performance and identifying troublesome behaviour.

Coaching, supporting, recognizing, and managing performance is the tough part of management, but it is an extremely important one. Organizations can only reach their strategic objectives if their personnel are coached and supported in their journey toward accomplishing their various strategic goals that add up to the organization's objectives.

Sources: Adapted from the book "Guide to Giving Effective Feedback," http://hbr.org/product/guide-to-giving-effective-feedback/an/10667-PDF-ENG, accessed 12 Nov 2012; Phoel, C.M., Grady, S., Gallo, A., Bielaszka-DuVernay, C., Manzoni, J-F., Butler, T., Barsoux, J.L., Erickson, T., and Krattenmaker, P. Guide to giving effective feedback. *Harvard Business Review (2011).*

reviews.[65] See Exhibit 11.9 for a list of topics that Meyer recommends for discussion in performance appraisal feedback sessions.

Finally, what people do with the performance feedback they receive really matters. A study of 1,361 senior managers found that managers who reviewed their 360-degree feedback with an executive coach (hired by the company) were more likely to set specific goals for improvement, ask their bosses for ways to improve, and subsequently improve their performance.[66]

Managers need to receive feedback as well as give it. HCL Technologies, an outsourcer of technology services, has team members rate their bosses, and the evaluations are made public on the company's intranet to hold top managers accountable. This was the *boss*'s idea.[67] A five-year study of 252 managers found that their performance improved dramatically if they met with their subordinates to discuss their 360-degree feedback ("You don't listen") and how they were going to address it ("I'll restate what others have said before stating my opinion"). Performance was dramatically lower for managers who never discussed their 360-degree feedback with subordinates and for managers who did not routinely do so (some managers did not review their 360-degree feedback with subordinates each year of the study). Why is discussing 360-degree feedback with subordinates so effective? These discussions help managers better understand their weaknesses, force them to develop a plan to improve, and demonstrate to the subordinates the managers' public commitment to improving.[68] In short, it helps to have people discuss their performance feedback with others, but it particularly helps to have them discuss their feedback with the people who provided it.

Keeping Qualified Workers

After Motorola's mobile devices division lost $1.2 billion in 2007, the company decided to split in half. In times of transition and uncertainty, it is easy for a company to lose valuable employees as job security decreases and people seek opportunities elsewhere. In an effort to retain its human resources, Motorola established an incentive program that offered bonuses to employees in key roles who remained on the job and to their supervisors for keeping them there.[69]

Compensation the financial and non-financial rewards that organizations give employees in exchange for their work

Employee separation the voluntary or involuntary loss of an employee

Job evaluation a process that determines the worth of each job in a company by evaluating the market value of the knowledge, skills, and requirements needed to perform it

Piecework a compensation system in which employees are paid a set rate for each item they produce

Commission a compensation system in which employees earn a percentage of each sale they make

Profit sharing a compensation system in which a company pays a percentage of its profits to employees in addition to their regular compensation

Employee stock ownership plan (ESOP) a compensation system that awards employees shares of company stock in addition to their regular compensation

Stock options a compensation system that gives employees the right to purchase shares of stock at a set price, even if the value of the stock increases above that price

LO6 Compensation and Employee Separation

Compensation includes both the financial and the nonfinancial rewards that organizations provide to employees in exchange for their work. **Employee separation** is a broad term covering the loss of an employee for any reason. *Involuntary separation* occurs when employers decide to terminate or lay off employees. *Voluntary separation* occurs when employees decide to quit or retire. Because employee separations affect recruiting, selection, training, and compensation, organizations should forecast the number of employees they expect to lose through terminations, layoffs, turnover, or retirements when doing human resource planning. The tax rate in Canada may be a surprise to many internationally recruited workers, as may be the overtime that many employees are required to contribute to the organization.

Let's learn more about compensation and employee separation by examining the ***6.1 compensation decisions that managers must make*** *as well as* ***6.2 terminations, 6.3 downsizing, 6.4 retirements,*** *and* ***6.5 turnover.***

6.1 Compensation Decisions

There are three basic kinds of compensation decisions: pay level, pay variability, and pay structure.[70]

Pay-level decisions are decisions about whether to pay workers at a level that is below, above, or at current market wages. Companies use job evaluation to set their pay structures. **Job evaluation** determines the worth of each job by determining the market value of the knowledge, skills, and requirements needed to perform it. After conducting a job evaluation, most companies try to pay the going rate, meaning the current market wage. There are always companies, however, whose financial situation causes them to pay considerably less than the current market wage. The child care industry, for example, has chronic difficulty filling jobs because it pays well below market wages. According to PayScale.com, while the director of a child care centre in Canada would make between $31,579 and $48,731, a child care worker would make $10 to $15 per hour ($19,000–$29,000). The pay for child care workers has gone up very little in the past 10 years.[71]

Some companies choose to pay above-average wages to attract and keep employees. *Above-market wages* can attract a larger, more qualified pool of job applicants, increase the rate of job acceptance, decrease the time it takes to fill positions, and increase the time that employees stay.[72]

Foreign workers in many parts of the world end up in low-paying jobs that disappear at the whim of the employer, with little in the way of security or benefits. Canada has a Seasonal Agricultural Workers Program that is considered by many a model of well-managed temporary immigration, and in the European Union, a third-country national (someone from outside the EU) who has held a legal temporary position for five years is entitled to permanent residency.[73]

Pay variability decisions concern the extent to which employees' pay varies with individual and organizational performance. Linking pay to performance is intended to increase employee motivation, effort, and job performance. Piecework, sales commissions, profit sharing, employee stock ownership plans, and stock options are common pay variability options. For instance, under **piecework** pay plans, employees are paid a set rate for each item produced up to some standard (e.g., 35 cents per item produced for output up to 100 units per day). Once productivity exceeds the standard, employees are paid a set amount for each unit of output over the standard (e.g., 45 cents for each unit above 100 units). Under a sales **commission** plan, salespeople are paid a percentage of the purchase price of items they sell. The more they sell, the more they earn.

Because pay plans such as piecework and commissions are based on individual performance, they can reduce the incentive that people have to work together. Therefore, companies also use group incentives (discussed in Chapter 10) and organizational incentives such as profit sharing, employee stock ownership plans, and stock options to encourage teamwork and cooperation.

With **profit sharing**, employees receive a portion of the organization's profits over and above their regular compensation. The more profitable the company, the more profit is shared. Employees at Proform Concrete Services Inc. of Red Deer, Alberta, share profits with the company. Proform awards 15 percent of the company's profits to its employees. The program is designed specifically to reward employees' loyalty and commitment.[74]

Employee stock ownership plans (ESOPs) compensate employees by awarding them shares of the company in addition to their regular compensation. By contrast, **stock options** give employees the right to purchase

How Do Options Work?

Options work like this. Let's say that you are awarded the right (or option) to buy 100 shares from the company for $5 a share. If the company's stock price rises to $15 a share, you can exercise your options and make $1,000. When you exercise your options, you pay the company $500 (100 shares at $5 a share), but because the stock is selling for $15 in the stock market, you can sell your 100 shares for $1,500 and make $1,000. Of course, as the company's profits and share values increase, stock options become even more valuable to employees. Stock options have no value, however, if the company's stock falls below the option "grant price," which is the price at which the options have been issued to you. For instance, the options you have on 100 shares of stock with a grant price of $5 aren't going to do you a lot of good if the company's stock is worth $2.50. Why exercise your stock options and pay $5 a share for stock that sells for $2.50 a share on the stock market? (Stock options are said to be "underwater" when the grant price is lower than the market price.)

The Canadian Press (J.P. Moczulski)

shares at a set price. Proponents of stock options argue that this gives employees and managers a strong incentive to work hard to make the company successful. If they do, the company's profits increase, as does its share price, and stock options increase in value. If they don't, profits stagnate or turn into losses, and stock options decrease in value or become worthless.

The incentive has to be more than just a piece of paper, however. A study carried out by the Toronto Stock Exchange found that ESOP companies' five-year profit growth was 123 percent higher, their net profit margins were 95 percent higher, and their productivity measured by revenue per employee was 24 percent higher than for non-ESOP companies, among other benefits.[75]

Pay structure decisions are concerned with internal pay distributions—that is, the extent to which people in the company receive very different levels of pay.[76] With *hierarchical pay structures,* there are big differences from one pay level to the next. The highest pay levels are for people near the top of the pay distribution. The basic idea behind hierarchical pay structures is that large differences in pay between jobs or organizational levels should motivate people to work harder to obtain those higher paying jobs. Many publicly owned companies have hierarchical pay structures by virtue of the huge amounts they pay their top managers and CEOs. For example, the average CEO now makes 364 times as much as the average worker. True, this is down from 525 times the pay of average workers just eight years ago. But with CEO pay packages averaging $18.8 million per year and average workers earning just $36,140, the difference is still vast and can have a significant detrimental impact on employee morale.[77]

By contrast, *compressed pay structures* typically have fewer pay levels and smaller differences in pay between levels. Pay is less dispersed and more similar across jobs in the company. The basic idea behind compressed pay structures is that similar pay levels should lead to higher levels of cooperation, feelings of fairness and common purpose, and better group and team performance.

So, should a company choose a hierarchical pay structure or a compressed one? Studies tend to indicate that there are significant problems with the hierarchical approach. The most damaging finding is that there appears to be little link between organizational performance and the pay of top managers.[78] Furthermore, studies of professional athletes indicate that hierarchical pay structures (e.g., paying superstars 40 to 50 times more than the lowest paid athlete on the team) hurt the performance of teams and individual players.[79] Likewise, managers are twice as likely to quit their jobs when their companies have strongly hierarchical pay structures (i.e., when they're paid dramatically less than the people above them).[80] It seems that hierarchical pay structures work best for independent work, where it's easy to determine the contributions of individual performers and little coordination with others is needed to get the job done. In other words, hierarchical pay structures work best when clear links can be drawn between individual performance and individual rewards. By contrast, compressed pay structures, in which everyone receives similar pay, seem to work best for work that requires employees to work together. Some companies are pursuing a middle ground, combining hierarchical and compressed pay structures by giving ordinary workers the chance to earn more through ESOPs, stock options, and profit sharing.

Wrongful discharge a legal doctrine that requires employers to have a job-related reason to terminate employees

Downsizing the planned elimination of jobs in a company

Outplacement services employment-counselling services offered to employees who are losing their jobs because of downsizing

6.2 Terminating Employees

Hopefully, the words "You're fired!" have never been directed at you. They are inappropriate and need to be relegated to the junkyard of antiquated business phrases. Employees are not property and should not be spoken to as if they are. No one should hear those words; there are many more professional terms to use such as downsizing, layoffs, staff reductions, redundancies (really a British term), and other more progressive terms. The *Ontario Employment Standards Act, 2000,* lists a number of expressions that are commonly used to describe termination of employment. These include "let go," "discharged," "dismissed," "fired," and "permanently laid off."[81]

During the worldwide economic and banking crisis of 2009, more than 473,200 Canadian workers were let go from their jobs in the first half of the year. Getting let go is a terrible thing, but many managers make it even worse by bungling the process, needlessly provoking the person who was let go and unintentionally inviting lawsuits. Although downsizing is never pleasant (and managers hate it nearly as much as employees), managers can do several things to minimize the problems inherent in laying off or discharging employees.

First, in most situations, discharge should not be the first option. Instead, employees should be given a chance to change their behaviour. When problems arise, employees should have ample warning and must be specifically informed as to the nature and seriousness of the trouble they're in. After being notified, they should be given sufficient time to change. If the problems continue, the employees should again be counselled about their job performance, what could be done to improve their performance, and the possible consequences if things don't change (e.g., written reprimand, suspension without pay, or, ultimately, discharge). Sometimes this is enough to solve the problem. If the problem isn't corrected after several rounds of warnings and discussions, however, the employee may be terminated.[82]

Inappropriate management

Second, employees should be terminated only for a good reason. Employers used to hire and un-hire employees under the legal principle of employment at will, which allowed them to do so for any reason, good, bad, or none at all. Similarly, employees could quit for a good reason, a bad reason, or no reason whenever they desired. As employees began contesting their discharges in court, however, the principle of wrongful discharge developed. **Wrongful discharge** is a legal doctrine that requires employers to have a job-related reason to terminate employees. In other words, as with other major human resource decisions, termination decisions must be made on the basis of job-related factors, such as consistently poor performance or violating company rules.

6.3 Downsizing

Downsizing is the planned elimination of jobs in a company. Whether it's because of cost cutting, declining market share, previous overaggressive hiring and growth, or outsourcing, companies typically eliminate jobs every year. Professor Marc Mentzer of the University of Saskatchewan analyzed data from 250 of Canada's largest companies. He found that downsizing is not always done for economic reasons or because the company needs to become more efficient. Contrary to common belief, decisions to downsize were unrelated to past performance. Profitable companies were no more likely to downsize than less profitable ones. Also, downsized companies were no more likely to be profitable than companies that did not.[83] Two-thirds of companies that downsize will downsize a second time within a year.

Another study of downsizing, this one over 15 years, found that downsizing 10 percent of a company's workforce produced only a 1.5 percent decrease in costs; that firms that downsized increased their stock price by only 4.7 percent over three years, compared to 34.3 percent for firms that did not; and that profitability and productivity were generally not improved by downsizing.[84] Downsizing can also result in the loss of skilled workers who will be expensive to replace when the company grows again.[85] Clearly, the best strategy is to conduct effective human resource planning and avoid downsizing altogether. Downsizing should always be a last resort.

Companies that do find themselves having to downsize to survive should train their managers in how to break the news to downsized employees. Also, senior managers should explain in detail why downsizing is necessary and should time the announcement so that employees hear it from the company and not from other sources such as news reports.[86] Finally, companies should do everything they can to help downsized employees find other work. One of the best ways to do this is to use **outplacement services** that provide counselling for employees faced with downsizing. Outplacement services often include advice and training in preparing résumés, getting ready for job interviews, and identifying job opportunities in other companies. In all instances, layoffs should be handled with as much empathy as possible, and organizations should do everything in their power to help people through the process.

How to Conduct Layoffs

1. Provide clear reasons and explanations for the layoffs.
2. To avoid laying off employees with critical or irreplaceable skills, knowledge, and expertise, get input from human resources, the legal department, and several levels of management.
3. Train managers in how to tell employees that they are being laid off (i.e., stay calm; make the meeting short; explain why, but don't be personal; and provide information about immediate concerns such as benefits, job search, and collecting personal goods).
4. Give employees the bad news early in the day, and try to avoid laying off employees before holidays.
5. Provide outplacement services and counselling to help laid-off employees find new jobs.
6. Communicate with survivors to explain how the company and their jobs will change.

Source: M. Boyle, "The Not-So-Fine Art of the Layoff," *Fortune*, 19 March 2001, 209.

Guillermo Perales Gonzalez/The Agency Collection/Getty Images

6.4 Retirement

Early retirement incentive programs (ERIPs) offer financial benefits to employees to encourage them to retire early. Companies use ERIPs to reduce the number of employees in the organization; to reduce costs by eliminating positions after employees retire; to reduce costs by replacing highly paid with lower paid, less experienced employees; or to create openings and job opportunities for people inside the company.

ERIPs can save companies money, but they can also pose a big problem for managers if they fail to accurately predict which employees—the good performers or the bad ones—and how many will retire early. Consultant Ron Nicol says: "The thing that doesn't work is just asking for volunteers. You get the wrong volunteers. Some of your best people will feel they can get a job anywhere. Or you have people who are close to retirement and are a real asset to the company."[87] A "bigger than expected" response to the University of Waterloo's cost-cutting, early retirement package resulted in the loss of 340 faculty and staff—about one-eighth of its employees, almost all of whom were senior faculty or senior administrators. This unexpected response to the ERIP offer represented a change that would normally occur over 10 years.[88]

Because of the problems associated with ERIPs, many companies are now offering **phased retirement**, in which employees transition to retirement by working reduced hours over a period of time before completely retiring. The advantage for employees is that they have more free time but continue to earn salaries and benefits without changing companies or careers. The advantage for companies is that it allows them to reduce salaries as well as hiring and training costs and retain experienced, valuable workers.[89] Phased retirement should be anticipated and become an ongoing part of the HR planning cycle, along with succession planning and employee career path development (as outlined in Section 2).

Early retirement incentive programs (ERIPs) programs that offer financial benefits to employees to encourage them to retire early

Phased retirement employees transition to retirement by working reduced hours over a period of time before completely retiring

Employee turnover loss of employees who voluntarily choose to leave the company

Functional turnover loss of poor-performing employees who voluntarily choose to leave a company

6.5 Employee Turnover

Employee turnover is the loss of employees who voluntarily choose to leave the company. In general, most companies try to keep the rate of employee turnover low to reduce recruiting, hiring, training, and replacement costs. Not all kinds of employee turnover are bad for organizations, however. In fact, some turnover can actually be good. For instance, **functional turnover** is the loss of poor-performing employees who choose to leave the organization.[90] Functional turnover gives the organization a chance to replace poor performers with better ones. One study found that simply replacing

Dysfunctional turnover loss of high-performing employees who voluntarily choose to leave a company

poor-performing leavers with average workers would increase the revenues produced by retail salespeople in an upscale department store by $112,000 per person per year.[91] By contrast, **dysfunctional turnover**, the loss of high performers who choose to leave, is a costly loss to the organization.

Employee turnover should be carefully analyzed to determine whether good or poor performers are choosing to leave the organization. If the company is losing too many high performers, managers should determine the reasons and find ways to reduce the loss of valuable employees. The company may have to raise salary levels, offer enhanced benefits, or improve working conditions to retain skilled workers. One of the best ways to influence functional and dysfunctional turnover is to link pay directly to performance. A study of four sales forces found that when pay was strongly linked to performance via sales commissions and bonuses, poor performers were much more likely to leave (i.e., functional turnover). By contrast, poor performers were much more likely to stay when paid large, guaranteed monthly salaries and small sales commissions and bonuses.[92]

Managing human resource systems is a complex and changing area. Students interested in a career in HR should check out one of the many national or provincial websites (www.hrpa.ca; www.bchrma.org; www.hrpnl.ca; www.hrmam.org; etc.) Also students should talk to their faculty about gaining student membership in their prospective provincial associations and pursuing a Certified Human Resources Professional (CHRP) designation (see www.chrp.ca). Many of the requisite knowledge areas can be covered in your courses at the university or college level to help you prepare for the national exam. The CHRP designation is a mark of distinction, and anyone interested in a career in HR should seriously consider enrolling in the program.

Go online at
www.nelson.com/4ltrpress/icanmgmt2
And access the essential Study Tools online for this chapter:

- **Flashcards**, to help you study
- **Interactive Quizzes**, to test your knowledge
- **Audio Chapter Summaries**, for chapter review
- **Crossword Puzzles and Beat the Clock**, to review key terms
- **What Would You Do? Cases**, for applying your knowledge to real-life situations
- **Self Assessments**, to learn about what kind of manager you are
- **Videos and Media Quizzing**, where you can watch a video about a real-life company and test yourself on what you've learned

Be sure to consult the Chapter Review Card at the back of the textbook.

12

Managing Individuals and a Diverse Workforce

LEARNING OUTCOMES

LO1 Describe diversity and explain why it matters.

LO2 Understand the special challenges that the dimensions of surface-level diversity pose for managers.

LO3 Explain how the dimensions of deep-level diversity affect individual behaviour and interactions in the workplace.

LO4 Explain the basic principles and practices that can be used to manage diversity.

Demographic projections are that Canada's population diversity will increase greatly by 2031, which will in turn have an impact on workplace diversity. In 2006, 20 percent of Canadians were foreign-born. If immigration levels continue as they are until 2031, roughly one in three Canadian workers will be foreign born.

The data tell us that 58 percent of those who arrived in Canada between 2001 and 2006 came from Asia and the Middle East and that almost all were in the 25 to 54 age group, injecting youth into Canada's society, including its labour market. Looking to the future, this trend is expected to continue, with South Asians, the largest visible minority group, expected to represent 28 percent of the visible minority population by 2031.[1] International immigration continues to fuel increases in Canada's population, especially in the Western provinces, signalling to managers that the face of Canada's workforce is changing and will continue to do so. Exhibit 12.1 shows the projected changes to Canada's population over the next decade.

Other significant changes should also be mentioned, including the dramatic growth in the number of women in the paid workforce—a prominent social trend in Canada over the past half-century. In 2009, 58.3 percent of women in Canada were employed—more than double the percentage of women employed in 1976.[2] As well, the employment rate of women with children has experienced a sharp increase: 73 percent of all women with children under 16 and living at home are now part of the employed workforce, compared to only 39 percent in 1976.[3]

Other demographic changes continue to draw attention, including the aging of the baby boomers. The proportion of Canadians over 65 continues to increase and is expected to represent between 23 and 25 percent of the Canadian population by 2036 (compared to 14.9 percent in 2012). This will affect the future composition of the Canadian workforce. In 2009, 69 percent of the Canadian population was considered to be working-age; by 2036 this is expected to decline to 60 percent.[4]

Diversity a variety of demographic, cultural, and personal differences among an organization's employees and customers

Diversity and Why It Matters

Diversity means variety. Therefore, **diversity** exists in an organization when there are a variety of demographic, cultural, and personal differences among the people who work there and the customers who do business there. At Xerox Research Institute of Canada (XRIC) in Mississauga, there are 100 to 150 employees from 30 different countries. "It's like a United Nations here," say Yiliang Wu, a Ph.D. who came to Canada from his native China in 1999 and is now a team leader at XRIC. "It is a wonderful place to work. The diversity is exciting and embracing. What counts here is the contribution you make, not where you came from."[5]

LO1 Diversity: Differences That Matter

You'll begin your exploration of diversity by learning ***1.1 that diversity is not employment equity,*** *and* ***1.2 how to build a business case for diversity.***

1.1 Diversity Is Not Employment Equity

A common misconception is that workplace diversity and employment equity are the same. However, these concepts differ in several critical ways, including their purpose, how they are practised, and the reactions they produce. In

Exhibit 12.1 Visible Minority Groups in Canada, 2001 and 2017

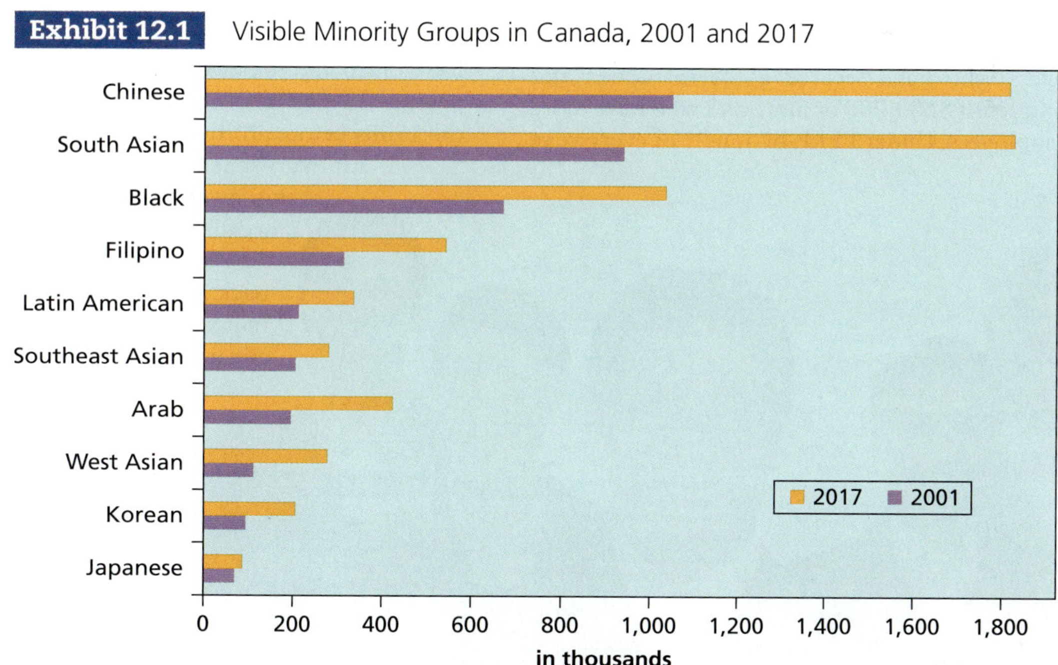

Source: Statistics Canada, "Visible Minority Groups in Canada, 2001 and 2017," *Canadian Demographics at a Glance*, 91-003-XWE 2007001. Released January 25, 2008. Available at http://www.statcan.gc.ca/pub/91-003-x/2007001/figures/4129878-eng.htm.

Employment equity an ongoing planning process used by an employer to eliminate barriers in an organization's employment procedures and to ensure appropriate representation of specific members of the workforce

Affirmative action purposeful steps taken by an organization to create employment opportunities for minorities and women

Canada, the term **employment equity** was introduced in 1984 to describe a planning process for achieving equality in all aspects of employment for four designated groups in Canada: women, Aboriginal peoples, persons with disabilities, and members of visible minorities.[6] In contrast, diversity exists in organizations where a variety of demographic, cultural, and personal differences exist among the people who work there and the customers who do business there. So, one key difference is that employment equity focuses more narrowly on demographics (gender, race, physical abilities), whereas diversity more broadly includes demographic as well as cultural and personal differences. A second difference is that employment equity is a process for actively creating diversity; however, diversity can exist even if organizations don't take purposeful steps to create it. For example, a McDonald's restaurant located near the University of British Columbia is more likely to have a more diverse group of employees than a McDonald's in Cochrane, Alberta.

A third important difference is that in Canada, certain employers are subject to the Employment Equity Act, passed in 1986, which contains two federal Employment Equity programs: the Legislated Employment Equity Program (LEEP), which applies to federally regulated employers and all federal departments; and the Federal Contractors Program (FCP), for employers who have secured a federal goods and services contract of $200,000 or more and who have more than 100 employees. Under LEEP, by June 1 of every year, employers must submit employment equity reports that detail the representation of the designated groups within their workforce. Similarly, under the FCP, contractors must certify in writing their commitment to employment equity in order to bid on large government contracts.[7] By contrast, there is no federal or provincial legislation to oversee diversity; organizations that pursue diversity goals do so voluntarily.

A common misconception is that workplace diversity and employment equity are the same.

Fourth, employment equity programs and diversity programs have different purposes. The purpose of employment equity is to

> *achieve equality in the workplace so that no person shall be denied employment opportunities or benefits for reasons unrelated to ability and in the fulfillment of goals, to correct the conditions of disadvantage in employment experienced by women, Aboriginal peoples, persons with disabilities, and visible minority people by giving effect to the principle that employment equity means more than treating persons in the same way but also requires special measures and the accommodation of differences.*[8]

In contrast, the general purpose of diversity programs is to create a positive work environment where no one is advantaged or disadvantaged, where "we" is everyone, where everyone can do his or her best work, where differences are respected and not ignored, and where everyone feels comfortable.

A distinction should be made between employment equity in Canada and affirmative action in the United States. **Affirmative action** refers to the purposeful steps taken by an organization to create employment opportunities for women and minorities; it includes programs that compensate for past discrimination, which was widespread in the 1960s before affirmative action legislation was passed. Affirmative action is required by law for private employers with 50 or more employees, and organizations that fail to uphold these laws may be required to hire, promote, or give back pay to those not hired or promoted; reinstate those who were wrongly terminated; pay legal fees and court costs for those who bring charges against them; and/or take other actions that make individuals whole by returning them to the condition or place they would have been had it not been for discrimination.[9] Thus, affirmative action is basically a punitive approach aimed

wavebreakmedia/Shutterstock.com

at organizations that have not achieved specific gender and race ratios in their workforces.[10]

Despite the overall success of affirmative action and employment equity in making workplaces much fairer than they used to be, the practice has drawn criticism from many people, especially when it comes to admissions quotas and hiring practices in institutions of higher education; government hiring practices; and the awarding of government contracts. Those who oppose these programs argue that giving preferential treatment to some groups at the expense of others is not fair; in particular, some Americans consider it unconstitutional.

1.2 Diversity Makes Good Business Sense

Those who support the idea of diversity in organizations often ignore its business aspects altogether, claiming instead that diversity is simply the right thing to do. Yet diversity actually makes good business sense in several ways: cost savings, attracting and retaining talent, and driving business growth.[11] The recent increase in senior executive positions such as "chief diversity officer" (CDO) suggests that more organizations are taking the business end of diversity seriously.[12]

Diversity experts have identified three strategic benefits of managing workplace diversity effectively[13]:

1. **Greater creativity and improved problem solving.** A workforce that has variances in demographic variables such as age, gender, and ethnicity/culture will also have diverse perspectives, skills, and talents. This aids in the performance of creative tasks and problem solving. In addition, employees who feel that diversity is supported in their organization tend to feel more valued and, as a result, tend to be more innovative. According to Marilyn Nagel, director of diversity at Cisco Systems Inc., "the link between innovation and diversity is clear. Companies that are more diverse regularly outperform companies that are not because they have stronger teamwork and a greater understanding of customers, partners, and suppliers."[14]
2. **Better insight into the needs of a diverse customer/client base.** As the market for goods and services continues to become more diverse, a diverse workforce with expanded cultural understanding becomes a competitive advantage for businesses that are intent on competing in the new global economy. Hyatt, the international hotel and resort company, understands firsthand that diversity among employees, customers, and suppliers is essential for success. Hyatt's vice president, Mark Demich, explains that "our employees mirror our guests, and since we operate all over the world, that means diversity and inclusion need to be part of our DNA. Companies that make diversity and inclusion an essential part of their business strategy are able to continually improve performance, productivity and customer satisfaction in the local and global marketplaces."[15]
3. **Enhanced ability to attract the best talent.** Companies achieve a competitive advantage when they optimize their human resources. They acquire that advantage when they hire and retain the best talent from an increasingly diverse labour market. Many companies today now understand that talented individuals are attracted to organizations that value their abilities and that respond to their unique needs; as a result, diversity has become an important part of recruitment efforts today. Diversity-friendly companies tend to attract better and more diverse job applicants.

The case for promoting workforce diversity is supported by research studies, including a 2011 *Forbes Insights* study of senior executives from companies that had in excess of $500 million in sales. That study found that 85 percent of companies agreed or strongly agreed that diversity is vital to innovation in the workplace.[16] A national survey of Canadians found that 77 percent of workers believe that cultural diversity contributes to innovation and creates a stronger business environment. Hadi Mahabadi, VP of the Xerox Research Centre of Canada, explains: "In the global economy of the 21st century, innovation will only thrive with the shared ideas of individuals with different backgrounds, areas of expertise and life experiences."[17]

In short, "diversity is no longer about counting heads; it's about making heads count," says Amy George, vice president of diversity and inclusion at PepsiCo.[18] Harvard Business School professor David Thomas agrees: "Where ten or twenty years ago, companies were asking, 'Will we be diverse?' today they must ask, 'How should we use diversity as a resource to be more effective as a business?'"[19] Ernest Hicks, who directs Xerox's corporate diversity office, says that "because we gain a competitive advantage by drawing on the experience, insight, and creativity of a well-balanced, diverse workforce, diversity enables Xerox to attract talent from the broadest possible pool of candidates. It creates more diverse work teams—facilitating diversity of thought and more innovative ideas—and it positions Xerox to attract a wider customer base and to address the needs of diverse customers."[20]

Overall, for many businesses today, the ability to manage and harness the benefits of today's diverse workforce is vital to remaining competitive in the changing global marketplace.

Diversity and Individual Differences

A survey that asked managers "What is meant by diversity to decision makers in your organization?" found that the following were most frequently mentioned: race, culture, gender, national origin, age, religion, and regional origin.[21] When managers describe workers this way, they are focusing on surface-level diversity.

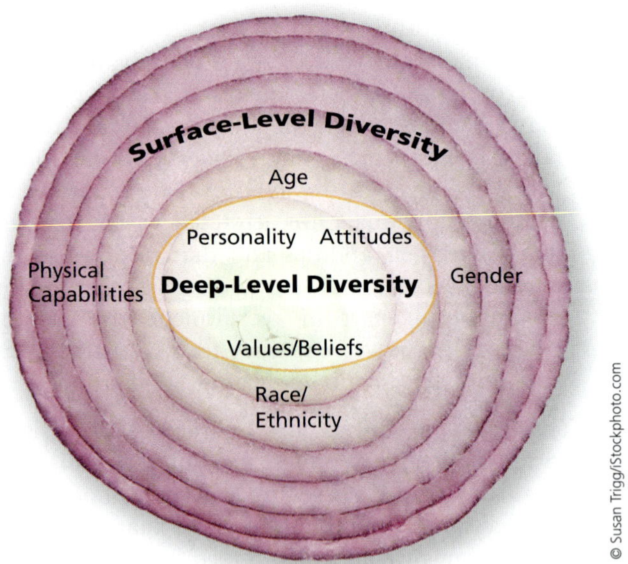

© Susan Trigg/iStockphoto.com

Surface-level diversity differences such as age, gender, race/ethnicity, and physical disabilities that are observable, typically unchangeable, and easy to measure

Deep-level diversity differences such as personality and attitudes that are communicated through verbal and nonverbal behaviours and are learned only through extended interaction with others

Social integration the degree to which group members are psychologically attracted to working with one another to accomplish a common objective

Age discrimination treating people differently (e.g., in hiring and firing, promotion, and compensation decisions) because of their age

Surface-level diversity relates to differences that are immediately observable, typically unchangeable, and easy to measure.[22] In other words, independent observers can usually agree on dimensions of surface-level diversity, such as another person's age, gender, race/ethnicity, or physical capabilities.

Most people start by using surface-level diversity to categorize or stereotype other people. But those initial categorizations typically give way to deeper impressions formed from knowledge of others' behaviour and psychological characteristics such as personality and attitudes.[23] When you think of others this way, you are focusing on deep-level diversity. **Deep-level diversity** consists of differences that are communicated through verbal and nonverbal behaviours and that are learned only through extended interaction with others.[24] Examples of deep-level diversity include personality differences, attitudes, beliefs, and values. In other words, as people in diverse workplaces get to know one another, the initial focus on surface-level differences such as age, race/ethnicity, gender, and physical capabilities is replaced by deeper, more complex knowledge of coworkers.

If managed properly, the shift from surface- to deep-level diversity can accomplish two things.[25] First, coming to know and understand one another better can result in reduced prejudice and conflict. Second, it can lead to stronger social integration. **Social integration** is the degree to which group members are psychologically attracted to working with one another to accomplish a common objective, or, as one manager put it, "working together to get the job done."

LO2 Surface-Level Diversity

Because age, gender, race/ethnicity, and physical disabilities are usually immediately observable, many managers and workers use these dimensions of surface-level diversity to form initial impressions and categorizations of coworkers, bosses, customers, or job applicants. Intentionally or not, sometimes those initial categorizations and impressions lead to decisions or behaviours that discriminate. Consequently, these dimensions of surface-level diversity pose special challenges for managers who are trying to create positive work environments where everyone feels comfortable and no one is advantaged or disadvantaged.

*Let's learn more about those challenges and the ways that **2.1 age, 2.2 gender, 2.3 race/ethnicity,** and **2.4 mental or physical disabilities** can affect decisions and behaviours in organizations.*

2.1 Age

Age discrimination is treating people differently (e.g., in hiring and firing, promotion, and compensation decisions) because of their age. A 2011 Ipso-Reid survey reports that one in three Canadians believe they've been the victim of age discrimination at work in a job interview, based on perceptions associated with their age.[26] Age discrimination can be levelled at younger as well as older workers; however, most often discussion in this area tends to focus on how older workers are sometimes seen as a burden, with younger candidates preferred in recruitment decisions. Age discrimination directed at older workers is often based on the assumption that "you can't teach an old dog new tricks," especially when it comes to computers and technology. In addition, some have the perception that older workers won't adapt to change, are sick more often, and, in general, are more expensive to employ than younger workers.

So, what's reality and what's myth? Do older employees actually cost more? In some ways, they do. The older people are and the longer they stay with a company, the more the company pays for salaries, pension plans, and vacation time. But older workers cost companies less, too, because they tend to show better judgment, care more about the quality of their work, and have a greater sense of loyalty to their employer. They are also less likely to quit, show up late, or be absent, the costs of which can be substantial. In fact, the myth of older workers being sick more often is not the case: studies show that younger workers, especially those with young children, take more sick days.[27] A survey by the Chicago outplacement firm Challenger, Gray & Christmas found that only 3 percent of employees age 50 and over changed jobs in any given year, compared to 10 percent of the entire workforce and 12 percent of workers aged 25 to 34. The study also found

Generational Assets

A mix of older and younger workers may be critical to a company's success in our fast-paced, interconnected global marketplace. Gen-Xers and particularly millennials are flexible; learn new technologies and skills easily; are comfortable with crossing boundaries of space, time, and class; and tend to value collaboration. Baby boomers, while they can be slower to adapt to change, have experience and knowledge, both of which are critical to a company's stability. The challenge is to overcome generational differences in values, work methods, and communication styles within work groups. Capitalizing on the different strong points of each group and training employees on these differences are essential for success.

Sources: W. Boddie, J. Contardo, and R. Childs, "The Future Workforce: Here They Come," *The Public Manager* 36 (winter 2007) 25–28; E. White, "Age is as Age Does; Making the Generation Gap Work for You," *The Wall Street Journal*, available online at http://online.wsj.com/article/SB121478926535514813.html [accessed 21 August 2008].

ranplett/E+/Getty Images (left); photomak/Shutterstock.com (right)

that while older workers make up about 14 percent of the workforce, they suffer only 10 percent of all workplace injuries and use fewer health care benefits than younger workers with school-age children.[28] As for the widespread belief that job performance declines with age, the scientific evidence clearly refutes this stereotype. Performance does not decline with age regardless of the type of job.[29]

The stereotype and perception of older workers has changed somewhat in recent years. A 2012 survey conducted with 500 hiring managers across a range of industries examined how managers view mature workers (defined as age 50 or above) and younger candidates, referred to as Millennials (i.e., born just before the milenium, from 1981 through 2000). It found that mature workers were considered more reliable (cited by 91 percent of respondents), more professional (88 percent), and better listeners (77 percent). Millennial workers, on the other hand, were thought to be more creative (74 percent), stronger networkers (73 percent) and more highly motivated (42 percent). Overall, these respondents said they were three times as likely to hire a mature worker as they were to hire a Millennial.[30]

Age will continue to be an important issue for managers as long as aging baby boomers continue to represent a substantial portion of the workforce. Those workers will be harder to replace when they exit the workforce. According to Statistics Canada, there is only one worker aged 25 to 34 years old for every three workers aged 55 or older; two decades ago, that ratio was reversed, at three younger workers for every older worker. As a result, employers will need to consider ways to maintain the skills of older workers, encourage older employees to stay at work, and make plans to prepare for when they leave. For example, making a commitment to provide ongoing training and development will help keep older workers engaged. It will also maintain their skills and enable them to master new skills as the economy changes. Reverse mentoring—where an experienced worker is trained by a younger mentor—can help support the professional development of both older and younger workers. Sue Black, head of Human Resources at Sodexo Canada, supports this practice: "We've found strong outcomes with reverse mentoring. It helps our older employees keep up with new trends, especially in technology, while also being able to share their wisdom with their younger mentor."[31] As well, allowing more part-time work and telecommuting may encourage older workers to stay on, extending their time in the workforce by placing lighter burdens on them.[32]

Gender discrimination treating people differently because of their gender

Glass ceiling the invisible barrier that prevents women and minorities from advancing to the top jobs in organizations

2.2 Gender

Gender discrimination occurs when people are treated differently because of their gender. Gender discrimination and racial/ethnic discrimination (discussed in the next section) are often associated with the so-called **glass ceiling**, the invisible barrier that prevents women and minorities from advancing to the top jobs in organizations.

To what extent do women face gender discrimination in the workplace? Statistics Canada reports that in 2011, men earned on average $956 per week while women earned $723 (see Exhibit 12.2 on page 206).[33] The fact that men continue to earn more than women is not new; what *is* concerning for many is the lack of progress in narrowing the earnings gap. Annual earnings of full-year, full-time women workers have held steady at 72 percent of men's earnings since the early 1990s; this contrasts with the preceding 20 years, during which there was a modest but steady narrowing of the earnings gap.[34]

A Conference Board of Canada study examined Canada's executive ranks from 1987 to 2009. It found

Exhibit 12.2 Average Earnings by Gender

Source: Statistics Canada, "Average Earnings by Sex and Work Pattern (All Earners)," http://www.statcan.gc.ca/tables-tableaux/sum-som/l01/cst01/labor01a-eng.htm.

that men are two to three times more likely than women to hold senior management positions, and 1.5 times more likely to hold posts in middle management, even though women make up almost half of Canada's workforce. Even more concerning for some is that the proportion of women in senior management changed very little during the time period studied. "Women have made great progress in many areas of society over the past 22 years, but not in the ranks of senior management positions," says the Conference Board's president and CEO, Anne Golden.[35] The statistics in business ownership are more encouraging—between 2001 and 2011, the number of self-employed females increased by 23 percent, compared with 14 percent for men. All in all, women have ownership in about 47 percent of small and medium-sized business enterprises (SMEs) and majority ownership in 16 percent of SMEs.[36]

Is gender discrimination the sole reason for the gender wage gap and for the slow rate at which women have been promoted to middle and upper management? Most economists agree that wage structures reflect a variety of human capital factors (such as experience, education, and tenure) and demographic characteristics (such as marital status and presence of children), as well as job characteristics (such as union status, part-time status, occupation, industry, and firm size).[37] In some instances, the slow progress appears to be due to career and job choices. Whereas men's career and job choices are often driven by the search for higher pay and advancement, women are more likely to choose jobs or careers that also give them a greater sense of accomplishment, more control over their work schedules, and easier movement in and out of the workplace.[38] Furthermore, women are historically much more likely than men to prioritize family over work at some point in their careers.

Beyond these reasons, however, it's likely that gender discrimination does play a role in women's slow progress into higher management. A national study of female executives found that even women who had climbed to the top of the corporate ladder believed that the glass ceiling still exists. Of those polled, 92 percent felt there was a divide in the opportunities for men and women to be promoted, and 72 percent felt that men were more likely to be given the opportunity to make important decisions.[39] As stated previously, there is an economic case for pursuing diversity in the workplace, and that includes gender diversity. According to Ann Golden, "increasing women's representation at the senior level is not simply a matter of justice or fairness—although it is that. And it is not simply a 'women's issue.' Companies that fail to integrate women's perspectives into their high-level decision making risk losing market share, competitive advantage, and profits."[40] So, what can companies do to make sure that women have the same opportunities for development and advancement as men? One strategy is mentoring, or pairing promising female executives with senior executives from whom they can seek advice and support. A vice president at a utility company says: "I think it's the single most critical piece to women advancing career-wise. In my experience you need somebody to help guide you and ... go to bat for you."[41] In fact, 91 percent of female executives have had a mentor at some point and feel their mentor was vital to their advancement.

The Golf Divide

For decades, golf has been known as the great executive pastime—the white male executive pastime. Today, however, many executive positions are held by women, who are less likely to be avid golfers, and techies and Silicon Valley executives, who prefer mountain biking, so corporate outings are becoming as diverse as their employees (soccer, cycling, etc.). Still, golf reigns as the activity of choice in many industries. And golf courses are considered ideal places to build and sustain business relationships. To get all types of businesspeople prepared to play, the PGA of America has a program called "Golf: For Business and for Life," which sponsors courses at colleges and universities. Also, the nonprofit Executive Women's Golf Association teaches the game to businesswomen, a growing number of whom are middle managers with executive aspirations.

Source: J. P. Newport and R. Adams, "Business Gold Changes Course," *The Wall Street Journal*, 26–27 May 2007, P1.

Another strategy is to make sure that male-dominated social activities don't unintentionally exclude women. Nearly half (47 percent) of women in the workforce believe that "exclusion from informal networks" makes it more difficult for them to advance their careers. By contrast, just 18 percent of CEOs thought this was a problem.[42] So it can be helpful to designate a "go-to person" other than their supervisor that women can talk to if they believe they are being held back or discriminated against because of their gender. Make sure this person has the knowledge and authority to conduct a fair and confidential internal investigation.[43]

2.3 Race/Ethnicity

Racial and ethnic discrimination occurs when people are treated differently because of their race or ethnicity. To what extent is racial and ethnic discrimination a factor in the workplace? And how is it addressed in the Canadian workplace? In Canada, the Canadian Human Rights Commission (CHRC) administers the Canadian Human Rights Act (CHRA) and is responsible for employers' compliance under the Employment Equity Act.

As noted previously, the role of visible minorities in Canada's workplace continues to expand in the face of an aging Canadian workforce and a lower birth rate. By 2031, Canada could be home to 14.4 million people belonging to a visible minority group, more than double the 5.3 million reported in 2006. The largest visible minority group, the South Asian population, could more than double from approximately 1.3 million in 2006 to 4.1 million by 2031, followed by the Chinese population, which is projected to grow from 1.3 million to 3 million.[44]

Racial and ethnic discrimination treating people differently because of their race or ethnicity

A national survey on career satisfaction and advancement of visible minorities in corporate Canada reported that visible minorities were more likely to perceive workplace barriers and lower levels of career satisfaction compared to white/Caucasian employees. Workplace barriers included the following: a perceived lack of fairness in terms of career advancement; inequality in performance standards; and fewer high-profile assignments. Given that career satisfaction is linked to productivity, the results are especially important for Canadian businesses—another reason to embrace diversity in the workplace.[45]

What accounts for the disparity between minority groups in the general population and their representation in management positions? Some studies have found that the disparities are due to pre-existing differences in training, education, and skills; when workers have similar skills, training, and education, they are much more likely to have similar jobs and salaries.[46]

Other studies, however, provide strong direct evidence of racial or ethnic discrimination in the workplace. For example, one study directly tested hiring discrimination by sending pairs of black and white males and pairs

The Judy Project

Judy Elder was a Toronto-based business leader who achieved great success at a relatively young age, reaching the top ranks of several large Canadian companies, including Microsoft Canada, IBM Canada, and Ogilvy One. She was known to be extremely passionate about the role women played in business, believing that there was plenty of room at the top for other women. After she passed away in 2002 at the age of 48, "The Judy Project—An Enlightened Leadership Forum for Executive Women," was established in her memory, in partnership with the Joseph L. Rotman School of Management at the University of Toronto. The annual week-long forum for a select group of senior executive women is a powerful and unique leadership-building experience led by CEOs and top academic thought leaders. "In a competitive environment," Colleen Moorehead, project cofounder and past president of E*Trade Canada, believes, "organizations thrive and grow on diversity of thinking and ideas. Selecting from 100% of available talent will always drive better results. Companies with diversity at the top, outperform their not so diverse peers where it counts, shareholder value. Corporate Canada can't afford to write-off 50% of its talent pool." The Judy Project's focus is to equip women to better navigate to the upper reaches of corporations while addressing the realities of the challenges that they face in seeking to be leaders of large organizations.

Courtesy of David Powell/Marketing Magazine

Sources: M. Johne, "Dynamic soul inspires program," *The Globe and Mail*, 14 June 2002; L. Bogomolny, "Melting the glass ceiling," Canadian Business Online, 24 April 2006.

Disability an activity limitation or participation restriction associated with a physical or mental condition or health problem

Disability discrimination treating people differently because of their disabilities

of Hispanic and non-Hispanic males to apply for the same jobs. Each pair went in with résumés with identical qualifications, and all were trained to present themselves in similar ways to minimize differences during interviews. The researchers found that the white males got three times as many job offers as the black males and that the non-Hispanic males got three times as many offers as the Hispanic males.[47]

Another study, which used similar methods to test hiring procedures at 149 different companies, found that whites received 10 percent more interviews than blacks. Half of the whites interviewed received job offers, but only 11 percent of the blacks. And when job offers were made, blacks were much more likely to be offered lower-level positions, while whites were more likely to be offered jobs at higher levels than the jobs they had applied for.[48]

Critics of these studies point out that it's nearly impossible to train different applicants to give identical responses in job interviews and that differences in interviewing skills may have somehow accounted for the results. However, British researchers found similar kinds of discrimination just by sending letters of inquiry to prospective employers. As in the other studies, the letters were identical except for the applicant's race. Employers often responded to letters from Afro-Caribbean, Indian, or Pakistani "applicants" by indicating that the positions had been filled. By contrast, they often responded to white, Anglo-Saxon "applicants" by inviting them to face-to-face interviews. Similar results were found with Vietnamese and Greek "applicants" in Australia.[49] In short, the evidence indicates that there is strong and persistent racial and ethnic discrimination in the hiring processes of many organizations.

What can companies do to make sure that people of all racial and ethnic backgrounds have the same opportunities?[50] They could start by looking at the numbers, comparing the hiring rates for whites to the hiring rates for racial and ethnic applicants. Then they could do the same thing for promotions within the company, and see if nonwhite workers quit at higher rates than white workers. Also, they could survey employees to compare white and nonwhite employees' satisfaction with jobs, bosses, and the company, as well as their perceptions regarding equal treatment. Next, if the numbers indicate racial or ethnic disparities, they could consider employing a private firm to test their hiring system by having applicants of different races with identical qualifications apply for company jobs.[51]

Another step companies can take is to eliminate unclear selection and promotion criteria. Vague criteria allow decision makers to focus on non-job-related characteristics that may lead unintentionally to employment discrimination. Selection and promotion criteria should spell out the specific knowledge, skills, abilities, education, and experience needed to perform a job well.

Finally, creating a culture that is visionary in its approach to diversity is key. It's not surprising that when it came time for PepsiCo to choose a new CEO, the board picked Indian-born Indra Nooyi. PepsiCo has a long history of diversity, stretching back to the end of the Second World War, when President Walter Mack hired Edward Boyd away from the National Urban League to head a team charged with launching a marketing program for African American consumers. In every part of the country where Boyd's team ran a marketing blitz, Pepsi sales increased, and soon Pepsi-Cola overtook market leader Coca-Cola in cities like Cleveland and Chicago. One of the most successful campaigns was a series of print advertisements titled "Leaders in Their Fields," which profiled the accomplishments of successful African American professionals. Pepsi's print campaign was the first to shun the stereotypical images of African Americans used in print and other advertisements. As you can see from PepsiCo's history, it takes a long time and a lot of effort to create a culture of diversity. But good hiring practices contribute to such an organizational culture and make it easier to achieve what PepsiCo has.[52]

AP Photo/Pepsi

2.4 Mental or Physical Disabilities

One in every seven Canadians is living with a disability. That is more than 4.4 million people.[53] A **disability** is defined as an activity limitation or participation restriction associated with a physical or mental condition or health problem.[54] In Canada, the most common types of disability involve pain, mobility, and agility—factors generally related to an aging population.[55] **Disability discrimination** occurs when people are treated differently because of their disability. To what extent is disability discrimination a factor in the workplace? According to the 2011 Annual Report on Disabilities, 26.1 percent of unemployed Canadian adults with a disability perceive that they have been refused work because of it.[56] In *The Business Case for Accessibility*, Bill Wilkerson summarizes the human resources potential of persons with disabilities in this way: "For far too many years, people with disabilities have been ignored in the marketplace. Yet this significant segment of the population is made up of many dedicated and talented people with much-needed abilities that have so far been under-utilized in the work environment."[57] Canadian statistics report that although 75.1 percent of working-age Canadians (those 14 to 64 years of age) were employed in 2006, only 53.5 percent of working-age Canadians with disabilities were.[58] In terms of income levels, individuals with disabilities earn less than people without disabilities, and women with disabilities earn far less than men with disabilities. Anna MacQuarrie, director of policy and programs for the Canadian Association for Community Living, says that "about 750,000 Canadians live with intellectual disabilities and they are predominantly among the poorest of the poor in Canada."[59]

Photo by Jim Wilkes/Toronto Star via Getty Images

What accounts for the disparities between the employment and income levels of able people and people with disabilities? One factor is that as a group, individuals with disabilities often have lower levels of education than those without, and corresponding lower levels of employment. But education alone does not explain the employment and income gaps that exist. "Even with education, people with disabilities do not achieve the same general labour market outcomes as those without. Other serious barriers include negative attitudes, inaccessible infrastructure, and the lack of various supports."[60] Studies show that as long as companies make reasonable accommodations for disabilities (e.g., changing procedures or equipment), people with disabilities perform their jobs just as well as able people. They also have better safety records and are no more likely to be absent or quit their jobs.[61]

What can companies do to make sure that people with disabilities have the same opportunities as everyone else? A good place to start is to commit to providing reasonable workplace accommodations to current and prospective employees with disabilities. Workplace modifications can be resource specific (e.g., job redesign, modified work schedules, computer aids) or physical/structural (e.g., handrails, modified workstations, accessible washrooms).[62] Accommodations for disabilities needn't be expensive. According to the Job Accommodation Network, 71 percent of accommodations cost employers $500 or less, and 20 percent of accommodations don't cost anything at all.[63]

Some of the accommodations described involve *assistive technology* that gives workers with disabilities the tools they need to overcome their disabilities. Providing workers with assistive technology is also an effective strategy for recruiting, retaining, and enhancing the productivity of people with disabilities. According to the National Council on Disability, 92 percent of workers with disabilities who

Workforce Health on the Decline

According to the Council for Disability Awareness, the general health of the American workforce is declining because of age and questionable lifestyle choices (poor diet, lack of exercise, etc.). Rising obesity rates are causing back pain, hip and knee injury (often leading to joint replacement), and diabetes. Claims for depression and other nervous disorders, chronic bronchitis, and asthma are also increasing. Many companies are finding ways to accommodate workers. American Express has made its cafeteria wheelchair accessible and has rearranged work schedules to coincide with the paratransit system. Sylvania has created flexible shifts for disabled employees, and General Motors enlists the help of an ergonomic specialist to help assign disabled workers to jobs that won't aggravate their ailments.

Source: M. P. McQueen, "Workplace Disabilities are on the Rise," *The Wall Street Journal*, 1 May 2007, D1.

gosphotodesign/Shutterstock.com

IBM Makes the Grade

IBM was recently ranked number 1 in *DiversityInc's* survey of the Top 10 Companies for People with Disabilities. In addition to education and recruitment programs, IBM provides a wide range of accommodations for its disabled workers. Ramps and power doors are installed for employees who use wheelchairs. Captioning devices, sign language interpreters, and note takers are available for deaf employees. Software programs that read text on a computer screen and audio transcripts of company publications are available for the blind. IBM has also formed Accommodation Assessment Teams to consult with employees to continue identifying and resolving unmet accommodations. IBM's efforts in training and mentoring programs for people with disabilities began when the company found itself constantly struggling to find precision machinists who could operate lathes and milling equipment. Eventually the company was able to find a trained and willing workforce in what some would consider an unlikely place—the National Technical Institute for the Deaf. This led IBM to hire employees with disabilities in other areas of the company. The company now estimates that between 4 and 6 percent of its workforce have disabilities.

Huntstock/Getty Images

Sources: "Accessibility at IBM: An Integrated Approach," IBM.com, n.d., http://www-03.ibm.com/able/access_ibm/execbrief.html#recruiting; "The DiversityInc Top 10 Companies for People with Disabilities," DiversityInc, May 6, 2010, http://www.diversityinc-digital.com/diversityincmedia/201006#pg38; C. Rash, "Hiring Disabled Veterans vs. Hiring Civilian Disabled People," Let's Talk About Work website, March 21, 2011, http://www.letstalkaboutwork.tv/hiring-disabled-veterans-vs-hiring-civilian-disabled-people.

use assistive technology report that it helps them work faster and better, 81 percent indicate that it helps them work longer hours, and 67 percent say that it is critical to getting a job.[64]

Finally, companies should actively recruit qualified workers with disabilities. In order to do so, Canadian employers need to overcome some misconceptions related to persons with disabilities.

Introverts and extraverts should be correctly matched to their jobs.

If an employer can move beyond these myths, hiring individuals with disabilities can make economic sense based on a simple equation: employers need skilled workers; persons with disabilities are a largely untapped human resource available to meet today's growing labour and skill shortages; and persons with disabilities are a large, growing consumer market.[65]

Myth:	Persons with disabilities can't keep up with other workers.
Reality:	90 percent of persons with disabilities rated average or better on job performance than their non-disabled colleagues.
Myth:	A person with a disability will miss a lot of work.
Reality:	86 percent of people with disabilities rated average or better on attendance than their non-disabled colleagues.
Myth:	A person with a disability will have more accidents on the job.
Reality:	98 percent of people with a disability rate average or better in work safety compared to their non-disabled colleagues.
Myth:	Persons with disabilities don't really want to work.
Reality:	Staff retention is 72 percent higher among persons with disabilities.

LO3 Deep-Level Diversity

As you learned in Section 2, people often use the dimensions of surface-level diversity to form initial impressions about others. Over time, however, initial impressions based on age, gender, race/ethnicity, and mental or physical disabilities give way to deeper impressions based on behaviour and psychological characteristics. When we think of others this way, we are focusing on deep-level diversity, or the differences that can be learned only through extended interaction with others—for example, differences in personality, attitudes, beliefs, and values. In short, recognizing deep-level diversity requires that we get to know and understand one another better. And that matters because it can result in less prejudice, discrimination, and conflict in the workplace. These changes can then lead to better *social integration*, defined as the degree to which organizational or group members are psychologically attracted to working with one another to accomplish a common objective.

Stop for a second and think about your current or previous manager. What words would you use to describe him or her? Is your boss introverted or extraverted? Agreeable or disagreeable? Organized or disorganized? When you describe your manager or others in this way, you are describing dispositions and personality.

A **disposition** is the tendency to respond to situations and events in a predetermined manner. **Personality** is the relatively stable set of behaviours, attitudes, and emotions displayed over time that makes people different from one another.[66] In other words, it is the person's core personality. In the past decade, personality research conducted in different cultures, different settings, and different languages has shown that five basic dimensions of personality account for most of the differences in people's behaviours, attitudes, and emotions. The *Big Five Personality Dimensions* are extraversion, emotional stability, agreeableness, conscientiousness, and openness to experience.[67]

Extraversion is the degree to which someone is active, assertive, gregarious, sociable, talkative, and energized by others. In contrast to extraverts, introverts are less active, prefer to be alone, and are shy, quiet, and reserved. For the best results in the workplace, introverts and extraverts should be correctly matched to their jobs.

Emotional stability is the degree to which someone is not angry, depressed, anxious, emotional, insecure, or excitable. People who are emotionally stable respond well to stress. In other words, they can maintain a calm, problem-solving attitude in even the toughest situations (e.g., conflict, hostility, dangerous conditions, or extreme time pressures). By contrast, emotionally unstable people find it difficult to handle the most basic demands of their work under only moderately stressful situations and become distraught, tearful, self-doubting, and anxious. Emotional stability is particularly important for high-stress jobs such as police work, firefighting, emergency medical treatment, and piloting planes.

Agreeableness is the degree to which someone is cooperative, polite, flexible, forgiving, good-natured, tolerant, and trusting. Basically, agreeable people are easy to work with and be around, whereas disagreeable people are distrusting and difficult to work with and be around.

Conscientiousness is the degree to which someone is organized, hard-working, responsible, persevering, thorough, and achievement oriented. Ninety-two studies across five occupational groups (professionals, police, managers, sales, and skilled/semiskilled jobs) with a combined total of 12,893 study participants indicated that, on average, conscientious people are inherently more motivated and are better at their jobs.[68]

Openness to experience is the degree to which someone is curious, broad-minded, and open to new ideas, things, and experiences; is spontaneous; and has a high tolerance for ambiguity. People in marketing, advertising, research, and other creative jobs need to be curious, open to new ideas, and spontaneous.

Which of the Big Five Personality Dimensions has the largest impact on behaviour in organizations? The cumulative results indicate that conscientiousness is related to job performance across five different occupational groups (professionals, police, managers, sales, and skilled/semiskilled jobs).[69] In short, people "who are dependable, persistent, goal directed, and organized tend to be higher performers on virtually any job; viewed negatively, those who are careless, irresponsible, low-achievement striving, and impulsive tend to be lower performers on virtually any job."[70] The results also indicate that extraversion is related to performance in jobs, such as sales and management, that involve significant interaction with others. In people-intensive jobs like these, it helps to be sociable, assertive, and talkative and to have energy and be able to energize others. Finally, people who are extraverted and open to experience seem to do much better in training. Being curious and open to new experiences as well as sociable, assertive, talkative, and full of energy helps people perform better in learning situations.[71]

Disposition the tendency to respond to situations and events in a predetermined manner

Personality the relatively stable set of behaviours, attitudes, and emotions displayed over time that makes people different from one another

Extraversion the degree to which someone is active, assertive, gregarious, sociable, talkative, and energized by others

Emotional stability the degree to which someone is not angry, depressed, anxious, emotional, insecure, and excitable

Agreeableness the degree to which someone is cooperative, polite, flexible, forgiving, good-natured, tolerant, and trusting

Conscientiousness the degree to which someone is organized, hardworking, responsible, persevering, thorough, and achievement oriented

Openness to experience the degree to which someone is curious, broad-minded, and open to new ideas, things, and experiences; is spontaneous; and has a high tolerance for ambiguity

How Can Diversity Be Managed?

How much should companies change their standard business practices to accommodate the diversity of their workers? What do you do when a talented top executive has a drinking problem that only seems to affect his behaviour at company social events or when entertaining clients, where he has made inappropriate advances toward female employees? What do you do when, despite aggressive company policies against racial discrimination, employees continue to tell racial jokes and publicly post cartoons displaying racial humour? And, since many people confuse diversity with employment equity, what do you do to make sure that your company's diversity practices and policies are viewed as benefiting all workers and not just some workers?

Questions like these make managing diversity one of the toughest challenges that managers face.[72] Nonetheless, there are steps companies can take to begin to address these issues.

Please Remain Stable

A well-known incident in which a JetBlue flight attendant lost his cool when dealing with a rude passenger illustrates what can happen when emotional stability is lacking in stressful situations. Moments after a JetBlue flight from Pittsburgh landed at New York's John F. Kennedy International Airport, a passenger stood up to retrieve his bags from the overhead bin while the plane was still moving—before the crew gave permission. When flight attendant Steven Slater told the passenger to remain seated, he refused. Slater approached the passenger just as he was pulling his bag down, striking Slater in the head. When Slater asked for an apology, the passenger cursed at him. Slater responded by cursing the passenger over the plane's public address system microphone, grabbing two beers from the beverage cart, and activating the emergency chute, which he used to slide out of the plane, head to the parking lot, and go home. Slater lost his job because of his inability to remain emotionally stable in this situation.

Source: A. Newman and R. Rivera, "Fed-Up Flight Attendant Makes Sliding Exit," *New York Times*, August 9, 2010, accessed May 28, 2011, http://www.nytimes.com/2010/08/10/nyregion/10attendant.html

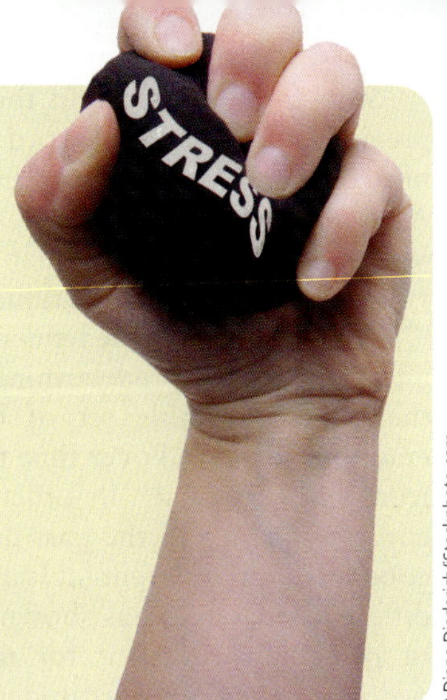

LO4 Managing Diversity

As discussed earlier, diversity programs try to create a positive work environment where no one is advantaged or disadvantaged, where "we" is everyone, where everyone can do his or her best work, where differences are respected and not ignored, and where everyone feels comfortable. *Let's begin to address those goals by learning about **4.1 different diversity paradigms, 4.2 diversity principles**, and **4.3 diversity training and practices**.*

4.1 Diversity Paradigms

There are several different methods or paradigms for managing diversity: the discrimination and fairness paradigm, the access and legitimacy paradigm, and the learning and effectiveness paradigm.[73] The *discrimination and fairness paradigm*, which is the most common method of approaching diversity, focuses on equal opportunity, fair treatment, recruitment of minorities, and strict compliance with the equal employment opportunity laws. Under this approach, success is usually measured by how well companies achieve recruitment, promotion, and retention goals for women, people of different racial/ethnic backgrounds, and other underrepresented groups. For example, one manager says:

> *If you don't measure something, it doesn't count. You measure your market share. You measure your profitability. The same should be true for diversity. There has to be some way of measuring whether you did, in fact, cast your net widely, and whether the company is better off today in terms of the experience of people of colour than it was a few years ago. I measure my market share and my profitability. Why not this?*[74]

The primary benefit of the discrimination and fairness paradigm is that it generally brings about fairer treatment of employees and increases demographic diversity. The primary limitation is that the focus of diversity remains on the surface-level dimensions of gender, race, and ethnicity.

The *access and legitimacy paradigm* focuses on the acceptance and celebration of differences to ensure that the diversity within the company matches the diversity found among primary stakeholders such as customers, suppliers, and local communities. This is similar to the *business growth* advantage of diversity discussed earlier in the chapter. The basic idea behind this approach is to attract a broader customer base by creating a more diverse workforce. "We are living in an increasingly multicultural country, and new ethnic groups are quickly gaining consumer power," says Ed Adams, vice president of human resources for Enterprise Rent-a-Car. "Our company needs a demographically more diverse workforce to help us gain access to these differentiated segments."[75] Consistent with this goal, he adds, "We want people who speak the same language, literally and figuratively, as our customers. We don't set quotas. We say [to our managers], 'Reflect your local market.'"[76] The primary benefit of this approach is that it establishes a clear business reason for diversity. Like the discrimination and fairness paradigm, however, it focuses only on surface-level diversity dimensions of gender, race, and ethnicity. Furthermore, employees who are assigned responsibility for customers and stakeholders on the basis of their gender, race, or ethnicity may eventually feel frustrated and exploited.

Whereas the discrimination and fairness paradigm focuses on assimilation (having a demographically representative workforce), and the access and legitimacy paradigm focuses on differentiation (having demographic differences inside the company match those of key customers and stakeholders), the *learning and effectiveness paradigm* focuses on integrating deep-level diversity differences, such as personality, attitudes, beliefs, and values, into the actual work of the organization. Aetna's 28,000 employees are diverse not only in terms of gender, ethnicity, and race, but also by age group, sexual orientation, work styles and levels, perspective, education, skills, and other characteristics. Raymond Arroyo, head of diversity at Aetna, says: "Diversity at Aetna means

Good Tip!

How to Create a Learning and Effectiveness Diversity Paradigm

1. Understand that a diverse workforce will embody different perspectives and approaches to work. Value variety of opinion and insight.
2. Recognize both the learning opportunities and the challenges that the expression of different perspectives presents for your organization.
3. Set high standards of performance for everyone.
4. Create an organizational culture that stimulates personal development.
5. Encourage openness and a high tolerance for debate. Support constructive conflict on work-related matters.
6. Create an organizational culture in which workers feel valued.
7. Establish a clear mission and make sure it is widely understood. This keeps discussions about work differences from degenerating into debates about the validity of individual perspectives.
8. Create a relatively egalitarian, nonbureaucratic structure.

Source: D. A. Thomas and R. J. Ely, "Making Differences Matter: A New Paradigm for Managing Diversity," *Harvard Business Review* 74, (September–October 1996); 79–90.

treating individuals individually, leveraging everyone's best, and maximizing the powerful potential of our workforce." He adds: "Part of a top diversity executive's role in any organization is to integrate diversity into every aspect of a business, including the workforce, customers, suppliers, products, services and even into the community a business serves."[77]

The learning and effectiveness paradigm is consistent with achieving organizational plurality. **Organizational plurality** describes a work environment where (1) all members are empowered to contribute in a way that maximizes the benefits to the organization, customers, and themselves, and (2) the individuality of each member is respected by not segmenting or polarizing people on the basis of their membership in a particular group.[78]

Organizational plurality a work environment where (1) all members are empowered to contribute in a way that maximizes the benefits to the organization, customers, and themselves, and (2) the individuality of each member is respected by not segmenting or polarizing people on the basis of their membership in a particular group

The learning and effectiveness diversity paradigm offers four benefits.[79] First, it values common ground. Dave Thomas of the Harvard Business School explains: "Like the fairness paradigm, it promotes equal opportunity for all individuals. And like the access paradigm, it acknowledges cultural differences among people and recognizes the value in those differences. Yet this new model for managing diversity lets the organization internalize differences among employees so that it learns and grows because of them. Indeed, with the model fully in place, members of the organization can say, 'We are all on the same team, with our differences—not despite them.'"[80]

Second, this paradigm distinguishes between individual and group differences. When diversity focuses only on differences between groups, such as females versus males, large differences within groups are ignored.[81] For example, think of the women you know at work. Now, think for a second about what they have in common. After that, think about how they're different. If your situation is typical, the list of differences should be just as long as the list of commonalities if not longer. In short, managers can achieve a greater understanding of diversity and their employees by treating them as individuals and by realizing that not all employees want the same things at work.[82]

Third, because the focus is on individual differences, the learning and effectiveness paradigm is less likely to encounter the conflict, backlash, and divisiveness sometimes associated with diversity programs that focus only on group differences. Ray Haines, a consultant who

© Robert Bremec/iStockphoto.com

IF YOU DON'T MEASURE SOMETHING, . . . IT DOESN'T COUNT.

RelaxFoto.de/E+/Getty Images

has helped companies deal with the aftermath of diversity programs that became divisive, says: "There's a large amount of backlash related to diversity training. It stirs up a lot of hostility, anguish, and resentment but doesn't give people tools to deal with [the backlash]. You have people come in and talk about their specific ax to grind."[83] Not all diversity programs are divisive or lead to conflict. But, by focusing on individual rather than group differences, the learning and effectiveness paradigm helps to minimize these potential problems.

Finally, unlike other diversity paradigms that simply focus on the value of being different (primarily in terms of surface-level diversity), the learning and effectiveness paradigm focuses on bringing different talents and perspectives *together* (i.e., deep-level diversity) to make the best organizational decisions and to produce innovative, competitive products and services.

4.2 Diversity Principles

Diversity paradigms are general approaches or strategies for managing diversity. Whichever diversity paradigm is chosen, diversity principles will help managers do a better job of *managing company diversity programs*.[84]

In a study of the Top 1,000 Canadian companies and employers filing employment equity reports, researchers at the Richard Ivey School of Business identified nine action areas for managing diversity.[85]

Linking diversity to strategic business goals. At Alberta-based Syncrude Canada, understanding of the strategic value of diversity is expressed by the following equation: high job satisfaction = motivation = going above and beyond in times of change and growth = breakthrough business performance. In general, larger organizations are more likely to include diversity in their mission statement, to have a diversity council (that includes executives), to link diversity to business strategy, and to have a clear understanding of how diversity links to economic performance.

Including diversity in human resource planning. Organizations that understand how diversity can contribute to success will make strides to incorporate diversity in human resource planning. For example, Xerox Corporation traced the career paths—specifically, the key jobs—taken by top executives as they advanced in the company, and then set goals for placing women and visible minorities on those same paths in order to ensure diversity in future top executive candidates.

Recruiting a diverse workforce. Organizations can ensure that recruiting materials (ads, brochures, website), recruiting processes, and the pools for identifying potential hires encourage a diverse set of applicants. Innoversity, a Canadian nonprofit organization that works to create opportunities for visible minorities, created a venue where artists and journalists from diverse ethnic groups could pitch their ideas to producers and broadcasters from across Canada. To meet its growing hiring needs, Suncor Energy now recruits around the world, including in countries such as Venezuela and South Africa.[86]

Selecting a diverse workforce. To facilitate diversity in the selection process, organizations should utilize structured interviews, assemble diverse teams to interview candidates, and identify ways that candidates can demonstrate job qualifications beyond traditional experiences. The

"We are all on the **same team,**

University of British Columbia trains recruitment managers on employment equity in the interview process, and Corus Entertainment Inc. forwards job openings to organizations representing the disabled, such as the Canadian National Institute for the Blind.[87]

Training and developing a diverse staff. Research shows that women and visible minorities are more likely to be chosen for management positions in organizations that provide more training and development opportunities. This highlights critical elements needed for career advancement among a diverse workforce. TD Bank, for example, offers a training curriculum to help foreign-educated professionals integrate into the workforce, and also offers a mentoring and internship program.[88]

© Yuri/iStockphoto.com

Monitoring the effectiveness of staffing for diversity. Organizations that fall under Canada's Employment Equity Act are required to submit statistics annually to the federal government. However, other firms may also collect data to assess the level of workforce diversity by tracking the diversity of applicants, new hires, promotions, and turnover rates.

Providing work-life flexibility and *Creating an inclusive working environment*. Organizations offering flexible organizational structures and benefits to employees create a more inclusive workplace environment for employees with a variety of family situations. An inclusive work environment has been linked to increased productivity and profitability. Flexibility benefits might include these: flexible work scheduling, work-at-home options, job sharing, reduced work hours, a compressed work week, part-time employment, and an on-site or company-supported dependent care centre.

Senior executive support for diversity. Support from senior management can be vital for creating and promoting workplace diversity. Home Depot Canada created a Diversity and Inclusion Committee in 2007, led by the VP of Human Resources, to measure recruitment activities in relation to diverse groups and to increase the number of disabled employees. Calgary-based Agrium Inc., a leading retail supplier of agricultural products, seeks to establish a long-term, formal diversity and inclusiveness strategy for the company with a program led by the CEO and supported by the in-house Diversity Council.[89]

Awareness training training designed to raise employees' awareness of diversity issues and to challenge the underlying assumptions or stereotypes they may have about others

4.3 Diversity Training and Practices

Organizations use diversity training and several common diversity practices to manage diversity. There are two basic types of diversity training programs. **Awareness training** is designed to raise employees' awareness of diversity issues, such as the five dimensions discussed in this chapter, and to get employees to challenge underlying assumptions or stereotypes they may have about others. L'Oréal Canada has developed a training program where baby boomers and Generation X and Y employees meet to discuss their different expectations in the workplace. They also work in mixed-generation teams to learn about and appreciate one another's strengths and aptitudes.[90] At Shell Canada, senior management teams participate in gender-in-the-workplace training sessions to increase awareness of how gender differences affect communication and leadership styles. Also,

with our **differences**—not despite them."

© Robert Churchill/iStockphoto.com

Skills-based diversity training training that teaches employees the practical skills they need for managing a diverse workforce, such as flexibility and adaptability, negotiation, problem solving, and conflict resolution

Diversity audits formal assessments that measure employee and management attitudes, investigate the extent to which people are advantaged or disadvantaged with respect to hiring and promotions, and review companies' diversity-related policies and procedures

Diversity pairing a mentoring program in which people of different cultural backgrounds, sexes, or races/ethnicities are paired together to get to know one another and change stereotypical beliefs and attitudes

all Shell employees are required to complete diversity awareness training, which covers topics such as cross-cultural communication, discrimination, and the business case for inclusiveness.[91]

By contrast, **skills-based diversity training** teaches employees the practical skills they need for managing a diverse workforce, such as flexibility and adaptability, problem solving, negotiation tactics, and conflict resolution.[92] The retail chain Canada Safeway Limited provides employees with hands-on training materials and a resource library on the company's diversity website, which is available on the company intranet. Similarly, KPMG Canada has introduced an online diversity training program, mandatory for all employees, that includes customized modules for employees, managers, and executive-level staff.[93]

Companies also use diversity audits, diversity pairing, and minority experiences for top executives to better manage diversity. **Diversity audits** are formal assessments that measure employee and management attitudes, investigate the extent to which people are advantaged or disadvantaged with respect to hiring and promotions, and review companies' diversity-related policies and procedures. Saskatchewan's electricity provider, SaskPower, measures the progress of its diversity-related recruitment goals through regular reporting to senior management. Similarly, the Royal Bank of Canada ensures that the company maintains a leadership role in diversity by preparing an annual diversity progress report in addition to its annual employment equity report.[94]

Earlier in the chapter you learned that *mentoring*—pairing a junior employee with a senior employee—is a common strategy for creating learning and promotional opportunities for women. Diversity pairing is a special kind of mentoring. In **diversity pairing**, people of different cultural backgrounds, sexes, or races/ethnicities are paired for mentoring. The hope is that stereotypical beliefs and attitudes will change as people get to know one another as individuals.[95] HSBC Bank Canada established an Aboriginal mentorship program that paired senior-level executives with Aboriginal employees. Ernst & Young Canada has developed a number of unique "reverse mentoring" programs, including one where junior-level LGBT (lesbian, gay, bisexual, transgendered) employees mentor senior executives on issues relating to generational differences and sexual orientation. As well, its Coaching Our Leaders program pairs partners with mentors who are visible minorities or women to facilitate greater understanding on issues related to religion, culture, or gender.[96]

In summary, population trends and related growth in immigration levels in Canada together suggest that managers must be aware of, and prepared to manage, the cultural diversity of the Canadian workforce. "Opportunities exist for senior managers who wish to move their firms ahead in the competition for the next generation of talent. By developing a diverse internal pipeline to build the diverse top management teams of the future, senior executives can move their companies to the forefront of the Canadian business community in the area of diversity and inclusiveness."[97]

Mixed Messages

Managers need to think twice before communicating to today's diverse workforce, to ensure they consider the cultural context of the listener, as variations exist in language, tone, phonetics, and verbal and nonverbal cues across cultures. For example, in Canada, shaking your head horizontally means "no," but in India a similar gesture signifies understanding or "yes." A "thumbs-up" in Canada can mean good job or good luck, but in Australia, Thailand, and Iraq it is perceived as an obscene gesture. Canadians are also known to be very even-toned in their speech, a sign of respect and professionalism; however, other cultures communicate in a much more animated and boisterous tone, which may be perceived by Canadians as anger or agitation. With workforce diversity nearing record levels in Canada, managers must take note of cultural differences in order to reduce communication gaps and misunderstandings.

Manfred Rutz/The Image Bank/Getty Images

Sources: S. Tatla, "Thumbs Up Not Always a Sign of Approval," *Financial Post*, April 28, 2010, http://www.financialpost.com/Thumbs+always+sign+approval/2961001/story.html; B. Koerner, "What Does a Thumbs Up Mean in Iraq?" Slate.com, March 28, 2003, http://slate.msn.com/id/2080812.

Go online at
www.nelson.com/4ltrpress/icanmgmt2
And access the essential Study Tools online for this chapter:

- **Flashcards**, to help you study
- **Interactive Quizzes**, to test your knowledge
- **Audio Chapter Summaries**, for chapter review
- **Crossword Puzzles and Beat the Clock**, to review key terms
- **What Would You Do? Cases**, for applying your knowledge to real-life situations
- **Self Assessments**, to learn about what kind of manager you are
- **Videos and Media Quizzing for Part 3**
  - Chapter 9: Modern Shed: Designing Adaptive Organizations
  - Chapter 10: Holden Outerwear: Leading Teams
  - Chapter 11: Barcelona Restaurant Group: Managing Human Resources
  - Chapter 12: Mitchell Gold + Bob Williams: Managing Diversity

Be sure to consult the Chapter Review Card at the back of the textbook.

13 Motivation

LEARNING OUTCOMES

LO1 Explain the basics of motivation.

LO2 Use equity theory to explain how employees' perceptions of fairness affect motivation.

LO3 Use expectancy theory to describe how workers' expectations about rewards, effort, and the link between rewards and performance influence motivation.

LO4 Explain how reinforcement theory works and how it can be used to motivate.

LO5 Describe the components of goal-setting theory and how managers can use them to motivate workers.

LO6 Discuss how the entire motivation model can be used to motivate workers.

What Is Motivation?

What makes people more satisfied and most productive at work? Is it money, benefits, opportunities for growth, interesting work, or something else altogether? And if people desire different things, how can a company manage to keep every different person motivated? It takes insight and hard work to motivate workers to join the company, perform well, and stay with the company. Professor Marylene Gagne, of the John Molson School of Business in Montreal, discusses the importance of both intrinsic and extrinsic motivation to managers.[1]

Motivation is the set of forces that initiates, directs, and makes people persist in their efforts to accomplish a goal.[2] *Initiation of effort* is concerned with the choices people make regarding how much effort they will put forth in their jobs ("Do I really knock myself out for these performance appraisals or just do a decent job?"). *Direction of effort* is concerned with the choices people make in deciding *where* to put forth effort in their jobs ("I should be spending time with my high-dollar accounts instead of learning this new computer system!"). *Persistence of effort* is concerned with the choices people make about how long they will put forth effort in their jobs before reducing or eliminating those efforts ("I'm only halfway through the project, and I'm exhausted. Do I plough through to the end, or just call it quits?"). Initiation, direction, and persistence are at the heart of motivation. A recent study of entrance scholarships at two Ontario universities found that they had little impact on how students performed throughout their postsecondary years. This suggests that the persistence that netted promising high school students their scholarships in the first place may not be further increased by financial aid from the university. This research provokes an interesting question: Would that persistence have been sustained in the absence of aid?[3]

LO1 Basics of Motivation

Motivation the set of forces that initiates, directs, and makes people persist in their efforts to accomplish a goal

Take your right hand and point the palm toward your face. Keep your thumb and pinky finger straight and bend the three middle fingers so the tips are touching your palm. Now rotate your wrist back and forth. If you were in the Regent Square Tavern that hand signal would tell waitress Marjorie Landale that you wanted a Yuengling beer. Marjorie, who isn't deaf, would not have understood that sign a few years ago. But with a university for the deaf nearby, the tavern always has its share of deaf customers, so she decided on her own to take classes in signing. At first, deaf customers would signal for a pen and paper to write out their orders. But after Marjorie signalled that she was learning to sign, "their eyes [would] light up, and they [would] finger-spell their order." Word quickly spread as the students started bringing in their friends, classmates, teachers, and hearing friends as well. Says Marjorie: "The deaf customers are patient with my amateur signing. They appreciate the effort."[4]

B

What would motivate an employee like Marjorie to voluntarily learn sign language? (Sign language is every bit as much of a language as French or Spanish.) She wasn't paid to take classes in her free time. She chose to do it on her own. And while she undoubtedly makes more tip money with a full bar than with an empty one, it's highly unlikely that she began her classes with the objective of making more money. Just what is it that motivates employees like Marjorie Landale?

Let's learn more about motivation by building a basic model of motivation out of ***1.1 effort and performance, 1.2 need satisfaction,*** *and* ***1.3 extrinsic and intrinsic rewards.*** *Then we'll discuss* ***1.4 how to motivate people with this basic model of motivation.***

Ryan Carter/Shutterstock.com

Michael Cheng is a highly motivated student. Only 23 years old, Surrey's Student Entrepreneur of 2012 has already established 11 start-ups, mostly in the fields of marketing and technology. One of his most recent start-ups is WittyCookie, a company that builds and helps maintain websites for small businesses. The company, founded in 2011, employs up to 40 people, including designers, developers, and videographers. More than 600 businesses subscribe for a modest monthly fee. "When people get a really good website for $20 a month," says Cheng, "they're usually very happy to recommend us to their friends and family."

Cheng is an undergraduate with SFU Surrey's School of Interactive Arts and Technology and a client of SFU's Venture Connection, an initiative designed to motivate and support entrepreneurship at the university. Cheng has recently received what may be his biggest motivation yet: he was selected for the 2013 cohort of The Next 36, a collaboration between government and private investors aimed at transforming Canada's most motivated postsecondary students into leading entrepreneurs. The students work in teams to conceive and develop ideas. Each team receives up to $80,000 to research, develop, prototype, and pilot a new venture in the mobile environment. They are also exposed to some of the country's key entrepreneurial leaders, such as Jim Pattison. "It's about trying to find the next Facebook, Instagram, Twitter, but here in Canada," Cheng says of The Next 36.

Source: Conner, S. (2013). "Success stories: Michael Cheng," *Vancouver Sun*, March 16, 2013. Available online at http://www.vancouversun.com/business/Working+city+success+stories/8109352/story.html#ixzz2NrQQRJkZ. Reprinted with permission.

Greg Epperson/Shutterstock.com

Needs the physical or psychological requirements that must be met to ensure survival and well-being

1.1 Effort and Performance

When most people think of work motivation, they think that working hard (effort) should lead to a good job (performance). Exhibit 13.1 shows a basic model of work motivation and performance, displaying this process. The first thing to notice about Exhibit 13.1 is that this is a basic model of work motivation *and* performance. In practice, it's almost impossible to talk about one without mentioning the other. Managers often assume that motivation is the only determinant of performance. This is evidenced when they say things like "Your performance was really terrible last quarter. What's the matter? Aren't you as motivated as you used to be?" In fact, motivation is just one of three primary determinants of job performance. In industrial psychology, job performance is frequently represented by this equation:

Job Performance = Motivation × Ability × Situational Constraints

In this formula, *job performance* is how well someone performs the requirements of the job. *Motivation,* as defined above, is effort, the degree to which someone works hard to do the job well. *Ability* is the degree to which workers possess the knowledge, skills, and talent they need to do a job well. And *situational constraints* are factors beyond the control of individual employees such as tools, policies, and resources that have an effect on job performance.

Exhibit 13.1 A Basic Model of Work Motivation and Performance

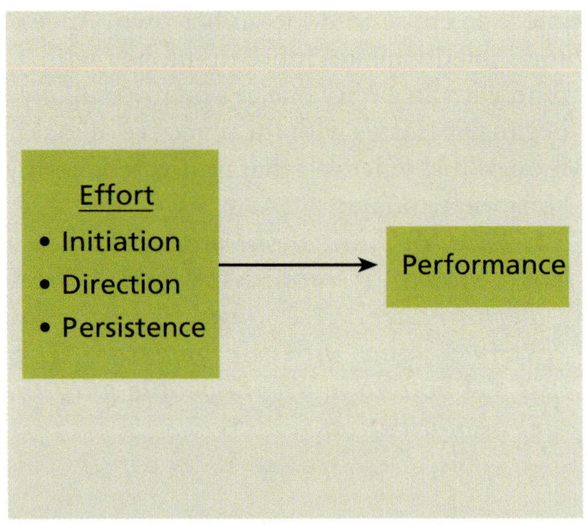

Since job performance is a multiplicative function of motivation times ability times situational constraints, job performance will suffer if any one of these components is weak. Does this mean that motivation doesn't matter? Not at all. It just means that all the motivation in the world won't translate into high performance when you have little ability and high situational constraints. So, while we will spend this chapter developing a model of work motivation, it is important to remember that ability and situational constraints affect job performance as well.

1.2 Need Satisfaction

In Exhibit 13.1, we started with a very basic model of motivation in which effort leads to job performance. But managers want to know, "What leads to effort?" Determining employee needs is the first step toward answering that question.

In this section, we look at some of the basic principles of need theories as they are useful for understanding human behaviour. Then we will discuss the shortcomings of need theory. **Needs** are the physical or psychological requirements we must meet to ensure our survival and well-being.[5] As shown on the left side of Exhibit 13.2, an unmet need creates an uncomfortable state of tension that must be resolved. For example, if you normally skip breakfast but then have to work through lunch, chances are you'll be so hungry by late afternoon that the only thing you'll be motivated to do is find something to eat. So, according to need theories, people are motivated by unmet needs. It follows that a need no longer motivates once it is met. Once it has been, people become satisfied, as shown on the right side of Exhibit 13.2.

Since people are motivated by unmet needs, managers must learn what those unmet needs are and address them. This is not always a straightforward task, because

Exhibit 13.2 Adding Need Satisfaction to the Model

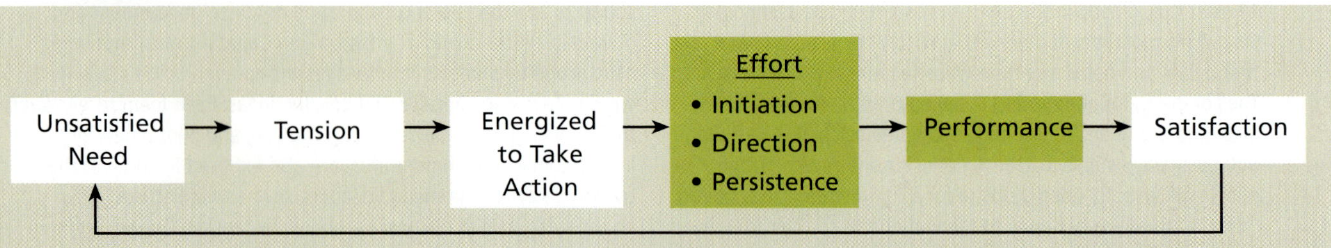

As shown on the left side of this exhibit, a person's unsatisfied need creates an uncomfortable, internal state of tension that must be resolved. So, according to needs theories, people are motivated by unmet needs. But once a need is met, it no longer motivates. When this occurs, people become satisfied, as shown on the right side of the exhibit.

different need theories suggest different needs categories. Consider three well-known needs theories. Maslow's Hierarchy of Needs suggests that people are motivated by five needs: *physiological* (food and water), *safety* (physical and economic), *belongingness* (friendship, love, social interaction), *esteem* (achievement and recognition), and *self-actualization* (realizing your full potential).[6] Alderfer's ERG Theory collapses Maslow's five needs into three: *existence* (safety and physiological needs), *relatedness* (belongingness), and *growth* (esteem and self-actualization).[7] McClelland's Learned Needs Theory suggests that people are motivated by the need for *affiliation* (to be liked and accepted), the need for *achievement* (to accomplish challenging goals), or the need for *power* (to influence others).[8]

Things become even more complicated when we consider the various predictions made by these theories. According to Maslow, needs are arranged in a hierarchy from low (physiological) to high (self-actualization), and people are motivated by their lowest unsatisfied need. As each need is met, they work their way up the hierarchy from physiological toward self-actualization needs. By contrast, Alderfer says that people can be motivated by more than one need at a time. Furthermore, he suggests that people are just as likely to move down the needs hierarchy as up, particularly when they are unable to achieve satisfaction at the next higher need level. McClelland argues that the degree to which particular needs motivate varies tremendously from person to person, with some people being motivated primarily by achievement and others by power or affiliation. McClelland also says that needs are learned, not innate. For instance, studies have found that children whose parents own a small business or hold a managerial position are much more likely to have a high need for achievement.[9]

Since people are motivated by unmet needs, managers must learn what those unmet needs are and address them.

So, with three different sets of needs and three very different ideas about how needs motivate, how do we provide a practical answer to managers who just want to know what leads to effort? Let's simplify the research a bit. To start, studies indicate that there are two basic needs categories.[10] As you would expect, *lower order needs* are concerned with safety and with physiological and existence requirements, whereas *higher order needs* are concerned with relationships (belongingness, relatedness, and affiliation), challenges and accomplishments (esteem, self-actualization, growth, and achievement), and influence (power). Studies generally show that there is a logical progression and that higher order needs will not motivate people as long as lower order needs remain unsatisfied.[11]

Imagine that you graduated from university six months ago and are still looking for your first job. With money running short (you're probably living on your credit cards and other peoples' couches) and the possibility of having to move back in with your parents looming (if that doesn't motivate you, what will?), your basic needs for food, shelter, and security drive your thoughts, behaviour, and choices at this point. But once you land that job, find a great place (of your own!) to live, and put some money in the bank, these basic needs should decrease in importance as you begin to think about making new friends and taking on challenging work assignments. In fact, once lower order needs are satisfied, it's difficult for managers to predict which higher order needs will motivate behaviour.[12] Some people will be motivated by affiliation, while others will be motivated by growth or esteem. Also, the relative importance of the various needs may change over time but not necessarily in a predictable pattern.

© Tom Grill/Corbis

WDG Photo/Shutterstock.com

Needs Classification of Different Theories

	MASLOW'S HIERARCHY	ALDERFER'S ERG	McCLELLAND'S LEARNED NEEDS
Higher-Order	Self-Actualization	Growth	Power
	Esteem	Relatedness	Achievement
	Belongingness		Affiliation
Lower-Order	Safety	Existence	
	Physiological		

Extrinsic reward a reward that is tangible, visible to others, and given to employees contingent on the performance of specific tasks or behaviours

Although popular, Maslow's needs hierarchy theory has been dismissed by most motivational experts. In general, research support for Maslow's theory is weak, mostly because it is somewhat rigid; that said, there is support for some sort of hierarchy of needs. There is disagreement about how quickly and for how long people fulfill their needs, and whether just one need is a motivator.[13] Why do we study something that is not perfect? Well, Maslow did not get everything right, but neither did he get it all wrong. Einstein did not get everything right either, but he could not have known about the boson particle. We learn more about human motivation as we progress in social sciences. Maslow deserves credit for bringing a positive approach to the study of human motivation and for laying some foundation for further topics of study, such as motivation crowding.[14]

1.3 Extrinsic and Intrinsic Rewards

So, what leads to effort? In part, needs do. But rewards are also important, and no discussion of motivation would be complete without considering them. So let's add two kinds of rewards—extrinsic and intrinsic—to the model in Exhibit 13.3.[15]

Extrinsic rewards are tangible and visible to others and are given to employees contingent on the performance of specific tasks or behaviours.[16] External agents (e.g., managers) determine and control the distribution, frequency, and amount of extrinsic rewards such as pay, company stock, benefits, and promotions. When IKEA, the home furniture chain, awarded its employees $80 million in bonuses, this was one example of motivating employees.[17] The same company opened a 37,000-square-metre store (about the size of six football fields!) in Winnipeg in early 2013, which included a 60-square-metre restaurant (the city's largest). In the run-up to the opening, it offered free meals to all the new staff.[18]

Companies offer extrinsic rewards in order to get people to do what they wouldn't otherwise do. Richard Yerema, managing editor of the Canada's Top 100 Employers project at Mediacorp Canada, says that a common thread that runs through forward-thinking companies is that they "create an ownership culture." "Money talks when it comes to attracting and retaining skilled labour," he says. "But decent wages and benefits don't form the whole bottom line when it comes to motivating employees." In fact, a motivated and productive workplace often hinges on nonfinancial strategies and incentives that boost morale, productivity, and quality of work life. So say human resources, workplace counselling, and other experts.[19]

Companies use extrinsic rewards to motivate people to perform four basic behaviours: join the organization, regularly attend their jobs, perform their jobs well, and stay with the organization.[20] Think about it. Would you show up to work every day to do the best job you can just out of the goodness of your heart? Very few people would. KPMG Canada, the accounting firm, now offers its employees paid sabbaticals, complete with benefits and a guaranteed job when they return. Deloitte & Touche LLP has a sabbatical program that offers staff from across Canada a chance to work in Mozambique, Egypt, Ghana, and Latin America, where they will work with nonprofits on projects. The longer an employee perseveres, the greater the rewards.[21] More than 20 of the 95 top-ranked employers in the Greater Toronto Area offer bonuses to *all* their employees. These bonuses are tied to performance, and these companies give all employees an opportunity to earn them, not just managers and company veterans. For example, McCarthy Tétrault, a legal firm in Toronto, used to offer more traditional, seniority-based bonuses at the end

Exhibit 13.3 Adding Rewards to the Model

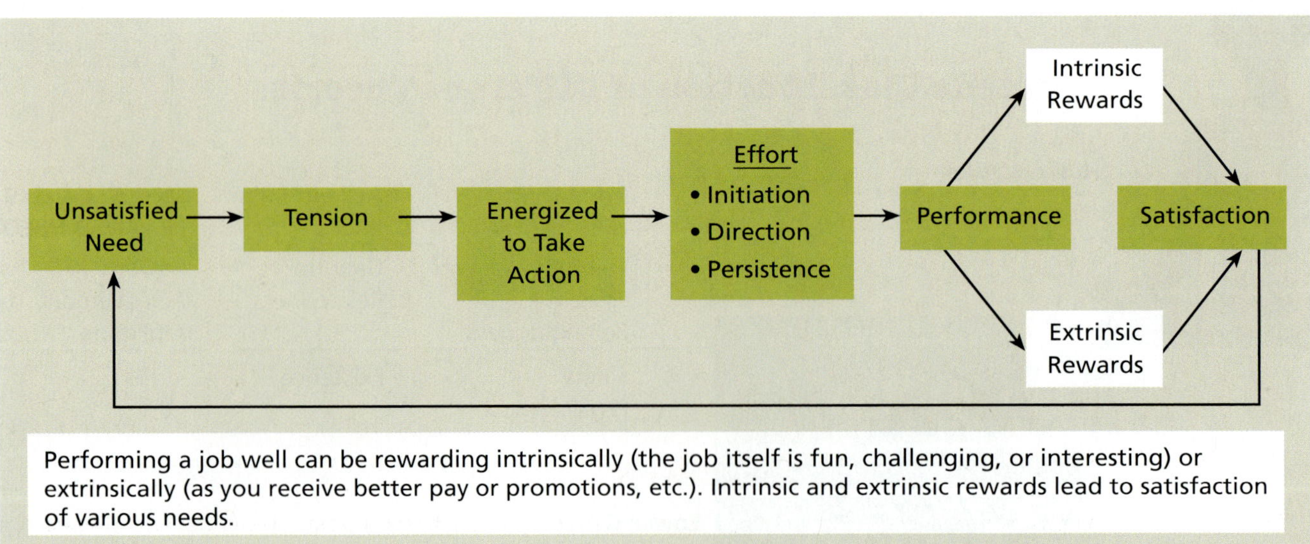

Performing a job well can be rewarding intrinsically (the job itself is fun, challenging, or interesting) or extrinsically (as you receive better pay or promotions, etc.). Intrinsic and extrinsic rewards lead to satisfaction of various needs.

Win–Win Motivation

Shari Adler took six months off from her job at Pfizer and spent it in Tanzania. But she wasn't on safari. She was working for the Tanzanian Ministry of Health. Adler reaped the benefits of Pfizer's paid volunteerism program, a strategy increasingly adopted by companies for a host of reasons. Younger workers want to see companies do more than write a cheque to help society. Moreover, meaningful volunteer opportunities help attract and retain workers who are motivated to use their job skills to help others in need. Paid volunteerism benefits companies, too, since employees return with broader perspectives, more independence and confidence, and new skills that can enhance their motivation and on-the-job performance. Salesforce.com, Microsoft, Timberland, PwC, Flatiron, and Eli Lilly are six other companies that will pay you to contribute your efforts towards positive social change.

Sources: Salvesen, A. (2012). "6 Companies That Will Pay You to Volunteer Abroad," GoOverSeas.Com, Published 07/23/2012. Available online at http://www.gooverseas.com/6-companies-will-pay-volunteer-abroad; S. E. Needleman, "The Latest Office Perk: Getting Paid to Volunteer," *The Wall Street Journal* 29 April 2008, D1.

of the year, near Christmas. The company has since moved toward a more performance-based model, one that takes into account individual and company performance.[22]

Intrinsic rewards are the natural rewards associated with performing a task or activity for its own sake. Setting aside the external rewards that management offers for doing something well, employees often find the activities or tasks they perform interesting and enjoyable. Examples of intrinsic rewards include a sense of accomplishment or achievement, a feeling of responsibility, the chance to learn something new or interact with others, or simply the fun that comes from performing an interesting, challenging, and engaging task.

A number of surveys suggest that extrinsic and intrinsic rewards are both important. One survey found that the most important rewards were good benefits and health insurance, job security, a week or more of vacation (all extrinsic rewards), interesting work, the opportunity to learn new skills, and independent work situations (all intrinsic rewards). Also, employee preferences for intrinsic and extrinsic rewards appear to be relatively stable. Studies conducted over the past three decades have consistently found that employees are twice as likely to indicate that important and meaningful work matters more to them than what they are paid.[23]

The Yukon Hospital Corp. (cited in the top 100 companies to work for in Canada), which operates facilities across the territory, allows its 170 full-time and 107 part-time workers to listen to music on the job. They're also kept up-to-date on developments and can provide feedback through a biweekly newsletter and suggestion box. Claude Balthazard of Ontario's Human Resources Professionals Association (HRPA) notes: "Usually the drivers of engagement at work are things like challenge, autonomy, stimulation, access to information, resources, and growth opportunities. Financial compensation is usually third or fourth down the list, but then again, it's the jobs that also have all that that tend to pay more."[24]

Intrinsic reward a natural reward associated with performing a task or activity for its own sake

1.4 Motivating with the Basics

Given the basic model of work motivation based on needs and rewards in Exhibit 13.3, what practical steps can managers take to motivate employees to increase their effort?

Well, *start by asking people what their needs are.* If managers don't know what workers' needs are, they won't be able to provide them with the opportunities and rewards that can satisfy those needs. At Polson Bourbonniere Financial Planning Group in Markham, Ontario, the competitive wages for the 14 financial planners and administrative staff are supplemented with flexible work hours, team-building events, and monthly cake breaks to recognize staff birthdays. "If you give somebody a raise, they're tickled for a day or two, but it doesn't really motivate you," says Susan Kelly, the firm's vice president of operations, noting that a low turnover rate—one person in the past 10 years has left the company—is a better indicator of people's satisfaction and motivation levels.[25]

Equity theory a theory that states that people will be motivated when they perceive that they are being treated fairly

Next, *satisfy lower order needs first*. Higher order needs will not motivate people as long as lower order needs remain unsatisfied. In practice, this means providing the equipment, training, and knowledge to create a safe workplace free of physical risks, as well as paying employees enough to provide financial security. Richard Yerema says that most forward-thinking companies "create an ownership culture."[26] Third, managers should *expect people's needs to change*. As some needs are satisfied or situations change, what motivated people before may not motivate them now. Similarly, what motivates people to accept a job (pay and benefits) may not necessarily motivate them once they actually have the job (the job itself, opportunities for advancement). Managers should also expect needs to change as people mature.[27] For older employees, benefits are as important as pay, which is always ranked as more important by younger employees. Older employees also rank job security as more important than personal and family time, which is more important to younger employees.[28]

Finally, *as needs change and lower order needs are satisfied, create opportunities for employees to satisfy higher order needs*. Recall that intrinsic rewards such as accomplishment, achievement, learning something new, and interacting with others are the natural rewards associated with performing a task or activity for its own sake. And intrinsic rewards generally correspond quite closely to higher order needs, which are concerned with relationships (belongingness, relatedness, affiliation) and challenges and accomplishments (esteem, self-actualization, growth, achievement). Therefore, one way for managers to meet employees' higher order needs is to create opportunities for employees to experience intrinsic rewards by providing challenging work, encouraging employees to take greater responsibility for their work, and giving employees the freedom to pursue tasks and projects they find naturally interesting.

How Perceptions and Expectations Affect Motivation

We've now seen that people are motivated to achieve intrinsic and extrinsic rewards. When employees believe that rewards are not fairly awarded, or when they don't believe they can achieve the performance goals the company has set for them, they won't be very motivated.

LO2 Equity Theory

Fairness—that is, what people perceive to be fair—is a critical issue in organizations. **Equity theory** says that people will be motivated at work when they *perceive* that they are being treated fairly. In particular, equity theory stresses the importance of perceptions. So, whatever the actual level of rewards people receive, they must also perceive that they are being treated fairly relative to others. As noted in Chapter 11, the average CEO now makes 364 times more than the average worker.[29] Many people believe that CEO pay is obscenely high and unfair. With the Big Five banks differing quite a lot in their profitability today, you would expect the compensation they offer their CEOs to vary as well—for them to receive different salaries, bonuses, and stock options. One would also expect to see different compensation philosophies at the different boards. Well, not so much. The following table has compiled the numbers for the 2011 fiscal year. The annualized returns for each of the bank stocks up to December 2011 are also included.

This table speaks to what's wrong with executive compensation. Should we pay every NHL player as if he is a star, or should we only pay the stars the big dollars?[30]

Change in China

In Chapter 8, you learned about Geert Hofstede's studies of cultural differences. Hofstede studied China in the 1980s, when he found Chinese workers to be motivated by money (high qualitative), collectivist, and ill-inclined to offer suggestions to a supervisor (high power distance). Not so for the Chinese worker of today, who is individualist, values leisure time alongside salary, has plenty of ideas about how the company can improve, and shares them in culturally sensitive ways. This is important information for Western companies seeking to hire and motivate workers in China, as they might respond better to a recognition dinner than a bonus or a plaque.

Source: K. King-Metters and R. Metters, "Misunderstanding the Chinese Worker," *The Wall Street Journal*, 7 July 2008, R11.

chungking/Shutterstock.com

	Firm	Total compensation	5-year total return
Ed Clark	TD	$11.38 million	5.5%
Gord Nixon	RBC	$11.17 million	2.7%
Bill Downe	BMO	$11.4 million	0.7%
Rick Waugh	BNS	$10.62 million	3.6%
Gerald McCaughey	CIBC	$10.6 million	0.8%

Gwyn Morgan, chairman of SNC-Lavalin Group Inc., the Montreal-based engineering company, takes the word "group" (in the company name) to heart. "When it comes to executive compensation, the board makes a point of regularly fine-tuning its pay policy according to what it believes are fair-minded, down-to-earth principles," he says. "The next thing we're going to do is examine longer periods of holding back incentive shares and putting more emphasis on long-term performance, even more than there has been." The point of this is to ensure that people in the company feel that everyone is being recognized equitably.[31]

Others, though, believe that CEO pay is fair because if it were easier to find good CEOs, then CEOs would be paid much less. Equity theory doesn't focus on objective equity (i.e., on the fact that CEOs make 364 times more than blue-collar workers). Instead, it posits that equity, like beauty, is in the eye of the beholder.

Let's learn more about equity theory by examining ***2.1 the components of equity theory, 2.2 how people react to perceived inequities,*** *and* ***2.3 how to motivate people using equity theory.***

2.1 Components of Equity Theory

The basic components of equity theory are inputs, outcomes, and referents. **Inputs** are the contributions that employees make to the organization. Inputs include education and training, intelligence, experience, effort, number of hours worked, and ability. **Outcomes** are what employees receive in exchange for their contributions to the organization. Outcomes include pay, fringe benefits, status symbols, and job titles and assignments. And, since perceptions of equity depend on comparisons, **referents** are those others with whom people compare themselves when determining whether they are being treated fairly. The referent can be a single person (comparing yourself with a coworker) or a generalized other (comparing yourself with "students in general," for example); it can also be yourself over time ("I was better off last year than I am this year"). Usually, people compare themselves with referents who hold the same job or a similar one, or who are otherwise similar in gender, race, age, tenure, or other characteristics.[32]

According to equity theory, employees compare their outcomes (the rewards they receive from the organization) to their inputs (their contributions to the organization). This comparison of outcomes to inputs is called the **outcome/input (O/I) ratio**.

$$\frac{\text{OUTCOMES}_{\text{SELF}}}{\text{INPUTS}_{\text{SELF}}} = \frac{\text{OUTCOMES}_{\text{REFERENT}}}{\text{INPUTS}_{\text{REFERENT}}}$$

After an *internal* comparison in which they compare their own outcomes to their own inputs, employees make an *external* comparison—that is, they compare their O/I ratio with the O/I ratio of a referent.[33] When people perceive that their O/I ratio is equal to the referent's O/I ratio, they conclude that they are being treated fairly; when people perceive that their O/I ratio is different from their referent's O/I ratio, they conclude that they are being treated inequitably or unfairly.

Inequity can take two forms: under-reward and over-reward. **Under-reward** occurs when your O/I ratio is worse than your referent's O/I ratio. In other words, you are getting fewer outcomes relative to your inputs than your referent is getting. When people perceive that they have been under-rewarded, they tend to experience anger or frustration.

By contrast, **over-reward** occurs when your O/I ratio is better than your referent's O/I ratio. In this case, you are getting more outcomes relative to your inputs than your referent is. In theory, when people perceive that they have been over-rewarded, they experience guilt. Not surprisingly, though, people have a very high tolerance for being over-rewarded. It takes a tremendous amount of overpayment before people decide that their pay or benefits are more than they deserve.

Inputs in equity theory, the contributions employees make to the organization

Outcomes in equity theory, the rewards employees receive for their contributions to the organization

Referents in equity theory, others with whom people compare themselves to determine if they have been treated fairly

Outcome/input (O/I) ratio in equity theory, an employee's perception of how the rewards received from an organization compare with the employee's contributions to that organization

Under-reward a form of inequity in which you are getting fewer outcomes relative to inputs than your referent is getting

Over-reward a form of inequity in which you are getting more outcomes relative to inputs than your referent

2.2 How People React to Perceived Inequity

What happens, then, when people perceive that they have been treated inequitably at work? Exhibit 13.4 (page 226) indicates that perceived inequity affects satisfaction. In the case of under-reward, this usually translates into frustration or anger; with over-reward, the reaction is guilt. These reactions lead to tension and a strong need to take action to restore equity in some way. At first, a slight inequity may not be strong enough to motivate an employee to take immediate action. But if the inequity persists or there are multiple inequities, tension may build over time until a point of intolerance is reached, and the person is energized to take action.[34]

When people perceive that they have been treated unfairly, they may try to restore equity by reducing inputs, increasing outcomes, rationalizing inputs or outcomes, changing the referent, or simply leaving. We will discuss

Exhibit 13.4 Adding Equity Theory to the Model

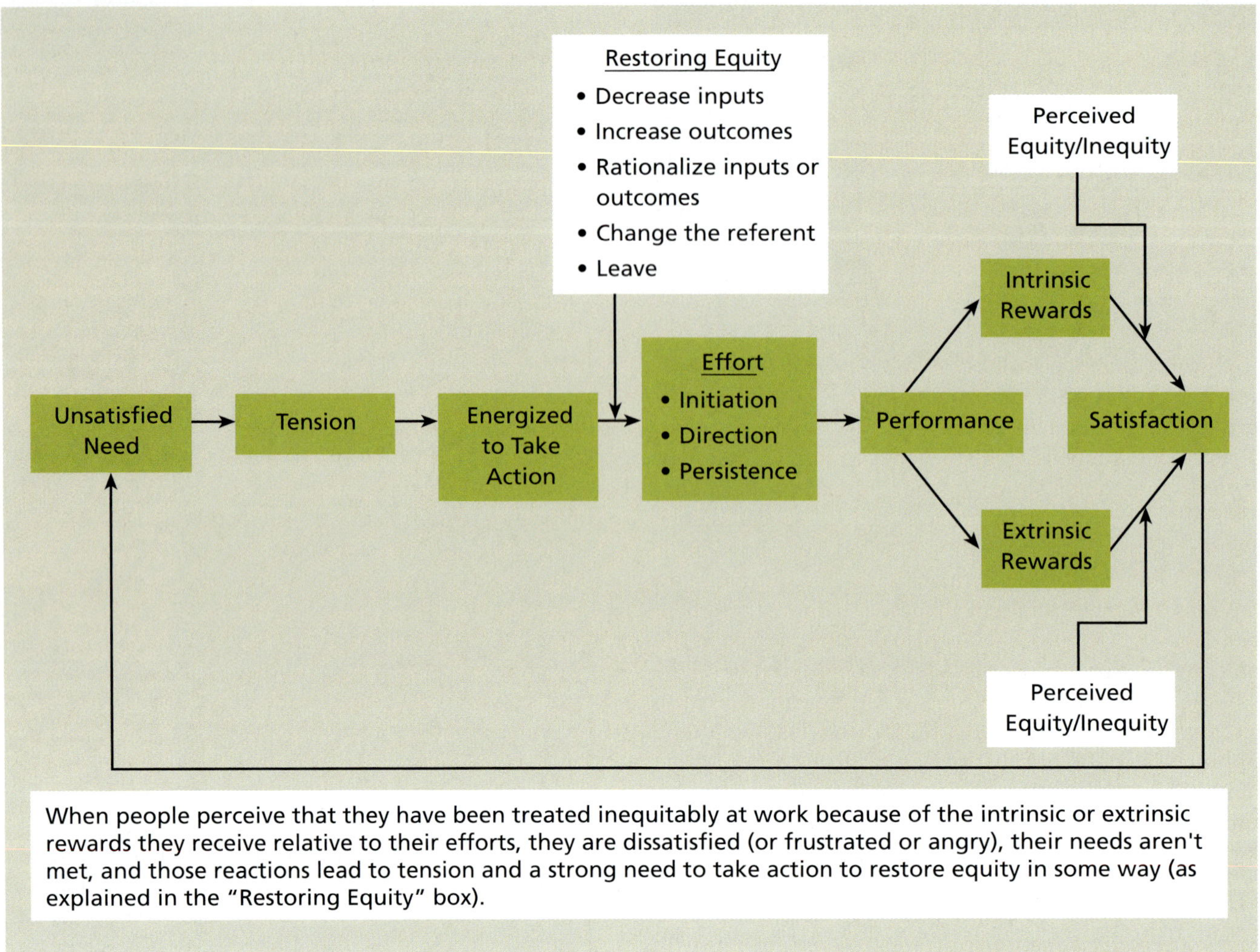

When people perceive that they have been treated inequitably at work because of the intrinsic or extrinsic rewards they receive relative to their efforts, they are dissatisfied (or frustrated or angry), their needs aren't met, and those reactions lead to tension and a strong need to take action to restore equity in some way (as explained in the "Restoring Equity" box).

these possible responses in terms of the inequity associated with under-reward, which is much more common than the inequity associated with over-reward.

People who perceive that they have been under-rewarded may try to restore equity by *decreasing or withholding their inputs* (i.e., effort). When General Motors Canada asked for billions in aid from Canadian and Ontario governments, it also planned to slash executive salaries by 10 percent and to cut benefits to hourly employees. Both the union and government felt that GM executives had not earned their (by some estimates) large salaries. Chrysler Canada requested aid from the federal and provincial governments. Ford Canada did not, but it was cutting salaries and closing plants. GM has closed down its Saturn plants and has eliminated its Pontiac division; Ford has closed its Mercury division; and several of the Big Three have closed their Canadian head offices. The outcomes from these decisions are not considered inequitable by the workers.[35]

Increasing outcomes is another way people try to restore equity. This might include asking for a raise or pointing out the inequity to the boss and hoping that he or she takes care of it. Sometimes, however, employees may go to external organizations such as labour unions, federal agencies, or the courts for help in increasing outcomes to restore equity.

Another method of restoring equity is to *rationalize or distort inputs or outcomes*. Instead of decreasing inputs or increasing outcomes, employees restore equity by making mental or emotional adjustments to their O/I ratios or the O/I ratios of their referents. Suppose that a company downsizes 10 percent of its workforce. It's likely that the survivors, the people who still have jobs, will be angry or frustrated with management because of the layoffs. If alternative jobs are difficult to find, however, these survivors may rationalize or distort their O/I ratios and conclude, "Well, things could be worse. At least I still have my job." Outcomes may be rationalized or distorted when other ways to restore equity aren't available. Small businesses, in particular, "are definitely trying a lot more creative approaches than they have in the past to try to attract and retain workers," says Dan Kelly, senior vice president of legislative affairs with the Canadian Federation of

Independent Business, which represents more than 107,000 small business owners. "In a restaurant, it could be a discount on products or services provided by the firm itself. I've heard of business owners so desperate for staff that they've taken employees into their homes, like an employee at one Dairy Queen in Royal, Alberta. There are restaurants in Canmore providing transportation for employees to and from work." Nothing can kill morale more than feeling "like you have no voice or are a cog in a wheel," says Mr. Kelly. Many small businesses are taking extra steps to ensure equitability in the job market.[36]

Changing the referent is another way to restore equity. In this case, people compare themselves to someone other than the referent they had been using for O/I ratio comparisons. Since people usually compare themselves to others who hold the same job or a similar one or who are otherwise similar (i.e., friends, family members, neighbours who work at other companies), they may change referents to restore equity when their personal situations change, such as a decrease in job status or pay.[37] Finally, when none of these methods are possible or restore equity, *employees may leave* by quitting their jobs, transferring, or increasing absenteeism.[38]

2.3 Motivating with Equity Theory

There are practical steps that managers can take to use equity theory to motivate employees. They can *start by looking for and correcting major inequities.* Among other things, equity theory makes us aware that an employee's sense of fairness is based on subjective perceptions. What one employee considers grossly unfair may not affect another employee's perceptions of equity at all. Although these different perceptions make it difficult for managers to create conditions that satisfy all employees, it's important that they do their best to take care of major inequities that can energize employees to take disruptive, costly, or harmful actions, such as decreasing inputs or leaving the company. Managers should look for major inequities and correct them whenever possible.

Second, managers can *reduce employees' inputs.* Increasing outcomes is often the first and only strategy that companies use to restore equity, yet reducing employee inputs is just as viable a strategy. In fact, with dual-career couples working 50-hour weeks, more and more employees are looking for ways to reduce stress and restore a balance between work and family. Consequently, it may make sense to ask employees to do less, not more; to have them identify and eliminate the 20 percent of their jobs that doesn't increase productivity or add value for customers; and to eliminate company-imposed requirements that really aren't critical to the performance of managers, employees, or the company (e.g., unnecessary meetings and reports).

Distributive justice the perceived degree to which outcomes and rewards are fairly distributed or allocated

Procedural justice the perceived fairness of the process used to make reward allocation decisions

Finally, managers should *make sure that decision-making processes are fair.* Equity theory focuses on **distributive justice**, the degree to which outcomes and rewards are fairly distributed or allocated. However, **procedural justice**, the fairness of the procedures used to make reward allocation decisions, is just as important.[39] Procedural justice matters because even when employees are unhappy with their outcomes (i.e., low pay), they're much less likely to be unhappy with company management if they believe that the procedures used to allocate outcomes were fair. For example, employees who are laid off tend to be hostile toward their employer when they perceive that the procedures leading to the layoffs were unfair. By contrast, employees who perceive layoff procedures as fair tend to continue to support and trust their employer.[40] Also, employees who perceive that outcomes were unfair (i.e., distributive injustice), but that the decisions and procedures leading to those outcomes were fair (i.e., procedural justice), are much more likely to seek constructive ways of restoring equity such as discussing these matters with their manager. By contrast, employees who perceive both distributive and procedural injustice may resort to more destructive tactics such as absenteeism, tardiness, withholding effort, or even sabotage and theft.[41] Among the companies that made the 12th annual *Globe and Mail* Top 100 list released in 2012 is the Great Little Box Co. (GLBC), a packaging manufacturer with its head office in Vancouver and with about 190 full-time workers. The GLBC was lauded for its no-cost programs and "exceptional" ability to engage workers. One novel Great Little Box program—which actually saves the company money—rewards employees who come up with company cost-savings ideas that are put into use by giving them a share of those savings. Now that's equity![42]

Fotosearch/Getty Images

Expectancy theory a theory that states that people will be motivated to the extent to which they believe that their efforts will lead to good performance, that good performance will be rewarded, and that they will be offered attractive rewards

Valence the attractiveness or desirability of a reward or outcome

Expectancy the perceived relationship between effort and performance

Instrumentality the perceived relationship between performance and rewards

LO3 Expectancy Theory

One of the hardest things about motivating people is that rewards that are attractive to some employees are unattractive to others. **Expectancy theory** says that people will be motivated to the extent that they believe their efforts will lead to good performance, that good performance will be rewarded, and that they will be offered attractive rewards.[43]

*Let's learn more about expectancy theory by examining **3.1 the components of expectancy theory** and **3.2 how to use expectancy theory as a motivational tool.***

3.1 Components of Expectancy Theory

Expectancy theory holds that people make conscious choices with regard to their motivation. The three factors that affect those choices are valence, expectancy, and instrumentality.

Valence is the attractiveness or desirability of various rewards or outcomes. Expectancy theory recognizes that the same reward or outcome—say, a promotion—will be highly attractive to some people, will be highly disliked by others, and will not make much difference one way or the other to still others. Accordingly, when people are deciding how much effort to put forth, expectancy theory says that they will consider the valence of all possible rewards and outcomes that they can receive from their jobs. The greater the sum of those valences, each of which can be positive, negative, or neutral, the more effort people will choose to put forth on the job.

Expectancy is the perceived relationship between effort and performance. When expectancies are strong, employees believe that their hard work and efforts will result in good performance, so they work harder. By contrast, when expectancies are weak, employees figure that no matter what they do or how hard they work, they won't be able to perform their jobs successfully, so they don't work as hard.

Instrumentality is the perceived relationship between performance and rewards. When instrumentality is strong, employees believe that improved performance will lead to more and better rewards, so they choose to work harder. When instrumentality is weak, employees don't believe that better performance will result in more or better rewards, so they choose not to work as hard.

Expectancy theory holds that for people to be highly motivated, all three variables—valence, expectancy, and instrumentality—must be high. Thus, expectancy theory can be represented by the following simple equation:

$$\text{Motivation} = \text{Valence} \times \text{Expectancy} \times \text{Instrumentality}$$

If any one of these variables (valence, expectancy, instrumentality) declines, overall motivation will decline as well.

Exhibit 13.5 incorporates the expectancy theory variables into our motivation model. Valence and instrumentality combine to affect employees' willingness to put forth effort (i.e., the degree to which they are energized to take action), while expectancy transforms intended effort ("I'm really going to work hard in this job") into actual effort. If you're offered rewards that you desire and you believe that you will in fact receive these rewards for good performance, you're highly likely to be energized to take action. However, you're not likely to actually exert effort unless you also believe that you can do the job (i.e., that your efforts will lead to successful performance).

Junial Enterprises/Shutterstock.com

3.2 Motivating with Expectancy Theory

Managers can take practical steps to use expectancy theory to motivate employees. First, they can *systematically gather information to find out what employees want from their jobs.* Individual managers can ask employees directly what they want from their jobs (see Subsection 1.4, "Motivating with the Basics"). But in addition to that, companies need to survey their employees regularly to determine their wants, needs, and dissatisfactions. Since people consider the valence of all the possible rewards and outcomes that they can receive from their jobs, regular identification of wants, needs, and dissatisfactions gives companies the chance to turn negatively valent rewards and outcomes into positively valent rewards and outcomes, thus raising overall motivation and effort. Therefore, employers should routinely survey employees not only to identify the range of rewards they value the most but also to understand the preferences of specific employees.

Second, managers can *take specific steps to link rewards to individual performance in a way that is clear and understandable to employees.* Unfortunately, most employees are extremely dissatisfied with the link between pay and performance in their organizations. In one study, based on a representative sample, 80 percent of the employees surveyed wanted to be paid according

Exhibit 13.5 Adding Expectancy Theory to the Model

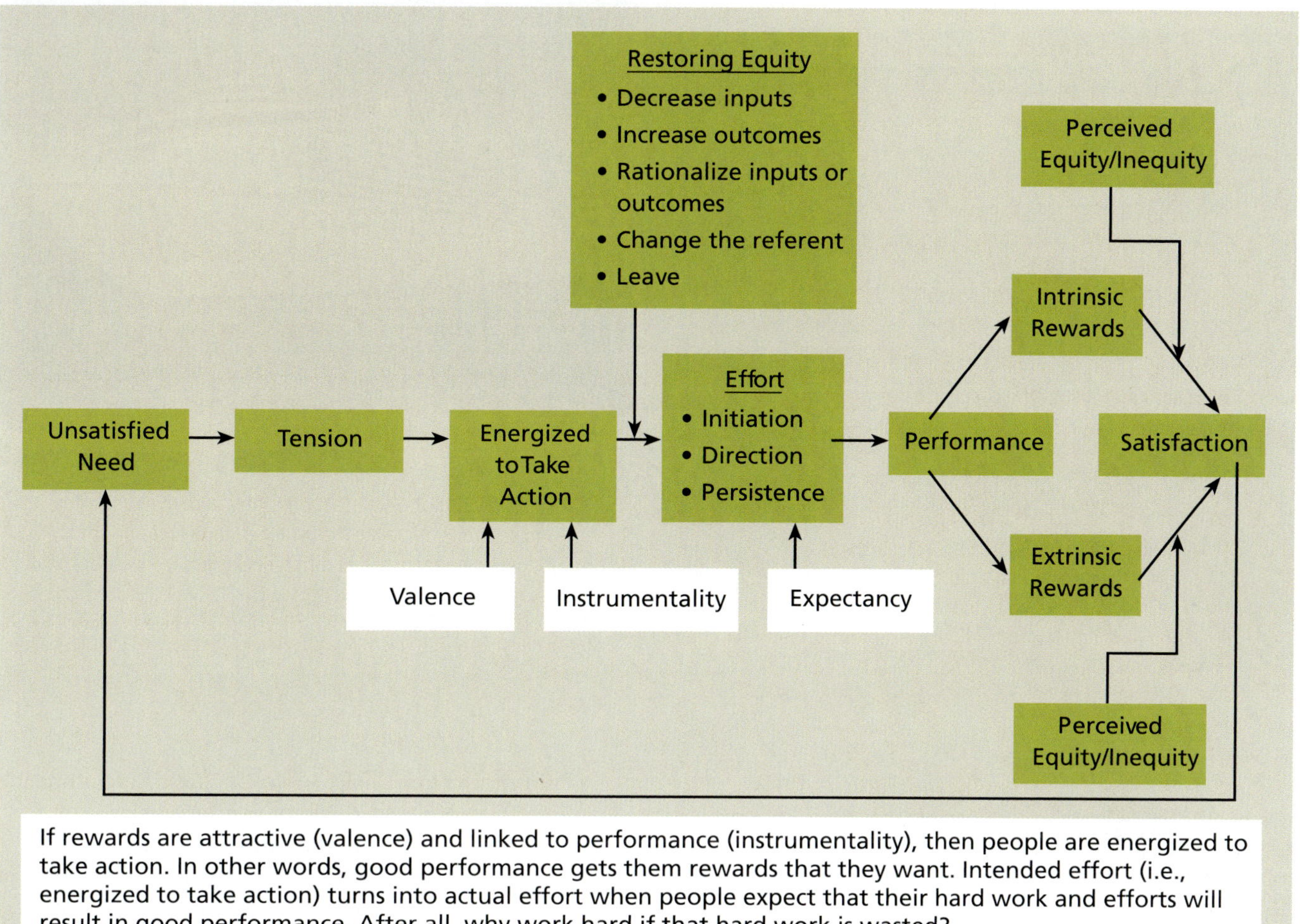

If rewards are attractive (valence) and linked to performance (instrumentality), then people are energized to take action. In other words, good performance gets them rewards that they want. Intended effort (i.e., energized to take action) turns into actual effort when people expect that their hard work and efforts will result in good performance. After all, why work hard if that hard work is wasted?

to a different kind of pay system. Moreover, only 32 percent of employees were satisfied with how their annual pay raises were determined, and only 22 percent were happy with the way the starting salaries for their jobs were determined.[44] One way to make sure that employees see the connection between pay and performance (see Chapter 11 for a discussion of compensation strategies) is for managers to publicize how pay decisions are made. This is especially important given that only 41 percent of employees know how their pay increases are determined.[45] As employees do more with less, more and more businesses are finding themselves challenged to find and retain good employees. It's the nonmonetary incentives that can set companies apart, says Marylka Empey, a certified management consultant in the Toronto area with Trinity Associates Inc. "A lot of research validates the fact that money does have its importance and place, but it does not sustain employees' feeling of engagement with an organization and the work they're doing. What their work is, how they're being managed, what the culture of the organization is—all that counts." Ms. Empey chairs the Human Resources Special Interest Group of the Canadian Association of Management Consultants.[46]

If managers want workers to have strong expectancies, they should empower them to make decisions.

Finally, managers should *empower employees to make decisions*. When valent rewards are linked to good performance, people should be energized to take action. But this works only if they also believe that their efforts will lead to good performance. One way that managers destroy the expectancy that hard work and effort will lead to good performance is by restricting what employees can do or by ignoring employees' ideas. In Chapter 9, you learned that *empowerment* is a feeling of intrinsic motivation, and that it arises when workers perceive their work to have meaning and perceive themselves to be competent, to have an impact, and to be capable of self-determination.[47] So if managers want workers to have strong expectancies, they should empower them to make decisions. Doing

Time to Get Serious About Rewarding Employees

A top performer in an organization was rewarded with a one-week Caribbean cruise—with company executives. This was not a reward: the prospect of going on a cruise, especially with senior management, was her idea of hell. "I don't like schmoozing, I don't like feeling trapped, why couldn't they just give me the money?" she asked. Rewards come in many extrinsic forms—bonuses, trips to conferences, praise, dinner events, plaques—and many intrinsic forms—the pleasure of completing something that met personal needs, or executing a job to the highest standard. Money can be effective, but the dollar amount must fit the circumstances and be appropriate for the amount of effort. Two team members received financial rewards for exceptional work. One did the work in a week and received $25. The other, who worked on a major project for a year, received $1,500. They were equally "blown away" by their bonuses.

One young professional's high performance earned him a clock radio—emblazoned with the company's logo. That irked him. "I am happy to work for them. But I resent them thinking they can come into my bedroom and wake me up."

James Nesterwitz/GetStock.com

The best reward: the satisfaction that you derive when you feel—and can tell yourself—that you've made an important contribution. You have made a difference.

Source: Moses, B. (2010). "Time to get serious about rewarding employees," *The Globe and Mail*, April 28; http://www.theglobeandmail.com/report-on-business/managing/barbara-moses/time-to-get-serious-about-rewarding-employees/article1549639/.

Reinforcement theory a theory that states that behaviour is a function of its consequences, that behaviours followed by positive consequences will occur more frequently, and that behaviours followed by negative consequences, or not followed by positive consequences, will occur less frequently

Reinforcement the process of changing behaviour by changing the consequences that follow behaviour

Reinforcement contingencies cause-and-effect relationships between the performance of specific behaviours and specific consequences

Schedule of reinforcement rules that specify which behaviours will be reinforced, which consequences will follow those behaviours, and the schedule by which those consequences will be delivered

so will motivate employees to take active rather than passive roles in their work.

How Rewards and Goals Affect Motivation

When used properly, rewards motivate and energize employees. When used incorrectly, they can demotivate, baffle, and even anger them. Goals are also supposed to motivate employees. But leaders who focus blindly on meeting goals at all costs often find that they destroy motivation.

LO4 Reinforcement Theory

Reinforcement theory says that behaviour is a function of its consequences, that behaviours followed by positive consequences (i.e., that are reinforced) will occur more frequently, and that behaviours followed by negative consequences, or not followed by positive consequences, will occur less frequently.[48] More specifically, **reinforcement** is the process of changing behaviour by changing the consequences that follow behaviour.[49]

Reinforcement has two parts: reinforcement contingencies and schedules of reinforcement. **Reinforcement contingencies** are the cause-and-effect relationships between the performance of specific behaviours and specific consequences. For example, if you get docked an hour's pay for being late to work, then a reinforcement contingency exists between a behaviour (being late to work) and a consequence (losing an hour's pay). A **schedule of reinforcement** is the set of rules regarding reinforcement contingencies such as which behaviours will be reinforced, which consequences will follow those behaviours, and the schedule by which those consequences will be delivered.[50]

Exhibit 13.6 (page 232) incorporates reinforcement contingencies and reinforcement schedules into our motivation model. First, notice that extrinsic rewards and the schedules of reinforcement used to deliver them are the primary method for creating reinforcement contingencies in organizations. In turn, those reinforcement contingencies directly affect valences (the attractiveness of rewards), instrumentality (the perceived link between rewards and performance), and effort (how hard employees will work).

*Let's learn more about reinforcement theory by examining **4.1 the components of reinforcement theory, 4.2 the different schedules for delivering reinforcement, and 4.3 how to motivate with reinforcement theory.***

4.1 Components of Reinforcement Theory

As just described, *reinforcement contingencies* are the cause-and-effect relationships between the performance of specific behaviours and specific consequences. There are four kinds of reinforcement contingencies: positive reinforcement, negative reinforcement, punishment, and extinction.

Positive reinforcement strengthens behaviour (i.e., increases its frequency) by following behaviours with desirable consequences. By contrast, **negative reinforcement** strengthens behaviour by withholding an unpleasant consequence when employees perform a specific behaviour. Negative reinforcement is also called avoidance learning because workers perform a behaviour to avoid a negative consequence. For example, at the Florist Network, company management instituted a policy of requiring good attendance for employees to receive their annual bonuses. Employee attendance improved significantly when excessive absenteeism threatened to result in the loss of $1,500 or more.[51] At Canada's SNC-Lavalin, employees who do not take any sick time receive a bonus of $1,500 just before Christmas. For every day that an employee is absent, $300 is deducted from that bonus.

Thinking about others, and what they want, can lead to more creative and useful ideas, according to new research. This finding has important implications for reinforcement, says Adam Grant, an associate professor at the University of Pennsylvania's Wharton School: "People who focus on others tend to be more creative than those who are just out for themselves, because focusing on others forces you to consider a wider range of perspectives."[52]

By contrast, **punishment** weakens behaviour (i.e., decreases its frequency) by following behaviours with undesirable consequences. For example, the standard disciplinary or punishment process in most companies is an oral warning ("Don't ever do that again"), followed by a written warning ("This letter is to discuss the serious problem you're having with ..."), followed by three days off without pay ("While you're at home not being paid, we want you to think hard about ..."), followed by being dismissed ("That was your last chance"). Although punishment can weaken behaviour, managers have to be careful to avoid the backlash that sometimes occurs when employees are punished at work. Frito-Lay began getting complaints from customers that they were finding potato chips with obscene messages written on them. Frito-Lay eventually traced the problem to a potato chip plant where supervisors had dismissed 58 out of the 210 workers for disciplinary reasons over a nine-month period. The remaining employees were so angry over what they saw as unfair treatment from management that they began writing the phrases on potato chips with felt-tipped pens.[53]

Extinction is a reinforcement strategy in which a positive consequence is no longer allowed to follow a previously reinforced behaviour. By removing the positive consequence, extinction weakens the behaviour, making it less likely to occur. Based on the idea of positive reinforcement, most companies give company leaders and managers substantial financial rewards when the company performs well. Based on the idea of extinction, you would then expect that leaders and managers would not be rewarded (i.e., removing the positive consequence) when companies perform poorly. If companies really want pay to reinforce the right kinds of behaviours, then rewards have to be removed when company management doesn't produce successful performance.

4.2 Schedules for Delivering Reinforcement

As mentioned earlier, *a schedule of reinforcement* is the set of rules regarding reinforcement contingencies such as which behaviours will be reinforced, which consequences will follow those behaviours, and the schedule by which those consequences will be delivered. There are two categories of reinforcement schedules: continuous and intermittent.

With **continuous reinforcement schedules**, a consequence follows every instance of a behaviour. For example, employees working on a piece-rate pay system earn money (consequence) for every part they manufacture (behaviour). The more they produce, the more they earn. By contrast, with **intermittent reinforcement schedules**, consequences are delivered after a specified or average time has elapsed or after a specified or average number of behaviours has occurred. As Exhibit 13.7 (page 233) shows, there are four types of intermittent reinforcement schedules. Two of these are based on time and are called *interval reinforcement schedules,* while the other two, known as *ratio schedules,* are based on behaviours.

Positive reinforcement reinforcement that strengthens behaviour by following behaviours with desirable consequences

Negative reinforcement reinforcement that strengthens behaviour by withholding an unpleasant consequence when employees perform a specific behaviour

Punishment reinforcement that weakens behaviour by following behaviours with undesirable consequences

Extinction reinforcement in which a positive consequence is no longer allowed to follow a previously reinforced behaviour, thus weakening the behaviour

Continuous reinforcement schedule a schedule that requires a consequence to be administered following every instance of a behaviour

Intermittent reinforcement schedule a schedule in which consequences are delivered after a specified or average time has elapsed or after a specified or average number of behaviours has occurred

Lambros Kazan/Shutterstock.com

Exhibit 13.6 Adding Reinforcement Theory to the Model

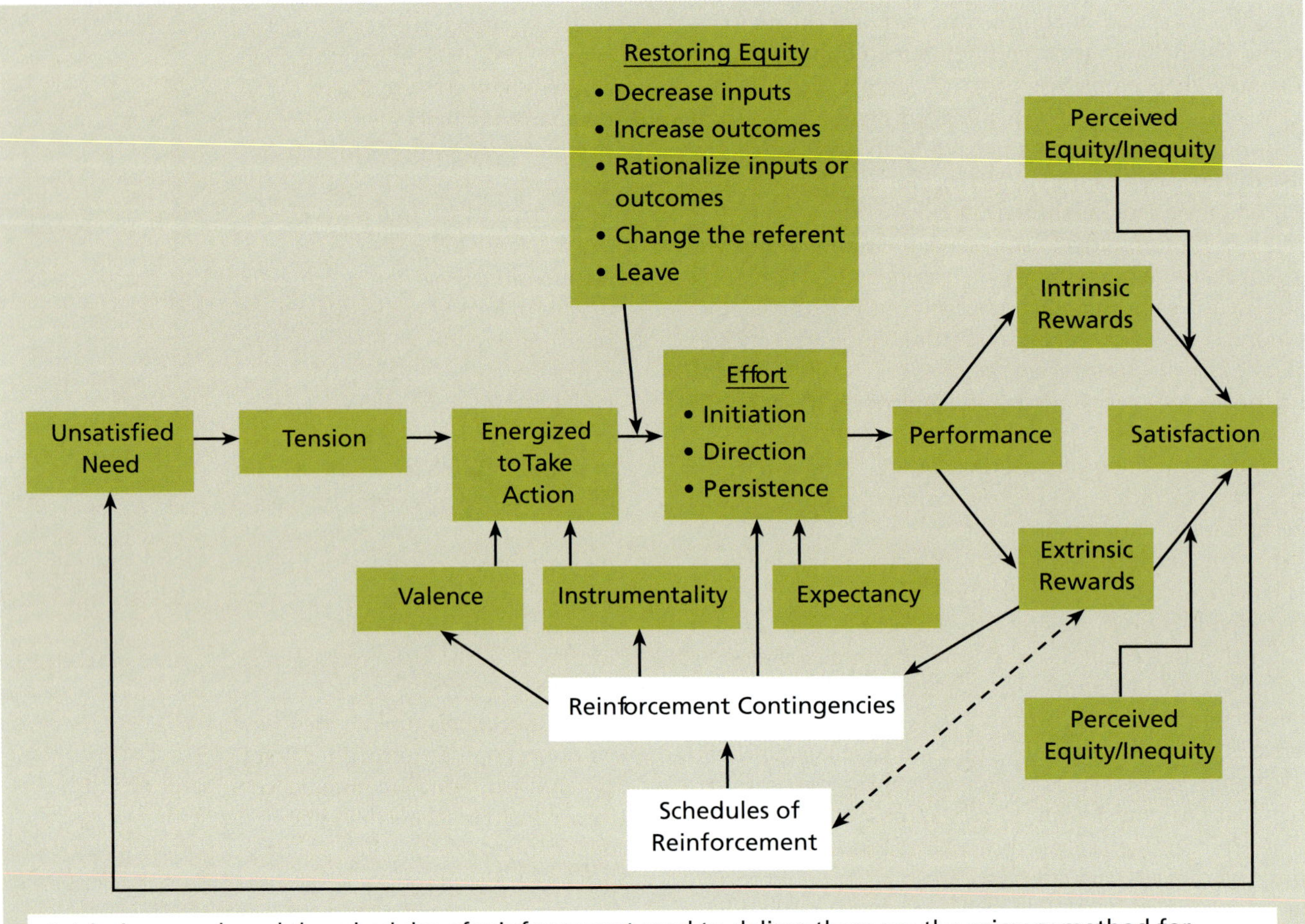

Extrinsic rewards and the schedules of reinforcement used to deliver them are the primary method for creating reinforcement contingencies in organizations. In turn, those reinforcement contingencies directly affect valences (the attractiveness of rewards), instrumentality (the perceived link between rewards and performance), and effort (how hard employees will work).

Fixed interval reinforcement schedule an intermittent schedule in which consequences follow a behaviour only after a fixed time has elapsed

Variable interval reinforcement schedule an intermittent schedule in which the time between a behaviour and the following consequences varies around a specified average

With **fixed interval reinforcement schedules**, consequences follow a behaviour only after a fixed time has elapsed. For example, most people receive their paycheques on a fixed interval schedule (e.g., once or twice per month). As long as they work (behaviour) during a specified pay period (interval), they get a paycheque (consequence). With **variable interval reinforcement schedules**, consequences follow a behaviour after different times, some shorter and some longer, that vary around a specified average time. On a 90-day variable interval reinforcement schedule, you might receive a bonus after 80 days or perhaps after 100 days, but the average interval between performing your job well (behaviour) and receiving your bonus (consequence) will be 90 days.

With **fixed ratio reinforcement schedules**, consequences are delivered following a specific number of behaviours. For example, a car salesperson might receive a $1,000 bonus after every 10 sales. Therefore, a salesperson with only 9 sales would not receive the bonus until he or she finally sold a 10th car.

With **variable ratio reinforcement schedules**, consequences are delivered following a different number of behaviours, sometimes more and sometimes less, that vary around a specified average number of behaviours. With a 10-car variable ratio reinforcement schedule, a salesperson might receive the bonus after 7 car sales, or after 12, 11, or 9 sales, but the average number of cars sold before receiving the bonus would be 10 cars.

Which reinforcement schedules work best? In the past, the standard advice was to use continuous reinforcement when employees were learning new behaviours because reinforcement after each success leads to faster learning. Similarly, the standard advice was to use intermittent reinforcement schedules to maintain behaviour after it is learned because intermittent rewards are supposed

Exhibit 13.7 Intermittent Reinforcement Schedules

	Fixed	Variable
Interval (Time)	Consequences follow behaviour after a fixed time has elapsed.	Consequences follow behaviour after different times, some shorter and some longer, that vary around a specific average time.
Ratio (Behaviour)	Consequences follow a specific number of behaviours.	Consequences follow a different number of behaviours, sometimes more and sometimes less, that vary around a specified average number of behaviours.

to make behaviour much less subject to extinction.[54] Research shows, however, that interval-based systems usually produce weak results, and that the continuous reinforcement, fixed ratio, and variable ratio schedules are almost equally effective.[55] In organizational settings, all three produce consistently large increases over noncontingent reward schedules. So managers should choose whichever of these three is easiest to use.

Managers are doing the best they can with the tools they have, but many of them have forgotten a tool that actually recognizes results and actions. That missing tool is acknowledgment, whichever reinforcement scheduled is used. "Managers need to simply acknowledge, in an appreciative tone, what the employee has done, without adding any judgment or any story about how it has helped the boss or the company."[56]

4.3 Motivating with Reinforcement Theory

What practical steps can managers take to use reinforcement theory to motivate employees? University business professor Fred Luthans, who has been studying the effects of reinforcement theory in organizations for more than a quarter of a century, says that there are five steps to motivating workers with reinforcement theory: *identify, measure, analyze, intervene,* and *evaluate* critical performance-related behaviours.[57]

Identify means identifying critical, observable, performance-related behaviours. These are the behaviours that are most important to successful job performance. In addition, they must also be easily observed so that they can be accurately measured. *Measure* means measuring the baseline frequencies of these behaviours. In other words, find out how often workers perform them. *Analyze* means analyzing the causes and consequences of these behaviours. Analyzing the causes helps managers create the conditions that produce these critical behaviours, and analyzing the consequences helps them determine whether these behaviours produce the results they want. *Intervene* means changing the organization by using positive and negative reinforcement to increase the frequency of these critical behaviours. *Evaluate* means evaluating the extent to which the intervention actually changed workers' behaviour. This is done by comparing behaviour after the intervention to the original baseline of behaviour before the intervention.

In addition to these five steps, managers should remember three other key things when motivating with reinforcement theory. The first of these is *don't reinforce the wrong behaviours.* Although reinforcement theory sounds simple, it's actually very difficult to put into practice. One of the most common mistakes is accidentally reinforcing the wrong behaviours. Sometimes managers reinforce behaviours that they don't want.

Fixed ratio reinforcement schedule an intermittent schedule in which consequences are delivered following a specific number of behaviours

Variable ratio reinforcement schedule an intermittent schedule in which consequences are delivered following a different number of behaviours, sometimes more and sometimes less, that vary around a specified average number of behaviours

Managers should also *correctly administer punishment at the appropriate time.* Many managers believe that punishment can change workers' behaviour and help them improve their job performance. Furthermore, managers believe that fairly punishing workers also lets other workers know what is or isn't acceptable.[58] A danger of using punishment is that it can produce a backlash against managers and companies. But if administered properly, punishment can weaken the frequency of undesirable behaviours without creating a backlash.[59] To be effective, the punishment must be strong enough to stop the undesired behaviour, and it must be administered objectively (the same rules applied to everyone), impersonally (without emotion or anger), consistently and contingently (each time improper behaviour occurs), and quickly (as soon as possible following the undesirable behaviour). In addition, managers should clearly explain what the appropriate behaviour is and why the employee is being punished. Employees typically respond well when punishment is administered this way.[60]

A penalty of US$250 for smoking in a hotel room was among the expenses charged to taxpayers by Bev Oda, Canada's former Minister of International Cooperation. The then-minister was dinged in 2010 for smoking in a hotel room during a trip to Washington, D.C. But the "punishment" for smoking has hit many hotel guests. In Edmonton a growing number of city hotels have banned smoking, and to enforce the policy, they are hitting scofflaws with fines up to $250. "They try everything," said Lori Bartlett, director of sales at Days Inn & Suites West Edmonton. "They push the screen

Trashing the Workweek

Giving employees freedom to go to a baseball game on Wednesday afternoon might seem like a risky way to motivate them. But the Results-Only Work Environment (ROWE) approach, pioneered at Best Buy by Cali Ressler and Jodi Thompson, taps into employees' need for independence in order to get them to perform at their best. Lauren Larose from Victoria, B.C., wrote to Ressler and Thompson stating that her first business co-op work term, with a government ministry, sucked. It was a great work environment, she said, but when her supervisor was out of the office she had nothing to do. The ROWE specialists responded that Lauren should try other communication (Twitter or texting) besides face-to-face taskings. They also suggested that Lauren mention to her supervisor that there were other projects that she would be interested in working on. "Self-motivation is something that all supervisors look for, and it sounds like you have it!" ROWE has boosted morale and productivity in many companies.

Sources: S. Westcott, "Beyond Flextime: Trashing the Workweek," *Inc.*, August 2008, 30–31; "Killing Time," Globe Life, March 31, 2009, http://www.theglobeandmail.com/report-on-business/killing-time/article1062282.

"That wasn't me barking, that was me giving a motivational speech."

Cartoonresource/Shutterstock.com

Pojoslaw/Shutterstock.com

Goal a target, objective, or result that someone tries to accomplish

Goal-setting theory a theory that states that people will be motivated to the extent to which they accept specific, challenging goals and receive feedback that indicates their progress toward goal achievement

out. They throw the butts out the window." The Sheraton and Four Points by Sheraton, divisions of Starwood Hotels & Resorts Worldwide Inc., have announced that their North American hotels will have a $200 smoking charge; Marriott International Hotels and Starwood's Westin Hotels are also non-smoking in North America. For many years now, the Westin in Edmonton has posted signs in its rooms advising of the smoking ban and of a $200 cleaning fee for breaking it. Perhaps that is punishment that works.[61]

Finally, managers should *choose the simplest and most effective schedule of reinforcement*. When choosing a schedule of reinforcement, managers need to balance effectiveness against simplicity. In fact, the more complex the schedule of reinforcement, the more likely it is to be misunderstood and resisted by managers and employees. Since continuous reinforcement, fixed ratio, and variable ratio schedules are about equally effective, continuous reinforcement schedules may be the best choice in many instances by virtue of their simplicity.

LO5 Goal-Setting Theory

The basic model of motivation with which we began this chapter showed that individuals feel tension after becoming aware of an unfulfilled need. Once they experience tension, they search for and select courses of action that they believe will eliminate this tension. In other words, they direct their behaviour toward something. This something is a goal. A **goal** is a target, objective, or result that someone tries to accomplish. **Goal-setting theory** says that people will be motivated to the extent they accept specific, challenging goals and receive feedback that indicates their progress toward goal achievement.

> One of the simplest, most effective ways to motivate workers is to assign them specific, challenging goals.

*Let's learn more about goal setting by examining **5.1** the components of goal-setting theory and **5.2** how to motivate with goal-setting theory.*

5.1 Components of Goal-Setting Theory

The basic components of goal-setting theory are goal specificity, goal difficulty, goal acceptance, and performance feedback.[62] **Goal specificity** is the extent to which goals are detailed, exact, and unambiguous. Specific goals, such as "I'm going to have a 3.0 average this semester," are more motivating than general goals, such as "I'm going to get better grades this semester."

Goal difficulty is the extent to which a goal is hard or challenging to accomplish. Difficult goals, such as "I'm going to have a 3.5 average and make the Dean's List this semester," are more motivating than easy goals, such as "I'm going to have a 2.0 average this semester."

Goal acceptance, which is similar to the idea of goal commitment discussed in Chapter 5, is the extent to which people consciously understand and agree to goals. Accepted goals, such as "I really want to get a 3.5 average this semester to show my parents how much I've improved," are more motivating than unaccepted goals, such as "My parents really want me to get a 3.5 average this semester, but there's so much more I'd rather do on campus than study!"

Performance feedback is information about the quality or quantity of past performance and indicates whether progress is being made toward the accomplishment of a goal. Performance feedback, such as "My prof said I need a 92 on the final to get an 'A' in that class," is more motivating than no feedback, "I have no idea what my grade is in that class." In short, goal-setting theory says that people will be motivated to the extent to which they accept specific, challenging goals and receive feedback that indicates their progress toward goal achievement.

How does goal setting work? To start, challenging goals focus employees' attention (i.e., direction of effort) on the critical aspects of their work and away from unimportant ones. Goals also energize behaviour. When faced with unaccomplished goals, employees typically develop plans and strategies to reach those goals. Goals also create tension between the goal (the desired future state of affairs) and where the employee or company is now (the current state of affairs). This tension can be satisfied only by achieving or abandoning the goal. Finally, goals influence persistence. Since goals only go away when they are accomplished, employees are more likely to persist in their efforts in the presence of goals. Exhibit 13.8 on page 236 incorporates goals into the motivation model by showing how they directly affect tension, effort, and the extent to which employees are energized to take action.

5.2 Motivating with Goal-Setting Theory

Managers can take practical steps to use goal-setting theory to motivate employees. One of the simplest and most effective ways to motivate workers is to *assign them specific, challenging goals.*

Second, managers should *make sure that workers truly accept organizational goals.* Specific, challenging goals won't motivate workers unless they really accept, understand, and agree to the organization's goals. For this to occur, people must see the goals as fair and reasonable. They must also trust management and believe that managers are using goals to clarify what is expected from them rather than to exploit or threaten them ("If you don't achieve these goals ..."). Participative goal setting, in which managers and employees generate goals together, can help increase trust and understanding and thus acceptance of goals. Furthermore, providing workers with training can help increase goal acceptance, particularly when workers don't believe they are capable of reaching the organization's goals.[63]

Goal specificity the extent to which goals are detailed, exact, and unambiguous

Goal difficulty the extent to which a goal is hard or challenging to accomplish

Goal acceptance the extent to which people consciously understand and agree to goals

Performance feedback information about the quality or quantity of past performance that indicates whether progress is being made toward the accomplishment of a goal

Finally, managers should *provide frequent, specific, performance-related feedback.* Once employees have accepted specific, challenging goals, they should receive frequent performance-related feedback so that they can track their progress toward goal completion. Feedback leads to stronger motivation and effort in three ways.[64] First: receiving specific feedback that indicates how well they're performing can encourage employees who don't have specific, challenging goals to set goals to improve their performance. Second: once people meet goals, performance feedback often encourages them to set higher, more difficult goals. Third: feedback lets people know whether they need to increase their efforts or change strategies in order to accomplish their goals. So to motivate employees with goal-setting theory, make sure they receive frequent performance-related feedback so that they can track their progress toward goal completion. Simple feedback benefits from immediacy and spontaneity. If you want to recognize an employee for going the extra mile, you need to do it immediately. Furthermore, you need to articulate to employees what it was about their performance that you most appreciated.

LO6 Motivating with the Integrated Model

We began this chapter by defining motivation as the set of forces that initiates, directs, and makes people persist in their efforts to accomplish a goal. We also asked the basic question that managers ask when they try to figure out how to motivate their workers: "What leads to effort?" The answer to that question is likely to be somewhat different for each employee, but the diagram on your Review Card for this chapter will help you begin to answer it by consolidating the practical advice from the theories reviewed in this chapter in one convenient location. If you're having difficulty figuring out why people aren't motivated where you work, check your Review Card for a useful, theory-based starting point.

Exhibit 13.8 Adding Goal-Setting Theory to the Model

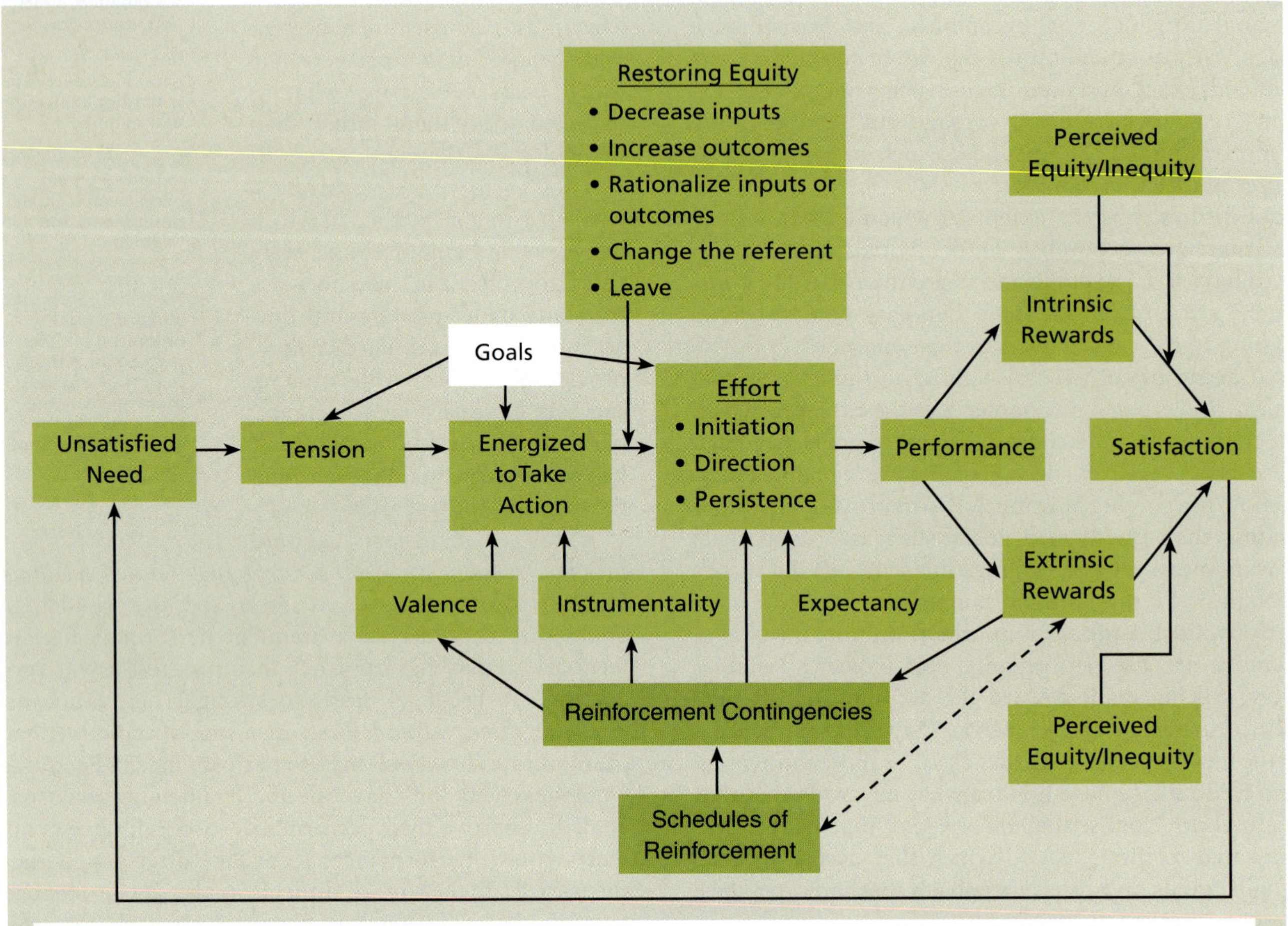

Restoring Equity
- Decrease inputs
- Increase outcomes
- Rationalize inputs or outcomes
- Change the referent
- Leave

Perceived Equity/Inequity

Intrinsic Rewards

Goals

Effort
- Initiation
- Direction
- Persistence

Unsatisfied Need

Tension

Energized to Take Action

Performance

Satisfaction

Extrinsic Rewards

Valence

Instrumentality

Expectancy

Reinforcement Contingencies

Perceived Equity/Inequity

Schedules of Reinforcement

Goals create tension between the goal, which is the desired future state of affairs, and where the employee or company is now, meaning the current state of affairs. This tension can be satisfied only by achieving or abandoning the goal. Goals also energize behaviour. When faced with unaccomplished goals, employees typically develop plans and strategies to reach those goals. Finally, goals influence persistence.

Go online at
www.nelson.com/4ltrpress/icanmgmt2
And access the essential Study Tools online for this chapter:

- **Flashcards**, to help you study
- **Interactive Quizzes**, to test your knowledge
- **Audio Chapter Summaries**, for chapter review
- **Crossword Puzzles and Beat the Clock**, to review key terms
- **What Would You Do? Cases**, for applying your knowledge to real-life situations
- **Self Assessments**, to learn about what kind of manager you are
- **Videos and Media Quizzing**, where you can watch a video about a real-life company and test yourself on what you've learned

Be sure to consult the Chapter Review Card at the back of the textbook.

14 Leadership

LEARNING OUTCOMES

LO1 Explain what leadership is.

LO2 Describe who leaders are and what effective leaders do.

LO3 Explain Fiedler's contingency theory.

LO4 Describe how path–goal theory works.

LO5 Explain the normative decision theory.

LO6 Discuss gender and leadership

LO7 Explain how visionary leadership (i.e., charismatic and transformational leadership) helps leaders achieve strategic leadership.

What Is Leadership?

If you've ever been in charge, or even just thought about it, chances are you've considered questions like these: Do I have what it takes to lead? What are the most important things leaders do? How can I transform a poorly performing department, division, or company? Do I need to adjust my leadership depending on the situation and the employee? Why doesn't my leadership inspire people? If you feel overwhelmed at the prospect of being a leader, you're not alone—millions of leaders in organizations around the world struggle with fundamental leadership issues on a daily basis.

How does an ensemble of 100 or more musicians, all playing different parts at different times on different instruments, manage to produce something as beautiful as Beethoven's Fifth Symphony? (If Gustav Mahler's Symphony of a Thousand is on the program, a lot more people might be involved!) The conductor, like a CEO, is responsible for managing all of this complexity and ensuring great output. But his or her job is about much more than keeping the beat with a baton. According to Dr. Ramona Wis, author of *The Conductor as Leader,* conductors must also build connections between people, inspire them with vision, command their trust, and persuade them to participate in the ensemble at their very best.[1]

Whether the end result is a stirring musical performance, the innovation of new products, feeding more people, or increased profits, **leadership** is the process of influencing others to achieve group or organizational goals. The knowledge and skills you'll learn in this chapter won't make the task of leadership less daunting, but they will help you navigate it.

Leadership the process of influencing others to achieve group or organizational goals

LO1 Leaders versus Managers

Henri Mintzberg of Montreal's McGill University spent a lifetime trying to understand what a manager does. His seminal work, *Management: Folk Lore and Fact*, helped define the difference between management and leadership. Managers make an endless series of decisions about doing things right. Leaders make decisions about doing the right thing.[2] In other words, leaders begin with the question, "What should we be doing?", while managers start with "How can we do what we're already doing better?" Leaders focus on vision, mission, goals, and objectives, while managers focus on productivity and efficiency. Managers see themselves as preservers of the status quo, while leaders see themselves as promoters of change and challengers of the status quo. Leaders, consequently, encourage creativity and risk taking. In 2013, Ashley Good of Canadian Engineers Without Borders was awarded the prestigious HBR/McKinsey Innovating Innovation Challenge with her "Fail Forward" message, referring to a "refreshing and bold practice that takes the tired mantra of 'embracing failure' and turns it into a way of life for an organization."[3] We can win by producing new products or designs that are a total embarrassment, says Good, and we need to "include phrases like 'the courage to fail' and 'learning means admitting failure'" in order to ultimately be successful.

> **Organizations are underled and overmanaged.**

Another difference is that managers take a relatively short-term perspective, while leaders take a long-term one. Also, managers are more concerned about *means,* that is, about *how* to get things done, while leaders are more concerned about *ends,* that is, about *what* gets done. Managers concern themselves with control and with limiting the choices of others, while leaders concern themselves with expanding people's choices and options.[4] Finally, managers solve problems so that others can do their work, while leaders inspire and motivate others to find their own solutions.

Although leaders are different from managers, organizations need both. Managers are vital to getting out the day-to-day work; leaders are vital to inspiring employees and setting the organization's long-term direction. For any organization, the key issue is whether it is properly led and properly managed. As Mintzberg said in summarizing up the difference between leaders and managers, organizations are underled and overmanaged. They do not pay enough attention to doing the right thing, and they pay too much attention to doing things right.[5]

LO2 Who Leaders Are and What Leaders Do

"I don't know if it is a marriage made in heaven," said Suncor's president, "but it is a match made in Canada." CEO Rick George was not shy about appealing to Canadian nationalism. The merger between Suncor Energy Inc. and Petro-Canada created the country's largest energy company. "This will truly be a flagship Canadian corporation," he told a Calgary news conference. He and his counterpart at Petro-Canada, the more introverted Ron Brenndenan, are now running Canada's largest energy company.[6]

Which one, George or Brenndenan, is likely to be more successful as a CEO? According to a survey of 1,542 senior managers, it's George, the extrovert. Forty-seven percent of those managers said that extroverts make better CEOs; 65 percent said that being an introvert hurts a CEO's chances of success.[7] Clearly, senior managers believe that extroverted CEOs are better leaders. But are they? Not necessarily. In fact, a rather high percentage of CEOs, 40 percent, are introverts. Canada's media giant Rogers Communications is led by a shy man: "Though friends know him as gregarious, Mr. Rogers has often been considered the shy son of Ted."[8] Yet he is the deputy chairman of Rogers and also serves as chairman of the trust that controls the family's voting shares.

Trait theory a leadership theory that holds that effective leaders possess a similar set of traits or characteristics

Traits relatively stable characteristics, such as abilities, psychological motives, or consistent patterns of behaviour

So, what makes a good leader? Does leadership success depend on who leaders are (i.e., whether they are introverts or extroverts), or on what leaders do and how they behave? *Let's learn more about who leaders are by investigating **2.1 leadership traits** and **2.2 leadership behaviours.***

2.1 Leadership Traits

Trait theory is one way to describe who leaders are. **Trait theory** posits that effective leaders possess similar characteristics. **Traits** are relatively stable characteristics, such as abilities, psychological motives, and patterns of behaviour. For example, according to trait theory, leaders are taller and more confident and have greater physical stamina (i.e., higher energy) than nonleaders. It is noteworthy that 14.5 percent of men are 183 centimetres tall or more, yet 58 *percent* of *Fortune* 500 CEOs are taller than that.[9] Trait theory is also known as the "great person" theory because early versions of it stated that leaders are born, not made. In other words, you either have the right stuff to be a leader or you don't. And if you don't, there is no way to get it.

For some time, it was thought that trait theory was faulty and that there are no consistent trait differences between leaders and nonleaders or between effective and ineffective leaders. However, more recent evidence suggests that "successful leaders are not like other people"—that they are indeed different from the rest of us.[10] Specifically, leaders are different from nonleaders in the following traits: drive, the desire to lead, honesty/integrity, self-confidence, emotional stability, cognitive ability, and knowledge of the business.[11]

Drive refers to a high level of effort and is characterized by achievement, motivation, initiative, energy, and tenacity. In terms of achievement and ambition, leaders always try to make improvements or achieve success in what they're doing. They have a strong desire to promote change or solve problems. Leaders typically have more energy—they have to, given the long hours they put in and followers' expectations that they be positive and upbeat. Leaders are also more tenacious than nonleaders and are better at overcoming obstacles and problems that would deter most of us.

Successful leaders also have a stronger *desire to lead*. They want to be in charge, and they think about ways to influence or convince others about what should or shouldn't be done. *Honesty/integrity* is also important to leaders. *Honesty*, being truthful with others, is a cornerstone of leadership. Leaders won't be trusted if they are dishonest. When they are honest, subordinates are willing to overlook other flaws. *Integrity* is the extent to which leaders do what they say they will do. Leaders may be honest and have good intentions, but they won't be trusted if they don't consistently deliver on what they promise.

Self-confidence, believing in one's abilities, also distinguishes leaders from nonleaders. Self-confident leaders are more decisive and assertive and are more likely to gain others' confidence. Moreover, self-confident

Don't Judge a Leader by Her Chanel

How much do physical traits affect our perception of a person's ability to lead? One study showed that female candidates tend to fare worse in elections than their male opponents because of their gender ... and worse yet if they are perceived as unattractive. Although it is just as easy to judge a leader by the clothes he or she is wearing as it is to judge a book by its cover, it is best to focus on whether a person has strong personal—rather than physical—traits, such as persistence, attention to detail, efficiency, analytical skills, and high standards. One clear trend in the past 10 years is that more women are setting up their own businesses. In 2010, over 900,000 of the 2.6 million self-employed workers in Canada were women according to Statistics Canada. Industry Canada's most recent estimates put the proportion of women-owned small businesses at 17 percent, which would represent about 187,000 firms. Between 2001 and 2013 the proportion of Canadian women employed in senior management positions rose 5 percent, and the proportion employed in natural and applied sciences rose 10 percent. A study by Catalyst, a women's advocacy group, found that women comprised 18.1 percent of senior officers and top earners at Canada's 500 largest companies in 2012.

THE CANADIAN PRESS/Jonathan Hayward

In mid-2013 the premiers of Nunavut, British Columbia, Alberta, Ontario, Quebec, and Newfoundland and Labrador were all females.

Sources: Statistics Canada, 2010, http://www.statcan.gc.ca/daily-quotidien/101209/dq101209a-eng.htm; J. Kwan, "Still Few women in Canada's Top Business Posts," *Yahoo Finance Canada*, February 20, 2013, http://ca.finance.yahoo.com/blogs/insight/still-few-women-canada-top-business-posts-212950873.html; H. Zubi, "Women-Owned Businesses: Canada Needs Moore Female Entrepreneurs," *Toronto Star*, May 16, 2013, http://www.thestar.com/business/small_busines/people/2013/01/30/women-ownedbusinesses–canada-needs-more-female-entrepreneurs.html; J.N. Schubert and M.A. Curran, "Stereotyping Effects in Candidate Evaluation: The Interaction of Gender and Attractiveness Bias," http://www3.niu.edu/~ti0jns1/mpsa2001_paper.htm; G. Anders, "Tough CEOs Often Most Successful, a Study Finds," *The Wall Street Journal*, http://online.wsj.com/article/SB119543240896797405.html.

leaders will admit mistakes because they view them as learning opportunities rather than as refutations of their capacity to lead. This means that leaders are also *emotionally stable.* Even when things go wrong, they remain even-tempered and consistent in their outlook and in the way they treat others. Leaders who can't control their emotions, who anger quickly or attack and blame others for mistakes, are unlikely to be trusted.

Leaders are also smart. They typically have strong *cognitive abilities.* This doesn't mean they are geniuses, but it does mean they have the capacity to analyze large amounts of seemingly unrelated, complex information and see patterns, opportunities, or threats where others might not. Finally, leaders know their stuff, which means they have superior technical knowledge about the businesses they run. Leaders who have a good *knowledge of the business* understand the key technological issues and challenges facing their companies. Studies indicate that more often than not, effective leaders have extensive experience in their industry. Kelsey Ramsden owns and runs a civil construction business. A 36-year-old mother of three, she grew up working for her father's road-building company—in fact, her first job was as a flag turner on the Alaska Highway. As a result, she knew how to play the game: "you must understand this complex business to be successful."[12] When the recession bit into the road construction business in 2009, "Ramsden did far more than avoid bankruptcy. She infused her company with a combination of size, sales growth, and profitability." All of this has ranked her #1 on the 2012 PROFIT/Chatelaine W100 list of Canada's Top Female Entrepreneurs.[13]

2.2 Leadership Behaviours

Thus far, you've read about who leaders *are*. It's hard to imagine a truly successful leader who lacks all of these qualities. But traits alone are not enough to make a successful leader. Leaders who have all of these traits (or many of them) must then take actions that encourage people to achieve group or organizational goals.[14] So we will now examine what leaders *do*, meaning the behaviours they perform or the actions they take to influence others to achieve group or organizational goals. When she interviewed the CEO of Procter & Gamble on the subject of leadership, Associated Press reporter Elise Amendola asked, "Are leaders born or made?" Debunking the "great person" theory, A.G. Lafley answered, "Clearly made. You choose to lead. You choose to want to make a difference, to make the world better in some meaningful way. Until that choice is made, you don't have a leader. You have a lump of clay."[15]

Initiating structure the degree to which a leader structures the roles of followers by setting goals, giving directions, setting deadlines, and assigning tasks

Researchers at the University of Michigan, Ohio State University, and the University of Texas examined the specific behaviours that leaders use to improve the satisfaction and performance of their subordinates. Hundreds of studies were conducted and hundreds of leader behaviours were examined. At all three universities, two basic leader behaviours emerged as central to successful leadership: initiating structure (called *job-centred leadership* at the University of Michigan, and *concern for production* at the University of Texas), and considerate leader behaviour (called *employee-centred leadership* at the University of Michigan and *concern for people* at the University of Texas).[16] These two leader behaviours form the basis for many of the leadership theories discussed in this chapter.

Initiating structure refers to the degree to which a leader structures the roles of followers by setting goals, giving directions, setting deadlines, and assigning tasks. A leader's ability to initiate structure primarily affects subordinates' job performance. VIA Rail and the Canadian Auto Workers Union (CAW) recently

Followers as Leaders

As more organizations become flatter, or adopt less hierarchical organizational structures, it is becoming increasingly clear that leaders and followers are dependent each other. One thing good leaders need is good followers. Barbara Kellerman of Harvard University outlines five different types of followers and urges leaders to understand what kinds of followers they have. Isolates and bystanders are not invested. They just do their jobs and tend to impede change. They can be useful for leaders who want to maintain the status quo but are otherwise dead weight. Good followers, by contrast, support a leader they've invested in. Consequently, they are good assets. Participants are self-motivated and driven to make a difference, and activists are eager and will go the extra mile, while diehards will support their leader even if it means going down with the ship. But leaders beware: these types of followers can be a liability if you have not inspired their loyalty. So followers are leaders, too. Williams states that followers demand leadership and trustworthiness and are fickle. Kellerman adds that "while they may lack authority, at least in comparison with their superiors, followers do not lack power and influence."

Sources: T. Williams, "What Every Leader Needs to Know About Followers," AZCentral .Com/Business & Enrepreneurship, 2013, http://yourbusiness.azcentral.com/leader -needsfollowers-17672.html; B. Kellerman, "What Every Leader Needs to Know About Followers," *Harvard Business Review* (December 2007): 84–91.

f9photos/Shutterstock.com

Consideration the extent to which a leader is friendly, approachable, and supportive and shows concern for employees

reached a tentative agreement, averting a strike. The three-year deal was achieved "after a difficult and challenging round of negotiations." This involved tough leadership, given that it dealt with workers' paycheques. The CAW represents 2,200 customer service, train service, and maintenance workers across Canada. According to CAW representative Bob Chernecki, "We feel just great about the settlement."[17]

© Shalom Ormsby/Photodisc/Jupiterimages

Consideration refers to the extent to which a leader is friendly, approachable, and supportive and shows concern for employees. Consideration primarily affects subordinates' job satisfaction. Specific consideration behaviours include listening to employees' problems and concerns, consulting with employees before making decisions, and treating employees as equals.[18] Canadian Tire CEO Stephen Wetmore knows about concern for people and relations within a company. The company's relationship with dealers (store owners) has not always been smooth when it comes to implementing change.

Canadian Tire long had a reputation for moving at a snail's pace, and both head office and its store owners realized that had to change. It took two years of negotiations to hammer out an agreement, which will last until 2020. Both sides say that because of their new relationship, Canadian Tire is positioned for success. According to Wetmore, "We've removed a lot of the procedural red tape that held up the speed of progress in an effort to make the relationship more streamlined and agile." In the past, when a product line was under review, it would take more than a year to make a decision after evaluating cost structure, quality, and capability. "You'd have an argument over here, disagreements over there and end up losing sight of the customer," says Wetmore, who adds that the company has now shaved months off the process and is working to get it down even more. But, he adds, the biggest benefit of the new consideration for people deal is that it has "rebuil[t] the trust between the organization and the dealers, which had eroded over the years."[19]

Researchers at Michigan, Texas, and Ohio generally agreed that initiating structure and consideration were basic leader behaviours, but they departed from one another with regard to how those two behaviours were related and which was more important. The Michigan studies indicated that the two were mutually exclusive behaviours on opposite ends of a continuum. In other words, leaders who wanted to be more considerate would have to do less initiating of structure (and vice versa). The Michigan studies also found that only considerate leader behaviours (i.e., employee-centred behaviours) were associated with successful leadership. By contrast, the researchers at Ohio and Texas found that initiating structure and showing consideration were independent behaviours—in other words, leaders could show consideration and initiate structure at the same time. Additional evidence confirms this finding.[20] The same researchers concluded that the most effective leaders excelled at both initiating structure and considerate leader behaviours.

This "high–high" approach can be seen in the upper right corner of the Blake/Mouton leadership grid, shown in Exhibit 14.1. Blake and Mouton used two leadership behaviours—concern for people (i.e., consideration) and concern for production (i.e., initiating structure)—to categorize five different leadership styles. In the exhibit, both behaviours are rated on a 9-point scale, with 1 representing "low" and 9 representing "high." Blake and Mouton suggest that a "high–high" or 9,9 leadership style is the best. They call this style *team management* because leaders who use it display a high concern for people (9) as well as a high concern for production (9).

By contrast, leaders use a 9,1 *authority-compliance* leadership style when they have a high concern for production and a low concern for people. A 1,9 *country club* style arises when leaders care about having a friendly and enjoyable work environment and don't really pay much attention to production or performance. Worst of all, according to the grid, is the 1,1 *impoverished* leader, who shows little concern for people or production and who does the bare minimum necessary to keep his or her job. Finally, the 5,5 *middle-of-the-road* style develops when leaders show a moderate amount of concern for both people and production.

Is the team management style, with its high concern for production and a high concern for people, really the best leadership style? Logically, it would seem so. Why wouldn't you want to show high concern for both people and production? Yet five decades of research indicates that there isn't one best leadership style. Rather, the best leadership style depends on the situation. In other words,

Exhibit 14.1 Blake/Mouton Leadership Grid

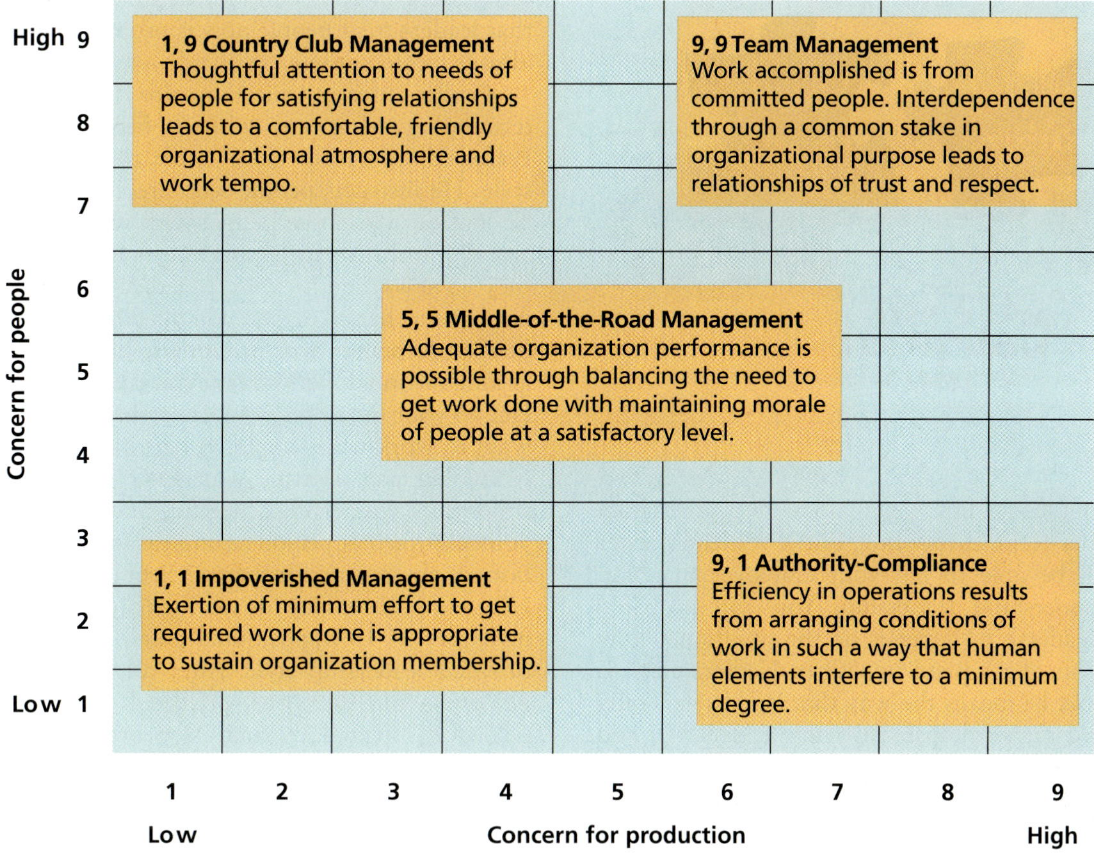

Source: R.R. Blake & A.A. McCanse, "The Leadership Grid (R)," Leadership Dilemmas—Grid Solutions (Houston: Gulf Publishing Company), 21. Copyright © 1991, by Scientific Methods, Inc. Reproduced by permission of Grid International, Inc.

there is no single combination of leadership behaviours that works well across all situations and employees.

Situational Approaches to Leadership

Situational factors constitute the third important perspective in leadership studies. We'll review three major situational approaches to leadership: Fiedler's contingency theory, House's path-goal theory, and Vroom and Yetton's normative decision model. All assume that the effectiveness of any **leadership style** depends on the situation.[21]

Situational leadership theories posit that there is no one best leadership style. Note, however, that Fiedler's contingency theory assumes (which the other two do not) that an individual's leadership style is difficult to change. According to him, then, leaders must be "matched" to a situation that fits their leadership style. In contrast, the other two situational theories assume that leaders are capable of adapting and adjusting their leadership styles to fit the demands of different situations.

LO3 Putting Leaders in the Right Situation: Fiedler's Contingency Theory

Fiedler's **contingency theory** states that in order to maximize work group performance, leaders must be matched to the right leadership situation.[22] The first basic assumption of Fiedler's theory is that leaders are effective when the work groups they lead perform well. So, instead of judging leaders' effectiveness by what the leaders do (i.e., initiating structure and consideration) or by who they are (i.e., trait theory), Fiedler assesses leaders in terms of the conduct and performance of the people they are leading. Second, Fiedler assumes that leaders are generally unable to change their style and that they are more effective when that style fits the situation. Third, he assumes that the success of a leader depends on the degree to which the he or she is able to influence the behaviour of group members. Note that it is the *group* behaviour and not the *leader* behaviour we are talking about here. In other words, besides traits, behaviours, and a favourable situation, leaders need the group's "permission" to lead.

Leadership style the way a leader generally behaves toward followers

Contingency theory a leadership theory that states that in order to maximize work group performance, leaders must be matched to the situation that best fits their leadership style

Let's learn more about Fiedler's contingency theory by examining 3.1 the least preferred coworker style, 3.2 situational favourableness, and 3.3 how to match leadership styles to situations.

3.1 Leadership Style: Least Preferred Coworker

When you are applying for a job right out of business school, your prospective employer will ask you some

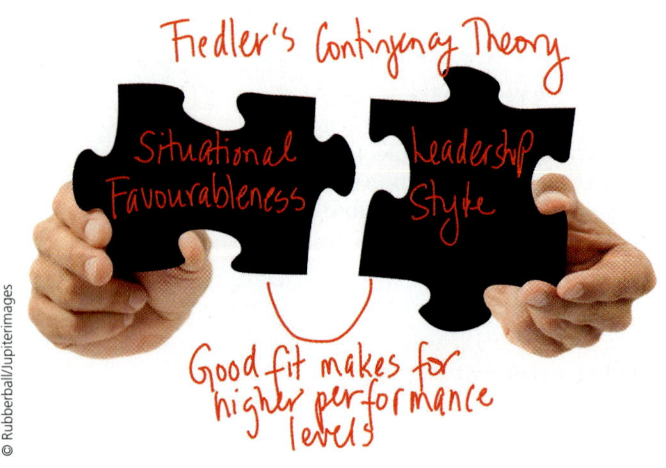

questions about leadership. We are going to be discussing this on a rather technical footing, but if you can master this, you will be able to tell your employer that you know and understand leadership. You will probably answer that leadership "depends on the situation." How will you explain that? Read on. When Fiedler refers to *leadership style,* he means the way that leaders generally behave toward their followers. Do the leaders yell and scream and blame others when things go wrong? Or do they correct mistakes by listening and then quietly but directly making their point? Do they let others make their own decisions and hold them accountable for the results? Or do they micromanage, insisting that all decisions be approved first by them? Fiedler also assumes that leadership styles are tied to leaders' underlying needs and personalities. Since personality and needs are relatively stable, he assumes that leaders are generally incapable of changing their leadership styles. In other words, the way that leaders treat people now is probably the way they've always treated others.

Fiedler uses a questionnaire (which uses arcane terminology—but stay with us here!) called the Least Preferred Coworker (LPC) scale to measure leadership style. He instructs people who are completing that scale to consider all of the people with whom they have ever worked and then to choose the one person with whom they have worked *least* well. Fiedler explains: "This does not have to be the person you liked least well, but should be the one person with whom you have the most trouble getting the job done."[23] How you describe this person is a clue to your own preferred leadership style—don't we all want to work with people we "get along with"?

Would you describe your LPC as pleasant, friendly, supportive, interesting, cheerful, and sincere? Or would you describe that person as unpleasant, unfriendly, hostile, boring, gloomy, and insincere? People who describe their LPC in a positive way (as scoring 64 and above on the full inventory of 18 oppositional pairs) have a *relationship-oriented* leadership style. After all, if they can still be positive about their least preferred coworker, they must be people-oriented. By contrast, people who describe their LPC in a negative way (as scoring 57 or below) have a *task-oriented* leadership style. Given a choice, they'll focus first on getting the job done and second on making sure everyone gets along. Finally, those with moderate scores (from 58 to 63) have a more flexible leadership style and can be somewhat relationship-oriented or somewhat task-oriented. We can see certain commonalities here with Exhibit 14.1.

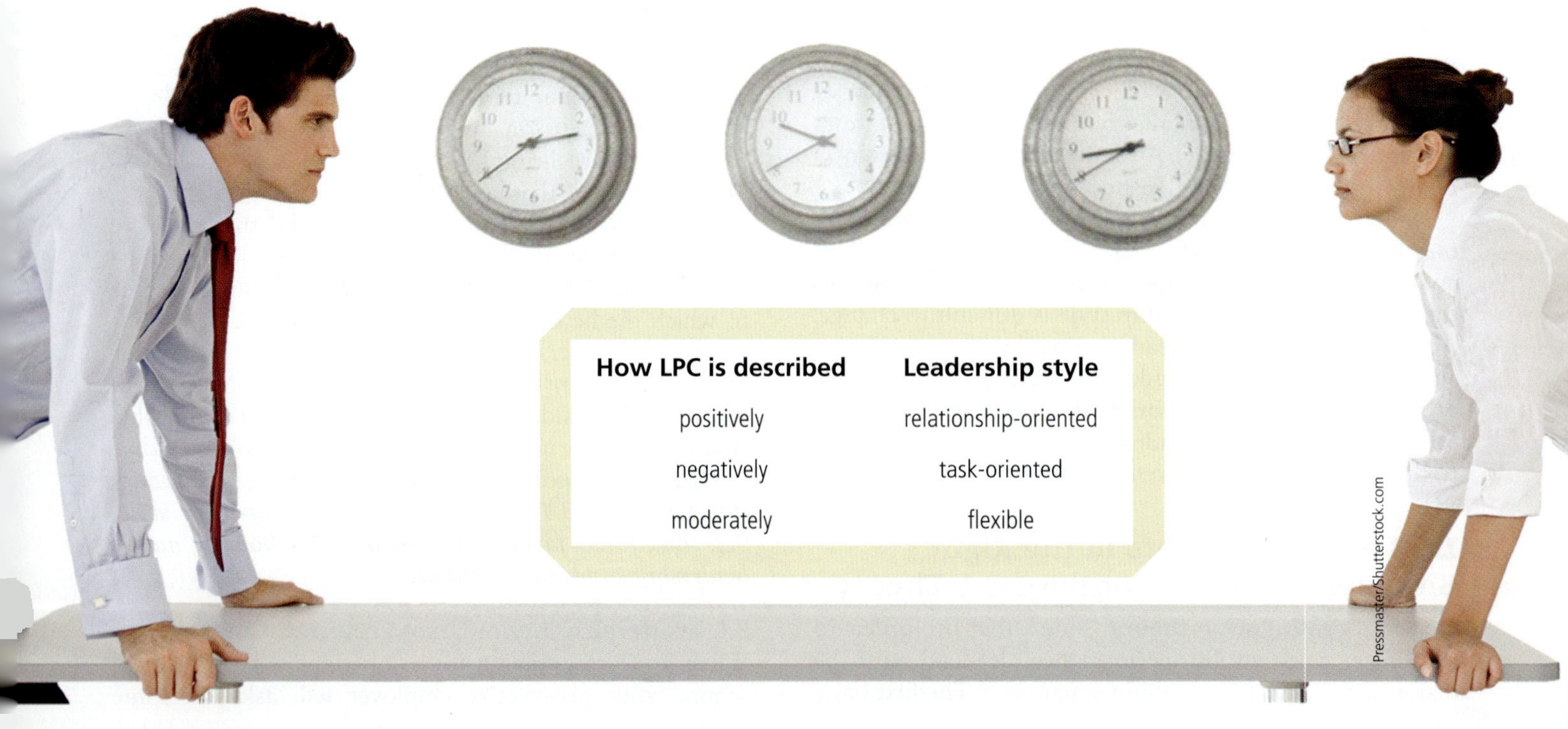

How LPC is described	Leadership style
positively	relationship-oriented
negatively	task-oriented
moderately	flexible

3.2 Situational Favourableness

Fiedler assumes that leaders will be more effective when their leadership styles are matched to the proper situation. Specifically, he defines **situational favourableness** as the degree to which a particular situation either allows or denies a leader the chance to influence the behaviour of group members.[24] In highly favourable situations, leaders find that their actions influence followers; in highly unfavourable situations, they have little or no success influencing the people they are trying to lead.

Three situational factors determine the favourability of a situation: leader–member relations, task structure, and position power. The most important situational factor is **leader–member relations**, which refers to how well followers respect, trust, and like their leaders. When leader–member relations are good, followers trust the leader and there is a friendly work atmosphere. **Task structure** is the degree to which the requirements of a subordinate's tasks are clearly specified. With highly structured tasks, employees have clear job responsibilities, goals, and procedures. **Position power** is the degree to which leaders are able to hire, fire, reward, and punish workers. The more influence leaders have over hiring, firing, rewards, and punishments, the greater their power.

Exhibit 14.2 shows how leader–member relations, task structure, and position power can be combined into eight situations that differ in their favourability to leaders. In general, Situation I, on the left side of Exhibit 14.2, is the most favourable situation for a leader. The followers like and trust their leader and know what to do because their tasks are highly structured. Also, the leader has the formal power to influence workers through hiring, firing, rewarding, and punishing them. Thus, in Situation I, it's relatively easy for the leader to influence his or her followers. By contrast, Situation VIII, on the right side of Exhibit 14.2, is the least favourable situation for a leader. The followers neither like nor trust their leader. Also, they are not sure what they're supposed to be doing because their tasks or jobs are highly unstructured. Finally, this leader finds it difficult to influence followers without the ability to hire, fire, reward, or punish them.

3.3 Matching Leadership Styles to Situations

After studying thousands of leaders and followers in hundreds of different situations, Fiedler found that the performances of relationship- and task-oriented leaders followed the pattern displayed in Exhibit 14.3 (page 246).

In moderately favourable situations, relationship-oriented leaders—those with high LPC scores—were better leaders (i.e., their groups performed more effectively). In these situations, the leader is liked somewhat, tasks are somewhat structured, and the leader has some position power. In such a situation, a relationship-oriented leader improves the most important of the three situational factors, which is leader–member relations. As a consequence, morale and performance improve.

By contrast, as Exhibit 14.3 shows, task-oriented leaders—those with low LPC scores—are better leaders in highly favourable and highly unfavourable situations. Task-oriented leaders do well in favourable situations where leaders are liked, tasks are structured, and the leader has the power to hire, fire, reward, and punish. In these situations, task-oriented leaders are in effect stepping on the gas of a well-tuned car. Their focus on performance sets the goal for the group, which then charges forward to meet it. But task-oriented leaders also do well in unfavourable situations, those in which leaders are disliked, tasks are unstructured, and the leader doesn't have the power to hire, fire, reward, and punish. In these situations, the task-oriented leader sets goals that focus attention on performance and that clarify what needs to be done, thus overcoming low task structure. This is enough to jump-start performance even if workers don't like or trust the leader.

Finally, although not shown in Exhibit 14.3, people with moderate LPC scores (who can be somewhat relationship-oriented or somewhat task-oriented) tend to do fairly well in all situations because they can adapt (or change) their behaviour to suit the situation. Typically, though, they don't perform quite as well as relationship-oriented or task-oriented leaders whose leadership styles are well matched to the situation.

Recall, though, that Fiedler assumes that leaders are incapable of changing their leadership style. Accordingly, the key to applying Fiedler's contingency theory in the workplace is to accurately assess leaders and then match

Situational favourableness the degree to which a particular situation either permits or denies a leader the chance to influence the behaviour of group members

Leader–member relations the degree to which followers respect, trust, and like their leaders

Task structure the degree to which the requirements of a subordinate's tasks are clearly specified

Position power the degree to which leaders are able to hire, fire, reward, and punish workers

Exhibit 14.2 Situational Favourableness

Leader–member relations	Good	Good	Good	Good	Poor	Poor	Poor	Poor
Task structure	High	High	Low	Low	High	High	Low	Low
Position power	Strong	Weak	Strong	Weak	Strong	Weak	Strong	Weak
Situation	I	II	III	IV	V	VI	VII	VIII
	Favourable			Moderately favourable			Unfavourable	

Exhibit 14.3 Matching Leadership Styles to Situations

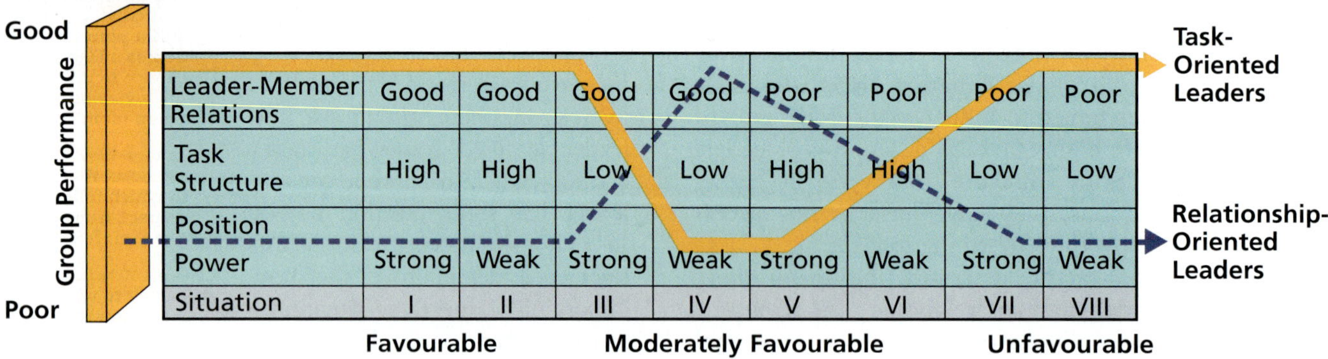

them to what they need to do to change the situation at hand. Of course, the theory won't work as well if leaders are attempting to change situational factors to fit their perceived leadership style rather than their real leadership style.[25] You will most likely be asked about your own personal leadership style in job interviews.

Path-goal theory a leadership theory that states that leaders can increase subordinate satisfaction and performance by clarifying and clearing the paths to goals and by increasing the number and kinds of rewards available for goal attainment

Source: F. E. Fiedler and M. M. Chemers, *Improving Leadership Effectiveness: The Leader Match Concept*, 2nd ed. (New York: John Wiley & Sons) 1984. Reproduced by permission of the authors.

© Jay P. Morgan/Workbook Stock/Getty Images

LO4 Adapting Leader Behaviour: Path-Goal Theory

In contrast to Fiedler's contingency theory, path-goal theory assumes that leaders can adapt their leadership styles to the situation at hand. Exhibit 14.4 (page 248) illustrates this process. As its name suggests, **path-goal theory** (as developed by the University of Toronto's John House) also posits that leaders can increase their followers' satisfaction and performance by clarifying and clearing the paths to goals and by increasing the number and kinds of rewards available for goal attainment. Put another way, leaders need to clarify how followers can achieve organizational goals, address the problems that prevent followers from achieving those goals, and then find more and varied rewards and satisfiers to motivate followers to achieve those goals.[26] Note that rewards are not necessarily monetary—indeed, they can be many different things (here, it would be useful to review Chapter 13 on motivation).

Leaders must meet two conditions if path clarification, path clearing, and rewards are to increase followers' motivation. First, the leader's behaviour must be a source of immediate or future satisfaction for followers. The things you do as a leader must please your followers today or lead to activities or rewards that will satisfy them in the future.

Second, leaders' behaviours must complement and not duplicate the characteristics of their followers' work environments. Thus, leaders' behaviours must offer something unique and valuable to followers beyond what they're already experiencing as they do their jobs and beyond what they can already do for themselves.

Let's learn more about path-goal theory by examining ***4.1 the four kinds of leadership styles that leaders use, 4.2 the subordinate and environmental contingency factors that determine when different leadership styles are effective,*** *and* ***4.3 the outcomes of path-goal theory in improving employee satisfaction and performance.***

4.1 Leadership Styles

As illustrated in Exhibit 14.4, the four leadership styles in path-goal theory are directive, supportive, participative, and achievement-oriented.[27] **Directive leadership** involves letting employees know precisely what is

Canadian CEO Chairs Clean Ontario Energy Task Force After Taking on Chinese Market

The leadership style needed for Asian countries, where female leaders can be seen as having weak position power, may require a relationship-oriented leader. Home Depot's Nova Scotia-born Annette Verschuren oversaw the company's Canadian operations growth from 19 stores in 1996 to 180 in 2011; she also led the company's entry into China. "We have expanded in North America and see China as a chance to grow," said Verschuren at a news conference in Beijing. "We see great opportunities to grow very aggressively." Clearly, Verschuren required a high LPC score to get the job done in China, and now she will need to change her leadership style once again as she heads up a new cutting-edge energy storage firm and chairs of the Clean Energy Task Force for Ontario. Verschuren was awarded the Order of Canada "for her contributions to Canada's retail industry and as a champion of corporate social responsibility" in 2011.

Sources: Nova Scotia Provincial News, "NS: Hall of Fame Recognizes Four Cape Breton Leaders," May 6, 2013, http://www.ns.dailybusinessbuzz.ca/Provincial-News/2013-05-06/article-3234620/NS%3A-Hall-of-Fame-recognizes-four-Cape-Breton-leaders/1; G. Pitts, "An Entrepreneurial Passion Renewed by Renewables," *Globe and Mail*, March 25, 2012, http://www.theglobeandmail.com/report-on-business/careers/careers-leadership/an-entrepreneurial-passion-renewed-by-renewables/article536404.

Annette Verschuren, former president of Home Depot's Asian and Canadian operations.

Photo by Dick Loek/Toronto Star via Getty Images

expected of them, giving them specific guidelines for performing their tasks, scheduling work, setting standards of performance, and making sure that people follow rules.

Supportive leadership involves being approachable, showing concern for employees and their welfare, treating them as equals, and creating a friendly climate. Supportive leadership is very similar to Blake and Mouton's considerate leader behaviour (see Exhibit 14.1). Supportive leadership often results in employee satisfaction with the job and with leaders. This leadership style may also result in improved performance when it increases employee confidence, lowers employee job stress, or improves relations and trust between employees and leaders.[28]

Good Tip!

How to Apply Path-Goal Theory

1. Clarify paths to goals.
2. Clear paths to goals by solving problems and removing roadblocks.
3. Increase the number and kinds of rewards/satisfaction available for goal attainment.
4. Do things that satisfy followers today or that will lead to future rewards or satisfaction.
5. Offer followers something unique and valuable beyond what they're experiencing or can already do for themselves.

Source: R. J. House and T. R. Mitchell, "Path-Goal Theory of Leadership," *Journal of Contemporary Business* 3 (1974): 81–97.

Participative leadership involves asking employees for suggestions and input before making decisions. Participation in decision making should help followers understand which goals are most important and clarify the paths to accomplishing them. When people participate in decisions, they become more committed to making them work: "Those who plan the battle don't battle the plan."

Achievement-oriented leadership entails setting challenging goals, having high expectations of employees, and displaying confidence that employees will assume responsibility and put forth extraordinary effort. Simon Cooper, president and COO of the Ritz-Carlton luxury hotel chain, uses the phrase "He who says it, does" to describe achievement-oriented leadership. He explains:

> *I use this phrase whenever someone convinces me that they can achieve something I consider to be unachievable. In the past I've been known to add focus to a goal by making a bet to see if they can make it—sometimes with amusing consequences. I remember being*

Directive leadership a leadership style in which the leader lets employees know precisely what is expected of them, gives them specific guidelines for performing tasks, schedules work, sets standards of performance, and makes sure that people follow standard rules and regulations

Supportive leadership a leadership style in which the leader is friendly and approachable, shows concern for employees and their welfare, treats them as equals, and creates a friendly climate

Participative leadership a leadership style in which the leader consults employees for their suggestions and input before making decisions

Achievement-oriented leadership a leadership style in which the leader sets challenging goals, has high expectations of employees, and displays confidence that employees will assume responsibility and put forth extraordinary effort

Exhibit 14.4 Path-Goal Theory

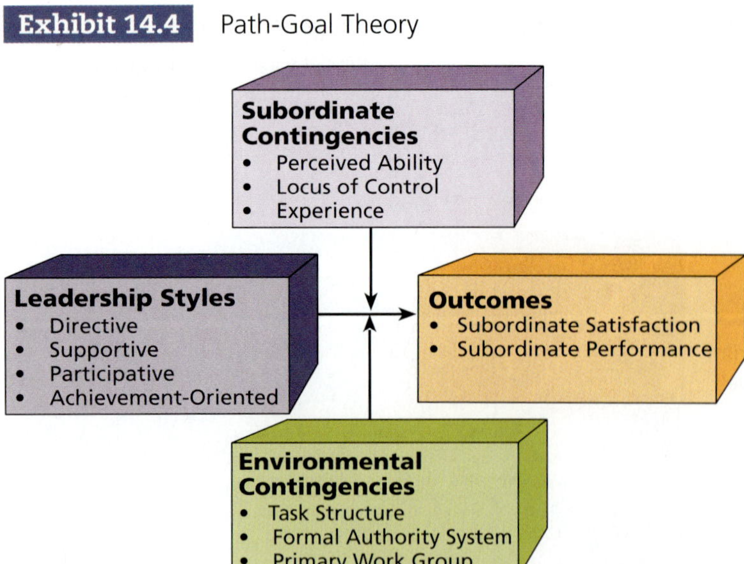

Source: R. J. House and T. R. Mitchell, "Path-Goal Theory of Leadership," *Journal of Contemporary Business* 3 (1974): 81–97.

at a mountain resort in Canada and proposing an incredible goal for the season. The team convinced me that they could achieve it, and I offered to jump into the lake if they did. It's a long story, but they made it. There's a great scene of a hole being cut in the ice and an ambulance on standby while I gave a whole new meaning to the term "dunking." The cognac [afterwards] was very welcome.[29]

Whatever leadership style you adopt, the ability to persuade and influence others is key to your success. As business becomes more global, and as the way people work changes, organizational structures are becoming flatter, or less hierarchical. This means that leaders must cross traditional boundaries and work with peers and subordinates alike in other divisions or even in other companies. Motivation is thus becoming far more important than direction. Whether you're a directive, supportive, participative, or achievement-oriented leader, your ability to bring others on board with your vision and plan is vital to good leadership.[30]

4.2 Subordinate and Environmental Contingencies

As shown in Exhibit 14.4, path-goal theory specifies that a leader's behaviours should be fitted to subordinates' characteristics. The theory identifies three kinds of contingencies relating to subordinates: perceived ability, experience, and locus of control. *Perceived ability* is simply how much ability subordinates believe they have for doing their jobs well. Subordinates who perceive they have a great deal of ability will be dissatisfied with directive leader behaviours.

Locus of control is a personality measure that indicates the extent to which people believe they have control over what happens to them in life. *Internals* believe that what happens to them, good or bad, is largely a result of their choices and actions. *Externals,* on the other hand, believe that what happens to them is caused by external forces beyond their control. Accordingly, externals are much more comfortable with a directive leadership style, while internals greatly prefer a participative leadership style because they like to have a say in what goes on at work.

Experienced employees are likely to react in a similar way. Since they already know how to do their jobs (or perceive that they do), they don't need or want close supervision. By contrast, subordinates with little experience or little perceived ability will welcome directive leadership.

Path-goal theory specifies that leader behaviours should complement rather than duplicate the characteristics of followers' work environments. In other words, a leader should use a leadership style that best responds to the characteristics of the environment as well as the characteristics of the people involved. There are three kinds of environmental contingencies: task structure, the formal authority system, and the primary work group. As in Fiedler's contingency theory, *task structure* refers to the degree to which the requirements of a subordinate's tasks are clearly specified. When task structure is low and tasks are unclear, directive leadership should be used because it complements the work environment. When task structure is high and tasks are clear, however, directive leadership is not needed because it duplicates what task structure provides. Alternatively, when tasks are stressful, frustrating, or dissatisfying, leaders should respond with supportive leadership.

The *formal authority system* is an organization's set of procedures, rules, and policies. When the formal authority system is unclear, directive leadership complements the situation by reducing uncertainty and increasing clarity. But when the formal authority system is clear, directive leadership is redundant and should not be used.

Primary work group refers to the amount of work-oriented participation or emotional support that is provided by an employee's immediate work group. Participative leadership should be used when tasks are complex and there is little existing work-oriented participation in the primary work group. When tasks are stressful, frustrating, or repetitive, supportive leadership is called for.

Maxim Petrichuk/Shutterstock.com

Exhibit 14.5 Path-Goal Theory: When to Use Directive, Supportive, Participative, or Achievement-Oriented Leadership

Directive Leadership	Supportive Leadership	Participative Leadership	Achievement-Oriented Leadership
Unstructured tasks	Structured, simple, repetitive tasks; stressful, frustrating tasks	Complex tasks	Unchallenging tasks
Workers with external locus of control	Workers lack confidence	Workers with internal locus of control	Workers with internal locus of control
Unclear formal authority system	Clear formal authority system	Workers not satisfied with rewards	
Inexperienced workers		Experienced workers	
Workers with low perceived ability		Workers with high perceived ability	Workers with high motivation

Finally, since keeping track of all of these subordinate and environmental contingencies can get a bit confusing, Exhibit 14.5 provides a summary of when directive, supportive, participative, and achievement-oriented leadership styles should be used. Above all, using path-goal theory means that a leader must be attuned and responsive to the sometimes changing complexities of his or her environment.

4.3 Outcomes

Does following path-goal theory improve subordinates' satisfaction and performance? Preliminary evidence suggests that it does.[31] In particular, people who work for supportive leaders are much more satisfied with their jobs and their bosses. Likewise, people who work for directive leaders are more satisfied with their jobs and bosses (but not quite as much as when their bosses are supportive) and perform their jobs better, too. Does adapting one's leadership style to subordinate and environmental characteristics improve subordinates' satisfaction and performance? At this point, because it is difficult to completely test this complex theory, it's too early to tell.[32] However, since the data clearly show that it makes sense for leaders to be both supportive *and* directive, it also makes sense that leaders could improve subordinates' satisfaction and performance by adding participative and achievement-oriented leadership styles to their capabilities as leaders.

LO5 Adapting Leader Behaviour: Normative Decision Theory

Many people believe that making tough decisions is at the heart of leadership. Yet experienced leaders will tell you that deciding *how* to make decisions is just as important. Vroom's **normative decision theory** (also known as the Vroom–Yetton–Jago model) helps leaders decide how much employee participation (from none to letting employees make the entire decision) should be used when making decisions.[33]

Normative decision theory **a theory that suggests how leaders can determine an appropriate amount of employee participation when making decisions**

*Let's learn more about normative decision theory by investigating **5.1 decision styles** and **5.2 decision quality and acceptance.***

5.1 Decision Styles

Unlike nearly all of the other leadership theories discussed in this chapter, which have specified *leadership* styles, the normative decision theory specifies five different *decision* styles, or ways of making decisions. (Refer back to Chapter 5 for a more complete review of decision making in organizations.) As shown in Exhibit 14.6 (page 250), those styles vary from *autocratic* (AI or AII) on the left, in which leaders make the decisions by themselves, to *consultative* (CI or CII), in which leaders share problems with subordinates but still make the decisions themselves, to *group* (GII) on the right, in which leaders share the problems with subordinates and then have the group make the decisions. GE Aircraft Engines uses this approach when making decisions. According to *Fast Company* magazine, "At GE/Durham, every decision is either an 'A' decision, a 'C' decision, or a 'G' decision. An 'A' decision is an Autocratic decision that the plant manager makes herself, without consulting anyone."[34] Plant manager Paula Sims says, "I don't make very many of those, and when I do make one, everyone at the plant knows it. I make maybe 10 or 12 a year."[35] "C" decisions are also made by the plant manager, but with Consultation of the people affected. "G" decisions, the most common type, are Group decisions by consensus among the people directly involved, with plenty

Exhibit 14.6 Normative Theory, Decision Styles, and Levels of Employee Participation

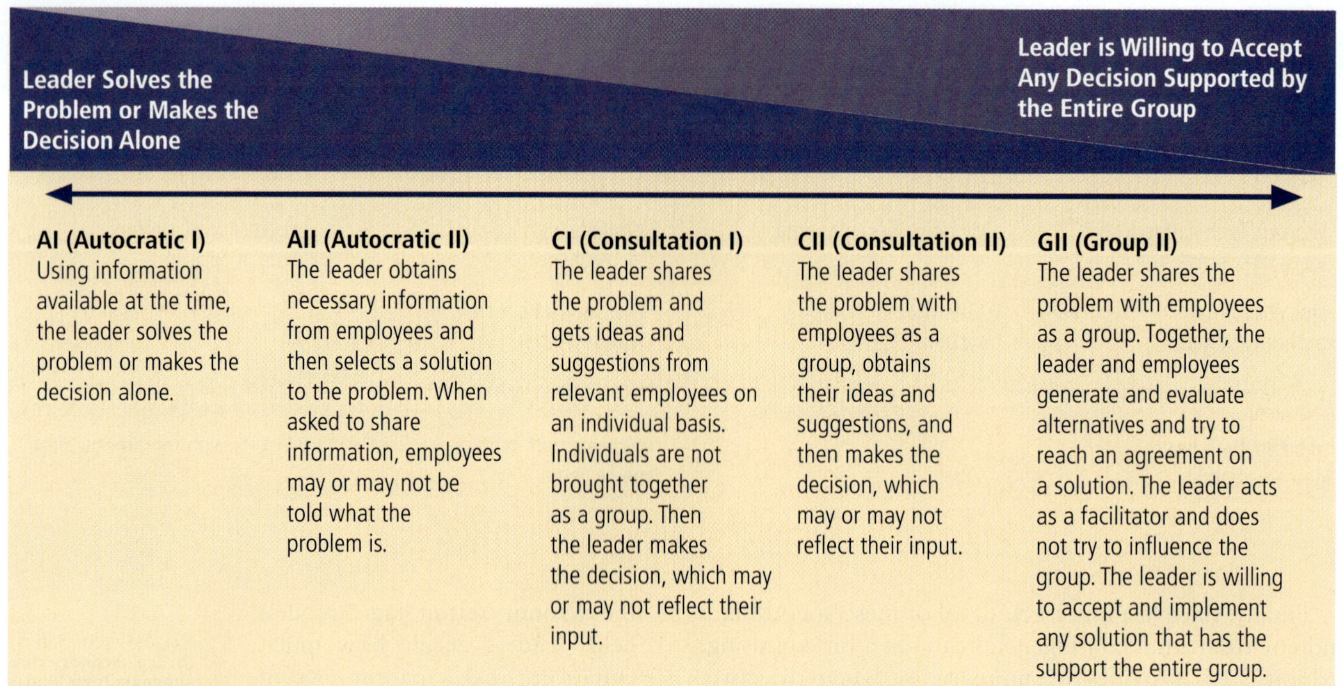

Source: Adapted from V.H. Vroom & P.W. Yetton, *Leadership and Decision Making* (Pittsburgh: University of Pittsburgh Press, 1973), 13.

of discussion. With "G" decisions, the view of the plant manager doesn't necessarily carry more weight than the views of those affected."[36]

5.2 Decision Quality and Acceptance

According to normative decision theory, using the right degree of employee participation improves the quality of decisions and the extent to which employees accept and are committed to decisions. Exhibit 14.7 lists the decision rules that normative decision theory uses to increase the quality of a decision and the degree to which employees accept and commit to a decision. The quality, leader information, subordinate information, goal congruence, and problem structure rules are used to increase decision quality. For example, the leader information rule states that a leader who doesn't have enough information to make a decision on his or her own should not use an autocratic decision style.

The commitment probability, subordinate conflict, and commitment requirement rules shown in Exhibit 14.7 are used to increase employee acceptance and commitment to decisions. For example, the commitment requirement rule says that if decision acceptance and commitment are important and the subordinates share the organization's goals, then you shouldn't use an autocratic or consultative style. In other words, if followers want to do what's best for the company and you need their acceptance and commitment to make a decision work, then use a group decision style and let them make the decision. As you can see, these decision rules help leaders improve decision quality and follower acceptance and commitment by eliminating decision styles that don't fit the particular decision or situation they're facing. Normative decision theory, like path-goal theory, is situational in nature.

The abstract decision rules in Exhibit 14.7 are then framed as yes/no questions, which makes the process of applying these rules more concrete. These questions are shown in the decision tree displayed in Exhibit 14.8 on page 252. You start at the left side of the model and answer the first question, "How important is the technical quality of this decision?", by choosing "high" or "low." Then you continue by answering each question as you proceed along the decision tree until you get to a recommended decision style.

Let's use the model to make the decision of whether to change from a formal business attire policy to a casual wear policy. The problem sounds simple, but it is actually more complex than you might think. Follow the yellow line in Exhibit 14.8 as we work through the decision in the discussion below.

*Problem: Change to Casual Wear?**

1. *Quality requirement: How important is the technical quality of this decision?* High. This question has to do with whether there are quality differences in the alternatives and whether those quality differences matter. In other words: Is there a lot at stake in this decision? Although most people would assume that quality isn't an issue here, it really is, given the overall positive changes that generally accompany changes to casual wear.

*Adapted from V.H. Vroom and P.W. Yetton, *Leadership and Decision Making* (Pittsburgh: University of Pittsburgh Press, 1973), 13.

Exhibit 14.7 Normative Theory Decision Rules

Decision Rules to Increase Decision Quality
Quality Rule. If the quality of the decision is important, then don't use an autocratic decision style.
Leader Information Rule. If the quality of the decision is important, and if the leader doesn't have enough information to make the decision on his or her own, then don't use an autocratic decision style.
Subordinate Information Rule. If the quality of the decision is important, and if the subordinates don't have enough information to make the decision themselves, then don't use a group decision style.
Goal Congruence Rule. If the quality of the decision is important, and subordinates' goals are different from the organization's goals, then don't use a group decision style.
Problem Structure Rule. If the quality of the decision is important, the leader doesn't have enough information to make the decision on his or her own, and the problem is unstructured, then don't use an autocratic decision style.
Decision Rules to Increase Decision Acceptance
Commitment Probability Rule. If having subordinates accept and commit to the decision is important, then don't use an autocratic decision style.
Subordinate Conflict Rule. If having subordinates accept the decision is important and critical to successful implementation and subordinates are likely to disagree or end up in conflict over the decision, then don't use an autocratic or consultative decision style.
Commitment Requirement Rule. If having subordinates accept the decision is absolutely required for successful implementation and subordinates share the organization's goals, then don't use an autocratic or consultative style.

Sources: Adapted from V.H. Vroom, "Leadership" in *Handbook of Industrial and Organizational Psychology*, ed. M. D. Dunnette (Chicago: Rand McNally, 1976); V. H. Vroom & A. G. Jago, *The New Leadership: Managing Participation in Organizations* (Englewood Cliffs, NJ: Prentice Hall, 1988).

2. *Commitment requirement: How important is subordinates' commitment to the decision?* High. Changes in culture, like dress codes, require subordinates' commitment or they fail.
3. *Leader's information: Do you have sufficient information to make a high-quality decision?* Yes. Let's assume that you've done your homework. Much has been written about casual wear, from how to make the change to the effects it has in companies (almost all positive).
4. *Commitment probability: If you were to make the decision by yourself, is it reasonably certain that your subordinate(s) would be committed to the decision?* No. Studies of casual wear find that employees' reactions are almost uniformly positive. Nonetheless, employees are likely to be angry if you change something as personal as clothing policies without consulting them.
5. *Goal congruence: Do subordinates share the organizational goals to be attained in solving this problem?* Yes. The goals that usually accompany a change to casual dress policies are a more informal culture, better communication, and less money spent on business attire.
6. *Subordinate information: Do subordinates have sufficient information to make a high-quality decision?* No. Most employees know little about casual wear policies or even what constitutes casual wear in most companies. Consequently, most companies have to educate employees about casual wear practices and policies before making a decision.
7. *CII is the answer:* With a CII, or consultative decision process, the leader shares the problem with employees as a group, obtains their ideas and suggestions, and then makes the decision, which may or may not reflect their input. So, given the answers to these questions (remember, different managers won't necessarily answer these questions the same way), the normative decision theory recommends that leaders consult with their subordinates before deciding whether to change to a casual wear policy.

How well does the normative decision theory work? A prominent leadership scholar has described it as the best supported of all leadership theories.[37] In general, the more managers violate the decision rules in Exhibit 14.7, the less effective their decisions are, especially with respect to subordinate acceptance and commitment.[38]

LO6 Gender and Leadership

Is there a difference between female leadership and male leadership? This is a complex question, and we will just scratch the surface here. "Elite-level leaders in business and government make significant and far-reaching decisions [that influence] many facets of society. However, relatively few of these powerful positions are held by women.[39]

Several studies reflect how "stereotypes, prejudice, and discrimination contribute to women's under-representation in elite leadership roles by both impacting perceptions of and responses to women as well as impacting the experiences of women themselves." There is also a "lack of

Exhibit 14.8 Normative Decision Theory Tree for Determining the Level of Participation in Decision Making

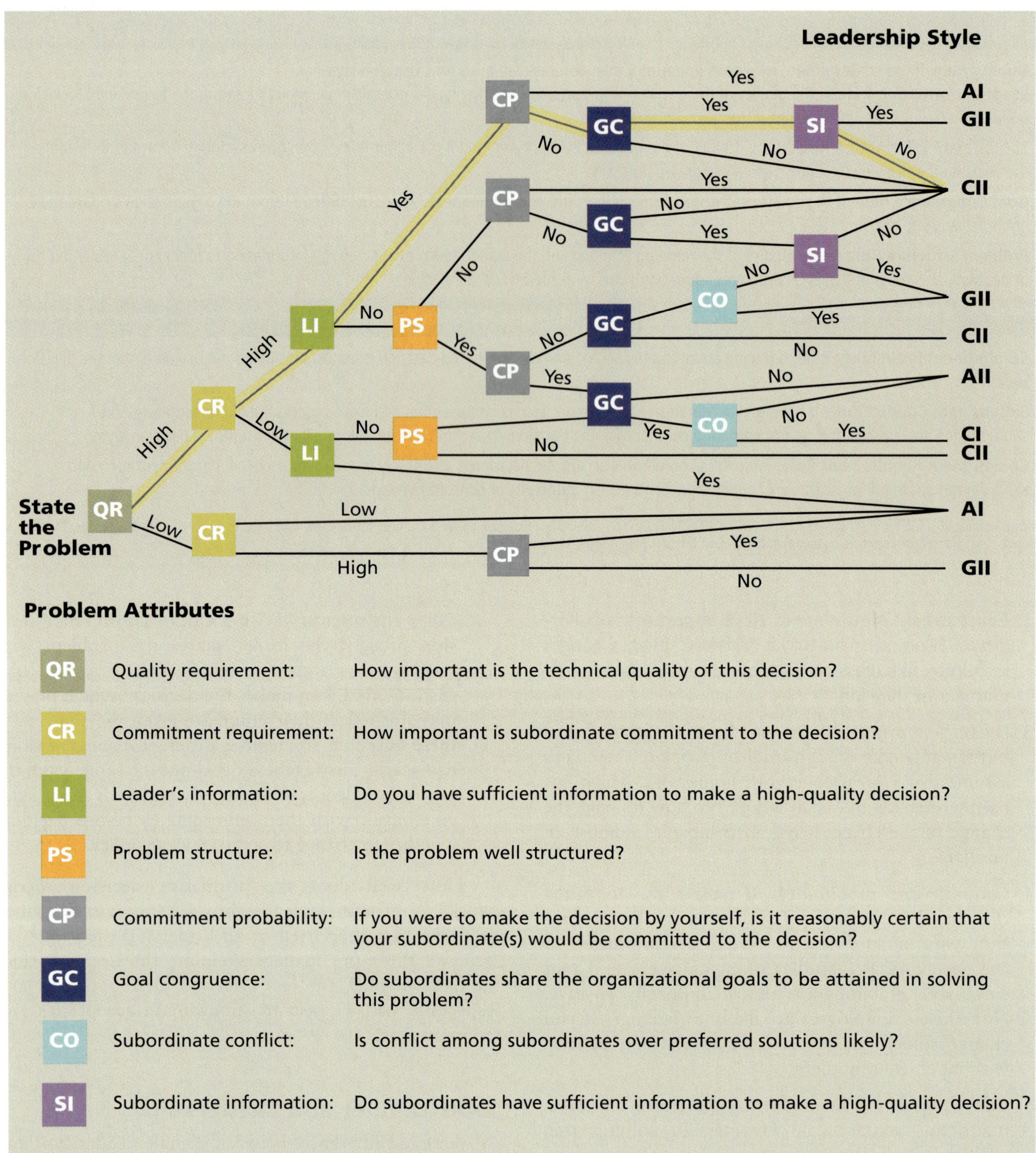

Source: Figure 9.3. Decision-Process Flow Chart for Both Individual and Group Problems from *Leadership and Decision-Making*, by Victor H. Vroom and Philip W. Yetton, © 1973. All rights controlled by the University of Pittsburgh Press, Pittsburgh, PA 15260. Adapted and used by permission of University of Pittsburgh Press.

parity between the sexes in leadership and there is empirical research that serves to illuminate obstacles to women's progress" (the glass ceiling).[40] Although the role of traits in understanding leadership emergence and effectiveness has been a controversial issue in the literature, "the extant research reveals that traits do play an important, albeit limited, role in leadership effectiveness."[41]

One study carried out on creativity and innovation management revealed that "employees report more innovative behaviour when the transformational leadership is displayed by male in comparison with female managers, confirming our gender bias hypothesis."[42] A separate experimental study "suggests that the romance of leadership does exist for both men and women but that the process of

"Casual Wear—Suit or Blue Jeans"

© Ashok Rodrigues/iStockphoto.com

pay allocation differs as a function of gender." Generally for a female leader, it is based on perceptions of her charisma and leadership ability rather than directly on company performance.[43] Warren Buffett of Berkshire Hathaway urges all men in business to fully employ "the talents of all its citizens ... We've seen what can be accomplished when we use 50% of our human capacity. If you visualize what 100% can do, you'll join me" in promoting and supporting female leaders.[44]

Strategic Leadership

Strategic leadership refers to the ability to anticipate, envision, maintain flexibility, think strategically, and work with others to initiate changes that will create a positive future for an organization.[45] This form of leadership captures how leaders inspire their companies to change and their followers to make extraordinary efforts to accomplish organizational goals.

LO7 Visionary Leadership

In Chapter 5, we defined vision as a statement of a company's purpose or reason for existing. Similarly, **visionary leadership** creates a positive image of the future that motivates organizational members and provides direction for future planning and goal setting.[46]

*Two kinds of visionary leadership are **6.1 charismatic leadership** and **6.2 transformational leadership**.*

7.1 Charismatic Leadership

Charisma is a Greek word meaning "divine gift." The ancient Greeks saw people with charisma as inspired by the gods and as capable of incredible accomplishments. German sociologist Max Weber (see Chapter 3.1) viewed charisma as a special bond between leaders and followers.[47] Weber wrote that the special qualities of charismatic leaders enable them to strongly influence followers. For example, Sergio Marchionne, a manager from Toronto, was the only person who could fix Fiat. It now turns out that he is the only person who can make Chrysler really drive. The young Marchionne attended the University of Toronto, then received a law degree from Osgoode Hall and an MBA from the University of Windsor. "He loves to talk, loves to gossip, can charm an audience in several languages, adores his mother, is quick with a put-down," says Eric Reguly. These are the attributes of a transformational leader, and Marchionne must now apply them to transform Chrysler. Chrysler needs "to clean up our act and move on from here," he says. "We'll certainly get better as we go through 2013."[48]

Weber also noted that charismatic leaders tend to emerge in times of crisis and that the radical solutions they propose enhance the admiration that followers feel for them. Indeed, charismatic leaders tend to have incredible influence over their followers, who may be inspired by their leaders and become fanatically devoted to them. From this perspective, charismatic leaders are often seen as larger-than-life or as more special than other employees of the company.

Strategic leadership the ability to anticipate, envision, maintain flexibility, think strategically, and work with others to initiate changes that will create a positive future for an organization

Visionary leadership leadership that creates a positive image of the future that motivates organizational members and provides direction for future planning and goal setting

The ancient Greeks saw people with charisma as inspired by the gods and capable of incredible accomplishments.

© Snezana Negovanovic/iStockphoto.com

Charismatic leadership the behavioural tendencies and personal characteristics of leaders that create an exceptionally strong relationship between them and their followers

Ethical charismatics charismatic leaders who provide developmental opportunities for followers, are open to positive and negative feedback, recognize others' contributions, share information, and have moral standards that emphasize the larger interests of the group, organization, or society

Unethical charismatics charismatic leaders who control and manipulate followers, do what is best for themselves instead of their organizations, want to hear only positive feedback, share only information that is beneficial to themselves, and have moral standards that put their interests before everyone else's

Transformational leadership leadership that generates awareness and acceptance of a group's purpose and mission and gets employees to see beyond their own needs and self-interests for the good of the group

Charismatic leaders have strong, confident, dynamic personalities that attract followers. This enables them to create strong bonds with their followers, who in turn trust their charismatic leaders, are loyal to them, and are inspired to work toward accomplishing their vision. Followers who become devoted to charismatic leaders may go to extraordinary lengths to please them. Thus, we can define **charismatic leadership** as the behavioural tendencies and personal characteristics of leaders that create an exceptionally strong relationship between them and their followers.

Charismatic leaders also

- articulate a clear vision for the future that is based on strongly held values or morals;
- model those values by acting in ways that are consistent with the vision;
- communicate high performance expectations to followers; and
- display confidence in followers' abilities to achieve the vision.[49]

Does charismatic leadership work? Studies indicate that it often does. In general, the followers of charismatic leaders are more committed and satisfied, are better performers, are more likely to trust their leaders, and simply work harder.[50] Nonetheless, charismatic leadership also has risks that are at least as large as its benefits. The problems are likely to occur with ego-driven charismatic leaders who take advantage of fanatical followers.

In general, there are two kinds of charismatic leaders: ethical charismatics and unethical charismatics.[51] **Ethical charismatics** provide developmental opportunities for followers, are open to positive and negative feedback, recognize others' contributions, share information, and have moral standards that emphasize the larger interests of the group, organization, or society.

By contrast, **unethical charismatics** control and manipulate followers, do what is best for themselves instead of their organizations, want to hear only positive feedback, share only information when it benefits themselves, and have moral standards that place their interests before everyone else's. Because followers can become just as committed to unethical as to ethical charismatics, unethical charismatics pose a tremendous risk for companies.

Exhibit 14.9 shows the stark differences between ethical and unethical charismatics with regard to several leader behaviours: exercising power, creating the vision, communicating with followers, accepting feedback, stimulating followers intellectually, developing followers, and living by moral standards. For example, ethical charismatics include followers' concerns and wishes when creating a company vision by having them participate in the development of that vision. By contrast, unethical charismatics develop a vision by themselves solely to meet their personal agendas. One unethical charismatic said that "the key thing is that it is my idea; and I am going to win with it at all costs."[52]

7.2 Transformational Leadership

Charismatic leadership involves articulating a clear vision, modelling values consistent with that vision, communicating high performance expectations, and establishing very strong relationships with followers. **Transformational leadership** goes even further than this by generating awareness and acceptance of a group's purpose and mission and by getting employees to see beyond their own needs and self-interest for the good of the group.[53] Like charismatic leaders, transformational leaders are visionary, but they transform their organizations by getting their followers to accomplish more than they intended and even more than they thought possible.

Transformational leaders make their followers feel that they are a vital part of the organization and help them see how their jobs fit with the organization's vision. By linking individual and organizational interests, transformational leaders encourage followers to make sacrifices for the organization. Followers willingly do so do so because they know they will prosper when the organization does.

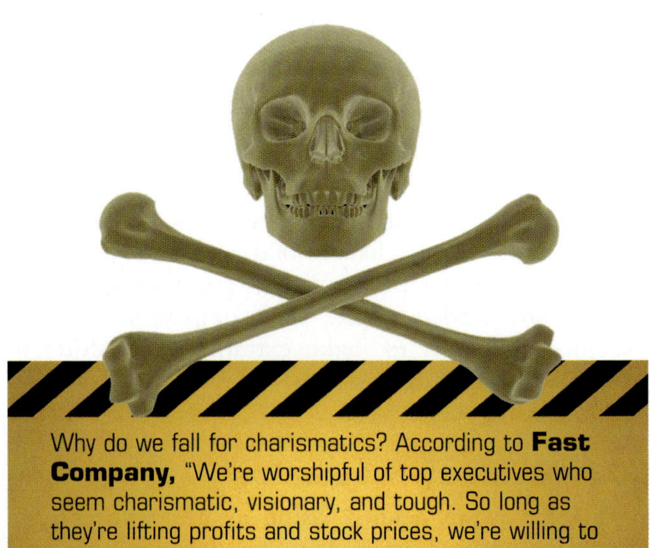

Why do we fall for charismatics? According to **Fast Company,** "We're worshipful of top executives who seem charismatic, visionary, and tough. So long as they're lifting profits and stock prices, we're willing to overlook that they can also be callous, cunning, manipulative, deceitful, verbally and psychologically abusive, remorseless, exploitative, self-delusional, irresponsible, and megalomaniacal."[54]

Lying in Luxury

In terms of cutting corners and dealing in self-interest it's hard to top the unethical charismatic behaviour of Conrad Black. Toronto artist George A. Walker engraved Black's story on 100 blocks of Canadian maple, which he hand-printed and hand-bound in an edition of 13 boxed copies—the same number of document boxes Black removed from his Toronto office on a fateful day in 2005. To spare himself the risk of saying anything libellous about a famously litigious man: "I haven't said anything about Lord Black or his troubles," he says. "I've just made pictures." Although Black "is still dealing with the messy legal aftermath of the crash of his newspaper empire, he is a popular fixture on Toronto's social circuit." Black served 37 months of a 42-month sentence in a Florida prison for fraud, which included purchasing an apartment from his company Hollinger in 2000 for $3 million and later sold for $9 million.

Sources: M. Wente, "Why Conrad Black Thinks the United States Is in Decline," *Globe and Mail*, May 17, 2013, http://www.theglobeandmail.com/news/world/why-conrad- black-thinks-the -united-states-is-in-decline/article12005862/?cmpid=rss1; Canadian Press, "Conrad Black Loses Bid to Have Remaining Convictions Dismissed," *Globe and Mail*, February 20, 2013, http://www .theglobeandmail.com/report-on-business/industry-news/the-law-page/conrad-black-loses-bid -to-have-remaining-convictions-dismissed/article8901488; R. Everett-Green, "Relive the Conrad Black Saga," *Globe and Mail*, 2013, http://www.theglobeandmail.com/arts/art-and-architecture/ relive-the-conrad-black-saga-carved-in-100-blocks-of-canadian-maple/article9615598.

Exhibit 14.9 Ethical and Unethical Charismatics

Charismatic Leader Behaviours	Ethical Charismatics	Unethical Charismatics
Exercising power	Power is used to serve others.	Power is used to dominate or manipulate others for personal gain.
Creating the vision	Followers help develop the vision.	Vision comes solely from leader and serves his or her personal agenda.
Communicating with followers	Two-way communication: Seek out viewpoints on critical issues.	One-way communication: Not open to input and suggestions from others.
Accepting feedback	Open to feedback. Willing to learn from criticism.	Inflated ego thrives on attention and admiration of sycophants. Avoid or punish candid feedback.
Stimulating followers	Want followers to think and question status quo as well as leader's views.	Don't want followers to think. Want uncritical, intellectually unquestioning acceptance of leader's ideas.
Developing followers	Focus on developing people with whom they interact. Express confidence in them and share recognition with others.	Insensitive and unresponsive to followers' needs and aspirations.
Living by moral standards	Follow self-guided principles that may go against popular opinion. Have three virtues: courage, a sense of fairness or justice, and integrity.	Follow standards only if they satisfy immediate self-interests. Manipulate impressions so that others think they are doing the right thing. Use communication skills to manipulate others to support their personal agenda.

Source: J.M. Howell & B. J. Avolio, "The Ethics of Charismatic Leadership: Submission or Liberation?" *Academy of Management Executive* 6, no. 2 (1992): 43–54.

Transactional leadership leadership based on an exchange process, in which followers are rewarded for good performance and punished for poor performance

Transformational leadership has four components: charismatic leadership or idealized influence, inspirational motivation, intellectual stimulation, and individualized consideration.[55]

Transformational leaders practise *charismatic leadership or idealized influence* by acting as role models for their followers. Because transformational leaders put others' needs ahead of their own and share risks with their followers, they are admired, respected, and trusted, and followers want to emulate them. Thus, in contrast to purely charismatic leaders (especially unethical charismatics), transformational leaders can be counted on to do the right thing and maintain high standards of ethical and personal conduct.

Regarding *inspirational motivation,* transformational leaders motivate and inspire followers by providing meaningful and challenging work. By clearly communicating expectations and demonstrating commitment to goals, transformational leaders help followers envision the future. This leads to greater enthusiasm and optimism about the future. Regarding *intellectual stimulation,* transformational leaders encourage followers to be creative and innovative, to question assumptions, and to look at problems and situations in new ways even if their ideas are different from the leader's.

Individualized consideration means that transformational leaders pay special attention to followers' individual needs by creating learning opportunities, accepting and tolerating individual differences, encouraging two-way communication, and being good listeners. Belinda Stronach has been a minister in Canada's federal Parliament *and* CEO of Magna Industries (Canada's largest auto parts supplier). At the age of 15, she was fighting with the engineers to ensure that the plant windows opened for employees. While travelling, she learned to think globally. "We'd go into a Russian plant, dark like something in a Dickens novel, with 150,000 workers, and sparks flying with no protection." She was Magna's CEO from 2001 to 2004, and she is credited with bringing stability, rather than innovation. She negotiated a win–win union contract (Magna's first) with the CAW. "I wasn't a great lover of auto parts, bumpers and door handles, but what did fascinate me, and still does, is the company culture." When she ran for political office, she was supported by Ed Lumley, a former federal Minister of Industry, and by former Ontario Premier Bill Davis. "She'd been great at human resources, negotiating compensation and health plans for employees," says Lumley, "and this was in a male-dominated business." Stronach is currently running the Belinda Stronach Foundation, which aims to improve the lives of girls, women, and Aboriginal youth.[56]

CP PHOTO/Fred Chartrand

Good Tip!

How to Reduce the Risks Associated with Unethical Charismatics

1. Have a clearly written code of conduct that is fairly and consistently enforced for all managers.
2. Recruit, select, and promote managers with high ethical standards.
3. Train leaders to value, seek, and use diverse points of view.
4. Train leaders and subordinates regarding ethical leader behaviours so that abuses can be recognized and corrected.
5. Reward people who exhibit ethical behaviours, especially ethical leader behaviours.

Sources: J. M. Burns, *Leadership* (New York: Harper & Row, 1978); B. M. Bass, "From Transactional to Transformational Leadership: Learning to Share the Vision," *Organizational Dynamics* 18 (1990): 19–36.

Finally, a distinction needs to be drawn between transformational leadership and transactional leadership. Transformational leaders use visionary and inspirational appeals to influence followers, whereas **transactional leadership** is based on an exchange process in which followers are rewarded for good performance and punished for poor performance. When leaders administer rewards fairly and offer followers rewards they want, followers often reciprocate with effort. A problem, however, is that transactional leaders often rely too heavily on discipline or threats to bring performance up to standards. This may work in the short run but is much less effective in the long run. Also, as discussed in Chapters 11 and 13, many leaders and organizations find it difficult to link pay practices to individual performance. That is why studies consistently show that transformational leadership is much more effective on average than transactional leadership. In Canada, Japan, the United States, and India, and at all organizational levels from first-level supervisors to upper-level executives, followers view transformational leaders as much better leaders and are much more satisfied when working for them. Furthermore, companies with transformational leaders have significantly better financial performance.[57]

15 Managing Communication

LEARNING OUTCOMES

LO1 Explain the role that perception plays in communication and communication problems.

LO2 Describe the communication process and the various kinds of communication in organizations.

LO3 Explain how managers can manage effective one-on-one communication.

LO4 Describe how managers can manage effective organization-wide communication.

What Is Communication?

It's estimated that managers spend over 80 percent of their day communicating with others.[1] Indeed, much of the basic management process—planning, organizing, leading, and controlling—cannot be performed without effective communication. The shift from an industrial economy to an information society has led to greater emphasis being placed on developing the soft skills that are critical for productive performance in current and future business leaders. Research studies on this topic support this trend, including a study that found that 75 percent of long-term job success depends on people skills, while only 25 percent depends on technical knowledge. The need for effective communication skills, which include listening, following instructions, conversing, and giving feedback, becomes even more critical for employees looking to progress in their careers, particularly in management. A study that examined the critical soft skills that employers want from their employees found that overwhelmingly, communication was one of the top two soft skills needed by employees in today's workplace.[2] Furthermore, across all industries, poor communication skills rank as the single most important reason why people do not advance in their careers.[3]

Communication is the process of transmitting information from one person or place to another.

Communication the process of transmitting information from one person or place to another

Perception the process by which individuals attend to, organize, interpret, and retain information from their environments

Perceptual filters the personality-, psychology-, or experience-based differences that influence people to ignore or pay attention to particular stimuli

LO1 Perception and Communication Problems

One study found that when *employees* were asked whether their supervisor gave recognition for good work, only 13 percent said their supervisor gave a pat on the back, and a mere 14 percent said their supervisor gave sincere and thorough praise. But when the *supervisors* of these employees were asked if they gave recognition for good work, 82 percent said they gave pats on the back, while 80 percent said that they gave sincere and thorough praise.[4] How could managers and employees have had such different perceptions of something as simple as praise?

Let's learn more about perception and communication problems by examining ***1.1 the basic perception process, 1.2 perception problems, 1.3 how we perceive others,*** *and* ***1.4 how we perceive ourselves.*** We'll also consider how all of these factors make it difficult for managers to achieve effective communication.

1.1 Basic Perception Process

As shown in Exhibit 15.1, **perception** is the process by which individuals attend to, organize, interpret, and retain information from their environments. And since communication is the process of transmitting information from one person or place to another, perception is obviously a key part of communication. Yet perception can also be a key obstacle to communication.

In today's workplace, people are often exposed to a wide variety of informational stimuli, including e-mails, direct conversations with coworkers, rumours heard over lunch, stories about the company in the press or transmitted via social media, or an online podcast of a speech from the CEO to all employees. Just being exposed to an informational stimulus, however, is no guarantee that an individual will pay attention to that stimulus. People experience stimuli through their own **perceptual filters**—the personality-, psychology-, or experience-based differences that influence them to ignore or pay attention to particular stimuli. Because of filtering, people exposed to the same information will often have different opinions on what they saw or heard. For example, a store manager may say to her employees, "The regional manager is coming to talk to us tomorrow." One of the employees may perceive that she said, "The regional manager is coming tomorrow to break some bad news to us." Another employee may think, "Head office must have noticed our sales are up, the regional manager is coming to congratulate us." Yet another employee may interpret this as, "The regional manager is really difficult to understand, he always seems to use jargon and obscure examples to try and get his point across." As shown in Exhibit 15.1, perceptual filters affect each part of the

Exhibit 15.1 Basic Perception Process

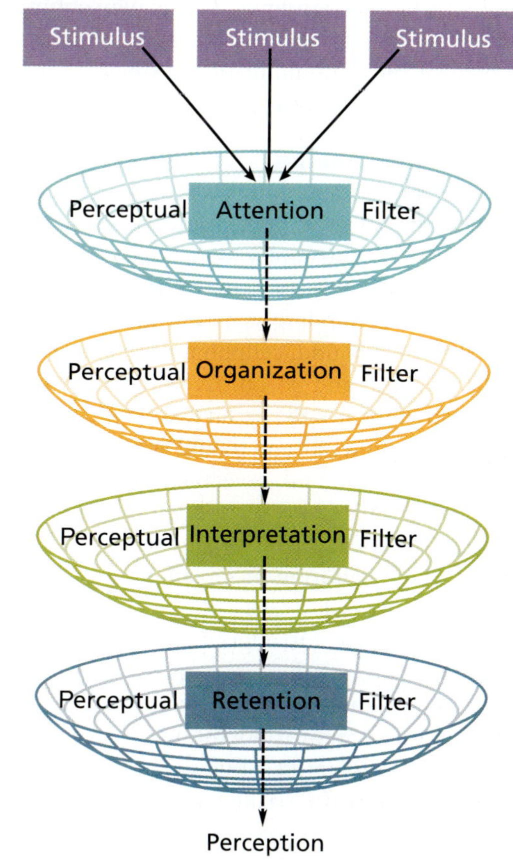

Robert Nicholas/OJO Images/Getty Images

Selective perception the tendency to notice and accept objects and information consistent with our values, beliefs, and expectations while ignoring or screening out or not accepting inconsistent information

Closure the tendency to fill in gaps of missing information by assuming that what we don't know is consistent with what we already know

Attribution theory a theory that states that we all have a basic need to understand and explain the causes of other people's behaviour

perception process: attention, organization, interpretation, and retention.

Attention is the process of noticing or becoming aware of particular stimuli. Because of perceptual filters, we attend to some stimuli and not others. *Organization* is the process of incorporating new information (from the stimuli that you notice) into your existing knowledge. Because of perceptual filters, we are more likely to incorporate new knowledge that is consistent with what we already know or believe. *Interpretation* is the process of attaching meaning to new knowledge. Because of perceptual filters, our preferences and beliefs strongly influence the meaning we attach to new information (e.g., "This must mean that top management supports our project"). Finally, *retention* is the process of remembering interpreted information. In other words, retention is what we recall and commit to memory after we have perceived something. Of course, perceptual filters also affect retention, that is, what we're likely to remember in the end.

In short, because of perception and perceptual filters, even when people are exposed to the same communications (e.g., organizational memos, discussions with managers or customers), they can end up with very different perceptions and understandings. This is why communication can be so difficult and frustrating for managers. Let's review some of the communication problems created by perception and perceptual filters.

1.2 Perception Problems

Two of the most common perception problems in organizations are selective perception and closure.

Employees are constantly bombarded with sensory stimuli while at work—by humming photocopiers, ringing phones, computers that ding as new e-mail arrives, people talking in the background, cellphones signalling new text or e-mail messages, and so on. As "limited processors," we cannot possibly notice, receive, and interpret all of this information. So we attend to and accept some stimuli, while screening out and rejecting others. **Selective perception** is the tendency to notice and accept objects and information consistent with our values, beliefs, and expectations while ignoring or screening out inconsistent information. A classic case of selective perception occurred when Apple introduced the iPhone 4, which has a metal antenna circling its edge. Since touching an antenna reduces signal reception, customers immediately began complaining about poor phone reception. Apple, however, hadn't encountered this problem in real-world testing, because it always cloaked its new phones in covers (so that they couldn't be photographed before product launch). Those covers prevented testers from touching the phone's antenna and experiencing the problem. Within days, "Antennagate" had become a public relations crisis for Apple as media sources began reporting the problem. In fact, after conducting lab tests, *Consumer Reports* magazine recommended that customers not buy the iPhone 4.[5] What made matters worse was that Apple denied the problem. Then CEO Steve Jobs said, "This has been blown so out of proportion that it's incredible. There is no Antennagate." The iPhone 4, he said, was "perhaps the best product made by Apple."[6] Furthermore, Jobs, who didn't think there was an issue (i.e., selective perception), instructed customers who e-mailed him about the issue to "avoid gripping it in the lower left corner in a way that covers both sides of the black strip in the metal [antenna] band, or simply use one of many available cases." Within ten days, Apple offered each of its iPhone 4 customers a free "bumper" (or case) that solved the problem by preventing contact with the antenna.[7]

Once we have initial information about a person, event, or process, **closure** is the tendency to fill in the gaps where information is missing, that is, to assume that what we don't know is consistent with what we already know. If employees are told that budgets must be cut by 10 percent, they may automatically assume that 10 percent of employees will lose their jobs, too, even if that isn't the case. Not surprisingly, when closure occurs, people sometimes fill in the gaps with inaccurate information. This, needless to say, can create problems for organizations.

1.3 Perceptions of Others

Attribution theory says that we all have a basic need to understand and explain the causes of other people's behaviour.[8] In other words, we need to know why

Maksim Shmeljov/Shutterstock.com

people do what they do. According to attribution theory, we use two general reasons or attributions to explain people's behaviour: an *internal attribution,* in which behaviour is thought to be voluntary or under the control of the individual, and an *external attribution,* in which behaviour is thought to be involuntary and outside of the control of the individual.

For example, have you ever seen someone changing a flat tire on the side of the road and thought to yourself, "What rotten luck—somebody's having a bad day"? If you did, you perceived the person through an external attribution known as the defensive bias. The **defensive bias** is the tendency for people to perceive themselves as personally and situationally similar to someone who is having difficulty or trouble.[9] And when we identify with the person in a situation, we tend to use external attributions (i.e., the situation) to explain the person's behaviour. For instance, since flat tires are common, it's easy to perceive ourselves in that same situation and to put the blame on external causes such as running over a nail.

Now, let's assume a different situation, this time in the workplace: A utility company worker places a ladder against a utility pole and then climbs up to do his work. As he's doing his work, he falls from the ladder and seriously injures himself.[10]

Answer this question: Who or what caused the accident? If you thought, "It's not the worker's fault. Anybody could fall from a tall ladder," then you're still operating from a defensive bias in which you see yourself as personally and situationally similar to someone who is having difficulty or trouble. In other words, you have made an external attribution by attributing the accident to an external cause, meaning the situation.

Most accident investigations, however, initially blame the worker (i.e., an internal attribution) and not the situation (i.e., an external attribution). Typically, 60 to 80 percent of workplace accidents each year are blamed on "operator error," that is, on the employees themselves. In reality, more complete investigations usually show that workers are responsible for only 30 to 40 percent of all workplace accidents.[11] Why are accident investigators so quick to blame workers? The reason is that they are committing the **fundamental attribution error**, which is the tendency to ignore external causes of behaviour and to attribute other people's actions to internal causes.[12] In other words, when investigators examine the possible causes of an accident, they're much more likely to assume that the accident was a function of the person and not the situation.

Which attribution—the defensive bias or the fundamental attribution error—are workers likely to make when something goes wrong? In general, employees and coworkers are more likely to perceive events and explain behaviour from a defensive bias. Because they do the work themselves and see themselves as similar to others who make mistakes, have accidents, or are otherwise held responsible for things that go wrong at work, employees and coworkers are likely to attribute problems to external causes such as failed machinery, poor support, or inadequate training. By contrast, because they are typically observers (who don't do the work themselves) and see themselves as situationally and personally different from workers, managers (i.e., bosses) tend to commit the fundamental attribution error and blame mistakes, accidents, and other things that go wrong on workers (i.e., an internal attribution).

Consequently, in most workplaces, when things go wrong, workers and managers can be expected to take opposite views. Therefore, together, the defensive bias, which is typically used by workers, and the fundamental attribution error, which is typically made by managers, present a significant challenge to effective communication and understanding in organizations.

Defensive bias the tendency for people to perceive themselves as personally and situationally similar to someone who is having difficulty or trouble

Fundamental attribution error the tendency to ignore external causes of behaviour and to attribute other people's actions to internal causes

Self-serving bias the tendency to overestimate our value by attributing successes to ourselves (internal causes) and attributing failures to others or the environment (external causes)

1.4 Self-Perception

The **self-serving bias** is the tendency to overestimate our value by attributing successes to ourselves (internal causes) and attributing failures to others or the environment (external causes).[13] The self-serving bias can make it especially difficult for managers to talk to employees about performance problems. In general, people have a need to maintain a positive self-image. This need is so strong that when people seek feedback at work, they typically want verification of their worth (rather than information about performance deficiencies) or assurance that mistakes or problems weren't their fault.[14] And when managerial communication threatens people's positive self-image, they can become defensive and emotional. They quit listening, and communication becomes ineffective. In the second half of this chapter, which focuses on improving communication, we'll explain ways in which managers can minimize this self-serving bias and improve effective one-on-one communication with employees.

LO2 Kinds of Communication

There are many kinds of communication—formal, informal, coaching/counselling, and nonverbal—but they all follow the same fundamental process.

Let's learn more about the different kinds of communication by examining ***2.1 the communication process, 2.2 formal communication channels, 2.3 informal communication channels, 2.4 coaching and counselling,*** *or* ***one-on-one communication,*** *and* ***2.5 nonverbal communication.***

2.1 The Communication Process

Earlier in the chapter, we defined *communication* as the process of transmitting information from one person or place to another. Exhibit 15.2 (page 262) displays a model of the communication process and its major components:

Exhibit 15.2 The Interpersonal Communication Process

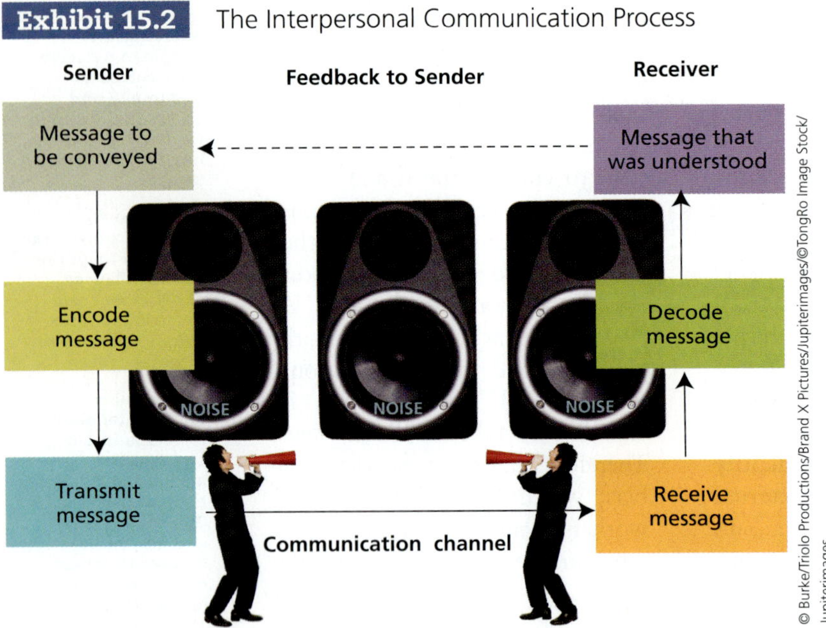

© Burke/Triolo Productions/Brand X Pictures/Jupiterimages/©TongRo Image Stock/Jupiterimages

Encoding putting a message into a written, verbal, or symbolic form that can be recognized and understood by the receiver

Decoding the process by which the receiver translates the written, verbal, or symbolic form of a message into an understood message

Feedback to sender in the communication process, a return message to the sender that indicates the receiver's understanding of the message

Noise anything that interferes with the transmission of the intended message

Jargon vocabulary particular to a profession or group

Formal communication channel the system of official channels that carry organizationally approved messages and information

the sender (message to be conveyed, encoding the message, transmitting the message); the receiver (receiving message, decoding the message, and the message that was understood); and noise, which interferes with the communication process.

The communication process begins when a *sender* thinks of a message he or she wants to convey to another person. The next step is to encode the message. **Encoding** means putting a message into a verbal (written or spoken) or symbolic form that can be recognized and understood by the receiver. The sender then *transmits the message* via *communication channels*. With some communication channels such as the telephone and face-to-face communication, the sender receives immediate feedback, whereas others such as e-mail, text messages, voice mail, or written correspondence, make the sender wait for the receiver to respond.

Unfortunately, because of technical difficulties (e.g., the battery dies in your mobile phone) or people-based transmission problems (e.g., forgetting to pass on the message), messages aren't always transmitted. If the message is transmitted and received, however, the next step is for the receiver to decode it. **Decoding** is the process by which the receiver translates the verbal or symbolic form of the message into an understood message. However, the message as understood by the receiver isn't always the same message that was intended by the sender. Because of different experiences or perceptual filters, receivers may attach a completely different meaning to a message than was intended.

The last step of the communication process occurs when the receiver gives the sender feedback. **Feedback to sender** is a return message to the sender that indicates the receiver's understanding of the message (of what the receiver was supposed to know, to do, or not to do). Feedback makes senders aware of possible miscommunications and enables them to continue communicating until the receiver understands the intended message.

Unfortunately, feedback doesn't always occur in the communication process. Complacency and overconfidence about the ease and simplicity of communication can lead senders and receivers to simply assume that they share a common understanding of the message and, consequently, not use feedback to improve the effectiveness of their communication. This is a serious mistake, especially since messages and feedback are always transmitted with and against a background of noise. **Noise** is anything that interferes with the transmission of the intended message, much like static on a radio station or a pop-up ad online. Noise can occur in any of the following situations:

- The sender isn't sure what message to communicate.
- The message is not clearly encoded.
- The wrong communication channel is chosen.
- The message is not received or decoded properly.
- The receiver doesn't have the experience or time to understand the message.

Jargon, which is vocabulary particular to a profession or group, is another form of noise that interferes with communication in the workplace. According to Carol Hymowitz of the *Wall Street Journal*, "a new crop of buzzwords usually sprouts every three to five years, or about the same length of time many top executives have to prove themselves. Although some of these words become overused and annoying, some can be useful in swiftly communicating, and spreading, new business concepts."

2.2 Formal Communication Channels

An organization's **formal communication channel** is the system of official channels that carry organizationally approved messages and information. Organizational objectives, rules, policies, procedures, instructions, commands, and requests for information are all transmitted via the formal communication system or "channel."

Annoying Business Jargon

It seems that every few years, new business buzzwords and jargon make the rounds. Some become increasingly annoying through overuse; others are destined to make their users sound hopelessly outdated. A recent *Forbes* magazine poll asked readers to weigh in with their opinions on some of the worst offenders in the workplace. Here are some of the top responses:

Igor Dutina/Shutterstock.com

Core competency. This expression refers to an organization's fundamental strength—even though that's not what the word "competent" means.
Buy-in. Asking for someone to "buy in" essentially means that you want someone to embrace an idea or a course of action that they were not actively involved in or a part of developing.
Scalable. A scalable business or activity is one that requires minimal effort or cost in order to gain additional output.
Boil the ocean. Essentially this means to waste time, since the assumption is that boiling the ocean would take a long time.
Leverage. The business world has converted this noun to a verb, to describe how a situation or environment can be controlled or manipulated to a company's advantage.
Think outside the box. This overused phrase can't seem to go away. It means approaching a problem from a unique or unconventional perspective.

Business communication should be clear, straightforward and devoid of industry jargon because when terms are overused, they lose their effectiveness. Case in point: the phrase "think outside the box"—a hall of famer—is considered by many to be so overused that it can lead to the opposite effect. As Daisy Yu, a Canadian business lawyer, points out, "it really doesn't encourage you to think outside the box when someone tells you that."

Sources: M. Mallet, B. Nelson, and C. Steiner, "The Most Annoying, Pretentious, and Useless Business Jargon," *Forbes*, January 26, 2012, http://www.forbes.com/sites/groupthink/2012/01/26/the-most-annoying-pretentious-and-useless-business-jargon; J. Schott, "The Most Annoying Corporate Buzzwords," *CEB Marketing and Communications*, August 13, 2012, http://www.executiveboard.com/marketing-blog/the-most-annoying-corporate-buzzwords; P. Wolchak, "The Most Overused Buzzwords—Survey," *Backbone Magazine*, November 24, 2009, http://www.backbonemag.com/Magazine/2009-12/most-overused-buzzwords-survey.aspx; CNW Newswire, "What Is the Buzz? Survey Reveals Most Overused Workplace Terms," http://www.newswire.ca/en/releases/archive/September2009/10/c3742.html; E. Wiltshire, "Buzzwords," *Lawyers Weekly*, November 27, 2009, http://www.lawyersweekly.ca/index.php?section=article&articleid=1048&rssid=4.

There are three formal communication channels: downward communication, upward communication, and horizontal communication.[15]

Downward communication flows from higher to lower levels in an organization. Downward communication is used to issue orders down the organizational hierarchy, to give organizational members job-related information, to give managers and workers performance reviews from upper managers, and to clarify organizational objectives and goals.[16]

Upward communication flows from lower levels to higher levels in an organization. Upward communication is used to give higher level managers feedback about operations, issues, and problems; to help higher level managers assess organizational performance and effectiveness; to encourage lower level managers and employees to participate in organizational decision making; and to give those at lower levels the chance to share their concerns with higher level authorities. As important as upward communication is, however, it is sometimes a challenge to get employees to voice their opinions or communicate to supervisors, managers, and higher-ups in the organization. A recent Canadian online poll found that about 44 percent of employees did not feel comfortable speaking their mind to their bosses.[17] This is unfortunate, since employee feedback is often vital to helping managers understand how they are being perceived and to creating a positive work environment.

Horizontal communication flows among managers and workers who are at the same organizational level, such as when a day shift nurse comes in at 7:30 a.m. for a half-hour discussion with the night nurse supervisor who leaves at 8:00 a.m. Horizontal communication helps facilitate coordination and cooperation between different parts of a company and allows coworkers to share relevant information. It also helps people at the same level resolve conflicts and solve problems without involving high levels of management. Studies show that communication breakdowns, which occur most often during horizontal communication, such as when patients are handed over from one nurse or doctor to another, are the largest source of medical errors in hospitals.[18]

Downward communication communication that flows from higher to lower levels in an organization

Upward communication communication that flows from lower to higher levels in an organization

Horizontal communication communication that flows among managers and workers who are at the same organizational level

Role Reversal

Nitin Kawale, president of Cisco Systems Canada, meets for regular mentoring sessions with Ioana Birleanu, a twenty-something Cisco business manager. What may be surprising is the role reversal taking place—Birleanu, a junior employee, is actually the mentor, teaching Kawale how to utilize the power of social media in external and internal communications. Reverse mentoring started a decade ago at General Electric Co. (GE), when then CEO Jack Welch asked hundreds of the company's seasoned managers to connect with younger employees. The concept was simple: pass ideas, expertise, and knowledge up the corporate ladder instead of the other way. The experiment at GE was a success, and now a host of companies are using reverse mentoring, including Best Buy Co., State Farm Life Insurance Co., and Procter & Gamble. Reverse mentoring can provide valuable benefits to both groups—senior employees often find themselves feeling re-energized and more motivated because of the interaction, younger workers appreciate the increased visibility it gives them among senior management, and overall it can help engage and improve relationships between different generations in the workplace. The biggest challenge in implementing reverse mentorship is getting senior employees, particularly senior-level managers, to accept the role reversal and learn how to be a "follower" instead of a "leader."

Zurijeta/Shutterstock.com

Sources: M. Johne, "Role Reversal: Mentoring from the bottom up," *The Globe and Mail*, 19 January 2012, available at: http://www.theglobeandmail.com/report-on-business/careers/career-advice/role-reversal-mentoring-from-the-bottom-up/article4171259/, T. Grant, "Role Reversal," *The Globe and Mail, Report on Business*, 11 July 2009; C. Wonderlic, "Reverse Mentoring, Old Dogs, New Tricks," 13 January, 2007, www.hr.com.

Informal communication channel ("grapevine") the transmission of messages from employee to employee outside of formal communication channels

In general, what can managers do to improve formal communication? First, decrease reliance on downward communication. Second, increase chances for upward communication by increasing personal contact with lower-level managers and workers. Third, encourage much better use of horizontal communication.

2.3 Informal Communication Channels

An organization's **informal communication channel**, sometimes called the **grapevine**, is the transmission of messages from employee to employee outside of formal communication channels. The grapevine arises out of curiosity, that is, the need to know what is going on in an organization and how it might affect you or others. To satisfy this curiosity, employees need a consistent supply of relevant, accurate, in-depth information about "who is doing what and what changes are occurring within the organization."[19] The office water cooler has long been considered the best place to learn company news and to swap stories with coworkers—including rumours and office gossip. However, in today's electronic age, e-mail, text messages, and social media are also considered part of the grapevine.

Grapevines arise out of informal communication networks such as a gossip or cluster chain. In a *gossip chain,* one highly connected individual shares information with many other managers and workers. By contrast, in a *cluster chain,* numerous people simply tell a few of their friends. The result in both cases is that information flows freely and quickly through the organization. Some believe that grapevines are a waste of employees' time, that they promote gossip and rumours that fuel political speculation, and that they are sources of highly unreliable, inaccurate information. Cy Charney, a management consultant and author of *The Instant Manager*, believes that for some employees, office gossip is a way to blow off steam. Thus it fills a need in the workplace.[20] Others believe that gossip can lead to a sense of camaraderie and create closer team relationships in a workplace, as coworkers who trade non-official knowledge often bond better. Studies clearly show that grapevines are highly accurate sources of information for

Andersen Ross/Blend Images/Jupiterimages

a number of reasons.[21] First, because grapevines typically carry "juicy" information that is interesting and timely, information spreads rapidly. Second, since information is typically spread by face-to-face conversation, receivers can send feedback to make sure they understand the message that is being communicated. This reduces misunderstandings and increases accuracy. Third, since most of the information in a company moves along the grapevine rather than formal communication channels, people can usually verify the accuracy of information by checking it out with others.

What can managers do to manage organizational grapevines? The very worst thing they can do is withhold information or try to punish those who share information with others. A better strategy is to embrace the grapevine and keep employees informed about possible changes and strategies. Failure to do so will just make things worse. And, in addition to using the grapevine to communicate with others, managers should not overlook the grapevine as a tremendous source of valuable information and feedback. In fact, information flowing through organizational grapevines is estimated to be 75 to 95 percent accurate.

2.4 Coaching and Counselling: One-on-One Communication

Coaching and counselling are two kinds of one-on-one communication. **Coaching** is communicating with someone for the direct purpose of improving the person's on-the-job performance or behaviour.[22] Coaching is also a valuable tool for retaining employees.

Around 52 percent of Canadian employers offer in-house coaches and trainers to aid in executive retention. According to Patty Prosser of Oi Partners, a talent management consulting company, "providing coaching to employees in how to become better managers is as important a signal of investing in their career development as are salary and benefit increases."[23] Tribute Communities, an Ontario-based home-building company, hired a workplace coach to help improve the quality of decision making, teamwork, and communication throughout the company. Eileen Chadnick, a certified coach, began by involving all employees in the development of a set of core values for the company; she then helped the company put those values in place through a year-long coaching initiative.[24]

Coaching communicating with someone for the direct purpose of improving the person's on-the-job performance or behaviour

Counselling communicating with someone about non-job-related issues that may be affecting or interfering with the person's performance

By contrast, **counselling** is communicating with someone about non-job-related issues such as stress, child care, health issues, retirement planning, or legal issues that may be affecting or interfering with the person's performance. Counselling does not mean that managers should try to be clinicians, even though an estimated 20 percent of employees are dealing with personal problems at any given time. Instead, managers should discuss specific performance problems, listen if the employee chooses to share personal issues, and then recommend that the employee call the company's Employee Assistance Program (EAP). EAPs are typically free when provided as part of a company's benefit package. In emergencies or times of crisis, EAPs can offer immediate counselling and support and provide referrals to organizations and professionals that can help employees and their family members address personal issues.

Gossip Makes the Business World Go Round

Gossip exists in virtually every workplace. Although it can create a distracting and potentially negative work environment, there are some ways that gossip can actually be beneficial and lead to better management. Some of the more common myths associated with office gossip? Many people believe that women gossip more than men; however, this may be because men do not admit they are gossiping and view their communication more as discussions or intelligence gathering. The assumption that most informal communication happens at the water cooler or at the photocopier is also misleading, as most people choose to share office gossip behind closed doors, to avoid the risk of being overheard. If you are a manager interested in how to best manage gossip in your work environment, you may want to consider taking a proactive approach by identifying the main sources of gossip or gatekeepers of informal communication within your organization. Managers have begun to realize that informal channels of communication can serve as an early warning system that yields useful information about an organization, and that they can help managers run less risk of being taken by surprise by developments. In addition, these unofficial channels may prove to be useful for testing the waters on new ideas or important announcements coming down the pipe. So, instead of steering clear of gossip, accept it as part of your organization's communication network, and if you can, embrace it for its benefits!

Source: G. Michelson, "Make Office Gossip Work For You," *Forbes*, 19 May 2011, available at: http://www.forbes.com/2011/05/19/make-office-gossip-work-for-you.html

Hey Coach!

Many organizations are investing in executive coaching to help their managers improve or modify their skills to fit their organization's changing needs. This is similar to what a sports coach might do with a star player—try and draw out his or her best game to improve the performance of the entire team. The return on investment for executive coaching can be quite substantial. According to a study of companies that used coaching services, 53 percent reported an increase in productivity, 48 percent saw quality improvements, and 61 percent noted improved job satisfaction. Even more impressive, the average return on investment for those who used coaching services was six times the initial cost of those programs.

Source: A. Holloway, "Mirror, mirror: executive coaching," *Canadian Business Online*, 8 May 2006, available at: http://www.canadianbusiness.com/managing/career/article.jsp?content=20060508_77300_77300

© Photodisc/Jupiterimages

Nonverbal communication any communication that doesn't involve words

Communication medium the method used to deliver an oral or written message

2.5 Nonverbal Communication

Nonverbal communication is any communication that doesn't involve words. Nonverbal communication almost always accompanies verbal communication and may either support and reinforce the verbal message or contradict it. The importance of nonverbal communication is well established. Researchers have estimated that as much as 93 percent of any message is transmitted nonverbally, with 55 percent coming from body language and facial expressions and 38 percent coming from the tone and pitch of the voice.[25] Since many nonverbal cues are unintentional, receivers often consider nonverbal communication to be a more accurate representation of what senders are thinking and feeling than the words they use.

In short, because nonverbal communication is so informative, especially when it contradicts verbal communication, managers need to learn how to monitor and control their nonverbal behaviour.

How to Improve Communication

When it comes to improving communication, managers face two primary tasks: managing one-on-one communication; and managing organization-wide communication.

LO3 Managing One-on-One Communication

You learned in Chapter 1 that on average, first-line managers spend 57 percent of their time with people; for middle managers, it is 63 percent, and for top managers, it's as much as 78 percent.[26] Clearly, managers spend a great deal of time in one-on-one communication with others.

Learn more about managing one-on-one communication by reading about how to ***3.1 choose the right communication medium, 3.2 be a good listener,*** *and* ***3.3 give effective feedback.***

3.1 Choosing the Right Communication Medium

Sometimes messages are poorly communicated simply because they are delivered using the wrong **communication medium**, which is the method used to deliver a message. For example, the wrong communication medium is being used when an employee returns from lunch, picks up the note left on her office chair, and learns she has been fired.

There are two general kinds of communication media: oral and written. *Oral communication* includes face-to-face and group meetings through telephone calls, videoconferencing, or any other means of sending and receiving spoken messages. Studies show that managers generally prefer oral communication over written because it provides the opportunity to ask questions about parts of the message they don't understand. Oral communication is also a rich communication medium because it allows managers to receive and assess the nonverbal communication that accompanies spoken messages (i.e., body language and facial expressions). Oral communication should not be used for all communication, however. In general, when the message is simple, such as a quick request or a presentation of straightforward information, a memo or an e-mail is often the better communication medium.

Written communication includes letters, memos, e-mails and texts. Although most managers still like and use oral communication, e-mail, because of its convenience and speed, has changed how managers communicate with workers, customers, and one another. For instance, because people read six times faster than they can listen, they usually can read 30 e-mail messages in 10 to 15 minutes.[27] By contrast, dealing with voice messages can take a considerable amount of time.

Furthermore, with e-mail accessible at the office, at home, and on the road (by laptop computer, cellphone, or Web-based e-mail), managers can use e-mail to stay in touch from anywhere at almost any time. And since e-mail and other written communications don't have to be sent and received simultaneously, messages can be sent and stored for reading at any time. Consequently, managers can send and receive many more messages using e-mail

Building Trust

Social psychologist Richard Nisbett, who studies cultural differences, affirms what many businesspeople have discovered—that for Asians, business starts by establishing relationships, whereas Westerners are more likely to get down to business first and then build the relationship. Dan Ryan, head of real estate management for EMC, a global provider of information technology services, was tasked with expanding EMC's business in India. The first step was to find a 46,500-square-metre facility, which was three times the size of EMC's current 15,300-square-metre office in Bangalore. So Ryan used a cross-cultural online resource, GlobeSmart, to learn about India's culture before communicating with Indian landlords. GlobeSmart advised building relationships first, before getting down to leasing details, such as price and business service amenities. So Ryan spent a significant amount of time with potential landlords, getting to know them and communicating his priorities. Once trust had been established, he explained how important it was for EMC to have an environmentally friendly building. Ryan says, "Building our relationship with the landlord first allowed us to get him to consider meeting those [environmental] standards. Now he's talking about doing all of his projects that way."

Sources: H. Alberts, "East versus West," *Forbes Asia*, May 11, 2009, 64–65; H. Aperian, "Helping Companies Bridge Cultures," *BusinessWeek Online*, September 8, 2008, accessed June 17, 2011, http://www.businessweek.com/technology/content/sep2008/tc2008095_508754.htm.

© FERRAN TRAITE SOLER/iStockphoto.com

than using oral communication, which requires people to get together in person or by phone or videoconference.

E-mail has its own drawbacks, however. One disadvantage is that it lacks the formality of paper memos and letters. It is easy to fire off an e-mail that is not well written or fully thought through. This is a particular problem in instances when we might be tempted to send a knee-jerk, emotional response to a message that has angered or confused us. Another drawback to e-mail is that it lacks nonverbal cues, making e-mails very easy to misinterpret. Kristin Byron, assistant professor of management at Syracuse University, says that "people perceive e-mails as more negative than they are intended to be, and even e-mails that are intended to be positive can be misinterpreted as more neutral." So take a minute to reflect before you hit *reply*.[28]

3.2 Listening

Are you a good listener? You probably think so. But in fact, most people, including managers, are terrible listeners, retaining only about 25 percent of what they hear.[29] You qualify as a poor listener if you frequently interrupt others, jump to conclusions about what people will say before they've said it, hurry the speaker to finish his or her point, are a passive listener (not actively working at your listening), or simply don't pay attention to what people are saying.[30] On this last point—attentiveness—college students were periodically asked to record their thoughts during a psychology course. On average, 20 percent of the students were paying attention (only 12 percent were actively working at being good listeners), 20 percent were thinking about sex, 20 percent were thinking about things they had done before class, and the remaining 40 percent were thinking about other things unrelated to the class (e.g., worries, lunch, the blond in the front row).[31]

Most people, including managers, are terrible listeners, retaining only about 25% of what they hear.

For a manager, how important is listening? According to Jim Treliving, Chairman of Boston Pizza International Inc., understanding and listening are the skills most responsible for his business success. With over 340 restaurants across Canada and annual sales over $1 billion, Treliving is a successful Canadian entrepreneur who believes that "if you are going to hire and work with a person, you have to have the ability to listen to them."[32] In general, about 45 percent of the total time you spend communicating with others is spent listening. Furthermore, listening is important for managerial and business success, even for those at the top of an organization. Listening is a more important skill for managers than ever, since Generation X employees tend to expect a high level

Supri Suharjoto/Shutterstock

of interaction with their supervisors. They want feedback on their performance, but they also want to offer feedback and know that it is heard.[33] In fact, managers with good listening skills are rated as better managers by their employees and are much more likely to be promoted.[34]

So, what can you do to improve your listening ability? First, understand the difference between hearing and listening. According to *Webster's New World Dictionary*, **hearing** is the act or process of perceiving sounds, whereas **listening** is making a conscious effort to hear. In other words, we react to sounds, such as bottles breaking or music being played too loud, because hearing is an involuntary physiological process. By contrast, listening is a voluntary behaviour. So if you want to be a good listener, you have to *choose* to be a good listener. Typically, that means choosing to be an active, empathetic listener.[35]

Active listening means assuming half the responsibility for successful communication by actively giving the speaker nonjudgmental feedback that shows you have accurately heard what he or she said. Active listeners make it clear from their behaviour that they are listening carefully to what the speaker has to say. Active listeners put the speaker at ease, maintain eye contact, and show the speaker that they are attentively listening by nodding and making short statements.

Several specific strategies can help you be a better active listener. First, *clarify responses* by asking the speaker to explain confusing or ambiguous statements. Second, when there are natural breaks in the speaker's delivery, use this time to paraphrase or summarize what has been said. *Paraphrasing* is restating what has been said in your own words. *Summarizing* is reviewing the speaker's main points or emotions. Paraphrasing and summarizing give the speaker the chance to correct the message if the active listener has attached the wrong meaning to it. Paraphrasing and summarizing also show the speaker that the active listener is interested in the speaker's message. Exhibit 15.3 lists specific statements that listeners can use to clarify responses, paraphrase, or summarize what has been said.

Active listeners also avoid evaluating the message or being critical until the message is complete. They recognize that their only responsibility during the transmission of a message is to receive it accurately and derive the intended meaning from it. Evaluation and criticism can take place after the message is accurately received. To be a good listener, you should avoid thinking about your response while someone is talking and turn all of your attention to listening. Finally, active listeners recognize that a large portion of any message is transmitted nonverbally and thus pay very careful attention to the nonverbal cues transmitted by the speaker.

Empathetic listening means understanding the speaker's perspective and personal frame of reference and giving feedback that conveys that understanding to the speaker. Empathetic listening goes beyond active

Good Tip!

Listen Up!

Author Robert W. Bly offers these tips to help you become a better listener:

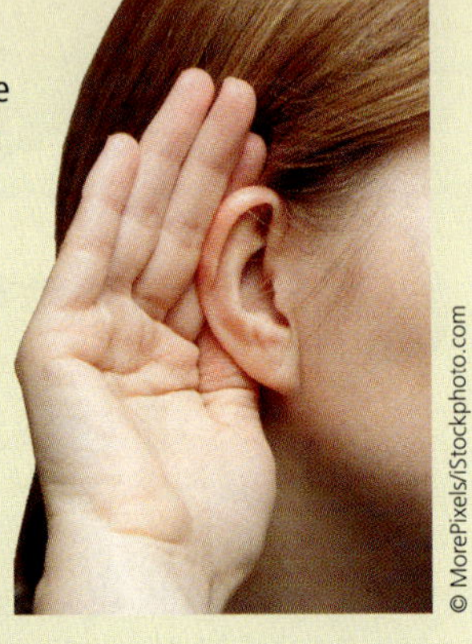
© MorePixels/iStockphoto.com

1. **Don't talk. Listen.** People appreciate a good listener more than a good talker. Why? People want a chance to get their thoughts and opinions across and a good listener lets them do that. If you interrupt or appear to not be listening, people will get the impression you aren't interested in what they are saying.
2. **Don't jump to conclusions.** Some people are tempted to tune out when they think they have the gist of the conversation, but that assumption can be dangerous.
3. **Listen "between the lines."** Concentrate on what is *not* being said as well as on what is being said. A lot of clues to meaning come from tone of voice, facial expressions, and gestures.
4. **Ask questions.** If you aren't sure what the speaker is saying, don't be afraid to ask that person questions or to repeat what the speaker has said in your own words to confirm that you heard correctly.
5. **Don't let yourself be distracted by the environment or the speaker's idiosyncrasies.** Paying too much attention to distractions (e.g., a strong accent, someone walking by) can break your concentration and cause you to miss an important point.
6. **Keep an open mind.** Don't listen only for statements that support your own opinions or beliefs.
7. **Provide feedback.** Make eye contact with the speaker, nod your head, maintain upright posture, interject an occasional comment (e.g., "I see") to demonstrate your understanding and attention.

Source: Bly, Robert W. *Magnetic selling: Develop the charm and charisma that attract customers and maximize sales.* New York: AMACOM, a Division of the American Management Association, 2006.

Exhibit 15.3 Clarifying, Paraphrasing, and Summarizing Responses for Active Listeners

Clarifying Responses	Paraphrasing Responses	Summarizing Responses
Could you explain that again?	What you're really saying is	Let me summarize . . . .
I don't understand what you mean.	If I understand you correctly	Okay, your main concerns are . . . .
I'm not sure how	In other words	To recap what you've said . . . .
I'm confused. Would you run through that again?	So your perspective is that	Thus far, you've discussed . . . .
	Tell me if I'm wrong, but what you seem to be saying is	

Source: E. Atwater, *I Hear You*, rev. ed. (New York: Walker, 1992).

listening because it depends on our ability to set aside our own attitudes or relationships so that we can see and understand things through someone else's eyes. Empathetic listening is just as important as active listening, especially for managers, because it helps build rapport and trust with others.

The key to being a more empathetic listener is to show your desire to understand and to reflect people's feelings. You can *show your desire to understand* by listening, that is, asking people to talk about what's most important to them and then giving them sufficient time to talk before responding or interrupting.

Reflecting feelings is also an important part of empathetic listening because it demonstrates that you understand the speaker's emotions. Unlike in active listening, during which you restate or summarize the informational content of what has been said, the focus is on the affective part of the message. As an empathetic listener, you can use the following statements to *reflect the speaker's emotions:*

- So, right now it sounds like you're feeling ...
- You seem as if you're ...
- Do you feel a bit ...?
- I could be wrong, but I'm sensing that you're feeling ...

In the end, says management consultant Terry Pearce, empathetic listening can be boiled down to these three steps. First, wait 10 seconds before you answer or respond. It will seem an eternity, but waiting prevents you from interrupting others and rushing your response. Second, to be sure you understand what the speaker wants, ask questions to clarify the speaker's intent. Third, only then should you respond first with feelings and then facts (notice that facts *follow* feelings).[36]

This section provides you with important tools to help you become a better listener. Applying them insincerely—or indiscriminately—may make you seem patronizing and derail your attempt to build better working relationships. Not everyone appreciates having what they said repeated back to them—even if you've repeated it in your own words. The key is to respond, rather than repeat or react, in a manner appropriate for the situation and the person with whom you're speaking.[37] The suggestions in Exhibit 15.3 are simply ways to learn the responses that typify active listening. You have to find your own voice to seem genuine.

Giving feedback does not give managers the right to personally attack workers.

3.3 Giving Feedback

In Chapter 11, you learned that performance appraisal feedback (i.e., judging) should be separated from developmental feedback (i.e., coaching).[38] We can now focus on the steps needed to communicate feedback one-on-one to employees.

To start, managers need to recognize that feedback can be constructive or destructive. **Destructive feedback** is disapproving without any intention of being helpful and almost always causes a negative or defensive reaction in the recipient. One study found that 98 percent of employees responded to destructive feedback from their bosses with either verbal aggression (two-thirds) or physical aggression (one-third).[39]

By contrast, **constructive feedback** is intended to be helpful, corrective, and/or encouraging. It is aimed at correcting performance deficiencies and motivating employees. For feedback to be constructive rather than destructive, it must be immediate, focused on specific behaviours, and problem-oriented. Immediate feedback is much more effective than delayed feedback because manager and worker can recall the mistake or incident more accurately and discuss it in detail. For example, if a worker is rude to a customer and the customer immediately reports the incident to management, and if the manager,

Hearing the act or process of perceiving sounds

Listening making a conscious effort to hear

Active listening assuming half the responsibility for successful communication by actively giving the speaker nonjudgmental feedback that shows you've accurately heard what he or she said

Empathetic listening understanding the speaker's perspective and personal frame of reference and giving feedback that conveys that understanding to the speaker

Destructive feedback feedback that disapproves without any intention of being helpful and almost always causes a negative or defensive reaction in the recipient

Constructive feedback feedback intended to be helpful, corrective, and/or encouraging

Online discussion forums the in-house equivalent of Internet newsgroups. By using Web- or software-based discussion tools that are available across the company, employees can easily ask questions and share knowledge with one another.

Wikis websites that allow employees across an organization to edit and update documents in a quick and easy way, facilitating collaboration and interdepartmental communication.

Televised/videotaped speeches and meetings speeches and meetings originally made to a smaller audience that are either simultaneously broadcast to other locations in the company or videotaped for subsequent distribution and viewing

Videoconferencing utilizes computer networks to transmit audio and video, allowing communication to take place at a distance.

in turn, immediately discusses the incident with the employee, there should be little disagreement over what was said or done. By contrast, it's unlikely that either the manager or the worker will be able to accurately remember the specifics of what occurred if the manager waits several weeks to discuss the incident. When that happens, it's usually too late to have a meaningful conversation.

Specific feedback focuses on particular acts or incidents that are clearly under the control of the employee. For instance, instead of telling an employee that he or she is "always late for work," it's much more constructive to say, "In the last three weeks, you have been 30 minutes late on four occasions and more than an hour late on two others." Furthermore, specific feedback isn't very helpful unless employees have control over the problems that the feedback addresses. Giving negative feedback about behaviours beyond someone's control is likely to be seen as unfair. Similarly, giving positive feedback about behaviours beyond someone's control may be viewed as insincere.

Last, *problem-oriented feedback* focuses on the problems or incidents associated with the poor performance rather than on the worker or the worker's personality. Giving feedback does not give managers the right to personally attack workers. Managers may be frustrated by a worker's poor performance, but the point of problem-oriented feedback is to draw attention to the problem in a nonjudgmental way so that the employee has enough information to correct it.

LO4 Managing Organization-Wide Communication

Although managing one-on-one communication is important, managers must also know how to communicate effectively with a larger number of people throughout an organization. According to studies by Watson Wyatt Research, there is a strong correlation between effective employee communication and financial success. Organizations that are highly effective in communication and change management are 2.5 times as likely to significantly outperform their peers as organizations that are not as highly effective in either of these areas.[40]

*Learn more about organization-wide communication by reading the following sections about **4.1 improving transmission by getting the message out** and **4.2 improving reception by finding ways to hear what others feel and think.***

4.1 Improving Transmission: Getting the Message Out

Several methods of electronic communication—e-mail, company intranets, online discussion forums, televised/videotaped speeches, and online podcasts—now make it easier for managers to communicate with people throughout the organization and get the message out.

Although we normally think of *e-mail,* or the transmission of messages via computers, as a means of one-on-one communication, it also plays an important role in organization-wide communication, allowing managers to keep employees up-to-date on changes and developments. On his first day as CEO of Diebold, which makes ATM machines, Thomas Swidarski e-mailed Diebold's 14,500 employees a message about improving customer loyalty, increasing the speed with which products were manufactured and delivered, and "providing quality products and outstanding service." Swidarski concluded his e-mail by writing that leading Diebold "does not rest with one person—it rests with each and every one of us."[41] Discussion forums are another means of electronically promoting organization-wide communication. **Online discussion forums** use Web or software-based discussion tools so that employees can easily ask questions and share knowledge with one another. The point is to share expertise and not duplicate solutions already discovered by others in the company. Furthermore, because online discussion forums remain online, they provide a historical database for people who are dealing with particular problems for the first time.

Wikis, or group-editable Web pages, are online tools that allow employees across an organization to update and publish content collaboratively. A host of organizations today are using wikis, including Sony's PlayStation team, who use wikis to update executives throughout the company about development stages for the video game console. Ned Lerner from Sony explains, "the marketing people can get a sense of what's coming their way, as well as the finance and legal people—anyone who needs to know the one-page overview of what's going on."[42]

Televised/videotaped speeches and meetings and online podcasts are a third electronic method of organization-wide communication. **Televised/videotaped speeches and meetings** are simply speeches and meetings originally made to a smaller audience that are either simultaneously broadcast to other locations in the company or videotaped for subsequent distribution and viewing. Cisco's CEO, John Chambers, tapes 10 to 15 videos each quarter to communicate with his employees and customers.[43]

Videoconferencing utilizes computer networks to transmit audio and video, allowing communication to take place at a distance; for companies that would ordinarily have to incur travel costs to get employees to a central meeting location, substantial savings can be realized using this method of communication.

Share and Tell

At Wardrop Engineering, a Canadian company with 13 locations across the country, communication with employees has always been a top priority, so it wasn't unusual when senior management embarked on a cross-country tour to connect with employees and gather their input to aid in the development of a new corporate vision. After meeting more than 700 employees and hearing so many great personal stories, the company's CEO and vice president of human resources wanted a way to connect their growing and diverse workforce, so they turned to technology as way to do so. An internal news service was developed and connected to the company's intranet, allowing staff at all levels of the organization to share stories and news – both personal and professional. For example, some employees were surprised to hear via the news service that the company's vice president of human resources was an avid runner and had qualified for the Boston Marathon. Employees working on international assignments were able to share stories and photos of projects they were working on with other employees who they did not regularly come into contact with. According to CEO Shayne Smith, the news service is a useful tool for sharing information and getting team members talking about personal and corporate wins, as well as celebrating the company's vision—"people, passion, and performance." According to company statistics, people-focused stories—as opposed to those with a business angle—are the most viewed stories on the site, which is a sure sign of employee engagement in an organization, according to G. Turchyn, vice president of business development.

Sources: M. Strutzenberger, "Stakeholder News Helps Global Engineering Firm Sustain Team Spirit, Says Far-Flung Employee," *Axiom News*, October 8, 2010, http://www.axiomnews.ca/node/1031; D. Harder, "Communication Pushes Firm to the Top," *Canadian HR Reporter*, October 20, 2008, http://www.hrreporter.com/issue?issueid=593; D. Hamel, "Wardrop's News Program Successful at Engaging Staff, Promoting Company Culture," *Axiom News*, May 2, 2008, http://www.axiomnews.ca/NewsArchives/2008/May/May02.html.

Maridav/Shutterstock.com

4.2 Improving Reception: Hearing What Others Feel and Think

When people think of "organization-wide" communication, they think of the CEO and top managers getting their message out to people in the company. But organization-wide communication also means finding ways to hear what people throughout the organization are feeling and thinking. This is important because most employees and managers are reluctant to share their thoughts and feelings with top managers. Surveys indicate that only 29 percent of first-level managers feel that their companies encourage employees to express their opinions openly. Another study of 22 companies found that 70 percent of the people surveyed were afraid to speak up about problems they knew existed at work.

Withholding information about organizational problems or issues is called **organizational silence**. Organizational silence occurs when employees believe that telling management about problems won't make a difference or that they'll be punished or hurt in some way for sharing such information.[44] Company hotlines, survey feedback, frequent informal meetings, surprise visits, and blogs are ways of overcoming organizational silence.

Organizational silence when employees withhold information about organizational problems or issues

Company hotlines phone numbers that anyone in the company can call anonymously to leave information for upper management

Surprise visits should also be used as an opportunity to encourage meaningful upward communication.

Company hotlines are phone numbers that anyone in the company can call anonymously to leave information for upper management. For example, Deloitte Touche Tohmatsu has a toll-free hotline for employees to call to report any kind of problem or issue within the

A Little Bird Told Me

Social media formats like Twitter, where users can post comments and opinions in an open forum (as long as they are contained in 140 characters or less) can be a powerful force when employees elect to include comments related to their workplace. When electronics retailer HMV fired hundreds of employees, including Poppy Rose Cleere, the company's online marketing and social media planner, they didn't expect the news to hit the public quite as quickly as it did. On hearing the news on that fateful day, Cleere immediately began tweeting—but not from her personal Twitter account. Instead she used HMV's official account. "There are over 60 of us being fired at once! Mass execution, of loyal employees who love the brand," Cleere tweeted. "Sorry we've been quiet for so long. Under contract, we've been unable to say a word, or—more importantly—tell the truth." "Under usual circumstances, we'd never dare to do such a thing as this. However, when the company you dearly love is being ruined … and those hard working individuals, who wanted to make HMV great again, have mostly been fired, there seemed to be no other choice."

The messages (which were all tagged #hmvXFactorFiring) were quickly deleted, but that did not stop the news from going viral, as users were quick to retweet the posts and capture screenshots of the comments. What can organizations learn from this incident? According to one observer, "Never fire the person in charge of your Twitter feed without revoking their access first."

Sources: E. Rowley, "HMV Staffer Claims Responsibility for Tweeting Mass Sacking," *The Telegraph*, January 31, 2013, http://www.telegraph.co.uk/finance/newsbysector/retailandconsumer/9839855/HMV-staffer-claims-responsibility-for-tweeting-mass-sacking.html; N. Evans, "Someone Had to Speak: HMV Employee Who Live Tweeted Firing of 60+ Staff from Chain's Official Twitter Revealed," *The Mirror*, February 1, 2013, http://www.mirror.co.uk/news/uk-news/hmvxfactorfiring-poppy-rose-cleere-behind-1568494; A. Samuel, "When HR Decisions Become Social Media Scandals," *Harvard Business Review*, February 8, 2013, http://blogs.hbr.org/samuel/2013/02/when-hr-decisions-become-socia.html.

Annette Shaff/Shutterstock.com

Survey feedback information that is collected by surveys from organizational members and then compiled, disseminated, and used to develop action plans for improvement

company. Hotlines are particularly important because 44 percent of employees will not report misconduct. Why not? The reason is twofold: they don't believe anything will be done, and they "fear that the report will not be kept confidential."[45]

Survey feedback is information that is collected by survey from organization members and then compiled, disseminated, and used to develop action plans for improvement. At Four Seasons Hotels and Resorts, an employee opinion survey is conducted once a year to ensure that management keeps its finger on the pulse of what it considers one of its greatest assets, its corporate culture.[46] Similarly, FedEx utilizes an online survey, which is completely anonymous, to enable all employees to evaluate their managers and the overall environment at FedEx, including benefits, incentives, and working conditions. The results are compiled and then given back to each FedEx work group to decide where changes and improvements need to be made and to develop specific action plans to address those problems.

Which Type of Leader Are You When It Comes to Social Media?

The following are the six basic categories that reflect the attitudes that business leaders have about social media.

Folly. Social media is a source of entertainment, nothing more. It does not have any value in business so it's not worth thinking about.

Fearful. Social media is a threat to productivity, intellectual capital, privacy, and management authority, and as such, it should be discouraged and/or prohibited in the workplace.

Flippant. There is nothing worth getting concerned about here. Let employees have access to social media and maybe something good will come of it.

Formulating. There is potential strategic value in social media, as long as the right approach is used to help capitalize on business opportunities and senior management is on board.

Forging. Social media is something the entire organization has embraced and uses to help gain business value from communities. Continued investment is under way to help continue the social media movement.

Fusing. This is the most advanced attitude. Leaders view social media as part of an overall focus on community collaboration and as an integral part of the organization's work. This *social* organization does not require a specific vision or strategy since all business strategy and execution already include community collaboration.

Source: A.J. Bradley and M.P. McDonald, "The Six Attitudes Leaders Take Towards Social Media," *Harvard Business Review*, 17 October 2011, available at: http://blogs.hbr.org/cs/2011/10/the_six_attitudes_leaders_take.html. Reprinted with permission.

Frequent *informal meetings* between top managers and lower-level employees are one of the best ways for top managers to hear what others feel and think. Many people assume that top managers are at the centre of everything that goes on in organizations, but top managers commonly feel isolated from most of their lower level managers and employees. Consequently, more and more top managers are scheduling frequent informal meetings with people throughout their companies.

Social media platforms are another way to hear what people are thinking and saying both inside and outside the organization. The grocery chain SUPERVALU has embraced the concept of social media for external as well as internal communication. Each store brand has its own Facebook page, and store directors use Twitter accounts to communicate with customers about individual stores. However, customers aren't the only audience for social media. Through the social media platform Yammer, store directors, corporate executives, and other employees within the organization are able to share best practices in real time, and a Twitter feed is used to share organizational news with investors, media bloggers, and others. Jeff Swanson, director of external communications, explains that "there are blurring lines on what social media means today. We see it as part marketing, part communications, part customer service."[47] Prior to using social media, there were limited opportunities for employees to send ideas upward to higher levels of management, and in cases where information was being shared, it was at a slow place and often filtered along the way. With Yammer, higher executives, including the CEO, are pleased with the quick turnaround of information, even when it is used to pose tough questions to company executives. Wayne Shurts, Chief Information Officer, explains: "One of the biggest lessons we learned: never underestimate the need for an employee to be heard and the value of listening."[48]

rui vale sousa/Shutterstock.com

Go online at
www.nelson.com/4ltrpress/icanmgmt2
And access the essential Study Tools online for this chapter:

- **Flashcards**, to help you study
- **Interactive Quizzes**, to test your knowledge
- **Audio Chapter Summaries**, for chapter review
- **Crossword Puzzles and Beat the Clock**, to review key terms
- **What Would You Do? Cases**, for applying your knowledge to real-life situations
- **Self Assessments**, to learn about what kind of manager you are
- **Videos and Media Quizzing for Part 4**
  - Chapter 13: Living Social Escapes: Motivating Employees
  - Chapter 14: Camp Bow Wow: Leadership
  - Chapter 15: Plant Fantasies: Managing Communication

Be sure to consult the Chapter Review Card at the back of the textbook.

16 Control

LEARNING OUTCOMES

LO1 Describe the basic control process.

LO2 Discuss the various methods that managers can use to maintain control.

LO3 Describe the behaviours, processes, and outcomes that today's managers are choosing to control in their organizations.

What Is Control?

For all companies, past success is no guarantee of future success. Even successful companies fall short, face challenges, and have to make changes. **Control** is a regulatory process of establishing standards to achieve organizational goals, comparing actual performance to the standards, and taking corrective action when necessary to restore performance to those standards. Control is not telling people what to do; it is working out, with the people in the firm, what the company goals should be. Control is achieved when behaviour and work procedures conform to standards and company goals are accomplished.[1] Control is not just an after-the-fact process, however. Preventive measures are also a form of control.

Basics of Control

Control is important because there is so much at stake when a company fails to meet standards. Maple Leaf Foods Inc. is a meat processing company headquartered in Toronto. The company employs around 23,500 people at its operations across Canada and in the United States, the United Kingdom, and Asia, with sales of $4.8 billion in 2012. Maple Leaf's internal control systems are augmented by external controls involving the Canadian Food Inspection Agency and provincial and local health authorities. But in August 2009, packaged meat products from Maple Leaf Foods were pinpointed as the source of a deadly, cross-Canada listeriosis outbreak that killed at least four people.

Michael McCain, CEO of Maple Leaf, said that the company has a culture of food safety with standards "well beyond" what regulators require. "This week, our best efforts failed," he said. "Tragically, our products have been linked to illness and loss of life." Linda Smith, a spokesperson for Maple Leaf, said that 100 percent of recalled meats products were removed within days of the recall. "There is a very active effort to work with all of the food distribution customers," she added, "but it is not as direct because there are customers, and then those customers have customers," involving thousands of accounts. Although part of the system broke down, other parts worked very well.

Certainly, some of the control standards failed at Maple Leaf; but other standards, for tracking through UPC/SSC codes and best-before dates, were extremely useful control tools in containing this tragedy. Control is now much better. The last of the lawsuits were settled and all the cheques to claimants were mailed out in 2012.

The point: loss of control, even for a short period, can have long-lasting effects.[2]

LO1 The Control Process

The basic control process ***1.1 begins with the establishment of clear standards of performance; 1.2 involves comparing performance to those standards; 1.3 takes corrective action, if needed, to repair performance deficiencies; 1.4 is a dynamic, cybernetic process; and 1.5 consists of three basic methods: feedback control, concurrent control, and feedforward control.*** *However, as much as managers would like,* ***1.6 control isn't always worthwhile or possible.***

Control a regulatory process of establishing standards to achieve organizational goals, comparing actual performance to the standards, and taking corrective action when necessary

Standards a basis of comparison for measuring the extent to which various kinds of organizational performance are satisfactory or unsatisfactory

1.1 Standards

The control process begins when managers set goals, such as satisfying 90 percent of customers or increasing sales by 5 percent. Companies then specify the performance standards that must be met to accomplish those goals. **Standards** are a basis of comparison for measuring the extent to which organizational performance is satisfactory or unsatisfactory. For example, many pizzerias use 30 to 40 minutes as the standard for delivery times. Since anything longer is viewed as unsatisfactory, they'll typically reduce the price if they can't deliver a hot pizza to you within that time period.

So how do managers set standards? How do they decide which levels of performance are satisfactory and which are not? To start with, a good standard must enable goal achievement. If you're meeting the standard but still not achieving company goals, the standard may have to be changed. There are many approaches to "standards." The Standards Council of Canada (SCC) is a federal Crown corporation whose mandate is to promote efficient and effective standardization in Canada. It oversees Canada's National Standards System. Located in Ottawa, the SCC reports to Parliament through the Minister of Industry. It is also part of the International Organization for Standards (ISO), which has 163 member countries. Because "International Organization for Standardization" would have different acronyms in different languages ("IOS" in English, "OIN" in French for Organisation Internationale de Normalisation), its founders decided to give it also a short, all-purpose name. They chose "ISO," derived from the Greek *isos*, meaning "equal." Whatever the country, whatever the language, the short form of the organization's name is always ISO.[3]

Companies also determine standards by listening to customers' comments, complaints, and suggestions, or by observing competitors' products and services. Standards are also sometimes set by government authorities. Although the Canadian Food Inspection Agency typically establishes food standards, some companies are not satisfied with the government's slow response to food safety concerns. In order to monitor and enforce quality

Maugli/Shutterstock

Bork/Shutterstock.com

Benchmarking the process of identifying outstanding practices, processes, and standards in other companies and adapting them to your company

Cybernetic the process of steering or keeping on course

Feedback control a mechanism for gathering information about performance deficiencies after they occur

standards, they have turned to private regulators such as GlobalGap. This organization is an offshoot of a Canadian program, Canada GAP. GlobalGap focuses on safety and sustainability for primary producers, including the agriculture, livestock, and aquaculture supply chains. GlobalGap has more than 130,000 producers representing 300 fruit products alone. BC Hothouse in Vancouver is a registered producer. Most meatpacking plants in Alberta and Ontario are also producer-members of GlobalGap. With private regulators, companies can move more quickly to prompt growers to comply with the standards, thereby improving food quality through the entire system.[4]

Standards can also be determined by benchmarking other companies. **Benchmarking** is the process of determining how well other companies (and not just competitors) are performing business functions or tasks. In other words, benchmarking is the process of determining other companies' standards. When setting standards by benchmarking, the first step is to determine what to benchmark. Companies can benchmark anything from cycle time (how fast) to quality (how well) to price (how much). The next step is to identify the companies against which to benchmark your standards. The last step is to collect data to determine other companies' performance standards.

1.2 Comparison to Standards

The next step in the control process is to compare actual performance to performance standards. The quality of the comparison largely depends on the measurement and information systems a company uses to keep track of performance. The better the system, the easier it is for companies to track their progress and identify problems that need to be fixed. One way for retailers to verify that performance standards are being met is to use mystery shoppers—that is, individuals who visit stores pretending to be customers but are really there to determine whether employees provide helpful customer service. The federal has government sent mystery shoppers to major airports to see how bilingual they are. Official Languages Commissioner Graham Fraser says that his office has used undercover observers to conduct checks. "We've looked at border services, we've done an audit of Air Canada's service to the public, and now we're looking at airports," Fraser said.

1.3 Corrective Action

The next step in the control process is to identify performance deviations, analyze those deviations, and then develop and implement programs to correct them.

Beta versions of software programs are a classic tool that developers use to monitor deviations from the standard. They can then take corrective action *before* the product is released on the market. Microsoft has an internal program called Software Quality Metrics (SQM) that company software developers use when creating new releases. SQM helps the developers determine how each change in the software code will affect the functionality of the program. It uses a system of comparison charts to show how the changes will affect users of new software.[5]

1.4 Dynamic, Cybernetic Process

As shown in Exhibit 16.1, control is a continuous, dynamic, cybernetic process. Control begins by setting standards, measuring performance, and then comparing performance to the standards. If the performance deviates from the standards, then managers and employees analyze the deviations and develop and implement corrective programs that (hopefully) achieve the desired performance by meeting the standards. Managers must repeat the entire process again and again in an endless feedback loop. Thus, control is not a one-time achievement or result. Rather, it continues over time (i.e., it is dynamic) and requires daily, weekly, and monthly attention from managers if performance levels are to be maintained at the standard. This constant attention is what makes control a cybernetic process. **Cybernetic** derives from the Greek word *kubernetes*, meaning "steersman"—that is, one who steers or keeps on course.[6] The control process shown in Exhibit 16.1 is cybernetic because constant attention to the feedback loop is necessary to keep the company's activities on course.

1.5 Feedback, Concurrent, and Feedforward Control

The three basic control methods are feedback control, concurrent control, and feedforward control. **Feedback control** is a mechanism for gathering information about performance deficiencies after they occur. This information is then used to correct performance deficiencies or prevent

Exhibit 16.1 Cybernetic Control Process

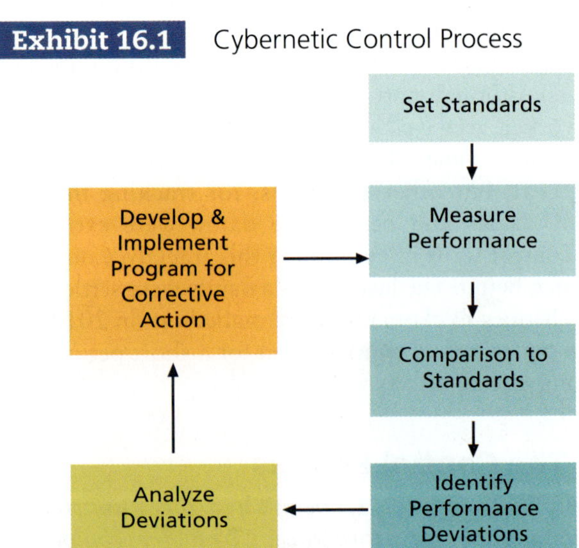

Source: Reprinted from H. Koontz & R. W. Bradspies, "Managing Through Feedforward Control: A Future Directed View," *Business Horizons*, June 1972, 25–36, with permission from Elsevier.

Alvov/Shutterstock.com

future deficiencies. Study after study has shown that feedback improves both individual and organizational performance. In most instances, any feedback is better than no feedback. If feedback has a downside, it's that it always occurs after the fact, after performance deficiencies have already occurred. Control can minimize the effects, but the damage is already done. The Canadian Aircraft Maintenance Engineer (AME) Licensing and Approved Training Organization (ATO) Systems are set by Transport Canada for private firms. This government organization is responsible for controls, regulations, standards, policies, and procedures for aircraft in Canada. Private firms then carry out maintenance work under a feedback control system.[7]

Concurrent control addresses the problems inherent in feedback control by gathering information about performance deficiencies as they occur. The Nike+ Running app tracks distance, pace, time, and calories burned with GPS, providing audio feedback as you run. After a runner installs a sensor in her shoes, it automatically uploads data via her smartphone to Nikeplus.com or Facebook so that she (and her friends) can see her runs, including her route and elevation. Runners can actually track their efforts every moment of their run and make changes on the fly.[8] Concurrent control is an improvement over feedback because it attempts to eliminate or shorten the delay between performance and feedback about the performance.

Feedforward control is a mechanism for gathering information about performance deficiencies *before* they occur. In contrast to feedback and concurrent control, which provide feedback on the basis of outcomes and results, feedforward control provides information about performance deficiencies by monitoring inputs, not outputs. Microsoft uses feedforward controls to try to prevent software problems before they occur. For example, when developing the latest version of its Windows 8 Operating System, Microsoft taught all of its experienced programmers new methods for writing more reliable software code *before* asking them to develop new features for the software. Microsoft has also developed new software testing tools that let the programmers thoroughly test the code they've written (i.e., input) before passing the code on to others to be used in beta testing and then in final products. To summarize, feedforward control seeks to prevent or minimize performance deficiencies before they happen.[9]

Concurrent control a mechanism for gathering information about performance deficiencies as they occur, thereby eliminating or shortening the delay between performance and feedback

Feedforward control a mechanism for monitoring performance inputs rather than outputs to prevent or minimize performance deficiencies before they occur

Control loss the situation in which behaviour and work procedures do not conform to standards

Good Tip!

Guidelines for Using Feedforward Control

1. Plan and analyze thoroughly.
2. Be discriminating as you select input variables.
3. Keep the feedforward system dynamic. Don't let it become a matter of habit.
4. Develop a model of the control system.
5. Collect data on input variables regularly.
6. Assess data on input variables regularly.
7. Take action on what you learn.

Sources: Skogestad, S., Postlethwaite. I. (2005). *Multivariable Feedback Control: Analysis and Design.* John Wiley & Sons; Hoboken, NJ; H. Koontz and R. W. Bradspies, "Managing through Feedforward Control: A Future Directed View," Business Horizons 15 (June 1972): 25–36.

1.6 Control Isn't Always Worthwhile or Possible

Control is achieved when behaviour and work procedures conform to standards and goals. By contrast, **control loss** occurs when behaviour and work procedures do not conform to standards.[10] Maintaining control is important because loss of control prevents organizations from achieving their goals. When control loss occurs, managers need to find out what, if anything, they could have done to prevent it. Usually, as discussed above, that means identifying deviations from standard performance, analyzing the causes of those deviations, and taking corrective action. Even so, implementing controls isn't

Automatic "Green"

The provincial government in British Columbia is promoting smart meters as a way for consumers to save money by monitoring and reducing their power usage. BC Hydro has said these meters will allow the distribution system to be used more efficiently and power failures to be identified and repaired more quickly.

Additionally, now you don't have to remember to turn down the thermostat when you leave the office in order to control energy costs. Software start-up companies are creating "green software" programs that keep tabs on your energy use, turn off lights automatically, and figure out when it is cheapest to use energy for flexible tasks such as cooling office space.

The convenience doesn't come cheap: This author was responsible for a project that installed more than $7 million in automated heating, ventilating, and cooling (HVAC) systems at UBC. Honeywell Canada provided the funding, on a payback basis, and everyone was a winner. The payback was guaranteed over a seven-year period and amounted to more than $1.2 million per year.

Sources: McInnes, C. (2013). "Dumb decisions plague B.C.'s smart meter rollout," *Vancouver Sun* Accessed online at http://www.vancouversun.com/opinion/columnists/Dumb+decisions +plague+smart+meter+rollout/7901930/story.html; J. Carlton, "To Cut Fuel Bills, Try High-Tech Help," *The Wall Street Journal*, 11 March 2008, B3.

Regulation costs the costs associated with implementing or maintaining control

Cybernetic feasibility the extent to which it is possible to implement each step in the control process

always worthwhile or possible. Let's look at regulation costs and cybernetic feasibility to see why.

To determine whether control is worthwhile, managers need to carefully assess **regulation costs**, which are the costs associated with implementing or maintaining control. If a control process costs more than an organization gains from its benefits, it may not be worthwhile. Thanks to technology, however, companies are finding it easier (i.e., more feasible) to control many more processes. For example, handwritten prescriptions can be difficult for pharmacists to read, but digital technology can be used to control the accuracy of prescriptions. Doctors can send prescriptions to the pharmacy electronically, and software can alert them to interactions with other drugs that might be harmful to a patient. Newfoundland and Labrador has started to link up 190 pharmacies in a provincial health department project. "A lot of drugs now do have serious interaction between them, and you obviously work with the pharmacy and doctors to try to avoid those," says St. John's pharmacist Chris Hollett. Remembers St. John's pharmacist Tom Healy: "We got a call from a drugstore in Conception Bay North that is also on the same centre of health information network, and he had a customer there who was trying to purchase a codeine product. But the prescription was also dispensed three days before, so we prevented a narcotic from being over dispensed." An Ontario pharmacy assistant discovered that chemotherapy drugs administered to more than 1,200 cancer patients in Ontario and New Brunswick were diluted. He had noticed that the electronic worksheet for calculating the dose for each patient was using the final concentration indicated on an old label. "It's just part of the process, it's part of our job, and it just happens that this check that we made had a broader impact than we certainly would have anticipated," Craig Woudsma said.[11]

Another factor to consider is **cybernetic feasibility**, which is the extent to which it is possible to implement each of the three steps in the control process. If one or more steps cannot be implemented, then maintaining effective control may be difficult or impossible.

How and What to Control

Soon after becoming CEO of Yahoo!, Marrisa Mayer told her 14,500 employees to start driving in to work every day—otherwise they could be terminated. Yoav Schwartz understood immediately why she set this new policy. The CEO of Uberflip, a 20-person start-up based in downtown Toronto, instituted a no-home-office policy just two years after founding the PDF-sharing technology company in 2009. "Over time, we noticed that people working from home were getting out of touch, or the outside developers were not keeping up-to-date with the changes in the organization," he says.[12]

However, not all companies agree. "Mobile workers can be among a company's more productive workers because they often work at different locations within the company or at a client's site," says Michael Thornburrow, senior vice president of corporate real estate at BMO Financial Group. And Richard Branson, the head of Virgin Group PLC, has said on the company's blog that not letting employees work outside the office is "old school thinking."

When you become a manager, what approach will you take to controlling your employees' behaviour?[13]

LO2 Control Methods

Managers can use five different methods to achieve control in their organizations: ***2.1 bureaucratic, 2.2 objective, 2.3 normative, 2.4 concertive,*** *and* ***2.5 self-control.***

Spencer Grant/GetStock.com

2.1 Bureaucratic Control

Bureaucratic control the use of hierarchical authority to influence employee behaviour by rewarding or punishing employees for compliance or noncompliance with organizational policies, rules, and procedures

Most people, when they think of managerial control, have in mind bureaucratic control. **Bureaucratic control** is top-down control—in other words, managers try to influence their employees' behaviour by rewarding (or punishing) them for complying (or not) with organizational policies, rules, and procedures. Most employees, though, would argue that bureaucratic managers emphasize punishment for noncompliance much more than rewards for compliance. For instance, when visiting the company's regional offices and managers, the president of a training company, who was known for his temper and for micromanaging others, would get some toilet paper from the restrooms and demand to know, "What's this?" When the managers answered "toilet paper," the president would scream that it was *two-ply* toilet paper that the company couldn't afford. When told of a cracked toilet seat in one of the women's washrooms, he said, "If you don't like sitting on that seat, you can stand up like I do!"[14]

Yet, as you learned in Chapter 2, bureaucratic management and control were created to prevent precisely this type of managerial behaviour. By encouraging managers to apply well-thought-out rules, policies, and procedures in an impartial, consistent manner to everyone in the organization, bureaucratic control is supposed to make companies more efficient, effective, and fair. Ironically, it often has just the opposite effect: managers who use bureaucratic control often emphasize following the rules above all else.

Another characteristic of bureaucratically controlled companies is that because of their rule- and policy-driven decision making, they are highly resistant to change and slow to respond to customers and competitors. Max Weber, the German sociologist who popularized the bureaucratic ideal,

Be Careful What You Say on Facebook

When a clothing retailer that employed a man who posted negative comments on his Facebook page about the death of Amanda Todd (the teen from Port Coquitlam, B.C., who committed suicide after being bullied on the Internet), it didn't hesitate to take action. The man was fired from his job at a London, Ontario, outlet of Mr. Big and Tall. The company CEO said the firm was taking the action it felt was appropriate. "The vast majority of people believe that what they say outside of the workplace is none of the employer's business," states David Doorey, Associate Professor of Labour and Employment Law at York University's School of Human Resource Management in Toronto. "But that's not true," he continues. "The employer can always fire you for whatever you say ... In a private workplace, there is no right to free expression."

Source: Davidson, J., (2012). "How an online posting can cost you your job." *CBC News*, Oct 18, 2012. Available online at http://www.cbc.ca/news/technology/story/2012/10/17/f-online-postings-job-dismissal.html.

© Marcin Winnicki/Dreamstime.com

Objective control the use of observable measures of worker behaviour or outputs to assess performance and influence behaviour

Behaviour control the regulation of the behaviours and actions that employees perform on the job

Output control the regulation of employees' results or outputs through rewards and incentives

Normative control the regulation of employees' behaviour and decisions through widely shared organizational values and beliefs

referred to bureaucracy as the "iron cage." He wrote that "once fully established, bureaucracy is among those social structures which are the hardest to destroy."[15]

2.2 Objective Control

In many companies, bureaucratic control has evolved into **objective control**, which is the use of observable measures of employee behaviour or output to assess performance and influence behaviour. Bureaucratic control focuses on whether policies and rules are followed, whereas objective control focuses on observing and measuring worker behaviour or output. There are two kinds of objective control: behaviour control and output control.

Behaviour control involves regulating behaviours and actions that people perform on the job. The basic assumption of behaviour control is that if you do the right things (i.e., perform the right behaviours) every day, then those things should lead to goal achievement. Behaviour control is still management-based, however, which means that managers are responsible for monitoring and rewarding employees for exhibiting desired behaviours and helping people overcome undesired behaviours. Companies that use global positioning satellite (GPS) technology to track where their employees are and what they're doing are using behaviour control.

GPS can be used in a multitude of ways. In Winnipeg, youths with multiple car-theft convictions were ordered by the court to wear ankle bracelets. In the first three years of the program, those ankle bracelets were tampered with 39 times. In one case, two chronic offenders stole a vehicle, cut off their GPS-tracking bracelets, and threw them out the window. One of the bracelets landed in the back seat of the stolen car, providing the police with their location.[16]

Instead of measuring what managers and employees do, **output control** measures the results of their efforts. Behaviour control regulates, guides, and measures how employees behave on the job; by contrast, output control gives managers and employees the freedom to behave as they see fit as long as they accomplish pre-specified, measurable results. Output control is often coupled with rewards and incentives.

There are three preconditions for output control and rewards to lead to improved business results. First, the output control measures must be reliable, fair, and accurate. Second, employees and managers must believe they can produce the desired results. If they don't, then the output controls won't affect their behaviour. Third, the rewards or incentives tied to output control measures must truly depend on achieving established standards of performance. This kind of output control can also be applied to CEOs. Robert Bell, CEO of Toronto's sprawling University Health Network, has part of his salary tied to a list of performance measures. "My compensation is dramatically at risk," he says. "If we don't accomplish what the board thinks we should accomplish, I don't get as much salary."[17]

2.3 Normative Control

Another way to control what goes on in an organization involves shaping the beliefs and values of its people. With **normative controls**, a company's widely shared values and beliefs guide employees' behaviour and decisions. High-end retailer Nordstrom, which plans to open five stores in Canada by 2016 (in Ottawa, Calgary, and Vancouver, plus two in Toronto) has one value that permeates the entire workforce from top to bottom: extraordinary customer service. On their very first day at Nordstrom, trainees begin their transformation to the "Nordstrom way" by reading the employee handbook. Sounds boring, doesn't it? But Nordstrom's handbook is printed on *one side* of a 3-by-5-inch note card (see Exhibit 16.2). That's it. No lengthy rules. No specifics about what behaviour is or is not appropriate. Just use your judgment.[18]

Companies that use normative controls are very careful about whom they hire. Many companies screen job applicants on the basis of their abilities; normatively controlled companies are just as likely to screen them for their attitudes and values. For example, before building stores in a new city, Nordstrom sends its human resource team into town to interview prospective employees. In a few cities, the company cancelled its expansion plans when it could not find enough applicants who embodied the service attitudes and values for which Nordstrom is known.[19]

Also, with normative controls, both managers and employees learn what they should and should not do by observing experienced employees and by listening to

Exhibit 16.2 Nordstrom's Employee Handbook

Welcome to Nordstrom's. We're glad to have you with our company. Our Number One goal is to provide outstanding customer service. Set both your personal and professional goals high. We have great confidence in your ability to achieve them.

Nordstrom Rules:

Rule #1: Use your good judgment in all situations. There will be no additional rules. Please feel free to ask your department manager, store manager, or division general manager any question at any time.

Sources: C. Kingsley, "Nordstrom's One and Only Rule," *Washington Post*, April 22, 2010, http://views.washingtonpost.com/leadership/panelists/2010/04/nordstroms-one-and-only-rule.html; M. Linderman, "Nordstrom's Employee Handbook—Short and Sweet," October 27, 2010, http://37signals.com/svn/posts/2632-nordstroms-employee-handbook-mdash-short-and-sweet.

the stories they tell about the company. At Nordstrom, many of these stories—which employees call "heroics"—have been inspired by the company motto, "Respond to Unreasonable Customer Requests!"[20] "Nordies," as Nordstrom employees call themselves, like to tell the story about a customer who just had to have a pair of burgundy Donna Karan slacks that had gone on sale, but she could not find her size. The sales associate who was helping her contacted five nearby Nordstrom stores, but none had the customer's size. So rather than leave the customer dissatisfied with her shopping experience, the sales associate went to her manager for petty cash and then went across the street and paid full price for the slacks at a competitor's store. She then resold them to the customer at Nordstrom's lower sale price.[21] Obviously, Nordstrom would quickly go out of business if this were the norm. Nevertheless, this story makes clear the attitude that drives employee performance at Nordstrom in ways that rules, behavioural guidelines, or output controls could not.

2.4 Concertive Control

Whereas normative controls are based on beliefs that are strongly held and widely shared throughout a company, **concertive controls** are based on beliefs that are shaped and negotiated by work groups.[22] Whereas normative controls are driven by strong organizational cultures, concertive controls usually arise when companies give autonomous work groups complete autonomy and responsibility for task completion. The most autonomous groups operate without managers and are completely responsible for controlling work group processes, outputs, and behaviour. Such groups do their own hiring, firing, worker discipline, work schedules, materials ordering, budget making and meeting, and decision making.

Concertive control is not established overnight. Highly autonomous work groups go through two phases as they develop concertive control. In the first phase, group members learn to work with one another, supervise one another's work, and develop the values and beliefs that will guide and control their behaviour. And because they develop these values and beliefs themselves, work group members feel strongly about following them.

In the steel industry, Nucor, which operates in Canada as the Harris Steel Canada Group, was long considered an upstart compared to the largest steel firms. Yet Nucor has managed to outlast many other mills; indeed, it has bought out many other mills in recent years. Nucor has a unique culture that gives real power to employees on the line and that fosters teamwork throughout the organization. This type of teamwork can be a difficult thing for a newly acquired group of employees to get used to. For example, at Nucor's first big acquisition, David Hutchins is a front-line supervisor or "lead man" in the rolling mill, where steel from the furnace is spread thin enough to be cut into sheets. Under the plant's previous ownership, if the guys doing the cutting got backed up, the guys doing the rolling—including Hutchins—would just take a break. He says, "We'd sit back, have a cup of coffee, and complain: 'Those guys stink.'" It took six months to convince the employees at the plant that the Nucor teamwork way was better than the old way. Now, Hutchins says, "At Nucor, we're not 'you guys' and 'us guys.' It's all of us guys. Wherever the bottleneck is, we go there, and everyone works on it."[23]

Concertive control the regulation of employees' behaviour and decisions through work group values and beliefs

Self-control (self-management) a control system in which managers and employees control their own behaviour by setting their own goals, monitoring their own progress, and rewarding themselves for goal achievement

The second phase in the development of concertive control is the emergence and formalization of objective rules to guide and control behaviour. The beliefs and values developed in the first phase usually develop into more objective rules as new members join teams. The clearer those rules, the easier it becomes for new members to figure out how and how not to behave. Concertive control is not established overnight.

Ironically, concertive control may lead to even higher expectations on employees than bureaucratic control. Under bureaucratic control, most employees only have to worry about pleasing the boss. But with concertive control, their behaviour has to satisfy the rest of the team. One team member says, "I don't have to sit there and look for the boss to be around; and if the boss is not around, I can sit there and talk to my neighbour or do what I want. Now the whole team is around me and the whole team is observing what I'm doing."[24] In addition, with concertive control, team members have a second, much more stressful role to perform—that of making sure their team members adhere to team values and rules.

2.5 Self-Control

Self-control, also known as **self-management**, is a control system in which managers and employees control their own behaviour.[25] Self-control does not result in anarchy, or a state in which everyone gets to do whatever he or she wants. In self-control or self-management, leaders and managers provide employees with clear boundaries within which they may guide and control their own goals and behaviours.[26] Leaders and managers also contribute to self-control by teaching others the skills they need to maximize and monitor their own work effectiveness. In turn, individuals who manage and lead themselves establish self-control by setting their own goals, monitoring their own progress, rewarding or punishing themselves for achieving or for not achieving their self-set goals, and constructing positive thought patterns that remind them of the importance of their goals and their ability to accomplish them.[27]

If you control for just one thing, such as costs, then other dimensions, like marketing, customer service, and quality are likely to suffer.

For example, let's assume you need to do a better job of praising and recognizing the good work that your staff does for you. You can use goal setting, self-observation, and self-reward to self-manage this behaviour. For

Balanced scorecard measurement of organizational performance from four equally important perspectives: finances, customers, internal operations, and innovation and learning

Suboptimization performance improvement in one part of an organization at the expense of decreased performance in another part

Cash flow analysis a type of analysis that predicts how changes in a business will affect its ability to take in more cash than it pays out

self-observation, use a memory app on your mobile smart device for "praise/recognition." Put an annotation or note on the app each time you praise or recognize someone (wait until the person has left before you do this). Keep track for a week. This serves as your baseline or starting point. Simply keeping track will probably increase how often you do this. After a week, assess your baseline or starting point, and then set a specific goal. For instance, if your baseline was twice a day, you might set a specific goal to praise or recognize others' work five times a day. Continue monitoring your performance with your app. Once you've achieved your goal every day for a week, give yourself a reward (perhaps a movie or lunch with a friend at a new restaurant) for achieving your goal.[28]

The components of self-management—self-set goals, self-observation, and self-reward—have their roots in the motivation theories you read about in Chapter 13. The key difference is that the goals, feedback, and rewards originate from employees themselves and not from their managers or organizations.

LO3 What to Control?

In the first section of this chapter, we discussed the basics of the control process and that control isn't always worthwhile or possible. In the second section, we looked at the various ways in which control can be obtained. In this third and final section, we address an equally important issue: "What should managers and the rest of the employees control?" The way a firm answers this question has important implications for most businesses.

If you control for just one thing, such as costs, then other dimensions, such as marketing, customer service, and quality, are likely to suffer. If you try to control for too many things, then managers and employees become confused about what's really important. In the end, successful companies find a balance that comes from doing three or four things right, such as managing costs, providing value, and keeping customers and employees satisfied.

*After reading this section, you should be able to explain **3.1 the balanced scorecard approach to control and how companies can achieve balanced control of company performance by choosing to control 3.2 budgets, cash flows, and economic value added; 3.3 customer defections; 3.4 quality;** and **3.5 waste and pollution.***

3.1 The Balanced Scorecard

Most companies measure performance using standard financial and accounting measures such as return on capital, return on assets, return on investments, cash flow, net income, and net margins. The **balanced scorecard** encourages managers to look beyond traditional financial measures to four different perspectives on company performance. How do customers see us (the customer perspective)? At what must we excel (the internal perspective)? Can we continue to improve and create value (the innovation and learning perspective)? How do we look to shareholders (the financial perspective)?[29]

The balanced scorecard has several advantages over traditional control processes that rely solely on financial measures. First, it forces managers at each level of the company to set specific goals and measure performance in each of the four areas. For example, Exhibit 16.3 shows that Nova Scotia Power Inc. uses different measures, at different levels in its organization, to determine whether it is meeting the standards it has set for itself. The four perspectives are financial, customer, internal, and learning and growth. *Financial* perspectives are very common in businesses: they include ROI, profitability ratios, debt ratios, and so forth. The *customer* perspectives include items such as getting 100 percent power 100 percent of the time—in other words, "What is the power outage rate, and how long do outages last?" *Internal* measures include items such as preventive maintenance; on-time performance; on-time, on-budget capital construction; and power frequency boundaries. *Learning and growth* perspectives deal with employee training, work-safe practices, innovations, and employee–management relations. Each of the corporation's strategic subunit (SBU), and subSBU (department) goals measures the four perspectives along the lines of the overall goals of Nova Scotia Power, which are to (1) cut costs, (2) build customer loyalty, (3) build the business, and (4) develop employee commitment.

The second major advantage of the balanced scorecard approach to control is that it minimizes the chances of **suboptimization**, which occurs when performance improves in one area but simultaneously decreases in others. As an example, Jon Meliones, chief medical director at a major children's hospital, says: "We could increase productivity ... by assigning more patients to a nurse, but doing so would raise the likelihood of errors—an unacceptable trade-off."[30]

Let's examine some of the ways that companies are controlling the four basic parts of the balanced scorecard: the financial perspective (budgets, cash flows, economic value added [EVA]); the customer perspective (customer defections); the internal perspective (total quality management); and the innovation and learning perspective (waste and pollution).

3.2 The Financial Perspective: Controlling Budgets, Cash Flows, and EVA

The traditional approach to controlling financial performance focuses on accounting tools such as cash flow analysis, balance sheets, income statements, financial ratios, and budgets. **Cash flow analysis** predicts how changes in a business will affect its ability to take in more cash

Exhibit 16.3 Nova Scotia Power Inc.'s Balanced Score Card

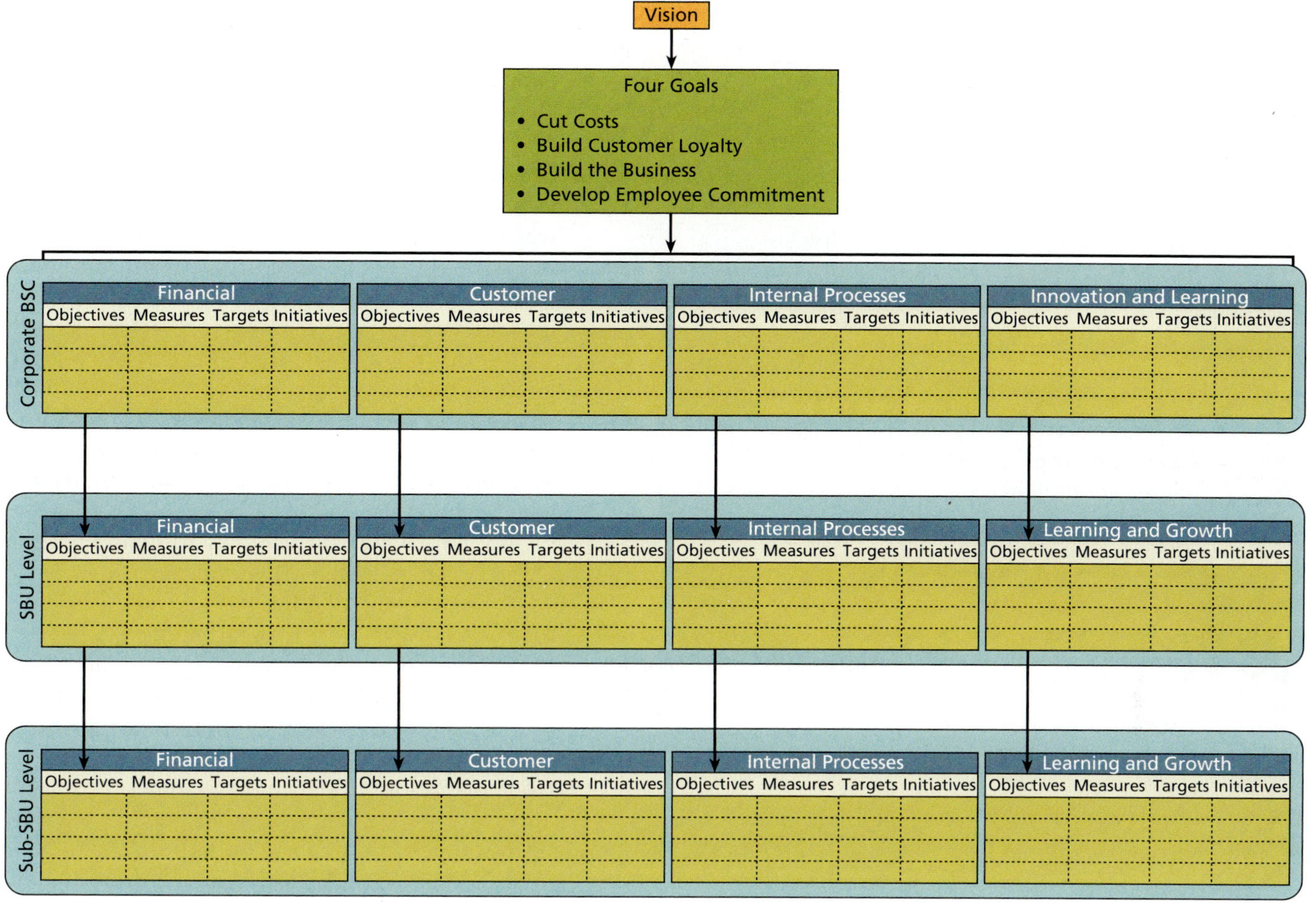

Source: Niven, P., 2006. Cascading the balanced scorecard: A case Study on Nova Scotia Power, Inc. http://www.scribd.com/doc/3489336/Cascading-the-Balanced-Scorecard-A-Case-Study-on-Nova-Scotia-Power. Accessed 19 June 2010. Reprinted by permission.

than it pays out. **Balance sheets** provide a snapshot of a company's financial position at a particular time (but not the future). **Income statements**, also called profit and loss statements, show what has happened to an organization's income, expenses, and net profit (income less expenses) over a period of time. **Financial ratios** are typically used to track a business's liquidity (cash), efficiency, and profitability over time compared to other businesses in its industry. Finally, **budgets** are used to project costs and revenues, prioritize and control spending, and ensure that expenses don't exceed available funds and revenues. The Financial Review Card bound in the back of this book contains tables that (a) show the basic steps or parts for cash flow analyses, balance sheets, and income statements; (b) list a few of the most common financial ratios and explain how they are calculated, what they mean, and when to use them; and (c) review the different kinds of budgets that managers can use to track and control company finances.

By themselves, none of these tools—cash flow analyses, balance sheets, income statements, financial ratios, or budgets—tell the whole financial story of a business. They must be used together when assessing a company's financial performance. Since these tools are reviewed in detail in your accounting and finance classes, only a brief overview is provided here. Still, these are necessary tools for controlling organizational finances and expenses, and they should be part of your business toolbox.

Though no one would dispute the importance of these four accounting tools, accounting research also indicates that the complexity and sheer amount of information contained in them can shut down the brain and glaze over the eyes of even the most experienced manager.[31] Sometimes there's simply too much information to make sense of. The balanced scorecard simplifies things by focusing on one simple question when it comes to finances: How do we look to shareholders? One way to answer that question is through something called economic value added.

Balance sheets accounting statements that provide a snapshot of a company's financial position at a particular time

Income statements accounting statements, also called "profit and loss statements," that show what has happened to an organization's income, expenses, and net profit over a period of time

Financial ratios calculations typically used to track a business's liquidity (cash), efficiency, and profitability over time compared to other businesses in its industry

Budgets quantitative plans through which managers decide how to allocate available money to best accomplish company goals

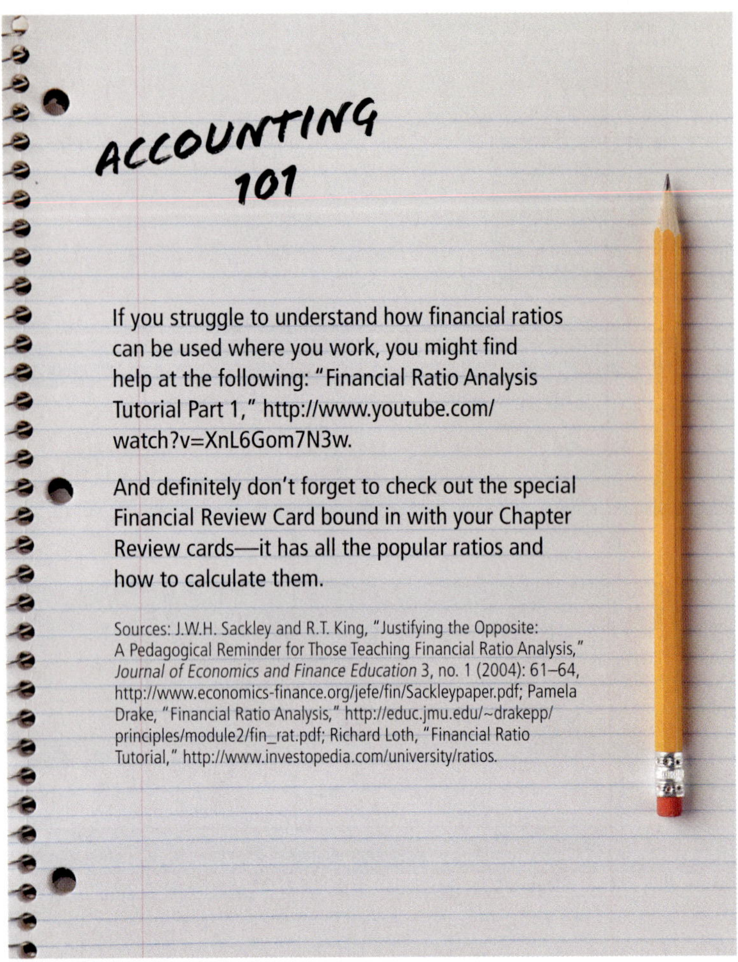

AER/Shutterstock

Economic value added (EVA) the amount by which company profits (revenues, minus expenses, minus taxes) exceed the cost of capital in a given year

Conceptually, **economic value added (EVA)** is not the same thing as profits. It is the amount by which profits exceed the cost of capital in a given year. It is based on the simple idea that capital is necessary to run a business and that capital comes at a cost. Although most people think of capital as cash, once it is invested (i.e., spent), capital is more likely to be found in a business in the form of computers, manufacturing plants, employees, raw materials, and so forth. And just as with the interest that a homeowner pays on a mortgage or that a college student pays on a student loan, there is a cost to that capital.

The most common costs of capital are the interest paid on long-term bank loans used to buy all those resources, the interest paid to bondholders (who lend organizations their money), and the dividends (cash payments) and growth in stock value that accrue to shareholders. EVA is positive when company profits (revenues minus expenses minus taxes) exceed the cost of capital in a given year. In other words, if a business is to truly grow, its revenues must be large enough to cover both short-term costs (annual expenses and taxes) and long-term costs (the cost of borrowing capital from bondholders and shareholders). If you're a bit confused, Clay Gillespie, portfolio manager with Vancouver-based Rogers Group Financial, states that when considering debt, "I would only recommend its use if your normal cash flow can pay the debt. Most individuals who use leverage get in trouble when they assume the investment can always pay the debt. This will not always be the case."[32]

Exhibit 16.4 shows how to calculate EVA. First, starting with a company's income statement, you calculate the net operating profit after taxes (NOPAT) by subtracting taxes owed from income from operations. (Remember, a quick review of an income statement is on the Financial Review Card bound at the back of your book.) The NOPAT shown in Exhibit 16.4 is $3,500,000. Second, identify how much capital the company has invested (i.e., spent). Total liabilities (what the company owes) less accounts payable and less accrued expenses (neither of which you pay interest on), provides a rough approximation of this amount. In Exhibit 16.4, total capital invested is $16,800,000. Third, calculate the cost (i.e., rate) paid for capital by determining the interest paid to bondholders (who lend organizations their money), which is usually somewhere between 5 and 8 percent, and the return that shareholders want in terms of dividends and stock price appreciation, which is historically about 13 percent. Take a weighted average of the two to determine the overall cost of capital. In your

Exhibit 16.4 Calculating Economic Value Added (EVA)

1. Calculate net operating profit after taxes (NOPAT).	$3,500,000
2. Identify how much capital the company has invested (i.e., spent).	$16,800,000
3. Determine the cost (i.e., rate) paid for capital (usually between 5 percent and 13 percent).	10%
4. Multiply capital used (Step 2) times cost of capital (Step 3).	(10% × $16,800,000) = $1,680,000
5. Subtract the total dollar cost of capital from net profit after taxes.	$3,500,000 NOPAT −$1,680,000 Total cost of capital $1,820,000 Economic value added

finance classes in future years you will learn more about the average weighted cost of capital, but these two facets (bond and dividends) will suffice for our example.

In Exhibit 16.4, the cost of capital is 10 percent. Fourth, multiply the total capital ($16,800,000) from Step 2 by the cost of capital (10 percent) from Step 3. In Exhibit 16.4, this amount is $1,680,000. Fifth, subtract the total dollar cost of capital in Step 4 from the NOPAT in Step 1. In Exhibit 16.4, this value is $1,820,000, which means that our example company has created economic value or wealth this year. If our EVA number had been negative, meaning that the company didn't make enough profit to cover the cost of capital from bondholders and shareholders, then the company would have destroyed economic value or wealth by taking in more money than it returned.[33]

Why is EVA so important? First and most important, because it includes the cost of capital, it shows whether a business, division, department, profit centre, or product is really paying for itself. The key is to make sure that managers and employees can see how their choices and behaviour affect the company's EVA.

Second, because EVA can easily be determined for subsets of a company such as divisions, regional offices, manufacturing plants, and sometimes even departments, it makes managers and employees at all levels pay much closer attention to their own segments of the business. When company offices were being refurbished at Genesco, a shoe company, a worker who had EVA training handed CEO Ben Harris $4,000 in cash. The worker explained that he now understood the effect his job had on the company's ability to survive and prosper. Since the company was struggling, he had sold the old doors that had been removed during remodelling so that the company could have the cash.[34] In other words, EVA motivates managers and employees to think like small business owners who must scramble to contain costs and generate enough business to meet their bills each month. And, unlike many kinds of financial controls, EVA doesn't specify what should or should not be done to improve performance. Thus, it encourages managers and employees to be creative in looking for ways to improve EVA performance.

Remember that EVA is the amount by which profits exceed the cost of capital in a given year. So the more that EVA exceeds the total dollar cost of capital, the better a company has used investors' money that year. Market value added (MVA) is simply the cumulative EVA created by a company over time. Thus, MVA indicates how much value or wealth a company has created or destroyed in total during its existence. The top ten Canadian companies by MVA and EVA are listed in Exhibit 16.5.

3.3 The Customer Perspective: Controlling Customer Defections

Customer defections a performance assessment in which companies identify which customers are leaving and measure the rate at which they are leaving

The second aspect of organizational performance that the balanced scorecard helps managers monitor is customers. It does so by forcing managers to address this question: "How do customers see us?" Unfortunately, most companies try to answer this question through customer satisfaction surveys, but these are often misleadingly positive. Most customers are reluctant to talk about their problems because they don't know who to complain to or think that complaining will not do any good. Companies are beginning to realize that social media, including chat groups and Facebook, are a source for gut reaction comments about them.[35]

Customer satisfaction surveys can be misleading because even very satisfied customers often switch to competitors. Studies indicate that companies may be farther ahead monitoring **customer defections**—that is, by identifying which customers are

© Tracy Hebden/Dreamstime.com; Bank of Canada.

Exhibit 16.5 Top 10 Canadian Companies by Market Value Added and Economic Value Added

	Market Value Added ($ 000)	Economic Value Added ($ 000)
Toronto-Dominion Bank	131,449,500	3,755,700
Bank of Nova Scotia	43,705,200	3,121,800
Royal Bank of Canada	105,732,000	1,762,200
Barrick Gold	90,121,200	3,466,200
Suncor Energy	13,597,200	755,400
Imperial Oil	7,640,400	636,700
Bank of Montreal	47,767,200	1,837,200
CIBC	33,954,900	1,787,100
Potash Corp. of Saskatchewan	22,287,600	2,476,400
Teck Resources	46,056,400	1,771,400

Sources: "The Top 1000," *Globe and Mail*, June 21, 2012; A.K. Sharma and S. Kumar, "Economic Value Added (EVA)—Literature Review and Relevant Issues," *International Journal of Economics and Finance* 30, no. 2 (2009), http://www.ccsenet.org/journal/index.php/ijef/article/download/5908/4688; H. Armitage and C. Ha, 2003, "The Pursuit of Value: EVA in Canada—An Uncertain Legacy," *Society of Management Accountants of Canada Magazine*; Stern Steward & Co., http://www.sternstewart.com.

abandoning them and at what rate. After all, customer defections have a great effect on profits.

Very few managers realize that landing a new customer costs ten times as much as keeping a current one. In fact, the cost of replacing old customers with new ones is so great that most companies could double their profits by increasing their customer retention rates by just 5 to 10 percent per year.[36] And if a company can keep a customer for life, the benefits are even greater.

The second reason to study customer defections is that customers who have left are much more likely than current customers to tell you what you were doing wrong. Finally, companies that understand why customers leave not only can take steps to fix ongoing problems, but also can identify which customers are likely to leave and make changes to prevent them from leaving.

3.4 The Internal Perspective: Controlling Quality

The third part of the balanced scorecard, the internal perspective, relates to the processes, decisions, and actions that managers and employees make within the organization. The internal perspective asks this question: "At what must we excel?" The internal perspective of the balanced scorecard usually leads managers to focus on quality.

Quality is typically defined and measured in three ways: excellence, value, and conformance to expectations.[37] When the company defines its quality goal as *excellence,* managers must try to produce a product or service of unsurpassed performance and features. For example, Singapore Airlines is the best airline in the world by almost any standard. It has also received various "best airline" awards from the *Pacific Asia Travel Association, Travel+Leisure, Business Traveller, Conde Nast Traveller,* and *Fortune.*[38] Many airlines try to cram passengers into every available inch on a plane; by contrast, Singapore Airlines delivers creature comforts to encourage repeat business and customers willing to pay premium prices. On its newer planes, the first-class cabin is divided into eight private mini-rooms, each with an unusually wide leather seat that folds down flat for sleeping, a 23-inch LCD TV that doubles as a computer monitor, and an adjustable table. These amenities and services are common in private jets but truly unique in the commercial airline industry.[39] Singapore Airlines was the first airline, in the 1970s, to introduce a choice of meals, complimentary drinks, and earphones in coach class. It was also the first to introduce worldwide video, news, telephone, and fax services and the first to feature personal video monitors for movies, news, documentaries, and games. Singapore Airlines has had AC power for laptop computers for some time, and recently it became the first airline to introduce on-board high-speed Internet access.

The Dreaded Mobile Contract

Alain Theriault tells of an experience that many of us have suffered through: the dreaded mobile contract. After dropping his BlackBerry into a swimming pool, he decided to "upgrade" to the latest iPhone (after he bought out his current contract with TELUS, which he did in order to change his phone). However, after waiting two weeks for delivery he was told he could not get the new Apple product—they were for "new" customers only.

"Find me a solution here my friend. The Bell guys are just on the other side of the corridor … but let's do a quick overview. The records show that I give you an average of $100/month on phone/data bills; that's $3600 on a 3 year contract, plus $300 for the phone, SO, that is a MINIMUM of $4000 that you guys are leaving on the table. I'm throwing you a lifeline here …"

"I can't …"

"Well tell your manager that he lost that … Thanks for your time and effort."

It can cost up to 10 times more to get new customers than to satisfy existing ones. Also, most companies pay bonuses to their salespeople based on *new* acquired business rather than paying bonuses to keep the existing ones.

Sources: Theriault, A. *The Startup Coach,* Available online at http://alaintheriault.com/startupcoaching/2010/08/customer-satisfaction-when-telus-chooses-to-leave-4k-on-the-table/; Customer Lifetime Value Calculator, http://hbsp.harvard.edu/multimedia/flashtools/cltv/; Sugars, B. (2012). "How to Calculate the Lifetime Value of a Customer," *Entrepreneur.* Available online at http://www.entrepreneur.com/article/224153.

MGMT TREND

Vertical Integration—Bucking the Trend or the New Trend?

According to an American Society for Quality (ASQ) 2013 Survey, one-third of respondents said they anticipated a shortage of parts due to a problem with a supplier this year. Wages in China and oil prices are up. Higher shipping costs, difficult communication, concerns about IP, long lead times, and concerns about quality have manufacturers rethinking. With all the buzz around "onshoring," one needs to consider whether vertical integration might be the next wave. Furthermore, many are worried about quality. GE, Apple, and Lenovo have announced investments in new North American facilities so that they can help regain control of quality.

Bao fan - Imaginechina via AP Images

Sources: Wiseman, P. (2013), "Vertical Integration – Bucking the Trend or the New Trend?" Technology Forecasters Inc. Available online at: http://www.techforecasters.com/archives/vertical-integration-bucking-the-trend-or-the-new-trend/; ASQ. (2013). "Suppliers confident, manufacturers concerned about supply chain after being burned in the past: ASQ Survey" Available Online at: http://www.asq.org/media-room/press-releases/2012/20121220-suppliers-manufacturers-survey.html

Value is the customer's perception that a product's quality is excellent for the price offered. At a higher price, customers may perceive the same product to be less of a value. When a company emphasizes value as its quality goal, managers must simultaneously control excellence, price, durability, and other features of a product or service that customers strongly associate with value. Loblaw currently operates under 22 different banners, including Independent, Zehrs, Superstore, Wholesale Club, Valuemart, No Frills, Maxi, Loblaws, and Provigo, and all of these operate on the principle of bringing maximum value to customers. Loblaw was always known for the quality, innovation, and value of its food offerings. In late 2009, however, Galen Weston said: "We are not delivering the right value for money. Our actual prices relative to Wal-Mart are significantly higher than we thought." Loblaw had to turn that around, and it did. It now offers Canada's strongest control label program (private label), one that includes President's Choice. People will pay extra for a product that has a high value but that, technically, is not a name brand. President's Choice has consistently beaten name brand rivals in taste and quality. In remarks accompanying record earnings released in Quarter 1 of 2013, executive chairman Galen G. Weston said that thanks to this simple "value" approach to business, "our fresh-led, customer-focused strategy is delivering results."[40]

When a company defines its quality goal as conformance to specifications, employees must base their decisions and actions on whether the services and products they offer measure up to the standard. In contrast to excellence and value-based definitions of quality, which can be somewhat ambiguous, measuring whether products and services are "in spec" is relatively easy. Although conformance to specifications (i.e., precise tolerances for a part's weight or thickness) is usually associated with manufacturing, it can be used equally well to control quality in nonmanufacturing jobs. Exhibit 16.6 (page 288) shows a checklist that a cook or restaurant owner would use to ensure quality when buying fresh fish.

Value customer perception that the product quality is excellent for the price offered

The way in which a company defines quality affects the methods and measures that employees use to control quality. Exhibit 16.7 (page 288) shows the advantages

Fred Lum/The Globe and Mail, © Copyright The Globe and Mail Inc.

Exhibit 16.6 Conformance to Specifications Checklist for Buying Fresh Fish

Quality Checklist For Buying Fresh Fish		
Fresh Whole Fish	**Acceptable**	**Not Acceptable**
Gills	✓ bright red, free of slime, clear mucus	✗ brown to greyish, thick, yellow mucus
Eyes	✓ clear, bright, bulging, black pupils	✗ dull, sunken, cloudy, grey pupils
Smell	✓ inoffensive, slight ocean smell	✗ ammonia, putrid smell
Skin	✓ opalescent sheen, scales adhere tightly to skin	✗ dull or faded colour, scales missing or easily removed
Flesh	✓ firm and elastic to touch, tight to the bone	✗ soft and flabby, separating from the bone
Belly cavity	✓ no viscera or blood visible, lining intact, no bone protruding	✗ incomplete evisceration, cuts or protruding bones, off-odour

Sources: "A Closer Look: Buy It Fresh, Keep It Fresh," *Consumer Reports Online*, [Online] available at http://www.seagrant.sunysb.edu/SeafoodTechnology/SeafoodMedia/cR02-2001/CR-SeafoodII020101.htm, 20 June 2005; "How To Purchase: Buying Fish," AboutSeaFood Web site, [Online] available at http://www.aboutseafood.com/faqs/purchase1.html, 20 June 2005.

and disadvantages associated with the excellence, value, and conformance-to-specification definitions of quality.

3.5 The Innovation and Learning Perspective: Controlling Waste and Pollution

The last part of the balanced scorecard, the innovation and learning perspective, addresses this question: "Can we continue to improve and create value?" Thus, the innovation and learning perspective involves continuous improvement in ongoing products and services (see Chapter 18); relearning and redesigning the processes by which products and services are created (see Chapter 7); and even things like waste and pollution minimization, an increasingly important area of innovation.

Exhibit 16.8 shows the four levels of waste minimization ranging from waste disposal, which produces the smallest minimization of waste, to waste prevention and reduction, which produces the greatest

Exhibit 16.7 Advantages and Disadvantages of Different Measures of Quality

Quality Measure	Advantages	Disadvantages
Excellence	Promotes clear organizational vision.	Provides little practical guidance for managers.
	Being/providing the "best" motivates and inspires managers and employees.	Excellence is ambiguous. What is it? Who defines it?
	Appeals to customers, who "know excellence when they see it."	Difficult to measure and control.
Value	Customers recognize differences in value.	Can be difficult to determine what factors influence whether a product/service is seen as having value.
	Easier to measure and compare whether products/services differ in value.	Controlling the balance between excellence and cost (i.e., affordable excellence) can be difficult.
Conformance to Specifications	If specifications can be written, conformance to specifications is usually measurable.	Many products/services cannot be easily evaluated in terms of conformance to specifications.
	Should lead to increased efficiency.	Promotes standardization, so may hurt performance when adapting to changes is more important.
	Promotes consistency in quality.	May be less appropriate for services, which are dependent on a high degree of human contact.

Source: C. A. Reeves and D. A. Bednar, "Defining Quality: Alternatives and Implications," *Academy of Management Review* 19 (1994): 419–445.

Exhibit 16.8 Four Levels of Waste Minimization

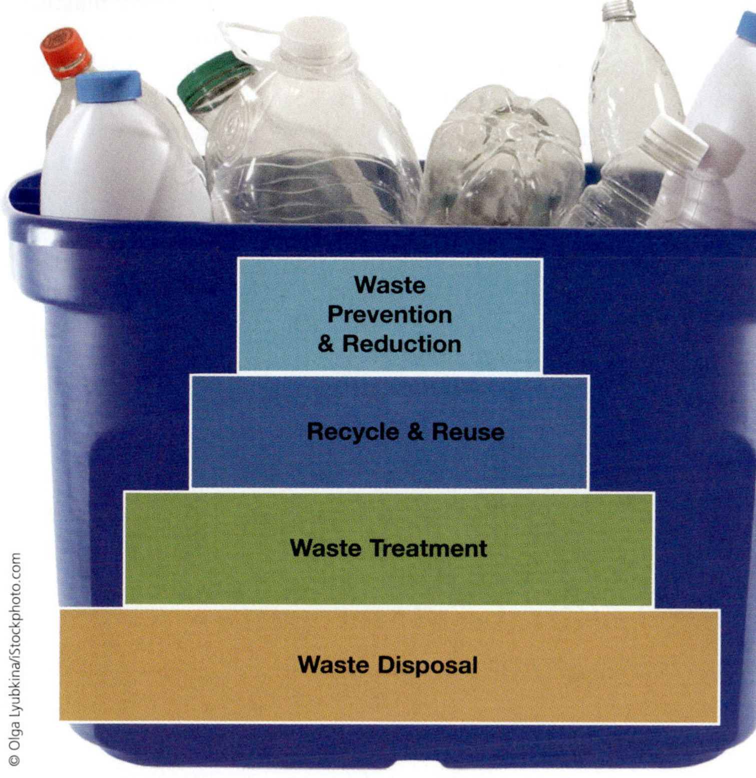

© Olga Lyubkina/Stockphoto.com

Source: Reprinted from D.R. May & B.L. Flannery, "Cutting Waste with Employee Involvement Teams," *Business Horizons*, September–October 1995, 28–38, with permission from Elsevier.

minimization.[41] The goal of the top level, *waste prevention and reduction,* is to prevent waste and pollution before they occur and to reduce them when they do occur. For example, United Parcel Service (UPS) uses a software program that helps drivers plan routes with only right turns to save driving time. The strategy also prevents environmental waste, since UPS saves more than 11 million litres of fuel each year and reduces CO_2 emissions by 31,000 metric tons.[42] There are three strategies for waste prevention and reduction:

1. **Good housekeeping.** Examples of this include performing regularly scheduled preventive maintenance for offices and plants and making sure that machines are running properly so that they don't use more fuel than necessary.
2. **Material/product substitution.** Examples include replacing toxic or hazardous materials with less harmful ones. As part of its Pollution Prevention Pays program, 3M Canada over the past 30 years has eliminated almost 100 million kilograms of pollutants and saved $1 billion by using benign substitutes for toxic solvents in its manufacturing processes.[43]
3. **Process modification.** Examples include changing steps or procedures to eliminate or reduce waste. Terracycle is a manufacturer of plant food made from the castings (i.e., droppings) of red worms that have feasted on various types of organic waste. But rather than package the plant food in new bottles, Terracycle packages its product in used beverage containers and ships the bottles in recycled boxes to the retailers. The company's entire process operation is 100 percent geared toward reducing or eliminating waste.[44]

At the second level of waste minimization, *recycle and reuse,* wastes are reduced by reusing materials as long as possible or by collecting materials for on- or off-site recycling. A growing trend in recycling is *design for disassembly*, where products are designed from the start for easy disassembly, recycling, and reuse once they are no longer usable. Alberta has been doing a lot to recycle. Albertans recycle standard-sized beer bottles (which are reused rather than recycled) and all other beverage containers. Containers are collected at privately owned for-profit bottle depots (as of 2012 there were more than 200 such bottle depots in Alberta).[45] Most of Alberta's larger municipalities have Blue Box recycling programs. In that province, curbside recycling of newsprint, cardboard, plastic packaging, and other nonfood household wastes is a municipal responsibility. Edmonton has citywide curbside recycling for single-family houses; it also recycles Christmas trees and construction waste. Higher levels of processing including large-scale composting and capturing methane to produce energy. In 2010, collection included multifamily buildings and businesses. It is expected that once the waste-to-biofuel plant is completed in 2013, Edmonton will divert 90 percent of its waste from landfills.[46] By contrast, Calgary currently collects recyclables only at private houses, and has no plans to introduce collection at condo and apartment buildings before 2015.[47]

At the third level of waste minimization, *waste treatment*, companies use biological, chemical, and other processes to turn potentially harmful wastes into harmless compounds or useful byproducts. For example, during "pickling," a process in the manufacture of steel sheets, the steel is bathed in an acid solution to clean impurities and oxides

Bakalusha/Shutterstock.com

(which would rust) from its surface. Fortunately, Magnetics International has found a safe and profitable way to treat the pickle juice, which it sprays into a 30-metre-high chamber at 650 degrees Celsius to form pure iron oxide, which can then be transformed into a useful magnetic powder for reuse in electric motors, stereo speakers, and refrigerator gaskets.[48]

The fourth and lowest level of waste minimization is waste disposal. Wastes that cannot be prevented, reduced, recycled, reused, or treated should be safely disposed of in processing plants or in environmentally secure landfills that prevent leakage and contamination of soil and underground water supplies. For example, with the average computer lasting just three years, approximately 60 million computers come out of service each year. But because of the lead in the monitors, toxic metals in the circuit boards, paint-coated plastic, and metal coatings that can contaminate ground water, old computers, tablets, and phones can't just be thrown away.[49] Hewlett Packard has started a unique computer disposal program that allows companies or individual computer users to recycle PCs and electronic equipment. HP has collected and recycled more than 315 million kilograms of used computer equipment and collected more than 97 million printer cartridges. The materials found in these old components can be used to make new HP products as well as new airplane parts, shoe soles, wagons, and fenceposts.[50] For more about this, visit Google HP Recycle Canada. HP makes no profit from this service.

Go online at
www.nelson.com/4ltrpress/icanmgmt2
And access the essential Study Tools online for this chapter:

- **Flashcards**, to help you study
- **Interactive Quizzes**, to test your knowledge
- **Audio Chapter Summaries**, for chapter review
- **Crossword Puzzles and Beat the Clock**, to review key terms
- **What Would You Do? Cases**, for applying your knowledge to real-life situations
- **Self Assessments**, to learn about what kind of manager you are
- **Videos and Media Quizzing**, where you can watch a video about a real-life company and test yourself on what you've learned

Be sure to consult the Chapter Review Card at the back of the textbook.

17

Managing Information in a Global World

LEARNING OUTCOMES

LO1 Explain the strategic importance of information.

LO2 Describe the characteristics of useful information (i.e., its value and costs).

LO3 Explain the basics of capturing, processing, and protecting information.

LO4 Describe how companies can access and share information and knowledge.

pairs well with

PSL Images/GetStock.com/© Tim Boyle/Getty Images

... if you're a dad in a hurry after work.

user telling the data mining software to look and test for specific patterns and relationships in a data set. Typically, this is done through a series of "what if?" questions or statements. For instance, a grocery store manager might instruct the data mining software to determine whether coupons placed in the Sunday paper increase or decrease sales. By contrast, with **unsupervised data mining**, the user simply tells the data mining software to uncover whatever patterns and relationships it can find in a data set. For example, State Farm Insurance used to have three pricing categories for car insurance, depending on one's driving record: *preferred* for the best drivers, *standard* for typical drivers, and *nonstandard* for the worst drivers. Now, however, it has moved to tiered pricing based on the 300 different kinds of driving records that its data mining software has been able to discover.[24]

Unsupervised data mining is especially good at identifying association or affinity patterns, sequence patterns, and predictive patterns. It can also identify what data mining technicians call data clusters.[25] **Association or affinity patterns** arise when two or more database elements tend to occur together in a significant way. Surprisingly, one company found that beer and diapers tended to be bought together between 5 and 7 p.m. The question, of course, was "why?" The answer, on further review, was fairly straightforward: fathers, who were told by their wives to buy some diapers on their way home, decided to pick up a six-pack for themselves, too.[26]

Sequence patterns occur when two or more database elements occur together in a significant pattern in which one of the elements precedes the other. StratBridge provides data mining capability to professional sports teams so that they can analyze their ticket sales in real time. Its StratTix software can help a team view up-to-the-minute seating charts to see which seats are selling and which are not. It also provides information about the people purchasing the tickets—for example, their geographic area and which source they used to purchase them (Ticketmaster, etc.). And it helps teams find the best time to market and promote games, and tells them which prices (at which times) will provide the best revenues. StratBridge has deals with most teams in the National Hockey League, so when you go to the Rogers Arena in Vancouver to watch the Canucks, you know you are getting the best seat at the best price.[27]

Predictive patterns are the opposite of association or affinity patterns. Association or affinity patterns look for database elements that seem to go together, whereas **predictive patterns** help identify database elements that are different.

The Hudson's Bay Company (HBC), Canada's oldest company, generates a tremendous amount of data, but for a long time it was spread across a number of operational systems. The implementation of a centralized data warehouse for its 500 stores, combined with database query manager programs, turned out to be an excellent investment. HBC is now able to ensure that the right inventory is in the right location at the right time. In addition, it is now making inventory and buying decisions based on analyses of detailed transaction data, and market basket analysis has uncovered product affinities that have led to more effective promotions. The new system has also cut down on fraud against the company.[28]

Data clusters occur when three or more database elements converge in a significant way. After analyzing several years' worth of repair and warranty claims, Ford Motor Company might find that, compared to cars built in its Mississauga plant, the cars it builds in Oakville (first element) are more likely to have problems with overtightened fan belts (second element) that break (third element) and result in overheated engines (fourth element), ruined radiators (fifth element), and payments for tow trucks (sixth element), which are paid for by Ford's three-year, 36,000 mile warranty.

Unsupervised data mining the process when the user simply tells the data mining software to uncover whatever patterns and relationships it can find in a data set

Association or affinity patterns when two or more database elements tend to occur together in a significant way

Sequence patterns when two or more database elements occur together in a significant pattern, but one of the elements precedes the other

Predictive patterns patterns that help identify database elements that are different

Data clusters when three or more database elements occur together (i.e., cluster) in a significant way

Protecting information the process of ensuring that data are reliably and consistently retrievable in a usable format for authorized users but no one else

Authentication making sure potential users are who they claim to be

Authorization granting authenticated users approved access to data, software, and systems

Data mining services and analyses are much more affordable than they used to be, within reach of most companies' budgets. And if it follows the path of most technologies, it will become even easier and cheaper to use in the future.

3.3 Protecting Information

Protecting information is the process of ensuring that data are reliably and consistently retrievable in a usable format for authorized users but no one else. Customers who purchase prescription medicines at CanadaDrugs.com, an online drugstore and health aid retailer, want to be confident that their medical and credit card information is available only to them, their pharmacist, and their doctor. Visit CanadaDrugs.com and click "Privacy Policy."

Companies like CanadaDrugs.com find it necessary to protect information because of the many security threats to data listed in Exhibit 17.3 (see page 302). People inside and outside companies can steal or destroy company data in various ways. For example, denial-of-service Web server attacks have brought down some of the busiest and best-run sites on the Internet; viruses and spyware/adware can spread quickly and result in data loss and business disruption; keystroke monitoring monitors and stores every mouse click and keystroke you make and sends that information to unauthorized users; and password-cracking software steals supposedly secure passwords. Finally, there is phishing, where fake but real-looking e-mails and websites trick users into sharing personal information (usernames, passwords, or account numbers).

Malware infects 30 percent of computers. A recently released report on computer viruses indicated that 48 percent of the 22 million computers scanned for the study were infected with malware. Over a million and a half were infected with crimeware or banker trojans. Also, only one-third were running behind a protected firewall (see below). Studies have found that the threats listed in Exhibit 17.3 are so widespread that automatic attacks will begin on an unprotected computer just 15 seconds after it connects to the Internet.[29]

As shown in the right-hand column of Exhibit 17.3, many steps can be taken to secure data and data networks. Some of the most important involve authentication and authorization, firewalls, antivirus software for PCs and e-mail servers, data encryption, and virtual private networks.[30] We will review those steps and then finish this section with a brief review of the dangers of wireless networks, which are exploding in popularity.

Two critical steps are required to ensure that data can be accessed by authorized users and no one else. One is **authentication**, that is, making sure users are who they claim to be.[31] The other is **authorization**, that is, granting authenticated users approved access to data, software,

You Are How You Type

A new form of biometrics involves identifying people by the way they type. Behavioural biometrics uses the unique characteristics of a person's typing for establishing identity. Keystroke dynamics technology offers security by enabling mobile devices to monitor and authenticate their users. Such devices are used so often in m-commerce that it must be possible to secure their data if they are lost or stolen. Biometric solutions to this problem are being developed that identify users based on their typing patterns. Several vendors are developing AI software that monitors your speed, how long you take to select keys, and the rhythm you use to key in your text. The more you use the software, the better it can identify *you* as the typist, making it nearly impossible for someone to hack into your computer. BioPassword is as accurate as finger and iris scans.

Sources: Behavioural Biometrics, (2013). The Biometrics Institute. Available online at http://www.biometricsinstitute.org/pages/types-of-biometrics.html; Ngugi, B., Kahn, B.K., and Tremaine, R. (2011). "Typing Biometrics: Impact of Human Learning on Performance Quality," *Journal of Data and Information Quality* 2(2), 22–29.

and systems.[32] When an ATM prompts you to enter your PIN number, the bank is authenticating that you are you. Once you've been authenticated, you are authorized to access your own funds and no one else's. Of course, as anyone who has lost a PIN or password or had one stolen knows, user authentication systems are not foolproof. In particular, users create security risks by not changing their default account passwords (such as birth dates) or by using weak passwords such as names ("Larry") or complete words ("football"), which are quickly guessed by password cracker software.[33]

All of this is why many companies are now turning to **two-factor authentication**, which is based on what users know, such as a password, and what they have, such as a secure ID card. For example, to log on to their computer accounts, employees at one company must enter a password, such as a four-digit PIN, plus a secure number that changes every 60 seconds and that is displayed on the tiny screen of the secure electronic ID they carry (about the size of a pack of gum). Other companies are turning to biometrics for authentication. With **biometrics** such as fingerprint recognition or iris scanning, users are identified by unique, measurable body features.[34] Of course, since some fingerprint scanners can be fooled by fingerprint moulds, some companies are taking security measures even further by requiring users to simultaneously scan their fingerprint *and* insert a secure, smart card containing a digital file of their fingerprint. This is another form of two-factor authentication.

Unfortunately, stolen or cracked passwords are not the only way for hackers and electronic thieves to gain access to an organization's computer resources. Unless special safeguards are put in place, every time corporate users are online there's literally nothing between their personal computer and the Internet (home users with high-speed DSL or cable Internet access face the same risks). Hackers can access files, run programs, and control key parts of computers if precautions aren't taken. To reduce these risks, companies use **firewalls**, which are hardware or software devices that sit between the computers in an internal organizational network and outside networks such as the Internet. Firewalls filter and check incoming and outgoing data. They also prevent company insiders from accessing unauthorized sites or from sending confidential company information to people outside the company. Firewalls also prevent outsiders from identifying and gaining access to company computers and data. If a firewall is working properly, the computers behind the company firewall literally cannot be seen or accessed by outsiders.

A **virus** is a program or piece of code that, without your knowledge, attaches itself to other programs on your computer and can trigger anything from a harmless flashing message to the reformatting of your hard drive to a systemwide network shutdown. You used to have to do or run something to get a virus—for example, double click on an infected e-mail attachment. Today's viruses are much more threatening. In fact, with some viruses, just being connected to a network can infect your computer. *Antivirus software for personal computers* scans e-mail, downloaded files, and computer hard drives, disk drives, and memory to detect and stop computer viruses from

Two-factor authentication authentication based on what users know, such as a password, and what they have in their possession, such as a secure ID card or key

Biometrics identifying users by unique, measurable body features, such as fingerprint recognition or iris scanning

Firewall a protective hardware or software device that sits between the computers in an internal organizational network and outside networks, such as the Internet

Virus a program or piece of code that, against your wishes, attaches itself to other programs on your computer and can trigger anything from a harmless flashing message to the reformatting of your hard drive to a system-wide network shutdown

Exhibit 17.3 Security Threats to Data and Data Networks

Security Problem	Source	Affects	Severity	The Threat	The Solution
Denial of service, Web server attacks, and corporate network attacks	Internet hackers	All servers	High	Loss of data, disruption of service, theft of service.	Implement firewall, password control, server-side review, threat monitoring, bug fixes; turn PCs off when not in use.
Password cracking software and unauthorized access to PCs	Local area network, Internet	All users, especially digital subscriber line and cable Internet users	High	Hackers take over PCs. Privacy can be invaded. Corporate users' systems are exposed to other machines on the network.	Close ports and firewalls, disable file and print sharing, and use strong passwords.
Viruses, worms, Trojan horses, and rootkits	E-mail, downloaded and distributed software	All users	Moderate to high	Monitor activities and cause data loss and file deletion. Compromise security by sometimes concealing their presence.	Use antivirus software and firewalls; control Internet access.
Spyware, adware, malicious scripts, and applets	Rogue Web pages	All users	Moderate to high	Invade privacy, intercept passwords, and damage files or file system.	Disable browser script support; use security, blocking, and spyware/adware software.
E-mail snooping	Hackers on your network and the Internet	All users	Moderate to high	People read your e-mail from intermediate servers or packets, or they physically access your machine.	Encrypt message, ensure strong password protection, and limit physical access to machines.
Keystroke monitoring	Trojan horses, people with direct access to PCs	All users	High	Records everything typed at the keyboard and intercepts keystrokes before password masking or encryption occurs.	Use antivirus software to catch Trojan horses, control Internet access to transmission, and implement system monitoring and physical access control.
Phishing	Hackers on your network and the Internet	All users, including customers	High	Fake, but real-looking, e-mails and Web sites that trick users into sharing personal information on what they wrongly thought was the company's website. This leads to unauthorized account.	Educate and warn users and customers about the dangers. Encourage both not to click on potentially fake URLs, which might take them to phishing websites. Instead, have them type your company's URL into the Web browser.
Spam	E-mail	All users and corporations	Mild to high	Clogs and overloads e-mail servers and inboxes with junk mail. HTML-based spam may be used for profiling and identifying users.	Filter known spam sources and senders on e-mail servers; have users create further lists of approved and unapproved senders on their personal computers.
Cookies	Websites you visit	Individual users	Mild to moderate	Trace Web usage and permit the creation of personalized Web pages that track behaviour and interest profiles.	Use cookie managers to control and edit cookies, and use ad blockers.

Sources: "Top 10 Security Threats," *PC Magazine*, April 10, 2007, 66; M. Sarrel, "Master End-User Security," *PC Magazine*, May 2008, 101; K. Bannan, "Look Out: Watching You, Watching Me," *PC Magazine*, July 2002, 99; A. Dragoon, "Fighting Phish, Fakes, and Frauds," *CIO*, 1 September 2004, 33; B. Glass, "Are You Being Watched?" *PC Magazine*, 23 April 2002, 54.

doing damage. However, this software is effective only to the extent that users of individual computers have and use up-to-date versions. With new viruses appearing all the time, users should update their antivirus software weekly or, even better, configure their virus software to automatically check for, download, and install updates. *Corporate antivirus software* automatically scans e-mail attachments such as Microsoft Word documents, graphics, and text files as they come across the company e-mail server. It also monitors and scans all file downloads across company databases and network servers. So, while antivirus software for personal computers prevents individual computers from being infected, corporate antivirus software for e-mail servers, databases, and network servers adds another layer of protection by preventing infected files from multiplying and being sent to others.

Another way of protecting information is to encrypt sensitive data. **Data encryption** transforms data into complex, scrambled digital codes that can be unencrypted only by authorized users who possess unique decryption keys. There is nothing like having the freedom to take your information with you. We take for granted that we can hop on a plane with our laptops, visit a major client in a distant city, and wow them with our comprehensive full-colour presentation. But wait a minute—what if we relax in the supposed safety of a private airport lounge, look away for only a second, and our laptop disappears? Canada's privacy laws require that businesses protect personal information in their possession from unauthorized access or disclosure by taking appropriate security measures. Across Canada, the number of reported break-and-enters into businesses continues to rise. Mercantile Mergers & Acquisitions Corporation of Toronto couldn't take that chance. As a brokerage firm specializing in the merger business in Canada, it needed encryption software to protect sensitive client information. Mercantile evaluated five commercial encryption software packages and picked one that suited its purposes, was within its budget, and provided a cost-effective solution.[35]

And with people increasingly gaining unauthorized access to e-mail messages—e-mail snooping—it's also important to encrypt sensitive e-mail messages and file attachments. You can use a system called "public key encryption" to do so. First, give copies of your "public key" to anyone who sends you files or e-mail. Have the sender use the public key, which is actually a piece of software, to encrypt files before sending them to you. The only way to decrypt the files is with a companion "private key" that you keep to yourself.

Although firewalls can protect personal computers and network servers connected to the corporate network, people away from their offices (e.g., salespeople, business travellers, telecommuters who work at home) who interact with their company networks via the Internet face a security risk. Because Internet data are not encrypted, packet sniffer software (see Exhibit 17.3) easily allows hackers to read everything sent or received except files that have been encrypted before sending. Previously, the only practical solution was to have employees dial in to secure company phone lines for direct access to the company network. Of course, with international and long-distance phone calls, the costs quickly added up. Now, **virtual private networks (VPNs)** have solved this problem by using software to encrypt all Internet data at both ends of the transmission process. Instead of making long-distance calls, employees connect to the Internet. But, unlike typical Internet connections in which Internet data packets are unencrypted, the VPN encrypts the data sent by employees outside the company computer network, decrypts the data when they arrive within the company network, and does the same when data are sent back to the computer outside the network.

Data encryption the transformation of data into complex, scrambled digital codes that can be unencrypted only by authorized users who possess unique decryption keys

Virtual private network (VPN) software that securely encrypts data sent by employees outside the company network, decrypts the data when they arrive within the company computer network, and does the same when data are sent back to employees outside the network

Secure sockets layer (SSL) encryption Internet browser-based encryption that provides secure off-site Web access to some data and programs

Many companies are now adopting Web-based **secure sockets layer (SSL) encryption** to provide secure off-site access to data and programs. If you've ever entered your credit card in a Web browser to make an online purchase, you've used SSL technology to encrypt and protect that information. SSL encryption is being used if a gold lock (Internet Explorer) or a gold key (Netscape) appears along the bottom of your Web browser. SSL encryption works the same way in the workplace. Managers and employees who aren't at the office simply connect to the Internet, open a Web browser, and then enter a user name and password to gain access to SSL-encrypted data and programs.

Finally, many companies now have wireless networks, which make it possible for anybody with a laptop and a wireless card to access the company network from anywhere in the office. Although wireless networks come equipped with security and encryption capabilities that, in theory, permit only authorized users to access the wireless network, those capabilities are easily bypassed with the right tools. Compounding the problem, many wireless networks are shipped with their security and encryption capabilities turned off for ease of installation.[36] Caution is important even when encryption is turned on because the WEP (Wired Equivalent Privacy) security protocol is easily compromised. If you work at home or are working on the go, extra care is critical because Wi-Fi networks in homes and public places such as hotel lobbies are among the most targeted by hackers.[37] See the Wi-Fi Alliance website at www.wi-fi.org for the latest information on wireless security and encryption protocols, which provide much stronger protection for your company's wireless network.

Executive information system (EIS) a data processing system that uses internal and external data sources to provide the information needed to monitor and analyze organizational performance

Intranets private company networks that allow employees to easily access, share, and publish information using Internet software

Corporate portal a hybrid of executive information systems and intranets that allows managers and employees to use a Web browser to gain access to customized company information and to complete specialized transactions

LO4 Accessing and Sharing Information and Knowledge

Today, information technologies allow companies to communicate data, share data, and provide data access to workers, managers, suppliers, and customers in ways that were unthinkable just a few years ago.

After reading this section, you should be able to explain how companies use IT to improve ***4.1*** ***internal access and sharing of information,*** ***4.2*** ***external access and sharing of information, and*** ***4.3*** ***the sharing of knowledge and expertise.***

© Goodshoot/Jupiterimages

4.1 Internal Access and Sharing

Executives, managers, and workers inside a company use three kinds of IT to access and share information: executive information systems, intranets, and portals. An **executive information system (EIS)** uses internal and external sources of data to provide managers and executives with the information they require to monitor and analyze organizational performance.[38] The purpose of an EIS is to provide accurate, complete, relevant, and timely information to managers.

Managers at **Colgate-Palmolive Canada**, which makes toothpaste, soap, and other home care products, as well as pet foods, use the company EIS, which they call the "dashboard," to see how well their company is running. Ruben Panizza, Colgate's Global IT Director of Business Intelligence, says that "these real-time dashboards are a change for people who are used to seeing a lot of numbers with their data. But they quickly realize they can use the information as it's presented in the dashboards to make faster decisions. In the past, executives relied on other people to get custom reports and data. Now, they can look at the information themselves. They see the real data as it is in the system much more easily and quickly. For the first time, many of the company's business leaders are running BI [business intelligence] tools—in this case, dashboards—to monitor the business to see what's going on at a high level."[39]

Intranets are private company networks that allow employees to access, share, and publish information using Internet software. Intranet websites are just like external websites, but the firewall separating the internal company network from the Internet permits only authorized internal access.[40] Companies typically use intranets to share information (e.g., about benefits) and to replace paper forms with online forms. Many company intranets are built on the Web model as it existed a decade ago. With more than 5,500 employees at its corporate head office and 475 retail outlets nationwide, Canadian Tire was looking to refresh its intranet site, known as inTIREnet. "Our employees require the ability to obtain information quickly and easily to make timely and well-informed decisions," says Laura Sousa, vice president of Enterprise IT and Governance at Canadian Tire. "Our new system ensures we have the most up-to-date and relevant information at our fingertips." Canadian Tire employees can now search documents, share information across the network, and receive daily corporate news updates. The new intranet has helped Canadian Tire increase communication among employees in the home office, while offering greater security measures and access to internal documents.[41]

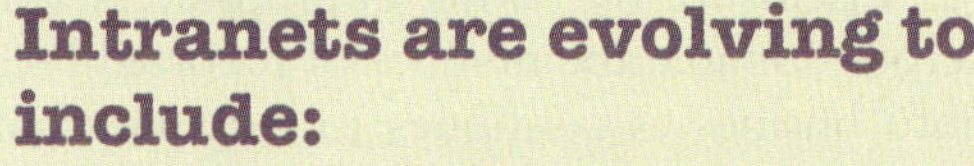

Intranets are evolving to include:

- collaboration tools, like wikis, where team members can post all relevant information for a project they're working on together
- customizable e-mail accounts
- presence awareness (whether someone you are looking for on the network is in the office, in a meeting, working from home, etc.)
- instant messaging
- simultaneous access to files for virtual team members

Finally, **corporate portals** are a hybrid of executive information systems and intranets. An EIS provides managers and executives with the information they need to monitor and analyze organizational performance, and intranets help companies distribute and publish information *and* forms within the company, whereas corporate portals allow company managers and employees to access customized information and complete specialized transactions using a Web browser. Hillman Group Canada sells the nuts, bolts, fasteners, keys, and key-cutting machines that you find in Home Depot, Lowes, Home Hardware, and nearly every other hardware store. Hillman's 1,800 employees produce products for 25,000 customers worldwide. The company's portal provides a real-time revenue report for every product it makes on a continuous basis,

Reasons Why Companies Build Intranets (aka Employee Portals)

Companies are committed to intranets and are working hard to increase their usability. Here are the main reasons cited by survey respondents for why their companies are implementing (or considering) intranets:

94%	Let employees find information
50%	Enable collaboration and information sharing
44%	Automate business processes
40%	Reduce costs
25%	Provide secure, remote access to company data via the Web
17%	Provide online training

Source: Data from Forrester Research, as reported by A. Blackman, "Dated and Confused: Corporate Intranets Should Be Invaluable Employee Tools, Too Bad They Often Aren't," *The Wall Street Journal*, 14 May 2007.

with updated production and sales numbers. This portal also offers 75 specialized reports, which are accessed by 800 managers and employees.[42]

4.2 External Access and Sharing

Companies were for a long time unable or reluctant to let outside groups have access to corporate information. Now, however, a number of information technologies—electronic data interchange, extranets, Web services, and the Internet—are making it easier for companies to share their data with external groups such as suppliers and customers. These same technologies are also reducing costs, increasing productivity by eliminating manual information processing, reducing data entry errors, improving customer service, and speeding communications.

With **electronic data interchange**, or **EDI**, two companies convert purchase and ordering information to a standardized format to enable direct electronic transmission of that information from one company's computer system to the other company's. For example, when an Apple Store associate drags an Apple iPod across the checkout scanner at the West Edmonton Mall, the store's computerized inventory system automatically reorders another iPod through the direct EDI connection that its computer has with Apple's manufacturing and shipping computer. No one at Apple or at Apple's main supplier, Foxconn, fills out paperwork. No one makes a phone call. There are no delays to wait to find out whether Apple has the iPod in stock. The transaction takes place instantly and automatically because the data from Apple and all of their manufacturing companies like Foxconn have been translated into a standardized, shareable, compatible format.

With EDI, the various purchasing and ordering applications in each company interact automatically without any human input. No one has to lift a finger to click a mouse, enter data, or hit the return key. An **extranet**, by contrast, allows a company to exchange information and conduct transactions by purposely providing outsiders with direct, Web browser–based access to authorized parts of its intranet or information system. Typically, user names and passwords are required to access an extranet.[43] For example, General Mills uses an extranet to provide Web-based access to its trucking database to 20 other companies that ship their products over similar distribution routes. This ensures that its distribution trucks don't waste money by running half empty (or make late deliveries to customers because they waited till they were full). When other companies are ready to ship products, they log on to General Mills' trucking database, check the availability, and then enter the shipping load, place, and pickup time. By sharing shipping capacity on its trucks, General Mills can run its trucks fully loaded all the time. In several test areas, General Mills saved 7 percent on shipping costs (nearly $2 million) in the first year. Expanding the program company-wide is producing even larger cost savings.[44]

Electronic data interchange (EDI) when two companies convert their purchase and ordering information to a standardized format to enable the direct electronic transmission of that information from one company's computer system to the other company's computer system

Extranets networks that allow companies to exchange information and conduct transactions with outsiders by providing them direct, Web-based access to authorized parts of a company's intranet or information system

Finally, companies are reducing paperwork and manual information processing by using the Internet to automate transactions with customers. This is similar to the way in which extranets are used to handle transactions with suppliers and distributors. For example, most airlines have automated the ticketing process by eliminating paper tickets altogether. Simply buy an e-ticket via the Internet, and then check yourself in online by printing your boarding pass from your personal computer or from a kiosk at the airport. Internet purchases, ticketless travel, and automated check-ins have fully automated the purchase of airline tickets. Use of self-service kiosks is also expanding. At the Canada Place Cruise Terminal in Vancouver, there are five car company kiosks to service the thousands of tourists who board Alaska cruise ships each year. For example, kiosks print rental agreements, permit upgrades to nicer cars, and allow customers to add additional drivers or buy extra insurance.[45]

In the long run, the goal is to link customer Internet sites with company intranets (or EDIs) and extranets so that everyone—all the employees and managers within a company as well as the suppliers and distributors outside the company—who is involved in providing a service or making a product for a customer is automatically notified when a purchase is made. Companies that use EDI, extranets, and the Internet to share data with customers

Knowledge the understanding that one gains from information

Decision support system (DSS) an information system that helps managers understand specific kinds of problems and potential solutions and analyze the impact of different decision options using "what if" scenarios

Expert system an information system that contains the specialized knowledge and decision rules used by experts and experienced decision makers so that nonexperts can draw on this knowledge base to make decisions

and suppliers achieve increases in productivity 2.7 times larger than those that don't.[46]

4.3 Sharing Knowledge and Expertise

At the beginning of the chapter, we distinguished between raw data, which consist of facts and figures, and information, which consists of useful data that influence someone's choices and behaviour. One more important distinction needs to be made—namely, data and information are not the same as knowledge. **Knowledge** is the understanding that one gains from information. Importantly, knowledge does not reside in information; it resides in people. That's why companies hire consultants and why family doctors refer patients to specialists. Unfortunately, it can be quite expensive to employ consultants, specialists, and experts. So companies have begun using two information technologies to capture and share the knowledge of consultants, specialists, and experts with other managers and workers: decision support systems and expert systems.

Whereas an executive information system (EIS) speeds up and simplifies the acquisition of information, a **decision support system (DSS)** helps managers understand problems and potential solutions by analyzing information using sophisticated models and tools.[47] Furthermore, whereas EIS programs are broad in scope and permit managers to retrieve all kinds of information about a company, DSS programs are usually narrow in scope and targeted toward helping managers solve specific kinds of problems. DSS programs have been developed to help managers pick the shortest and most efficient routes for delivery trucks, select the best combinations of stocks for investors, and schedule the flow of inventory through complex manufacturing facilities.

It's important to understand that DSS programs don't replace managerial decision making; they *improve* it by furthering managers' and workers' understanding of the problems they face and the solutions that might work. Although used by just 2 percent of physicians, medical DSS programs hold the promise of helping doctors make more accurate patient diagnoses. A British study of 88 cases misdiagnosed or initially misdiagnosed (to be correctly diagnosed much later) found that a medical DSS made the right diagnosis 69 percent of the time.[48] With a medical DSS, doctors enter patient data, such as age, gender, weight, and medical symptoms. The medical DSS then produces a list of diseases and conditions, ranked by probability, low or high, or by medical specialty, such as cardiology or oncology. For instance, when emergency room physician Dr. Harold Cross treated a 10-year-old boy who had been ill with nausea and dizziness for two weeks, he wasn't sure what was wrong because the boy had a healthy appetite, no abdominal pain, and just one brief headache. However, when the medical DSS that Dr. Cross used suggested a possible problem in the back of the boy's brain, he ordered an MRI scan that revealed a tumour, which was successfully removed two days later. Says Dr. Cross: "My personal knowledge of the literature and physical findings would not have prompted me to suspect a brain tumor."[49]

Expert systems are created by capturing the specialized knowledge and decision rules used by experts and experienced decision makers. They permit nonexpert employees to draw on this expert knowledge base to make decisions. Most expert systems work by using a collection of "if–then" rules to sort through information and recommend a course of action. For example, let's say that you're using your Bank of Montreal MasterCard or your TD Visa card to help your spouse celebrate a promotion. After dinner and a movie, the two of you stroll by a travel office with a Montreal poster in its window. Thirty minutes later, caught up in the moment, you find yourselves at the airport ticket counter trying to purchase last-minute tickets to Montreal. But there's just one problem. VISA didn't approve your purchase. In fact, the ticket counter agent is now on the phone with a VISA customer service agent.

What brought your weekend escape to Montreal to a temporary halt? It was an expert system that VISA calls "Authorizer's Assistant."[50] The first "if–then" rule that prevented your purchase was the rule "*if* a purchase is much larger than the cardholder's regular

AntonSokolov/Shutterstock.com

People have knowledge. Computers contain data and information.

William Manning/GetStock.com

spending habits, *then* deny approval of the purchase." This if–then rule, just one of 3,000, is built into Royal Bank's VISA transaction-processing system, which handles thousands of purchase requests per second. Now that the VISA customer service agent is on the line, he or she is prompted by the Authorizer's Assistant to ask the ticket counter agent to examine your identification. You hand over your driver's licence and another credit card to prove that you're you. Finally, your ticket purchase is approved. Why? Because you met the last series of "if–then" rules: *if* the purchaser can provide proof of identity and *if* the purchaser can provide personal information that isn't common knowledge, *then* approve the purchase.

Go online at
www.nelson.com/4ltrpress/icanmgmt2
And access the essential Study Tools online for this chapter:

- **Flashcards**, to help you study
- **Interactive Quizzes**, to test your knowledge
- **Audio Chapter Summaries**, for chapter review
- **Crossword Puzzles and Beat the Clock**, to review key terms
- **What Would You Do? Cases**, for applying your knowledge to real-life situations
- **Self Assessments**, to learn about what kind of manager you are
- **Videos and Media Quizzing**, where you can watch a video about a real-life company and test yourself on what you've learned

Be sure to consult the Chapter Review Card at the back of the textbook.

18

Managing Service and Manufacturing Operations

LEARNING OUTCOMES

LO1 Discuss the kinds of productivity and their importance in managing operations.

LO2 Explain the role that quality plays in managing operations.

LO3 Explain the essentials of managing a service business.

LO4 Describe the different kinds of manufacturing operations.

LO5 Explain why and how companies should manage inventory levels.

Managing for Productivity and Quality

Furniture manufacturers, hospitals, restaurants, automakers, airlines, and many other kinds of businesses struggle to find ways to produce quality products and services efficiently and then deliver them in a timely manner. Managing the daily production of goods and services, or operations management, is a key part of a manager's job. But an organization's success depends on the quality of its products and services as well as on its productivity.

Take the airline industry as an example. An airline's profitability rests on being able to achieve a delicate balance: filling seats to achieve as close to capacity as possible, and increasing the utilization of aircraft by flying them more hours in the day, all the while keeping costs as low as possible without sacrificing safety or quality. Canada's WestJet has made a name for itself as Canada's low-cost airline and is now this country's second largest carrier. The company has modelled itself on US-based Southwest Airlines. Its success can be attributed to its commitment to cost control, high-growth revenue, and customer service. WestJet keeps its costs low by flying a single type of aircraft (the Boeing 737), by creating cost efficiencies in employee training, maintenance, and purchasing, and by keeping ground-handling charges low through subcontracting. WestJet's strategy has been to focus wherever possible on airports with competitive cost terms, as well as on niche routes where it is the only carrier to offer nonstop service and short-haul flights. This has allowed it to reduce some costly in-flight amenities.[1] Want a meal on your flight? You can buy snacks à la carte or, better yet, pack your own meal. Need a pillow or blanket? You can purchase these for seven dollars. Want to visit the airport lounge? For $25 you can enter one of the open access lounges that WestJet has partnered with across the country.[2] As a result of its no-frills strategy, WestJet's costs are an estimated 30 percent lower on domestic flights than those of its rival, Air Canada. Thus, WestJet has been able to do more for less and to benefit from higher productivity.[3] In 2012, WestJet reported record annual results with increases in revenue, capacity, operating margins, and net earnings; it also marked its eighth consecutive year of profitability. Also in 2012, WestJet was the only Canadian airline and one of only two North American airlines to make *Aviation Week*'s top ten list of international airlines—an airline industry ranking that compares airline performance in five major operational categories.[4]

The Canadian Press Images/Bayne Stanley

LO1 Productivity

At their core, organizations are production systems. Companies combine inputs such as labour, raw materials, capital, and knowledge to produce outputs in the form of finished products or services. **Productivity** is a measure of performance that indicates how many inputs it takes to produce or create an output.

$$\text{Productivity} = \frac{\text{Outputs}}{\text{Inputs}}$$

The fewer inputs it takes to create an output (or the greater the output from one input), the higher the productivity. For example, a car's gas mileage is a common measure of productivity. A car that gets 60 kilometres (output) per litre (input) is more productive and fuel-efficient than a car that gets 40 kilometres per litre.

Productivity a measure of performance that indicates how many inputs it takes to produce or create an output

*Let's examine **1.1 why productivity matters** and **1.2 the different kinds of productivity**.*

1.1 Why Productivity Matters

Why does productivity matter? Higher productivity—that is, doing more with less—results in lower costs, lower prices, faster service, higher market share, and higher profits. For example, every second saved in the drive-through lane at a fast food restaurant increases sales by 1 percent. With up to 70 percent of all fast food restaurant sales coming from the drive-through window, it's no wonder that Wendy's (average drive-through time: 129.75 seconds), McDonald's (188.83), and Burger King (201.33) continue to look for ways to shorten the time it takes to process a drive-through order.[5] Productivity matters so much at a drive-through that McDonald's has experimented with outsourcing, using a call centre in California to take drive-through orders at a select group of McDonald's franchises around the United States. During the 10 seconds it takes for a car

© DNY59/iStockphoto.com

Partial productivity a measure of performance that indicates how much of a particular kind of input it takes to produce an output

to pull away from the microphone at a drive-through, a call centre operator can take the order of a different customer at another restaurant, even if it is thousands of miles away.[6] McDonald's continues to look for ways to improve its drive-through efficiency, especially in many of its busiest locations. For example, it has introduced a two-lane system where vehicles are split into two ordering lanes to place their orders, and then funnelled back into one line for payment and order pickup. The bottom line—more efficient service can lead to more sales and lower labour costs.[7]

The productivity of a country's businesses matters because it is mainly productivity that determines living standards and quality of life. Productivity and living standards are tightly linked.[8] Companies that do more with less can raise employee wages without increasing prices or sacrificing normal profits. For households, that translates into additional income without loss of purchasing power. For businesses, higher productivity means profit growth; for governments, additional tax revenues can support health care, education, and/or social services.[9] Another benefit of productivity is that it makes products more affordable or better. The richest countries are the ones that manufacture products and deliver services most effectively.[10]

Small improvements in productivity sustained for an extended time can result in significant increases in living standards; that is why economists and the business community closely monitor changes in productivity levels and productivity growth (See Exhibit 18.1). In 2012, the Conference Board of Canada reported that Canada ranked 13th among its 16 peer countries in labour productivity. Canada's productivity level had fallen to 80 percent of the US level, after reaching a high of 91 percent in the mid-1980s.[11] Experts point to business factors as the reason for Canada's lower productivity relative to that of the United States—specifically, to reduced investments in equipment, lower levels of innovation, a smaller high-tech industry, less worker training, and smaller production facilities.[12] Historically, Canada has lagged behind other, larger countries in labour productivity growth. In 2012, Canada's labour productivity growth rate was 0.8 percent—not an impressive number by historical standards. However, other countries performed worse: Canada's ranking relative to its peer countries improved, earning it fifth place (a "B" grade") among them.[13]

The topic of productivity will continue to draw attention in Canada because

> *an improvement of even one percentage point in the annual growth rate of productivity, sustained for an extended period, can significantly improve the daily lives of Canadians. It can mean a more comfortable home, a more luxurious car, improved health services, more leisure or a cleaner environment. The upcoming decades will increasingly highlight this fact. Canada's aging society will increasingly depend on growth in productivity to maintain and improve its standard of living and quality of life.*[14]

1.2 Kinds of Productivity

Two common measures of productivity are partial productivity and multifactor productivity. **Partial productivity** indicates how much of a particular kind of input it takes to produce an output:

$$\text{Partial productivity} = \frac{\text{Outputs}}{\text{Single kind of input}}$$

The Pitfalls of Multitasking

Multitasking—or doing multiple tasks *at the same time*—may seem like a positive trait for an employee, and the answer to increasing productivity, but this is not necessarily the case. Multitasking is part of our everyday lives, both personal and professional, yet 97 percent of people are hopeless at it. How effective can you be answering e-mail, reviewing a report, and being attentive at a meeting—all at the same time? According to the *Harvard Business Review*, multitaskers often accomplish less, miss information, and reduce their efficiency by as much as 40 percent. The term multitasking itself is considered to be a misnomer, when you consider that many individuals who believe they are multitasking are actually simply switching tasks, as our brain chooses which information to process. It takes an average of 15 minutes for a person to reorient to a task after being distracted by another task. Many individuals in the workplace find themselves constantly moving from project to project, depending on who is demanding their time or offering a distraction. Often, the result is that tasks do not get completed before people move on to the next one, which causes a ripple effect as workers get off track and miss deadlines.

Sources: Anita Bruzzese, "Break the Multitasking Habit," *USA Today*, December 21, 2011, http://usatoday30.usatoday.com/money/jobcenter/workplace/bruzzese/story/2011-12-21/multitasking-diverts-you-fromcompleting-tasks/52132902/1; D. Gulati, "Multitasking's Real Victims," *Harvard Business Review*, July 18, 2012, http://blogs.hbr.org/cs/2012/07/multitaskings_real_victims.html; C. Deeb, "Multitasking Effects on a Worker's Performance," *Small Business Chronicle*, http://smallbusiness.chron.com/multitasking-effectsworkers-performance-32339.html; P. Atchley, "You Can't Multitask, So Stop Trying," *Harvard Business Review*, December 21, 2010, http://blogs.hbr.org/cs/2010/12/you_cant_multi-task_so_stop_tr.html.

Labour is one kind of input that is often used when determining partial productivity. *Labour productivity* typically indicates the cost of the labour it takes to produce an output (or the number of hours of labour). In other words, the lower the labour cost per unit of output, or the less labour time it takes to produce a unit of output, the higher the labour productivity. Automakers often measure labour productivity by determining the average number of hours of labour it takes to completely assemble a car. Lower labour costs give automakers an average cost advantage, which is important in this highly competitive industry. In the United States, the most productive automakers are Toyota and Chrysler. Both companies assemble a vehicle with 30.4 hours of labour.[15] Interestingly, when you compare the productivity of the three NAFTA countries, Canada, United States, and Mexico, the good news for Canada is that our average assembly productivity is 20.71 hours per vehicle, compared to 23.06 in the United States and 28.03 in Mexico.[16]

Partial productivity assesses how efficiently companies use only one input, such as labour, when creating outputs. Multifactor productivity is an overall measure of productivity; it assesses how efficiently companies use *all* the inputs it takes to make outputs. Specifically, **multifactor productivity** indicates how much labour, capital, materials, and energy it takes to produce an output.[17]

Multifactor productivity an overall measure of performance that indicates how much labour, capital, materials, and energy it takes to produce an output

$$\text{Multifactor Productivity} = \frac{\text{Outputs}}{(\text{Labour} + \text{Capital} + \text{Materials} + \text{Energy})}$$

In assessing multifactor productivity (MFP) in Canada, once again, the United States is used for comparison. Research by Statistics Canada on past economic trends (to help forecast future economic growth) has found that Canada is lagging behind the United States in MFP. In 1999, the Canadian aggregate MFP was 80.3 percent of the American one. Between 1961 to 2008, there was a 0.3 percent increase in Canadian MFP, which was essentially no growth. Statistics Canada reports that "the slowdown in labour productivity after 2000 was almost entirely accounted for by the factors that determine multifactor growth—technology, innovation, firm organization, scale and capacity utilization effect." Industries that contributed to declines in business MFP were mining, oil and gas extraction, and manufacturing; those associated with growth included finance, insurance, and real estate.[18]

Managers should use both multiple and partial productivity measures. MFP indicates a company's overall productivity relative to its competitors. In the end, that is what counts most. However, MFP measures don't indicate the specific contributions that labour, capital, materials, and energy make to overall productivity. To analyze the contributions of these individual components, managers need to use partial productivity measures. Doing so can help them determine which factors need to be adjusted or in which areas adjustment would make the most difference in overall productivity.

LO2 Quality

With the average new car costing more than $30,000, buyers want to make sure they're getting good quality for their money. As part of an annual study of new vehicle quality, J.D. Power and Associates monitors and reports on the number of problems per 100 vehicles experienced by customers in the first 90 days of ownership. Fortunately, as indicated by the number of problems per 100 cars (PP100), today's cars are of much higher quality than they used to be. In 1981, Japanese cars averaged 240 PP100, while General Motors cars averaged 670, Ford 740, and Chrysler 870. In other words, as measured by PP100, the quality of North American cars was two to three times poorer than that of Japanese cars. Over the past few decades, though, quality in the North American auto industry has improved dramatically, as evidenced by the most recent J.D. Power and Associates Survey of initial car quality, which reported an overall industry average of 102 PP100. A number of manufacturers had scores under 100, meaning less than one problem per car. The "winners" in this regard included Lexus (73 PP100), Cadillac (80 PP100), Honda (83 PP100), and General Motors (99). Toyota Canada's assembly plant in Cambridge, Ontario, was also the recipient of several J.D. Powers Quality Awards, including the 2012 Gold Medal (Best in the Americas) and the 2011 Platinum Award (Best in World), becoming the first Toyota plant outside of Japan to win the global top

Exhibit 18.1 Standard of Living and Labour Productivity in Canada

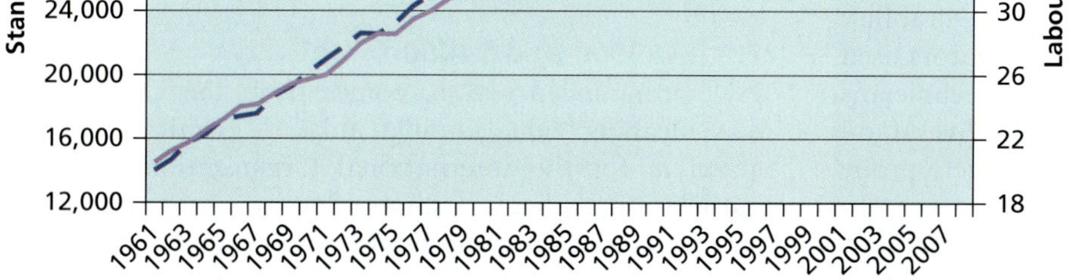

Source: Conference Board of Canada. (2013). Labour productivity growth; http://www.conferenceboard.ca/hcp/details/economy/measuring-productivity-canada.aspx. Reprinted by permission of the Conference Board of Canada.

Quality a product or service free of deficiencies, or the characteristics of a product or service that satisfy customer needs

honour. "Companies have learned quality manufacturing techniques from top competitors, and they're using higher quality materials than in the past. Everybody in the industry knows that if they don't keep improving, they're going to fall behind."[19]

The American Society for Quality offers two meanings for **quality**. It can mean a product or service free of deficiencies, or a product or service that satisfies customer needs.[20] Today's cars are of higher quality than those produced 20 years ago in both senses. Not only do they have fewer problems per 100 cars, but they also have a larger number of standard features (air bags, anti-lock brakes, power windows and locks, cruise control, air conditioning), as well as a plethora of available options (GPS navigational systems, satellite radio, Bluetooth and USB connectivity, rearview camera, blind spot monitoring) to address the changing needs of today's drivers.

In this part of the chapter, you will learn about ***2.1 quality-related characteristics for products and services, 2.2 ISO 9000 and 14000, 2.3 the Baldrige National Quality Award,*** *and* ***2.4 total quality management.***

2.1 Quality-Related Characteristics for Products and Services

Quality products usually have three characteristics: reliability, serviceability, and durability.[21] A breakdown occurs when a product quits working or doesn't do what it was designed to do. The longer it takes for a product to break down, or the longer the time between breakdowns, the more reliable the product. Consequently, many companies define product *reliability* in terms of the average time between breakdowns.

Serviceability refers to how easy or difficult it is to fix a product. The easier it is to maintain a working product or fix a broken product, the more serviceable that product is. Western Digital sells the WD RE4 2TB hard drive, an extremely fast two-terabyte hard drive that customers can use for gaming, multimedia, and video applications. This particular product is so reliable that the estimated mean time between breakdowns is 1.2 million hours, or more than 137 years.[22]

A product breakdown assumes that a product can be repaired. However, some products don't break down—they fail. *Product failure* means that products can't be repaired, only replaced. *Durability* is defined as the mean time to failure. Thus, durability is a quality characteristic that applies to products that cannot be repaired. Durability is often crucial for products such as the defibrillators used by doctors, nurses, and emergency medical technicians to restart patients' hearts. Imagine the lost lives (and lawsuits) that would occur if this equipment were prone to frequent failure.

High-quality *products* are characterized by reliability, serviceability, and durability. *Services* are not as easy to evaluate using the same criteria. For example, once a lawn service has mowed your lawn, the job is done until the mowers return the next week to do it again. Also, services don't have serviceability—that is, they can't be maintained or fixed. If a service wasn't performed correctly, all you can do is have it performed again. Finally, the quality of service often depends on how the service provider interacts with the customer. Was the service provider friendly, rude, helpful? Five characteristics typically distinguish a quality service: reliability, tangibles, responsiveness, assurance, and empathy.[23]

Dikiiy/Shutterstock.com

Studies have found that *service reliability* matters more to customers than anything else when they are buying services. When you take your clothes to the dry cleaner, you don't want them returned with cracked buttons or wrinkles down the front. If your dry cleaner gives you back perfectly clean and pressed clothes every time, it's providing a reliable service.

Also, although services themselves are not tangible (you can't see or touch them), they are provided in tangible places. *Tangibles* relate to the offices, equipment, and personnel involved with the delivery of a service. One of the best examples of the effect of tangibles on perceptions of quality is the restroom. When you eat at a fancy restaurant, you expect clean, if not upscale, restrooms. How different is your perception of a business—say, a gas station—if it has clean restrooms rather than filthy ones?

Responsiveness refers to the promptness and willingness with which service providers give good service (your dry cleaner returning your laundry perfectly clean and pressed in a day or an hour). *Assurance* refers to the customer's confidence that service providers will be knowledgeable, courteous, and trustworthy. *Empathy* is the extent to which service providers give individual attention and care to customers' concerns and problems.

2.2 ISO 9000 and 14000

ISO, pronounced *eye-so*, comes from the Greek word *isos*, meaning "equal, similar, alike, or identical." It is the acronym for the International Organization for Standardization, the world's largest developer of international standards for companies and organizations that want to ensure their products and services meet customer standards and that quality is consistently improved. This agency develops and publishes standards that facilitate the international exchange of goods and services.[24] **ISO 9000** is a series of five international standards, from ISO 9000 to ISO 9004, for achieving consistency in quality management and quality assurance in companies throughout the world. **ISO 14000** is a series of international standards for managing, monitoring, and minimizing an organization's harmful effects on the environment.[25] (For more on environmental quality and issues, see Section 3.5 of Chapter 16 on controlling waste and pollution.)

The ISO 9000 and 14000 standards can be used for manufacturing any kind of product or delivering any kind of service. The ISO 9000 standards don't describe how to make a better-quality car, computer, or widget. Instead, they describe how companies can extensively document (and thereby standardize) the steps they take to create and improve the quality of their products. Studies have found that customers clearly prefer to buy from companies that are ISO 9000 certified. Companies, for their part, believe that ISO 9000 certification will help them keep customers who might otherwise switch to competitors who already have it. ISO 9000 certification is increasingly becoming a prerequisite for doing business.[26]

To become ISO certified (a process that can take months), a company must show that it is following its own procedures for improving production, updating design plans and specifications, keeping machinery in top condition, educating and training workers, and satisfactorily dealing with customer complaints.[27] An accredited third party oversees ISO certification, in much the same way that a certified public accountant verifies that a company's financial accounts are up-to-date and accurate. Once a company has been certified as ISO 9000 compliant, the accredited third party issues an ISO 9000 certificate, which the company can use in its advertising and publications. Continued ISO 9000 certification is not guaranteed, however. Accredited third parties conduct periodic audits to ensure that the company is still following quality procedures. If it is not, its certification is suspended or cancelled.

2.3 Baldrige National Quality Award

The Baldrige National Quality Award, which is administered by the US government's National Institute for Standards and Technology, is given "to recognize U.S. companies for their achievements in quality and business performance and to raise awareness about the importance of quality and performance excellence as a competitive edge."[28] Each year, up to three awards may be given in these categories: manufacturing, service, small business, education, health care, and not-for-profit.

The cost of applying for the Baldrige Award includes a $150 eligibility fee, an application fee ($7,000 for manufacturing and service companies, $3,500 for small businesses), and a site visitation fee ($20,000 to $35,000 for manufacturing firms, $10,000 to $17,000 for small businesses).[29] It costs so much to apply because companies that do get a great deal of information about their business that will be useful even if they don't win. At a minimum, each company that applies receives an extensive report based on 300 hours of assessment from at least eight business and quality experts. Organizations receiving a site visit can benefit from up to 1,000 hours of in-depth review; however, additional fees do apply.

Businesses that apply for the Baldrige Award are placed on a 1,000-point scale that encompasses seven criteria (see Exhibit 18.2).[30] "Results" is clearly the most important of these (450 points).

ISO 9000 a series of five international standards, from ISO 9000 to ISO 9004, for achieving consistency in quality management and quality assurance in companies throughout the world

ISO 14000 a series of international standards for managing, monitoring, and minimizing an organization's harmful effects on the environment

Exhibit 18.2 Criteria for the Baldrige National Quality Award

2009–2010 Categories/Items	Point Values
1 LEADERSHIP	**120**
1.1 Senior Leadership	70
1.2 Governance and Social Responsibilities	50
2 STRATEGIC PLANNING	**85**
2.1 Strategy Development	40
2.2 Strategy Deployment	45
3 CUSTOMER	**85**
3.1 Customer Engagement	40
3.2 Voice of the Customer	45
4 MEASUREMENT, ANALYSIS, AND KNOWLEDGE MANAGEMENT	**90**
4.1 Measurement, Analysis, and Improvement of Organizational Performance	45
4.2 Management of Information, Information Technology, and Knowledge	45
5 WORKFORCE FOCUS	**85**
5.1 Workforce Engagement	45
5.2 Workforce Environment	40
6 PROCESS MANAGEMENT	**85**
6.1 Work Systems	35
6.2 Work Processes	50
7 RESULTS	**450**
7.1 Product Outcomes	100
7.2 Customer-Focused Outcomes	70
7.3 Financial and Market Outcomes	70
7.4 Workforce-Focused Outcomes	70
7.5 Process Effectiveness Outcomes	70
7.6 Leadership Outcomes	70
TOTAL POINTS 1,000	

Source: "Criteria for Performance Excellence," *Baldrige National Quality Program 2009-2010*, [Online] available at http://www.nist.gov/baldrige/publications/upload/2009_2010_Business_Nonprofit_Criteria.pdf.

Total quality management (TQM) an integrated, principle-based, organization-wide strategy for improving product and service quality

Customer focus an organizational goal to concentrate on meeting customers' needs at all levels of the organization

Customer satisfaction an organizational goal to provide products or services that meet or exceed customers' expectations

Continuous improvement an organization's ongoing commitment to constantly assess and improve the processes and procedures used to create products and services

Variation a deviation in the form, condition, or appearance of a product from the quality standard for that product

Companies must also show that they have achieved superior quality in terms of products and services, customers, financial performance and market share, treatment of employees, organizational effectiveness, and leadership and social responsibility. This emphasis on results is what differentiates the Baldrige Award from the ISO 9000 standards. The Baldrige Award indicates the extent to which companies have actually achieved world-class quality. The ISO 9000 standards simply indicate whether a company is following the management system it put in place to improve quality. In fact, ISO 9000 certification covers less than 10 percent of the requirements for the Baldrige Award.[31] Most companies that apply for the Baldrige Award do it to grow, prosper, and stay competitive.[32]

2.4 Total Quality Management

Total quality management (TQM) is an integrated, organization-wide strategy for improving product and service quality.[33] TQM is not a specific tool or technique but a philosophy or overall approach to management. It is based on three principles: customer focus and satisfaction, continuous improvement, and teamwork.[34]

Most economists, accountants, and financiers argue that companies exist to earn profits for shareholders. By contrast, TQM suggests that customer focus and customer satisfaction should be a company's primary goals. **Customer focus** means that the entire organization, from top to bottom, should be focused on meeting customers' needs. The result of that customer focus should be **customer satisfaction**, which occurs when the company's products or services meet or exceed customers' expectations. At companies where TQM is taken seriously, such as Enterprise Rent-a-Car, paycheques and promotions depend on keeping customers satisfied.[35] Enterprise measures customer satisfaction with a detailed survey called the Enterprise Service Quality index. Enterprise not only ranks each branch office by operating profits and customer satisfaction but also makes promotions to higher-paying jobs contingent on above-average customer satisfaction scores.

Continuous improvement refers to an ongoing commitment to increase product and service quality by constantly assessing and improving the processes and procedures used to create those products and services. Besides higher customer satisfaction, continuous improvement is usually associated with reduced variation. **Variation** is a deviation in the form, condition, or appearance of a product from the quality standard for that product. The less a product varies from the quality standard, or the more consistently a company's products

R2D2 vs. Rosie from *The Jetsons*

Reducing the risk of germs and infectious diseases is critical in a hospital, particularly when potentially deadly bugs such a *C. difficile* and norovirus increase the threat to vulnerable patients, hospital workers, and visitors alike. Enter Trudi the robot, a device that can disinfect a hospital room, using powerful ultraviolet rays to kill germs and viruses. The 1.65-metre-tall robot (think R2D2 from Star Wars or Rosie from *The Jetsons*) is able to use its sensors to size up a room and determine how much exposure is required to disinfect it, which can be anywhere from 15 minutes to an hour. Vancouver General Hospital is one of the first hospitals in Canada to test out the Tru-D Smart UVC machine, and so far the results have been good. Since UV light is used to sterilize medical equipment, it's only natural that the application be extended to other areas. Although the device cannot move on its own, it may only be a matter of time before a fully automated version is available.

Sources: J. Keller, "Vancouver Hospital First in Canada to Use Bug-Killing Robot Armed with UV Light," *Times Colonist*, February 1, 2013, http://www.timescolonist.com/life/health/vancouver-hospital-first-in-canada-to-use-bug-killing-robot-armed-with-uvlight-1.64456; Canadian Press, "Germ-killing UV robot Tested at Vancouver hospital," February 1, 2013, http://www.cbc.ca/news/canada/british-columbia/story/2013/02/01/bc-germ-killing-robot.html.

Mark Ralston/AFP/Getty Images

meet a quality standard, the higher the quality. Companies like General Electric continually strive to improve their product quality, adopting principles like Six Sigma in an effort to reduce the amount of variation or defects in their products. Six Sigma is a data-driven methodology that strives to eliminate defects from products and services to the tune of six standard deviations between the mean and the nearest specification limit—in other words, as close to zero defects as possible. To achieve Six Sigma Quality, a process must produce no more than 3.4 defects per million opportunities.[36]

The third principle of TQM is teamwork. **Teamwork** means collaboration between managers and nonmanagers, across business functions, and between the company and its customers and suppliers. Put simply, quality improves when everyone in the company is given (a) the incentive to work together, and (b) the responsibility and authority to make improvements and solve problems. At Toronto's Sunnybrook Hospital, teamwork has been the key to success in a number of departments, including the Odette Cancer Centre and the Department of Medical Imaging. Health care teams in these areas include surgeons, nurses, technicians, and administrative assistants, all of whom focus on achieving an important goal—reducing wait times for cancer surgery patients. Team members work together to ensure that the process is as efficient as possible; for example, a special "nurse navigator" acts as a sort of traffic control centre for cancer care. All aspects of the diagnostic imaging process are studied, including the booking process and no-show rates, to ensure that all available imaging slots are being utilized. As a result of these efforts, wait times at Sunnybrook Hospital are now well below the provincial average.[37]

Customer focus and satisfaction, continuous improvement, and teamwork mutually reinforce one another to improve quality throughout a company. Customer-focused continuous improvement is necessary to increase customer satisfaction. At the same time, continuous improvement depends on teamwork from different functional and hierarchical parts of the company.

Managing Operations

At the start of this chapter, you learned that operations management means managing the daily production of goods and services. Then you learned that to manage production, you must oversee the factors that affect productivity and quality. In this part of the chapter, you will learn about managing operations in service and manufacturing businesses. The chapter ends with a discussion of inventory management, which is a key factor in a company's profitability.

LO3 Service Operations

Imagine that your digital camera suddenly stops working just as you are about to head out for spring break. You've got two choices. You can run to the closest Best Buy and buy a new camera, or you can try and have it fixed at Best Buy's repair department. Either way, you hope to end up with the same thing—a working camera. However, the first choice—getting a new digital camera—involves buying a physical product (a good); whereas the second—dealing with the repair department—involves buying a service.

Services differ from goods in several ways. First, goods are produced or made, but services are performed. In other words, services are almost always labour-intensive: someone has to perform the service for you. A repair shop could sell you the parts you need to repair your digital camera, but you would end up with a broken camera and no technician to make the repairs. Second, goods are tangible, but services are intangible. You can touch and see that new camera, but you can't touch or see the service provided by the technician who fixed your camera. All you can "see" is that the camera is working again. Third, services are perishable and not storable. If you don't use them when they're available, they're wasted. If the camera repair department is backlogged on repair jobs, you'll just have to wait until next week to get yours repaired. You can't store an unused service and use it when you like. By contrast, you can purchase a good, such as motor oil, and store it until you're ready to use it.

Because services are different from goods, managing a service operation is different from managing a manufacturing or production operation. *Let's look at 3.1 the service–profit chain and 3.2 service recovery and empowerment.*

Teamwork collaboration between managers and non-managers, across business functions, and between companies, customers, and suppliers

Rasch/Shutterstock.com

Service recovery restoring customer satisfaction to strongly dissatisfied customers

3.1 The Service–Profit Chain

A key assumption in the service business is that success depends on how well employees—that is, service providers—deliver their services to customers. But success actually begins with how well management treats service employees, as the service–profit chain demonstrates (see Exhibit 18.3).[38]

The key concept behind the service–profit chain is *internal service quality*, meaning the quality of treatment that employees receive from a company's internal service providers such as management, payroll and benefits, human resources, and so forth. Vancity, Canada's largest credit union, believes strongly that connecting directly with employees is vital for senior managers. It places a lot of emphasis on internal communications—specifically, on listening to employees. Vancity's culture centres on the concept that success starts with employees. Employees are not an afterthought; instead, they are a key group that the organization strives to impress every day. In fact, one performance measure that determines compensation for top executives at Vancity is results from employee surveys.[39]

Success begins with how well management treats service employees.

As depicted in Exhibit 18.3, good internal service leads to employee satisfaction and service capability. *Employee satisfaction* develops when companies treat employees in a way that meets or exceeds their expectations. In other words, the better employees are treated, the more satisfied they are, and the more likely they are to give high-value service that satisfies customers.

How employers treat employees is important because it affects service capability. *Service capability* is an employee's perception of his or her ability to serve customers well. When an organization serves its employees in ways that help them do their jobs well, employees, in turn, are more likely to believe that they can and ought to provide high-value service to customers.

Finally, according to the service–profit chain shown in Exhibit 18.3, *high-value service* leads to *customer satisfaction* and *customer loyalty*, which, in turn, leads to *long-term profits and growth*. What's the link between customer satisfaction and loyalty, on the one hand, and profits, on the other? To start, the average business keeps only 70 to 90 percent of its existing customers each year. No big deal, you say? Just replace leaving customers with new customers. Well, there's one significant problem with that solution: it costs ten times as much to find a new customer as it does to keep an existing customer. Also, new customers typically buy only 20 percent as much as established customers. In fact, keeping existing customers is so cost-effective that most businesses could double their profits simply by keeping 5 percent more customers per year![40]

Exhibit 18.3 Service-Profit Chain

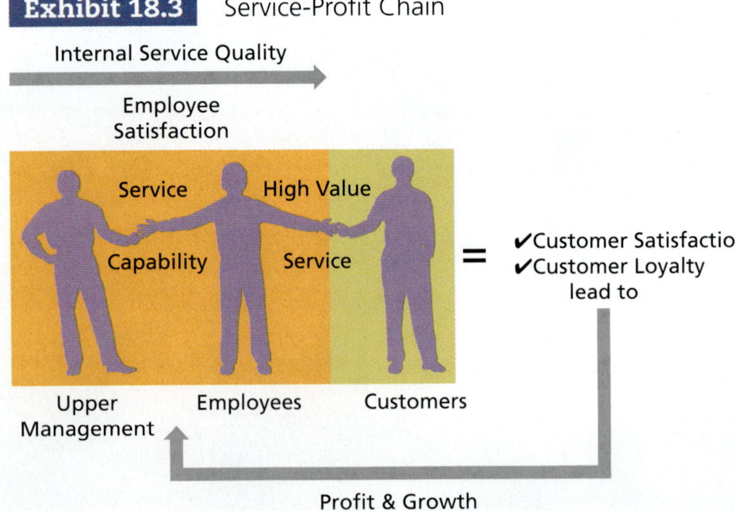

Sources: R. Hallowell, L.A. Schlesinger, and J. Zornitsky, "Internal Service Quality, Customer and Job Satisfaction: Linkages and Implications for Management," *Human Resource Planning* 19 (1996): 20–31; J.L. Heskett, T.O. Jones, G.W. Loveman, W.E. Sasser, Jr., and L.A. Schlesinger, "Putting the Service-Profit Chain to Work," *Harvard Business Review* (March-April 1994): 164–174.

3.2 Service Recovery and Empowerment

When mistakes are made, when problems occur, and when customers become dissatisfied with the service they've received, service businesses must switch from the process of service delivery to the process of **service recovery**, or restoring customer satisfaction to strongly dissatisfied customers.[41] Service recovery sometimes requires service employees not only to fix whatever mistake was made but also to perform service acts that delight highly dissatisfied customers by far surpassing their expectations of fair treatment. For example, an executor of a family estate called a Vancouver branch of Vancity Credit Union requesting access to a deceased family member's safety deposit box. The executor lived on Vancouver Island, so an appointment was made to have the box removed. However, on the day of the appointment, the branch kept the executor waiting more than 40 minutes only to discover that the safety deposit box was located at another branch. Needless to say, the executor was not happy about what he thought was a wasted trip. The manager, however, recognizing that the branch was entirely at fault, refunded the executor $100 to cover ferry costs and his wasted time as well as the $140 in administrative costs for removing the security box.[42]

Unfortunately, when mistakes occur, service employees often don't have the discretion to resolve customer complaints. Customers who want service employees to correct or make up for poor service are often told, "I'm not allowed to do that," "I'm just following company rules," or "I'm sorry, only managers are allowed to make changes of any kind." In other words, company rules prevent them from engaging in acts of service recovery meant to turn dissatisfied customers back into satisfied customers. The result is frustration for customers and service employees and lost customers for the company.

Now, however, many companies are empowering their service employees.[43] In Chapter 9, you learned that *empowering workers* means permanently passing decision-making authority and responsibility from managers to workers. With respect to service recovery, empowering workers means giving service employees the authority and responsibility to make decisions that immediately solve customer problems.[44] As part of Vancity's Service Recovery Program, employees are encouraged to "own" complaints and are empowered to take action and make decisions. Customer complaints and their resolution are tracked electronically. Each quarter, the Sales and Outstanding Service Committee reviews the feedback.[45] Empowering service workers does entail some costs, but these are usually less than the company's savings from retaining customers.

LO4 Manufacturing Operations

Toyota makes cars, and Dell does computers. Shell produces gasoline, Bombardier makes aircraft, and Molson makes beer. The *manufacturing operations* of these companies all produce physical goods. But not all manufacturing operations, especially these, are the same. *Let's learn how various manufacturing operations differ in terms of* ***4.1 the amount of processing that is done to produce and assemble a product*** *and* ***4.2 the flexibility to change the number, kind, and characteristics of products that are produced.***

4.1 Amount of Processing in Manufacturing Operations

Manufacturing operations can be classified according to the amount of processing or assembly that occurs after a customer order is received. The highest degree of processing occurs in **make-to-order operations**. A make-to-order operation does not start processing or assembling products until it receives a customer order. In fact, some make-to-order operations may not even order parts until a customer order is received. Not surprisingly, make-to-order operations produce or assemble highly specialized or customized products for customers.

For example, Dell has one of the most advanced make-to-order operations in the computer business. Because Dell has no finished goods inventory and no component parts inventory, its computers always have the latest, most advanced components, and Dell can pass on price cuts to customers. Plus, Dell can customize all of its orders, big and small. So whether you're ordering 5,000 personal computers for your company or just one personal computer for your home, Dell doesn't make the computers until you order them.

Make-to-order operation a manufacturing operation that does not start processing or assembling products until a customer order is received

Assemble-to-order operation a manufacturing operation that divides manufacturing processes into separate parts or modules that are combined to create semicustomized products

Make-to-stock operation a manufacturing operation that orders parts and assembles standardized products before receiving customer orders

A moderate degree of processing occurs in **assemble-to-order operations**. A company using an assemble-to-order operation divides its manufacturing or assembly process into separate parts or modules. The company orders parts and assembles modules ahead of customer orders. Then, based on actual customer orders or on research forecasting what customers will want, those modules are combined to create semicustomized products. For example, when a customer orders a new car, General Motors may have already ordered the basic parts or modules it needs from suppliers. Based on sales forecasts, GM may already have ordered enough tires, air-conditioning compressors, brake systems, and seats from suppliers to accommodate nearly all customer orders on a particular day. Special orders from customers and car dealers are then used to determine the final assembly checklist for particular cars as they move down the assembly line.

The lowest degree of processing occurs in **make-to-stock operations** (also called build-to-stock). Because the products are standardized, meaning each product is exactly the same as the next, a company using a make-to-stock operation starts ordering parts and assembling finished products before receiving customer orders. Customers

What Qualifies as "Made in Canada?"

Some Canadian food manufacturers are becoming frustrated with the Canadian government's new "Product of Canada" and "Made in Canada" food labelling rules. For example, Ontario-based Chapman's Ice Cream has Canadian employees, uses milk from Canadian cows, and has its packaging made in Canada, yet the company doesn't qualify for the "Product of Canada" label because it uses some imported ingredients that are not available in Canada (cocoa beans, cane sugar, pineapple). Company president Penny Chapman says, "It's just plain stupid." According to her, although refined sugar and sweeteners are available in Canada, using those ingredients would price their ice cream out of the market.

Source: CBC News, "'Made in Canada' Rules Under Review," CBC News, 22 May 2010.

Thomas M Perkins/Shutterstock.com

Claudio Bravo/Shutterstock.com

Manufacturing flexibility the degree to which manufacturing operations can easily and quickly change the number, kind, and characteristics of products they produce

Continuous-flow production a manufacturing operation that produces goods at a continuous, rather than a discrete, rate

Line-flow production manufacturing processes that are pre-established, occur in a serial or linear manner, and are dedicated to making one type of product

Batch production a manufacturing operation that produces goods in large batches in standard lot sizes

then purchase these standardized products—such as Rubbermaid storage containers, microwave ovens, and vacuum cleaners—at retail stores or directly from the manufacturer. Because parts are ordered and products are assembled before customers order the products, make-to-stock operations are highly dependent on the accuracy of sales forecasts. If sales forecasts are incorrect, make-to-stock operations may end up building too many or too few products, or they may make products with the wrong features or without the features that customers want. These disadvantages are leading many companies to move from make-to-stock to assemble-to-order systems.

4.2 Flexibility of Manufacturing Operations

A second way to categorize manufacturing operations is by **manufacturing flexibility**, meaning the degree to which manufacturing operations can easily and quickly change the number, kind, and characteristics of products they produce. Flexibility allows companies to respond quickly to changes in the marketplace (i.e., competitors and customers) and to reduce the lead time between ordering and final delivery of products. There is often a tradeoff between flexibility and cost, however, with the most flexible manufacturing operations frequently having higher costs per unit and the least flexible operations having lower costs per unit.[46] Some common manufacturing operations, arranged in order from least flexible to most flexible, are continuous-flow production, line-flow production, batch production, and job shops.

Most production processes generate finished products at a discrete rate. A product is completed, and then—perhaps a few seconds, minutes, or hours later—another is completed, and so on. By contrast, in **continuous-flow production**, products are produced continuously rather than at a discrete rate. Like a water hose that is never turned off and just keeps on flowing, production of the final product never stops. Liquid chemicals and petroleum products are examples of continuous-flow production. Because of their complexity, continuous-flow production processes are the most standardized and least flexible manufacturing operations.

Line-flow production processes are pre-established, occur in a serial or linear manner, and are dedicated to making one type of product. Line-flow production processes are inflexible because typically, they are dedicated to manufacturing one kind of product. Consider the process required for a bottling plant that produces beer. The production steps are serial, meaning they must occur in a particular order: sterilize bottle; fill with beer; cap bottles; check for underfilling and missing caps; apply label; inspect a final time; then place bottles in cases, cases on pallets, and pallets on delivery trucks.[47]

Batch production involves the manufacture of large batches of different products in standard lot sizes. This production method is being used increasingly by restaurant chains. To ensure consistency in the taste and quality of their products, many restaurants have central kitchens, or commissaries, that produce batches of food such as mashed potatoes, stuffing, macaroni and cheese, rice, quiche filling, and chili, in volumes ranging from 10 to 200 litres. These batches are then delivered to restaurants, which serve the food to customers.

Finally, **job shops** are small manufacturing operations that handle special manufacturing processes or jobs. In contrast to batch production, which handles large batches of different products, job shops typically handle very small batches, some as small as one product or process per batch. Basically, each job in a job shop is different, and once a job is done, the job shop moves on to a completely different job or manufacturing process, most likely for a different customer. According to Shawn Doucette, vice president of Ontario-based Precision Components, "job shops require workers who are multi-talented which allows them to instinctively apply greater attention to detail, providing more value in every job. It also allows for a little bit of excitement, to keep the entrepreneurial fire stoked by birthing new designs, techniques and processes to make today's complex high precision parts competitive."[48]

LO5 Inventory

In 2006, when SUVs and pickup trucks accounted for nearly 80 percent of its sales, Chrysler was reluctant to stop making them, even after consumer demand dried up. Despite a lack of orders for SUVs and pickups, Chrysler kept building cars—cars that people didn't want—and ended up with nearly a four-month supply of inventory. In addition to what was already on dealer lots, the automaker had 50,000 vehicles sitting in random storage lots across the US Midwest.[49] In the automobile industry, excess inventory can cause a downward spiral. When automobile manufacturers continue to produce inventory just to keep factories running, production does not match "real" demand, and this leads to discounting by auto dealers and incentives offered by manufacturers. In some cases, brand image becomes tarnished.[50]

Inventory is the amount and number of raw materials, parts, and finished products a company has in its possession. Over the past few years, North American automakers have experienced a wild ride, so to speak, in the form of the worst automotive sales results since the 1990s. Inventory management has become even more critical for them. Faced with a crisis, slowly over time, America's six biggest automakers—Nissan, Honda, GM, Ford, Chrysler, and Toyota—have all managed to maintain their inventories at adequate levels. Ford Motor Co. sales analyst George Pipas explains that "auto manufacturers have been pretty disciplined about gauging demand and keeping inventory under control. You can't just put the business on cruise control anymore."[51]

*In this section, you will learn about **5.1 the different types of inventory, 5.2 how to measure inventory levels, 5.3 the costs of maintaining an inventory,** and **5.4 the different systems for managing inventory.***

Photo by Tim Boyle/Getty Images

5.1 Types of Inventory

Exhibit 18.4 (page 320) shows the four kinds of inventory a manufacturer stores: raw materials, component parts, work-in-process, and finished goods. The flow of inventory through a manufacturing plant begins when the purchasing department buys raw materials from vendors. **Raw material inventories** are the basic inputs in the manufacturing process. For example, to begin making a car, automobile manufacturers purchase raw materials such as steel, iron, aluminum, copper, rubber, and unprocessed plastic.

Next, raw materials are fabricated or processed into **component parts inventories**, meaning the basic parts used in manufacturing a product. For example, in an automobile plant, steel is fabricated or processed into a car's body panels, and steel and iron are melted and shaped into engine parts such as pistons and engine blocks. Some component parts are purchased from vendors rather than fabricated in-house.

The component parts are then assembled to make unfinished **work-in-process inventories**, which are also known as partially finished goods. This process is also called *initial assembly.* For example, steel body panels are welded to one another and to the frame of the car to make a "unibody," which comprises the unpainted interior frame and exterior structure of the car. Likewise, pistons, camshafts, and other engine parts are inserted into the engine block to create a working engine.

Next, all the work-in-process inventories are assembled to create **finished goods inventories**, which are the final outputs of the manufacturing process. This process is also called *final assembly.* For a car, the engine, wheels, brake system, suspension, interior, and electrical system are assembled into a car's painted unibody to make the working automobile, which is the factory's finished product. In the last step in the process, the finished goods are sent to field warehouses, distribution centres, or wholesalers, and then to retailers for final sale to customers.

5.2 Measuring Inventory

As you'll learn below, uncontrolled inventory can generate huge costs for a manufacturing operation. Consequently, managers need good measures of inventory to prevent inventory costs from becoming too large. Three basic measures of inventory are average aggregate inventory, weeks of supply, and inventory turnover.

Job shops manufacturing operations that handle custom orders or small batch jobs

Inventory the amount and number of raw materials, parts, and finished products that a company has in its possession

Raw material inventories the basic inputs in a manufacturing process

Component parts inventories the basic parts used in manufacturing that are fabricated from raw materials

Work-in-process inventories partially finished goods consisting of assembled component parts

Finished goods inventories the final outputs of manufacturing operations

Exhibit 18.4 Types of Inventory

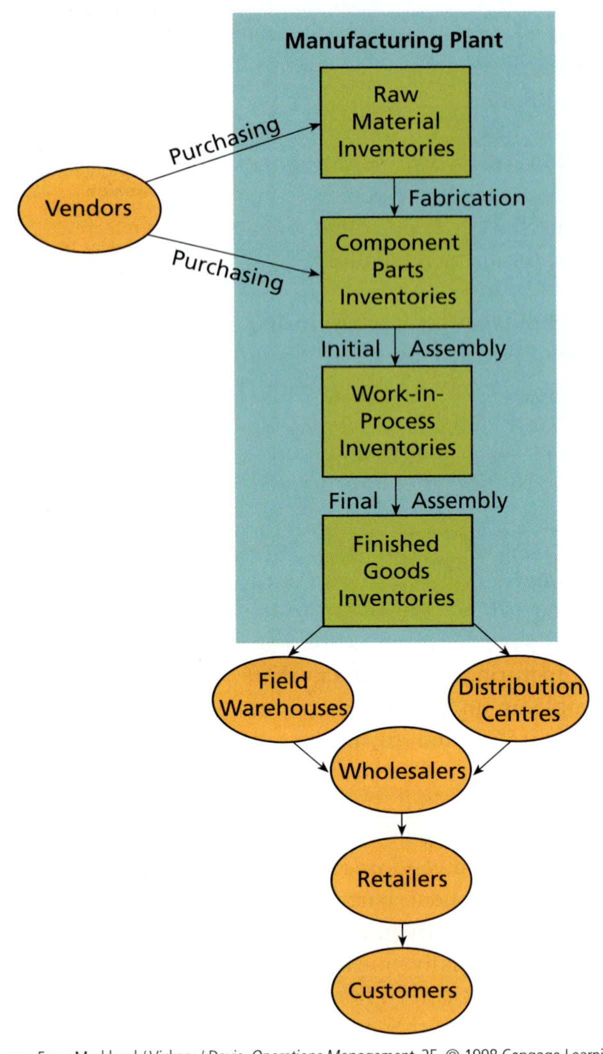

Source: From Markland / Vickery / Davis. *Operations Management*, 2E. © 1998 Cengage Learning.

© Anderson Ross/Brand X Pictures/Jupiterimages

Average aggregate inventory average overall inventory during a particular time period

Stockout the situation when a company runs out of finished product

If you ever worked in a retail store and had to take inventory, you probably weren't too excited about the process of counting every item in the store and storeroom. It's an extensive task that's a bit easier today because of bar codes that mark items and computers that can count and track them. Nonetheless, inventories still differ from day to day depending on when in the month or week they're taken. Because of such differences, companies often measure **average aggregate inventory**, which is the average overall inventory during a particular time period. Average aggregate inventory for a month can be determined by simply averaging the inventory counts at the end of each business day for that month. One way companies know whether they're carrying too much or too little inventory is to compare their average aggregate inventory to the industry average for aggregate inventory. For example, 72 days of inventory is the average for the automobile industry.

Inventory is also measured in terms of *weeks of supply*, meaning the number of weeks it would take for a company to run out of its current supply of inventory. In general, there is an acceptable number of weeks of inventory for a particular kind of business. Too few weeks of inventory on hand, and a company risks a **stockout**—running out of inventory. Competition in the retail hardware and home improvement industry has heated up over the past few years in Canada. One of the newest entrants into Canada, Lowe's, is squaring off against Canadian Tire, RONA, and fellow US rival Home Depot, which has been in Canada since 1994. For more than a decade, Lowe's significantly outperformed its key rival Home Depot, posting higher sales and larger profits and opening more stores. Home Depot, however, is catching up, because unlike Lowe's, it has done a better job of avoiding stockouts. After a particularly stormy winter, Home Depot's profits rose twice as fast as Lowe's, and its same-store sales rose four times as fast. The key was Home Depot's strong sales of snow blowers, shovels, salt, and other winter items that were in high demand. Lowe's, meanwhile, ran out of these products and lost sales.[52]

Another common inventory measure, **inventory turnover**, is the number of times per year that a company sells or "turns over" its average inventory. For example, if a company keeps an average of 100 finished products in inventory each month, and it sells 1,000 products this year, then it has turned its inventory 10 times this year.

In general, the higher the number of inventory turns, the better. In practice, a high turnover means that a company can continue its daily operations with just a small amount of inventory on hand. Let's take two companies, A and B, which have identical inventory levels (520,000 parts and raw materials) over the course of a year. If company A turns its inventories 26 times a year, it will completely replenish its inventory every two weeks and have an average inventory of 20,000 parts and raw materials. By contrast, if company B turns its inventories only twice a year, it will completely replenish its inventory every 26 weeks and have an average inventory of 260,000 parts and raw materials. So, because it turns its inventory more often, company A has 92 percent less inventory on hand at any one time than company B.

The average number of inventory turns across all kinds of manufacturing plants is approximately eight per year, although the average can be higher or lower for different industries.[53] For example, whereas the average auto company turns its entire inventory 13 times per year, some of the best auto companies more than double that rate, turning their inventory 27.8 times per year, or once every two weeks.[54] Turning inventory more frequently than the industry average can cut an auto company's costs by several hundred million dollars per year.

In the consumer technology industry, competition is fierce and effective supply chain management—in particular, inventory turnover—can make or break a company. Recently, Gartner Inc., a global information technology research company, published its list of the top 25 supply chain companies. Apple Computers was ranked the number one supply chain in the world, turning over its inventory 74 times in a year—an astonishing once every five days. For a company that sells hundreds of millions of products all over the world, this is a major competitive advantage, since the company does not need to stockpile goods in any large quantities. The next two companies in Apple's category were Dell and Samsung, which turned over their inventory approximately once every 10 and 21 days respectively.[55]

5.3 Costs of Maintaining an Inventory

Maintaining an inventory results in four kinds of costs: ordering, setup, holding, and stockout. **Ordering cost** is not the cost of the inventory itself but the costs associated with ordering the inventory. It includes the costs of completing paperwork, manually entering data into a computer, making phone calls, getting competing bids, correcting mistakes, and simply determining when and how much new inventory should be reordered. For example, ordering costs are relatively high in the restaurant business because 80 percent of food service orders (which is how restaurants reorder food supplies) are processed manually. It's estimated that the food industry could save $6.6 billion if all restaurants converted to electronic data interchange (see Chapter 17).[56]

Setup cost is the cost of changing or adjusting a machine so that it can produce a different kind of inventory.[57] For example, 3M uses the same production machinery to make several kinds of industrial tape, and it must adjust the machines whenever it switches from one kind of tape to another. There are two kinds of setup costs: downtime and lost efficiency. *Downtime* occurs whenever a machine is not being used to process inventory. If it takes five hours to switch a machine from processing one kind of inventory to another, then five hours of downtime have occurred. Downtime is costly because companies earn an economic return only when machines are actively turning raw materials

Inventory turnover the number of times per year that a company sells or "turns over" its average inventory

Ordering cost the costs associated with ordering inventory, including the cost of data entry, phone calls, obtaining bids, correcting mistakes, and determining when and how much inventory to order

Setup cost the costs of downtime and lost efficiency that occur when a machine is changed or adjusted to produce a different kind of inventory

©Stockbyte/Jupiterimages

Sharp Turns

How long do cars stay on dealers' lots? The new-vehicle "turn rate"—that is, the number of days a car sits on a dealer's lot before being sold—is a good indication of economic stability. The average retail turn rate for all vehicles is on average 63 days. In Canada, the automotive industry was happy to report that the turn rate reached a low of 51 days in October 2009 (12 days lower than in October 2008)—proof that the automobile industry was showing signs of economic recovery. Compact and midsize vehicle categories were in the top ten segments that had turn rates lower than the industry average. For example, the Ford Escape, Chevrolet Equinox, and Honda CR-V and Toyota RAV4, all part of the compact CUV (crossover utility vehicle) segment, had a turn rate below 50 days.

Sources: A. Wilson, "No More Push: How the Detroit 3 Finally Stopped Overproducing," *Automotive News*, 8 February 2010; "'Turn Rate' Indicates Economic Recovery: J.D. Power," *Canadian Driver News*, November 17, 2009; H. Elliott, "Most Popular 2010 Cars," *Forbes*, December 15, 2009.

Holding cost the cost of keeping inventory until it is used or sold, including storage, insurance, taxes, obsolescence, and opportunity costs

Stockout costs the costs incurred when a company runs out of a product, including transaction costs to replace inventory and the loss of customers' goodwill

Economic order quantity (EOQ) a system of formulas that minimizes ordering and holding costs and helps determine how much and how often inventory should be ordered

Just-in-time (JIT) inventory system an inventory system in which component parts arrive from suppliers just as they are needed at each stage of production

Kanban a ticket-based JIT system that indicates when to reorder inventory

into parts or parts into finished products. The second setup cost is *lost efficiency*. Recalibrating a machine to its optimal settings after a switchover typically takes some time. It may take several days of fine-tuning before a machine finally produces the number of high-quality parts that it is supposed to. So, each time a machine has to be changed to handle a different kind of inventory, setup costs (downtime and lost efficiency) rise.

Holding cost, also known as *carrying* or *storage cost*, is the cost of keeping inventory until it is used or sold. Holding cost includes the cost of storage facilities, insurance to protect inventory from damage or theft, inventory taxes, and obsolescence (i.e., the cost of holding inventory that is no longer useful to the company), as well as the opportunity cost of spending money on inventory that could have been spent elsewhere in the company. It's estimated that US airlines have a total of $60 billion worth of airplane parts in stock for maintenance, repair, and overhauling their planes at any one time. The holding cost for managing, storing, and purchasing these parts is nearly $12.5 billion—or roughly one-fifth of the cost of the parts themselves.[58]

Stockout costs are the costs incurred when a company runs out of a product, as happened to Apple when it failed to have enough iPods for the holiday shopping season. There are two basic kinds of stockout costs. First, the company incurs the transaction costs of overtime work, shipping, and the like in trying to quickly replace out-of-stock inventories with new inventories. The second and perhaps more damaging cost is the loss of customers' goodwill when a company cannot deliver the products it promised.

5.4 Managing Inventory

Inventory management has two basic goals. The first is to avoid running out of stock and thus angering and dissatisfying customers. Consequently, this goal seeks to increase inventory to a safe level that won't risk stockouts. The second goal is to maintain a minimum level of inventory. This goal is achieved by efficiently reducing inventory levels and costs as much as possible without impairing daily operations. The following inventory management techniques—economic order quantity (EOQ), just-in-time inventory (JIT), and materials requirement planning (MRP)—are different ways of balancing these competing goals.

Economic order quantity (EOQ) is a system of formulas that together help determine how much and how often inventory should be ordered. EOQ takes into account the overall demand (D) for a product while trying to minimize ordering costs (O) and holding costs (H). The formula for EOQ is

$$EOQ = \sqrt{\frac{2DO}{H}}$$

For example, if a factory uses 40,000 litres of paint a year (D), ordering costs (O) are $75 per order, and holding costs (H) are $4 per litre, then the optimal quantity to order is 1,225 litres:

$$EOQ = \sqrt{\frac{2(40{,}000)(75)}{4}} = 1{,}225$$

And, with 40,000 litres of paint being used per year, the factory uses approximately 110 litres per day:

$$\frac{40{,}000 \ litres}{365 \ days} = 110$$

Consequently, the factory would order 1,225 new litres of paint approximately every 11 days:

$$\frac{1{,}225 \ litres}{110 \ litres \ per \ day} = 11.1 \ days$$

EOQ formulas try to *minimize* holding and ordering costs. The just-in-time (JIT) approach to inventory management attempts to *eliminate* holding costs by reducing inventory levels to near zero. With a **just-in-time (JIT) inventory system**, component parts arrive from suppliers just as they are needed at each stage of production. When parts arrive just in time, the manufacturer has little inventory on hand and thus avoids the costs associated with holding it.

To have just the right amount of inventory arrive at just the right time requires a tremendous amount of coordination between manufacturers and suppliers. One way to promote tight coordination under JIT is close proximity. Most parts suppliers for Toyota's JIT system at its Georgetown, Kentucky, plant are located within 200 miles of the plant. Furthermore, parts are picked up from suppliers and delivered to Toyota as often as 16 times a day.[59] A second way to promote close coordination under JIT is to have a shared information system that allows a manufacturer and its suppliers to know the quantity and kinds of parts inventory each has in stock. Generally, factories and suppliers facilitate information sharing by using the same part numbers and names.

Manufacturing operations and their parts suppliers can also facilitate close coordination by using the Japanese system of kanban. **Kanban**, which is Japanese for "sign," is a simple ticket-based system that indicates when it is time to reorder inventory. Suppliers attach kanban cards to batches of parts. Then, when an assembly-line worker uses the first part out of a batch, the kanban card is removed. The cards are then collected, sorted, and quickly returned to the supplier, who begins resupplying the factory with parts that match the order information on the kanban cards. Because prices and batch sizes are typically agreed to ahead of time, kanban tickets greatly reduce paperwork and ordering costs.[60]

A third method for managing inventory is **materials requirement planning (MRP)**. MRP is a production and inventory system that, from beginning to end, precisely determines the production schedule, production batch sizes, and inventories needed to complete final products. The three key parts of MRP systems are the master production schedule, the bill of materials, and inventory records. The *master production schedule* is a detailed schedule that indicates the quantity of each item to be produced, the planned delivery dates for those items, and the time by which each step of the production process must be completed in order to meet those delivery dates. Based on the quantity and kind of products set forth in the master production schedule, the *bill of materials* identifies all the necessary parts and inventory, the quantity or volume of inventory to be ordered, and the order in which the parts and inventory should be assembled. *Inventory records* indicate the kind, quantity, and location of inventory that is on hand or that has been ordered. When inventory records are combined with the bill of materials, the resulting report indicates what to buy, when to buy it, and what it will cost to order. Today, nearly all MRP systems are available in the form of powerful, flexible computer software.[61]

Which inventory management system should you use? EOQ formulas are intended for use with **independent demand systems**, in which the level of one kind of inventory does not depend on another. For example, because inventory levels for automobile tires are unrelated to the inventory levels of women's dresses, Sears could use EOQ formulas to calculate separate optimal order quantities for dresses and tires. By contrast, JIT and MRP are used with **dependent demand systems**, in which the level of inventory depends on the number of finished units to be produced. For example, if Yamaha makes 1,000 motorcycles a day, then it will need 1,000 seats, 1,000 gas tanks, and 2,000 wheels and tires each day. So, when optimal inventory levels depend on the number of products to be produced, use a JIT or MRP management system.

Materials requirement planning (MRP) a production and inventory system that determines the production schedule, production batch sizes, and inventory needed to complete final products

Independent demand system an inventory system in which the level of one kind of inventory does not depend on another

Dependent demand system an inventory system in which the level of inventory depends on the number of finished units to be produced

Go online at
www.nelson.com/4ltrpress/icanmgmt2
And access the essential Study Tools online for this chapter:

- **Flashcards**, to help you study
- **Interactive Quizzes**, to test your knowledge
- **Audio Chapter Summaries**, for chapter review
- **Crossword Puzzles and Beat the Clock**, to review key terms
- **What Would You Do? Cases**, for applying your knowledge to real-life situations
- **Self Assessments**, to learn about what kind of manager you are
- **Videos and Media Quizzing for Part 5**
  - Chapter 16: Barcelona Restaurant Group: Managing Quality and Performance
  - Chapter 17: Numi Organic Tea: The Value Chain, IT, and E-Business: Sustainable Supply Chain
  - Chapter 18: Quality and Performance: Small Company, Tall Order

Be sure to consult the Chapter Review Card at the back of the textbook.

End Notes

Chapter 1

1. J. Johnson, "Dunkin' Donuts Ordered to Pay $16.4 Million to Quebec Franchisees," *Financial Post*, June 25, 2012, http://business.financialpost.com/2012/06/25/dunkin-donuts-ordered-to-pay-16-4m-to-quebec-franchisees; Canadian Press, "Dunkin' Donuts to Appeal Verdict Giving ex-Quebec Franchisees $16.4 Million," *Canadian Business*, June 25, 2012, http://www.canadianbusiness.com/article/88919--dunkin-donuts-to-appeal-verdict-giving-ex-quebec-franchisees-16-4-million, http://thechronicleherald.ca/business/110859-dunkin-donuts-to-appeal-verdict-giving-franchisees-164-million; S. Silcoff, "Court Rules in Favour of Dunkin' Donuts Franchisees," *Globe and Mail*, June 25, 2012, http://www.theglobeandmail.com/report-on-business/court-rules-in-favour-of-dunkin-donuts-franchisees/article4369753.
2. U.S. Commercial Service, "Market Report on Management Consulting Services," http://www.buyusa.gov/canada/en/marketintelligenceforusfirms.html; http://www.globaltrade.net/f/market-research/text/Canada/Business-Support-Services-Management-Consulting-in-Canada.html; http://www.cmc-canada.ca/Media/PublicSectorDrivingVibrantCanadianConsultingMarket.cfm.
3. D. Dale, "Jim Treliving: The Loving Dragon," *Toronto Star*, March 15, 2010, http://www.thestar.com/business/article/779809--jim-treliving-the-loving-dragon; H. Schachter, "Dragon's Den Co-star Says Use Your Head—and Your Heart—to Make Decisions," *Globe and Mail*, 25 September 2012, http://www.theglobeandmail.com/report-on-business/careers/management/dragons-den-co-star-says-use-your-head-and-your-heart-to-make-decisions/article4567463; http://www.bpincomefund.com/Files/Documents/jimbio.pdf.
4. *Shouldice Hernia Center Newsletter* 11, no. 1, http://www.shouldice.com/newsletter.htm.
5. K. Jaher, "Wal-Mart Seeks New Flexibility in Worker Shifts," *Wall Street Journal*, January 3, 2007, A1.
6. D.A. Wren, A.G. Bedeian, and J.D. Breeze, "The Foundations of Henri Fayol's Administrative Theory," *Management Decision* 40 (2002): 906–18.
7. S. Totilo, "The Unexpected Gamer Who Runs EA," *Kotaku*, http://kotaku.com/5568591/the-unexpected-gamer-who-runs-ea, accessed November 29, 2012; EA Executives, http://www.ea.com/executives.
8. H. Fayol, *General and Industrial Management* (London: Pittman and Sons, 1949).
9. R. Stagner, "Corporate Decision Making," *Journal of Applied Psychology* 53 (1969): 1–13.
10. D.W. Bray, R.J. Campbell, and D.L. Grant, *Formative Years in Business: A Long-Term AT&T Study of Managerial Lives* (New York: Wiley, 1993).
11. "Retail Profile: Core Values, Planning, and Perspective Key to Success of Lululemon," *Canadian Retailer*, January–February 2010, 20.
12. A. Lashinsky, "Search and Enjoy," *Fortune*, January 22, 2007, 70.
13. "2010 Olympic and Paralympic Winter Games," http://www.tourismvancouver.com/visitors/vancouver/2010_olympics/2010_olympics; "The Vancouver 2010 Olympic Winter Games: By the Numbers," http://www.vancouver2010.com/olympic-news/n/news/the-vancouver-2010-olympic-winter-games-by-the-numbers_297556Ko.html; M. Cernetig, "A Glitch-Free Games?", *National Post*, August 12, 2009; M. Cernetig, "It's our party so let's enjoy the moment," *Vancouver Sun*, http://www.canada.com/vancouversun/news/westcoastnews/story.html?id=262b307d-183c-4a18-a16f-0cf8cd602611&k=54906; Canadian Tourism Commission, "2010 Media FAQ," http://mediacentre.canada.travel/media-faq; City of Vancouver http://www.tourismvancouver.com; Dan Richards, "Olympian-Like Effort Key to Achieving One's Financial Goals," http://www.theglobeandmail.com/globe-investor/investment-ideas/features/experts-podium/olympian-like-effort-key-to-achieving-ones-financial-goals/article1468538.
14. C. Cornell, "Running Room Goes South," *Profit Magazine*, April 2004, http://www.profitguide.com/manage-grow/success-stories/running-room-goes-south-28444.
15. B. O'Keefe and D. Burke, "Meet the CEO of the Biggest Company on Earth," *Fortune*, September 27, 2010, 80–94.
16. H.S. Jonas III, R.E. Fry, and S. Srivastva, "The Office of the CEO: Understanding the Executive Experience," *Academy of Management Executives* 4 (1990): 36–47.
17. R. Williams, "CEO Failures: How On-Boarding Can Help," 2 May 2010, available at: http://www.psychologytoday.com/blog/wired-success/201005/ceo-failures-how-boarding-can-help.
18. "Why Corporate Boardrooms Are in Turmoil," *Wall Street Journal*, September 16, 2006, A7.
19. M. Porter, J. Lorsch, and N. Nohria, "Seven Surprises for New CEOS," *Harvard Business Review* (October 2004): 62.
20. M. Murray, "As Huge Firms Keep Growing, CEOs Struggle to Keep Pace," *Wall Street Journal*, February 8, 2001, A1.
21. Q. Huy, "In Praise of Middle Managers," *Harvard Business Review* (September 2001): 72–79.
22. Coalition for Secure and Trade-Efficient Borders, Canadian Manufacturers, and Exporters (CME), "Rethinking Our Borders: A New North American Partnership," http://www.cme-mec.ca/pdf/Coalition_Report0705_Final.pdf; University of Waterloo, Department of Economics, and Wilfrid Laurier University, Department of Econonics (2011), "Border Delays Re-emerging Priority: Within-Country Dimensions for Canada," *Canadian Public Policy*, http://utpjournals.metapress.com/content/r2278402k31t6436/fulltext.pdf; "New International Trade Crossing Study: Border Delays Cost U.S. and Canada $30 Billion Every Year" (April 2011), http://www.mirsnews.com/pdfs/

pdfs/Press_Releases/1304089398_Dric2.pdf; Alexander Moens and Nachum Gabler, "Measuring the Costs of the Canada–US border (August 2012), http://www.fraserinstitute.org/uploadedFiles/fraser-ca/Content/research-news/research/publications/measuring-the-costs-of-the-canada-us-border.pdf.

23. http://www.hp.com/canada/portal/smb/success_stories/stories/harry_rosen.html.
24. T. Seideman, "Harnessing the Giant," *World Trade* 15 (2002): 28–29.
25. J. Adamy, "A Menu of Options: Restaurants Have a Host of Ways to Motivate Employees to Provide Good Service," *Wall Street Journal,* October 30, 2006, R1–R6.
26. S. Tully, "What Team Leaders Need to Know," *Fortune,* February 20, 1995, 93.
27. B. Francella, "In a Day's Work," *Convenience Store News,* September 25, 2001, 7.
28. L. Liu and A. McMurray, "Frontline Leaders: The Entry Point for Leadership Development in the Manufacturing Industry," *Journal of European Industrial Training* 28, nos. 2–4 (2004): 339–52.
29. "What Makes Teams Work?" *Fast Company,* 1 November 2000, 109.
30. K. Hultman, "The 10 Commandments of Team Leadership," *Training and Development,* February 1, 1998, 12–13.
31. L. Landro, "The Informed Patient: Bringing Surgeons Down to Earth—New Programs Aim to Curb Fear That Prevents Nurses from Flagging Problems," *Wall Street Journal*, November 16, 2005, D1.
32. N. Steckler and N. Fondas, "Building Team Leader Effectiveness: A Diagnostic Tool," *Organizational Dynamics* (Winter 1995): 20–34.
33. Tully, "What Team Leaders Need to Know."
34. Tully, "What Team Leaders Need to Know."
35. H. Mintzberg, *The Nature of Managerial Work* (New York: Harper and Row, 1973).
36. P. Hales, "What Do Managers Do? A Critical Review of the Evidence," *Journal of Management Studies* 23, no. 1 (1986): 88–115.
37. "Canada's Top 100 Employers," http://www.canadastop100.com/index.html; "Employer Review, Mountain Equipment Co-op," http://www.eluta.ca/top-employer-mountain-equipment-co-op.
38. Francella, "In a Day's Work."
39. D. Deveau, "Blog Helps Boost Morale," Canwest News Service, November 5, 2009, http://www.thestarphoenix.com/entertainment/Blog+helps+boost+morale/2023946/story.html.
40. A. Lashinsky, "The Decade of Steve," *Fortune*, November 23, 2009, 114.
41. J. Kohane, "Spirited Female CEOs Bottle Success," *Business Edge* 23, no. 5 (March 17, 2005), http://www.businessedge.ca/archives/article.cfm/spirited-female-ceos-bottle-success-8786.
42. M. Langley, "Changing Gears," *Wall Street Journal,* December 22, 2006, A1.
43. J. Welch and G. Khermouch, "Can GM Save an Icon?" *Business Week,* April 8, 2002, 60.
44. L. Greenblatt, "Beatles Sales of iTunes Hit New Milestone," *Music Mix*, January 14, 2011.
45. L.A. Hill, *Becoming a Manager: Mastery of a New Identity* (Boston: Harvard Business School Press, 1992).
46. R.L. Katz, "Skills of an Effective Administrator," *Harvard Business Review* (September–October 1974): 90–102.
47. A. Bartlett and S. Ghoshal, "Changing the Role of Top Management: Beyond Systems to People," *Harvard Business Review* (May–June 1995): 132–42.
48. L. Schmidt and J.E. Hunter, "Development of a Causal Model of Process Determining Job Performance," *Current Directions in Psychological Science* 1 (1992): 89–92.
49. J.B. Miner, "Sentence Completion Measures in Personnel Research: The Development and Validation of the Miner Sentence Completion Scales," in *Personality Assessment in Organizations,* ed. H.J. Bernardin and D.A. Bownas (New York: Praeger, 1986), 147–46.
50. M.W. McCall, Jr., and M.M. Lombardo, "What Makes a Top Executive?", *Psychology Today,* February 1983, 26–31; E. van Velsor and J. Brittain, "Why Executives Derail: Perspectives Across Time and Cultures," *Academy of Management Executive* (November 1995): 62–72.
51. McCall and Lombardo, "What Makes a Top Executive?"
52. P. Wallington, "Management2 Toxic!" *Financial Mail,* 28 July 2006, 48.
53. J. Sandberg, "Overcontrolling Bosses Aren't Just Annoying; They're Also Inefficient," *Wall Street Journal,* March 30, 2005, B1.
54. J. Hogan, J. Hogan, J., R.B. Kaiser, and S. Zedeck, "Management Derailment," 2011, *APA Handbook of Industrial and Organizational Psychology,* Vol. 3, http://psycnet.apa.org/books/12171/015,
55. D.L. DeVries and R.B. Kaiser, "Going Sour in the Suite: What You Can Do About Executive Derailment," workshop presented at the Maximizing Executive Effectiveness meeting of the Human Resources Planning Society, Miami, (2003, November).
56. R. Hogan and R.B. Kaiser, "What We Know About Leadership," *Review of General Psychology* 9 (2005): 169–80.
57. R. Hogan, *Personality and the Fate of Organizations* (Hillsdale: Lawrence Erlbaum, 2007), 106.
58. Hogan, Hogan, and Kaiser, "Management Derailment."
59. J. Pfeffer, *The Human Equation: Building Profits by Putting People First* (Boston: Harvard Business School Press, 1996); Pfeffer, *Competitive Advantage Through People: Unleashing the Power of the Work Force* (Boston: Harvard Business School Press, 1994).
60. D. Sankey, "You Need 'Skin' in the Game to Win," *Financial Post,* May 13, 2009, http://www.canada.com/story_print.html?id=0975cd7e-a92d-46f2-92d7-575b7b24cdbd&sponsor=
61. "Watson Wyatt's Human Capital Index: Human Capital as a Leading Indicator of Shareholder Value," 2001–2 Survey Report, http://www.blindspot.ca/PDFs/HumanCapitalIndex.pdf.
62. I. Fulmer, B. Gerhart, and K. Scott, "Are the 100 Best Better? An Empirical Investigation of the Relationship between Being a 'Great Place to Work' and Firm Performance," *Personnel Psychology* (Winter 2003): 965–93.
63. B. Schneider and D.E. Bowen, "Employee and Customer Perceptions of Service in Banks: Replication and Extension," *Journal of Applied Psychology* 70 (1985): 423–33; B. Schneider, J.J. Parkington, and V.M. Buxton, "Employee and Customer Perceptions of Service in Banks," *Administrative Science Quarterly* 25 (1980): 252–67.

Chapter 2

1. C.S. George, Jr., *The History of Management Thought* (Englewood Cliffs: Prentice Hall, 1972).
2. A. Erman, *Life in Ancient Egypt* (London: Macmillan, 1984).
3. S.A. Epstein, *Wage Labor and Guilds in Medieval Europe* (Chapel Hill: University of North Carolina Press, 1991).
4. R. Braun, *Industrialization and Everyday Life,* trans. S. Hanbury-Tenison (Cambridge: Cambridge University Press, 1990).
5. J.B. White, "The Line Starts Here: Mass-Production Techniques Changed the Way People Work and Live Throughout the World," *Wall Street Journal,* January 11, 1999, R25.
6. R.B. Reich, *The Next American Frontier* (New York: Times Books, 1983).
7. J. Mickelwait and A. Wooldridge, *The Company: A Short History of a Revolutionary Idea* (New York: Modern Library, 2003).
8. H. Kendall, "Unsystematized, Systematized, and Scientific Management," in *Scientific Management: A Collection of the More Significant Articles Describing the Taylor System of Management,* ed. C. Thompson (Easton: Hive, 1972), 103–31.
9. US Congress, House, Special Committee, *Hearings to Investigate the Taylor and Other Systems of Shop Management,* Vol. 3 (Washington: GPO, 1912).
10. A. Derickson, "Physiological Science and Scientific Management in the Progressive Era: Frederic S. Lee and the Committee on Industrial Fatigue," *Business History Review* 68 (1994): 483–514.
11. US Congress, House, Special Committee, 1912.
12. F.W. Taylor, *The Principles of Scientific Management* (New York: Elibron Classics, 1911), 26.
13. C.D. Wrege and R.M. Hodgetts, "Frederick W. Taylor's 1899 Pig Iron Observations," *Academy of Management Journal* 43 (2000): 1283–91; J.R. Hough and M.A. White, "Using Stories to Create Change: The Object Lesson of Frederick Taylor's 'Pig-Tale,'" *Journal of Management* 27, no. 5 (2001): 585.
14. George, *History of Management Thought.*
15. D. Ferguson, "Don't Call It 'Time and Motion Study,'" *IIE Solutions* 29, no. 5 (1997): 22–23.
16. P. Peterson, "Training and Development: The View of Henry L. Gantt (1861–1919)," *SAM Advanced Management Journal* (Winter 1987): 20–23.
17. H. Gantt, "Industrial Efficiency," *National Civic Federation Report of the 11th Annual Meeting,* New York, January 12, 1991, 103.
18. M. Weber, *The Theory of Economic and Social Organization,* trans. A. Henderson and T. Parsons (New York: Free Press, 1947).
19. H. Verney, "Un grand ingénieur: Henri Fayol," *La fondateur de la doctrine administrative: Henri Fayol* (Paris: Dunod, 1925), as cited in Wren, "Henri Fayol As Strategist."
20. D.A. Wren, A.G. Bedeian, and J.D. Breeze, "The Foundations of Henri Fayol's Administrative Theory," *Management Decision* 40 (2002): 906–18.
21. Mary Parker Follett, *Mary Parker Follett—Prophet of Management: A Celebration of Writings from the 1920s,* ed. P. Graham (Boston: Harvard Business School Press, 1995).
22. D. Linden, "The Mother of Them All," *Forbes,* January 16, 1995, 75.
23. M. Losey, "HR Comes of Age," *HRMagazine* 43, no. 3 (1998): 40–53.
24. J.H. Smith, "The Enduring Legacy of Elton Mayo," *Human Relations* 51, no. 3 (1998): 221–49.
25. E. Mayo, *The Human Problems of an Industrial Civilization* (New York: Macmillan, 1933).
26. Mayo, *Human Problems.*
27. "Hawthorne Revisited: The Legend and the Legacy," *Organizational Dynamics* (Winter 1975): 66–80.
28. E. Mayo, *The Social Problems of an Industrial Civilization* (Boston: Harvard Graduate School of Business Administration, 1945), 65–67.
29. C.I. Barnard, *The Functions of the Executive* (Cambridge, MA: Harvard University Press, 1938), 4.
30. J. Fuller and A. Mansour, "Operations Management and Operations Research: A Historical and Relational Perspective," *Management Decision* 41 (2003): 422–26.
31. D. Ashmos and G. Huber, "The Systems Paradigm in Organization Theory: Correcting the Record and Suggesting the Future," *Academy of Management Review* 12 (1987): 607–21; F. Kast and J. Rosenzweig, "General Systems Theory: Applications for Organizations and Management," *Academy of Management Journal* 15 (1972): 447–65; D. Katz and R. Kahn, *The Social Psychology of Organizations* (New York: Wiley, 1966).
32. R. Mockler, "The Systems Approach to Business Organization and Decision Making," *California Management Review* 11, no. 2 (1968): 53–58.
33. F. Luthans and T. Stewart, "A General Contingency Theory of Management," *Academy of Management Review* 2, no. 2 (1977): 181–95.

Chapter 3

1. C. Simpson, "Sony's 2013 TVs: Everything You Need to Know," *PCWorld,* May 29, 2013, http://www.pcworld.idg.com.au/article/463061/sony_2013_tvs_everything_need_know. I. Kane, "Sony's Newest Display Is a Culture Shift," *Wall Street Journal,* May 8, 2008, B1.
2. E. Romanelli and M.L. Tushman, "Organizational Transformation as Punctuated Equilibrium: An Empirical Test," *Academy of Management Journal* 37 (1994): 1141–66.
3. C. Williams, A. Kondra, and C. Vibert, *Management*, 2nd Canadian Ed. (Toronto: Nelson, 2008).
4. Government of Canada, Canadian Dairy Information Centre, http://www.dairyinfo.gc.ca/pdf/histprod.pdf.
5. B. Stone, "Revenue at Craigslist Is Said to Top $100 Million," *New York Times*, June 9, 2009, http://www.nytimes.com/2009/06/10/technology/internet/10craig.html?_r=1&ref=craigslist.
6. J. Falls, "What the *Wall Street Journal* Has, Few Will Match," *Social Media Explorer*, October 30, 2009, 2010, http://www.socialmediaexplorer.com/2009/10/30/what-the-wall-street-journal-has-few-will-match; S. Ladurantaye, "Slow Online Ad Sales Hurt Publishers," *Globe and Mail.com,* May 10, 2012, https://secure.globeadvisor.com/servlet/ArticleNews/story/gam/20120510/RBNEWSPAPERSDIGITALLADURANTAYEATL.
7. K. Yamagishi, "Japanese Makers Forge $1 Billion LCD Alliance," CNET News, August 31, 2004, http://news.cnet.com/Japanese-makers-forge-1-billion-LCD-

alliance/2100-1041_3-5331665.html?tag=mncol; E. Ogg, "Flat-Panel TV Makers Sing the Discount Blues," CNET News, March 7, 2007, http://news.cnet.com/Flat-panel-TV-makers-sing-the-discount-blues/2100-1041_3-6165022.html.

8. "Consumer Products Brief—Kraft Foods Inc.: Price of Maxwell House Coffee to Rise 14% As Costs Increase," *Wall Street Journal,* December 15, 2004, A16.

9. Conference Board of Canada, "Economics Blog," http://www2.conferenceboard.ca/weblinx/ibc/Default.htm.

10. Dr. S. Shaw, "Who Wants to Go Shopping?" *TechlifeMag.ca*, November 2007, http://www.techlifemag.ca/728.htm. VIP Concierge and Errand Service, http://www.vipedmonton.net/corporateconcierge.htm; J. Bond, C. Thompson, E. Galinsky, and D. Prottas, "Highlights of the *National Study of the Changing Workforce*," Families and Work Institute, 2002, http://www.familiesandwork.org/site/research/summary/nscw2002summ.pdf.

11. Industry Canada Website, "Privacy in the Digital Economy," http://www.ic.gc.ca/eic/site/ecic-ceac.nsf/eng/h_gv00045.html; Canadian Centre for Occupational Health and Safety, "Legislation, Bill C-45 Overview," http://www.ccohs.ca/oshanswers/legisl/billc45.html; Province of Manitoba, "Employment Standards," February 18, 2010, http://www.gov.mb.ca/labour/standards/doc,unpaid-leave,factsheet.pdf; J. Koop and D. Kirby, "Canada: Increase in Climate Change Litigation in the U.S. Courts Could Spill Over into Canada," *Mondaq*, November 24, 2009, http://www.mondaq.com/canada/article.asp?articleid=89816; P. Webster, "The (Legal) Heat Is On: Why Companies Should Reveal Climate Impact," *Canadian Business Online*, March 26, 2007; http://www.canadianbusiness.com/after_hours/lifestyle_activities/article.jsp?content=20070326_85382_85382.

12. R. Johnston and S. Mehra, "Best-Practice Complaint Management," *Academy of Management Experience* 16 (November 2002): 145–54.

13. D. Smart and C. Martin, "Manufacturer Responsiveness to Consumer Correspondence: An Empirical Investigation of Consumer Perceptions," *Journal of Consumer Affairs* 26 (1992): 104.

14. C. Binkley, "Lucky Numbers: Casino Chain Mines Data on Its Gamblers, and Strikes Pay Dirt," *Wall Street Journal*, May 4, 2000, A1; "Harrah's Hits Customer Loyalty Jackpot," *SAS Customer Success*, http://www.sas.com; T. Mullaney, "Harrah's," *BusinessWeek*, November 24, 2003, 94; "Caesars Entertainment," http://www.caesars.com/corporate/index.html.

15. S.A. Zahra and S.S. Chaples, "Blind Spots in Competitive Analysis," *Academy of Management Executive* 7 (1993): 7–28.

16. M. Frazier, "You Suck: Dyson, Hoover, and Oreck Trade Accusations in Court, on TV as Brit Upstart Leaves Rivals in Dust," *Advertising Age,* July 25, 2005, 1.

17. M. Rekei, "Waiting for Target: Canadian Retailers Retrench," *Macleans.ca*, October 30, 2012, http://www2.macleans.ca/2012/10/30/retailers-retrench; H. Shaw, "Are Sears Canada's Days Numbered? Poor Results Could Have U.S. Retailers Circling Soon," *Financial Post*, January 8, 2012, http://business.financialpost.com/2013/01/08/are-sears-canadas-days-numbered-poor-results-could-have-u-s-retailers-circling-soon; J. Pachner, "WalMart's Secret Weapon," *Canadian Business*, October 1, 2012, 40–43.

18. K.G. Provan, "Embeddedness, Interdependence, and Opportunism in Organizational Supplier-Buyer Networks," *Journal of Management* 19 (1993): 841–56.

19. C. Unninayar and N.P. Sindt, "Diamonds an Industry in Transition: Sometimes the Speed of Change Is Alarming," *Couture International Jeweler,* August–September 2003, 68–75; N. Gaouette, "Israel's Diamond Dealers Tremble," *Christian Science Monitor,* June 1, 2001, http://www.csmonitor.com/2001/0601/p6s1.html.

20. N. Shirouzu, "Chain Reaction—Big Three's Outsourcing Plan: Make Parts Suppliers Do It," *Wall Street Journal,* June 10, 2004, A1.

21. J. McCracken and P. Glader, "New Detroit Woe: Makers of Parts Won't Cut Prices: Some Can't Afford To," *Wall Street Journal,* March 2, 2007, A1, A15.

22. D. Birch, "Staying on Good Terms," *Supply Management,* April 12, 2001, 36.

23. S. Parker and C. Axtell, "Seeing Another Viewpoint: Antecedents and Outcomes of Employee Perspective Taking," *Academy of Management Journal* 44 (2001): 1085–1100; B.K. Pilling, L.A. Crosby, and D.W. Jackson, "Relational Bonds in Industrial Exchange: An Experimental Test of the Transaction Cost Economic Framework," *Journal of Business Research* 30 (1994): 237–51.

24. "Carmakers Eye Economy with Unease," *USA Today,* May 24, 2004, B6.

25. Health Canada, "Toy Safety," http://www.hc-sc.gc.ca/hl-vs/iyh-vsv/prod/toys-jouets-eng.php; Government of Canada, "Regulations Amending the Hazardous Products (Toys) Regulations," *Canada Gazette*, http://www.gazette.gc.ca/rp-pr/p1/2009/2009-06-20/html/reg5-eng.html; Canadian Toy Association, http://www.cdntoyassn.com/index.cfm.

26. B. Clarkson, "LCBO Campaign Tackles Elephant in the Room," *Toronto Sun*, December 10, 2009, http://www.torontosun.com/news/torontoandgta/2009/12/10/12104056-sun.html; http://www.torontosun.com/news/torontoandgta/2009/12/09/12098991.html; M. Kuburas, "LCBO Deflates Elephant in the Room," *Media in Canada*, December 2, 2009, http://ads.strategyonline.ca/articles/news/20091207/lcboelephant.html.

27. Canadian Press, "Environmental Group Seeks Forest Product Boycott," *Business Edge* 1, no. 11 (May 27, 2004), http://www.businessedge.ca/archives/article.cfm/environmental-group-seeks-forest-product-boycott-6108; M. DeSouza, CanWest Global News Service, "Greenpeace Blasts Boreal Forest Destruction," September 25, 2008, http://www.theprovince.com/Greenpeace+blasts+boreal+forest+destruction/836502/story.html.

28. N.E. Boudette and J.A. White, "At GM, Curbing Inventories Calls for Juggling Act," *Wall Street Journal,* 8 January 2007, A1. http://www.detroitproject.com/readmore/wsj_010803.htm.

29. C. Hymowitz, "Top Marketing Officers Find Getting Together Helps Them Do the Job," *Wall Street Journal,* January 11, 2005, B1.

30. D.F. Jennings and J.R. Lumpkin, "Insights Between Environmental Scanning Activities and Porter's Generic Strategies: An Empirical Analysis," *Journal of Management* 4 (1992): 791–803.

31. V. Vara, "Software Giants Seek Friends Among Hackers," *Wall Street Journal,* August 3, 2006, B1.

32. S.E. Jackson and J.E. Dutton, "Discerning Threats and Opportunities," *Administrative Science Quarterly* 33 (1988): 370–87.

33. B. Thomas, S.M. Clark, and D.A. Gioia, "Strategic Sensemaking and Organizational Performance: Linkages Among Scanning, Interpretation, Action, and Outcomes," *Academy of Management Journal* 36 (1993): 239–70.

34. R. Daft, J. Sormunen, and D. Parks, "Chief Executive Scanning, Environmental Characteristics, and Company Performance: An Empirical Study," *Strategic Management Journal* 9 (1988): 123–39; V. Garg, B. Walters, and R. Priem, "Chief Executive Scanning Emphases, Environmental Dynamism, and Manufacturing Firm Performance," *Strategic Management Journal* 24 (2003): 725–44; D. Miller and P.H. Friesen, "Strategy-Making and Environment: The Third Link," *Strategic Management Journal* 4 (1983): 221–35.

35. P. Grant, "Comcast Plans Major Rollout of Phone Service Over Cable *Wall Street Journal*, January 10, 2005, B1.

36. D. Butcher, "Smartphones to Have 23 Percent Market Share by 2013: Study," *Mobile Marketer*, March 10, 2009, http://www.mobilemarketer.com/cms/news/research/2798.html; "Global Market for Smartphones and PDAs Worth $153.3 Billion in 2014," Electronics.ca Research Network Press Release, September 11, 2009, http://www.electronics.ca/presscenter; J. Kinkaid, "Apple Has Sold 450,000 iPads, 50 million iPhones to Date," *TechCrunch*, April 8, 2010, http://techcrunch.com/2010/04/08/apple-has-sold-450000-ipads-50-million-iphones-to-date.

37. Gartner Report, "Market Share: Mobile Phones by Region and Country, 3Q12," November 13, 2012, http://www.gartner.com/resId=2236115.

38. A. Harrington, N. Hira, and C. Tkaczyk, "Hall of Fame: If Making the 100 Best List Is an Enormous Accomplishment, Consider How Tough It Is to Repeat the Feat Every Single Year," *Fortune*, January 24, 2005, 94; "SAS Makes the *Fortune* 'Hall of Fame,'" http://www.sas.com/news/fortune2011.html.

39. P. Elmer-DeWitt, "Mine, All Mine; Bill Gates Wants a Piece of Everybody's Action, but Can He Get It?" *Time*, June 5, 1995.

40. D.M. Boje, "The Storytelling Organization: A Study of Story Performance in an Office-Supply Firm," *Administrative Science Quarterly* 36 (1991): 106–26.

41. S. Walton and J. Huey, *Sam Walton: Made in America* (New York: Doubleday, 1992).

42. A. Davis, "Sky High: How WestJet Got There—and How You Can, Too," *Profit Magazine*, February 2004, http://www.profitguide.com/manage-grow/success-stories/sky-high-2841; http://www.canadianbusiness.com/profit_magazine/article.jsp?content=20040213_171556_4580; P. Quinn, "WestJet Locks in Top Spot on Corporate Culture Honour Roll," *Financial Post*, January 30, 2008, http://www.financialpost.com/working/story.html?id=241844.

43. D.R. Denison and A.K. Mishra, "Toward a Theory of Organizational Culture and Effectiveness," *Organization Science* 6 (1995): 204–23.

44. Davis, "Sky High"; J. Kirby, "WestJet's Plan to Crush Air Canada," *Maclean's*, April 30, 2009, http://www2.macleans.ca/2009/04/30/westjet%E2%80%99s-plan-to-crush-air-canada;

45. "Most Admired Corporates: #2—Four Seasons," *Financial Post*, December 3, 2008, http://www.financialpost.com/working/story.html?id=1024072.

46. J. Sorenson, "The Strength of Corporate Culture and the Reliability of Firm Performance," *Administrative Science Quarterly* 47 (2002): 70–91.

47. A. Zuckerman, "Strong Corporate Cultures and Firm Performance: Are There Tradeoffs?" *Academy of Management Executive* (November 2002): 158.

48. *McDonald's Summary Annual Report* 2005, 2–4; D. Stires, "McDonald's Keeps Right on Cooking," *Fortune*, May 17, 2004, 102.

49. E. Schein, *Organizational Culture and Leadership*, 2nd ed. (San Francisco: Jossey-Bass, 1992).

50. M. Parker, "M&A and Corporate Culture," *Canadian Business Online*, July 4, 2007. http://www.canadianbusiness.com/columnists/marty_parker/article.jsp?content=20070619_150029_6476.

51. C. Leung, "Book Values," *Canadian Business Online*, October 10, 2005, http://www.canadianbusiness.com/companies/article.jsp?content=20051010_71494_71494.

52. "Employer Review: Yellow Pages Group Co.," *Eluta.ca*.

53. M. Parker, "Creating a Responsive and Adaptive Culture," *Canadian Business Online*, July 18, 2007, http://www.canadianbusiness.com/columnists/marty_parker/article.jsp?content=20070710_125841_4696.

54. M. Parker, "M&A and Corporate Culture," *Canadian Business Online*, July 4, 2007, http://www.canadianbusiness.com/columnists/marty_parker/article.jsp?content=20070619_150029_6476.

55. S. Islam, "Execs See Link to Bottom Line," *Vancouver Sun*, September 25, 2009, http://www.vancouversun.com/business/execs+link+bottom+line/1177050/story.html; A. Wahl, "Culture Shock: A Survey of Canadian Executives Reveals That Corporate Culture Is in Need of Improvement," http://www.waterstonehc.com/node/168; see also http://www.waterstonehc.com/news-events/news/canadas-10-most-admired-corporate-cultures-2011-announced-today.

56. C. Leung, "Culture Club: Effective Corporate Cultures," *Canadian Business Online*, October 9, 2006, http://www.canadianbusiness.com/business-strategy/culture-club-effective-corporate-cultures/ https://getinfo.de/app/Culture-club-Effective-corporate-cultures-can-create/id/BLSE%3ARN196634445.

Chapter 4

1. Ethics Research Center, *2011 National Business Ethics Survey: "Workplace Ethics in Transition*, http://www.ethics.org/nbes/files/FinalNBES-web.pdf.

2. Ethics Research Center, *2011 National Business Ethics Survey.*

3. Ethics Research Center, *2011 National Business Ethics Survey.*

4. Deloitte LLP, "Social Networking and Reputational Risk in the Workplace: 2009 Ethics and Workplace Survey," http://www.slideshare.net/opinionwatch/social-networking-and-reputational-risk-in-the-workplace-deloitte-survey-july-09.

5. LRN, "LRN Ethics Study: Employee Engagement," 2007, http://www.ethics.org/files/u5/LRNEmployeeEngagement.pdf.

6. Deloitte LLP, "Trust in the WorkPlace: 2010 Ethics and Workplace Survey," http://www.deloitte.com/view/en_US/us/About/Ethics-Independence/8aa3cb51ed812210VgnVCM100000ba42f00aRCRD.htm.

7. Deloitte LLP, "Trust in the WorkPlace."

8. Association of Certified Fraud Examiners, "Report to the Nations on Occupational Fraud and Abuse, 2012 Global Fraud Survey," http://www.acfe.com/uploadedFiles/ACFE_Website/Content/rttn/2012-report-to-nations.pdf.
9. S.L. Robinson and R.J. Bennett, "A Typology of Deviant Workplace Behaviors: A Multidimensional Scaling Study," *Academy of Management Journal* 38 (1995): 555–72.
10. J. Norman, "Cultivating a Culture of Honesty," *Orange County Register*, 23 October 2006.
11. Norman, "Cultivating a Culture of Honesty"
12. Centre for Retail Research, "The First Worldwide Shrinkage Survey," http://www.retailresearch.org/grtb_globaltrends.php; H. Shaw, "Workers steal 33% of all goods that go missing at retailers: survey," *Financial Post*, 31 October 2012, http://business.financialpost.com/2012/10/31/workers-steal-33-of-all-goods-that-go-missing-at-retailers-survey.
13. ACFE, 2012 Report.
14. Retail Council of Canada, "The New Face of Organized Crime," *Retail Organized Crime Report and Recommendations*, 2008, http://members.retailcouncil.org/advocacy/lp/issues/asr/2008_ROC_Report.pdf.
15. CBC News, "Almost 1 in 5 Violent Incidents Occurs in Workplace: StatsCan," February 16, 2007; Statistics Canada, Canadian Centre for Justice Statistics Profile Series, *Criminal Victimization in the Workplace* by Sylvain Leseleuc (Ottawa: Statistics Canada, 2007).
16. W. Cragg and K. McKague, "Compendium of Ethics Codes and Instruments of Corporate Responsibility," Schulich School of Business, York University, Toronto, 2003; http://www.yorku.ca/csr/_files/file.php?fileid=fileCDOICwJiei&filename=file_Codes_Compendium_Jan_2007.pdf.
17. "1991 Federal Sentencing Guidelines as a Paradigm for Ethics Training," *Journal of Business Ethics* 29, nos. 1–2 (2001): 77–84.
18. K. Tyler, "Do the Right Thing: Ethics Training Programs Help Employees Deal with Ethical Dilemmas," *HR Magazine* 50 (February 2005), http://www.highbeam.com/doc/1G1-129557302.html. http://www.shrm.org/hrmagazine/articles/0205/0205tyler.asp.
19. L.A. Hays, "A Matter of Time: Widow Sues IBM over Death Benefits," *Wall Street Journal*, July 6, 1995.
20. S. Morris and R. McDonald, "The Role of Moral Intensity in Moral Judgments: An Empirical Investigation," *Journal of Business Ethics* 14 (1995): 715–26; B. Flannery and D. May, "Environmental Ethical Decision Making in the U.S. Metal Finishing Industry," *Academy of Management Journal* 43 (2000): 642–62.
21. L. Kohlberg, "Stage and Sequence: The Cognitive Developmental Approach to Socialization," in *Handbook of Socialization Theory and Research*, ed. D.A. Goslin (Chicago: Rand McNally, 1969); L. Trevino, "Moral Reasoning and Business Ethics: Implications for Research, Education, and Management," *Journal of Business Ethics* 11 (1992): 445–59.
22. L. Trevino and M. Brown, "Managing to Be Ethical: Debunking Five Business Ethics Myths," *Academy of Management Executive* 18 (May 2004): 69–81.
23. L.T. Hosmer, "Trust: The Connecting Link Between Organizational Theory and Philosophical Ethics," *Academy of Management Review* 20 (1995): 379–403.
24. M.R. Cunningham, D.T. Wong, and A.P. Barbee, "Self Presentation Dynamics on Overt Integrity Tests: Experimental Studies of the Reid Report," *Journal of Applied Psychology* 79 (1994): 643–58; J. Wanek, P. Sackett, and D. Ones, "Toward an Understanding of Integrity Test Similarities and Differences: An Item Level Analysis of Seven Tests," *Personnel Psychology* 56 (Winter 2003): 873–94.
25. H.J. Bernardin, "Validity of an Honesty Test in Predicting Theft Among Convenience Store Employees," *Academy of Management Journal* 36 (1993): 1097–108.
26. J.M. Collins and F.L. Schmidt, "Personality, Integrity, and White Collar Crime: A Construct Validity Study," *Personnel Psychology* (1993): 295–311.
27. W.C. Borman, M.A. Hanson, and J.W. Hedge, "Personnel Selection," *Annual Review of Psychology* 48 (1997): 299–337.
28. P.E. Murphy, "Corporate Ethics Statements: Current Status and Future Prospects," *Journal of Business Ethics* 14 (1995): 727–40.
29. Canadian Tire, "Our Code of Business Conduct," http://corp.canadiantire.ca/EN/AboutUs/Documents/code_of_business_conduct.pdf.
30. S.J. Harrington, "What Corporate America Is Teaching About Ethics," *Academy of Management Executive* 5 (1991): 21–30.
31. L. Bogomolny, "Good Housekeeping: How to Ensure Your Code of Ethics Is Effective," *Canadian Business Online*, March 1, 2004, http://www.canadianbusiness.com/article.jsp?content=20040301_58731_58731.
32. L.A. Berger, "Train All Employees to Solve Ethical Dilemmas," *Best's Review—Life Health Insurance Edition* 95 (1995): 70–80.
33. Lockheed Martin, "Leaders Guide 2013, Lockheed Martin 2013 Ethics Awareness Training," , http://www.lockheedmartin.ca/content/dam/lockheed/data/corporate/documents/ethics/2013-EAT-Leaders-Guide.pdf. http://www.lockheedmartin.com/data/assets/corporate/documents/ethics/2008_EAT_Leaders_Guide.pdf.
34. L. Trevino, G. Weaver, D. Gibson, and B. Toffler, "Managing Ethics and Legal Compliance: What Works and What Hurts," *California Management Review* 41, no. 2 (1999): 131–51.
35. Boeing, "Ethics and Business Conduct Home," http://www.boeing.com/companyoffices/aboutus/ethics/hotline.html#howto.
36. Trevino, et al., "Managing Ethics."
37. Bogomolny, "Good Housekeeping."
38. Ethics Research Center, "Workplace Ethics in Transition."
39. Ethics Research Center, "2009 National Business Ethics Survey," http://www.ethics.org/nbes/files/nbes-final.pdf.
40. 2011 National Business Ethics Survey, "Workplace Ethics in Transition."
41. G. Weaver and L. Trevino, "Integrated and Decoupled Corporate Social Performance: Management Commitments, External Pressures, and Corporate Ethics Practices," *Academy of Management Journal* 42 (1999): 539–52; G. Weaver, L. Trevino, and P. Cochran, "Corporate Ethics Programs as Control Systems: Influences of Executive Commitment and Environmental Factors," *Academy of Management Journal* 42 (1999): 41–57.
42. J. Salopek, "Do the Right Thing," *Training and Development* 55 (July 2001): 38–44.
43. Ethics Research Center, 2011 National Business Ethics Survey, http://www.ethics.org/nbes/files/FinalNBES-web.pdf;

Ethics Research Center, 2009 National Business Ethics Survey, http://www.ethics.org/nbes/files/nbes-final.pdf.

44. M.P. Miceli and J.P. Near, "Whistleblowing: Reaping the Benefits," *Academy of Management Executive* 8 (1994): 65–72.

45. M. Master and E. Heresniak, "The Disconnect in Ethics Training," *Across the Board* 39 (September 2002): 51–52.

46. H.R. Bower, *Social Responsibilities of the Businessman* (New York: Harper and Row, 1953).

47. "Beyond the Green Corporation," *BusinessWeek,* January 29, 2007.

48. S.L. Wartick and P.L. Cochran, "The Evolution of the Corporate Social Performance Model," *Academy of Management Review* 10 (1985): 758–69.

49. J. Nocera, "The Paradox of Businesses as Do-Gooders," *New York Times,* February 3, 2007, C1.

50. S. Waddock, C. Bodwell, and S. Graves, "Responsibility: The New Business Imperative," *Academy of Management Executive* 16 (2002): 132–48.

51. T. Donaldson and L.E. Preston, "The Stakeholder Theory of the Corporation: Concepts, Evidence, and Implications," *Academy of Management Review* 20 (1995): 65–91.

52. M.B.E. Clarkson, "A Stakeholder Framework for Analyzing and Evaluating Corporate Social Performance," *Academy of Management Review* 20 (1995): 92–117.

53. B. Agle, R. Mitchell, and J. Sonnenfeld, "Who Matters to CEOs? An Investigation of Stakeholder Attributes and Salience, Corporate Performance, and CEO Values," *Academy of Management Journal* 42 (1999): 507–25.

54. J. Wingrove, "Finger Lickin' Tofu: KFC Goes Vegan," *Globe and Mail*, June 4, 2008.

55. A.B. Carroll, "A Three-Dimensional Conceptual Model of Corporate Performance," *Academy of Management Review* 4 (1979): 497–505.

56. J. Lublin and M. Murrary, "CEOs Leave Faster Than Ever Before as Boards, Investors Lose Patience," *Wall Street Journal Interactive,* October 27, 2000.

57. Lublin and Murrary, "CEOs Leave Faster."

58. L. Cameron, "Rumble at the Tim's Drive-Thru," *Canadian Business*, January 18, 2010, 13.

59. T. Howard, "Low-Carb Message Not Popular, but Sales Are Up," *USA Today,* December 8, 2003, 10B.

60. Sears Canada http://www.sears.ca/content/corporate-info/social-responsibility/in-your-community/scouts-canada.

61. R. Spence, "What a Bargain: Do Successful Entrepreneurs Owe a Debt to the World?" *Profit Magazine*, December 2009.

62. K. Scannell, "Witness Says Police-Vest Maker Ignored Safety Concerns," *Wall Street Journal,* November 15, 2004, C1.

63. L. Story, "Disney to Test Character Toys for Lead Paint," *New York Times*, September 10, 2007.

64. A. McWilliams and D. Siegel, "Corporate Social Responsibility: A Theory of the Firm Perspective," *Academy of Management Review* 26, no. 1 (2001): 117–27; H. Haines, "Noah Joins Ranks of Socially Responsible Funds," *Dow Jones News Service*, October 13, 1995. A meta-analysis of 41 different studies also found no relationship between corporate social responsibility and profitability. Though not reported in the meta-analysis, when confidence intervals are placed around its average sample-weighted correlation of .06, the lower confidence interval includes zero, leading to the conclusion that there is no relationship between corporate social responsibility and profitability. See M. Orlitzky, "Does Firm Size Confound the Relationship Between Corporate Social Responsibility and Firm Performance?" *Journal of Business Ethics* 33 (2001): 167–80; S. Ambec and P. Lanoie, "Does It Pay to Be Green? A Systematic Overview," *Academy of Management Perspectives*, 22 (2008): 45–62.

65. M. Orlitzky, "Payoffs to Social and Environmental Performance," *Journal of Investing* 14 (2005): 48–51.

66. M. Orlitzky, F. Schmidt, and S. Rynes, "Corporate Social and Financial Performance: A Meta-analysis," *Organization Studies* 24 (2003): 403–41.

67. Orlitzky, "Payoffs to Social and Environmental Performance."

68. G. Reynolds, "Can Honda Bring Corporate-Style Jet Travel to the Masses?", *Popular Mechanics,* March 4, 2010, http://www.popularmechanics.com/technology/aviation/news/hondajet_air_travel.

69. Orlitzky et al., "Corporate Social and Financial Performance."

70. A. Murray and A. Strassel, "Environment (A Special Report); Ahead of the Pack: GE's Jeffrey Immelt on Why It's Business, Not Personal," *Wall Street Journal*, March 24, 2008, R3.

71. K. Kranhold, "Greener Postures: GE's Environment Push Hits Business Realities: CEO's Quest to Reduce Emissions Irks Clients; The Battle of the Bulbs," *Wall Street Journal*, September 14, 2007, A1.

72. "Ecoimagination Is GE," 2008 Ecoimagination Annual Report, http://ge.ecoimagination.com.

73. K. Brown, "Chilling at Ben & Jerry's: Cleaner, Greener," *Wall Street Journal*, April 15, 2004, B1.

Chapter 5

1. L.A. Hill, *Becoming a Manager: Master a New Identity* (Boston: Harvard Business School Press, 1992).

2. J. Jargon, "General Mills Sees Wealth via Health," *Wall Street Journal*, February 25, 2008, A9, General Mills Global Responsibility 2012 Report, http://www.generalmills.com/~/media/Files/CSR/csr_2012.ashx.

3. E.A. Locke and G.P. Latham, *A Theory of Goal Setting and Task Performance* (Englewood Cliffs: Prentice Hall, 1990).

4. M.E. Tubbs, "Goal-Setting: A Meta-Analytic Examination of the Empirical Evidence," *Journal of Applied Psychology* 71 (1986): 474–83.

5. J. Bavelas and E.S. Lee, "Effect of Goal Level on Performance: A Trade-Off of Quantity and Quality," *Canadian Journal of Psychology* 32 (1978): 219–40.

6. D. Pollard, "Christine Sinclair Named QMI Agency's Canadian Female Athlete of the Year," *Toronto Sun*, December 19, 2012, http://www.torontosun.com/2012/12/19/christine-sinclair-named-qmi-agencys-female-athlete-of-the-year; G. Granger, "Burnaby's Christine Sinclair Helps Canada Chase Olympic Soccer Dream," *Burnaby News Leader*, January 25, 2012, http://www.burnabynewsleader.com/news/138056178.html; L. Ewing, "Christine Sinclair Named Canada's Female Athlete of Year," *Globe and Mail*, December 27, 2012, http://www.theglobeandmail.com/sports/soccer/christine-sinclair-named-canadas-female-athlete-of-year/article6735502.

7. Harvard Management Update, "Learn by 'Failing Forward,'" *Globe and Mail,* October 31, 2000, B17.
8. C.C. Miller, "Strategic Planning and Firm Performance: A Synthesis of More Than Two Decades of Research," *Academy of Management Performance* 37 (1994): 1649–65.
9. H. Mintzberg, "Rethinking Strategic Planning," *Long Range Planning* 27 (1994): 12–30; H. Mintzberg, "The Pitfalls of Strategic Planning," *California Management Review* 36 (1993): 32–47.
10. J.D. Stoll, "GM Sees Brighter Future," *Wall Street Journal*, January 18, 2008, A3; D. Welch, "Live Green or Die," *BusinessWeek*, May 26, 2008, 36–41; L. Greenemeier, "GM's Chevy Volt to Hit the Streets of San Francisco and Washington D.C.," *60-Second Science Blog*, February 5, 2009, http://www.scientificamerican.com; "Electric Vehicles Expected in the Next Two Years [photos]" CNET, July 16, 2010, http://news.cnet.com/2300-11128_3-10004136.html?tag=mncol.
11. Mintzberg, "Pitfalls of Strategic Planning."
12. Locke and Latham, *Theory of Goal Setting.*
13. A. King, B. Oliver, B. Sloop, and K. Vaverek, *Planning and Goal Setting for Improved Performance: Participant's Guide* (Cincinnati: Thomson Executive, 1995).
14. H. Klein and M. Wesson, "Goal and Commitment and the Goal-Setting Process: Conceptual Clarification and Empirical Synthesis," *Journal of Applied Psychology* 84 (1999): 885–86.
15. B. Scudamore, "Simplicity Breeds Success," *Profit Magazine*, October 2008, http://www.profitguide.com/manage-grow/strategy-operations/simplicity-breeds-success-29454.
16. Scudamore, "Simplicity Breeds Success."
17. K. Linbaugh and N.E. Boudette, "Fiat Models to Drive Chrysler," *Wall Street Journal*, October 27, 2009, http://online.wsj.com/article/SB125659536562909009.html?mg=com; B. Vlasic and N. Bunkley, "Party's Over: A New Tone for Chrysler," *New York Times*, November 4, 2009, 2010, http://www.nytimes.com/2009/11/05/business/05auto.html.
18. A. Bandura and D.H. Schunk, "Cultivating Competence, Self-Efficacy, and Intrinsic Interest Through Proximal Self-Motivation," *Journal of Personality and Social Psychology* 41 (1981): 586–98.
19. Locke and Latham, *Theory of Goal Setting.*
20. M.J. Neubert, "The Value of Feedback and Goal Setting over Goal Setting Alone and Potential Moderators of This Effect: A Meta-Analysis," *Human Performance* 11 (1998): 321–35.
21. E.H. Bowman and D. Hurry, "Strategy Through the Option Lens: An Integrated View of Resource Investments and the Incremental-Choice Process," *Academy of Management Review* 18 (1993): 760–82.
22. M. Lawson, "In Praise of Slack: Time Is of the Essence," *Academy of Management Executive* 15 (2000): 125–35.
23. "Google's Mission Is to Organize the World's Information and Make It Universally Accessible and Useful," http://www.google.sh/intl/en/corporate.
24. D. Forest and F. David, "It's Time to Redraft Your Mission Statement," *Journal of Business Strategy*, January–February 2003, 11–14, http://www.esf.edu/for/germain/David_8_12.pdf.
25. http://www.starbucks.com/about-us/company-information/mission-statement.
26. "Our Starbucks Mission Statement," http://www.lululemon.com/about/culture; "Legion Mission Statement," http://legion.ca/Home/mission_e.cfm.
27. S. Fife, "Break the Competitive Roadblock: Three Canadian Success Stories," *Canadian Business Online*, May 18, 2007, http://www.canadianbusiness.com/innovation/article.jsp?content=20070518_094759_4716; Leadership and Management Development Council of British Columbia, "Magnotta: Breaking New Ground with Innovative Marketing Strategies," December 2005, http://www.ic.gc.ca/eic/site/061.nsf/eng/rd02457.html. http://www.leadershipmanagement.bc.ca/pdf/MagnottaWinery_Eng[1].pdf; Magnotta.com, http://www.magnotta.com/About.aspx.
28. Industry Canada, Small Business Policy Branch, "Blue Falls Manufacturing: Turning Market Knowledge into a Competitive Edge," November 2006, http://www.ic.gc.ca/eic/site/061.nsf/eng/..%5Cvwapj%5Cbluefallsmanufacturing_eng.pdf%5C$file%5Cbluefallsmanufacturing_eng.pdf.
29. CBC News, "61% of Companies Monitor Workers' Web Surfing: Survey," April 19, 2007, http://www.cbc.ca/technology/story/2007/04/19/work-websurfing.html?ref=rss.
30. M. Geist, "Computer and E-mail Workplace Surveillance in Canada: The Shift from Reasonable Expectation of Privacy to Reasonable Surveillance," *Canadian Bar Review* 82, no. 2 (August 2003). http://www.terremoto.ca/privacy/geist_report.pdf; and S. Gaudin, "Study: 54% of Companies Ban Facebook, Twitter, at Work," *Computerworld*, October 6, 2009, http://www.computerworld.com/s/article/print/9139020/Study_54_of_companies_ban_Facebook_Twitter_at_work?taxonomyName=Web+Apps&taxonomyId=169.
31. Adapted from quality procedure at G & G Manufacturing, Cincinnati, Ohio.
32. N. Humphrey, "References a Tricky Issue for Both Sides," *Nashville Business Journal* 11 (May 8, 1995), 1A.
33. K.R. MacCrimmon, R.N. Taylor, and E.A. Locke, "Decision Making and Problem Solving," in *Handbook of Industrial and Organizational Psychology,* ed. M.D. Dunnette (Chicago: Rand McNally, 1976), 1397–453.
34. J. Jargon, "As Profit Cools, Starbucks Plans Price Campaign," *Wall Street Journal*, April 30, 2009, B3.
35. J. Jargon, "As Profit Cools, Starbucks Plans Price Campaign.
36. *Consumers Reports Buying Guide: 2006,* 129–31.
37. P. Djang, "Selecting Personal Computers," *Journal of Research on Computing in Education* 25 (1993): 327.
38. Cushman & Wakefield Healy & Baker, "European Cities Monitor" (2010), http://www.berlinpartner.de/fileadmin/chefredaktion/documents/pdf_Presse/European_Investment_Monitor_2007.pdf; European Cities Monitor 2010, http://www.europeancitiesmonitor.eu/wp-content/uploads/2010/10/ECM-2010-Full-Version.pdf.
39. K. Blanchard, "The Critical Role of Teams," March 2006, http://www.kenblanchard.com/img/pub/pdf_critical_role_teams.pdf.
40. L. Pelled, K. Eisenhardt, and K. Xin, "Exploring the Black Box: An Analysis of Work Group Diversity, Conflict, and Performance," *Administrative Science Quarterly* 44, no. 1 (March 1, 1999): 1.
41. I.L. Janis, *Groupthink* (Boston: Houghton Mifflin, 1983).

42. C.P. Neck and C.C. Manz, "From Groupthink to Teamthink: Toward the Creation of Constructive Thought Patterns in Self-Managing Work Teams," *Human Relations* 47 (1994): 929–52; J. Schwartz and M.L. Wald, "'Groupthink' Is 30 Years Old, and Still Going Strong," *New York Times,* March 9, 2003, 5.

43. C. Ferraris and R. Carveth, "NASA and the Columbia Disaster: Decision-Making by Groupthink?", Proceedings of the 2003 Association for Business Communication Annual Convention, http://businesscommunication.org/wp-content/uploads/2011/04/03ABC03.pdf.

44. C. Gallo, "How to Run a Meeting Like Google," *Business Week Online,* September 8, 2006, 15; P. Cohan, "4 Reasons Marissa Mayer's No-At-Home-Work Policy Is an Epic Fail," *Forbes*, February 26, 2013, http://www.forbes.com/sites/petercohan/2013/02/26/4-reasons-marissa-mayers-no-at-home-work-policy-is-an-epic-fail; http://www.forbes.com/sites/petercohan/2013/02/26/4-reasons-marissa-mayers-no-at-home-work-policy-is-an-epic-fail.

45. A. Mason, W. A. Hochwarter, and K. R. Thompson, "Conflict: An Important Dimension in Successful Management Teams," *Organizational Dynamics* 24 (1995): 20.

46. C. Olofson, "So Many Decisions, So Little Time: What's Your Problem?" *Fast Company*, 1 October 1999, 62.

47. A. Edmondson, "The Psychology of Conflict, and 4 Ways to Work It Out," *Fast Company*, June 5, 2012, http://www.fastcompany.com/1839408/psychology-conflict-and-4-ways-work-it-out.

48. R. Cosier and C.R. Schwenk, "Agreement and Thinking Alike: Ingredients for Poor Decisions," *Academy of Management Executive* 4 (1990): 69–74.

49. K. Jenn and E. Mannix, "The Dynamic Nature of Conflict: A Longitudinal Study of Intragroup Conflict and Group Performance," *Academy of Management Journal* 44, no. 2 (2001): 238–51; R.L. Priem, D.A. Harrison, and N.K. Muir, "Structured Conflict and Consensus Outcomes in Group Decision Making," *Journal of Management* 21 (1995): 691–710.

50. A. Van De Ven and A.L. Delbecq, "Nominal Versus Interacting Group Processes for Committee Decision Making Effectiveness," *Academy of Management Journal* 14 (1971): 203–12.

51. A.R. Dennis and J.S. Valicich, "Group, Sub-Group, and Nominal Group Idea Generation: New Rules for a New Media?", *Journal of Management* 20 (1994): 723–36.

52. R.B. Gallupe and W.H. Cooper, "Brainstorming Electronically," *Sloan Management Review,* Fall 1993, 27–36.

53. Gallupe and Cooper, "Brainstorming Electronically."

54. G. Kay, "Effective Meetings Through Electronic Brainstorming," *Management Quarterly* 35 (1995): 15.

Chapter 6

1. D. Travlos, "The iPad will Mirror the iPod's Market Dominance: Here's Why and Why it Matters," *Forbes,* July 13, 2012), http://www.forbes.com/sites/darcytravlos/2012/07/13/the-ipad-will-mirror-the-ipods-market-dominance-heres-why-and-why-it-matters; E. Spence, (2013) "BlackBerry Must Ignore Market Share," *Forbes,* January 30, 2013, http://www.forbes.com/sites/ewanspence/2013/01/30/blackberry-must-ignore-market-share.

2. C. Jones, "Apple's iPad Market Share Slips Farther Below 50%," *Forbes,* February 2, 2013, http://www.forbes.com/sites/chuckjones/2013/02/02/apples-ipad-market-share-slips-farther-below-5.

3. M. O'Mara, "BlackBerry's smartphone market share declined more than 33% in 2012: Gartner," *Financial Post,* February 13, 2013, http://business.financialpost.com/2013/02/13/blackberry-smartphone-market-share-declined-44-in-fourth-quarter-gartner/?__lsa=8d7e-0d45.

4. L. Kahney, "Inside Look at the Birth of the iPod," *Wired,* July 21, 2004, http://www.wired.com/news/culture/0,64286-0.html; http://www.apple-history.com/?page=gallery&model=ipod; K. Hall, "Sony's iPod Assault Is No Threat to Apple," *BusinessWeek,* March 13, 2006, 53; N. Wingfield, "SanDisk Raises Music-Player Stakes," *Wall Street Journal,* August 21, 2006, B4; "Growing Louder: Microsoft Plods after iPod Like a Giant—Powerful, Determined, Untiring," *Winston-Salem Journal,* November 15, 2006, D1–D2; A. Athavaley and R.A. Guth, "How the Zune Is Faring So Far with Consumers," *Wall Street Journal,* December 12, 2006, D1, D7; P. Cruz, "US Top Selling Computer Hardware for January 2007," Bloomberg.com, http://www.bloomberg.com/apps/news?pid=conewsstory&refer=conews&tkr=AAPL:US&sid=ap0bqJw2VpwI; J. Raphael, "Motorola's 2GHz Android Phone Means Business," *PCWorld*, June 11, 2010, http://www.pcworld.com/businesscenter/article/198636/motorolas_2ghz_android_phone_means_business.html; I. Fried, "Microsoft Claims Android Steps on Its Patents," CNET News, April 27, 2010, http://news.cnet.com/8301-13860_3-20003602-56.html; M. Ruhfass, "Bell Canada Now Offering RIM BlackBerry Pearl 3G 9100," Mobileburn.com, June 5, 2010, http://www.mobileburn.com/news.jsp?Id=9631.

5. J. Barney, "Firm Resources and Sustained Competitive Advantage," *Journal of Management* 17 (1991): 99–120; J. Barney, "Looking Inside for Competitive Advantage," *Academy of Management Executive* 9 (1995): 49–61.

6. J. Snell, "Apple's Home Run," *Macworld,* November 2006, 7.

7. D. Etherington, "Charting the iTunes Store's Path To 25 Billion Songs Sold, 40 Billion Apps Downloaded and Beyond," *Techcrunch.com*, February 6, 2013, http://techcrunch.com/2013/02/06/charting-the-itunes-stores-path-to-25-billion-songs-sold-40-billion-apps-downloaded-and-beyond.

8. L. Rao. "iTunes Downloads: 100M Movies, 450M TV Episodes, 35M Books, 11.7M Songs," *TechCrunch,* September 1, 2010, http://www.techcrunch.com/2010/09/01itunes-downloads-100-million-movies-35-million-books-11-7-billion-songs.

9. R. Levine, "Napster's Ghost Rises," *Fortune,* March 6, 2006, 30; "30 Products for 30 Years," *MacWorld,* June 2006, 15–16.

10. S. Hart and C. Banbury, "How Strategy-Making Processes Can Make a Difference," *Strategic Management Journal* 15 (1994): 251–69.

11. R.A. Burgelman, "Fading Memories: A Process Theory of Strategic Business Exit in Dynamic Environments," *Administrative Science Quarterly* 39 (1994): 24–56; R.A. Burgelman and A.S. Grove, "Strategic Dissonance," *California Management Review* 38 (1996): 8–28.

12. R. Burgelman and A. Grove, "Strategic Dissonance," *California Management Review* (Winter 1996): 8–28.

13. E. Smith and M. Peers, "Cost Cutting Is an Uphill Fight at Warner Music," *Wall Street Journal,* May 24, 2004, B1.

14. A. Fiegenbaum, S. Hart, and D. Schendel, "Strategic Reference Point Theory," *Strategic Management Journal* 17 (1996): 219–35.
15. L. Barth, "Most and Least Reliable Brands," *Consumer Reports*, October 31, 2012, http://www.consumerreports.org/cro/news/2012/10/most-and-least-reliable-new-cars-by-brand/index.htm.
16. S. Segan and E. Griffith, "The Best (and Worst) Tech Support in America," *PC Magazine,* July 29, 2008, http://www.pcmag.com/article2/0,2817,2326603,00.asp.
17. D.J. Collis, "Research Note: How Valuable Are Organizational Capabilities?", *Strategic Management Journal* 15 (1994): 143–52.
18. CBC News, "Ottawa T & T Supermarket Opens to Huge Crowds," October 28, 2009, http://www.cbc.ca/canada/ottawa/story/2009/10/28/ottawa-091028.html.
19. H. Thomas, "An Analysis of the Environment and Competitive Dynamics of Management Education," *Journal of Management Development* 26, no. 1 (2007): 9–21, http://www.emeraldinsight.com/journals.htm?articleid=1585399&show=abstract.
20. G.C. Peng and M.E. Nunes (2007) "Using PEST Analysis as a Tool for Refining and Focusing Contexts for Information Systems Research," 6th European Conference on Research Methodology for Business and Management Studies, Lisbon, 2007, Portugal, 229–36, http://ssrn.com/abstract=1417274
21. A. Fiegenbaum and H. Thomas, "Strategic Groups as Reference Groups: Theory, Modeling, and Empirical Examination of Industry and Competitive Strategy," *Strategic Management Journal* 16 (1995): 461–76.
22. R.K. Reger and A.S. Huff, "Strategic Groups: A Cognitive Perspective," *Strategic Management Journal* 14 (1993): 103–24.
23. CBC News, "RONA-Revy Home Centre Combo to Create Home Improvement Giant," May 14, 2001, http://www.cbc.ca/money/story/2001/05/14/ronaremy_tmc010514.html; RONA, http://www.rona.ca; CBC News, "Lowe's Says Canadian Expansion "On Track,'" September 21, 2006, http://www.cbc.ca/money/story/2006/09/21/lowes.html.
24. TimbrMart, http://www.timbr.com.
25. Canac, http://www.canac-marquis.com/Canac-Marquis-Grenier/client/fr/Accueil/Accueil.asp
26. "Auto Source Loses Money But Gains Experience," *Automotive Marketing,* May 1994, 20; Steven E. Bachand, "There's a Lot More to Canadian Tire," *Business Quarterly,* Spring 1995, 30–33, 36–39; Ian Brown, *Freewheeling: The Feuds, Broods, and Outrageous Fortunes of the Billes Family and Canada's Favourite Company* (Toronto: HarperCollins, 1989); "Trouble in Tireland," *Canadian Business,* November 1989, 95–109; "Canadian Tire's Journey South Is Uphill All the Way," *Business Week,* February 6, 1984, 88H.
27. N. Pupo, (2010), *The Shifting Landscape of Work* (2010), http://books.google.ca/books?hl=en&lr=&id=Y0x9eqhJsUgC&oi=fnd&pg=.
28. "Canadian Tire Releases Business Sustainability Results for Third Quarter of 2012," http://corp.canadiantire.ca/EN/MAD/BusinessSustainability/Documents/Q3%20Business%20Sustainability%20Online%20Report_FINAL%20ENG.pdf; F. Kopun, "Canadian Tire Adds Bling," *Toronto Star,* December 10, 2012, http://www.thestar.com/life/homes/2012/12/10/canadian_tire_adds_bling.html.
29. M. Lubatkin, "Value-Creating Mergers: Fact or Folklore?", *Academy of Management Executive* 2 (1988): 295–302; M.H. Lubatkin and P.J. Lane, "Psst ... The Merger Mavens Still Have It Wrong!", *Academy of Management Executive* 10 (1996): 21–39.
30. M. Lubatkin and S. Chatterjee, "Extending Modern Portfolio Theory into the Domain of Corporate Diversification: Does It Apply?", *Academy of Management Journal* 37 (1994): 109–36.
31. "Who We Are," 3M, http://solutions.3m.com/wps/portal/3M/en_US/our/company/information/about-us.
32. "About Samsung," http://www.samsung.com/us/aboutsamsung/index.html.
33. J.A. Pearce II, "Selecting Among Alternative Grand Strategies," *California Management Review* (Spring 1982): 23–31.
34. W.M. Bulkeley, "Staples Offers $3.6 Billion for Dutch Rival," *Wall Street Journal,* February 20, 2008, A8.
35. "Subaru Archives Homepage," *Cars101.com,* http://www.cars101.com/subaru_archives.html.
36. J.A. Pearce II, "Retrenchment Remains the Foundation of Business Turnaround," *Strategic Management Journal* 15 (1994): 407–17.
37. E. Taylor and C. Rauwald, "Daimler Scores Profit on Its Own," *Wall Street Journal,* February 15, 2008, C7.
38. S. Krashinsky, "Labatt Strikes Back Against Molson with Hockey Night Deal," *Globe and Mail,* January 18, 2013, http://www.theglobeandmail.com/report-on-business/industry-news/marketing/labatt-strikes-back-against-molson-with-hockey-night-deal/article7499966.
39. K. Gallinger, "An Ex-Car Salesman Asks: Is My Old Job Ethical?", *Toronto Star,* November 17, 2012, http://www.thestar.com/life/2012/11/17/an_excar_salesman_asks_is_my_old_job_ethical.html.
40. M. Hartley, "A Tale of Two Video Game Industries—Quebec vs. British Columbia," *Financial Post,* October 12, 2012, http://business.financialpost.com/2012/10/15/a-tale-of-two-video-game-industries/?__lsa=8b7a-9259.
41. P. Wonacott, "Wal-Mart, Others Demand Lowest Prices, Managers Scramble to Slash Costs," *Wall Street Journal,* November 13, 2003, A1.
42. M. Veverka, "Bigger and Better: Costco's Costly Expansion Is About to Pay Off—for Shoppers and Shareholders," *Barron's,* May 12, 2003, 28.
43. L. Tischler, "The Price Is Right," *Fast Company,* November 1, 2003, 83.
44. R.E. Miles and C.C. Snow, *Organizational Strategy, Structure, and Process* (New York: McGraw-Hill, 1978); S. Zahra and J.A. Pearce, "Research Evidence on the Miles-Snow Typology," *Journal of Management* 16 (1990): 751–68; W.L. James and K.J. Hatten, "Further Evidence on the Validity of the Self Typing Paragraph Approach: Miles and Snow Strategic Archetypes in Banking," *Strategic Management Journal* 16 (1995): 161–68.
45. H. Greenberg, "Rivals Won't Let Tempur-Pedic Rest," *Wall Street Journal,* February 16–17, 2008, B3.
46. M. Chen, "Competitor Analysis and Interfirm Rivalry: Toward a Theoretical Integration," *Academy of Management Review* 21 (1996): 100–34; J.C. Baum and H.J. Korn, "Competitive Dynamics of Interfirm Rivalry," *Academy of Management Journal* 39 (1996): 255–91.
47. J.C. Baum and H.J. Korn, "Competitive Dynamics of Interfirm Rivalry," *Academy of Management Journal* 39 (1996): 255–91.

48. S. Leung, "Wendy's Sees Green in Salad Offerings—More Sophistication, Ethnic Flavors Appeal to Women, Crucial to Building Market Share," *Wall Street Journal,* April 24, 2003, B2.
49. M. Stopa, "Wendy's New-Fashioned Growth: Buy Hardee's," *Crain's Detroit Business,* October 21, 1996.
50. K. Crowe and H. Shachter, "The Paradox of the Canadian Diet," CBC News, January 20, 2004, http://www.cbc.ca/news/background/food/paradox.html.
51. Subway, http://www.subway.com, July 29, 2008; N. Torres, "2007 Franchise of the Year," *Entrepreneur.com,* http://www.entrepreneur.com/magazine/entrepreneur/2007/january/172060.html; J. Jargon, (2011). "Subway Runs Past McDonald's Chain", *Wall Street Journal (Online),* March 8, 2011, http://online.wsj.com/article/SB10001424052748703386704576186432177464052.html.
52. "Frequently Asked Questions, Subway Restaurants," http://www.subway.com/ContactUs/CustServFAQs.aspx.
53. S. Leung, "Fast Food Budgets Don't Buy Consumer Loyalty," *Wall Street Journal,* July 24, 2010, B4.
54. D. Ketchen, Jr., C. Snow, and V. Street, "Improving Firm Performance by Matching Strategic Decision-Making Processes to Competitive Dynamics," *Academy of Management Executive* 18 (2004): 29–43.
55. R. Mudhar, "Amazon Launches Kindle ereaders in Canada," *Toronto Star,* July 15, 2013, http://www.thestar.com/life/technology/2013/01/23/amazon_launches_kindle_ereaders_in_canada.html.
56. H. McCraken, "E-Reader Price Wars: You Out There, Sony?", *PCWorld,* http://www.pcworld.com/article/199628/ereader_price_wars_you_out_there_sony.html?tk=hp_new.

Chapter 7

1. "Swedes to Use Body Heat to Warm Offices," ABC News, Accessed 11 Aug 13 at http://www.abc.net.au/news/2008-01-11/commuters-body-heat-to-warm-swedish-office/1009918; E. Yerger, "Company in Sweden Uses Body Heat to Warm Office Building," *PopFi,* http://www.popfi.com/2008/01/14/company-to-use-body-heat-to-warm-office-building-2; D. Chazan, "Office Block Warmed by Body Heat," BBC News, http://news.bbc.co.uk/2/hi/science/nature/7233123.stm.
2. T.M. Amabile, R. Conti, H. Coon, J. Lazenby, and M. Herron, "Assessing the Work Environment for Creativity," *Academy of Management Journal* 39 (1996): 1154–84.
3. Amabile et al., "Assessing the Work Environment."
4. A.H. Van de Ven and M.S. Poole, "Explaining Development and Change in Organizations," *Academy of Management Review* 20 (1995): 510–40.
5. Amabile et al., "Assessing the Work Environment."
6. "Thinking About Tomorrow," *Wall Street Journal,* January 28, 2008, R1.
7. G. Athanassakos, "Can Canada Go the Way of Greece?", *Globe and Mail,* September 6, 2012, http://m.theglobeandmail.com/globe-investor/investment-ideas/can-canada-go-the-way-of-greece/article4179962/?service=mobile.
8. P. Anderson and M.L. Tushman, "Managing Through Cycles of Technological Change," *Research/Technology Management,* May–June 1991, 26–31.
9. R.N. Foster, *Innovation: The Attacker's Advantage* (New York: Summitt, 1986).
10. J. Burke, *The Day the Universe Changed* (Boston: Little, Brown, 1985).
11. "Industry Snapshot," *Time,* December 5, 2005, 110; W. Symonds, "Kodak: Is This the Darkest Hour?", *BusinessWeek Online,* August 8, 2006, 3.
12. S. Gee, "Digital Camera Sales Slump as People Use Smartphones to Take Snaps," *The Telegraph* (London), 2012, http://www.telegraph.co.uk/technology/news/9361867/Digital-camera-sales-slump-as-people-use-smartphones-to-take-snaps.html.
13. M.L. Tushman, P.C. Anderson, and C. O'Reilly, "Technology Cycles, Innovation Streams, and Ambidextrous Organizations: Organization Renewal Through Innovation Streams and Strategic Change," in *Managing Strategic Innovation and Change,* ed. M.L. Tushman and P. Anderson (New York: Oxford University Press, 1997), 3–23.
14. "Blu Capabilities Still Up in the Air," *Home Media Magazine,* http://www.nxtbook.com/nxtbooks/questex/hom041308/#/2.
15. W. Abernathy and J. Utterback, "Patterns of Industrial Innovation," *Technology Review* 2 (1978): 40–47.
16. C. Hartley, "Consumers Less Likely to Buy Single-Function Electronics, While Plans to Purchase Multi-Function Devices Are on the Rise, Accenture Survey Finds" *Globe Investor,* January 7, 2013, http://www.theglobeandmail.com/globe-investor/news-sources/?date=20130107&archive=bwire&slug=20130107005334.
17. National Research Council of Canada, "NRC Helps Reinforce Tough Vehicle Emission Standards," April 7, 2007, http://www.nrc-cnrc.gc.ca/eng/achievements/highlights/2007/laser_induced_incandescence.html.
18. N.E. Boudette, E. Taylor, and L. Etter, "GM Expands Links to Ethanol," *Wall Street Journal,* January 14, 2008, A6.
19. A. Cremer and L. Frost, "'Everyone's a Bit Lost': Carmakers Think Outside the Box as Electric Dreams Shatter," *Financial Post,* March 13, 2008, http://business.financialpost.com/2013/03/08/everyones-a-bit-lost-carmakers-think-outside-the-box-as-electric-dreams-shatter/?__lsa=02fa-2dbc.
20. M. Schilling, "Technological Lockout: An Integrative Model of the Economic and Strategic Factors Driving Technology Success and Failure," *Academy of Management Review* 23 (1998): 267–84; M. Schilling, "Technology Success and Failure in Winner-Take-All Markets: The Impact of Learning Orientation, Timing, and Network Externalities," *Academy of Management Journal* 45 (2002): 387–98.
21. S. McBride and Y.I. Kane, "As Toshiba Surrenders: What's Next for DVDs?", *Wall Street Journal,* February 18, 2008, http://online.wsj.com/article/SB120321618700574049.html?mod=MKTW; Y.I. Kane, "Toshiba Regroups After Losing DVD War," *Wall Street Journal*, February 20, 2008, http://online.wsj.com/article/SB120342115442976687.html?mod= googlenews; B. Coxworth, "Transparent, Flexible Memory Chips Could Replace Flash Memory in Electronic Devices," *Gizmag,* April 2, 2012, http://www.gizmag.com/transparent-flexible-flash-replacement-chip/22031.
22. Amabile et al., "Assessing the Work Environment."
23. Amabile et al., "Assessing the Work Environment."
24. M. Csikszentmihalyi, *Flow: The Psychology of Optimal Experience* (New York: Harper and Row, 1990).
25. V. Vara, "Pleasing Google's Tech-Savvy Staff," *Wall Street Journal,* March 18, 2008, B6.

26. A. Oreskovic, "Yahoo's Work-from-Home Ban Squanders Benefits Spurred by Telecommuting," *Financial Post,* March 13, 2013, http://business.financialpost.com/2013/03/15/yahoo-work-from-home-ban.
27. S. Kirsner, "Adobe Idol," *Fast Company,* May 2007, 95.
28. K. Capell, "Thinking Simple at Philips," *Business Week,* December 11, 2006, 50.
29. K. Goetz, "How 3M Gave Everyone Days Off and Created an Innovation Dynamo," *Fast Company,* June 6, 2011, http://www.fastcodesign.com/1663137/how-3m-gave-everyone-days-off-and-created-an-innovation-dynamo.
30. K.M. Eisenhardt, "Accelerating Adaptive Processes: Product Innovation in the Global Computer Industry," *Administrative Science Quarterly* 40 (1995): 84–110.
31. Eisenhardt, "Accelerating Adaptive Processes."
32. E. Masamitsu, "This Is My Job: Parachute Tester," *Popular Mechanics* 185 (June 2008): 174.
33. C. Salter, "Ford's Escape Route," *Fast Company,* October 1, 2004, 106.
34. L. Kraar, "25 Who Help the U.S. Win: Innovators Everywhere Are Generating Ideas to Make America a Stronger Competitor," *Fortune,* March 22, 1991.
35. M.W. Lawless and P.C. Anderson, "Generational Technological Change: Effects of Innovation and Local Rivalry on Performance," *Academy of Management Journal* 39 (1996): 1185–217.
36. G. Graff, "Plastics Firm Unlocks Value of Early Supplier Involvement," *Purchasing,* June 14, 2007, 5.
37. K. Kelly, "Older Harry Rates a PG-13: The Awkward, Lovelorn Hero of 'Goblet of Fire' May Lose Kids, Gain Broader Audience," *Wall Street Journal,* November 16, 2005, B1.
38. B. Baumohl and W. Cole, "The Perils of Having Way More Than Enough," *Time,* January 13, 1997, 58; S. Forest, "Incredible Universe: Lost in Space," *BusinessWeek,* March 4, 1996, http://www.businessweek.com/1996/10/b346580.htm.
39. P. Strebel, "Choosing the Right Change Path," *California Management Review* (Winter 1994): 29–51.
40. W. Weitzel and E. Jonsson, "Reversing the Downward Spiral: Lessons from W.T. Grant and Sears Roebuck," *Academy of Management Executive* 5 (1991): 7–22.
41. Weitzel and Jonsson, "Reversing the Downward Spiral."
42. T. Van Alphen, "Unions Must Change Quickly to Survive, Says Secret Report by CEP/CAW," *Toronto Star,* January 26, 2012, http://www.thestar.com/news/gta/2012/01/26/unions_must_change_quickly_to_survive_says_secret_report_by_cepcaw.html.
43. T. Reed, "What's Wrong with Ford and GM Shares?", *CNBC,* March 13, 2013, http://www.cnbc.com/id/100549938.
44. K. Lewin, *Field Theory in Social Science: Selected Theoretical Papers* (New York: Harper, 1951).
45. Lewin, *Field Theory in Social Science.*
46. Lewin, *Field Theory in Social Science.*
47. A.B. Fisher, "Making Change Stick," *Fortune*, April 17, 1995, 121.
48. J.P. Kotter and L.A. Schlesinger, "Choosing Strategies for Change," *Harvard Business Review* (March–April 1979): 106–14; Harvard Business School Press, *Managing Change to Reduce Resistance* (Cambridge, MA: Harvard Business School Press, 2005).
49. D. Sewell, "P&G Open to Outside Ideas, but No Kitty Swiffers," *Report on Business,* January 4, 2010, http://www.eternalcode.com/pg-open-to-outside-ideas-but-no-kitty-swiffers/
50. J. Neff, "P&G (Canada) Will Put 'up to' 20% of Budget in Digital in the Great North," May 21, 2008, http://customerlistening.typepad.com/customer_listening/2008/05/pg-canada-will.html.
51 PG.com, "Management Perspectives," July 18, 2013, http://www.pg.com/en_CA/company/who_we_are/letter_penner.shtml.
52. B. Orwall, "Disney Decides It Must Draw Artists into Computer Age," *Wall Street Journal,* October 23, 2003, A1.
53. J.P. Kotter, "Leading Change: Why Transformation Efforts Fail," *Harvard Business Review* 73, no. 2 (March–April 1995): 59.
54. A. Wahl, "Q&A: Celestica's Craig Muhlhauser," *Canadian Business*, 2008, http://www.canadianbusiness.com/business-strategy/qa-celesticas-craig-muhlhauser.
55. H. Miller, "Celestica Fills BlackBerry Gap with Aerospace," *Bloomberg News*, 2013, http://www.bloomberg.com/news/2013-04-24/celestica-fills-blackberry-gap-with-aerospace-corporate-canada.html.
56. E. Byron, "P&G Makes a Bigger Play for Men," *Wall Street Journal,* August 28, 2009, http://online.wsj.com/article/SB124096436192766099.html.
57. Byron, "P&G Makes a Bigger Play."
58. P. Engardio and J. McGregor, "Lean and Mean Gets Extreme," *Business Week*, March 23, 2009, 60, http://www.thefreelibrary.com/+LEAN+AND+MEAN+GETS+EXTREME-a01611821658.
59. Miller, "Celestica Fills BlackBerry Gap With Aerospace."
60. R. Carrick, "Rising from the Stock Market Rubble," *Globe and Mail,* June 21, 2008, B15;
61. W. Dabrowski, "Celestica Buoyed by Smartphone Market Potential," *Toronto Star*, April 24, 2009, B4, http://www.thestar.com/business/2009/04/24/celestica_buoyed_by_smartphone_market_potential.html.
62. Harvard Business School Press, *The Results-Driven Manager: Getting People on Board* (Cambridge, MA: Havard Business School Press, 2005).
63. M. Ihlwan, L. Armstrong, and M. Eidam, "Hyundai: Kissing Clunkers Goodbye," *Business Week,* 17 May 2004, 46.
64. J.D. Power and Associates, "J.D. Power and Associates Reports: Domestic Brands Surpass Imports in Initial Quality for the First Time in IQS History," *Autoblog,* June 17, 2010, http://www.theautochannel.com/news/2010/06/17/483121.html.
65. Harvard Business School Press, *The Results-Driven Manager.*
66. Ihlwan, Armstrong, and Eidam, "Hyundai: Kissing Clunkers Goodbye."
67. P. Ingrassia, "Why Hyundai Is an American Hit," *Wall Street Journal,* September 14, 2009, A13, http://online.wsj.com/article/SB10001424052970203917304574410692912072328.html.
68. Ingrassia, "Why Hyundai Is an American Hit."
69. Ingrassia, "Why Hyundai Is an American Hit."
70. W.J. Rothwell, R. Sullivan, and G.M. McLean, *Practicing Organizational Development: A Guide for Consultants* (San Diego: Pfeiffer, 1995).

71. R.N. Ashkenas and T.D. Jick, "From Dialogue to Action in GE WorkOut: Developmental Learning in a Change Process," in *Research in Organizational Change and Development* 6, ed. W.A. Pasmore and R.W. Woodman (Greenwich: JAI, 1992), 267–87.

72. T. Stewart, "GE Keeps Those Ideas Coming," *Fortune*, August 12, 1991, 40.

73. Stewart, "GE Keeps Those Ideas Coming."

74. Rothwell, Sullivan, and McLean, *Practicing Organizational Development.*

75. Rothwell, Sullivan, and McLean, *Practicing Organizational Development.*

Chapter 8

1. F. Jacob and G. Strube, *Why Go Global? The Multinational Imperative* (Berlin: Springer, 2008), 2–33.

2. UN Conference on Trade and Development, "World Investment Report, 2006," http://www.unctad.org/en/docs/wir2006annexes_en.pdf.

3. G. Samor, "Steelmaker Girds for Growth—Gerdau of Brazil Looks to Bulk Up Further in United States Market," *Wall Street Journal,* April 5, 2005, B2.

4. J. Partridge, "Molson Coors SABMiller Brew Up $10 billion Venture," *Globe and Mail*, October 9, 2009, http://www.theglobeandmail.com/report-on-business/molson-coors-sabmiller-brew-up-10-billion-venture/article1084185; R. Blackwell, "Brewing a Recipe for Success," *Globe and Mail,* August 23, 2012, http://www.theglobeandmail.com/report-on-business/careers/careers-leadership/brewing-a-recipe-for-success/article573391.

5. "Sapporo Acquisition of Sleeman on Tap," *CBCNews/Business*, August 11, 2008, http://www.cbc.ca/news/business/story/2006/08/11/sapporo-sleeman.html.

6. J. Miller, "China's Low Fruit Prices Highlight EU's Vulnerabilities over Trade," *Wall Street Journal,* December 26, 2006, A4.

7. GreenFacts, "Table 5: Applied Tariffs on Ethanol in Selected Countries," http://www.greenfacts.org/en/biofuels/figtableboxes/tarifs-ethanol.htm; Canada News Centre, "Canada Poised to Become 'Tariff-Free Zone' for Manufacturers Thanks to Budget 2010," March 9, 2010, http://news.gc.ca/web/article-eng.do?m=/index&nid=517449.

8. "Determination of Total Amounts and Quota Period for Tariff-Rate Quotas for Raw Cane Sugar and Certain Imported Sugars, Syrups, and Molasses," *Federal Register,* April 15, 2002, 18162.

9. J. Sparshott, "U.S. Sugar Growers Fear Losses from Free-Trade Push," *Washington Times,* March 24, 2005, C07.

10. World Trade Organization, "Understanding the WTO," http://www.wto.org/english/thewto_e/whatis_e/tif_e/agrm9_e.htm.

11. D. Poulin and K. Boame, "Mad Cow Disease and Beef Trade," November 12, 2009, http://www.statcan.gc.ca/pub/11-621-m/11-621-m2003005-eng.htm; S. Kosinski, "Canada Imports into the US," June 21, 2010, http://www.foragebeef.ca/app33/foragebeef/index_body.jsp.

12. P. Lemieux, "Bombardier's Gain Is the Taxpayer's Loss—FP Comment," July 22, 2008, http://www.pierrelemieux.org/artbombardier.html; A. Lampert, "Americans Frown, Embraer Scraps with Bombardier and We Pick Up the Tab," August 14, 2008, http://www.canada.com/story.html?id=4ba12685-83d0-47e9-988c-a13cb5a019cb; CBC News, 2 April 2009. "A Transportation Giant Evolves," April 2, 2009, http://www.cbc.ca/canada/montreal/story/2009/04/02/f-bombardier-indepth-0402.html.

13. "Rocky Receives Customs Clarification on Imported Boots," *FN,* March 31, 2003.

14. H. Blodget, "How to Solve China's Piracy Problem: A Dozen Ideas: Maybe One Will Work," *Slate,* April 12, 2005, http://slate.msn.com/id/2116629.

15. "The History of the European Union," *Europa—The European Union Online,* http://europa.eu/about-eu/eu-history.

16. "The History of the European Union," *Europa,* http://europa.eu/about-eu/countries/index_en.htm.

17. D. Luhnow, "Crossover Success: How NAFTA Helped Wal-Mart Reshape the Mexican Market," *Wall Street Journal,* August 31, 2001, A1.

18. L.H. Teslik, "NAFTA's Economic Impact," Council on Foreign Relations, http://www.cfr.org/publication/15790/naftas_economic_ impact.html#4.

19. Office of the United States Trade Representative, "US Trade with the CAFTA-DR Countries," July 2011, http://www.ustr.gov/about-us/press-office/fact-sheets/2011/may/us-trade-cafta-dr-countries.

20. UNASUR, Union of South American Nations, http://www.comunidadandina.org/ingles/sudamerican.htm.

21. "Selected Basic ASEAN Indicators", *Association of Southeast Nations*, http://www.asean.org/news/item/selected-key-indicators; *Association of Southeast Nations*, http://www.asean.org/images/2013/resources/statistics/SKI/table2.pdf; "ASEAN Free Trade Area (AFTA)," *Association of Southeast Nations*, http://www.asean.org/communities/asean-economic-community/item/asean-free-trade-area-afta-an-update.

22. Asia Pacific Economic Cooperation, "Member Economies," http://www.apec.org/about-us/about-apec/member-economies.aspx; Asia-Pacific Economic Cooperation, "Frequently Asked Questions (FAQs," http://www.apec.org/FAQ.aspx.

23. "The Big Mac Index," *The Economist,* http://www.economist.com/blogs/dailychart/2011/07/big-mac-index.

24. World Trade Organization, "Freer Trade Cuts the Cost of Living," http://www.wto.org/english/thewto_e/whatis_e/10ben_e/10b04_e.htm.

25. MTV Brasil, http://mtv.uol.com.br; MTV China, http://mtvchina.com; MTV India, http://www.mtvindia.com/sillypoint/sourav.php.

26. A. Sundaram and J.S. Black, "The Environment and Internal-Organization of Multinational Enterprises," *Academy of Management Review* 17 (1992): 729–57.

27. H.S. James, Jr., and M. Weidenbaum, *When Businesses Cross International Borders: Strategic Alliances and Their Alternatives* (Westport: Praeger, 1993).

28. J.T. Areddy, "China's Export Machine Threatened by Rising Costs," *Wall Street Journal,* June 30, 2008, A1.

29. J.D. Stoll, N. Shirouzu, and N.E. Boudette, "Detroit Sets Bold Goal: Exporting U.S. Cars," *Wall Street Journal,* April 8, 2008, A1.

30. Fuji Xerox, "Company Profile," http://www.fujixerox.co.jp/eng/company/profile.html.

31. "Arrow, Shell Seal a Venture," *Wall Street Journal,* September 15, 2008, http://online.wsj.com/article/SB122144583046434931.html.

32. "Joint Ventures," *Encyclopedia of Business*, 2nd ed., http://www.referenceforbusiness.com/encyclopedia/Int-Jun/Joint-Ventures.html#WHY_JOINT_VENTURES_FAIL.

33. M.W. Hordes, J.A. Clancy, and J. Baddaley, "A Primer for Global Start-Ups," *Academy of Management Executive* (May 1995): 7–11.

34. D. Pavlos, J. Johnson, J. Slow, and S. Young, "Micromultinationals: New Types of Firms for the Global Competitive Landscape," *European Management Journal* 21, no. 2 (April 2003): 164; B.M. Oviatt and P.P. McDougall, "Toward a Theory of International New Ventures," *Journal of International Business Studies* (Spring 1994): 45; S. Zahra, "A Theory of International New Ventures: A Decade of Research," *Journal of International Business Studies* (January 2005): 20–28.

35. M. Copeland, "The Mighty Micro-Multinational," *Business 2.0,* July 1, 2006, 106.

36. *TokyoPrices.com,* July 16, 2009,http://www.tokyoprices.com/coke-prices-in-tokyo-japan.

37. D. Lynch, "Developing Nations Poised to Challenge USA as King of the Hill," *USA Today,* February 8, 2007, B1; N. Srinivas, "Of Carats and Calories," *Economic Times,* December 29, 2006.

38. F. Vogelstein, "How Intel Got Inside," *Fortune,* October 4, 2004, 127.

39. P. Dvorak, "Why Multiple Headquarters Multiply," *Wall Street Journal,* November 19, 2007, B1; J.L. Yang, "Making Mergers Work," *Fortune,* November 26, 2007, 42.

40. Netherlands Foreign Investment Agency, "Customer Care in the Netherlands," http://www.nfia.com/solutions.php?pageid=11 (content no longer available online).

41. J. Oetzel, R. Bettis, and M. Zenner, "How Risky Are They?" *Journal of World Business* 36, no. 2 (Summer 2001): 128–45.

42. K.D. Miller, "A Framework for Integrated Risk Management in International Business," *Journal of International Business Studies* (2nd Quarter 1992): 311.

43. A. Osborn and D. Gauthier-Villars, "Twisty Road: Renault Deal in Russia Shows Kremlin Tactics," *Wall Street Journal,* March 21, 2008, A1.

44. "Chapter 1: Political Outlook," *UAE Business Forecast Report* (2007 1st Quarter): 5–10.

45. I. Brat, "Going Global by Going Green," *Wall Street Journal,* February 26, 2008, B1.

46. M. Tomz, J.L. Goldstein, and D. Rivers, "Do We Really Know That the WTO Increases Trade?" *American Economic Review* 97, no. 5 (2007): 2005–18.

47. G. Hofstede, "The Cultural Relativity of the Quality of Life Concept," *Academy of Management Review* 9 (1984): 389–98; G. Hofstede, "The Cultural Relativity of Organizational Practices and Theories," *Journal of International Business Studies* (Fall 1983): 75–89; G. Hofstede, "The Interaction Between National and Organizational Value Systems," *Journal of Management Studies* (July 1985): 347–57; M. Hoppe, "An Interview with Geert Hofstede," *Academy of Management Executive* (February 2004): 75–79; G.K. Stephens and C.R. Greer, "Doing Business in Mexico: Understanding Cultural Differences," *Organizational Dynamics*, Special Report, 1998.

48. R.L. Tung and A. Verbeke, "Beyond Hofstede and GLOBE: Improving the Quality of Cross-Cultural Research," *Journal of International Business Studies* 41 (2010): 1259–74; J.C. Singh, R.J. House, and F.C. Brodbeck, *Culture and Leadership, Across the World: The GLOBE Book of In-Depth Studies of 25 Societies* (Mahwah: LEA, 2012); G. Hofstede, "What Did GLOBE Really Measure? Researchers' Minds Versus Respondents' Minds," *Journal of International Business Studies 37* (2006): 882–96.

49. R. Hodgetts, "A Conversation with Geert Hofstede," *Organizational Dynamics* (Spring 1993): 53–61.

50. T. Lenartowicz and K. Roth, "Does Subculture Within a Country Matter? A Cross-Cultural Study of Motivational Domains and Business Performance in Brazil," *Journal of International Business Studies* 32 (2001): 305–25.

51. M. Janssens, J.M. Brett, and F.J. Smith, "Confirmatory Cross-Cultural Research: Testing the Viability of a Corporation-Wide Safety Policy," *Academy of Management Journal* 38 (1995): 364–82.

52. J.S. Black, M. Mendenhall, and G. Oddou, "Toward a Comprehensive Model of International Adjustment: An Integration of Multiple Theoretical Perspectives," *Academy of Management Review* 16 (1991): 291–317; R.L. Tung, "American Expatriates Abroad: From Neophytes to Cosmopolitans," *Columbia Journal of World Business,* June 22, 1998, 125; A. Harzing, "The Persistent Myth of High Expatriate Failure Rates," *International Journal of Human Resource Management* 6 (1995): 457–75; A. Harzing, "Are Our Referencing Errors Undermining Our Scholarship and Credibility? The Case of Expatriate Failure Rates," *Journal of Organizational Behavior* 23 (2002): 127–48; N. Forster, "The Persistent Myth of High Expatriate Failure Rates: A Reappraisal," *International Journal of Human Resource Management* 8 (1997): 414–33; A. McMullen, "Canada Tops Global Expats Survey of Best Countries," *National Post*, December 2, 2009, http://www2.canada.com/story.html?id=2292837.

53. W.W. Maddux, A.D. Galinsky, and C.T. Tadmor, "Be a Better Manger: Live Abroad," *Harvard Business Review,* September 9, 2010.

54. Canadian Bureau for International Education, http://www.cbie-bcei.ca/wp-content/uploads/2011/10/20100520_WorldOfLearningReport_e.pdf.

55. J. Black, "The Right Way to Manage Expats," *Harvard Business Review* 77 (March–April 1999): 52; C. Joinson, "No Returns," *HR Magazine,* November 1, 2002, 70.

56. Information for Canadian Students Planning to Study Abroad, http://www.cicic.ca/409/Information_for_Canadian_Students.canada.

57. C. Joinson, "No Returns," *HR Magazine,* November 2002, 70.

58. J.S. Black and M. Mendenhall, "Cross-Cultural Training Effectiveness: A Review and Theoretical Framework for Future Research," *Academy of Management Review* 15 (1990): 113–36.

59. K. Essick, "Executive Education: Transferees Prep for Life, Work in Far-Flung Lands," *Wall Street Journal,* November 12, 2004, A6.

60. P.W. Tam, "Culture Course—'Awareness Training' Helps U.S. Workers Better Know Their Counterparts in India," *Wall Street Journal,* May 25, 2004, B1.

61. W. Arthur, Jr., and W. Bennett, Jr., "The International Assignee: The Relative Importance of Factors Perceived to Contribute to Success," *Personnel Psychology* 48 (1995): 99–114; B. Cheng, "Home Truths About

Foreign Postings; To Make an Overseas Assignment Work, Employers Need More Than an Eager Exec with a Suitcase," *BusinessWeek Online*, July 14, 2002, http://www.businessweek.com/careers/content/jul2002/ca20020715_9110.htm.

62. E. Gaydos, "Five Hard Lessons in Global Talent Management," *Mobility*, 2010, http://www.sri-2000.com/resources.html.
63. Prudential Real Estate and Relocation Services Intercultural Group, "OAI: Overseas Assignment Inventory," May 11, 2011, http://www.prudential.com/view/page/public/14394.
64. D. Eschbach, G. Parker, and P. Stoeberl, "American Repatriate Employees' Retrospective Assessments of the Effects of Cross-Cultural Training on Their Adaptation to International Assignments," *International Journal of Human Resource Management* 12 (2001): 270–87; "Culture Training: How to Prepare Your Expatriate Employees for Cross-Cultural Work Environments," *Managing Training & Development*, February 1, 2005.
65. J. Areddy, "Deep Inside China, American Family Struggles to Cope," *Wall Street Journal*, August 2, 2005, A1.

Chapter 9

1. "Sony Corp. Info: Organizational Data SONY Group Organizational Chart Summary, as of June 1, 2013," http://www.sony.net/SonyInfo/CorporateInfo/Data/organization.html.
2. M. Hammer and J. Champy, *Reengineering the Corporation: A Manifesto for Business Revolution* (New York: Harper and Row, 1993).
3. "Strength in Structure," *Procter & Gamble*, http://www.pg.com/en_US/company/global_structure_operations/corporate_structure.shtml; *P&G Annual Report 2012*, http://annualreport.pg.com/annualreport2012/index.shtml; "Pampers: The Birth of P&G's First 10-Billion-Dollar Brand," June 27, 2012, http://news.pg.com/blog/10-billion-dollar-brand/pampers-birth-pgs-first-10-billion-dollar-brand, A. Alexander, "P&G reorganizes global business units into industry-based sectors," *Drugstore News*, 6 June 2013, available at: http://drugstorenews.com/article/pg-reorganizes-global-business-units-industry-based-sectors, http://news.pg.com/press-release/pg-corporate-announcements/procter-gamble-announces-organization-changes.
4. J.G. March and H.A. Simon, *Organizations* (New York: John Wiley, 1958).
5. United Technologies Corporation, "2012 Annual Report," http://2012ar.utc.com/assets/pdfs/UTCAR12_Full_Report.pdf.
6. United Technologies Corporation, "2012 Annual Report."
7. Saputo, "Annual Information Form," June 7, 2011, http://www.saputo.com/uploadedFiles/Saputo/investors-and-medias/financial-documents/AIF_EN_2011.pdf.
8. L.R. Burns, "Adoption and Abandonment of Matrix Management Programs: Effects of Organizational Characteristics and Interorganizational Networks," *Academy of Management Journal* 36 (1993): 106–38.
9. H. Fayol, *General and Industrial Management*, trans. C. Storrs (London: Pitman, 1949).
10. M. Weber, *The Theory of Social and Economic Organization*, trans. and ed. A.M. Henderson and T. Parsons (New York: Free Press, 1947).
11. Fayol, *General and Industrial Management*.
12. K. Moore, "Murray Martin Talks to Karl Moore," *Globe and Mail*, April 6, 2010, http://www.theglobeandmail.com/report-on-business/murray-martin-talks-to-karl-moore/article1525148.
13. A. Lopez-Pacheco, "Letting Go the Day-to-Day: It Starts with Building the Right Team," *Financial Post*, May 16, 2010, http://www.financialpost.com/Letting+starts+with+building+right+team/3038099/story.html.
14. M. Stern, "10 Worst Leadership Habits," *Canadian Business*, May 1, 2008: 63–65, http://www.michaelstern.com/coaching/10_Worst_Leadership_Habits.pdf; http://www.canadianbusiness.com/managing/career/article.jsp?content=20080312_198703_198703.
15. D. Ovsey, "Technology and Bedside Manners Key to Elective Healthcare Success," *Financial Post*, March 23, 2012, http://business.financialpost.com/2012/03/23/technology-and-bedside-manners-key-to-elective-healthcare-success/.
16. S. Bowness, "Healthy Leadership: Trillium Motivates from the Ground Up," *Canadian Business Online*, January 8, 2007, http://www.canadianbusiness.com/technology-news/healthy-leadership-trillium-motivates-from-the-ground-up.
17. E.E. Lawler, S.A. Mohrman, and G.E. Ledford, *Creating High Performance Organizations: Practices and Results of Employee Involvement and Quality Management in Fortune 1000 Companies* (San Francisco: Jossey-Bass, 1995).
18. B. Harding, "Globe and Mail Update," *Globe and Mail*, April 7, 2009, http://m.theglobeandmail.com/report-on-business/brett-harding/article884122/?service=mobile.
19. S. Curry, "Retention Getters," *Incentive*, April 1, 2005.
20. J. Jargon, "McDonald's Tackles Repair of 'Broken' Service," *Wall Street Journal*, April 10, 2013, http://online.wsj.com/article/SB1000142412788732401070457841490171017564 8.html.
21. B. Duffy, "Fast and Furious," *Bloomberg BusinessWeek*, May 9, 2011, http://www.businessweek.com/magazine/content/11_20/b4228064581642.htm.
22. R.W. Griffin, *Task Design* (Glenview: Scott, Foresman, 1982).
23. F. Herzberg, *Work and the Nature of Man* (Cleveland: World Press, 1966).
24. J.R. Hackman and G.R. Oldham, *Work Redesign* (Reading: Addison-Wesley, 1980).
25. T. Burns and G.M. Stalker, *The Management of Innovation* (London: Tavistock, 1961).
26. Hammer and Champy, *Reengineering the Corporation*.
27. Hammer and Champy, *Reengineering the Corporation*.
28. J.D. Thompson, *Organizations in Action* (New York: McGraw-Hill, 1967).
29. J.B. White, "'Next Big Thing': Re-Engineering Gurus Take Steps to Remodel Their Stalling Vehicles," *Wall Street Journal Interactive*, November 26, 1996.
30. White, "Next Big Thing."
31. G.M. Spreitzer, "Individual Empowerment in the Workplace: Dimensions, Measurement, and Validation," *Academy of Management Journal* 38 (1995): 1442–65.
32. M. Schrage, "I Know What You Mean: And I Can't Do Anything about It," *Fortune*, April 2, 2001, 186.
33. K.W. Thomas and B.A. Velthouse, "Cognitive Elements of Empowerment," *Academy of Management Review* 15 (1990): 666–81.

34. G.G. Dess, A.M.A. Rasheed, K.J. McLaughlin, and R.L. Priem, "The New Corporate Architecture," *Academy of Management Executive* 9 (1995): 7–18.
35. D.E. Diliger, "Report Details iPad 2 Components, 5 Million Unit Supply." *Apple Insider*, http://www.appleinsider.com/articles/11/01/30/report_details_ipad_2_components_5_million_unit_supply.html.
36. C.C. Snow, R.E. Miles, and H.J. Coleman, Jr., "Managing 21st Century Network Organizations," *Organizational Dynamics* (Winter 1992): 5–20.

Chapter 10

1. B. Dumaine, "The Trouble with Teams," *Fortune*, September 5, 1994, 86–92; G.M. Parker, *Team Players and Teamwork: New Strategies for Developing Successful Collaborations* (San Francisco: Jossey-Bass, 2010).
2. J. Hoerr, "The Payoff from Teamwork—the Gains in Quality Are Substantial—So Why Isn't It Spreading Faster?" *BusinessWeek*, July 10, 1989, 56.
3. J.R. Katzenback and D.K. Smith, *The Wisdom of Teams* (Boston: Harvard Business School Press, 1993).
4. S.E. Gross, *Compensation for Teams* (New York: American Management Association, 1995); B.L. Kirkman and B. Rosen, "Beyond Self-Management: Antecedents and Consequences of Team Empowerment," *Academy of Management Journal* 42 (1999): 58–74; G. Stalk and T.M. Hout, *Competing Against Time: How Time-Based Competition Is Reshaping Global Markets* (New York: Free Press, 1990); S.C. Wheelwright and K.B. Clark, *Revolutionizing New Product Development* (New York: Free Press, 1992).
5. J. Marquez, "Hewitt-BP Split May Signal End of 'Lift and Shift' Deals," *Workforce Management*, December 29, 2006, 3.
6. R.D. Banker, J.M. Field, R.G. Schroeder, and K.K. Sinha, "Impact of Work Teams on Manufacturing Performance: A Longitudinal Field Study," *Academy of Management Journal* 39 (1996): 867–90.
7. C. Fishman, "The Anarchist's Cookbook: John Mackey's Approach to Management Is Equal Parts Star Trek and 1970s Flashback," *Fast Company*, July 1, 2004, 70.
8. J.L. Cordery, W.S. Mueller, and L.M. Smith, "Attitudinal and Behavioral Effects of Autonomous Group Working: A Longitudinal Field Study," *Academy of Management Journal* 34 (1991): 464–76; T.D. Wall, N.J. Kemp, P.R. Jackson, and C.W. Clegg, "Outcomes of Autonomous Workgroups: A Long-Term Field Experiment," *Academy of Management Journal* 29 (1986): 280–304.
9. Whole Foods Market, "Declaration of Interdependence," http://www.wholefoodsmarket.com/mission-values/core-values/declaration-interdependence.
10. Whole Foods Market, "Declaration of Interdependence."
11. A. Erez, J. Lepine, and H. Elms, "Effects of Rotated Leadership and Peer Evaluation on the Functioning and Effectiveness of Self-Managed Teams: A Quasi-Experiment," *Personnel Psychology* 55, no. 4 (2002): 929.
12. C. Stephenson, "Leveraging Diversity to Maximum Advantage: The Business Case for Appointing More Women to Boards," *Ivey Business Journal*, September–October 2004, 1–5.
13. R. Liden, S. Wayne, R. Jaworski, and N. Bennett, "Social Loafing: A Field Investigation," *Journal of Management* 30 (2004): 285–304.
14. J. George, "Extrinsic and Intrinsic Origins of Perceived Social Loafing in Organizations," *Academy of Management Journal* 35 (1992): 191–202.
15. T.T. Baldwin, M.D. Bedell, and J.L. Johnson, "The Social Fabric of a Team-Based M.B.A. Program: Network Effects on Student Satisfaction and Performance," *Academy of Management Journal* 40 (1997): 1369–97.
16. D. Johnson, "Teams at Work," *HRMagazine*, May 1, 1999, 30.
17. R. Wageman, "Critical Success Factors for Creating Superb Self-Managing Teams," *Organizational Dynamics* 26, no. 1 (1997): 49–61.
18. D.A. Harrison, S. Mohammed, J.E. McGrath, A.T. Florey and S.W. Vanderstoep, "Time Matters in Team Performance: Effects of Member Familiarity, Entrainment, and Task Discontinuity on Speed and Quality," *Personnel Psychology* 56, no. 3 (August 2003): 633–69.
19. R.T. King, Jr., "Jeans Therapy: Levi's Factory Workers Are Assigned to Teams, and Morale Takes a Hit," *Wall Street Journal*, May 20, 1998, A1.
20. D.S. Staples, I.K. Wong, and A.F. Cameron, "Best Practices for Virtual Team Effectiveness," *Virtual Teams: Projects, Protocols, and Processes* (2004): 160–85.
21. Kirkman and Rosen, "Beyond Self-Management."
22. S. Easton and G. Porter, "Selecting the Right Team Structure to Work in Your Organization," in *Handbook of Best Practices for Teams*, vol. 1, ed. G.M. Parker (Amherst: Irwin, 1996).
23. R.J. Recardo, D. Wade, C.A. Mention, and J. Jolly, *Teams* (Houston: Gulf, 1996).
24. D.R. Denison, S.L. Hart, and J.A. Kahn, "From Chimneys to Cross-Functional Teams: Developing and Validating a Diagnostic Model," *Academy of Management Journal* 39, no. 4 (1996): 1005–23.
25. J. Morgan, "Cessna Aims to Drive SCM to Its Very Core: Here Are 21 Steps and Tools It's Using to Make This Happen," *Purchasing*, June 6, 2002, 31.
26. A.M. Townsend, S.M. DeMarie, and A.R. Hendrickson, "Virtual Teams: Technology and the Workplace of the Future," *Academy of Management Executive* 13, no. 3 (1998): 17–29.
27. J. Hyatt, "MySQL: Workers in 25 countries with no HQ," *Fortune*, June 1, 2006, http://money.cnn.com/2006/05/31/magazines/fortune/mysql_greatteams_fortune/index.htm.
28. A.M. Townsend, S.M. DeMarie, and A.R. Hendrickson, "Are You Ready for Virtual Teams?" *HR Magazine* 41, no. 9 (1996): 122–26.
29. J.B. Arbaugh, "Do Undergraduates and MBAs Differ Online?: Initial Conclusions From the Literature," *Journal of Leadership and Organizational Studies*, May 1, 2010: 129–42.
30. R.S. Wellins, W.C. Byham, and G.R. Dixon, *Inside Teams* (San Francisco: Jossey-Bass, 1994).
31. Townsend, DeMarie, and Hendrickson, "Virtual Teams."
32. W.F. Cascio, "Managing a Virtual Workplace," *Academy of Management Executive* 14 (2000): 81–90.
33. R. Katz, "The Effects of Group Longevity on Project Communication and Performance," *Administrative Science Quarterly* 27 (1982): 245–82.
34. D. Mankin, S.G. Cohen, and T.K. Bikson, *Teams and Technology: Fulfilling the Promise of the New Organization* (Cambridge, MA: Harvard Business School Press, 1996).

35. A.P. Ammeter and J.M. Dukerich, "Leadership, Team Building, and Team Member Characteristics in High Performance Project Teams," *Engineering Management* 14, no. 4 (2002): 3–11.
36. K. Lovelace, D. Shapiro, and L. Weingart, "Maximizing Cross-Functional New Product Teams' Innovativeness and Constraint Adherence: A Conflict Communications Perspective," *Academy of Management Journal* 44 (2001): 779–93.
37. L. Holpp and H.P. Phillips, "When Is a Team Its Own Worst Enemy?", *Training,* September 1, 1995, 71.
38. D.A. Cook, "Models of Interprofessional Learning in Canada," *Journal of Interprofessional Care* 19, no. 1 (2005): 107–15
39. S. Asche, "Opinions and Social Pressure," *Scientific American* 193 (1995): 31–35.
40. G. Smith, "How Nucor Steel Rewards Performance and Productivity," *Business Know How,* http://www.businessknowhow.com/manage/nucor.htm; "Nucor Agrees to Buy Harris Steel of Canada for $1.07 Billion," *New York Times,* January 2, 2010, http://www.nytimes.com/2007/01/03/business/03steel.html.
41. S.G. Cohen, G.E. Ledford, and G.M. Spreitzer, "A Predictive Model of Self-Managing Work Team Effectiveness," *Human Relations* 49, no. 5 (1996): 643–76.
42. P. Dunn, and A. Shome, "Cultural Crossvergence and Social Desirability Bias: Ethical Evaluations by Chinese and Canadian Business Students," *Journal of Business Ethics* 85, no. 4 (2009): 527–43.
43. K. Bettenhausen and J.K. Murnighan, "The Emergence of Norms in Competitive Decision-Making Groups," *Administrative Science Quarterly* 30 (1985): 350–72.
44. R. Simpson, J. Sturges, A. Woods, and Y. Altman, "Career Progress and Career Barriers: Women MBA Graduates in Canada and the UK," *Career Development International* 9, no. 5 (2004): 459–77.
45. G.T. Lemmon, "Malala, Others on Front Lines in Fight for Women," CNN, January 10, 2013, http://www.cnn.com/2013/01/09/opinion/lemmon-malala-girls-rights/index.html.
46. World Economic Forum, "The Global Gender Gap Report 2012," http://www.weforum.org/issues/global-gender-gap.
47. M.E. Shaw, *Group Dynamics* (New York: McGraw-Hill, 1981).
48. S.E. Jackson, "The Consequences of Diversity in Multidisciplinary Work Teams," in *Handbook of Work Group Psychology,* ed. M.A. West (Chichester: Wiley, 1996).
49. A.M. Isen and R.A. Baron, "Positive Affect as a Factor in Organizational Behavior," in *Research in Organizational Behavior* 13, ed. L.L. Cummings and B.M. Staw (Greenwich: JAI, 1991), 1–53.
50. C.R. Evans and K.L. Dion, "Group Cohesion and Performance: A Meta Analysis," *Small Group Research* 22, no. 2 (1991): 175–86.
51. R. Stankiewicsz, "The Effectiveness of Research Groups in Six Countries," in *Scientific Productivity,* ed. F.M. Andrews (Cambridge: Cambridge University Press, 1979), 191–221.
52. F. Rees, *Teamwork from Start to Finish* (San Francisco: Jossey-Bass, 1997).
53. S.M. Gully, D.S. Devine, and D.J. Whitney, "A Meta-Analysis of Cohesion and Performance: Effects of Level of Analysis and Task Interdependence," *Small Group Research* 26, no. 4 (1995): 497–520.
54. E. Matson, "Four Rules for Fast Teams," *Fast Company,* August 1996, 87.
55. F. Tschan and M.V. Cranach, "Group Task Structure, Processes and Outcomes," in *Handbook of Work Group Psychology,* ed. M.A. West (Chichester: Wiley, 1996).
56. D.E. Yeatts and C. Hyten, *High Performance Self Managed Teams* (Thousand Oaks: Sage, 1998); H.M. Guttman and R.S. Hawkes, "New Rules for Strategic Development," *Journal of Business Strategy* 25, no. 1 (2004): 34–39.
57. Yeatts and Hyten, *High Performance Self Managed Teams*; Guttman and Hawkes, "New Rules"; J. Colquitt, R. Noe, and C. Jackson, "Justice in Teams: Antecedents and Consequences of Procedural Justice Climate," *Personnel Psychology,* April 1, 2002, 83.
58. A. Rassuli and J.P. Manzer, "'Teach Us to Learn': Multivariate Analysis of Perception of Success in Team Learning," *Journal of Education for Business* 81, no. 1 (2005): 21–27.
59. D.S. Kezsbom, "Re-opening Pandora's Box: Sources of Project Team Conflict in the '90s," *Industrial Engineering* 24, no. 5 (1992): 54–59.
60. A.C. Amason, W.A. Hochwarter, and K.R. Thompson, "Conflict: An Important Dimension in Successful Management Teams," *Organizational Dynamics* 24 (1995): 20.
61. A.C. Amason, "Distinguishing the Effects of Functional and Dysfunctional Conflict on Strategic Decision Making: Resolving a Paradox for Top Management Teams," *Academy of Management Journal* 39, no. 1 (1996): 123–48.
62. K.M. Eisenhardt, J.L. Kahwajy, and L.J. Bourgeois III, "How Management Teams Can Have a Good Fight," *Harvard Business Review* 75, no. 4 (July–August 1997): 77–85.
63. Eisenhardt et al., "How Management Teams."
64. C. Nemeth and P. Owens, "Making Work Groups More Effective: The Value of Minority Dissent," in *Handbook of Work Group Psychology,* ed. M.A. West (Chichester: Wiley, 1996).
65. J.M. Levin and R.L. Moreland, "Progress in Small Group Research," *Annual Review of Psychology* 9 (1990): 72–78; S.E. Jackson, "Team Composition in Organizational Settings: Issues in Managing a Diverse Work Force," in *Group Processes and Productivity,* ed. S. Worchel, W. Wood, and J. Simpson (Beverly Hills: Sage, 1992).
66. Eisenhardt, et al., "How Management Teams."
67. B.W. Tuckman, "Development Sequence in Small Groups," *Psychological Bulletin* 63, no. 6 (1965): 384–99.
68. Gross, *Compensation for Teams.*
69. J.F. McGrew, J.G. Bilotta, and J.M. Deeney, "Software Team Formation and Decay: Extending the Standard Model for Small Groups," *Small Group Research* 30, no. 2 (1999): 209–34.
70. McGrew et al., "Software Team Formation."
71. L. Lee-Kelley, J. Crossman, and A. Cannings, "A Social Interaction Approach to Managing the 'Invisibles' of Virtual Teams," *Industrial Management and Data Systems* 104, no. 8 (2004): 650–57.
72. McGrew et al., "Software Team Formation."

73. J.R. Hackman, "The Psychology of Self-Management in Organizations," in *Psychology and Work: Productivity, Change, and Employment,* ed. M.S. Pallak and R. Perloff (Washington: APA, 1986), 85–136.
74. A. O'Leary-Kelly, J.J. Martocchio, and D.D. Frink, "A Review of the Influence of Group Goals on Group Performance," *Academy of Management Journal* 37, no. 5 (1994): 1285–301.
75. Smith, "How Nucor Steel Rewards Performance."
76. A. Zander, "The Origins and Consequences of Group Goals," in *Retrospections on Social Psychology,* ed. L. Festinger (New York: Oxford University Press, 1980), 205–35.
77. M. Erez and A. Somech, "Is Group Productivity Loss the Rule or the Exception? Effects of Culture and Group-Based Motivation," *Academy of Management Journal* 39, no. 6 (1996): 1513–37.
78. S. Sherman, "Stretch Goals: The Dark Side of Asking for Miracles," *Fortune,* 13 November 1995, 231.
79. S. Kerr and S. Landauer, "Using Stretch Goals to Promote Organizational Effectiveness and Personal Growth: General Electric and Goldman Sachs," *Academy of Management Executive* (November 2004): 134–38.
80. K.R. Thompson, W.A. Hochwarter, and N.J. Mathys, "Stretch Targets: What Makes Them Effective?", *Academy of Management Executive* 11, no. 3 (1997): 48–60.
81. Parker, *Team Players and Teamwork.*
82. Dumaine, "The Trouble with Teams."
83. G.A. Neuman, S.H. Wagner, and N.D. Christiansen, "The Relationship Between Work-Team Personality Composition and the Job Performance of Teams," *Group and Organization Management* 24, no. 1 (1999): 28–45.
84. M.A. Campion, G.J. Medsker, and A.C. Higgs, "Relations Between Work Group Characteristics and Effectiveness: Implications for Designing Effective Work Groups," *Personnel Psychology* 46, no. 4 (1993): 823–50.
85. B.L. Kirkman and D.L. Shapiro, "The Impact of Cultural Values on Employee Resistance to Teams: Toward a Model of Globalized Self-Managing Work Team Effectiveness," *Academy of Management Review* 22, no. 3 (1997): 730–57.
86. C. Fishman, "Engines of Democracy:" *Fast Company,* October 1, 1999, 174.
87. J. Bunderson and K. Sutcliffe, "Comparing Alternative Conceptualizations of Functional Diversity in Management Teams: Process and Performance Effects," *Academy of Management Journal* 45 (2002): 875–93.
88. J. Barbian, "Getting to Know You," *Training,* June 2001: 60–63.
89. J. Hackman, "New Rules for Team Building—the Times Are Changing," *Optimize,* July 1, 2002, 50.
90. J. Christenson, G. Innes, D. McKnight, and B. Boychuk, "Safety and Efficiency of Emergency Department Assessment of Chest Discomfort," *Canadian Medical Association Journal* 170, no. 1 (2004): 1803-7; C.S. Burke, E. Salas, K. Wilson-Donnelly, and H. Priest, "How to Turn a Team of Experts into an Expert Medical Team: Guidance from the Aviation and Military Communities," *British Medical Journal* 13, no. 1 (2004): 96–104.
91. Joinson, "Teams at Work."
92. K. Mollica, "Stay Above the Fray: Protect Your Time—and Your Sanity—by Coaching Employees to Deal with Interpersonal Conflicts on Their Own," *HRMagazine,* April 2005, 111.
93. S. Caudron, "Tie Individual Pay to Team Success," *Personnel Journal* 73, no. 10 (October 1994): 40.
94. Caudron, "Tie Individual Pay."
95. Gross, *Compensation for Teams,* 85.
96. G. Ledford, "Three Case Studies on Skill-Based Pay: An Overview," *Compensation and Benefits Review* 23, no. 2 (1991): 11–24.
97. J.R. Schuster and P.K. Zingheim, *The New Pay: Linking Employee and Organizational Performance* (New York: Lexington, 1992).
98. S.G. Cohen and D.E. Bailey, "What Makes Teams Work: Group Effectiveness Research from the Shop Floor to the Executive Suite," *Journal of Management* 23, no. 3 (1997): 239–90.
99. S. Berglas, "How to Keep A Players Productive," *Harvard Business Review*, September 2006, 1–8.
100. R. Allen and R. Kilmann, "Aligning Reward Practices in Support of Total Quality Management," *Business Horizons* 44 (May 2001): 77–85.

Chapter 11

1. Canada, Department of Justice, Canada Labour Code, http://laws-lois.justice.gc.ca/eng/acts/L-2.
2. Government of Canada, Canadian Charter of Rights and Freedoms, 2010, http://laws.justice.gc.ca/en/charter.
3. W. Chow, "Fire Hall 6 to Be Renovated to Accommodate Firefighters" (2011), *Burnaby NewsLeader*, http://www.burnabynewsleader.com/news/124782979.html; "Female Firefighters All Off the Job," *Vancouver Province*, March 22, 2006, http://www.canada.com/theprovince/news/story.html?id=7817f631-f71c-4f55-8630-8589aebd718b; CBC News, "Female Firefighters Walk Off Job in B.C. City, Alleging Harassment," March 21, 2006, http://www.cbc.ca/canada/story/2006/03/21/firefighters-richmond060321.html#ixzz0sZm4R3eU; K. Bryce, "Nanaimo Fire Department Hires Its First Professional Female Firefighter," *Nanaimo Daily News*, May 27, 2010, http://www2.canada.com/nanaimodai lynews/news/story.html?id=e43e59e9-2a9d-448f-8775-84d6d2c6734c.
4. Women's Legal Education and Action Fund, "Supreme Court Decides Fitness Test Discriminates Against B.C. Woman Firefighter," September 9, 1999, http://www.leaf.ca/media/releases/BCGSEU_Media_Release_September_9_1999.pdf.
5. Government of Canada, Canadian Human Rights Commission, http://www.chrc-ccdp.gc.ca/eng.
6. Province of British Columbia, "Work-Safe BC: Regulation and Related Materials," 2010, http://www2.worksafebc.com/publications/OHSRegulation/Home.asp.
7. Canadian Bar Association, B.C. Branch, "Sexual Harassment," 2013, http://cbabc.org/For-the-Public/Dial-A-Law/Scripts/Employment-and-Social-Benefits/271.
8. B. Etherington, ed., "Systematic Inequality and Workplace Culture: Challenging the Institutionalization of Sexual Harassment," *Canadian Labour and Employment Law Journal* 3 (1993), http://personnel.mcgill.ca/files/colleen.sheppard/Systemic_Inequality_Workplace.pdf; *Alpaerts v. Obront* [1993] OJ #732 (QL) (OCJGD), http://www.isthatlegal.ca/index.php?name=jurisdiction2.small_claims_court_law_ontario.

9. D.A. Lubin, "Courts Won't Tolerate Toxic Management," *Metro Canada,* February 17, 2010, http://metronews.ca/news/178046/courts-wont-tolerate-toxic-management.

10. D.A. Lublin, "Is Your Boss Just Tough, or a Bully?", *Globe and Mail,* August 8, 2012, http://www.theglobeandmail.com/report-on-business/careers/career-advice/life-at-work/is-your-boss-just-tough-or-a-bully/article4469548.

11. Lublin, "Is Your Boss Just Tough."

12. A. Sagan, "Defence Team in RCMP Harassment Case Plans to Strike Down Discrimination Claims," August 2, 2012, http://www.theglobeandmail.com/news/british-columbia/defence-team-in-rcmp-harassment-case-plans-to-strike-down-discrimination-claims/article4459487/.

13. E. Peirce, C.A. Smolinski, and B. Rosen, "Why Sexual Harassment Complaints Fall on Deaf Ears," *Academy of Management Executive* 12, no. 3 (1998): 41–54.; H. Burnett-Nichols, "Sexual Harassment Best Practices: University Community as Partners," March 8, 2010, http://www.universityaffairs.ca/sexual-hrassment-best-practices.aspx; "BCIT Harassment and Discrimination Policies," 2010, http://www.bcit.ca/harassment; "SFU Human Rights Policy," 2013, http://www.sfu.ca/humanrights.html; UBC Equity Office, http://equity.ubc.ca/who/message-from-the-associate-vice-president-equity.

14. Province of Ontario, "The New Mandate of the Ontario Human Rights Commission," http://www.ohrc.on.ca/en/ontario-human-rights-commission-200910%E2%80%93201112-business-plan/mandate; http://www.isthatlegal.ca/index.php?name=jurisdiction2.small_claims_court_law_ontario; Simon Fraser University, "Protocol for Investigation: Human Rights Policy (GP18)," April 30, 2008, http://www.sfu.ca/humanrights/guides-protocols/investigation-protocol.html; S. Katz, "Sexual Relations Between Students and Faculty: A Look at the Sexual Harassment Policies at Canadian Universities," January 10, 2010, http://www.universityaffairs.ca/sexual-relations-between-students-faculty.aspx.

15. M. Ryval, "40 Who Dared to Say 'We Can Make This Work,'" *Globe and Mail,* March 31, 2009, http://www.theglobeandmail.com/incoming/40-who-dared-to-say-we-can-make-this-work/article4193201.

16. R.D. Gatewood and H.S. Field, *Human Resource Selection* (Fort Worth: Dryden, 1998).

17. Gatewood and Field, *Human Resource Selection.*

18. E. White, "Job Ads Loosen Up, Get Real," *Wall Street Journal,* March 12, 2007, B3.

19. *British Columbia (Public Service Employee Relations Commission)* v. BCGSEU, [1999] 3 S.C.R. 3 9 September 1999, http://scc.lexum.org/decisia-scc-csc/scc-csc/scc-csc/en/item/1724/index.do.

20. V. Catano et al., *Recruitment and Selection in Canada* (Toronto: Nelson Education, 2009), 118; Ontario Human Rights Commission, "Sexual Harassment: Know Your Rights," 2010, http://www.ohrc.on.ca/en/issues/sexual_harassment.

21. M. Belcourt, K.J. McBey, Y. Hong, and M. Yap, *Strategic Human Resource Planning,* 5th ed. (Nelson: Toronto, 2013).

22. W.L. Gardner, B.J. Reithel, R.T. Foley, C.C. Cogliser, and F.O. Walumbsa, "Effects of Realistic Recruitment and Vertical and Horizontal Individualism—Collectivism," *Management Communication Quarterly* 22, no. 3 (2009): 437–72.

23. J. Breaugh and M. Starke, "Research on Employee Recruitment: So Many Studies, So Many Remaining Questions," *Journal of Management* 26 (2000): 405–34.

24. M. Granovetter, "Optimal Social-Networking Strategy Is a Function of Socioeconomic Conditions," *Psychological Science* 74, no. 5 (2012), http://pss.sagepub.com/content/early/2012/11/02/0956797612446708.full.pdf+html.

25. "Website Offers Retirees a New Lease on Working Life," *Vancouver Sun*, March 24, 2007, http://www.canada.com/vancouversun/news/archives/story.html?id=f1da0cd8-766d-4985-ac6a-aaccccde8a33.

26. J.T. Areddy, "China's Top Innovator Baidu Out-Googles Google," *Wall Street Journal,* July 25, 2008, http://online.wsj.com/article/SB121692051761181653.html.

27. "Internet Recruitment Report," NAS Insights, http://www.nasrecruitment.com/our-thinking/nas-insights/.

28. K. Maher, "Corporations Cut Middlemen and Do Their Own Recruiting," *Wall Street Journal*, January 14, 2003, B10.

29. Government of Alberta, Human Rights Commission, "A Recommended Guide for Pre-Employment Inquiries," 2013, http://www.albertahumanrights.ab.ca/publications/bulletins_sheets_booklets/sheets/hr_and_employment/pre_employment_inquiries_guide.asp.

30. M.N. Wexler, "Successful Resume Fraud: Conjectures on the Origins of Amorality in the Workplace," *Journal of Human Values* 12, no. 2 (2006): 137–52.

31. S. Adler, "Verifying a Job Candidate's Background: The State of Practice in a Vital Human Resources Activity," *Review of Business* 15, no. 2 (1993–94): 3–8.

32. V. Catano et al., *Recruitment and Selection in Canada* (Toronto: Nelson Education, 2009), 326.

33. *Wallace v. United Grain Growers Ltd.,* [1997] 3 S.C.R. 701, http://scc.lexum.org/decisia-scc-csc/scc-csc/scc-csc/en/item/1557/index.do.

34. M. Le, T. Nguyen, and B. Kleiner, "Legal Counsel: Don't Be Sued for Negligent Hiring," *Nonprofit World*, May 1, 2003, 14–15.

35. "Why It's Critical to Set a Policy on Background Checks for New Hires," *Managing Accounts Payable*, September 2004, 6; J. Schramm, "Future Focus: Background Checking," *HR Magazine*, January 2005.

36. C. Cohen, "Reference Checks," *CA Magazine*, November 2004, 41.

37. J. Teitel, "Fired over Facebook: The Consequences of Discussing Work Online, *Western Journal of Legal Studies* 2, no. 2 (2012): 1–22; M. Shaw, "Air Canada Workers May Be Fired over Facebook Comments," *Toronto Sun*, February 12, 2013, http://www.torontosun.com/2013/02/13/air-canada-workers-may-be-fired-over-facebook-comments; A. Frank, "Your Facebook Status Can Cost You Your Job," Monster.ca, 2013, http://career-advice.monster.ca/in-the-workplace/leaving-a-job/fired-over--facebook-comments-canada/article.aspx; M. Fitzgibbon, "Social Media and Background Checks," September 3, 2009, http://www.slaw.ca/2009/09/03/social-media-background-checks; BackCheck, "Criminal Record Check for Employment Screening," 2010, http://www.backcheck.ca; CBC News, "NDP Candidate in B.C. Election Quits over Racy Photos in Facebook," April 20, 2009, http://www.cbc.ca/canada/bcvotes2009/story/2009/04/20/bc-election-lam-facebook.html.

38. R. Blackwell, "Answering the Hiring Question with Psychological Testing," *Globe and Mail,* November 1, 2011, http://www.theglobeandmail.com/report-on-business/careers/

answering-the-hiring-question-with-psychological-testing/article4199936.

39. J. Hunter, "Cognitive Ability, Cognitive Aptitudes, Job Knowledge, and Job Performance," *Journal of Vocational Behavior* 29 (1986): 340–62.

40. F.L. Schmidt, "The Role of General Cognitive Ability and Job Performance: Why There Cannot Be a Debate," *Human Performance* 15 (2002): 187–210.

41. K. Murphy, "Can Conflicting Perspectives on the Role of *g* in Personnel Selection Be Resolved?", *Human Performance* 15 (2002): 173–86.

42. J.R. Glennon, L.E. Albright, and W.A. Owens, *A Catalog of Life History Items* (Greensboro: Richardson Foundation, 1966).

43. Gatewood and Field, *Human Resource Selection.*

44. I. Kotlyar and K. Ades, "HR Technology: Assessment Technology Can Help Match the Best Applicant to the Right Job," *HR Magazine*, May 1, 2002, 97.

45. F. Kuschnereit, "Improving the Accuracy of Biodata Questionnaires" (Saint John: University of New Brunswick, 2001), http://dspace.hil.unb.ca:8080/xmlui/bitstream/handle/1882/42937/MQ68253.pdf?sequence=1.

46. T.T. Pittinsky and B. Welle, "Negative Outgroup Leader Actions Increase Liking for Ingroup Leaders: An Experimental Test of Intergroup Leader-Enhancement Effects," *Group Processes Intergroup Relations* 11, no. 4 (2008): 513–23; G.G. Manley, J. Benavidez, and K. Dunn, "Development of a Personality Biodata Measure to Predict Ethical Decision Making," *Journal of Managerial Psychology* 22, no. 7 (2007): 664–82.

47. A. Furnham, *The Psychology of Behaviour at Work: The Individual and the Organization,* 2nd ed. (New York: Psychology Press, 2012); A. Furnham, *Personality and Intelligence at Work: Exploring and Explaining Individual differences at Work* (New York: Psychology Press, 2008).

48. M.S. Taylor and J.A. Sniezek, "The College Recruitment Interview: Topical Content and Applicant Reactions," *Journal of Occupational Psychology* 57 (1984): 157–68.

49. R. Burnett, C. Fan, S.J. Motowidlo, and T. DeGroot, "Interview Notes and Validity," *Personnel Psychology* 51, no. 10 (1998): 375–96; M.A. Campion, D.K. Palmer, and J.E. Campion, "A Review of Structure in the Selection Interview," *Personnel Psychology* 50, no. 3 (1997): 655–702.

50. Campion et al., "A Review of Structure."

51. T. Judge, "The Employment Interview: A Review of Recent Research and Recommendations for Future Research," *Human Resource Management Review* 10, no. 4 (2000): 383–406.

52. J. Cortina, N. Goldstein, S. Payne, K. Davison, and S. Gilliland, "The Incremental Validity of Interview Scores Over and Above Cognitive Ability and Conscientiousness Scores," *Personnel Psychology* 53, no. 2 (2000): 325–51.

53. S. Livingston, T.W. Gerdel, M. Hill, B. Yerak, C. Melvin, and B. Lubinger, "Ohio's Strongest Companies All Agree That Training Is Vital to Their Success," *Cleveland Plain Dealer*, May 21, 1997, 30S; Rigzone, "Today's Trends: U.S., Canadian E&P Spending Estimates Rise," June 18, 2010, http://www.rigzone.com/news/article.asp?a_id=94873; Canadian Society for Training and Development, "Investing in People," 2010, http://c.ymcdn.com/sites/www.cstd.ca/resource/resmgr/iip/metastudy.pdf.

54. Oil Spill Training Company, http://the-oil-spill-training-company.software.informer.com; CBC News, "BP Oil Spill Price Tag Hits $2 Billion," June 21, 2010, http://www.cbc.ca/world/story/2010/06/21/bp-oil-well-cost.html.

55. S. Overby, "The World's Biggest Classroom," *CIO*, February 1, 2002, http://www.cio.com/article/30830/Dow_Chemical_The_World_s_Biggest_Classroom.

56. M. Totty, "Better Training Through Gaming," *Wall Street Journal*, April 25, 2005, R6.

57. J. Borzo, "Almost Human: Using Avatars for Corporate Training, Advocates Say, Can Combine the Best Parts of Face-to-Face Interaction and Computer-Based Learning," *Wall Street Journal*, 24 May 2004, R4.

58. D.L. Kirkpatrick, "Four Steps to Measuring Training Effectiveness," *Personnel Administrator* 28 (1983): 19–25.

59. L. Gills and A. Bailey, "ROI Case Study Methodology: Putting the Pieces Together," *Canadian Society for Training and Development,* 2009, http://c.ymcdn.com/sites/www.cstd.ca/resource/resmgr/iip/metastudy.pdf.

60. J. Stack, "The Curse of the Annual Performance Review," *Inc.*, March 1, 1997, 39.

61. D. Murphy, "Are Performance Appraisals Worse Than a Waste of Time? Book Derides Unintended Consequences," *San Francisco Chronicle*, September 9, 2001, W1.

62. U.J. Wiersma and G.P. Latham, "The Practicality of Behavioral Observation Scales, Behavioral Expectation Scales, and Trait Scales," *Personnel Psychology* 39 (1986): 619–28; U.J. Wiersma, P.T. Van Den Berg, and G.P. Latham, "Dutch Reactions to Behavioral Observation, Behavioral Expectation, and Trait Scales," *Group and Organization Management* 20 (1995): 297–309.

63. D.J. Schleicher, D.V. Day, B.T. Mayes, and R.E. Riggio, "A New Frame for Frame-of-Reference Training: Enhancing the Construct Validity of Assessment Centers," *Journal of Applied Psychology* (August 2002): 735–46.

64. H.H. Meyer, "A Solution to the Performance Appraisal Feedback Enigma," *Academy of Management Executive* 5, no. 1 (1991): 68–76; G.C. Thornton, "Psychometric Properties of Self-Appraisals of Job Performance," *Personnel Psychology* 33 (1980): 263–71.

65. A. Waldman, L.E. Atwater, and D. Antonioni, "Has 360 Feedback Gone Amok?", *Academy of Management Executive* 12, no. 2 (1998): 86–94.

66. J. Smither, M. London, R. Flautt, Y. Vargas, and I. Kucine, "Can Working with an Executive Coach Improve Multisource Feedback Ratings over Time? A Quasi-Experimental Field Study," *Personnel Psychology* (Spring 2003): 21–43.

67. J. McGregor, "The Employee Is Always Right," *BusinessWeek,* November 8, 2007, http://www.businessweek.com/globalbiz/content/nov2007/gb2007118_541063.htm.

68. A. Walker and J. Smither, "A Five-Year Study of Upward Feedback: What Managers Do with Their Results Matters," *Personnel Psychology* (Summer 1999): 393–422.

69. W. Wong, "Motorola Introduces Worker Retention Incentives," *Chicago Tribune,* April 3, 2008; B. Nussbaum, "Motorola Splits in Two," *Bloomberg BusinessWeek,* March 26, 2008, http://www.businessweek.com/innovate/NussbaumOnDesign/archives/2008/03/motorola_splits.html

70. G.T. Milkovich and J.M. Newman, *Compensation*, 4th ed. (Homewood: Irwin, 1993).

71. Pay Scale Canada, "Hourly Rate Snapshot for Child Care / Day Care Worker," http://www.payscale.com/research/CA/Job=Child_Care_%2F_Day_Care_Worker/Hourly_Rate.

72. M.L. Williams and G.F. Dreher, "Compensation System Attributes and Applicant Pool Characteristics," *Academy of Management Journal* 35, no. 3 (1992): 571–95.

73. J.H. Carens, "Live-in Domestics, Seasonal Workers, and Others Hard to Locate on the Map of Democracy," *Journal of Political Philosophy—Special Issue: Philosophy, Politics, and* Society 16, no. 4 (2008): 419–45.

74. Proform Concrete Services Inc., "Profit Sharing Retirement Savings Program (PSRSP)," http://www.proformconcrete.com/.

75. C. Jensen, "Research and Legislation on ESOPs Could Have Positive Effects for Canada," *Axiom News*, January 19, 2009, http://www.axiomnews.ca/node/457.

76. M. Bloom, "The Performance Effects of Pay Dispersion on Individuals and Organizations," *Academy of Management Journal* 42, no. 1 (1999): 25–40.

77. AFL-CIO, "2007 Trends in CEO Pay," http://www.aflcio.org/Corporate-Watch/CEO-Pay-and-You; C. Hymowitz, "Pay Gap Fuels Worker Woes," *Wall Street Journal*, April 28, 2008, B8.

78. W. Grossman and R.E. Hoskisson, "CEO Pay at the Crossroads of Wall Street and Main: Toward the Strategic Design of Executive Compensation," *Academy of Management Executive* 12, no. 1 (1998): 43–57.

79. M. Bloom, "Performance Effects," 2010, http://www.keepjobsincanada.ca; "Canada Lost 129,000 Jobs in January: StatsCan," CBC News, February 6, 2009, http://www.cbc.ca/money/story/2009/02/06/januaryjobs.html#ixzz0sbRAATYf.M.

80. M. Bloom and J.G. Michel, "The Relationships Among Organizational Context, Pay Dispersion, and Managerial Turnover," *Academy of Management Journal* 45 (2002): 33–42.

81. *Ontario Employment Standards Act 2000*, http://www.e-laws.gov.on.ca/html/statutes/english/elaws_statutes_00e41_e.htm; Ontario Ministry of Labour, "Termination of Employment Defined," http://www.labour.gov.on.ca/english/es/pubs/guide/termination.php.

82. P. Michal-Johnson, *Saying Good-Bye: A Manager's Guide to Employee Dismissal* (Glenview: Scott, Foresman, 1985).

83. M. Mentzer, "Study Suggests Downsizing Is a Fad That Does More Damage Than Good," *Canadian Journal of Administrative Sciences* 8, no. 12 (1996): 23–42, http://announcements.usask.ca/news/archive/1996/10/downsizing_stud.html.

84. J.R. Morris, W.F. Cascio, and C.E. Young, "Downsizing After All These Years: Questions and Answers About Who Did It, How Many Did It, and Who Benefited from It," *Organizational Dynamics* 27, no. 3 (1999): 78–87.

85. K. Maher, "Hiring Freezes Cushion New Layoffs," *Wall Street Journal*, January 24, 2008, A13.

86. K.E. Mishra, G.M. Spreitzer, and A.K. Mishra, "Preserving Employee Morale During Downsizing," *Sloan Management Review* 39, no. 2 (1998): 83–95.

87. J. Hilsenrath, "Adventures in Cost Cutting," *Wall Street Journal*, May 10, 2004, R1.

88. University of Waterloo, "Early Retirement for 340," 2010, http://newsrelease.uwaterloo.ca/news.php?id=521.

89. M. Willett, "Early Retirement and Phased Retirement Programs for the Public Sector," *Benefits and Compensation Digest*, April 2005, 31.

90. D.R. Dalton, W.D. Todor, and D.M. Krackhardt, "Turnover Overstated: The Functional Taxonomy," *Academy of Management Review* 7 (1982): 117–23.

91. J.R. Hollenbeck and C.R. Williams, "Turnover Functionality Versus Turnover Frequency: A Note on Work Attitudes and Organizational Effectiveness," *Journal of Applied Psychology* 71 (1986): 606–11.

92. C.R. Williams, "Reward Contingency, Unemployment, and Functional Turnover," *Human Resource Management Review* 9 (1999): 549–76.

Chapter 12

1. S. Proudfoot, "Immigrants Boost Population Growth: StatsCan," *CanWest News Service National Post*, March 26, 2009, http://www.migrationexpert.com/canada/visa/canadian_immigration_news/2009/mar/1/580/canadas_population_continues_to_grow_thanks_to_immigration. Statistics Canada, "Study: Projected Trends to 2031 for the Canadian Labour Force," August 17, 2011, http://www.statcan.gc.ca/daily-quotidien/110817/dq110817b-eng.htm; Statistics Canada, "Canada Year Book 2011," Cat. no. 11-402-X, http://www.statcan.gc.ca/pub/11-402-x/2011000/pdf/ethnic-ethnique-eng.pdf.

2. Statistics Canada, "Women in Canada: Paid Work," *The Daily*, December 9, 2010, http://www.statcan.gc.ca/daily-quotidien/101209/dq101209a-eng.htm; V. Ferrao, "Paid work," *Women in Canada: A Gender-based Statistical Report, http://www.statcan.gc.ca/pub/89-503-x/2010001/article/11387-eng.htm.*

3. M. Almay, Statistics Canada, "Women in Canada: Work Chapter Updates," http://www5.statcan.gc.ca/bsolc/olc-cel/olc-cel?catno=89F0133X&lang=eng.

4. Statistics Canada, "Population Count and Population Growth in Canada," http://www.statcan.gc.ca/pub/91-520-x/2010001/aftertoc-aprestdm1-eng.htm; Statistics Canada, "Population Projections for Canada, Provinces, and Territories 2009 to 2036, http://www.statcan.gc.ca/pub/91-520-x/91-520-x2010001-eng.pdf.

5. T. Belford, "Corporations Embrace Canada's Diverse Workforce," Can-West News Service, December 4, 2009, http://www.ottawacitizen.com/about-ottawa-citizen/Newcomers+strive+speak+office/2725088/Corporations+embrace+Canada+diverse+worceforce/2286018/story.html.

6. Human Resources and Skills Development Canada, "What Is Employment Equity?", http://www.chrc-ccdp.ca/eng/content/employment-equity#1.

7. HRSDC, "What Is Employment Equity?"

8. "*Employment Equity Act* Annual Report—2007," http://www.hrsdc.gc.ca/eng/labour/publications/equality/annual_reports/2007/page03.shtml.

9. Equal Employment Opportunity Commission, "Federal Laws Prohibiting Job Discrimination Questions and Answers," http://www.eeoc.gov/facts/qanda.html.

10. A.P. Carnevale and S.C. Stone, *The American Mosaic: An In-Depth Report on the Future of Diversity at Work* (New York: McGraw-Hill, 1995).

11. E. Orenstein, "The Business Case for Diversity," *Financial Executive*, May 2005, 22–25; G. Robinson and K. Dechant, "Building a Business Case for Diversity," *Academy of Management Executive* 11, no. 3 (1997): 21–31.

12. R. Rodriguez, "Diversity Finds Its Place," *HRMagazine* 51, August 2008, http://www.shrm.org/Publications/hrmagazine/EditorialContent/Pages/0806rodriguez.aspx.

13. A. Konrad, "Managing for Diversity and Inclusiveness: Results of the 2004–05 Ivey Strategic Diversity and Inclusiveness Survey," Richard Ivey School of Business, http://www.ivey.uwo.ca/cmsmedia/35546/Konrad_Report_07.pdf.

14. T. Worth, "The Business Case for Diversity: How Companies Keep Their Competitive Edge," *California Diversity*, November 2009, http://www.californiadiversitymagazine.org/the-business-case-for-diversity/#respond.

15. "Hyatt: Diversity and Inclusion," http://www.hyattdiversity.com/hyatt-in-action.

16. "Global Diversity and Inclusion Fostering Innovation Through a Diverse Workforce," *Forbes Insights*, July 2011, http://images.forbes.com/forbesinsights/StudyPDFs/Innovation_Through_Diversity.pdf.

17. Xerox News Room, "Canadians Name Diversity as Key Ingredient in Formula for Innovation Success," September 25, 2007, http://en-news.xerox.ca/news/CAN_News_9_25_2007.

18. R. Rodriguez, "Diversity Finds Its Place: More Organizations Are Dedicating Senior-Level Executives to Drive Diversity Initiatives for Bottom-Line Effect," *HR Magazine*, August 2006; Society for Human Resource Management, http://www.shrm.org.

19. C. Hymowitz, "The New Diversity," *Wall Street Journal*, November 14, 2005, R1.

20. "Diversity at Work: Public Relations Make a Difference for Global Giants," *Public Relations Society of America*, October 1, 2010, http://www.prsa.org/Intelligence/Tactics/Articles/view/8828/1021/Diversity_at_work_Public_relations_makes_a_difference.

21. M.R. Carrell and E.E. Mann, "Defining Workplace Diversity Programs and Practices in Organizations," *Labor Law Journal* 44 (1993): 743–64.

22. D.A. Harrison, K.H. Price, and M.P. Bell, "Beyond Relational Demography: Time and the Effects of Surface- and Deep-Level Diversity on Work Group Cohesion," *Academy of Management Journal* 41 (1998): 96–107.

23. D. Harrison, K. Price, J. Gavin, and A. Florey, "Time, Teams, and Task Performance: Changing Effects of Surface- and Deep-Level Diversity on Group Functioning," *Academy of Management Journal* 45 (2002): 1029–45.

24. Harrison, Price, and Bell, "Beyond Relational Demography."

25. Harrison, Price, and Bell, "Beyond Relational Demography."

26. "Young Canadians Most Likely to Say They've Been the Victim of Age Discrimination at Work or in an Interview," July 23, 2012, http://www.ipsos-na.com/download/pr.aspx?id=11807.

27. S. Baille-Ruder, "Hiring Older Workers," *Profit Magazine*, December 2004, http://www.shrm.org/Publications/hrmagazine/EditorialContent/2013/0813/Pages/0813-older-workers.aspx.

28. A. Fisher, "Wanted: Aging Baby-Boomers," *Fortune*, September 30, 1996, 204.

29. G.M. McEvoy and W.F. Cascio, "Cumulative Evidence of the Relationship Between Employee Age and Job Performance," *Journal of Applied Psychology* 74 (1989): 11–17.

30. A. Bednarz, "Hiring Preferences Favor Mature Workers over Millenials: Study," *Network World*, 9 October 2012, http://www.networkworld.com/news/2012/100912-mature-workers-263193.html?page=1.

31. M. Johne, "Don't Sweep Older Workers Under the Rug," *Globe and* Mail, June 27, 2012, http://www.theglobeandmail.com/report-on-business/careers/business-education/dont-sweep-older-workers-under-the-rug/article4374579.

32. D. Bloom and D. Canning, "How Companies Must Adapt for an Aging Workforce," *Harvard Business Review, HBR Blog Network,* December 3, 2012, http://blogs.hbr.org/cs/2012/12/how_companies_must_adapt_for_a.html.

33. Human Resources and Skills Development Canada, "Indicators of Well Being in Canada," http://www4.hrsdc.gc.ca/.3ndic.1t.4r@-eng.jsp?iid=18#M_2.

34. M. Drolet, "Why Has the Gender Age Gap Narrowed?", Statistics Canada, *Perspectives on Labour and Income,* Spring 2011, http://www.statcan.gc.ca/pub/75-001-x/2011001/pdf/11394-eng.pdf.

35. L. Chenier and E. Wohlbold, "Women in Senior Management: Where Are They?", Conference Board of Canada, August 11, 2011, http://www.conferenceboard.ca/e-library/abstract.aspx?did=4416; R. Wright, "Women in Senior Management: Progress Is Glacial," November 10, 2011, http://www.conferenceboard.ca/insideedge/2011/nov2011/nov10-womenseniormgmnt.aspx; "Women Still Missing in Action from Senior Management Positions in Canadian Organizations," News Release, Conference Board of Canada, December 29, 2012, http://www.conferenceboard.ca/press/newsrelease/11-08-31/women_still_missing_in_action_from_senior_management_positions_in_canadian_organizations.aspx.

36. Industry Canada, "Key Small Business Statistics," July 2012, www.google.ca/url?sa=t&rct=j&q=&esrc=s&source=web&cd=2&ved=0CEAQFjAB&url=http%3A%2F%2Fwww.ic.gc.ca%2Feic%2Fsite%2F061.nsf%2Fvwapj%2FKSBS-PSRPE_July-Juillet2012_eng.pdf%2F%24FILE%2FKSBS-PSRPE_July-Juillet2012_eng.pdf&ei=nKg3UeLiLOWVyAGH-oDgCQ&usg=AFQjCNFc4_qXfbNtQNQkKA9PuNX1aQ_8lw&sig2=pNeAfdXgQpcEdrGfJwvEUw&bvm=bv.43287494,d.aWc.

37. J. Cool, "Wage Gap Between Women and Men," Library of Parliament, July 29, 2010, http://www.parl.gc.ca/Content/LOP/ResearchPublications/2010-30-e.htm.

38. J.R. Hollenbeck, D.R. Ilgen, C. Ostroff, and J.B. Vancouver, "Sex Differences in Occupational Choice, Pay, and Worth: A Supply-Side Approach to Understanding the Male-Female Wage Gap," *Personnel Psychology* 40 (1987): 715–44.

39. Y. Zacharias, "Women Execs Believe Glass Ceiling Still an Impediment in Canada: Study," *Vancouver Sun*, December 11, 2012, http://www.vancouversun.com/business/Women+execs+believe+glass+ceiling+still+impediment+Canada+study/7684710/story.html.

40. CBC News, "Women's Glass Ceiling Remains," August, 31, 2011, http://www.cbc.ca/news/business/story/2011/08/31/women-executive-conference-board.html.

41. B.R. Ragins, B. Townsend, and M. Mattis, "Gender Gap in the Executive Suite: CEOs and Female Executives Report on Breaking the Glass Ceiling," *Academy of Management Executive* 12 (1998): 28–42.

42. N. Lockwood, "The Glass Ceiling: Domestic and International Perspectives," *HRMagazine*, 2004 Research Quarterly, 2–10.

43. T.B. Foley, "Discrimination Lawsuits Are a Small-Business Nightmare: A Guide to Minimizing the Potential Damage," *Wall Street Journal*, September 28, 1998, 15.

44. L. Whittington, "Visible Minorities Increasing in Canada," *Toronto* Star, May 17, 2012 http://www.thestar.com/news/canada/2012/05/17/visible_minorities_increasing_in_canada.html.

45. Ryerson University Media Release, "Catalyst and Ryerson University Release New Study of More Than 17,000 Seasoned Professionals," June 28, 2007, http://www.catalyst.org/media/catalyst-and-ryerson-university-release-new-study-more-17000-seasoned-professionals.

46. D.A. Neal and W.R. Johnson, "The Role of Premarket Factors in Black-White Wage Differences," *Journal of Political Economy* 104, no. 5 (1996): 869–95.

47. M. Fix, G. Galster, and R. Struyk, "An Overview of Auditing for Discrimination," in *Clear and Convincing Evidence: Testing for Discrimination in America,* ed. M. Fix and R. Struyk (Washington: Urban Institute Press, 1993).

48. M. Bendick, Jr., C.W. Jackson, and V.A. Reinoso, "Measuring Employment Discrimination Through Controlled Experiments," in *African-Americans and Post-Industrial Labor Markets*, ed. J.B. Stewart (New Brunswick: Transaction, 1997), 77–100.

49. P.B. Riach and J. Rich, "Measuring Discrimination by Direct Experimental Methods: Seeking Gunsmoke," *Journal of PostKeynesian Economics* 14, no. 2 (Winter 1991–92): 143–50.

50. A.P. Brief, R.T. Buttram, R.M. Reizenstein, and S.D. Pugh, "Beyond Good Intentions: The Next Steps Toward Racial Equality in the American Workplace," *Academy of Management Executive* 11 (1997): 59–72.

51. L.E. Wynter, "Business and Race: Federal Agencies, Spurred on by Nonprofit Groups, Are Increasingly Embracing the Use of Undercover Investigators to Identify Discrimination in the Marketplace," *Wall Street Journal*, July 1, 1998, B1.

52. S. Capparell, *The Real Pepsi Challenge: The Inspirational Story of Breaking the Color Barrier in American Business* (New York: Reed Elsevier, 2007).

53. Canadian Press, "1 in 7 Canadians Live with Disability: Statscan," December 3, 2007, http://www.thestar.com/article/282097.

54. Statistics Canada, "Participation and Activity Limitation Survey 2006: Technical and Methodological Report," http://www.statcan.gc.ca/pub/89-628-x/89-628-x2007001-eng.htm#1.

55. Canadian Press, "More Disabled People in Canada: Report," December 28, 2009, http://www.cbc.ca/health/story/2009/12/28/disabled-reportcanada.html?ref=rss.

56. Government of Canada's Annual Report on Disability Issues 2010, http://www12.hrsdc.gc.ca/p.5bd.2t.1.3ls@-eng.jsp?pid=3875.

57. B. Wilkerson, *The Business Case for Accessibility* (Toronto: Queen's Printer, November 2001), http://www.ilcanada.ca/upload/documents/information_sheet_2007_1of4.pdf.

58. Human Resources and Skills Development Canada, "2009 Federal Disability Report," http://www.gov.mb.ca/dio/pdf/2009_fdr.pdf.

59. Canadian Press, "More Disabled People in Canada."

60. Human Resources and Skills Development Canada, "2009 Federal Disability Report."

61. R. Greenwood and V.A. Johnson, "Employer Perspectives on Workers with Disabilities," *Journal of Rehabilitation* 53 (1987): 37–45.

62. Greenwood and Johnson, "Employer Perspectives."

63. Office of Disability Employment Policy, "Low Cost Accommodation Solutions," http://www.hreonline.com/HRE/view/story.jhtml?id=26670972.

64. National Council on Disability, "Study on the Financing of Assistive Technology Devices and Services for Individuals with Disabilities: A Report to the President and the Congress of the United States," http://www.ncd.gov/publications/1993/Mar41993.

65. Government of British Columbia, "Workable Solutions: An Initiative of the Minister's Council on Employment for Persons with Disabilities," http://www.mhr.gov.bc.ca/epwd/docs/Handbook.pdf.

66. R.B. Cattell, "Personality Pinned Down," *Psychology Today* 7 (1973): 40–46; C.S. Carver and M.F. Scheier, *Perspectives on Personality* (Boston: Allyn and Bacon, 1992).

67. J.M. Digman, "Personality Structure: Emergence of the Five-Factor Model," *Annual Review of Psychology* 41 (1990): 417–40; M.R. Barrick and M.K. Mount, "The Big Five Personality Dimensions and Job Performance: A Meta-Analysis," *Personnel Psychology* 44 (1991): 1–26.

68. Barrick and Mount, "The Big Five Personality Dimensions"; M.K. Mount and M.R. Barrick, "The Big Five Personality Dimensions: Implications for Research and Practice in Human Resource Management," *Research in Personnel and Human Resources Management* 13 (1995): 153–200; M.K. Mount and M.R. Barrick, "Five Reasons Why the 'Big Five' Article Has Been Frequently Cited," *Personnel Psychology* 51 (1998): 849–57; D.S. Ones, M.K. Mount, M.R. Barrick, and J.E. Hunter, "Personality and Job Performance: A Critique of the Tett, Jackson, and Rothstein (1991) Meta-Analysis," *Personnel Psychology* 47 (1994): 147–56.

69. Barrick and Mount, "The Big Five Personality Dimensions and Job Performance."

70. Mount and Barrick, "Five Reasons Why."

71. Mount and Barrick, "Five Reasons Why."

72. Staff, "The Diverse Work Force," *Inc.*, January 1993, 33.

73. D.A. Thomas and R.J. Ely, "Making Differences Matter: A New Paradigm for Managing Diversity," *Harvard Business Review* 74 (September–October 1996): 79–90.

74. D.A. Thomas and S. Wetlaufer, "A Question of Color: A Debate on Race in the U.S. Workplace," *Harvard Business Review* 75 (September–October 1997), 118–32.

75. Thomas and Ely, "Making Differences Matter."

76. A. Fisher, "How You Can Do Better on Diversity," *Fortune*, November 15, 2004, 60.

77. Aetna, "2005 Diversity Annual Report," www.aetna.com.

78. J.R. Norton and R.E. Fox, *The Change Equation: Capitalizing on Diversity for Effective Organizational Change* (Washington: APA, 1997).

79. Norton and Fox, *The Change Equation.*

80. Thomas and Ely, "Making Differences Matter."

81. R.R. Thomas, Jr., *Beyond Race and Gender: Unleashing the Power of Your Total Workforce by Managing Diversity* (New York: AMACOM, 1991).

82. Thomas, *Beyond Race and Gender.*
83. S. Lubove, "Damned If You Do, Damned If You Don't," *Forbes*, December 15, 1997, 122.
84. L.S. Gottfredson, "Dilemmas in Developing Diversity Programs," in *Diversity in the Workplace*, ed. S.E. Jackson and Associates (New York: Guildford, 1992).
85. A. Konrad, C. Maurer, and Y. Yang, "Managing for Diversity and Inclusiveness: Results of the 2004–5 Ivey Strategic Diversity and Inclusiveness Survey," Richard Ivey School of Business, University of Western Ontario, http://www.ivey.uwo.ca/faculty/Konrad_Report_07.pdf.
86. "Forest Company Keys into Aboriginal Workforce," *Vancouver Sun*, April 5, 2008, http://www.canada.com/vancouversun/news/story.html?id=041ec56f-7401-4c40-bd09-e743548f69b2.
87. R. Caballero and R. Yerema, "Canada's Best Diversity Employers," March 23, 2010; UBC Employer Review, http://www.eluta.ca/diversity-at-university-of-british-columbia; http://www.eluta.ca/diversity-at-corus-entertainment.
88. "Forest Company Keys into Aboriginal Workforce," *Vancouver Sun.*
89. Caballero and Yerema, "Canada's Best Diversity Employers."
90. Caballero and Yerema, "Canada's Best Diversity Employers."
91. Caballero and Yerema, "Canada's Best Diversity Employers."
92. Carnevale and Stone, *The American Mosaic.*
93. Caballero and Yerema, "Canada's Best Diversity Employers."
94. Caballero and Yerema, "Canada's Best Diversity Employers."
95. J.R. Joplin and C.S. Daus, "Challenges of Leading a Diverse Workforce," *Academy of Management Executive* 11 (1997): 32–47.
96. Caballero and Yerema, "Canada's Best Diversity Employers."
97. Konrad, Maurer, and Yang, "Managing for Diversity and Inclusiveness."

Chapter 13

1. M. Gagne and E. Deci, "Self-Determination Theory and Work Motivation," *Journal of Organizational Behaviour* 26 (2005): 331–62.
2. J. P. Campbell and R.D. Pritchard, "Motivation Theory in Industrial and Organizational Psychology," in *Handbook of Industrial and Organizational Psychology*, ed. M.D. Dunnette (Chicago: Rand McNally, 1976).
3. Higher Education Quality Council of Ontario, http://www.heqco.ca/en-CA/Pages/Home.aspx.
4. P. Thomas, "Waitress Makes the Difference in Bringing Deaf to Pittsburgh," *Wall Street Journal Interactive Edition*, March 2, 1999.
5. E.A. Locke, "The Nature and Causes of Job Satisfaction," in *Handbook of Industrial and Organizational Psychology*, ed. M.D. Dunnette (Chicago: Rand McNally, 1976).
6. A.H. Maslow, "A Theory of Human Motivation," *Psychological Review* 50 (1943): 370–96.
7. C.P. Alderfer, *Existence, Relatedness, and Growth: Human Needs in Organizational Settings* (New York: Free Press, 1972).
8. D.C. McClelland, "Toward a Theory of Motive Acquisition," *American Psychologist* 20 (1965): 321–33; D.C. McClelland and D.H. Burnham, "Power Is the Great Motivator," *Harvard Business Review* 54, no. 2 (1976): 100–10.
9. J.H. Turner, "Entrepreneurial Environments and the Emergence of Achievement Motivation in Adolescent Males," *Sociometry* 33 (1970): 147–65.
10. L.W. Porter, E.E. Lawler III, and J.R. Hackman, *Behavior in Organizations* (New York: McGraw-Hill, 1975).
11. C. Ajila, "Maslow's Hierarchy of Needs Theory: Applicability to the Nigerian Industrial Setting," *IFE Psychology* (1997): 162–74.
12. M.A. Wahba and L.B. Birdwell, "Maslow Reconsidered: A Review of Research on the Need Hierarchy Theory," *Organizational Behavior and Human Performance* 15 (1976): 212–40; J. Rauschenberger, N. Schmitt, and J.E. Hunter, "A Test of the Need Hierarchy Concept by a Markov Model of Change in Need Strength," *Administrative Science Quarterly* 25 (1980): 654–70.
13. K. Dye, A.J. Mills, and T.G. Weatherbee, (2005). "Maslow: Man Interrupted: Reading Management Theory in Context," *Management Decisions* 43, no. 10 (2005): 1375-95; C.P. Alderfer, R.E. Kaplan, and K.K. Smith, "The Effect of Relatedness Need Satisfaction on Relatedness Desires", *Administrative Science Quarterly,* 19 (1974): 507–32; M.A. Wahba and L.B. Bridwell, "Maslow Reconsidered: A Review of Research on the Need Hierarchy Theory," *Organizational Behavior and Human Performance* 15 (1976): 212–40; J. Rauschenberger, N. Schmitt, and J.E. Hunter, "A Test of the Need Hierarchy Concept by a Markov Model of Change in Need Strength," *Administrative Science Quarterly* 25 (1980): 654–70.
14. B. Irlenbusch and D. Sliwka, "Incentives, Decision Frames, and Motivation Crowding Out—An Experimental Investigation," *IZA Discussion Paper No. 1758,* September 2005, http://papers.ssrn.com/sol3/papers.cfm?abstract_id=822866; A.M. Bertelli, "Motivation Crowding and the Federal Civil Servant: Evidence from the US Internal Revenue Service", *International Public Management Journal* 9, no. 1 (2006), http://www.tandfonline.com/doi/abs/10.1080/10967490600625191.
15. E.E. Lawler III and L.W. Porter, "The Effect of Performance on Job Satisfaction," *Industrial Relations* 7 (1967): 20–28.
16. Porter, Lawler, and Hackman, *Behavior in Organizations.*
17. IKEA, "IKEA: Home Is the Most Important Place in the World," September 28, 2008, http://www.ikea.com.
18. G. Kirbyson, "IKEA's Restaurant Ready for Big Opening," *Winnipeg Free Press*, November 23, 2012, http://www.winnipegfreepress.com/business/IKEAs-restaurant-ready-for-big-opening-180615321.html.
19. M. Habib, "Motivation Without Money? You Bet", *Globe and Mail*, November 23, 2010, http://www.theglobeandmail.com/report-on-business/small-business/sb-managing/human-resources/motivation-without-money-you-bet/article1315526.
20. Porter, Lawler, and Hackman, *Behavior in Organizations.*

21. J.S. Lublin, "Creative Compensation: A CEO Talks About His Company's Innovative Pay Ideas—Free Ice Cream, Anyone?", *Wall Street Journal*, April 10, 2006, R6; Tavia Grant, "Worst of Times Might Be Best of Times to Take Off," *Globe and Mail*, April 4, 2009, http://yoursabbatical.com/2009/04/04/worst-of-times-might-be-best-of-times-to-take-off; T. Amabile and S. Kramer, "What Makes Work Worth Doing?", *HBR Blog Network / HBS Faculty,* August 31, 2012, http://blogs.hbr.org/hbsfaculty/2012/08/what-makes-work-worth-doing.html.

22. B. Smith, "Bonuses That Are Available to All Motivate Staff," *Globe and Mail*, November 19, 2012, http://www.theglobeandmail.com/report-on-business/careers/top-employers/bonuses-that-are-available-to-all-motivate-staff/article5434755.

23. C. Caggiano, "What Do Workers Want?", *Inc.*, November 1992, 101–4; Families and Work Institute, "National Study of the Changing Workforce," http://www.familiesandwork.org/3w/research/downloads/3wes.pdf.

24. Habib, "Compensation: Motivation Without Money?"

25. Habib, "Compensation: Motivation Without Money?"

26. Habib, "Compensation: Motivation Without Money?"

27. R. Kanfer and P. Ackerman, "Aging, Adult Development, and Work Motivation," *Academy of Management Review* (2004): 440–58.

28. E. White, "The New Recruits: Older Workers," *Wall Street Journal,* January 14, 2008, B3.

29. AFL-CIO, "2007 Trends in CEO Pay," http://www.aflcio.org/corporatewatch/paywatch/pay/index.cfm.

30. T. Bradley, "Can I Join the Club?", *Steady Hand Blog*, March 8, 2012, http://www.steadyhand.com/cgi-bin/search/index.cgi?query=http%3A%2F%2Fwww.steadyhand.com%2Findustry%2F2012%2F03%2F08%2Fcan+_i_join_the_club.

31. T. Krisher, "GM CEO's Compensation Rises 44 per cent in 2012 to $11.1 Million as Automaker Changes Pay Mix," 2013, http://www.canadianbusiness.com/business-news/gm-ceos-compensation-rises-44-per-cent-in-2012-to-11-1-million-with-bigger-stock-awards; B. Marotte, "SNC-Lavalin: Engineering a Fair-Minded Pay Policy," *Globe and Mail*, August 23, 2012, http://m.theglobeandmail.com/report-on-business/careers/management/board-games/snc-lavalin-engineering-a-fair-minded-pay-policy/article4330684/?service=mobile.

32. C.T. Kulik and M.L. Ambrose, "Personal and Situational Determinants of Referent Choice," *Academy of Management Review* 17 (1992): 212–37.

33. J.S. Adams, "Toward an Understanding of Inequity," *Journal of Abnormal Social Psychology* 67 (1963): 422–36.

34. R.A. Cosier and D.R. Dalton, "Equity Theory and Time: A Reformulation," *Academy of Management Review* 8 (1983): 311–19; M.R. Carrell and J.E. Dittrich, "Equity Theory: The Recent Literature, Methodological Considerations, and New Directions," *Academy of Management Review* 3 (1978): 202–9.

35. "GM, Chrysler Ask for Billions in Canadian Aid," CBC News, February 21, 2009, http://www.cbc.ca/money/story/2009/02/20/carbailouts.html.

36. Habib, "Compensation: Motivation without money?"

37. C. Chen, J. Choi, and S. Chi, "Making Justice Sense of Local-Expatriate Compensation Disparity," *Academy of Management Journal* (2002): 807–17.

38. K. Aquino, R.W. Griffeth, D.G. Allen, and P.W. Hom, "Integrating Justice Constructs into the Turnover Process: A Test of a Referent Cognitions Model," *Academy of Management Journal* 40, no. 5 (1997): 1208–27.

39. R. Folger and M.A. Konovsky, "Effects of Procedural and Distributive Justice on Reactions to Pay Raise Decisions," *Academy of Management Journal* 32 (1989): 115–30; M.A. Konovsky, "Understanding Procedural Justice and Its Impact on Business Organizations," *Journal of Management* 26 (2000): 489–512.

40. E. Barret-Howard and T.R. Tyler, "Procedural Justice as a Criterion in Allocation Decisions," *Journal of Personality and Social Psychology* 50 (1986): 296–305; Folger and Konovsky, "Effects of Procedural and Distributive Justice."

41. R. Folger and J. Greenberg, "Procedural Justice: An Interpretive Analysis of Personnel Systems," in *Research in Personnel and Human Resources Management*, Vol. 3, ed. K. Rowland and G. Ferris (Greenwich: JAI, 1985); R. Folger, D. Rosenfield, J. Grove, and L. Corkran, "Effects of 'Voice' and Peer Opinions on Responses to Inequity," *Journal of Personality and Social Psychology* 37 (1979): 2253–61; E.A. Lind & T.R. Tyler, *The Social Psychology of Procedural Justice* (New York: Plenum, 1988); Konovsky, "Understanding Procedural Justice."

42. Habib, "Compensation: Motivation without money?"

43. V.H. Vroom, *Work and Motivation* (New York: Wiley, 1964); L.W. Porter and E.E. Lawler III, *Managerial Attitudes and Performance* (Homewood: Dorsey Press and Richard D. Irwin, 1968).

44. P.V. LeBlanc and P.W. Mulvey, "How American Workers See the Rewards of Work," *Compensation and Benefits Review* 30 (February 1998): 24–28.

45. A. Fox, "Companies Can Benefit When They Disclose Pay Processes to Employees," *HR Magazine* 47 (July 2002): 25.

46. Habib, "Compensation: Motivation Without Money?"

47. K.W. Thomas and B.A. Velthouse, "Cognitive Elements of Empowerment," *Academy of Management Review* 15 (1990): 666–81.

48. E.L. Thorndike, *Animal Intelligence* (New York: Macmillan, 1911).

49. B.F. Skinner, *Science and Human Behavior* (New York: Macmillan, 1954); B.F. Skinner, *Beyond Freedom and Dignity* (New York: Bantam, 1971); B.F. Skinner, *A Matter of Consequences* (New York: NYU Press, 1984).

50. A.M. Dickinson and A.D. Poling, "Schedules of Monetary Reinforcement in Organizational Behavior Management: Latham and Huber Revisited," *Journal of Organizational Behavior Management* 16, no. 1 (1992): 71–91.

51. R. Ho, "Attending to Attendance," *Wall Street Journal Interactive*, December 7, 1998.

52. W. Immen, "Want to Be Really Creative? Stop Thinking About Yourself," *Globe and Mail,* March 18, 2011, http://www.theglobeandmail.com/report-on-business/careers/career-advice/want-to-be-really-creative-stop-thinking-about-yourself/article573600.

53. D. Grote, "Manager's Journal: Discipline Without Punishment," *Wall Street Journal*, May 23, 1994, A14.

54. J.B. Miner, *Theories of Organizational Behavior* (Hinsdale: Dryden, 1980).

55. Dickinson and Poling, "Schedules of Monetary Reinforcement."

56. H. Schachter, "Making Your Words of Praise Heard," *Globe and Mail*, January 27, 2013, http://www.theglobeandmail.com/report-on-business/careers/management/making-your-words-of-praise-heard/article7868035.

57. F. Luthans and A.D. Stajkovic, "Reinforce for Performance: The Need to Go Beyond Pay and Even Rewards," *Academy of Management Executive* 13, no. 2 (1999): 49–57.

58. K.D. Butterfield, L.K. Trevino, and G.A. Ball, "Punishment from the Manager's Perspective: A Grounded Investigation and Inductive Model," *Academy of Management Journal* 39 (1996): 1479–512.

59. R.D. Arvey and J.M. Ivancevich, "Punishment in Organizations: A Review, Propositions, and Research Suggestions," *Academy of Management Review* 5 (1980): 123–132.

60. R.D. Arvey, G.A. Davis, and S.M. Nelson, "Use of Discipline in an Organization: A Field Study," *Journal of Applied Psychology* 69 (1984): 448–60; M.E. Schnake, "Vicarious Punishment in a Work Setting," *Journal of Applied Psychology* 71 (1986): 343–45.

61. S. Kilpatrick, "Bev Oda: Penalty for Smoking in a Hotel Room Among Expenses MP Charged to Taxpayers," *Maclean's Magazine*, September 8, 2012, http://www2.macleans.ca/2012/09/08/bev-oda-penalty-for-smoking-in-a-hotel-room-among-expenses-mp-charged-to-taxpayers; B. Mah, "Smoking Can Add $250 to Your City Hotel Bill," *Edmonton Journal*, March 1, 2012, http://www.canada.com/edmontonjournal/news/story.html?id=696d72a7-605b-40b0-8bff-c4c031ffa5cd.

62. E.A. Locke and G.P. Latham, *Goal Setting: A Motivational Technique That Works* (Englewood Cliffs: Prentice-Hall, 1984); E.A. Locke and G.P. Latham, *A Theory of Goal Setting and Task Performance* (Englewood Cliffs: Prentice-Hall, 1990).

63. G.P. Latham and E.A. Locke, "Goal Setting—a Motivational Technique That Works," *Organizational Dynamics* 8, no. 2 (1979): 68.

64. Latham and Locke, "Goal Setting."

Chapter 14

1. R. Wis, The Conductor as Leader: Principles of Leadership Applied to Life on the Podium (Napierville: GIA, 2006). See also C.W. Elkins, Conducting Her Destiny: The Making of a Maestra, 2008, http://books.google.ca/books?hl=en&lr=&id=i Mq0ASIiHYAC&oi=fnd&pg=PR4&dq=CANADIAN+BOOKS+ON+LEADERSHIP+AND+CONDUCTING+ORCHESTRAS&ots=8FAaYPgiio&sig=1nkZhW23UeQtEElHRhaw5lNYB00#v=onepage&q&f=false.

2. W. Bennis, "Why Leaders Can't Lead," Training and Development Journal 43, no. 4 (1989); H. Mintzberg, "The Manager's Job: Folklore and Fact," in Managing People and Organizations, ed. John J. Garbarro (Cambridge: Harvard Business School Publications, 1992), http://www.uu.edu/personal/bnance/318/mintz.html; "The Man Who Invented Management: Why Peter Drucker's Ideas Still Matter," Business Week, November 2005, http://www.businessweek.com/magazine/content/05_48/b3961001.htm; H. Mintzsberg, Managers, Not MBAs: A Hard Look at the Soft Practice of Managing and Management Development (San Francisco: Berrett-Koehler, 2006); H. Mintzberg, "Proven Models: 10 Managerial Roles," 2010, http://www.provenmodels.com/88/ten-managerial-roles/mintzberg,-henry.

3. A. Good, "Fail Forward wins the HBR/McKinsey Innovating Innovation Challenge," 2013, http://failforward.org/author/ashleygood; L. Buchanan, "How the Creative Stay Creative," Inc., June 2008, 102–3.

4. A. Zaleznik, "Managers and Leaders: Are They Different?" Harvard Business Review 55 (1977): 76–78; A. Zaleznik, "The Leadership Gap," Washington Quarterly 6 (1983): 32–39.

5. Bennis, "Why Leaders Can't Lead."

6. J. Lewis, "Rick George Recalls the Suncor-Petro Canada Merger," Alberta Oil, The Business of Energy, January 2013, http://www.albertaoilmagazine.com/2013/01/rick-george-remembers-the-petro-canada-merger-with-suncor; L. MacDonald, "Is Suncor's Merger with Petro-Canada About to Pay Off?", Globe and Mail, January 17, 2011, http://m.theglobeandmail.com/globe-investor/is-suncors-merger-with-petro-canada-about-to-pay-off/article563691/?service=mobile; CBC News, "Suncor, Petro-Canada Announce Merger," March 23, 2009, http://www.cbc.ca/money/story/2009/03/23/suncor-petro-canada-merge.html#ixzz 0sCN0BOJn.

7. D. Jones, "Not All Successful CEOs are Extroverts," USA Today, June 7, 2006, B1.

8. Canadian Press, "Rogers CEO Nadir Mohamed Stepping Down," CBC News, February 15, 2013, http://www.cbc.ca/news/business/story/2013/02/15/business-rogers-ceo-resigns.html; G. Robertson, "How a Shy Guy and Matt Damon Are Helping Kids, One by One," Globe and Mail, October 31, 2009, http://www.theglobeandmail.com/globe-investor/how-a-shy-guy-and-matt-damon-are-helping-kids-one-by-one/article1278592.

9. M. Gladwell, "Why Do We Love Tall Men?" Gladwell.Com, http://www.gladwell.com/blink/blink_excerpt2.html.

10. R.J. House and R.M. Aditya, "The Social Scientific Study of Leadership: Quo Vadis?", Journal of Management 23 (1997): 409–73; T. Judge, R. Illies, J. Bono, and M. Gerhardt, "Personality and Leadership: A Qualitative and Quantitative Review," Journal of Applied Psychology (August 2002): 765–82; S.A. Kirkpatrick and E.A. Locke, "Leadership: Do Traits Matter?", Academy of Management Executive 5, no. 2 (1991): 48–60.

11. House and Aditya, "The Social Scientific Study"; Kirkpatrick and Locke, "Leadership: Do Traits Matter?"

12. E. Beaton, "Kelsey Ramsden's Shift into Moving Earth for an All-New Client Base Has Landed Her Atop the W100 Ranking," Profit Guide.Com, October 1, 2012, http://www.profitguide.com/manage-grow/strategy-operations/different-dirt-w100-profile-41320.

13. Beaton, "Kelsey Ramsden's Shift."

14. Kirkpatrick and Locke, "Leadership: Do Traits Matter?"

15. E. Amendola, "P&G CEO Wields High Expectations, but No Whip," USA Today, http://www.usatoday.com/money/companies/management/2007-02-19-exec-pandg-usat_x.htm?loc=insterstitialskip.

16. E.A. Fleishman, "The Description of Supervisory Behavior," Journal of Applied Psychology 37 (1953): 1–6; L.R. Katz, New Patterns of Management (New York: McGraw-Hill, 1961).

17. Canadian Press, "VIA Rail Strike Averted," June 27, 2010, http://www.cbc.ca/consumer/story/2010/06/27/via-strike-averted.html#ixzz0sCVFjl8o.

18. K. Miller, Organizational Communication: Approaches and Processes, 6th ed. (Wadsworth: Boston, 2011).

19. J. Beer, "I500: Canadian Tire Rolls Out New Focus on Innovation," Canadian Business, May 12, 2013, http://www.canadianbusiness.com/list-and-rankings/canadian-tire-rolls-out-new-focus-on-innovation.
20. P. Weissenberg and M.H. Kavanagh, "The Independence of Initiating Structure and Consideration: A Review of the Evidence," Personnel Psychology 25 (1972): 119–30.
21. R.J. House and T.R. Mitchell, "Path-Goal Theory of Leadership," Journal of Contemporary Business 3 (1974): 81–97; F.E. Fiedler, "A Contingency Model of Leadership Effectiveness," in Advances in Experimental Social Psychology, ed. L. Berkowitz (New York: Academic Press, 1964); V.H. Vroom and P.W. Yetton, Leadership and Decision Making (Pittsburgh: University of Pittsburgh Press, 1973); P. Hersey and K.H. Blanchard, The Management of Organizational Behavior, 4th ed. (Englewood Cliffs: Prentice Hall, 1984); S. Kerr and J.M. Jermier, "Substitutes for Leadership: Their Meaning and Measurement," Organizational Behavior and Human Performance 22 (1978): 375–403.
22. F.E. Fiedler and M.M. Chemers, Leadership and Effective Management (Glenview: Scott, Foresman, 1974); F.E. Fiedler and M.M. Chemers, Improving Leadership Effectiveness: The Leader Match Concept, 2nd ed. (New York: John Wiley, 1984).
23. Fiedler and Chemers, Improving Leadership Effectiveness.
24. F.E. Fiedler, "The Effects of Leadership Training and Experience: A Contingency Model Interpretation," Administrative Science Quarterly 17, no. 4 (1972): 455; F.E. Fiedler, A Theory of Leadership Effectiveness (New York: McGraw-Hill, 1967).
25. L.S. Csoka and F.E. Fiedler, "The Effect of Military Leadership Training: A Test of the Contingency Model," Organizational Behavior and Human Performance 8 (1972): 395–407.
26. House and Mitchell, "Path-Goal Theory of Leadership."
27. House and Mitchell, "Path-Goal Theory of Leadership."
28. B.M. Fisher and J.E. Edwards, "Consideration and Initiating Structure and Their Relationships with Leader Effectiveness: A Meta-Analysis," Proceedings of the Academy of Management, August 1988, 201–5.
29. M. Copeland, K. Crawford, J. Davis, S. Hamner, C. Hawn, R. Howe, P. Kaihla, M. Maier, O. Malik, D. McDonald, C. Null, E. Schonfeld, O. Thomas, and G. Zachary, "My Golden Rule," Business 2.0, December 1, 2005, 108.
30. E. White, "Art of Persuasion Becomes Key," Wall Street Journal, May 19, 2008, B5.
31. J.C. Wofford and L.Z. Liska, "Path-Goal Theories of Leadership: A Meta-Analysis," Journal of Management 19 (1993): 857–76.
32. House and Aditya, "The Social Scientific Study of Leadership."
33. V.H. Vroom and A.G. Jago, The New Leadership: Managing Participation in Organizations (Englewood Cliffs: Prentice Hall, 1988).
34. C. Fishman, "How Teamwork Took Flight: This Team Built a Commercial Engine—and Self-Managing GE Plant—from Scratch," Fast Company, October 1, 1999, 188.
35. Fishman, "How Teamwork Took Flight."
36. Fishman, "How Teamwork Took Flight."
37. G.A. Yukl, Leadership in Organizations, 3rd ed. (Englewood Cliffs: Prentice Hall, 1995).
38. B.M. Bass, Bass and Stogdill's Handbook of Leadership: Theory, Research, and Managerial Applications (New York: Free Press, 1990).
39. C.L. Hoyt, "Women, Men, and Leadership: Exploring the Gender Gap at the Top," Social and Personality Psychology Compass 4, no. 7 (2010): 484–98.
40. C.L. Hoyt, "Women, Men, and Leadership: Exploring the Gender Gap at the Top," Social and Personality Psychology Compass 4, no. 7 (2010): 484–98.
41. S.J. Zaccaro, L.M.V. Gulick, and V.P. Khare, "Personality and Leadership," in Leadership at the Crossroads: Leadership and Psychology, Vol. 1, ed. C.L. Hoyt, G.R. Goethals, and D.R. Forsyth (Westport: Praeger, 2008), 1–10.
42. M. Reuvers, M.L. Van Engen, C.J. Vinkenburg, E. Wilson-Evered, "Transformational Leadership and Innovative Work Behaviour: Exploring the Relevance of Gender Differences," Creativity and Innovation Management 17, no. 3 (2008): 227–44.
43. C. Kulich, M.K. Ryan, S.A. Haslam, "Where Is the Romance for Women Leaders? The Effects of Gender on Leadership Attributions and Performance-Based Pay," Applied Psychology 56, no. 4 (2007): 582–601.
44. W. Buffett, "Warren Buffett Is Bullish ... on Women," Fortune, May 2, 2013, http://money.cnn.com/2013/05/02/leadership/warren-buffett-women.pr.fortune/index.html; A. Steinbrecher, "Warren Buffett Says We Need More Women in Business, and a New Study Shows He's Right," 2013, http://www.policymic.com/articles/42421/warren-buffett-says-we-need-more-women-in-business-and-a-new-study-shows-he-s-right.
45. R.D. Ireland and M.A. Hitt, "Achieving and Maintaining Strategic Competitiveness in the 21st Century: The Role of Strategic Leadership," Academy of Management Executive 13, no. 1 (1999): 43–57.
46. P. Thoms and D.B. Greenberger, "Training Business Leaders to Create Positive Organizational Visions of the Future: Is It Successful?", Academy of Management Journal (Best Papers and Proceedings 1995): 212–16.
47. M. Weber, The Theory of Social and Economic Organizations, trans. R.A. Henderson and T. Parsons (New York: Free Press, 1947).
48. D. Buss, "Profit Drop Is 'One-Off Event' for Chrysler, Marchionne Says," Forbes, April 29, 2013, http://www.forbes.com/sites/dalebuss/2013/04/29/chrysler-profit-tumble-reminds-that-every-launch-is-important; "Why Marchionne Should Fold Fiat into Chrysler," Globe and Mail, April 25, 2013; Eric Reguly, Globe and Mail, http://www.the globeandmail.com/report-on-business/rob-magazine/ceo-of-the-year/article1375887.
49. D.A. Waldman and F.J. Yammarino, "CEO Charismatic Leadership: Levels-of-Management and Levels-of-Analysis Effects," Academy of Management Review 24, no. 2 (1999): 266–85.
50. K.B. Lowe, K.G. Kroeck, and N. Sivasubramaniam, "Effectiveness Correlates of Transformational and Transactional Leadership: A Meta-Analytic Review of the MLQ Literature," Leadership Quarterly 7 (1996): 385–425.
51. J.M. Howell and B.J. Avolio, "The Ethics of Charismatic Leadership: Submission or Liberation?", Academy of Management Executive 6, no. 2 (1992): 43–54.
52. Howell and Avolio, "The Ethics of Charismatic Leadership."
53. B.M. Bass, "From Transactional to Transformational Leadership: Learning to Share the Vision,"

Organizational Dynamics 4, no. 8 (1991): 19–31, http://strandtheory.org/images/From_transactional_to_transformational_-_Bass.pdf.

54. A. Deutschman, "Is Your Boss a Psychopath?", Fast Company, July 2005, 44.
55. B.M. Bass, A New Paradigm of Leadership: An Inquiry into Transformational Leadership (Alexandra: U.S. Army Research Institute for the Behavioral and Social Sciences, 1996).
56. A. Lowe, "Belinda Stronach Explains Why She Gives to Charity," Globe and Mail, October 25, 2011, http://www.theglobeandmail.com/life/giving/video-belinda-stronach-explains-why-she-gives-to-charity/article608551; Sylvia Fraser, "The Belinda Stronach Defence," Toronto Life, February 2006, http://www.belindastronach.com/pdf/Toronto%20Life%20February%202006.pdf; Postmedia News, "Belinda Stronach Quits Politics for Magna," Financial Post, April 11, 2007, http://www.canada.com/nationalpost/news/story.html?id=3f2efd7c-0d10-477c-bf2c-4bb4ecda3abd&k=96098.
57. B.M. Bass, "From Transactional to Transformational Leadership."

Chapter 15

1. E.E. Lawler III, L.W. Porter, and A. Tannenbaum, "Managers' Attitudes toward Interaction Episodes," *Journal of Applied Psychology* 52 (1968): 423–39; H. Mintzberg, *The Nature of Managerial Work* (New York: Harper and Row, 1973).
2. M.M. Robles, "Executive Perceptions of the Top 10 Soft Skills Needed in Today's Workplace," *Business Communication Quarterly* 75 no. 4 (December 2012): 453–65.
3. M.M. Robles, "Executive Perceptions of the Top 10 Soft Skills Needed in Today's Workplace."
4. E.E. Jones and K.E. Davis, "From Acts to Dispositions: The Attribution Process in Person Perception," in *Advances in Experimental and Social Psychology* 2, ed. L. Berkowitz (New York: Academic Press, 1965), 219–66; R.G. Lord and J.E. Smith, "Theoretical, Information-Processing, and Situational Factors Affecting Attribution Theory Models of Organizational Behavior," *Academy of Management Review* 8 (1983): 50–60.
5. "Lab Tests: Why Consumer Reports Can't Recommend the iPhone 4," *Consumer Reports*, July 12, 2010, accessed June 12, 2011, http://news.consumerreports.org/electronics/2010/07/apple-iphone-4-antenna-issues-signal-strength-att-network-gsm.html.
6. G. Fowler and I. Sherr, "A Defiant Steve Jobs Confronts 'Antennagate'," *WallStreet Journal*, July 17, 2010, B1.
7. J. Topolsky, "Apple Responds to iPhone 4 Reception Issues: You're Holding the Phone the Wrong Way," Engadget.com, June 24, 2010, accessed June 12, 2011, http://www.engadget.com/2010/06/24/apple-responds-over-iphone-4-reception-issues-youre-holding-the/.
8. H.H. Kelly, *Attribution in Social Interaction* (Morristown: General Learning, 1971).
9. J.M. Burger, "Motivational Biases in the Attribution of Responsibility for an Accident: A Meta-Analysis of the Defensive-Attribution Hypothesis," *Psychological Bulletin* 90 (1981): 496–512.
10. D.A. Hofmann and A. Stetzer, "The Role of Safety Climate and Communication in Accident Interpretation: Implications for Learning from Negative Events," *Academy of Management Journal* 41, no. 6 (1998): 644–57.
11. C. Perrow, *Normal Accidents: Living with High-Risk Technologies* (New York: Basic, 1984).
12. A.G. Miller and T. Lawson, "The Effect of an Informational Opinion on the Fundamental Attribution Error," *Journal of Personality and Social Psychology* 47 (1989): 873–96; J.M. Burger, "Changes in Attribution Errors over Time: The Ephemeral Fundamental Attribution Error," *Social Cognition* 9 (1991): 182–93.
13. F. Heider, *The Psychology of Interpersonal Relations* (New York: Wiley, 1958); D.T. Miller and M. Ross, "Self-Serving Biases in Attribution of Causality: Fact or Fiction?" *Psychological Bulletin* 82 (1975): 213–25.
14. J.R. Larson, Jr., "The Dynamic Interplay Between Employees' Feedback-Seeking Strategies and Supervisors' Delivery of Performance Feedback," *Academy of Management Review* 14, no. 3 (1989): 408–22.
15. G.L. Kreps, *Organizational Communication: Theory and Practice* (New York: Longman, 1990).
16. Kreps, *Organizational Communication.*
17. E. Beaton, "Frankly Speaking: Why It Pays to Tell Your Bosses What You Really Think of Them," *Globe and Mail*, March 19, 2010, http://www.theglobeandmail.com/report-on-business/frankly-speaking/article1505364.
18. L. Landro, "The Informed Patient: Hospitals Combat Errors at the 'Hand-Off,'" *Wall Street Journal*, June 28, 2006, D1.
19. J. Sandberg, "Ruthless Rumors and the Managers Who Enable Them," *Wall Street Journal*, October 29, 2003, B1.
20. D. Therrien, "Rid Your Office of Backstabbers: How Good Managers Can Control Counterproductive Workplace Gossip," *Canadian Business Online*, November 22, 2004, http://www.canadianbusiness.com/business-strategy/rid-your-office-of-backstabbers-how-good-managers-can-control-counterproductive-workplace-gossip; http://www.canadianbusiness.com/managing/article.jsp?content=20041122_63827_63827.
21. J. Sandberg, "Ruthless Rumors and the Managers Who Enable Them."
22. D.T. Hall, K.L. Otazo, and G.P. Hollenbeck, "Behind Closed Doors: What Really Happens in Executive Coaching," *Organizational Dynamics* 27, no. 3 (1999): 39–53.
23. J. Hollon, "Half of Companies Report Higher Turnover Than Last Year," *TLTN*, 23 May 2013, http://www.tlnt.com/2013/05/23/survey-half-of-companies-report-higher-turnover-than-last-year; W. Immen, "Hanging On to the Best and Brightest in Lean Times," *Globe and Mail*, August 23, 2012, http://m.theglobeandmail.com/report-on-business/careers/career-advice/hanging-on-to-the-best-and-brightest-in-lean-times/article4325562/?service=mobile.
24. V. Galt, September 15, 2007). "Managing Change: Coach Them, Don't Boss Them," *Globe and Mail*, September 15, 2007, B17.
25. A. Mehrabian, "Communication Without Words," *Psychology Today* 3 (1968): 53; A. Mehrabian, *Silent Messages* (Belmont: Wadsworth, 1971); R. Harrison, *Beyond Words: An Introduction to Nonverbal Communication* (Upper Saddle River: Prentice Hall, 1974); A. Mehrabian, *Non-Verbal Communication* (Chicago: Aldine, 1972).
26. C.A. Bartlett and S. Ghoshal, "Changing the Role of Top Management: Beyond Systems to People," *Harvard Business Review* (May–June 1995): 132–42.
27. T. Andrews, "E-Mail Empowers, Voice-Mail Enslaves," *PC Week*, April 10, 1995, E11.

28. A. Rawlins, "There's a Message in Every Email," *Fast Company,* September 2007, http://www.fastcompany.com/60320/there's-message-every-email.
29. R.G. Nichols, "Do We Know How to Listen? Practical Helps in a Modern Age," in *Communication Concepts and Processes*, ed. J. DeVitor (Englewood Cliffs: Prentice Hall, 1971); P.V. Lewis, *Organizational Communication: The Essence of Effective Management* (Columbus: Grid, 1975).
30. R.G. Nichols, "Do We Know How to Listen? Practical Helps in a Modern Age."
31. E. Atwater, *I Hear You*, rev. ed. (New York: Walker, 1992).
32. T. Pittaway, "Dragons' Den: Fly Like a Dragon," *Profit Magazine*, October 2008, http://www.profitguide.com/manage-grow/success-stories/dragons-den-fly-like-a-dragon-29444; "Boston Pizza Quick Facts," http://www.bostonpizza.com/assets/mediacentre/documents/pdf/Boston_Pizza_Quick_Facts.pdf.
33. C. Gallo, "Why Leadership Means Listening," *BusinessWeek Online* January 31, 2007, http://www.businessweek.com/smallbiz/content/jan2007/sb20070131_192848.htm.
34. B.D. Seyber, R.N. Bostrom, and J.H. Seibert, "Listening, Communication Abilities, and Success at Work," *Journal of Business Communication* 26 (1989): 293–303.
35. Atwater, *I Hear You*.
36. J. Sandberg, "Not Communicating with Your Boss? Count Your Blessings," *Wall Street Journal,* May 22, 2007, B1.
37. P. Sellers, A. Diba, and E. Florian, "Get Over Yourself—Your Ego Is Out of Control—You're Screwing Up Your Career," *Fortune*, April 30, 2001, 76.
38. H.H. Meyer, "A Solution to the Performance Appraisal Feedback Enigma," *Academy of Management Executive* 5, no. 1 (1991): 68–76.
39. C. Hymowitz, "Executives Who Build Truth-Telling Cultures Learn Fast What Works," *Wall Street Journal,* June 12, 2006, B1.
40. The 2011–2012 Change and Communication ROI Study Report "Clear Direction in a Complex World: How Top Companies Create Clarity, Confidence, and Community to Build Sustainable Performance," January 2012, http://www.towerswatson.com/en/Insights/IC-Types/Survey-Research-Results/2012/01/2011-2012-Change-and-Communication-ROI-Study-Report.
41. C. Hymowitz, "Diebold's New Chief Shows How to Lead After a Sudden Rise," *Wall Street Journal*, May 8, 2006, B1.
42. R. King, "No Rest for the Wiki," *Bloomberg Business Week*, April 26, 2010, http://www.businessweek.com/technology/content/mar2007/tc20070312_740461.htm.
43. A. Lashinsky, "Lights! Camera! Cue the CEO!" *Fortune*, August 21, 2006, 27.
44. E.W. Morrison, "Organizational Silence: A Barrier to Change and Development in a Pluralistic World," *Academy of Management Review* 25 (2000):706-725.
45. K. Maher, "Global Companies Face Reality of Instituting Ethics Programs," *Wall Street Journal*, November 9, 2004, B8.
46. "Four Seasons Hotels and Resorts Named to FORTUNE List of the '100 Best Companies to Work For,'" January 16, 2008, http://www.reuters.com/article/2013/01/16/four-seasons-hotels-idUSnPnCG43386+160+PRN20130116.
47. D. Orgel, "Supervalu's Strategic Approach to Social Media," *Supermarket News*, November 7, 2011, http://supermarketnews.com/viewpoints/supervalu_strategic_1107.
48. P. Desmond, "CIO 100: Supervalu Uses Social Media to Connect with Employees and Spur Turnaround," August 12, 2012, http://www.nttcom.tv/2012/08/22/supervalu-uses-social-media-to-connect-with-employees-and-spur-turnaround.

Chapter 16

1. H.R. Kerzner, *Project Management: A Systems Approach to Planning, Scheduling, and Controlling* (Hoboken: John Wiley, 2013); "National Standard of Canada for Psychological Health and Safety in the Workplace Released," http://www.csa.ca/cm/ca/en/search/article/national-standard-of-canada-psychological-health-and-safety-in-the-workplace; R. Leifer and P.K. Mills, "An Information Processing Approach for Deciding upon Control Strategies and Reducing Control Loss in Emerging Organizations," *Journal of Management* 22 (1996): 113–37.
2. Canadian Press, "Maple Leaf Foods Posts $14.8-million Loss in 'Very Difficult' Quarter," *Financial Post,* May 13, 2013, http://business.financialpost.com/2013/05/02/maple-leaf-foods-posts-14-8-million-loss-in-very-difficult-quarter; "Maple Leaf Foods Reports Results for Fourth Quarter and Year-End 2012," http://investor.mapleleaf.ca/phoenix.zhtml?c=88490&p=irol-newsArticle&ID=1789261&highlight=; Canadian Food Inspection Agency, "Health Hazard Alert: Certain Ready-to-Eat Deli Meat Products Produced at Establishment 97b May Contain Listeria Monocytogenes," August 19, 2008, http://news.gc.ca/web/article-eng.do?crtr.sj1D=&mthd=advSrch&crtr.mnthndVl=&nid=415369&crtr.dpt1D=&crtr.tp1D=&crtr.lc1D=&crtr.yrStrtVl=2008&crtr.kw=&crtr.dyStrtVl=26&crtr.aud1D=&crtr.mnthStrtVl=2&crtr.yrndVl=&crtr.dyndVl=; "Maple Leaf Foods Product Recall List," *Windsor Star,* August 25, 2008, http://www.canada.com/windsorstar/story.html?id=b5abf899-4f68-4465-925c-7da9a29c03f7; *The Gazette* (Montreal), "Deadly Listeriosis Outbreak Traced to Maple Leaf Meats," August 24, 2008, http://www.canada.com/montrealgazette/news/story.html?id=7365606e-e710-4cad-a883-a9bb390b3487; CBC News, "Meat Recall Could Cost Millions More," August 28, 2008, http://www.cbc.ca/canada/toronto/story/2008/08/25/maple-leaf-listeria.html#ixzz0sDiXnjOl864db14b8; "Deadly Outbreak Officially Tied to Maple Leaf Meats," *Globe and Mail*, August 28, 2008, http://v1.theglobeandmail.com/servlet/story/RTGAM.20080823.wvmaplerecall0823/VideoStory/Front/?pid=RTGAM.20080823.wlisteriosis_0813; CTV News, "Maple Leaf Foods Plant Linked to Listeria Outbreak," August 23, 2008, http://www.ctv.ca/CTVNews/TopStories/20080823/recall_listeria_080823.
3. "About the Standards Council of Canada," http://www.scc.ca/en/about-scc.
4. Global Food Safety Resource, 2013, http://www.globalfoodsafetyresource.com/globalgap.html; GLOBAL G.A.P., http://www1.globalgap.org/north-america/front_content.php?i dcat=249; J.W. Miller, "Private Food Standards Gain Favor," *Wall Street Journal,* March 11, 2008, B1; "GlobalGap Passes Producer Landmark," May 27, 2010, http://www.fruitnet.com/content.aspx?ttid=14&cid=6819; CBC News, "BC Hot House Changes Labeling on Mexican Produce," April 23, 2008, http://www.cbc.ca/canada/british-columbia/story/2008/04/23/bc-bchothouse-mexican-brand.html#ixzz0sHTUArJ0.
5. [MS-SQMCS2]: Software Quality Metrics (SQM) Client-to-Service Version 2 Protocol (2013), "No Changes to

the Meaning, Language, or Formatting of the Technical Content," http://msdn.microsoft.com/en-us/library/hh554414.aspx.

6. N. Wiener, *Cybernetics; or Control and Communication in the Animal and the Machine* (New York: Wiley, 1948).
7. AME Licensing and Training, 2013, http://www.tc.gc.ca/eng/civilaviation/standards/maintenance-aarpb-menu-2534.htm.
8. "More from Your Run," http://nikeplus.nike.com/plus/products/gps_app.
9. A. Jesdanun, "Microsoft's Windows 8.1 offers free upgrade after Windows 8 complaints," http://www.commercialappeal.com/news/2013/may/14/microsofts-windows-81-offers-free-upgrade-after/?print=1.
10. R. Leifer and P.K. Mills, "An Information Processing Approach for Deciding upon Control Strategies and Reducing Control Loss in Emerging Organizations," *Journal of Management* 22, no. 1 (2013): 113–37.
11. "Newfoundland and Labrador Pharmacy Network to Limit Drug Errors, Abuse," http://www.cbc.ca/news/canada/newfoundland-labrador/story/2010/05/27/nl-pharmacy-network-527.html; M. Babbage, M. (2013). "Ontario Pharmacy Assistant Who Found Chemo Errors 'Not a Hero,' He Says," Canadian Press, http://www.theglobeandmail.com/news/national/ontario-pharmacy-assistant-who-found-chemo-errors-not-a-hero-he-says/article11773549/.
12. L. Kane, "Examining the Work-from-Home Debate," *Toronto Star,* http://www.thestar.com/business/personal_finance/2013/03/01/examing_the_workfromhome_debate.html.
13. B. Marotte, "Out of Office Reply: Canadian Firms Split on Value of Telecommuting," *Globe and Mail,* April 26, 2013, http://www.theglobeandmail.com/report-on-business/careers/the-future-of-work/out-of-office-reply-canadian-firms-split-on-value-of-telecommuting/article11566700/.
14. S. Shellenbarger, "Is the Awful Behavior of Some Bad Bosses Rooted in Their Past?", *Wall Street Journal,* May 17, 2000, B1.
15. M. Weber, *The Protestant Ethic and the Spirit of Capitalism* (New York: Scribner's, 1958).
16. K. Ramlakhan and L. Peterson, "Car Thieves Try to Break Leash: 39 Cases of Tampering with GPS Bracelet Since 2008," *Winnipeg Free Press*, January 2, 2012, http://www.winnipegfreepress.com/special/opensecrets/car-thieves-try-to-break-leash-39-cases-of-tampering-with-gps-bracelet-since-2008-136526038.html; CBC News, "GPS Bracelets Lead to Arrests of 2 Chronic Car Thieves," December 22, 2009, http://www.cbc.ca/canada/manitoba/story/2009/12/22/mb-police-chase-winnipeg.html#ixzz0sHg4DPzz.
17. CBC, *The Fifth Estate*, "Reaction to 'Rate My Hospital' in Toronto," April 12, 2013, http://www.cbc.ca/fifth/2012-2013/2013/04/reaction-to-rate-my-hospital-in-toronto.html; J. McFarland, "Hospitals Raise Caution over Uniform Pay-for-Performance Rules," *Globe and Mail*, April 29, 2010, http://www.theglobeandmail.com/news/national/hospitals-raise-caution-over-uniform-pay-for-performance-rules/article1529878.
18. Canadian Press, "Toronto to Get Second Nordstrom Location in Canadian Expansion," *Financial Post*, http://business.financialpost.com/2013/04/08/nordstrom-canada-toronto; "Nordstrom Expands Canadian Footprint to Yorkdale Mall," CBC News, April 8, 2013, http://www.cbc.ca/news/business/story/2013/04/08/business-nordstrom-yorkdale.html; A. DeFelice, "A Century of Customer Love: Nordstrom Is the Gold Standard for Customer Service Excellence," *CRM Magazine,* June 1, 2005, 42, http://www.destinationcrm.com/Articles/Editorial/Magazine-Features/A-Century-of-Customer-Love-42958.aspx; Nordstrom, "International Shopping," http://shop.nordstrom.com/c/6025407/...6pbo%3D6008488.
19. R.T. Pascale, "Nordstrom: Respond to Unreasonable Customer Requests!," *Planning Review* 2 (May–June 1994): 17.
20. Pascale, "Nordstrom."
21. Pascale, "Nordstrom."
22. J.R. Barker, "Tightening the Iron Cage: Concertive Control in Self-Managing Teams," *Administrative Science Quarterly* 38 (1993): 408–37.
23. N. Byrnes, "The Art of Motivation," *Business Week,* May 1, 2006, 56–62; D. Crofts and R. Delaney, "Nucor Buys Canada's Harris Steel for $1.07 Billion," *Bloomberg News*, January 3, 2007, http://www.bloomberg.com/apps/news?pid=newsarchive&sid=atc7t4wqgN1Q&refer=us.
24. Barker, "Tightening the Iron Cage."
25. S.F. Premeaux and A.G. Bedeian, "Breaking the Silence: The Moderating Effects of Self-Monitoring in Predicting Speaking Up in the Workplace," *Journal of Management Studies* 40, no. 6 (2003): 1537–62; C. Manz and H. Sims, "Leading Workers to Lead Themselves: The External Leadership of Self-Managed Work Teams," *Administrative Science Quarterly* 32 (1987): 106–28.
26. P.L. Nesbit, "The Role of Self-Reflection, Emotional Management of Feedback, and Self-Regulation Processes in Self-Directed Leadership Development," *Human Resource Development Review* 11, no. 2 (2012): 203–22; J. Slocum and H.A. Sims, "Typology for Integrating Technology, Organization, and Job Design," *Human Relations* 33 (1980): 193–212.
27. C.C. Manz and H.P. Sims, Jr., "Self-Management as a Substitute for Leadership: A Social Learning Perspective," *Academy of Management Review* 5 (1980): 361–67.
28. A. Moritz, "5 Apps That Help Improve Memory and Overall Cognition," *Brainscape,* September 8, 2012, http://blog.brainscape.com/2012/08/apps-memory-cognition; C. Parker, (2012). "Best Android apps for improving memory," May 9, 2012, http://www.androidauthority.com/best-android-apps-improving-memory-83632/; C. Manz and C. Neck, *Mastering Self-Leadership,* 3rd ed. (Upper Saddle River: Pearson, Prentice Hall, 2004).
29. R.S. Kaplan and D.P. Norton, "Using the Balanced Scorecard as a Strategic Management System," *Harvard Business Review* (January–February 1996): 75–85; R.S. Kaplan and D.P. Norton, "The Balanced Scorecard: Measures That Drive Performance," *Harvard Business Review* (January–February 1992): 71–79; P. Niven, "Cascading the Balanced Scorecard: A Case Study on Nova Scotia Power, Inc.," http://www.scribd.com/doc/3489336/Cascading-the-Balanced-Scorecard-A-Case-Study-on-Nova-Scotia-Power.
30. J. Meliones, "Saving Money, Saving Lives," *Harvard Business Review* (November–December 2000): 57–65.
31. M.H. Stocks and A. Harrell, "The Impact of an Increase in Accounting Information Level on the Judgment Quality of Individuals and Groups," *Accounting, Organizations, and Society*, October–November 1995, 685–700.

32. J. Chevreau, "When Does It Pay to Borrow to Invest?", *Financial Post* (2013), http://www.financialpost.com/money/wealthyboomer/story.html?id=a251451b-7717-42a0-962f-b1b30a0c3b74.

33. G. Colvin, "America's Best and Worst Wealth Creators: The Real Champions Aren't Always Who You Think," *Fortune*, December 18, 2000, 207; "Introducing the Wealth Added Framework (Relative Wealth Added (RWA) and Wealth Added Index (WAI)," August 2009, http://sternstewart.com/rankings/SSGlobal1000/Introducing%20the%20Wealth%20Added%20Framework.pdf.

34. E. Varon, "Implementation Is Not for the Meek," *CIO*, November 15, 2002, http://www.cio.com/article/31510/Strategic_Planning_Implementation_Is_Not_for_the_Meek.

35. B. Turnbull, "Tweet for Satisfaction," *Toronto Star,* July 15, 2009, http://www.thestar.com/life/2009/07/15/tweet_for_satisfaction.html.

36. C.B. Furlong, "12 Rules for Customer Retention," *Bank Marketing 5* (January 1993): 14.

37. E.E. Bowen, B.D. Bowen, and D.E. Headley, "Development of a Model of Airline Consumer Satisfaction," *Aviation Technology Faculty and Staff Publications*, Purdue University, 2013, http://docs.lib.purdue.edu/authors.html; C.A. Reeves and D.A. Bednar, "Defining Quality: Alternatives and Implications," *Academy of Management Review* 19 (1994): 419–45.

38. "Our Achievements," Singapore Airlines, http://www.singaporeair.com.

39. S. Holmes, "Creature Comforts at 30,000 feet," *Business Week*, December 18, 2006, 138.

40. H. Shaw, "Loblaw Execs Reveal Company Problems" *Financial Post*, 2009, http://www.financialpost.com/story.html?id=65573c81-1600-48e0-88fb-8ca878b8c87c&k=0; "Loblaw Profit Soars, Vows More Aid to Bangladesh Victims," *CBCNews,* May 1, 2013, http://www.cbc.ca/news/business/story/2013/05/01/business-loblaws-profit.html; http://www.weston.ca/en/Loblaw-Companies-Ltd.aspx; "Loblaw Net Earnings Soar in Q1," *Montreal Gazette,* May 1, 2013, http://www.montrealgazette.com/business/Loblaw+earnings+soar/8320448/story.html#ixzz2Tru3CQsq; "Loblaw Net Profits Soar 40% in Q1, Raises Dividend," *Ottawa Citizen,* http://www.ottawacitizen.com/business/Loblaw+profits+ soar+raises+dividend/8320590/story.html#ixzz2TrvKCqFf.

41. D.R. May and B.L. Flannery, "Cutting Waste with Employee Involvement Teams," *Business Horizons*, September–October 1995, 28–38.

42. J. Carlton, "To Cut Fuel Bills, Try High-Tech Help," *Wall Street Journal,* March 11, 2008, B3.

43. M. Warner, "Plastic Potion No. 9," *Fast Company,* September 2008, 88.

44. B. Burlingham, "The Coolest Little Start-Up in America," *Inc.*, July 2006, 78–85.

45. Alberta Environment and Sustainable Resource Development, http://environment.alberta.ca/02785.html.

46. City of Edmonton, "Waste-to-Biofuels Facility Turning Garbage into Fuel," http://www.edmonton.ca/for_residents/garbage_recycling/biofuels-facility.aspx.

47. "Recycling at Calgary Condos Grows Niche Company," CBC News, May 12, 2013, http://www.cbc.ca/news/canada/calgary/story/2010/10/20/calgary-condominium-recycling-company.html.

48. J. Szekely and G. Trapaga, "From Villain to Hero (Materials Industry's Waste Recovery Efforts)," *Technology Review*, January 1, 1995, 30.

49. Intel, "The End of the Road: Schools and Computer Recycling," http://www.intel.com/education/recycling_computers/recycling.htm.

50. B. Rose, "Where Old Computers Go: While Too Many Are Dumped Illegally, Sr. Center Salvages Thousands," *Press Democrat*, June 18, 2001, D1.

Chapter 17

1. R. Lenzner, "The Reluctant Entrepreneur," *Forbes*, September 11, 1995, 162–66.

2. H. Thompson, "Slash the Bundle: How to Cut Your Internet-Phone Bill." *Globe and Mail*, October 10, 2012, http://www.theglobeandmail.com/technology/gadgets-and-gear/gadgets/slash-the-bundle-how-to-cut-your-internet-phone-bill/article4602005.

3. D. Tencer, "15 Countries with the Highest Broadband Internet Penetration Rate," *Huffington Post Canada*, February 8, 2013, http://www.huffingtonpost.ca/2012/08/02/broadband-internet-penetration-oecd_n_1730332.html.

4. M. Geist, "Canada's Digital Divide Likely to Widen," *Toronto Star*, April 5, 2013, http://www.thestar.com/authors.geist_michael.html. /2013/04/05/canadas_digital_divide_likely_to_widen_geist.html.

5. F. Suarez and G. Lanzolla, "The Half-Truth of First-Mover Advantage," *Harvard Business Review* 83, no. 4 (2005): 121–27, 134; R.D. Buzzell and B.T. Gale, *The PIMS Principles: Linking Strategy to Performance* (New York: Free Press, 1987); M. Lambkin, "Order of Entry and Performance in New Markets," *Strategic Management Journal* 9 (1988): 127–40.

6. F. Suarez and G. Lanzolla, "The Role of Environmental Dynamics in Building a First Mover Advantage Theory," *Academy of Management Review* 32, no. 2 (2007): 377–92; G.L. Urban, T. Carter, S. Gaskin, and Z. Mucha, "Market Share Rewards to Pioneering Brands: An Empirical Analysis and Strategic Implications," *Management Science* 32 (1986): 645–59.

7. S. Nassauer, "'I Hate My Room,' the Traveler Tweeted, Ka-Boom! An Up-Grade!", *Wall Street Journal*, June 24, 2010.

8. J. McKinnell, (2013). "Hotel for Pets, and People Too," *MacLean's,* http://www2.macleans.ca/2013/01/30/hotel-for-pets-and-people-too.

9. A. Donnelly, "Updated: NextBus Lets TTC Riders Track Buses by GPS", *National Post*, July 11, http://news.nationalpost.com/2011/07/11/nextbus-lets-ttc-riders-track-buses-by-gps.

10. L. Tischler, "Tech for Toques," *Fast Company*, May 1, 2006, 68; Squirrel Systems, "O'Charley's Names Squirrel Systems as Enterprise Support Partner of the Year," http://www.squirrelsystems.com/Company/News.

11. D. Voss, *Supply Freight Sustainability* (East Lansing: Michigan State University Press, 2013); R. Pastore, "Cruise Control," *CIO,* February 1, 2003, 60–66.

12. Pastore, "Cruise Control."

13. C. Quintanilla and L. Claman, "Acxiom Corporation—Chmn. and Pres. Interview," *CNBC/Dow Jones Business Video*, November 21, 2002.

14. A. Hui, "CERN Puts the World's First Website Back Online" *Globe and Mail*, May 1, 2013,

http://www.theglobeandmail.com/technology/cern-puts-the-worlds-first-website-back-online/article11656855.

15. J.D. Shiers, "Lessons Learnt from WLCG Service Deployment" (2011), http://www.gridpp.ac.uk/papers/WLCGdeployment-Shiers-paper-CHEP07.pdf; M. Górski, (2013) "10 years of WLCG—Epiphany 2013," epiphany.ifj.edu.pl/current/pres/day1_mg_epiphany_wlcg.pdf.
16. J. Stroller, "Why Cold Canada Is Becoming a Hot Spot for Data Centres," *Globe and Mail,* December 20, 2012, http://www.theglobeandmail.com/report-on-business/economy/canada-competes/why-cold-canada-is-becoming-a-hot-spot-for-data-centres/article6598555.
17. V. Beal, "Why Putting Your Data Center in Canada Makes Sense", *CIO.com*, October 8, 2012, http://www.cio.com/article/718251/Why_Putting_Your_Data_Center_in_Canada_Makes_Sense.
18. G. Murphy, "B.C. Hydro Responds to Attack on Its Smart Meter Technology," *Victoria News,* February 22, 2013, http://www.vicnews.com/opinion/letters/192524881.html; T. Knauss, "Niagara Mohawk Meters to Send Readings by Radio," *Post-Standard Syracuse*, September 17, 2002, A1.
19. S. Lubar, *Infoculture: The Smithsonian Book of Information Age Inventions* (Boston: Houghton, Mifflin, 1993).
20. J. MacDougall, "Why Radio Frequency Identification Makes Me Nervous" *National Post,* May 25, 2013, http://life.nationalpost.com/2013/05/25/jane-macdougall-rfids-make-me-nervous.
21. B. Worthen, "Bar Codes on Steroids," *CIO,* December 15, 2002, 53.
22. M. Stone, "Scanning for Business," *PC Magazine*, May 10, 2005, 117.
23. N. Rubenking, "Hidden Messages," *PC Magazine*, May 22, 2001, 86.
24. A. Carter and D. Beucke, "A Good Neighbor Gets Better," *BusinessWeek*, June 20, 2005, 16.
25. Rubenking, "Hidden Messages."
26. G. Saitz, "Naked Truth—Data Miners, Who Taught Retailers to Stock Beer Near Diapers, Find Hidden Sales Trends," *Star-Ledger*, August 1, 2002, 41.
27. M. Overfelt, "A Better Way to Sell Tickets," *Fortune Small Business*, December 1, 2006, 76; R. Leth, "Sports Buzz in Toronto," April 3, 2013, http://globalnews.ca/video/458041/sports-buzz-in-toronto.
28. Teradata, "Hudson's Bay Company: Nailing Fraud and Raising ROI," 2013, http://www.teradata.com/customers/Retail-Hudsons-Bay.
29. D. Danchev, "Report: 48% of 22 Million Scanned Computers Infected with Malware," *ZDNet,* January 27, 2010, http://www.zdnet.com/blog/security/report-48-of-22-million-scanned-computers-infected-with-malware/5365; T. Samson, "Malware Infects 30 Percent of Computers in U.S,," *InfoWorld,* 2010, http://www.infoworld.com/t/cyber-crime/malware-infects-30-percent-of-computers-in-us-199598; B. Gottesman and K. Karagiannis, "A False Sense of Security," *PC Magazine*, February 22, 2005, 72.
30. F.J. Derfler, Jr., "Secure Your Network," *PC Magazine*, June 27, 2000, 183–200.
31. "Authentication," *Webopedia.com,* http://www.webopedia.com/TERM/a/authentication.html.
32. "Authorization," Webopedia.com, http://www.webopedia.com/TERM/a/authorization.html.
33. L. Seltzer, "Password Crackers," *PC Magazine*, February 12, 2002, 68.
34. B. Grimes, "Biometric Security," *PC Magazine*, April 22, 2003, 74.
35. Mercantile Mergers and Acquisitions Corporation, http://www.mercantilemergersacquisitions.com/aboutus/mark-borkowski.html; R. Carrick, "Storing Your Financial Data the Safe Way" *Globe and Mail*, September 6, 2012, http://www.theglobeandmail.com/globe-investor/personal-finance/storing-your-financial-data-the-safe-way/article4325109; C. Payette, "Mercantile Mergers Locks and Loads with Drive Crypt," 2009, http://www.theglobeandmail.com/technology/mercantile-mergers-locks-and-loads-with-drive-crypt/article1157409; C. Atchison, "Security: Stop, Thief?", 2008, *Profit Magazine*, October 2008, http://www.profitguide.com/manage-grow/strategy-operations/security-stop-thief-29453.
36. R. Gann, "How to Secure a Wireless Network: Top Tips for Securing Your Businesses Wireless Network," 2012, *TechRadar,* http://www.techradar.com/news/internet/how-to-secure-a-wireless-network-1075710.
37. J. DeAvila, "Wi-Fi Users, Beware: Hot Spots are Weak Spots," *Wall Street Journal,* January 16, 2008, D1.
38. J. van den Hoven, "Executive Support Systems and Decision Making," *Journal of Systems Management* 47, no. 8 (March–April 1996): 48.
39. D. Hannon, "Colgate-Palmolive Empowers Senior Leaders with Executive Dashboards," *InsiderProfiles*, April 1, 2011, http://insiderprofiles.wispubs.com/article.aspx?Articled=5720.
40. "Intranet," *Webopedia.com,* http://www.webopedia.com/TERM/i/intranet.html.
41. Microsoft Office System Customer Solution Case Study, "Canadian Tire Rolls Out SharePoint® for Worker Collaboration" 2012, http://www.itreportcanada.ca/itpublic/Canadian_Tire_Rolls_Out_SharePoint.pdf; S. Holz, "Bring Your Intranet Into the 21st Century," *Communication World,* January–February 2008, 14–18.
42. J. Ericson, "The Hillman Group Leverages Consolidated Reporting, Geographic Analysis to Support Its Hardware Manufacturing/Distribution Leadership," *Business Intelligence Review*, March 1, 2007, 12.
43. "Extranet," Webopedia.com, available online at http://www.webopedia.com/TERM/E/extranet.html.
44. S. Hamm, D. Welch, W. Zellner, F. Keenan, and F. Engardio, "Down but Hardly Out: Downturn Be Damned, Companies Are Still Anxious to Expand Online," *BusinessWeek*, March 26, 2001, 126.
45. R. Ruggero, "Alaska Cruise Port Info for Vancouver, Canada," 2009, http://suite101.com/article/alaska-cruise-port-info-for-vancouver-canada-a109149.
46. Hamm et al., "Down but Hardly Out."
47. K.C. Laudon, J.P. Laudon, and M.E. Brabston, *Management Information Systems: Managing the Digital Firm* (6th Canadian ed.) (Toronto: Pearson Canada 2013).
48. J. Borzo, "Software for Symptoms," *Wall Street Journal*, May 23, 2005, R10.
49. Borzo, "Software for Symptoms."
50. R. Hernandez, "American Express Authorizer's Assistant," *Business Rules Journal*, http://bizrules.com/advice.htm.

Chapter 18

1. WestJet, "1999 Initial Public Offering Prospectus," http://www.westjet.com/pdf/investorMedia/financialReports/062899prospectus.pdf.
2. WestJet, "InFlight Experience," http://www.westjet.com/guest/en/experience/inflightExperience/buyOnBoard.shtml.
3. C. Sorensen, "WestJet's Big Plans to Conquer Air Canada and Then the World," *Maclean's*, May 27, 2010, http://www2.macleans.ca/2010/05/27/ready-for-takeoff/2.
4. WestJet, "Management's Discussion and Analysis of Financial Results 2012," http://www.westjet.com/guest/en/media-investors/2012-annual-report/WestJet-MDA-2012.pdf.
5. S. Oches, "2012 QSR Drive-Thru Study," *QSR Magazine Special Report,* October 2012, http://www.qsrmagazine.com/content/2012-qsr-drive-thru-study-average-service-time.
6. M. Richtel, "The Long-Distance Journey of a Fast-Food Order," *New York Times,* April 11, 2006, http://www.nytimes.com/2006/04/11/technology/11fast.html?ei=5090&en=fba08e17788e24c9&ex=1302408000&pagewanted=all.
7. Oches, "2012 QSR Drive-Thru Survey."
8. "Solving (Almost) Canada's Productivity Puzzle," CBC News, August 11, 2009, http://www.cbc.ca/money/story/2009/08/10/f-productivity-statistics-canada-study.html.
9. TD Economics Topic Paper, "Canada's Productivity Challenge," October 5, 2005, http://www.td.com/document/PDF/economics/topic/td-economics-topic-el1005-prod.pdf.
10. "Solving (Almost) Canada's Productivity Puzzle."
11. How Canada Performs, "Labour Productivity Growth," March 2013, http://www.conferenceboard.ca/hcp/details/economy/measuring-productivity-canada.aspx.
12. "Solving (Almost) Canada's Productivity Puzzle."
13. How Canada Performs, "Labour Productivity Growth."
14. D. Shaw, "Productivity: Its Increasing Influence over Canadians' Standard of Living and Quality of Life Industry," Library of Parliament, Infrastructure and Resources Division, November 5, 2009, 4, http://www2.parl.gc.ca/Content/LOP/ResearchPublications/prb0315-e.pdf.
15. B. Koenig, "Toyota and Chrysler Lead in Auto-Plant Efficiency," *Bloomberg*, June 5, 2008, http://www.bloomberg.com/apps/news?sid=aWdVR3oRciow&pid=newsarchive.
16. J. Stanford, "Productivity in the North American Auto Assembly Industry 1998-2007," *Canadian Auto Workers,* January 2009, http://www.caw.ca/assets/images/Productivity_in_N_American_Auto_Assembly_CAW_Jan_09.pdf.
17. Bureau of Labor Statistics, "Multifactor Productivity," http://stats.bls.gov/bls/productivity.htm.
18. J. Baldwin and W. Gu, "The Canadian Productivity Review: Productivity Performance in Canada, 1961 to 2008: An Update on Long-term Trends," August 2009, http://www.statcan.gc.ca/pub/15-206-x/15-206-x2009025-eng.pdf.
19. M. Rechtin, "Porsche, Hyundai Score Big Gains in J.D. Power Quality Survey," *Auto Week,* June 7, 2006, http://www.autoweek.com/apps/pbcs.dll/article?AID=/20060608/FREE/60607007/1041&te; T. Krisher, "Toyota Plant, Lexus, Tops in J.D. Power Quality Study," *Ottawa Citizen*, June 21, 2012, http://www.ottawacitizen.com/cars/Toyota+plant+Lexus+tops+Power+quality+study/6818401/story.html.
20. American Society for Quality, "Quality Glossary—Q," http://www.asq.org/glossary/q.html.
21. R.E. Markland, S.K. Vickery, and R.A. Davis, "Managing Quality" (Chapter 7), *Operations Management: Concepts in Manufacturing and Services* (Cincinnati: South-Western, 1998).
22. "WD Launches High-Performance, 7200 Rpm 2Tb Hard Drives for Desktop and Enterprise Systems," *Western Digital,* September 1, 2009, http://www.wdc.com.
23. L.L. Berry and A. Parasuraman, *Marketing Services* (New York: Free Press, 1991).
24. International Organization for Standardization, "FAQs—General," http://www.iso.org/iso/home/faqs/faqs_general_information_on_iso.htm.
25. International Organization for Standardization, "ISO 9000 and ISO 14000," http://www.iso.org/iso/home/standards/management-standards/iso_9000.htm; http://www.iso.org/iso/home/standards/management-standards/iso14000.htm.
26. J. Briscoe, S. Fawcett, and R. Todd, "The Implementation and Impact of ISO 9000 Among Small Manufacturing Enterprises," *Journal of Small Business Management* 43 (July 1, 2005): 309.
27. R. Henkoff, "The Not New Seal of Quality (ISO 9000 Standard of Quality Management)," *Fortune*, June 28, 1993, 116.
28. National Institute of Standards and Technology, "Frequently Asked Questions about the Malcolm Baldrige National Quality Award," http://www.nist.gov/public_affairs/factsheet/baldfaqs.cfm.
29. National Institute of Standards and Technology, "Baldrige Award Application Forms," http://www.baldrige.nist.gov/PDF_files/2008_Award_Application_Forms.pdf.
30. Baldridge National Quality Program 2008, "Criteria for Performance Excellence," http://www.quality.nist.gov/PDF_files/2008_Business_Criteria.pdf.
31. Baldridge National Quality Program 2008, "Criteria for Performance Excellence."
32. Baldridge National Quality Program 2008, "Criteria for Performance Excellence."
33. J.W. Dean, Jr., and J. Evans, *Total Quality: Management, Organization, and Strategy* (St. Paul: West, 1994).
34. J.W. Dean, Jr., and D.E. Bowen, "Management Theory and Total Quality: Improving Research and Practice Through Theory Development," *Academy of Management Review* 19 (1994): 392–418.
35. R. Allen and R. Kilmann, "Aligning Reward Practices in Support of Total Quality Management," *Business Horizons*, May 1, 2001, 77.
36. General Electric, "What is Six Sigma?", http://www.ge.com/en/company/companyinfo/quality/whatis.htm.
37. "A Team Approach to Reducing Waiting Times," *Globe and Mail,* December 3, 2012, http://www.theglobeandmail.com/life/health-and-fitness/advsunnybrook/sunnybrookfeatures/a-team-approach-to-reducing-wait-times/article5913697.
38. R. Hallowell, L.A. Schlesinger, and J. Zornitsky, "Internal Service Quality, Customer and Job Satisfaction: Linkages and Implications for Management," *Human Resource*

Planning 19 (1996): 20–31; J.L. Heskett, T.O. Jones, G.W. Loveman, W.E. Sasser, Jr., and L.A. Schlesinger, "Putting the Service-Profit Chain to Work," *Harvard Business Review* (March–April 1994): 164–74.

39. A. Wahl, "Best Workplaces 2006: On the Money—Vancity," *Canadian Business Online*, April 10, 2006, http://www.canadianbusiness.com/business-strategy/the-best-workplaces-in-canada.
40. R. Eder, "Customer-Easy Doesn't Come Easy," *Drug Store News*, October 21, 2002, 52.
41. L.L. Berry and A. Parasuraman, "Listening to the Customer—The Concept of a Service-Quality Information System," *Sloan Management Review* 38, no. 3 (Spring 1997): 65; C.W.L. Hart, J.L. Heskett, and W.E. Sasser, Jr., "The Profitable Art of Service Recovery," *Harvard Business Review* (July–August 1990): 148–56.
42. Vancity Credit Union, "2002–2003 Accountability Report," https://www.vancity.com/lang/fr/AboutUs/OurBusiness/OurReports/AccountabilityReport/0203AccountabilityReport/CommitmentThree.
43. D.E. Bowen and E.E. Lawler III, "The Empowerment of Service Workers: What, Why, How, and When," *Sloan Management Review* 33 (Spring 1992): 31–39; D.E. Bowen and E.E. Lawler III, "Empowering Service Employees," *Sloan Management Review* 36 (Summer 1995): 73–84.
44. Bowen and Lawler III, "The Empowerment of Service Workers."
45. Vancity Credit Union, "2002–2003 Accountability Report."
46. G.V. Frazier and M.T. Spiggs, "Achieving Competitive Advantage Through Group Technology," *Business Horizons* 39 (1996): 83–88.
47. "The Top 100 Beverage Companies: The List," *Beverage Industry*, July 2001, 30.
48. C. Li, "Canadian Job Shops: Getting Better All the Time," *Canadian Metalworking*, June 20, 2012, http://www.canadianmetalworking.com/daily-news/canadian-job-shopsgetting-better-all-the-time-67895.html.
49. S. Silke Carty, "Chrysler Wrestles with High Levels of Inventory as Unsold Vehicles Sit on Lots," *USA Today*, November 2, 2006, http://www.usatoday.com/money/autos/2006-11-02-chrysler-high-inventory_x.htm?loc=interstitialskip; J.D. Stoll, "Chrysler Maintains Plan to Cut Production as Inventory Rises," *Wall Street Journal*, August 24, 2006, http://www.wsj.com.
50. A. Wilson, "No More Push: How Detroit Stopped Overproducing," *Automotive News*, February 8, 2010, http://www.autonews.com/apps/pbcs.dll/article?AID=/20100208/RETAIL03/302089951.
51. N. Martinez, "Automakers Inventory Levels Kept at Bay Despite Extremely Dismal Sales," *Automotive News*, October 20, 2008, http://wot.motortrend.com/6301021/auto-news/automakers-inventory-levels-kept-at-bay-despite-extremely-dismal-sales/index.html.
52. M. Bustillo, "For Lowe's, Landscape Begins to Shift," *Wall Street Journal*, February 24, 2011, B3.
53. D. Drickhamer, "Reality Check," *Industry Week*, November 2001, 29; Inventory Tables, *Industry Week*, http://www.industryweek.com/uncategorized10/inventory-tables.
54. D. Drickhamer, "Zeroing In on World-Class," *Industry Week*, November 2001, 36; Inventory Tables, *Industry Week*, http://www.industryweek.com/uncategorized10/inventory-tables.
55. A. Madrigal, "Wow! Apple Turns Over Its Inventory Once Every 5 Days," *The Atlantic*, May 31, 2012, http://www.theatlantic.com/technology/archive/2012/05/wow-apple-turns-over-its-inventory-once-every-5-days/257915; Gartner Announces Rankings of Its 2012 Supply Chain Top 25, May 22, 2012, http://www.gartner.com/newsroom/id/2023116.
56. *EFR-Central.com*, "Welcome," http://www.efr-central.com/aboutefr.html.
57. J.R. Henry, "Minimized Setup Will Make Your Packaging Line S.M.I.L.E.," *Packaging Technology and Engineering*, February 1, 1998, 24.
58. J. Donoghue, "The Future Is Now," *Air Transport World*, April 1, 2001, 78.
59. N. Shirouzu, "Why Toyota Wins Such High Marks on Quality Surveys," *Wall Street Journal*, March 15, 2001, A1.
60. Shirouzu, "Why Toyota Wins."
61. G. Gruman, "Supply on Demand: Manufacturers Need to Know What's Selling Before They Can Produce and Deliver Their Wares in the Right Quantities," *Info World*, April 18, 2005.

Index

Note: Entries in bold indicate key terms in the text.

O

P

T

CHAPTER IN REVIEW

Management

Minerva Studio/Shutterstock.com

LO1

management
Getting work done through others. (p. 3)

efficiency
Getting work done with a minimum of effort, expense, or waste. (p. 3)

effectiveness
Accomplishing tasks that help fulfill organizational objectives. (p. 3)

LO2

planning (management functions)
Determining organizational goals and a means for achieving them. (p. 4)

organizing
Deciding where decisions will be made, who will do what jobs and tasks, and who will work for whom. (p. 4)

leading
Inspiring and motivating workers to work hard to achieve organizational goals. (p. 5)

controlling
Monitoring progress toward goal achievement and taking corrective action when needed. (p. 5)

LO3

top managers
Executives responsible for the overall direction of the organization. (p. 6)

middle managers
Managers responsible for setting objectives consistent with top management's goals and for planning and implementing subunit strategies for achieving these objectives. (p. 7)

first-line managers
Managers who train and supervise the performance of nonmanagerial employees who are directly responsible for producing the company's products or services. (p. 8)

team leaders
Managers responsible for facilitating team activities toward accomplishing a goal. (p. 8)

LO4

figurehead role
The interpersonal role managers play when they perform ceremonial duties. (p. 10)

leader role
The interpersonal role managers play when they motivate and encourage workers to accomplish organizational objectives. (p. 10)

liaison role
The interpersonal role managers play when they deal with people outside their units. (p. 10)

monitor role
The informational role managers play when they scan their environment for information. (p. 10)

disseminator role
The informational role managers play when they share information with others in their departments or companies. (p. 10)

spokesperson role
The informational role managers play when they share information with people outside their departments or companies. (p. 10)

LO1 Management Is ...

Good management is working through others to accomplish tasks that help fulfill organizational objectives as efficiently as possible.

LO2 Management Functions

Henri Fayol's classic management functions are known today as planning, organizing, leading, and controlling. Planning is determining organizational goals and a means for achieving them. Organizing is deciding where decisions will be made, who will do what jobs and tasks, and who will work for whom. Leading is inspiring and motivating workers to work hard to achieve organizational goals. Controlling is monitoring progress toward goal achievement and taking corrective action when needed. Studies show that performing the management functions well leads to better managerial performance.

LO3 Kinds of Managers

There are four different kinds of managers. Top managers are responsible for creating a context for change, developing attitudes of commitment and ownership, creating a positive organizational culture through words and actions, and monitoring their company's business environments. Middle managers are responsible for planning and allocating resources, coordinating and linking groups and departments, monitoring and managing the performance of subunits and managers, and implementing the changes or strategies generated by top managers. First-line managers are responsible for managing the performance of nonmanagerial employees, teaching them how to do their jobs, and making detailed schedules and operating plans based on middle management's intermediate-range plans. Team leaders are responsible for facilitating team performance, fostering good relationships among team members, and managing external relationships.

LO4 Managerial Roles

Managers perform interpersonal, informational, and decisional roles in their jobs. In fulfilling the interpersonal role, managers act as figureheads by performing ceremonial duties, as leaders by motivating and encouraging workers, and as liaisons by dealing with people outside their units. In performing their informational role, managers act as monitors by

Exhibit 1.3 Mintzberg's Managerial Roles

Interpersonal Roles
- Figurehead
- Leader
- Liaison

Informational Roles
- Monitor
- Disseminator
- Spokesperson

Decisional Roles
- Entrepreneur
- Disturbance Handler
- Resource Allocator
- Negotiator

Top to bottom: EDHAR/Shutterstock.com; R. Gino Santa Maria/Shutterstock.com; © Tuomas Kujansuu/iStockphoto.com

Source: Reprinted by permission of *Harvard Business Review* (an exhibit) from "The Manager's Job: Folklore and Fact," By Mintzberg, H. *Harvard Business Review,* July-August 1975.

Minerva Studio/Shutterstock.com

entrepreneur role
The decisional role managers play when they adapt themselves, their subordinates, and their units to change. (p. 11)

disturbance handler role
The decisional role managers play when they respond to severe problems that demand immediate action. (p. 11)

resource allocator role
The decisional role managers play when they decide who gets what resources. (p. 12)

negotiator role
The decisional role managers play when they negotiate schedules, projects, goals, outcomes, resources, and employee raises. (p. 12)

LO5

technical skills
The specialized procedures, techniques, and knowledge required to get the job done. (p. 12)

human skills
The ability to work well with others. (p. 13)

conceptual skills
The ability to see the organization as a whole, understand how the different parts affect one another, and recognize how the company fits into or is affected by its environment. (p. 13)

motivation to manage
An assessment of how enthusiastic employees are about managing the work of others. (p. 13)

scanning their environment for information, as disseminators by sharing information with others in the company, and as spokespeople by sharing information with people outside their departments or companies. In fulfilling decisional roles, managers act as entrepreneurs by adapting their units to incremental change, as disturbance handlers by responding to larger problems that demand immediate action, as resource allocators by deciding resource recipients and amounts, and as negotiators by bargaining with others about schedules, projects, goals, outcomes, and resources.

LO5 What Companies Look for in Managers

Companies do not want one-dimensional managers. They want managers with a balance of skills. Managers need the knowledge and abilities to get the job done (technical skills), must be able to work effectively in groups and be good listeners and communicators (human skills), must be able to assess the relationships between the different parts of the company and the external environment and position their companies for success (conceptual skills), and should want to assume positions of leadership and power (motivation to manage). Technical skills are most important for lower-level managers, human skills are equally important at all levels of management, and conceptual skills and motivation to manage increase in importance as managers rise through the managerial ranks.

LO6 Mistakes Managers Make

Another way to understand what it takes to be a manager is to look at some common mistakes managers make. One of the more common mistakes made by managers was being insensitive to others through their abrasive, intimidating, and bullying management style. Other common mistakes included betraying a trust, being overly political and ambitious, and being unable to delegate.

LO7 The Transition to Management: The First Year

Managers often begin their jobs by using more formal authority and less people management skill. However, most managers find that being a manager has little to do with "bossing" their subordinates. After six months on the job, the managers were surprised at the fast pace and heavy workload and that "helping" their subordinates was viewed as interference. After a year on the job, most of the managers had come to think of themselves not as doers but as managers who get things done through others. And, because they finally realized that people management was the most important part of their job, most of them had abandoned their authoritarian approach for one based on communication, listening, and positive reinforcement.

LO8 Competitive Advantage through People

Why does management matter? Well-managed companies are competitive because their workforces are smarter, better trained, more motivated, and more committed. Furthermore, companies that practise good management consistently enjoy greater sales revenues, profits, and stock market performance than companies that don't. Finally, good management matters because good management leads to satisfied employees who, in turn, provide better service to customers. Because employees tend to treat customers the same way that their managers treat them, good management can improve customer satisfaction.

How to Use the Card

1. Look over the card to preview the new concepts you'll be introduced to in the chapter.
2. Read the chapter to fully understand the material.
3. Go to class (and pay attention).
4. Review the card one more time to make sure you've registered the key concepts.
5. Don't forget, this card is only one of many MGMT learning tools available to help you succeed in your management course.

CHAPTER IN REVIEW

History of Management

WitR/Shutterstock.com

LO1 The Origins of Management

Management as a field of study is just 125 years old, but management ideas and practices have actually been used since 6000 BCE. From the ancient Sumerians to sixteenth-century Europe, there are historical antecedents for each of the functions of management discussed in this textbook: planning, organizing, leading, and controlling. However, there was no compelling need for managers until systematic changes in the nature of work and organizations occurred during the last two centuries. As work shifted from families to factories, from skilled labourers to specialized, unskilled labourers, from small, self-organized groups to large factories employing thousands under one roof, and from unique, small batches of production to large, standardized mass production, managers were needed to impose order and structure, to motivate and direct large groups of workers, and to plan and make decisions that optimized overall company performance by effectively coordinating the different parts of organizational systems.

LO2 Scientific Management

Scientific management involved studying and testing different work methods to identify the best, most efficient ways to complete a job. According to Frederick W. Taylor, the father of scientific management, managers should follow four scientific management principles. First, study each element of work to determine the one best way to do it. Second, scientifically select, train, teach, and develop workers to reach their full potential. Third, cooperate with employees to ensure that the scientific principles are implemented. Fourth, divide the work and the responsibility equally between management and workers. Above all, Taylor felt these principles could be used to align managers and employees by determining a fair day's work, what an average worker could produce at a reasonable pace, and a fair day's pay (what management should pay workers for that effort). Taylor felt that incentives were one of the best ways to align management and employees.

Frank and Lillian Gilbreth are best known for their use of motion studies to simplify work. Whereas Taylor used time study to determine a fair day's work based on how long it took a "first-class man" to complete each part of his job, Frank Gilbreth used film cameras and microchronometers to conduct motion studies to improve efficiency by eliminating unnecessary or repetitive motions. Henry Gantt is best known for the Gantt chart, which graphically indicates when a series of tasks must be completed to perform a job or project; but he also developed ideas regarding pay-for-performance plans (where workers were rewarded for producing more but were not punished if they didn't) and worker training (all workers should be trained and their managers should be rewarded for training them).

LO2

scientific management
Thoroughly studying and testing different work methods to identify the best, most efficient way to complete a job. (p. 20)

soldiering
When workers deliberately slow their pace or restrict their work outputs. (p. 21)

motion study
Breaking each task or job into its separate motions and then eliminating those that are unnecessary or repetitive. (p. 22)

time study
Timing how long it takes good workers to complete each part of their jobs. (p. 22)

Gantt chart
A graphic chart that shows which tasks must be completed at which times in order to complete a project or task. (p. 23)

LO3 Bureaucratic and Administrative Management

Today, we associate bureaucracy with inefficiency and red tape. Yet German sociologist Max Weber thought that bureaucracy—that is, running organizations on the basis of knowledge, fairness, and logical rules and procedures—would accomplish organizational goals much more efficiently than monarchies and patriarchies, where decisions were based on personal or family connections, personal gain, and arbitrary decision making. Bureaucracies are characterized by seven elements: qualification-based hiring; merit-based promotion; chain of command; division of labour; impartial application of rules and procedures; recording rules, procedures, and decisions in writing; and separating managers from owners. Nonetheless, bureaucracies are often inefficient and can be highly resistant to change.

The Frenchman Henri Fayol, whose ideas were shaped by his twenty-plus years of experience as a CEO, is best known for developing 5 management functions (planning, organizing, coordinating, commanding, and controlling) and 14 principles of management (division of work, authority and responsibility, discipline, unity of command, unity of direction, subordination of individual interests to the general interest, remuneration, centralization, scalar chain, order, equity, stability of tenure of personnel, initiative, and esprit de corps). He is also known for his belief that management could and should be taught to others.

LO3

bureaucracy
The exercise of control on the basis of knowledge, expertise, or experience. (p. 24)

WitR/Shutterstock.com

LO4

integrative conflict resolution
An approach to dealing with conflict in which both parties deal with the conflict by indicating their preferences and then working together to find an alternative that meets the needs of both. (p. 26)

organization
A system of consciously coordinated activities or forces created by two or more people. (p. 30)

LO4 Human Relations Management

Unlike most people who view conflict as bad, Mary Parker Follett believed that it should be embraced rather than avoided. Of the three ways of dealing with conflict—domination, compromise, and integration— she argued that the latter was the best because it focuses on developing creative methods for meeting conflicting parties' needs.

Elton Mayo is best known for his role in the Hawthorne Studies at the Western Electric Company. In the first stage of the Hawthorne Studies, production went up because the increased attention paid to the workers in the study and their development into a cohesive work group led to significantly higher levels of job satisfaction and productivity. In the second stage, productivity dropped because the workers had already developed strong negative norms. The Hawthorne Studies demonstrated that workers' feelings and attitudes affected their work, that financial incentives weren't necessarily the most important motivator for workers, and that group norms and behaviour play a critical role in behaviour at work.

Chester Barnard emphasized the critical importance of willing cooperation in organizations and said that managers could gain workers' willing cooperation through three executive functions: securing essential services from individuals (through material, nonmaterial, and associational incentives), unifying the people in the organization with a clear purpose, and providing a system of communication. Barnard maintains that it is better to induce cooperation through incentives, clearly formulated organizational objectives, and effective communication throughout the organization than to impose it using managerial authority.

LO5

system
A set of interrelated elements or parts that function as a whole. (p. 32)

subsystems
Smaller systems that operate in the context of a larger system. (p. 32)

synergy
When two or more subsystems working together can produce more than they can working apart. (p. 32)

closed systems
Systems that can sustain themselves without interacting with their environment. (p. 32)

open systems
Systems that can sustain themselves only by interacting with their environment, on which they depend for their survival. (p. 32)

contingency approach
Holds that there are no universal management theories and that the most effective management theory or idea depends on the kinds of problems or situations that managers are facing at a particular time and place. (p. 32)

LO5 Operations, Information, Systems, and Contingency Management

Operations management uses a quantitative or mathematical approach to find ways to increase productivity, improve quality, and manage or reduce costly inventories. The manufacture of standardized, interchangeable parts, the graphical and computerized design of parts, and the accidental discovery of just-in-time management were some of the most important historical events in operations management.

Throughout history, organizations have pushed for and quickly adopted new information technologies that reduce the cost or increase the speed with which they can acquire, store, retrieve, or communicate information. Some of the most important technologies that have revolutionized information management have been paper and the printing press in the fourteenth and fifteenth centuries, the manual typewriter in 1850, cash registers in 1879, the telephone in the 1880s, time clocks in the 1890s, the personal computer in the 1980s, and the Internet in the 1990s.

A system is a set of interrelated elements or parts that function as a whole. Organizational systems obtain inputs from both general and specific environments. Managers and workers then use their management knowledge and manufacturing techniques to transform those inputs into outputs that, in turn, provide feedback to the organization. Organizational systems must also address the issues of synergy, open *versus* closed systems, and entropy.

Finally, the contingency approach to management clearly states that there are no universal management theories. The most effective management theory or idea depends on the kinds of problems or situations that managers or organizations are facing at a particular time. This means that management is much harder than it looks.

Organizational Environments and Cultures

Tom Wang/Shutterstock.com

LO1

external environments
All events outside a company that have the potential to influence or affect it. (p. 35)

environmental change
The rate at which a company's general and specific environments change. (p. 35)

stable environment
An environment in which the rate of change is slow. (p. 35)

dynamic environment
An environment in which the rate of change is fast. (p. 35)

punctuated equilibrium theory
A theory according to which companies go through long, simple periods of stability (equilibrium), followed by short periods of dynamic, fundamental change (revolution), and ending with a return to stability (new equilibrium). (p. 35)

environmental complexity
The number of external factors in the environment that affect organizations. (p. 36)

simple environment
An environment with few environmental factors. (p. 36)

complex environment
An environment with many environmental factors. (p. 36)

resource scarcity
The abundance or shortage of critical organizational resources in an organization's external environment. (p. 37)

uncertainty
Extent to which managers can understand or predict which environmental changes and trends will affect their businesses. (p. 37)

LO2

general environment
The economic, technological, sociocultural, and political trends that indirectly affect all organizations. (p. 37)

specific environment
The customers, competitors, suppliers, industry regulations, and advocacy groups that are unique to an industry and directly affect how a company does business. (p. 37)

business confidence indices
Indices that show managers' level of confidence about future business growth. (p. 38)

technology
The knowledge, tools, and techniques used to transform input into output. (p. 39)

LO3

competitors
Companies in the same industry that sell similar products or services to customers. (p. 41)

competitive analysis
A process for monitoring the competition that involves identifying competition, anticipating their moves, and determining their strengths and weaknesses. (p. 41)

suppliers
Companies that provide material, human, financial, and informational resources to other companies. (p. 42)

supplier dependence
The degree to which a company relies on a supplier because of the importance of the supplier's product to the company and the difficulty of finding other sources for that product. (p. 42)

LO1 Changing Environments

Environmental change, complexity, and resource scarcity are the basic components of external environments. Environmental change is the rate at which conditions or events affect change in a business. Environmental complexity is the number and intensity of external factors in an external environment. Resource scarcity is the scarcity or abundance of resources available in the external environment. As rates of environmental change increase, as the environment becomes more complex, and as resources become scarce, managers become less confident that they can understand, predict, and react effectively to the trends affecting their businesses. According to punctuated equilibrium theory, companies experience periods of stability followed by short periods of dynamic, fundamental change, followed by a return to periods of stability.

LO2 General Environment

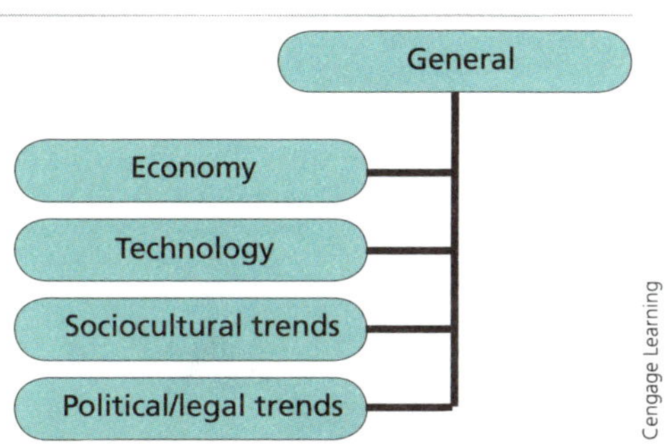

Cengage Learning

The general environment consists of events and trends that affect all organizations. Because the economy influences basic business decisions, managers often use economic statistics and business confidence indices to predict future economic activity. Changes in technology, which transforms inputs into outputs, can be a benefit or a threat to a business. Sociocultural trends such as changing demographic characteristics affect how companies run their businesses, whether they are competing domestically or in international markets. Similarly, sociocultural changes in behaviour, attitudes, and beliefs affect the demand for a business's products and services. Court decisions and new federal and provincial laws have imposed much greater political/legal responsibility on companies. The best way to manage legal responsibilities is to educate managers and employees about laws and regulations as well as potential lawsuits in domestic or foreign markets that could affect a business.

LO3 Specific Environment

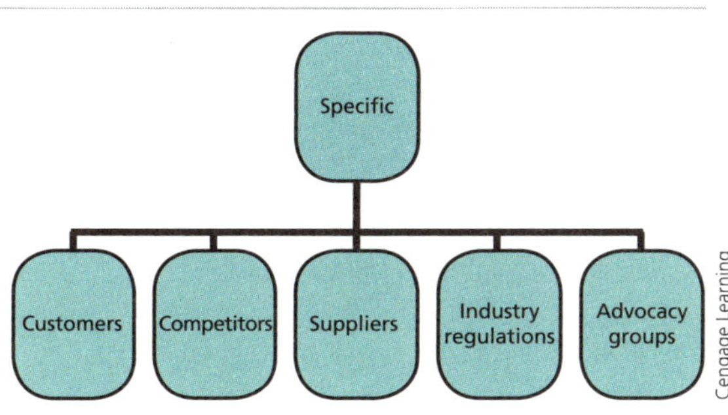

Cengage Learning

The specific environment is made up of the five components shown here. Companies can monitor customers' needs by identifying customer problems after they occur or by anticipating problems before they occur. Because they tend to focus on well-known competitors, managers often underestimate their competition or do a poor job of identifying future competitors. Suppliers and buyers are very dependent on each other, and that dependence sometimes leads to opportunistic behaviour, in which one benefits at the expense of the other. Regulatory agencies affect businesses by creating rules and then enforcing them. Advocacy groups cannot regulate organizations' practices, but through public communications, media advocacy, and product boycotts, they try to convince companies to change their practices.

Tom Wang/Shutterstock.com

buyer dependence
The degree to which a supplier relies on a buyer because of the importance of that buyer to the supplier and the difficulty of finding other buyers for its products. (p. 42)

opportunistic behaviour
A transaction in which one party in the relationship benefits at the expense of the other. (p. 42)

relationship behaviour
Mutually beneficial, long-term exchanges between buyers and suppliers. (p. 43)

industry regulation
Regulations and rules that govern the business practices and procedures of specific industries, businesses, and professions. (p. 43)

advocacy groups
Groups of concerned citizens who band together to try to influence the business practices of specific industries, businesses, and professions. (p. 43)

public communications
An advocacy group tactic that relies on voluntary participation by the news media and the advertising industry to get the advocacy group's message out. (p. 43)

media advocacy
An advocacy group tactic that involves framing issues as public issues; exposing questionable, exploitative, or unethical practices; and forcing media coverage by buying media time or creating controversy that is likely to receive extensive news coverage. (p. 43)

product boycott
An advocacy group tactic that involves protesting a company's actions by convincing consumers not to purchase its product or service. (p. 44)

LO4

environmental scanning
Searching the environment for important events or issues that might affect an organization. (p. 44)

cognitive maps
Graphic depictions of how managers believe environmental factors relate to possible organizational actions. (p. 45)

internal environment
The events and trends inside an organization that affect management, employees, and organizational culture. (p. 46)

organizational culture
The values, beliefs, and attitudes shared by members of the organization. (p. 46)

LO5

organizational stories
Stories told by members to make sense of events and changes in an organization and to emphasize culturally consistent assumptions, decisions, and actions. (p. 47)

organizational heroes
People celebrated for their qualities and achievements within an organization. (p. 47)

company vision
A business's purpose or reason for existing. (p. 47)

consistent organizational culture
When a company actively defines and teaches organizational values, beliefs, and attitudes. (p. 48)

LO4 Making Sense of Changing Environments

Managers use a three-step process to make sense of external environments: environmental scanning, interpreting information, and acting on it. Managers scan their environments based on their organizational strategies, their need for up-to-date information, and their need to reduce uncertainty. When managers identify environmental events as threats, they take steps to protect the company from harm. When managers identify environmental events as opportunities, they formulate alternatives for taking advantage of them to improve company performance. Using cognitive maps can help managers visually summarize the relationships between environmental factors and the actions they might take to deal with them.

LO5 Organizational Cultures: Creation, Success, and Change

Organizational culture is the set of key values, beliefs, and attitudes shared by members of an organization. Organizational cultures are often created by company founders and then sustained by telling organizational stories and celebrating organizational heroes. Adaptable cultures that promote employee involvement, make clear the organization's strategic purpose and direction, and actively define and teach organizational values and beliefs can help companies achieve higher sales growth, return on assets, profits, quality, and employee satisfaction. Organizational cultures exist on three levels: the surface level, where cultural artifacts and behaviours can be observed; just below the surface, where values and beliefs are expressed; and deep below the surface, where unconsciously held assumptions and beliefs exist. Managers can begin to change company cultures by focusing on the top two levels.

CHAPTER IN REVIEW

Ethics and Social Responsibility

iQoncept/Shutterstock.com

LO1 Workplace Deviance

Ethics is the set of moral principles or values that define right and wrong. Workplace deviance is behaviour that violates important organizational norms about right and wrong and that harms the organization or its workers. There are four different types of workplace deviance. Production deviance and property deviance harm the company, whereas political deviance and personal aggression harm individuals within the company.

LO2 North American Ethics Guidelines and Legislation

At the present time there is no national ethics legislation in Canada; however, an International Code of Ethics was released in 1997 to act as a guideline for Canadian businesses. Under the US Sentencing Commission Guidelines, companies can be prosecuted and fined up to $300 million for employees' illegal actions.

LO3 Influences on Ethical Decision Making

Three factors influence ethical decisions: the ethical intensity of the decision, the moral development of the manager, and the ethical principles used to solve the problem. Ethical intensity is strong when decisions have large, certain, immediate consequences and when we are physically or psychologically close to those affected by the decision. There are three phases of moral maturity. At the preconventional level, decisions are made for selfish reasons. At the conventional level, decisions conform to societal expectations. At the postconventional level, internalized principles are used to make ethical decisions. Each of these phases has two steps within it. Managers can use a number of different principles when making ethical decisions: self-interest, personal virtue, religious injunctions, government requirements, utilitarian benefits, individual rights, and distributive justice.

LO4 Practical Steps to Ethical Decision Making

Employers can increase their chances of hiring ethical employees by testing all job applicants. Most large companies now have corporate codes of ethics. In addition to offering general rules, ethics codes must also provide specific, practical advice. Ethics training seeks to increase employees' awareness of ethical issues; make ethics a serious, credible factor in organizational decisions; and teach employees a practical model of ethical decision making. The most important factors in creating an ethical business climate are the personal examples set by company managers, the involvement of management in the company ethics program, a reporting system that encourages whistle blowers to report potential ethics violations, and fair but consistent punishment of violators.

LO5 To Whom Are Organizations Socially Responsible?

Social responsibility is a business's obligation to benefit society. According to the shareholder model, a company's only social responsibility is to maximize shareholder wealth by maximizing company profits. According to the stakeholder model, companies must satisfy the needs and interests of multiple corporate stakeholders, not just shareholders. The needs of primary stakeholders, on which the organization relies for its existence, take precedence over those of secondary stakeholders.

Primary		Secondary
Governments	Suppliers Local	Media
Employees	Shareholders	Special Interest Groups
Customers	Communities	Trade Associations

LO1

ethics
The set of moral principles or values that defines right and wrong for a person or group. (p. 51)

ethical behaviour
Behaviour that conforms to a society's accepted principles of right and wrong. (p. 51)

workplace deviance
Unethical behaviour that violates organizational norms about right and wrong. (p. 51)

production deviance
Unethical behaviour that hurts the quality and quantity of work produced. (p. 51)

property deviance
Unethical behaviour aimed at the organization's property or products. (p. 52)

employee shrinkage
Employee theft of company merchandise. (p. 52)

political deviance
Using one's influence to harm others in the company. (p. 52)

personal aggression
Hostile or aggressive behaviour toward others. (p. 52)

LO3

ethical intensity
The degree of concern people have about an ethical issue. (p. 54)

magnitude of consequences
The total harm or benefit derived from an ethical decision. (p. 54)

social consensus
Agreement on whether behaviour is bad or good. (p. 54)

probability of effect
The chance that something will happen and then harm others. (p. 54)

temporal immediacy
The time between an act and the consequences the act produces. (p. 54)

proximity of effect
The social, psychological, cultural, or physical distance between a decision maker and those affected by his or her decisions. (p. 54)

concentration of effect
The total harm or benefit that an act produces on the average person. (p. 55)

preconventional level of moral development
The first level of moral development, in which people make decisions based on selfish reasons. (p. 55)

conventional level of moral development
The second level of moral development, in which people make decisions that conform to societal expectations. (p. 55)

postconventional level of moral development
The third level of moral development, in which people make decisions based on internalized principles. (p. 55)

principle of long-term self-interest
An ethical principle that holds that you should never take any action that is not in your or your organization's long-term self-interest. (p. 56)

principle of personal virtue
An ethical principle that holds that you should never do anything that is not honest, open, and truthful and that you would not be glad to see reported in the newspapers or on TV. (p. 56)

principle of religious injunctions
An ethical principle that holds that you should never take any action that is not kind and that does not build a sense of community. (p. 56)

iQoncept/Shutterstock.com

principle of government requirements
An ethical principle that holds that you should never take any action that violates the law, for the law represents the minimal moral standard. (p. 56)

principle of utilitarian benefits
An ethical principle that holds that you should never take any action that does not result in greater good for society. (p. 56)

principle of individual rights
An ethical principle that holds that you should never take any action that infringes on others' agreed-upon rights. (p. 56)

principle of distributive justice
An ethical principle that holds that you should never take any action that harms the least fortunate among us: the poor, the uneducated, the unemployed. (p. 56)

LO4

overt integrity test
A written test that estimates job applicants' honesty by directly asking them what they think or feel about theft or about punishment of unethical behaviours. (p. 57)

personality-based integrity test
A written test that indirectly estimates job applicants' honesty by measuring psychological traits, such as dependability and conscientiousness. (p. 57)

whistle-blowing
Reporting others' ethics violations to management or legal authorities. (p. 59)

social responsibility
A business's obligation to pursue policies, make decisions, and take actions that benefit society. (p. 60)

LO5

shareholder model
A view of social responsibility that holds that an organization's overriding goal should be to maximize profit for the benefit of shareholders. (p. 60)

stakeholder model
A theory of corporate responsibility that holds that management's most important responsibility, long-term survival, is achieved by satisfying the interests of multiple corporate stakeholders. (p. 61)

stakeholders
Persons or groups with a "stake" or legitimate interest in a company's actions. (p. 61)

primary stakeholder
Any group on which an organization relies for its long-term survival. (p. 61)

secondary stakeholder
Any group that can influence or be influenced by a company and can affect public perceptions about its socially responsible behaviour. (p. 61)

LO6

economic responsibility
The expectation that a company will make a profit by producing a valued product or service. (p. 62)

legal responsibility
A company's social responsibility to obey society's laws and regulations. (p. 62)

ethical responsibility
A company's social responsibility not to violate accepted principles of right and wrong when conducting its business. (p. 62)

discretionary responsibility
The expectation that a company will voluntarily serve a social role beyond its economic, legal, and ethical responsibilities. (p. 62)

LO7

social responsiveness
Refers to a company's strategy for responding to stakeholders' economic, legal, ethical, or discretionary expectations concerning social responsibility. (p. 63)

reactive strategy
A social responsiveness strategy in which a company does less than society expects. (p. 63)

defensive strategy
A social responsiveness strategy in which a company admits responsibility for a problem but does the least required to meet societal expectations. (p. 63)

accommodative strategy
A social responsiveness strategy in which a company accepts responsibility for a problem and does all that society expects to solve that problem. (p. 64)

proactive strategy
A social responsiveness strategy in which a company anticipates responsibility for a problem before it occurs and does more than society expects to address the problem. (p. 64)

LO6 For What Are Organizations Socially Responsible?

Companies can best benefit their stakeholders by fulfilling their economic, legal, ethical, and discretionary responsibilities. Being profitable, or meeting one's economic responsibility, is a business's most basic social responsibility. Legal responsibility consists of following a society's laws and regulations. Ethical responsibility means not violating accepted principles of right and wrong when doing business. Discretionary responsibilities are social responsibilities beyond basic economic, legal, and ethical responsibilities.

Cengage Learning

LO7 Responses to Demands for Social Responsibility

Social responsiveness is a company's response to stakeholders' demands for socially responsible behaviour. There are four social responsiveness strategies. When a company uses a reactive strategy, it denies responsibility for a problem. When it uses a defensive strategy, it takes responsibility for a problem but does the minimum required to solve it. When a company uses an accommodative strategy, it accepts responsibility for problems and does all that society expects to solve them. Finally, when a company uses a proactive strategy, it does much more than expected to solve social responsibility problems.

LO8 Social Responsibility and Economic Performance

Does it pay to be socially responsible? Sometimes it costs, and sometimes it pays. Overall, there is no clear relationship between social responsibility and economic performance. Consequently, managers should not expect an economic return from socially responsible corporate activities. If your company chooses to practise a proactive or accommodative social responsibility strategy, it should do so to better society and not to improve its financial performance.

CHAPTER IN REVIEW

Planning and Decision Making

Echo/Cultura/Getty Images

LO1

planning
Choosing a goal and developing a strategy to achieve that goal. (p. 69)

LO2

S.M.A.R.T. goals
Goals that are specific, measurable, attainable, realistic, and timely. (p. 71)

goal commitment
The determination to achieve a goal. (p. 71)

action plan
The specific steps, people, and resources needed to accomplish a goal. (p. 71)

proximal goals
Short-term goals or subgoals. (p. 72)

distal goals
Long-term or primary goals. (p. 72)

options-based planning
Maintaining flexibility by making small, simultaneous investments in many alternative plans. (p. 73)

slack resources
A cushion of extra resources that can be used with options-based planning to adapt to unanticipated change, problems, or opportunities. (p. 73)

LO3

strategic plans
Overall company plans that clarify how the company will serve customers and position itself against competitors over the next two to five years. (p. 74)

vision statement
A statement of a company's purpose and the ultimate destination it hopes to reach, acting as a guide to individuals in an organization. (p. 74)

mission statement
A broad statement of an organization's purpose that distinguishes the organization from others of a similar type. (p. 74)

tactical plans
Plans created and implemented by middle managers that specify how the company will use resources, budgets, and people over the next six months to two years to accomplish specific goals within its mission. (p. 74)

management by objectives (MBO)
A four-step process in which managers and employees discuss and select goals, develop tactical plans, and meet regularly to review progress toward goal accomplishment. (p. 75)

operational plans
Day-to-day plans, developed and implemented by lower-level managers, for producing or delivering the organization's products and services over a 30-day to six-month period. (p. 75)

single-use plans
Plans that cover unique, one-time-only events. (p. 75)

standing plans
Plans used repeatedly to handle frequently recurring events. (p. 75)

policy
A standing plan that indicates the general course of action that should be taken in response to a particular event or situation. (p. 75)

LO1 Benefits and Pitfalls of Planning

Planning is choosing a goal and developing a method for achieving it. Planning is one of the best ways to improve organizational and individual performance. It encourages people to work harder (intensified effort), to work hard for extended periods (persistence), to engage in behaviours directly related to goal accomplishment (directed behaviour), and to think of better ways to do their jobs (task strategies). However, planning also has three potential pitfalls. Companies that are overly committed to their plans may be slow to adapt to environmental changes. Planning is based on assumptions about the future, and when those assumptions are wrong, plans can fail. Finally, planning can fail when planners are detached from the implementation of plans.

LO2 How to Make a Plan That Works

There are five steps to making a plan that works: (1) Set S.M.A.R.T. goals—goals that are **S**pecific, **M**easurable, **A**ttainable, **R**ealistic, and **T**imely. (2) Develop commitment to the goals. Managers can increase workers' goal commitment by encouraging worker participation in goal setting, making goals public, and getting top management to show support for workers' goals. (3) Develop action plans for goal accomplishment. (4) Track progress toward goal achievement by setting both proximal and distal goals and by providing workers with regular performance feedback. (5) Maintain flexibility by keeping options open.

Exhibit 5.1 How to Make a Plan That Works

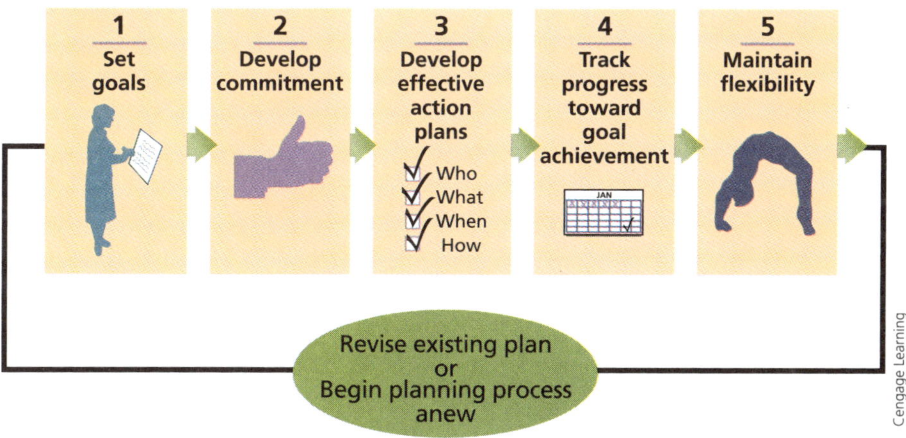

Cengage Learning

LO3 Planning from Top to Bottom

Proper planning requires that the goals at the bottom and middle of the organization support the objectives at the top of the organization. The goals at the top will be longer range than those at the bottom, as shown here. Top management develops strategic plans, which start with the creation of an organizational vision and mission. Middle managers use techniques such as management by objectives (MBO) to develop tactical plans that direct behaviour, efforts, and priorities. Finally, lower level managers develop operational plans that guide daily activities in producing or delivering an organization's products and services. There are three kinds of operational plans: single-use plans, standing plans (policies, procedures, and rules and regulations), and budgets.

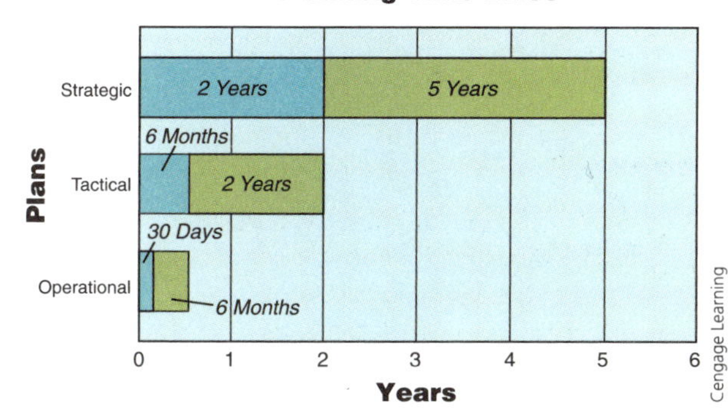

Cengage Learning

Echo/Cultura/Getty Images

procedure
A standing plan that indicates the specific steps that should be taken in response to a particular event. (p. 75)

rules and regulations
Standing plans that describe how a particular action should be performed or what must happen or not happen in response to a particular event. (p. 76)

budgeting
Quantitative planning through which managers decide how to allocate available money to best accomplish company goals. (p. 76)

decision making
The process of choosing a solution from available alternatives. (p. 76)

rational decision making
A systematic process of defining problems, evaluating alternatives, and choosing optimal solutions. (p. 76)

LO4

problem
A gap between a desired state and an existing state. (p. 76)

decision criteria
The standards used to guide judgments and decisions. (p. 76)

absolute comparisons
A process in which each criterion is compared to a standard or ranked on its own merits. (p. 77)

relative comparisons
A process in which each criterion is compared directly to every other. (p. 77)

maximizing
Choosing the best alternative. (p. 79)

satisficing
Choosing a "good enough" alternative. (p. 79)

LO5

groupthink
A barrier to good decision making caused by pressure within a group for members to agree with one another. (p. 80)

c-type conflict (cognitive conflict)
Disagreement that focuses on problem- and issue-related differences of opinion. (p. 81)

a-type conflict (affective conflict)
Disagreement that focuses on individual or personal issues. (p. 81)

devil's advocacy
A decision-making method in which an individual or a subgroup is assigned the role of a critic. (p. 81)

nominal group technique
A decision-making method that begins and ends by having group members quietly write down and evaluate ideas to be shared with the group. (p. 81)

Delphi technique
A decision-making method in which members of a panel of experts respond to questions and to one another until reaching agreement on an issue. (p. 82)

brainstorming
A decision-making method in which group members build on one another's ideas to generate as many alternative solutions as possible. (p. 82)

electronic brainstorming
A decision-making method in which group members use computers to build on one another's ideas and generate many alternative solutions. (p. 82)

production blocking
A disadvantage of face-to-face brainstorming in which a group member must wait to share an idea because another member is presenting an idea. (p. 82)

evaluation apprehension
Fear of what others will think of your ideas. (p. 82)

LO4 Steps and Limits to Rational Decision Making

Rational decision making is a six-step process in which managers define problems, evaluate alternatives, and compute optimal solutions. Step 1 is identifying and defining the problem. Problems are gaps between desired and existing states. Managers won't begin the decision-making process unless they are aware of the gap, motivated to reduce it, and possess the necessary resources to fix it. Step 2 is defining the decision criteria used to judge alternatives. In Step 3, an absolute or relative comparison process is used to rate the importance of the decision criteria. Step 4 involves generating many alternative courses of action (i.e., solutions). Potential solutions are assessed in Step 5 by systematically gathering information and evaluating each alternative against each criterion. In Step 6, criterion ratings and weights are used to compute the optimal value for each alternative course of action. Rational managers then choose the alternative with the highest optimal value.

The rational decision-making model describes how decisions should be made in an ideal world without limits. However, bounded rationality recognizes that managers' limited resources, incomplete and imperfect information, and limited decision-making capabilities restrict their decision-making processes in the real world.

LO5 Using Groups to Improve Decision Making

When groups view problems from multiple perspectives, use more information, have a diversity of knowledge and experience, and become committed to solutions they help choose, they can produce better solutions than individual decision makers. However, group decisions can suffer from these disadvantages: groupthink, slowness, discussions dominated by just a few individuals, and unfelt responsibility for decisions. Group decisions work best when group members encourage c-type conflict. Group decisions don't work as well when groups become mired in a-type conflict. The devil's advocacy and dialectical inquiry approaches improve group decisions because they bring structured c-type (cognitive) conflict into the decision-making process. By contrast, the nominal group technique and the Delphi technique both improve decision making by reducing a-type (affective) conflict. Because it overcomes the problems of production blocking and evaluation apprehension, electronic brainstorming is more effective than face-to-face brainstorming.

CHAPTER IN REVIEW

6 Organizational Strategy

Photo By RJ Sangosti/The Denver Post via Getty Images

LO1

resources
The assets, capabilities, processes, information, and knowledge that an organization uses to improve its effectiveness and efficiency, create and sustain competitive advantage, and fulfill a need or solve a problem. (p. 85)

competitive advantage
Providing greater value for customers than competitors can. (p. 85)

sustainable competitive advantage
A competitive advantage that other companies have tried unsuccessfully to duplicate and have, for the moment, stopped trying to duplicate. (p. 86)

valuable resource
A resource that allows companies to improve efficiency and effectiveness. (p. 86)

rare resources
Resources that are not controlled or possessed by many competing firms. (p. 86)

imperfectly imitable resources
Resources that are impossible or extremely costly or difficult for other firms to duplicate. (p. 86)

nonsubstitutable resource
A resource that produces value or competitive advantage and has no equivalent substitutes or replacements. (p. 87)

LO2

competitive inertia
A reluctance to change strategies or competitive practices that have been successful in the past. (p. 87)

strategic dissonance
A discrepancy between a company's intended strategy and the strategic actions managers take when implementing that strategy. (p. 87)

situational (SWOT) analysis
An assessment of the strengths and weaknesses in an organization's internal environment and the opportunities and threats in its external environment. (p. 87)

distinctive competence
What a company can make, do, or perform better than its competitors. (p. 88)

core capabilities
The internal decision-making routines, problem-solving processes, and organizational cultures that determine how efficiently inputs can be turned into outputs. (p. 88)

PEST
An acronym that stands for the Political, Economic, Social/Demographic and Technological factors that affect a company and shape the company's strategy. (p. 89)

strategic group
A group of companies within an industry that top managers choose to compare, evaluate, and benchmark strategic threats and opportunities. (p. 89)

core firms
The central companies in a strategic group. (p. 89)

secondary firms
The firms in a strategic group that follow strategies related to but somewhat different from those of the core firms. (p. 89)

strategic reference points
The strategic targets managers use to measure whether a firm has developed the core competencies it needs to achieve a sustainable competitive advantage. (p. 90)

LO1 Sustainable Competitive Advantage

Firms can use their resources to create and sustain a competitive advantage, that is, to provide greater value for customers than competitors can. A competitive advantage becomes sustainable when other companies cannot duplicate the benefits it provides and have, for now, stopped trying.

LO2 Strategy-Making Process

The first step in strategy-making is determining whether a strategy needs to be changed to sustain a competitive advantage. The second step is to conduct a situational analysis that examines internal strengths and weaknesses as well as external threats and opportunities. The third step involves choosing a strategy. Strategic reference point theory suggests that when companies are performing better than their strategic reference points, top management will typically choose a risk-averse strategy. When performance is below strategic reference points, risk-seeking strategies are more likely to be chosen.

LO3 Corporate-Level Strategies

Corporate-level strategies, such as portfolio strategy and grand strategies, help managers determine what businesses they should be in. Portfolio strategy focuses on lowering business risk by being in multiple, unrelated businesses and by investing the cash flows from slow-growth businesses into faster growing businesses. One portfolio strategy is the BCG matrix. The most successful way to use the portfolio approach to corporate strategy is to reduce risk through related diversification.

The three kinds of grand strategies are growth, stability, and retrenchment/recovery. Companies can grow externally by merging with or acquiring other companies, or they can grow internally through direct expansion or creating new businesses. Companies choose a stability strategy when their external environment changes very little or after they have dealt with periods of explosive growth. Retrenchment strategy—shrinking the size or scope of a business—is used to turn around poor performance. If retrenchment works, it is often followed by a recovery strategy that focuses on growing the business again.

LO4 Industry-Level Strategies

Industry-level strategies focus on how companies choose to compete in their industry; they are shown in the chart below. The five industry forces determine an industry's overall attractiveness to corporate investors and its potential for long-term profitability. Together, a high level of these elements combine to increase competition and decrease profits. The three positioning strategies can help companies protect themselves from the negative effects of industry-wide competition. The four adaptive strategies help companies adapt to changes in the external environment. Defenders want to defend their current strategic positions. Prospectors look for new market opportunities by bringing innovative new products to market. Analyzers minimize risk by following the proven successes of prospectors. Reactors do not follow a consistent strategy but instead react to changes in their external environment after they occur.

Industry-Level Strategies

Five Industry Forces	Positioning Strategies	Adaptive Strategies
Character of rivalry	Cost leadership	Defenders
Threat of new entrants	Differentiation	Prospectors
Threat of substitute products or services	Focus	Analyzers
Bargaining power of suppliers		Reactors
Bargaining power of buyers		

Photo By RJ Sangosti/The Denver Post via Getty Images

LO3

diversification
A strategy for reducing risk by owning a variety of items (stocks or, in the case of a corporation, types of businesses) so that the failure of one stock or one business does not doom the entire portfolio. (p. 92)

portfolio strategy
A corporate-level strategy that minimizes risk by diversifying investment among various businesses or product lines. (p. 92)

acquisition
The purchase of a company by another company. (p. 92)

unrelated diversification
Creating or acquiring companies in completely unrelated businesses. (p. 92)

BCG matrix
A portfolio strategy, developed by the Boston Consulting Group, that categorizes a corporation's businesses by growth rate and relative market share and helps managers decide how to invest corporate funds. (p. 93)

star
A company with a large share of a fast-growing market. (p. 93)

question mark
A company with a small share of a fast-growing market. (p. 93)

cash cow
A company with a large share of a slow-growing market. (p. 93)

dog
A company with a small share of a slow-growing market. (p. 93)

related diversification
Creating or acquiring companies that share similar products, manufacturing, marketing, technology, or cultures. (p. 94)

grand strategy
A broad corporate-level strategic plan used to achieve strategic goals and guide the strategic alternatives that managers of individual businesses or subunits may use. (p. 94)

growth strategy
A strategy that focuses on increasing profits, revenues, market share, or the number of places in which the company does business. (p. 94)

stability strategy
A strategy that focuses on improving the way in which the company sells the same products or services to the same customers. (p. 95)

retrenchment strategy
A strategy that focuses on turning around very poor company performance by shrinking the size or scope of the business. (p. 95)

recovery
The strategic actions taken after retrenchment to return to a growth strategy. (p. 95)

LO5 Firm-Level Strategies

Firm-level strategies are concerned with direct competition between firms. Market commonality and resource similarity determine whether firms are in direct competition and thus likely to attack each other and respond to each other's attacks. In general, the more markets in which there is product, service, or customer overlap, and the greater the resource similarity between two firms, the more intense the direct competition between them. Market entries and exits are the most important kinds of attacks and responses.

Exhibit 6.6 Porter's Five Industry Forces

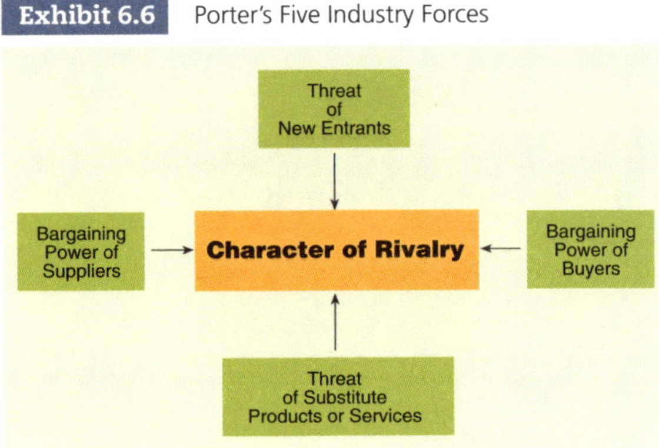

Source: Reprinted with permission of Simon & Schuster Publishing Group from the Free Press edition of *COMPETITIVE STRATEGY: Techniques for Analyzing Industries and Competitors*, by Michael E. Porter. Copyright © 1980, 1998 by The Free Press. All rights reserved.

LO4

industry-level strategy
A corporate strategy that addresses the question "How should we compete in this industry?". (p. 95)

character of the rivalry
A measure of the intensity of competitive behaviour between companies in an industry. (p. 95)

threat of new entrants
A measure of the degree to which barriers to entry make it easy or difficult for new companies to get started in an industry. (p. 96)

threat of substitute products or services
A measure of the ease with which customers can find substitutes for an industry's products or services. (p. 96)

bargaining power of suppliers
A measure of the influence that suppliers of parts, materials, and services to firms in an industry have on the prices of these inputs. (p. 96)

bargaining power of buyers
A measure of the influence that customers have on a firm's prices. (p. 96)

cost leadership
The positioning strategy of producing a product or service of acceptable quality at consistently lower production costs than competitors can, so that the firm can offer the product or service at the lowest price in the industry. (p. 96)

differentiation
The positioning strategy of providing a product or service that is sufficiently different from competitors' offerings that customers are willing to pay a premium price for it. (p. 97)

focus strategy
The positioning strategy of using cost leadership or differentiation to produce a specialized product or service for a limited, specially targeted group of customers in a particular geographic region or market segment. (p. 97)

defenders
Those who adopt an adaptive strategy aimed at defending strategic positions by seeking moderate, steady growth and by offering a limited range of high-quality products and services to a well-defined set of customers. (p. 97)

prospectors
Those who adopt an adaptive strategy that seeks fast growth by searching for new market opportunities, encouraging risk taking, and being the first to bring innovative new products to market. (p. 97)

analyzers
Those who adopt an adaptive strategy that seeks to minimize risk and maximize profits by following or imitating the proven successes of prospectors. (p. 97)

reactors
Those who take an adaptive strategy of not following a consistent strategy, but instead reacting to changes in the external environment after they occur. (p. 98)

LO5

firm-level strategy
A corporate strategy that addresses the question "How should we compete against a particular firm?" (p. 98)

direct competition
The rivalry between two companies that offer similar products and services, acknowledge each other as rivals, and react to each other's strategic actions. (p. 98)

market commonality
The degree to which two companies have overlapping products, services, or customers in multiple markets. (p. 99)

resource similarity
The extent to which a competitor has similar amounts and kinds of resources. (p. 99)

attack
A competitive move designed to reduce a rival's market share or profits. (p. 100)

response
A competitive countermove, prompted by a rival's attack, to defend or improve a company's market share or profit. (p. 100)

CHAPTER IN REVIEW

Innovation and Change

ssuaphotos/Shutterstock.com

LO1

organizational innovation
The successful implementation of creative ideas in organizations. (p. 103)

creativity
The production of novel and useful ideas. (p. 103)

organizational change
A difference in the form, quality, or condition of an organization over time. (p. 103)

technology cycle
A cycle that begins with the birth of a new technology and ends when that technology reaches its limits and is replaced by a newer, substantially better technology. (p. 103)

S-curve pattern of innovation
A pattern of technological innovation characterized by slow initial progress, then rapid progress, and then slow progress again as a technology matures and reaches its limits. (p. 103)

innovation streams
Patterns of innovation over time that can create sustainable competitive advantage. (p. 105)

technological discontinuity
A scientific advance or a unique combination of existing technologies creates a significant breakthrough in performance or function. (p. 105)

discontinuous change
The phase of a technology cycle characterized by technological substitution and design competition. (p. 105)

technological substitution
The purchase of new technologies to replace older ones. (p. 105)

design competition
Competition between old and new technologies to establish a new technological standard or dominant design. (p. 105)

dominant design
A new technological design or process that becomes the accepted market standard. (p. 105)

technological lockout
When a new dominant design (i.e., a significantly better technology) prevents a company from competitively selling its products or makes it difficult to do so. (p. 107)

incremental change
The phase of a technology cycle in which companies innovate by lowering costs and improving the functioning and performance of the dominant technological design. (p. 107)

LO2

creative work environments
Workplace cultures in which workers perceive that new ideas are welcomed, valued, and encouraged. (p. 108)

flow
A psychological state of effortlessness, in which you become completely absorbed in what you're doing and time seems to pass quickly. (p. 108)

experiential approach to innovation
An approach to innovation that assumes a highly uncertain environment and uses intuition, flexible options, and hands-on experience to reduce uncertainty and accelerate learning and understanding. (p. 109)

design iteration
A cycle of repetition in which a company tests a prototype of a new product or service, improves on that design, and then builds and tests the improved prototype. (p. 109)

LO1 Why Innovation Matters

Exhibit 7.1 S-Curves and Technological Innovation

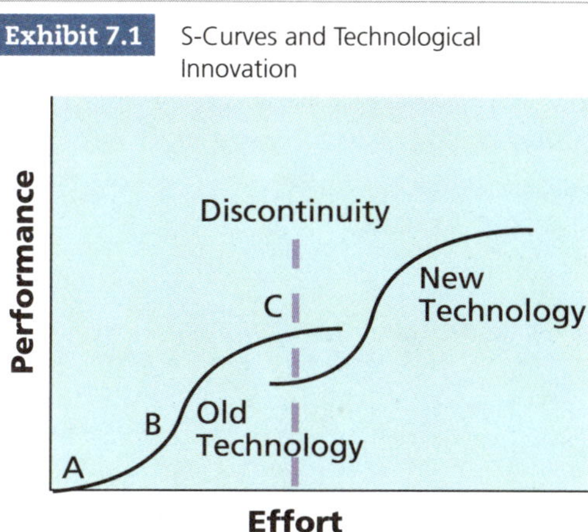

Source: R.N. Foster, *Innovation: The Attacker's Advantage* (New York: Summit, 1986).

Technology cycles typically follow an S-curve pattern of innovation. Early in the cycle, technological progress is slow, and improvements in technological performance are small. As a technology matures, however, performance improves quickly. Finally, as the limits of a technology are reached, only small improvements occur. At this point, significant improvements in performance must come from new technologies. The best way to protect a competitive advantage is to create a stream of innovative ideas and products. Innovation streams begin with technological discontinuities that create significant breakthroughs in performance or function. Technological discontinuities are followed by discontinuous change, in which customers purchase new technologies and companies compete to establish the new dominant design. Dominant designs emerge because of critical mass, because they solve a practical problem, or because of the negotiations of independent standards bodies. Because technological innovation both enhances and destroys competence, companies that bet on the wrong design often struggle, while companies that bet on the eventual dominant design usually prosper. When a dominant design emerges, companies focus on incremental change, lowering costs and making small but steady improvements in the dominant design. This focus continues until the next technological discontinuity occurs.

LO2 Managing Innovation

To successfully manage innovation streams, companies must manage the sources of innovation and learn to manage innovation during both discontinuous and incremental change. Since innovation begins with creativity, companies can manage the sources of innovation by supporting a work environment in which creative thoughts and ideas are welcomed, valued, and encouraged. Creative work environments provide challenging work; offer organizational, supervisory, and work group encouragement; allow significant freedom; and remove organizational impediments to creativity.

Discontinuous and incremental change require different strategies, as shown below. Companies that succeed in periods of discontinuous change typically follow an experiential approach to innovation. The experiential approach assumes that intuition, flexible options, and hands-on experience can reduce uncertainty and accelerate learning and understanding. A compression approach to innovation works best during periods of incremental change. This approach assumes that innovation can be planned using a series of steps and that compressing the time it takes to complete those steps can speed up innovation.

ssuaphotos/Shutterstock.com

product prototype
A full-scale, working model that is being tested for design, function, and reliability. (p. 109)

testing
The systematic comparison of different product designs or design iterations. (p. 109)

milestones
Formal project review points used to assess progress and performance. (p. 110)

multifunctional teams
Work teams composed of people from different departments. (p. 110)

compression approach to innovation
An approach to innovation that assumes that incremental innovation can be planned using a series of steps and that compressing those steps can speed innovation. (p. 111)

generational change
Change based on incremental improvements to a dominant technological design such that the improved technology is fully backward compatible with the older technology. (p. 111)

LO3

organizational decline
A large decrease in organizational performance that occurs when companies don't anticipate, recognize, neutralize, or adapt to the internal or external pressures that threaten their survival. (p. 112)

LO4

change forces
Forces that produce differences in the form, quality, or condition of an organization over time. (p. 113)

resistance forces
Forces that support the existing state of conditions in organizations. (p. 113)

resistance to change
Opposition to change resulting from self-interest, misunderstanding and distrust, a low tolerance for change, and time and cost factors. (p. 113)

unfreezing
Getting the people affected by change to believe that change is needed. (p. 114)

change intervention
The process used to get workers and managers to change their behaviour and work practices (p. 114)

refreezing
Supporting and reinforcing new changes so that they stick. (p. 114)

coercion
Using formal power and authority to force others to change. (p. 115)

results-driven change
Change created quickly by focusing on the measurement and improvement of results. (p. 117)

General Electric workout
A three-day meeting in which managers and employees from different levels and parts of an organization quickly generate and act on solutions to specific business problems. (p. 117)

organizational development
A philosophy and collection of planned change interventions designed to improve an organization's long-term health and performance. (p. 118)

change agent
The person formally in charge of guiding a change effort. (p. 118)

Exhibit 7.5 General Steps for Organizational Development Interventions

1. Entry	A problem is discovered and the need for change becomes apparent. A search begins for someone to deal with the problem and facilitate change.
2. Startup	A change agent enters the picture and works to clarify the problem and gain commitment to a change effort.
3. Assessment & feedback	The change agent gathers information about the problem and provides feedback about it to decision makers and those affected by it.
4. Action planning	The change agent works with decision makers to develop an action plan.
5. Intervention	The action plan, or organizational development intervention, is carried out.
6. Evaluation	The change agent helps decision makers assess the effectiveness of the intervention.
7. Adoption	Organizational members accept ownership and responsibility for the change, which is then carried out through the entire organization.
8. Separation	The change agent leaves the organization after first ensuring that the change intervention will continue to work.

Source: W. J. Rothwell, R. Sullivan, and G. M. McLean, *Practicing Organizational Development: A Guide for Consultants* (San Diego: Pfeiffer & Co., 1995).

LO3 Organizational Decline: The Risk of Not Changing

The five-stage process of organizational decline begins when organizations don't recognize the need for change. In the blinded stage, managers fail to recognize the changes that threaten their organization's survival. In the inaction stage, management recognizes the need to change but doesn't act, hoping that the problems will correct themselves. In the faulty action stage, management focuses on cost cutting and efficiency rather than facing up to the fundamental changes needed to ensure survival. In the crisis stage, failure is likely unless fundamental reorganization occurs. Finally, in the dissolution stage, the company is dissolved through bankruptcy proceedings; by selling assets to pay creditors; or through the closing of stores, offices, and facilities. If companies recognize the need to change early enough, however, dissolution may be avoided.

Five Stages of Organizational Decline

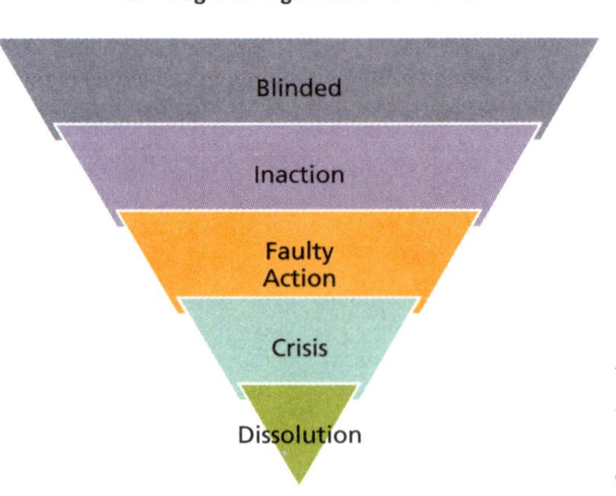

Cengage Learning

LO4 Managing Change

The basic change process involves unfreezing, change, and refreezing. Resistance to change stems from self-interest, misunderstanding, and distrust as well as a general intolerance for change. It can be managed through education and communication, participation, negotiation, top management support, and coercion. Knowing what not to do is as important as knowing what to do to achieve successful change. Managers should avoid these errors when leading change: not establishing urgency, not creating a guiding coalition, lacking a vision, undercommunicating the vision, not removing obstacles to the vision, not creating short-term wins, declaring victory too soon, and not anchoring changes in the corporation's culture. Finally, managers can use a number of change techniques. Results-driven change and the GE workout reduce resistance to change by getting change efforts off to a fast start. Organizational development is a collection of planned change interventions (large system, small group, person-focused), guided by a change agent, that are designed to improve an organization's long-term health and performance.

CHAPTER IN REVIEW

8 Global Management

watcharakun/Shutterstock.com

LO1

global business
The buying and selling of goods and services by people from different countries. (p. 121)

multinational corporation
A corporation that owns businesses in two or more countries. (p. 121)

foreign direct investment
A method of investment in which a company builds a new business or buys an existing business in a foreign country. (p. 121)

trade barriers
Government-imposed regulations that increase the cost and restrict the number of imported goods. (p. 122)

protectionism
A government's use of trade barriers to shield domestic companies and their workers from foreign competition. (p. 122)

tariff
A direct tax on imported goods. (p. 122)

nontariff barriers
Nontax methods of increasing the cost or reducing the volume of imported goods. (p. 122)

quota
A limit on the number or volume of imported products. (p. 122)

voluntary export restraints
Voluntarily imposed limits on the number or volume of products exported to a particular country. (p. 122)

government import standard
A standard ostensibly established to protect the health and safety of citizens but, in reality, often used to restrict imports. (p. 122)

subsidies
Government loans, grants, and tax deferments given to domestic companies to protect them from foreign competition. (p. 123)

customs classification
A classification assigned to imported products by government officials that affects the size of the tariff and imposition of import quotas. (p. 123)

General Agreement on Tariffs and Trade (GATT)
A worldwide trade agreement that reduced and eliminated tariffs, limited government subsidies, and established protections for intellectual property. (p. 123)

World Trade Organization (WTO)
The successor to GATT, the only international organization dealing with the global rules of trade between nations. Its main function is to ensure that trade flows as smoothly, predictably, and freely as possible. (p. 123)

regional trading zones
Areas in which tariff and nontariff barriers on trade between countries are reduced or eliminated. (p. 123)

Maastricht Treaty of Europe
A regional trade agreement between most European countries. (p. 124)

North American Free Trade Agreement (NAFTA)
A regional trade agreement between the United States, Canada, and Mexico. (p. 124)

Central America Free Trade Agreement (CAFTA-DR)
A regional trade agreement between Costa Rica, the Dominican Republic, El Salvador, Guatemala, Honduras, Nicaragua, and the United States. (p. 124)

Union of South American Nations (UNASUR)
A regional trade agreement between Argentina, Brazil, Paraguay, Uruguay, Venezuela, Bolivia, Colombia, Ecuador, Peru, Guyana, Suriname, and Chile. (p. 124)

LO1 Global Business, Trade Rules, and Trade Agreements

Today, there are more than 77,000 multinational corporations worldwide. Historically, tariffs and nontariff trade barriers such as quotas, voluntary export restraints, government import standards, government subsidies, and customs classifications have made buying foreign goods much harder or more expensive than buying domestically produced products. In recent years, however, worldwide trade agreements such as GATT, along with regional trading agreements like the Maastricht Treaty of Europe, NAFTA, CAFTA-DR, UNASUR, ASEAN, and APEC have substantially reduced tariffs as well as nontariff barriers to international trade. Companies have responded by investing in growing markets in Asia, Eastern Europe, and Latin America. Consumers have responded by purchasing products based on value rather than geography.

LO2 Consistency or Adaptation?

Global business requires a balance between global consistency and local adaptation. Global consistency means using the same rules, guidelines, policies, and procedures in each location. Managers at company headquarters like global consistency because it simplifies decisions. Local adaptation means adapting standard procedures to differences in markets. Local managers prefer a policy of local adaptation because it gives them more control. Not all businesses need the same combination of global consistency and local adaptation. Some thrive by emphasizing global consistency and ignoring local adaptation. Others succeed by ignoring global consistency and emphasizing local adaptation.

LO3 Forms of Global Business

The phase model of globalization says that, as companies move from a domestic to a global orientation, they use these organizational forms in sequence: exporting, cooperative contracts (licensing and franchising), strategic alliances, and wholly owned affiliates. Yet not all companies follow the phase model. For example, global new ventures are global from their inception.

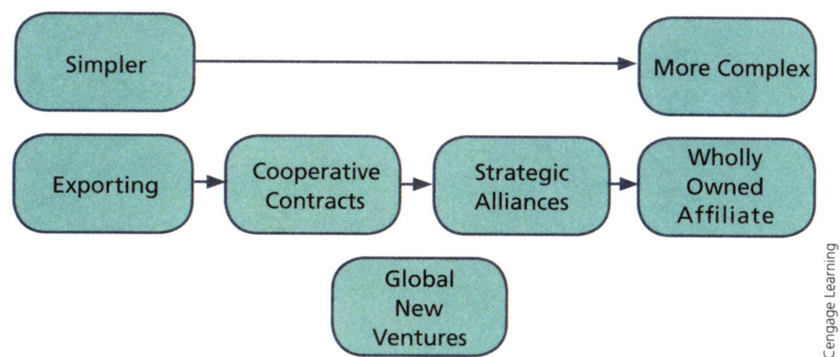

Cengage Learning

LO4 Finding the Best Business Climate

The first step in deciding where to take your company global is finding an attractive business climate. Be sure to look for a growing market where consumers have strong purchasing power and foreign competitors are weak. When locating an office or manufacturing facility, consider both qualitative and quantitative factors. In assessing political risk, be sure to examine both political uncertainty and policy uncertainty. If the location you choose has considerable political risk, you can avoid it, try to control the risk, or use a cooperation strategy.

watcharakun/Shutterstock.com

LO5 Becoming Aware of Cultural Differences

National culture is the set of shared values and beliefs that affects the perceptions, decisions, and behaviour of the people from a particular country. The first step in dealing with culture is to recognize meaningful differences such as those relating to individualism, masculinity, uncertainty avoidance, and short-term/long-term orientation. Cultural differences should be carefully interpreted because they are based on generalizations rather than specific individuals. Adapting managerial practices to cultural differences is difficult because policies and practices can be perceived differently in different cultures. Another difficulty is that cultural values may be changing in many parts of the world. Consequently, when companies try to adapt management practices to cultural differences, they need to be sure they are not using outdated assumptions about a country's culture.

LO6 Preparing for an International Assignment

Many expatriates return prematurely from international assignments because of poor performance. This is much less likely to happen if employees receive linguistic and cross-cultural training, such as documentary training, cultural simulations, or field experiences, before going on assignment. Adjustment of expatriates' spouses and families, which is the most important determinant of success in international assignments, can be improved through adaptability screening and intercultural training.

Exhibit 8.5 Hofstede's Five Cultural Dimensions

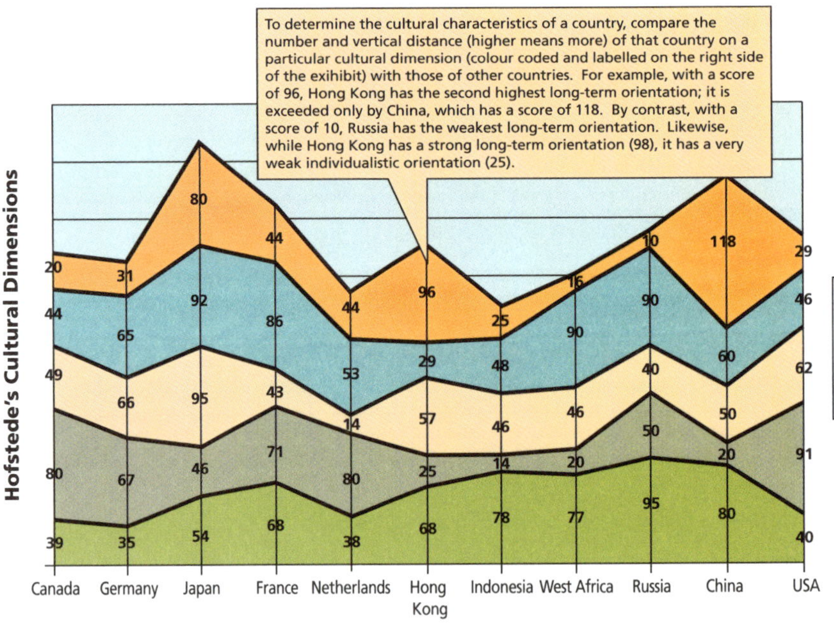

Source: G. H. Hofstede, "Cultural Contraints in Management Theories," *Academy of Management Executive* 7, no. 1 (1993): 81–94.

Association of Southeast Asian Nations (ASEAN)
A regional trade agreement between Brunei Darussalam, Cambodia, Indonesia, Lao PDR, Malaysia, Myanmar, the Philippines, Singapore, Thailand, and Vietnam. (p. 125)

Asia-Pacific Economic Cooperation (APEC)
A regional trade agreement between Australia, Canada, Chile, the People's Republic of China, Hong Kong, Japan, Mexico, New Zealand, Papua New Guinea, Peru, Russia, South Korea, Taiwan, the United States, and all members of ASEAN, except Cambodia, Lao PDR, and Myanmar. (p. 125)

LO2

global consistency
When a multinational company has offices, manufacturing plants, and distribution facilities in different countries and runs them all using the same rules, guidelines, policies, and procedures. (p. 127)

local adaptation
When a multinational company modifies its rules, guidelines, policies, and procedures to adapt to differences in foreign customers, governments, and regulatory agencies. (p. 127)

LO3

exporting
Selling domestically produced products to customers in foreign countries. (p. 127)

cooperative contract
An agreement in which a foreign business owner pays a company a fee for the right to conduct that business in his or her country. (p. 128)

licensing
An agreement in which a domestic company, the licensor, receives royalty payments for allowing another company, the licensee, to produce the licensor's product, sell its service, or use its brand name in a specified foreign market. (p. 128)

franchise
A collection of networked firms in which the manufacturer or marketer of a product or service, the franchisor, licenses the entire business to another person or organization, the franchisee. (p. 128)

strategic alliance
An agreement in which companies combine key resources, costs, risk, technology, and people. (p. 129)

joint venture
A strategic alliance in which two existing companies collaborate to form a third, independent company. (p. 129)

wholly owned affiliates
Foreign offices, facilities, and manufacturing plants that are 100 percent owned by the parent company. (p. 130)

global new ventures
New companies that are founded with an active global strategy and have sales, employees, and financing in different countries. (p. 130)

LO4

purchasing power
A comparison of the relative cost of a standard set of goods and services in different countries. (p. 130)

political uncertainty
The risk of major changes in political regimes that can result from war, revolution, death of political leaders, social unrest, or other influential events. (p. 133)

policy uncertainty
The risk associated with changes in laws and government policies that directly affect the way foreign companies conduct business. (p. 133)

LO5

national culture
The set of shared values and beliefs that affects the perceptions, decisions, and behaviour of the people from a particular country. (p. 135)

ethnocentrism
Generally judging and interpreting people and mannerisms of another culture solely by the values and standards of our own culture. (p. 135)

culture shock
The disorientation we might feel when experiencing an unfamiliar way of life due to a business trip to a new country, or to a move between social environments, if we get posted on an international assignment to a new, unfamiliar country. (p. 136)

LO6

expatriate
Someone who lives and works outside his or her native country. (p. 137)

CHAPTER IN REVIEW

Designing Adaptive Organizations

Adriano Castelli/Shutterstock.com

LO1 Departmentalization

There are five traditional departmental structures: functional, product, customer, geographic, and matrix. Functional departmentalization is based on the different business functions or types of expertise used to run a business. Product departmentalization is organized according to the different products or services a company sells. Customer departmentalization focuses its divisions on the different kinds of customers a company has. Geographic departmentalization is based on the different geographic areas or markets in which the company does business. Matrix departmentalization is a hybrid form that combines two or more forms of departmentalization, the most common being the product and functional forms. There is no single best departmental structure. Each structure has advantages and disadvantages.

LO2 Organizational Authority

Organizational authority is determined by the chain of command, line versus staff authority, delegation, and the degree of centralization in a company. The chain of command vertically connects every job in the company to higher levels of management and makes clear who reports to whom. Managers have line authority to command employees below them in the chain of command but have only staff, or advisory, authority over employees not below them in the chain of command. Managers delegate authority by transferring to subordinates the authority and responsibility needed to do a task; in exchange, subordinates become accountable for task completion. In centralized companies, most authority to make decisions lies with managers in the upper levels of the company. In decentralized companies, much of the authority is delegated to the workers closest to problems, who can then make the decisions necessary for solving the problems themselves.

Exhibit 9.8 Delegation: Responsibility, Authority, and Accountability

Manager

Subordinate

Responsibility →

Authority →

← Accountability

Monkey Business Images/Shutterstock.com

Source: C. D. Pringle, D. F. Jennings, and J. G. Longenecker, *Managing Organizations: Functions and Behaviours* © 1990. Adapted by permission of Pearson Education, Inc., Upper Saddle River, NJ

LO3 Job Design

Companies use specialized jobs because they are economical and easy to learn and don't require highly paid workers. However, specialized jobs aren't motivating or particularly satisfying for employees. Companies have used job rotation, job enlargement, job enrichment, and the job characteristics model to make specialized jobs more interesting and motivating. The goal of the job characteristics model is to make jobs intrinsically

LO1

organizational structure
The vertical and horizontal configuration of departments, authority, and jobs within a company. (p. 141)

organizational process
The collection of activities that transform inputs into outputs that customers value. (p. 141)

departmentalization
Subdividing work and workers into separate organizational units responsible for completing particular tasks. (p. 142)

functional departmentalization
Organizing work and workers into separate units responsible for particular business functions or areas of expertise. (p. 142)

product departmentalization
Organizing work and workers into separate units responsible for producing particular products or services. (p. 143)

customer departmentalization
Organizing work and workers into separate units responsible for particular kinds of customers. (p. 143)

geographic departmentalization
Organizing work and workers into separate units responsible for doing business in particular geographic areas. (p. 144)

matrix departmentalization
A hybrid organizational structure in which two or more forms of departmentalization, most often product and functional, are used together. (p. 144)

simple matrix
A form of matrix departmentalization in which managers in different parts of the matrix negotiate conflicts and resources. (p. 146)

complex matrix
A form of matrix departmentalization in which managers in different parts of the matrix report to matrix managers, who help them sort out conflicts and problems. (p. 146)

LO2

authority
The right to give commands, take action, and make decisions to achieve organizational objectives. (p. 146)

chain of command
The vertical line of authority that clarifies who reports to whom throughout the organization. (p. 146)

span of control
The number of individuals who report directly to a manager. (p. 147)

unity of command
A management principle that workers should report to just one boss. (p. 147)

line authority
The right to command immediate subordinates in the chain of command. (p. 147)

staff authority
The right to advise, but not command, others who are not subordinates in the chain of command. (p. 147)

line function
An activity that contributes directly to creating or selling the company's products. (p. 147)

staff function
An activity that does not contribute directly to creating or selling the company's products, but instead supports line activities. (p. 147)

Adriano Castelli/Shutterstock.com

motivating. For this to happen, jobs must be strong on five core job characteristics (skill variety, task identity, task significance, autonomy, and feedback), and workers must experience three critical psychological states (knowledge of results, responsibility for work outcomes, and meaningful work). If jobs aren't internally motivating, they can be redesigned by combining tasks, forming natural work units, establishing client relationships, vertical loading, and opening feedback channels.

LO4 Intra-Organizational Processes

Today, companies are using re-engineering and empowerment to change their intra-organizational processes. Re-engineering changes an organization's orientation from vertical to horizontal and its work processes by decreasing sequential and pooled interdependence and by increasing reciprocal interdependence. Re-engineering promises dramatic increases in productivity and customer satisfaction, but it has been criticized as simply an excuse to cut costs and lay off workers. Empowering workers means taking decision-making authority and responsibility from managers and giving it to workers. Empowered workers develop feelings of competence and self-determination and believe that their work has meaning and impact.

LO5 Inter-Organizational Processes

Organizations are using modular and virtual organizations to change inter-organizational processes. Because modular organizations outsource all noncore activities to other businesses, they are less expensive to run than traditional companies. However, modular organizations require extremely close relationships with suppliers, may result in a loss of control, and could create new competitors if the wrong business activities are outsourced. Virtual organizations participate in a network in which they share skills, costs, capabilities, markets, and customers. Virtual organizations can reduce costs, respond quickly, and, if they can successfully coordinate their efforts, produce outstanding products and services.

delegation of authority
The assignment of direct authority and responsibility to a subordinate to complete tasks for which the manager is normally responsible. (p. 147)

centralization of authority
The location of most authority at the upper levels of the organization. (p. 148)

decentralization
The location of a significant amount of authority in the lower levels of the organization. (p. 148)

standardization
Solving problems by consistently applying the same rules, procedures, and processes. (p. 149)

LO3

job design
The number, kind, and variety of tasks that individual workers perform in doing their jobs. (p. 149)

job specialization
A job composed of a small part of a larger task or process. (p. 149)

job rotation
Periodically moving workers from one specialized job to another to give them more variety and the opportunity to use different skills. (p. 149)

job enlargement
Increasing the number of different tasks that a worker performs within one particular job. (p. 149)

job enrichment
Increasing the number of tasks in a particular job and giving workers the authority and control to make meaningful decisions about their work. (p. 150)

job characteristics model (JCM)
An approach to job redesign that seeks to formulate jobs in ways that motivate workers and lead to positive work outcomes. (p. 150)

internal motivation
Motivation that comes from the job itself rather than from outside rewards. (p. 150)

skill variety
The number of different activities performed in a job. (p. 151)

task identity
The degree to which a job, from beginning to end, requires the completion of a whole and identifiable piece of work. (p. 151)

task significance
The degree to which a job is perceived to have a substantial impact on others inside or outside the organization. (p. 151)

autonomy
The degree to which a job gives workers the discretion, freedom, and independence to decide how and when to accomplish the job. (p. 151)

feedback
The amount of information the job provides to workers about their work performance. (p. 151)

mechanistic organization
An organization characterized by specialized jobs and responsibilities; precisely defined, unchanging roles; and a rigid chain of command based on centralized authority and vertical communication. (p. 152)

organic organization
An organization characterized by broadly defined jobs and responsibility; loosely defined, frequently changing roles; and decentralized authority and horizontal communication based on task knowledge. (p. 152)

LO4

intra-organizational process
The collection of activities that take place within an organization to transform inputs into outputs that customers value. (p. 152)

re-engineering
Fundamental rethinking and radical redesign of business processes to achieve dramatic improvements in critical measures of performance, such as cost, quality, service, and speed. (p. 153)

task interdependence
The extent to which collective action is required to complete an entire piece of work. (p. 153)

pooled interdependence
Work completed by having each job or department independently contribute to the whole. (p. 153)

sequential interdependence
Work completed in succession, with one group's or job's outputs becoming the inputs for the next group or job. (p. 154)

reciprocal interdependence
Work completed by different jobs or groups working together in a back-and-forth manner. (p. 154)

empowering workers
Permanently passing decision-making authority and responsibility from managers to workers by giving them the information and resources they need to make and carry out good decisions. (p. 155)

empowerment
Feelings of intrinsic motivation, in which workers perceive their work to have impact and meaning and perceive themselves to be competent and capable of self-determination. (p. 155)

LO5

inter-organizational process
A collection of activities that take place among companies to transform inputs into outputs that customers value. (p. 155)

modular organization
An organization that outsources noncore business activities to outside companies, suppliers, specialists, or consultants. (p. 155)

virtual organization
An organization that is part of a network in which many companies share skills, costs, capabilities, markets, and customers to collectively solve customer problems or provide specific products or services. (p. 156)

CHAPTER IN REVIEW

Leading Teams

Photo by Marianne Helm/Getty Images

LO1

work team
A small number of people with complementary skills who hold themselves mutually accountable for pursuing a common purpose, achieving performance goals, and improving interdependent work processes. (p. 159)

cross-training
Training team members to do all or most of the jobs performed by the other team members. (p. 159)

social loafing
Behaviour in which team members withhold their efforts and fail to perform their share of the work. (p. 160)

groupthink
When members of highly cohesive groups feel intense pressure not to disagree with one another so that the group can approve a proposed solution. (p. 160)

LO2

traditional work group
A group composed of two or more people who work together to achieve a shared goal. (p. 162)

employee involvement team
Team that provides advice or makes suggestions to management concerning specific issues. (p. 162)

semiautonomous work group
A group that has the authority to make decisions and solve problems related to the major tasks of producing a product or service. (p. 163)

self-managing team
A team that manages and controls all of the major tasks of producing a product or service. Students will also see this referred to as self-directed work teams (see the highlighted box below for an example). (p. 163)

self-designing team
A team that has the characteristics of self-managing teams but also controls team design, work tasks, and team membership. (p. 163)

cross-functional team
A team composed of employees from different functional areas of the organization. (p. 163)

virtual team
A team composed of geographically and/or organizationally dispersed coworkers who use telecommunication and information technologies to accomplish an organizational task. (p. 163)

project team
A team created to complete specific, one-time projects or tasks within a limited time. (p. 165)

LO3

norms
Informally agreed-on standards that regulate team behaviour. (p. 165)

cohesiveness
The extent to which team members are attracted to a team and motivated to remain in it. (p. 166)

forming
The first stage of team development, in which team members meet one another, form initial impressions, and begin to establish team norms. (p. 169)

LO1 The Good and Bad of Using Teams

In many industries, teams are growing in importance because they help organizations respond to specific problems and challenges. Teams have been shown to increase customer satisfaction, product and service quality, and employee job satisfaction. Although teams can produce significant improvements in these areas, using teams does not guarantee these positive outcomes. Teams and teamwork have the disadvantages of initially high turnover and social loafing (especially in large groups). Teams also share many of the advantages (multiple perspectives, generation of more alternatives, and more commitment) and disadvantages (groupthink, time, poorly run meetings, domination by a few team members, and weak accountability) of group decision making. Teams should be used for a clear purpose: when the work requires that people work together, when rewards can be provided for both teamwork and team performance, when ample resources can be provided, and when teams can be given clear authority over their work.

Advantages and Disadvantages of Teams

Advantages	Disadvantages
Customer satisfaction	Initially high employee turnover
Product and service quality	Social loafing
Speed and efficiency in product development	Disadvantages of group decision making (groupthink, inefficient meetings, domination by a minority, lack of accountability)
Employee job satisfaction	
Better decision making and problem solving (multiple perspectives, more alternative solutions, increased commitment to decisions)	

Exhibit 10.1 When to Use and When Not to Use Teams

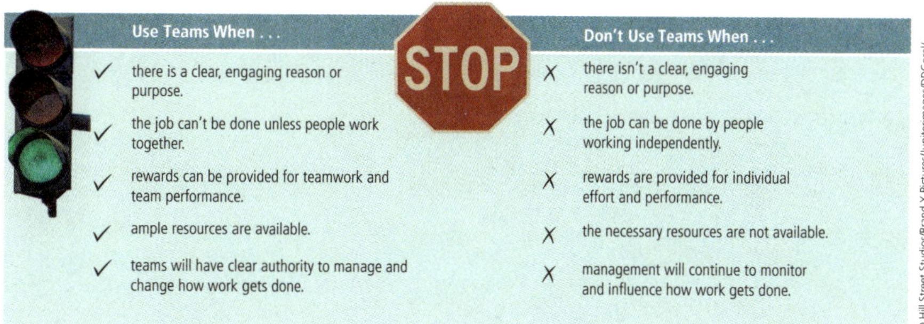

Use Teams When . . .	Don't Use Teams When . . .
✓ there is a clear, engaging reason or purpose.	X there isn't a clear, engaging reason or purpose.
✓ the job can't be done unless people work together.	X the job can be done by people working independently.
✓ rewards can be provided for teamwork and team performance.	X rewards are provided for individual effort and performance.
✓ ample resources are available.	X the necessary resources are not available.
✓ teams will have clear authority to manage and change how work gets done.	X management will continue to monitor and influence how work gets done.

© Hill Street Studios/Brand X Pictures/Jupiterimages/DDCoral/Shutterstock

Source: R. Wageman, "Critical Success Factors for Creating Superb Self-Managing Teams," *Organizational Dynamics* 26, no. 1 (1997): 49–61.

LO2 Kinds of Teams

Companies use different kinds of teams to make themselves more competitive. Autonomy is the key dimension that makes teams different. Traditional work groups (which execute tasks) and employee involvement groups (which make suggestions) have the lowest levels of autonomy. Semiautonomous work groups (which control major, direct tasks) have more autonomy, while self-managing teams (which control all direct tasks) and self-designing teams (which control membership and how tasks are done) have the highest levels of autonomy. Cross-functional, virtual, and project teams are common but are not easily categorized in terms of autonomy. Cross-functional teams combine employees from different functional areas to help teams attack problems from multiple perspectives and generate more ideas and solutions. Virtual teams use telecommunications and information technologies to bring coworkers together, regardless of physical location or time zone. Virtual teams reduce travel and work time, but communication may suffer since team members don't work face-to-face. Finally, project teams are used for specific, one-time projects or tasks that must be completed within a limited time. Project teams reduce communication barriers and promote flexibility; teams and team members are reassigned to their departments or new projects as old projects are completed.

Photo by Marianne Helm/Getty Images

storming
The second stage of development, characterized by conflict and disagreement, in which team members disagree over what the team should do and how it should do it. (p. 169)

norming
The third stage of team development, in which team members begin to settle into their roles, group cohesion grows, and positive team norms develop. (p. 170)

performing
The fourth stage of team development, in which performance improves because the team has matured into an effective, fully functioning team. (p. 170)

adjourning
The final stage of Bruce Tuckman's model of team development, in which a company wraps up the team and takes any lessons learned forward to other teams (with three important substages; de-norming, de-storming, and de-forming). (p. 170)

LO3 Work Team Characteristics

The most important characteristics of work teams are team norms, cohesiveness, size, conflict, and development. Norms let team members know what is expected of them and can influence team behaviour in positive and negative ways. Positive team norms are associated with organizational commitment, trust, and job satisfaction. Team cohesiveness helps teams retain members, promotes cooperative behaviour, increases motivation, and facilitates team performance. Attending team meetings and activities, creating opportunities to work together, and engaging in nonwork activities can increase cohesiveness. Team size has a curvilinear relationship with team performance: teams that are very small or very large do not perform as well as moderate-sized teams of six to nine members. Teams of this size are cohesive and small enough for team members to get to know one another and contribute in a meaningful way but are large enough to take advantage of team members' diverse skills, knowledge, and perspectives. Conflict and disagreement are inevitable in most teams. The key to dealing with team conflict is to maximize cognitive conflict, which focuses on issue-related differences, and minimize affective conflict, the emotional reactions that occur when disagreements become personal rather than professional. As teams develop and grow, they pass through four stages of development: forming, storming, norming, and performing. If a team is not managed well, its performance may decline after a period of time as the team regresses through the stages of de-norming, de-storming, and de-forming.

How Teams Can Have a Good Fight

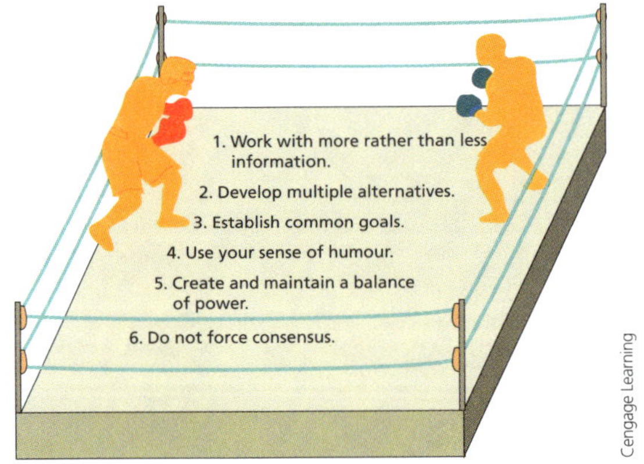

Source: K. M. Eisenhardt, J. L. Kahwajy, and L. J. Bourgeois III, "How Management Teams Can Have a Good Fight," *Harvard Business Review* 75, no. 4 (July-August 1997): 77–85.

LO4

structural accommodation
The ability to change organizational structures, policies, and practices in order to meet stretch goals. (p. 172)

bureaucratic immunity
The ability to make changes without first getting approval from managers or other parts of an organization. (p. 172)

individualism–collectivism
The degree to which a person believes that people should be self-sufficient and that loyalty to one's self is more important than loyalty to team or company. (p. 172)

team level
The average level of ability, experience, personality, or any other factor on a team. (p. 172)

team diversity
The variances or differences in ability, experience, personality, or any other factor on a team. (p. 173)

interpersonal skills
Skills, such as listening, communicating, questioning, and providing feedback, that enable people to have effective working relationships with others. (p. 174)

skill-based pay
Compensation system that pays employees for learning additional skills or knowledge. (p. 175)

gainsharing
A compensation system in which companies share the financial value of performance gains, such as productivity, cost savings, or quality, with their workers. (p. 175)

LO4 Enhancing Work Team Effectiveness

Companies can make teams more effective by setting team goals and managing how team members are selected, trained, and compensated. Team goals provide a clear focus and purpose, reduce the incidence of social loafing, and lead to higher team performance 93 percent of the time. Extremely difficult stretch goals can be used to motivate teams as long as teams have autonomy, control over resources, structural accommodation, and bureaucratic immunity. Not everyone is suited for teamwork. When selecting team members, companies should select people who have a preference for teamwork (individualism–collectivism) and should consider team level (average ability on a team) and team diversity (different abilities on a team). Organizations that successfully use teams provide thousands of hours of training to make sure that teams work. The most common types of team training are for interpersonal skills, decision-making and problem-solving skills, conflict resolution, technical training to help team members learn multiple jobs (i.e., cross training), and training for team leaders. Employees can be compensated for team participation and accomplishments in three ways: skill-based pay, gainsharing, and nonfinancial rewards.

CHAPTER IN REVIEW

Managing Human Resource Systems

fotoscool/Shutterstock.com

LO1

human resource management (HRM)
The process of finding, developing, and keeping the right people to form a qualified workforce. (p. 177)

bona fide occupational qualification (BFOQ)
An exception in employment law that permits sex, age, religion, and the like to be used when making employment decisions, but only if they are "reasonably necessary to the normal operation of that particular business." (p. 177)

sexual harassment
A form of discrimination in which unwelcome sexual advances, requests for sexual favours, or other verbal or physical conduct of a sexual nature occur while performing one's job; another form of sexual harassment is when employment outcomes, such as hiring, promotion, or simply keeping one's job, depend on whether an individual submits to sexual harassment. (p. 179)

hostile work environment
A form of harassment in which unwelcome and demeaning behaviour creates an intimidating and offensive work environment. (p. 179)

LO2

human resources planning
An umbrella term that encompasses overarching philosophies, policies, and practices that are in line with the organization's strategy. (p. 180)

recruiting
The process of developing a pool of qualified job applicants. (p. 180)

job analysis
A purposeful, systematic process for collecting information on the important work-related aspects of a job in line with the organization's strategic direction. (p. 180)

job description
A written description of the basic tasks, duties, and responsibilities required of an employee holding a particular job to help the organization realize its strategy. (p. 181)

job specifications
A written summary of the qualifications needed to successfully perform a particular job to enable the organization to reach its organizational objectives. (p. 181)

internal recruiting
The process of developing a pool of qualified job applicants from people who already work in the company. (p. 182)

succession planning
Deals with evaluating the needs that are required in future years in terms of staffing to replace people who retire, or who may leave, and to provide personnel for needed strategic growth requirements. (p. 182)

external recruiting
The process of developing a pool of qualified job applicants from outside the company. (p. 182)

realistic job previews
A tool used to explain to potential new employees both the positive and negative aspects of a new job. (p. 182)

LO1 Employment Legislation

Human resource management is subject to numerous major federal employment laws and subject to review by several federal agencies. In general, these laws indicate that sex, age, religion, colour, national origin, race, disability, and pregnancy may not be considered in employment decisions unless these factors reasonably qualify as BFOQs.

Exhibit 11.1 The Human Resource Management Process

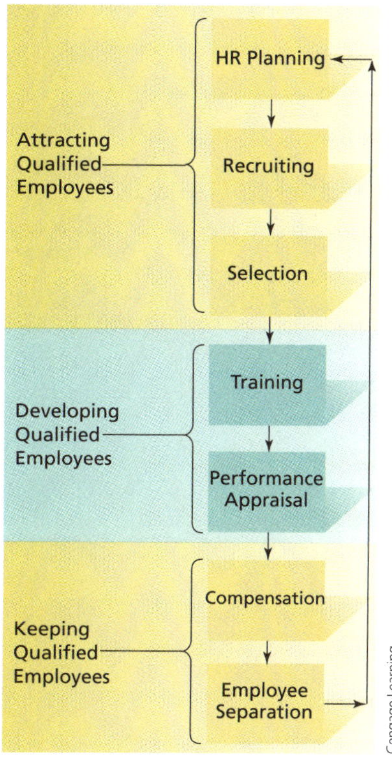

LO2 HR Planning

Recruiting is the process of finding qualified job applicants. The first step in recruiting is to conduct a job analysis, which is used to write a job description of basic tasks, duties, and responsibilities and to write job specifications indicating the knowledge, skills, and abilities needed to perform the job. Whereas internal recruiting involves finding qualified job applicants from inside the company, external recruiting involves finding qualified job applicants from outside the company.

Importance of Job Analysis to Human Resource Management

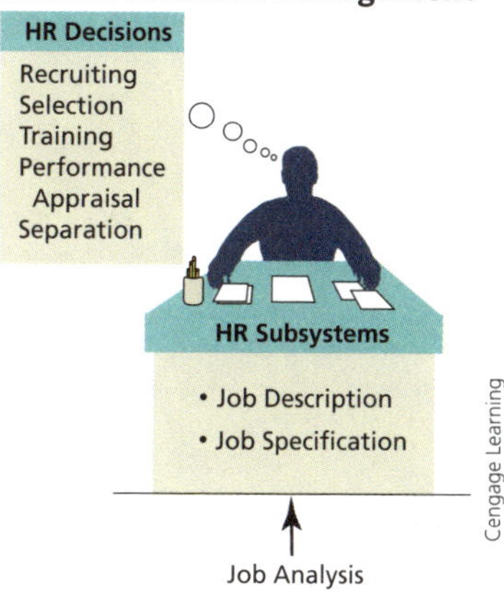

fotoscool/Shutterstock.com

LO3

selection
The process of gathering information about job applicants to decide who should be offered a job. (p. 183)

validation
The process of determining how well a selection test or procedure predicts future job performance. The better or more accurate the prediction of future job performance, the more valid a test is said to be. (p. 183)

employment references
Sources such as previous employers or coworkers who can provide job-related information about job candidates. (p. 183)

background checks
Procedures used to verify the truthfulness and accuracy of information that applicants provide about themselves and to uncover negative, job-related background information not provided by applicants. (p. 185)

specific ability tests (aptitude tests)
Tests that measure the extent to which an applicant possesses the particular kind of ability needed to do a job well. (p. 185)

cognitive ability tests
Tests that measure the extent to which applicants have abilities in perceptual speed, verbal comprehension, numerical aptitude, general reasoning, and spatial aptitude. (p. 186)

biographical data (biodata)
Extensive surveys that ask applicants questions about their personal backgrounds and life experiences. (p. 186)

work sample tests
Tests that require applicants to perform tasks that are actually done on the job. (p. 186)

assessment centres
A series of managerial simulations, graded by trained observers, that are used to determine applicants' capability for managerial work. (p. 186)

interviews
A selection tool in which company representatives ask job applicants job-related questions to determine whether they are qualified for the job. (p. 187)

unstructured interviews
Interviews in which interviewers are free to ask the applicants anything they want. (p. 187)

structured interviews
Interviews in which all applicants are asked the same set of standardized questions, usually including situational, behavioural, background, and job knowledge questions. (p. 187)

LO4

training
Developing the skills, experience, and knowledge employees need to perform their jobs or improve their performance. (p. 189)

needs assessment
The process of identifying and prioritizing the learning needs of employees. (p. 189)

LO3 Selection

Selection is the process of gathering information about job applicants to decide who should be offered a job. Accurate selection procedures are valid, are legally defendable, and improve organizational performance. Application forms and résumés are the most common selection devices. Managers should check references and conduct background checks even though previous employers are often reluctant to provide such information for fear of being sued for defamation. Unfortunately, without this information, other employers are at risk of negligent hiring lawsuits. Selection tests generally do the best job of predicting applicants' future job performance. The three kinds of job interviews are unstructured, structured, and semistructured interviews.

LO4 Training

Training is used to give employees the job-specific skills, experience, and knowledge they need to do their jobs or improve their job performance. To make sure training dollars are well spent, companies need to determine specific training needs, select appropriate training methods, and then evaluate the training.

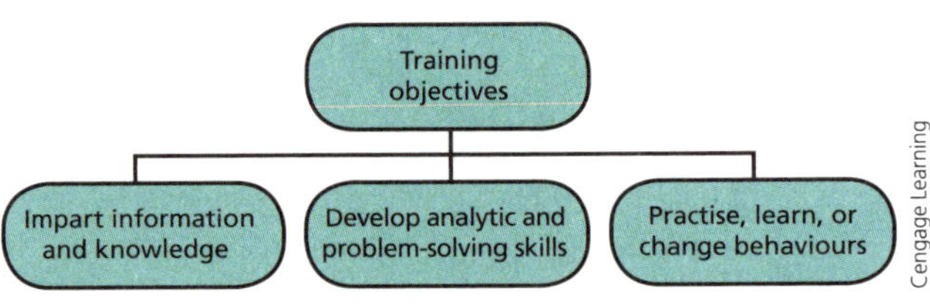

LO5 Performance Appraisal

The keys to successful performance appraisal are accurately measuring job performance and effectively sharing performance feedback with employees. Organizations should develop good performance appraisal scales; train raters how to accurately evaluate performance; and impress upon managers the value of providing feedback in a clear, consistent, and fair manner, as well as setting goals and monitoring progress toward those goals.

LO5

performance appraisal
The process of assessing how well employees are doing their jobs. (p. 190)

objective performance measures
Measures of job performance that are easily and directly counted or quantified. (p. 191)

behavioural observation scales (BOSs)
Rating scales that indicate the frequency with which workers perform specific behaviours that are representative of the job dimensions critical to successful job performance. (p. 191)

rater training
Training performance appraisal raters in how to avoid rating errors and increase rating accuracy. (p. 191)

360-degree feedback
A performance appraisal process in which feedback is obtained from the boss, subordinates, peers and coworkers, and the employees themselves. (p. 192)

fotoscool/Shutterstock.com

LO6 Compensation and Employee Separation

Compensation includes both the financial and the nonfinancial rewards that organizations give employees in exchange for their work. There are three basic kinds of compensation decisions: pay level, pay variability, and pay structure. Employee separation is the loss of an employee, which can occur voluntarily or involuntarily. Companies use downsizing and early retirement incentive programs to reduce the number of employees in the organization and lower costs. However, companies generally try to keep the rate of employee turnover low to reduce costs associated with finding and developing new employees. Functional turnover, on the other hand, can be good for organizations.

Kinds of Compensation Decisions

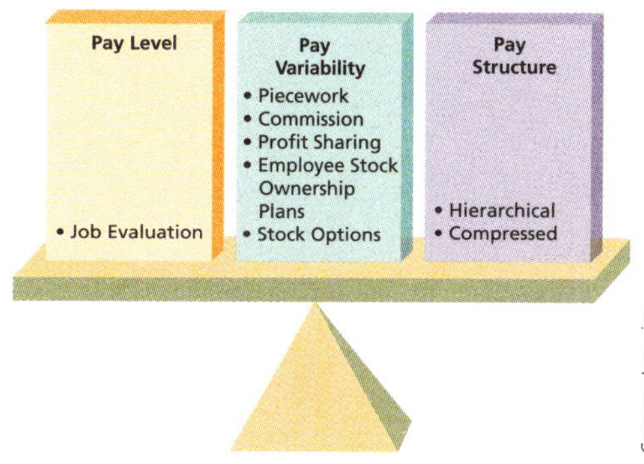

Cengage Learning

LO6

compensation
The financial and nonfinancial rewards that organizations give employees in exchange for their work. (p. 194)

employee separation
The voluntary or involuntary loss of an employee. (p. 194)

job evaluation
A process that determines the worth of each job in a company by evaluating the market value of the knowledge, skills, and requirements needed to perform it. (p. 194)

piecework
A compensation system in which employees are paid a set rate for each item they produce. (p. 194)

commission
A compensation system in which employees earn a percentage of each sale they make. (p. 194)

profit sharing
A compensation system in which a company pays a percentage of its profits to employees in addition to their regular compensation. (p. 194)

employee stock ownership plan (ESOP)
A compensation system that awards employees shares of company stock in addition to their regular compensation. (p. 194)

stock options
A compensation system that gives employees the right to purchase shares of stock at a set price, even if the value of the stock increases above that price. (p. 194)

wrongful discharge
A legal doctrine that requires employers to have a job-related reason to terminate employees. (p. 196)

downsizing
The planned elimination of jobs in a company. (p. 196)

outplacement services
Employment-counselling services offered to employees who are losing their jobs because of downsizing. (p. 196)

early retirement incentive programs (ERIPs)
Programs that offer financial benefits to employees to encourage them to retire early. (p. 197)

phased retirement
Employees transition to retirement by working reduced hours over a period of time before completely retiring. (p. 197)

employee turnover
Loss of employees who voluntarily choose to leave the company. (p. 197)

functional turnover
Loss of poor-performing employees who voluntarily choose to leave a company. (p. 197)

dysfunctional turnover
Loss of high-performing employees who voluntarily choose to leave a company. (p. 198)

fotoscool/Shutterstock.com

Notes

CHAPTER IN REVIEW

Managing Individuals and a Diverse Workforce

maredonna8888/Shutterstock.com

LO1

diversity
A variety of demographic, cultural, and personal differences among an organization's employees and customers. (p. 201)

employment equity
An ongoing planning process used by an employer to eliminate barriers in an organization's employment procedures and to ensure appropriate representation of specific members of the workforce. (p. 202)

affirmative action
Purposeful steps taken by an organization to create employment opportunities for minorities and women. (p. 202)

surface-level diversity
Differences such as age, gender, race/ethnicity, and physical disabilities that are observable, typically unchangeable, and easy to measure. (p. 204)

deep-level diversity
Differences such as personality and attitudes that are communicated through verbal and nonverbal behaviours and are learned only through extended interaction with others. (p. 204)

social integration
The degree to which group members are psychologically attracted to working with one another to accomplish a common objective. (p. 204)

LO2

age discrimination
Treating people differently (e.g., in hiring and firing, promotion, and compensation decisions) because of their age. (p. 204)

gender discrimination
Treating people differently because of their gender. (p. 205)

glass ceiling
The invisible barrier that prevents women and minorities from advancing to the top jobs in organizations. (p. 205)

racial and ethnic discrimination
Treating people differently because of their race or ethnicity. (p. 207)

disability
An activity limitation or participation restriction associated with a physical or mental condition or health problem. (p. 208)

disability discrimination
Treating people differently because of their disabilities. (p. 208)

LO3

disposition
The tendency to respond to situations and events in a predetermined manner. (p. 211)

personality
The relatively stable set of behaviours, attitudes, and emotions displayed over time that makes people different from one another. (p. 211)

extraversion
The degree to which someone is active, assertive, gregarious, sociable, talkative, and energized by others. (p. 211)

emotional stability
The degree to which someone is not angry, depressed, anxious, emotional, insecure, and excitable. (p. 211)

LO1 Diversity: Differences That Matter

Diversity exists in organizations when there are demographic, cultural, and personal differences among the people who work there and the customers who do business there. A common misconception is that workplace diversity and employment equity are the same. However, employment equity is more narrowly focused on demographics; while diversity is broader in focus (going beyond demographics), voluntary, and more positive in that it encourages companies to value all kinds of differences. Employment equity and diversity thus differ in purpose, practice, and the reactions they produce. Diversity makes good business sense in terms of cost savings, attracting and retaining talent, and driving business growth (improving marketplace understanding and promoting higher-quality problem solving).

General Purpose of Diversity Programs

- No one is advantaged or disadvantaged.
- "We" is everyone.
- Everyone can do his or her best work.
- Differences are respected and not ignored.
- Everyone feels comfortable.

Source: T. Roosevelt, "From Affirmative Action to Affirming Diversity," *Harvard Business Review* 68, no. 2 (1990): 107–117.

LO2 Surface-Level Diversity

Age, gender, race/ethnicity, and physical and mental disabilities are dimensions of surface-level diversity. Because those dimensions are (usually) easily observed, managers and workers tend to rely on them to form initial impressions and stereotypes. Sometimes this can lead to age, gender, racial/ethnic, or disability discrimination (i.e., treating people differently) in the workplace. In general, older workers, women, people of colour or different national origins, and people with disabilities are much less likely to be hired or promoted than white males. This disparity is often due to incorrect beliefs or stereotypes such as "job performance declines with age," or "women aren't willing to travel on business," or "workers with disabilities aren't as competent as able workers." To reduce discrimination, companies can determine the hiring and promotion rates for different groups, train managers to make hiring and promotion decisions on the basis of specific criteria, and make sure that everyone has equal access to training, mentors, reasonable work accommodations, and assistive technology. Finally, companies need to designate a go-to person that employees can talk to if they believe they have suffered discrimination.

LO3 Deep-Level Diversity

Deep-level diversity matters because it can reduce prejudice, discrimination, and conflict while increasing social integration. It consists of dispositional and personality differences that can be learned only through extended interaction with others. Research conducted in different cultures, settings, and languages indicates that there are five basic dimensions of personality: extraversion, emotional stability, agreeableness, conscientiousness, and openness to experience. Of these, conscientiousness is perhaps the most important because conscientious workers tend to be better performers on virtually any job. Extraversion is also related to performance in jobs that require significant interaction with others.

LO4 Managing Diversity

The three paradigms for managing diversity are the discrimination and fairness paradigm (equal opportunity, fair treatment, strict compliance with the law), the access and legitimacy paradigm (matching internal diversity to external diversity), and the learning and effectiveness paradigm (achieving organizational plurality by integrating deep-level diversity into the work of the organization). Unlike the other paradigms, which focus on surface-level differences, the learning and effectiveness program values common ground, distinguishes between individual and group differences, minimizes conflict and divisiveness, and focuses on bringing different talents and perspectives together. What principles can companies use when managing diversity? Link diversity to strategic business

maredonna8888/Shutterstock.com

agreeableness
The degree to which someone is cooperative, polite, flexible, forgiving, good-natured, tolerant, and trusting. (p. 211)

conscientiousness
The degree to which someone is organized, hardworking, responsible, persevering, thorough, and achievement oriented. (p. 211)

openness to experience
The degree to which someone is curious, broad-minded, and open to new ideas, things, and experiences; is spontaneous; and has a high tolerance for ambiguity. (p. 211)

LO4

organizational plurality
A work environment where (1) all members are empowered to contribute in a way that maximizes the benefits to the organization, customers, and themselves, and (2) the individuality of each member is respected by not segmenting or polarizing people on the basis of their membership in a particular group. (p. 213)

awareness training
Training designed to raise employees' awareness of diversity issues and to challenge the underlying assumptions or stereotypes they may have about others. (p. 215)

skills-based diversity training
Training that teaches employees the practical skills they need for managing a diverse workforce, such as flexibility and adaptability, negotiation, problem solving, and conflict resolution. (p. 216)

diversity audits
Formal assessments that measure employee and management attitudes, investigate the extent to which people are advantaged or disadvantaged with respect to hiring and promotions, and review companies' diversity-related policies and procedures. (p. 216)

diversity pairing
A mentoring program in which people of different cultural backgrounds, sexes, or races/ethnicities are paired together to get to know one another and change stereotypical beliefs and attitudes. (p. 216)

goals. Include diversity in human resource planning. Recruit a diverse workforce. Select a diverse workforce. Train and develop a diverse staff. Monitor the effectiveness of staffing for diversity. Provide work–life flexibility. Create an inclusive working environment. Encourage senior executive support for diversity. The two types of diversity training are awareness training and skills-based diversity training. Companies also manage diversity through diversity audits and diversity pairing.

Paradigms for Managing Diversity

Diversity Paradigm	Focus	Success Measured by	Benefits	Limitations
Discrimination & fairness	Equal opportunity Fair treatment Recruitment of minorities Strict compliance with laws	Recruitment, promotion, and retention goals for underrepresented group	Fairer treatment Increased demographic diversity	Focus on surface-level diversity
Access & legitimacy	Acceptance and celebration of differences	Diversity in company matches diversity of primary stakeholders	Establishes a clear business reason for diversity	Focus on surface-level diversity
Learning & effectiveness	Integrating deep-level differences into organization	Valuing people on the basis of individual knowledge, skills, and abilities	Values common ground Distinction between individual and group differences Less conflict, backlash, and divisiveness Bringing different talents and perspectives together	Focus on deep-level diversity is more difficult to measure and quantify

Motivation

Greg Epperson/Shutterstock.com

LO1 Basics of Motivation

Motivation is the set of forces that initiates, directs, and makes people persist in their efforts over time to accomplish a goal. Managers often confuse motivation and performance, but job performance is a multiplicative function of motivation times ability times situational constraints. Needs are the physical or psychological requirements that must be met to ensure survival and well-being. Different motivational theories (Maslow's Hierarchy of Needs, Alderfer's ERG Theory, and McClelland's Learned Needs Theory) specify a number of different needs. However, studies show that there are only two general kinds of needs: lower order needs and higher order needs. Both extrinsic and intrinsic rewards motivate people.

Motivating to Increase Effort

- Start by asking people what their needs are.
- Satisfy lower order needs first.
- Expect people's needs to change.
- As needs change and lower order needs are satisfied, satisfy higher order needs by looking for ways to allow employees to experience intrinsic rewards

LO2 Equity Theory

The basic components of equity theory are inputs, outcomes, and referents. After an internal comparison in which they compare their outcomes (O) to their inputs (I), employees make an external comparison in which they compare their O/I ratio with the O/I ratio of a referent, a person who works in a similar job or is otherwise similar. When their O/I ratio is equal to the referent's O/I ratio, employees perceive that they are being treated fairly. But, when their O/I ratio is different from their referent's O/I ratio, they perceive that they have been treated inequitably or unfairly. There are two kinds of inequity: under-reward and over-reward. Under-reward, which occurs when a referent's O/I ratio is better than the employee's O/I ratio, leads to anger or frustration. Over-reward, which occurs when a referent's O/I ratio is worse than the employee's O/I ratio, can lead to guilt but only when the level of over-reward is extreme.

LO3 Expectancy Theory

Expectancy theory holds that three factors affect the conscious choices people make about their motivation: valence, expectancy, and instrumentality. Expectancy theory holds that all three factors must be high for people to be highly motivated. If any one of these factors declines, overall motivation will decline too.

Motivating with Expectancy Theory

- Systematically gather information to find out what employees want from their jobs.
- Take specific steps to link rewards to individual performance in a way that is clear and understandable to employees.
- Empower employees to make decisions if management really wants them to believe that their hard work and effort will lead to good performance.

LO4 Reinforcement Theory

Reinforcement theory says that behaviour is a function of its consequences. Reinforcement has two parts: reinforcement contingencies and schedules of reinforcement. The four kinds of reinforcement contingencies are positive reinforcement and negative reinforcement, which strengthen behaviour, and punishment and extinction, which weaken behaviour. There are two kinds of reinforcement schedules, continuous and intermittent; intermittent schedules, in turn, can be divided into fixed and variable interval schedules and fixed and variable ratio schedules.

LO1

motivation
The set of forces that initiates, directs, and makes people persist in their efforts to accomplish a goal. (p. 219)

needs
The physical or psychological requirements that must be met to ensure survival and well-being. (p. 220)

extrinsic reward
A reward that is tangible, visible to others, and given to employees contingent on the performance of specific tasks or behaviours. (p. 222)

intrinsic reward
A natural reward associated with performing a task or activity for its own sake. (p. 223)

LO2

equity theory
A theory that states that people will be motivated when they perceive that they are being treated fairly. (p. 224)

inputs
In equity theory, the contributions employees make to the organization. (p. 225)

outcomes
In equity theory, the rewards employees receive for their contributions to the organization. (p. 225)

referents
In equity theory, others with whom people compare themselves to determine if they have been treated fairly. (p. 225)

outcome/input (O/I) ratio
In equity theory, an employee's perception of how the rewards received from an organization compare with the employee's contributions to that organization. (p. 225)

under-reward
A form of inequity in which you are getting fewer outcomes relative to inputs than your referent is getting. (p. 225)

over-reward
A form of inequity in which you are getting more outcomes relative to inputs than your referent. (p. 225)

distributive justice
The perceived degree to which outcomes and rewards are fairly distributed or allocated. (p. 227)

procedural justice
The perceived fairness of the process used to make reward allocation decisions. (p. 227)

LO3

expectancy theory
A theory that states that people will be motivated to the extent to which they believe that their efforts will lead to good performance, that good performance will be rewarded, and that they will be offered attractive rewards. (p. 228)

valence
The attractiveness or desirability of a reward or outcome. (p. 228)

expectancy
The perceived relationship between effort and performance. (p. 228)

instrumentality
The perceived relationship between performance and rewards. (p. 228)

Greg Epperson/Shutterstock.com

LO4

reinforcement theory
A theory that states that behaviour is a function of its consequences, that behaviours followed by positive consequences will occur more frequently, and that behaviours followed by negative consequences, or not followed by positive consequences, will occur less frequently. (p. 230)

reinforcement
The process of changing behaviour by changing the consequences that follow behaviour. (p. 230)

reinforcement contingencies
Cause-and-effect relationships between the performance of specific behaviours and specific consequences. (p. 230)

schedule of reinforcement
Rules that specify which behaviours will be reinforced, which consequences will follow those behaviours, and the schedule by which those consequences will be delivered. (p. 230)

positive reinforcement
Reinforcement that strengthens behaviour by following behaviours with desirable consequences. (p. 231)

negative reinforcement
Reinforcement that strengthens behaviour by withholding an unpleasant consequence when employees perform a specific behaviour. (p. 231)

punishment
Reinforcement that weakens behaviour by following behaviours with undesirable consequences. (p. 231)

extinction
Reinforcement in which a positive consequence is no longer allowed to follow a previously reinforced behaviour, thus weakening the behaviour. (p. 231)

continuous reinforcement schedule
A schedule that requires a consequence to be administered following every instance of a behaviour. (p. 231)

intermittent reinforcement schedule
A schedule in which consequences are delivered after a specified or average time has elapsed or after a specified or average number of behaviours has occurred. (p. 231)

fixed interval reinforcement schedule
An intermittent schedule in which consequences follow a behaviour only after a fixed time has elapsed. (p. 232)

variable interval reinforcement schedule
An intermittent schedule in which the time between a behaviour and the following consequences varies around a specified average. (p. 232)

fixed ratio reinforcement schedule
An intermittent schedule in which consequences are delivered following a specific number of behaviours. (p. 232)

variable ratio reinforcement schedule
An intermittent schedule in which consequences are delivered following a different number of behaviours, sometimes more and sometimes less, that vary around a specified average number of behaviours. (p. 232)

LO5

goal
A target, objective, or result that someone tries to accomplish. (p. 234)

LO5 Goal-Setting Theory

A goal is a target, objective, or result that someone tries to accomplish. Goal-setting theory says that people will be motivated to the extent to which they accept specific, challenging goals and receive feedback that indicates their progress toward goal achievement. The basic components of goal-setting theory are goal specificity, goal difficulty, goal acceptance, and performance feedback. Goal specificity is the extent to which goals are detailed, exact, and unambiguous. Goal difficulty is the extent to which a goal is hard or challenging to accomplish. Goal acceptance is the extent to which people consciously understand and agree to goals. Performance feedback is information about the quality or quantity of past performance and indicates whether progress is being made toward the accomplishment of a goal.

Exhibit 13.8 Adding Goal-Setting Theory to the Model

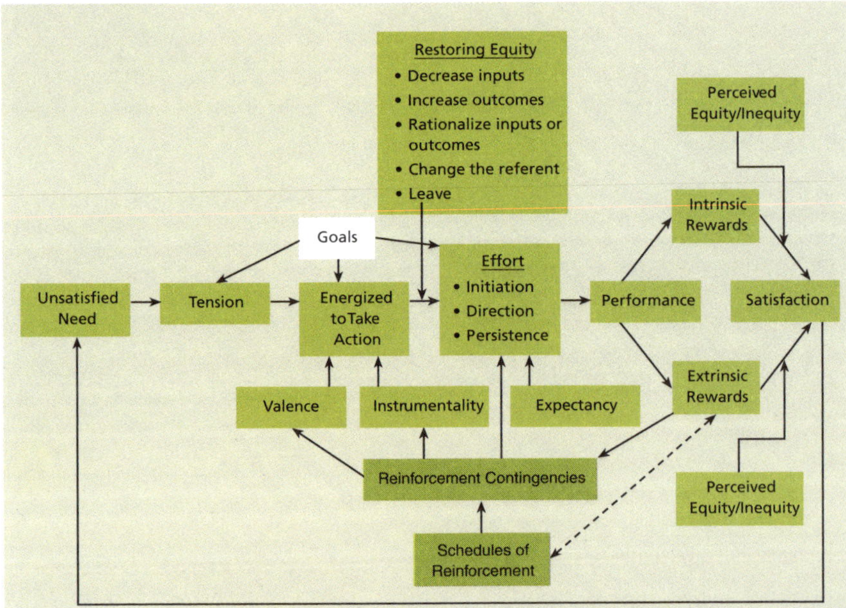

Goals create tension between the goal, which is the desired future state of affairs, and where the employee or company is now, meaning the current state of affairs. This tension can be satisfied only by achieving or abandoning the goal. Goals also energize behaviour. When faced with unaccomplished goals, employees typically develop plans and strategies to reach those goals. Finally, goals influence persistence.

Cengage Learning

goal-setting theory
A theory that states that people will be motivated to the extent to which they accept specific, challenging goals and receive feedback that indicates their progress toward goal achievement. (p. 234)

goal specificity
The extent to which goals are detailed, exact, and unambiguous. (p. 235)

goal difficulty
The extent to which a goal is hard or challenging to accomplish. (p. 235)

goal acceptance
The extent to which people consciously understand and agree to goals. (p. 235)

performance feedback
Information about the quality or quantity of past performance that indicates whether progress is being made toward the accomplishment of a goal. (p. 235)

CHAPTER IN REVIEW

Leadership

Mikael Damkier/Shutterstock.com

LO1

leadership
The process of influencing others to achieve group or organizational goals. (p. 239)

LO2

trait theory
A leadership theory that holds that effective leaders possess a similar set of traits or characteristics. (p. 240)

traits
Relatively stable characteristics, such as abilities, psychological motives, or consistent patterns of behaviour. (p. 240)

initiating structure
The degree to which a leader structures the roles of followers by setting goals, giving directions, setting deadlines, and assigning tasks. (p. 241)

consideration
The extent to which a leader is friendly, approachable, and supportive and shows concern for employees. (p. 242)

leadership style
The way a leader generally behaves toward followers. (p. 243)

LO3

contingency theory
A leadership theory that states that in order to maximize work group performance, leaders must be matched to the situation that best fits their leadership style. (p. 243)

situational favourableness
The degree to which a particular situation either permits or denies a leader the chance to influence the behaviour of group members. (p. 245)

leader–member relations
The degree to which followers respect, trust, and like their leaders. (p. 245)

task structure
The degree to which the requirements of a subordinate's tasks are clearly specified. (p. 245)

position power
The degree to which leaders are able to hire, fire, reward, and punish workers. (p. 245)

LO1 Leaders versus Managers

Management is getting work done through others; leadership is the process of influencing others to achieve group or organizational goals. Leaders are different from managers. The primary difference is that leaders are concerned about doing the right thing, while managers are concerned about doing things right. Organizations need both managers and leaders. But in general, companies are overmanaged and underled.

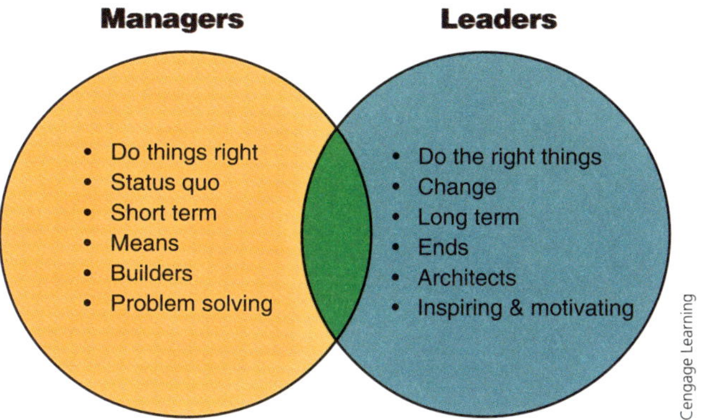

LO2 Who Leaders Are and What Leaders Do

Trait theory says that effective leaders possess traits or characteristics that differentiate them from nonleaders. Those traits are drive, the desire to lead, honesty/integrity, self-confidence, emotional stability, cognitive ability, and knowledge of the business. These traits alone aren't enough for successful leadership; leaders who have many or all of them must also behave in ways that encourage people to achieve group or organizational goals. Two key leader behaviours are initiating structure, which improves subordinate performance, and consideration, which improves subordinate satisfaction. There is no ideal combination of these behaviours. The best leadership style depends on the situation.

LO3 Putting Leaders in the Right Situation: Fiedler's Contingency Theory

Fiedler's theory assumes that leaders are effective when their work groups perform well, that leaders are unable to change their leadership styles, that leadership styles must be matched to the proper situation, and that favourable situations permit leaders to influence group members. According to the Least Preferred Coworker (LPC) scale, there are two basic leadership styles. People who describe their LPC in a positive way have relationship-oriented leadership styles. By contrast, people who describe their LPC in a negative way have task-oriented leadership styles. Situational favourableness, which occurs when leaders can influence followers, is determined by leader–member relations, task structure, and position power. In general, relationship-oriented leaders with high LPC scores are better leaders under moderately favourable situations, while task-oriented leaders with low LPC scores are better leaders in highly favourable and unfavourable situations. Since Fiedler assumes that leaders are incapable of changing their leadership styles, the key is to accurately measure and match leaders to situations or to teach leaders how to change situational factors. Although matching or placing leaders in appropriate situations works well, re-engineering situations to fit leadership styles doesn't because of the complexity of the model, which makes it difficult for people to understand.

Mikael Damkier/Shutterstock.com

Exhibit 14.1 Blake/Mouton Leadership Grid

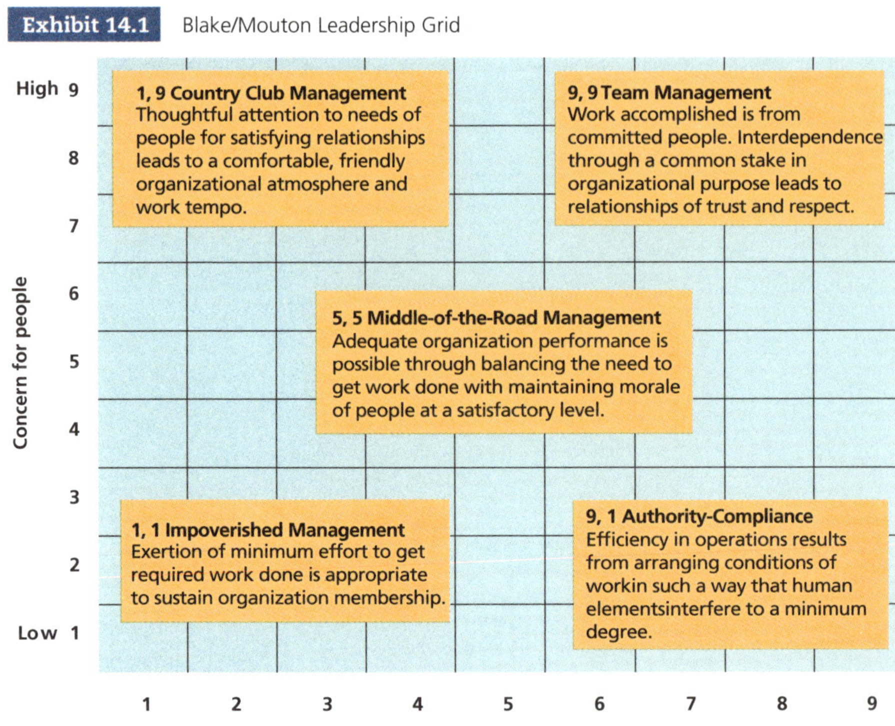

Source: R.R. Blake & A.A. McCanse, "The Leadership Grid (R)," *Leadership Dilemmas—Grid Solutions* (Houston: Gulf Publishing Company), 21. Copyright © 1991, by Scientific Methods, Inc. Reproduced by permission of Grid International, Inc.

LO4 Adapting Leader Behaviour: Path-Goal Theory

Path-goal theory states that leaders can increase subordinate satisfaction and performance by clari-fying and clearing the paths to goals and by increasing the number and kinds of rewards available for goal attainment. For this to work, however, leader behaviour must be a source of immediate or future satisfaction for followers and must complement and not duplicate the characteristics of followers' work environments. In contrast to Fiedler's contingency theory, path-goal theory assumes that leaders can and do change their leadership styles (directive, supportive, participative, and achievement-oriented), depending on their subordinates (experience, perceived ability, internal or external locus of control) and the environment in which those subordinates work (task structure, formal authority system, primary work group).

Exhibit 14.4 Path-Goal Theory

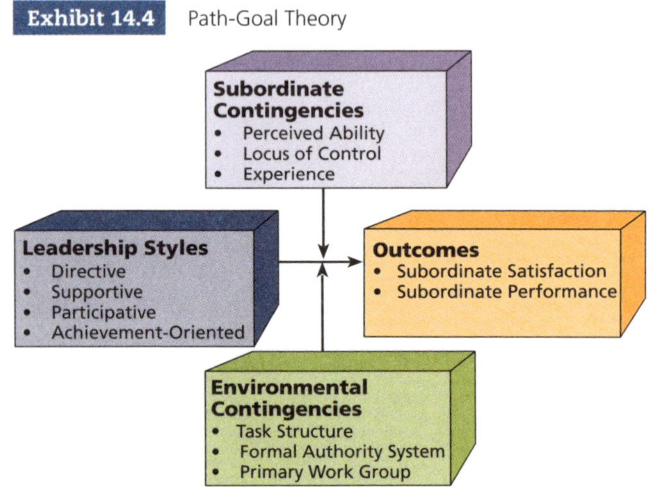

Source: R. J. House and T. R. Mitchell, "Path-Goal Theory of Leadership," *Journal of Contemporary Business* 3 (1974): 81–97.

LO4

path-goal theory
A leadership theory that states that leaders can increase subordinate satisfaction and performance by clarifying and clearing the paths to goals and by increasing the number and kinds of rewards available for goal attainment. (p. 246)

directive leadership
A leadership style in which the leader lets employees know precisely what is expected of them, gives them specific guidelines for performing tasks, schedules work, sets standards of performance, and makes sure that people follow standard rules and regulations. (p. 246)

supportive leadership
A leadership style in which the leader is friendly and approachable, shows concern for employees and their welfare, treats them as equals, and creates a friendly climate. (p. 247)

participative leadership
A leadership style in which the leader consults employees for their suggestions and input before making decisions. (p. 247)

achievement-oriented leadership
A leadership style in which the leader sets challenging goals, has high expectations of employees, and displays confidence that employees will assume responsibility and put forth extraordinary effort. (p. 247)

Mikael Damkier/Shutterstock.com

LO5 Adapting Leader Behaviour: Normative Decision Theory

The normative decision theory helps leaders decide how much employee participation should be used when making decisions. Using the right degree of employee participation improves the quality of decisions and the extent to which employees accept and are committed to decisions. The theory specifies five different decision styles or ways of making decisions: autocratic (AI or AII), consultative (CI or CII), and group (GII). The theory improves decision quality via the decision rules of quality, leader information, subordinate information, goal congruence, and problem structure. The theory improves employee commitment and acceptance via the decision rules of commitment probability, subordinate conflict, and commitment requirement. These decision rules help leaders improve decision quality and follower acceptance and commitment by eliminating decision styles that don't fit the decision or situation they're facing. Normative decision theory then operationalizes these decision rules in the form of yes/no questions, as shown in the decision tree displayed in Exhibit 14.8.

LO5

normative decision theory
A theory that suggests how leaders can determine an appropriate amount of employee participation when making decisions. (p. 249)

LO6 Gender and Leadership

"Stereotypes, prejudice, and discrimination contribute to women's under-representation in elite leadership roles by both impacting perceptions of and responses to women as well as impacting the experiences of women themselves."[1] The role of traits in understanding leadership emergence and effectiveness has been a controversial issue in the literature.

A study by Reuvers et al. showed that "employees report more innovative behaviour when the transformational leadership is displayed by male in comparison with female managers, confirming our gender bias hypothesis."[2] In a separate experimental study, Kulich et al. suggested "that the romance of leadership does exist for both men and women but that the process of pay allocation differs as a function of gender." Generally for a female leader, it is based on perceptions of her charisma and leadership ability rather than directly on company performance.[3] We must do all we can to promote and support female leaders.

LO6

strategic leadership
The ability to anticipate, envision, maintain flexibility, think strategically, and work with others to initiate changes that will create a positive future for an organization. (p. 253)

LO7 Visionary Leadership

Strategic leadership requires visionary, charismatic, and transformational leadership. Visionary leadership creates a positive image of the future that motivates organizational members and provides direction for future planning and goal setting. Charismatic leaders have strong, confident, dynamic personalities that attract followers, enable the leader to create strong bonds, and inspire followers to accomplish the leader's vision. Followers of ethical charismatic leaders work harder, are more committed and satisfied, are better performers, and are more likely to trust their leaders. Followers can be just as supportive and committed to unethical charismatics, who can pose a tremendous risk for companies. Unethical charismatics control and manipulate followers and do what is best for themselves instead of their organizations. Transformational leadership goes beyond charismatic leadership by generating awareness and acceptance of a group's purpose and mission and by getting employees to see beyond their own needs and self-interests for the good of the group. The four components of transformational leadership are charisma or idealized influence, inspirational motivation, intellectual stimulation, and individualized consideration.

LO7

visionary leadership
Leadership that creates a positive image of the future that motivates organizational members and provides direction for future planning and goal setting. (p. 253)

charismatic leadership
The behavioural tendencies and personal characteristics of leaders that create an exceptionally strong relationship between them and their followers. (p. 254)

ethical charismatics
Charismatic leaders who provide developmental opportunities for followers, are open to positive and negative feedback, recognize others' contributions, share information, and have moral standards that emphasize the larger interests of the group, organization, or society. (p. 254)

unethical charismatics
Charismatic leaders who control and manipulate followers, do what is best for themselves instead of their organizations, want to hear only positive feedback, share only information that is beneficial to themselves, and have moral standards that put their interests before everyone else's. (p. 254)

transformational leadership
Leadership that generates awareness and acceptance of a group's purpose and mission and gets employees to see beyond their own needs and self-interests for the good of the group. (p. 254)

transactional leadership
Leadership based on an exchange process, in which followers are rewarded for good performance and punished for poor performance. (p. 256)

[1] C.L. Hoyt, "Women, Men, and Leadership: Exploring the Gender Gap at the Top," *Social and Personality Psychology Compass* 4, no. 7 (2010): 484–98.

[2] M. Reuvers, M.L. Van Engen, C.J. Vinkenburg, E. Wilson-Evered, "Transformational Leadership and Innovative Work Behaviour: Exploring the Relevance of Gender Differences," *Creativity and Innovation Management* 17, no. 3 (2008): 227–44.

[3] C. Kulich, M.K. Ryan, S.A. Haslam, "Where Is the Romance for Women Leaders? The Effects of Gender on Leadership Attributions and Performance-Based Pay," *Applied Psychology* 56, no. 4 (2007): 582–601.

Mikael Damkier/Shutterstock.com

Notes

Managing Communication

Robert Nicholas/OJO Images/Getty Images

LO1

communication
The process of transmitting information from one person or place to another. (p. 259)

perception
The process by which individuals attend to, organize, interpret, and retain information from their environments. (p. 259)

perceptual filters
The personality-, psychology-, or experience-based differences that influence people to ignore or pay attention to particular stimuli. (p. 259)

selective perception
The tendency to notice and accept objects and information consistent with our values, beliefs, and expectations while ignoring or screening out or not accepting inconsistent information. (p. 260)

closure
The tendency to fill in gaps of missing information by assuming that what we don't know is consistent with what we already know. (p. 260)

attribution theory
A theory that states that we all have a basic need to understand and explain the causes of other people's behaviour. (p. 260)

defensive bias
The tendency for people to perceive themselves as personally and situationally similar to someone who is having difficulty or trouble. (p. 261)

fundamental attribution error
The tendency to ignore external causes of behaviour and to attribute other people's actions to internal causes. (p. 261)

self-serving bias
The tendency to overestimate our value by attributing successes to ourselves (internal causes) and attributing failures to others or the environment (external causes). (p. 261)

LO2

encoding
Putting a message into a written, verbal, or symbolic form that can be recognized and understood by the receiver. (p. 262)

decoding
The process by which the receiver translates the written, verbal, or symbolic form of a message into an understood message. (p. 262)

feedback to sender
In the communication process, a return message to the sender that indicates the receiver's understanding of the message. (p. 262)

noise
Anything that interferes with the transmission of the intended message. (p. 262)

jargon
Vocabulary particular to a profession or group. (p. 262)

formal communication channel
The system of official channels that carry organizationally approved messages and information. (p. 262)

downward communication
Communication that flows from higher to lower levels in an organization. (p. 263)

upward communication
Communication that flows from lower to higher levels in an organization. (p. 263)

LO1 Perception and Communication Problems

Perception is the process by which people attend to, organize, interpret, and retain information from their environments. Perception is not a straightforward process. Because of perceptual filters such as selective perception and closure, people exposed to the same information stimuli often end up with very different perceptions and understandings. Perception-based differences can also lead to differences in the attributions (internal or external) that managers and workers make when explaining workplace behaviour. In general, workers are more likely to explain behaviour from a defensive bias, in which they attribute problems to external causes (i.e., the situation). Managers, on the other hand, tend to commit the fundamental attribution error, attributing problems to internal causes (i.e., the worker associated with a mistake or error). Consequently, when things go wrong, it's common for managers to blame workers and for workers to blame the situation or context in which they do their jobs. Finally, this problem is compounded by a self-serving bias that leads people to attribute successes to internal causes and failures to external causes. So, when workers receive negative feedback from managers, they may become defensive and emotional and not hear what their managers have to say. In short, perceptions and attributions represent a significant challenge to effective communication and understanding in organizations.

Exhibit 15.1 Basic Perception Process

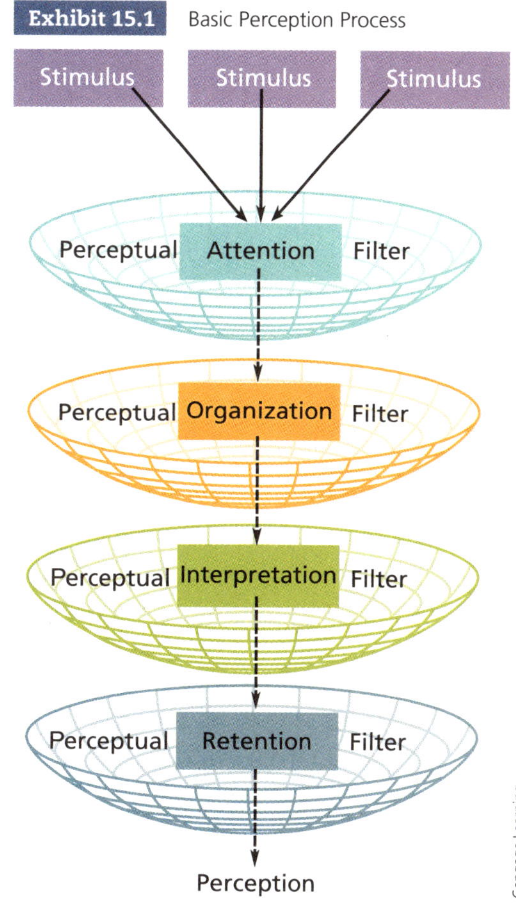

LO2 Kinds of Communication

Organizational communication depends on the communication process, formal and informal communication channels, one-on-one communication, and nonverbal communication. The major components of the communication process are the sender, the receiver, noise, and feedback. Senders often mistakenly assume that they can pipe their intended messages directly into receivers' heads with perfect clarity. Formal communication channels such as downward, upward, and horizontal communication carry organizationally approved messages and information. By contrast, the informal communication channel, called the "grapevine," arises out of curiosity and is carried out through gossip or cluster chains.

Robert Nicholas/OJO Images/ Getty Images

horizontal communication
Communication that flows among managers and workers who are at the same organizational level. (p. 263)

informal communication channel ("grapevine")
The transmission of messages from employee to employee outside of formal communication channels. (p. 264)

coaching
Communicating with someone for the direct purpose of improving the person's on-the-job performance or behaviour. (p. 265)

counselling
Communicating with someone about non-job-related issues that may be affecting or interfering with the person's performance. (p. 265)

nonverbal communication
Any communication that doesn't involve words. (p. 266)

LO3

communication medium
The method used to deliver an oral or written message. (p. 266)

hearing
The act or process of perceiving sounds. (p. 268)

listening
Making a conscious effort to hear. (p. 268)

active listening
Assuming half the responsibility for successful communication by actively giving the speaker nonjudgmental feedback that shows you've accurately heard what he or she said. (p. 268)

empathetic listening
Understanding the speaker's perspective and personal frame of reference and giving feedback that conveys that understanding to the speaker. (p. 268)

destructive feedback
Feedback that disapproves without any intention of being helpful and almost always causes a negative or defensive reaction in the recipient. (p. 269)

constructive feedback
Feedback intended to be helpful, corrective, and/or encouraging. (p. 269)

LO4

online discussion forums
The in-house equivalent of Internet newsgroups. By using Web- or software-based discussion tools that are available across the company, employees can easily ask questions and share knowledge with one another. (p. 270)

Wikis
Websites that allow employees across an organization to edit and update documents in a quick and easy way, facilitating collaboration and interdepartmental communication. (p. 270)

televised/videotaped speeches and meetings
Speeches and meetings originally made to a smaller audience that are either simultaneously broadcast to other locations in the company or videotaped for subsequent distribution and viewing. (p. 270)

videoconferencing
Utilizes computer networks to transmit audio and video, allowing communication to take place at a distance. (p. 270)

There are two kinds of one-on-one communication. Coaching is used to improve on-the-job performance while counselling is used to communicate about non-job-related issues affecting job performance. Nonverbal communication, such as kinesics and paralanguage, accounts for as much as 93 percent of a message's content and understanding.

Exhibit 15.2 The Interpersonal Communication Process

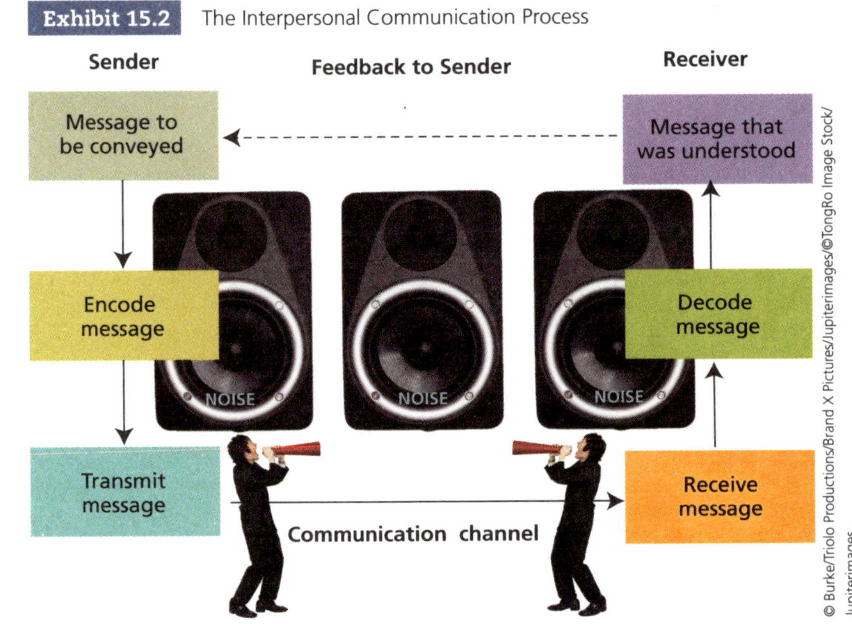

© Burke/Triolo Productions/Brand X Pictures/Jupiterimages/©TongRo Image Stock/ Jupiterimages

LO3 Managing One-on-One Communication

One-on-one communication can be managed by choosing the right communication medium, being a good listener, and giving effective feedback. Managers generally prefer oral communication because it provides the opportunity to ask questions and assess nonverbal communication. Oral communication is best suited to complex, ambiguous, or emotionally laden topics. Written communication is best suited for delivering straightforward messages and information. Listening is important for managerial success, but most people are terrible listeners. To improve your listening skills, choose to be an active listener (clarify responses, paraphrase, and summarize) and an empathetic listener (show your desire to understand, reflect feelings). Feedback can be constructive or destructive. To be constructive, feedback must be immediate, focused on specific behaviours, and problem-oriented.

LO4 Managing Organization-Wide Communication

Managers need methods for managing organization-wide communication and for making themselves accessible so that they can hear what employees throughout their organizations are feeling and thinking. E-mail, online discussion forums, wikis, televised/videotaped speeches and conferences, podcasts, and videoconferences make it much easier for managers to improve message transmission and get the message out. By contrast, anonymous company hotlines, survey feedback, and frequent informal meetings help managers avoid organizational silence and improve reception by giving them the opportunity to hear what others in the organization feel and think. Monitoring social media sites is another way to find out what people are saying and thinking about your organization.

organizational silence
When employees withhold information about organizational problems or issues. (p. 271)

company hotlines
Phone numbers that anyone in the company can call anonymously to leave information for upper management. (p. 271)

survey feedback
Information that is collected by surveys from organizational members and then compiled, disseminated, and used to develop action plans for improvement. (p. 272)

CHAPTER IN REVIEW

Control

Bork/Shutterstock.com

LO1

control
A regulatory process of establishing standards to achieve organizational goals, comparing actual performance to the standards, and taking corrective action when necessary. (p. 275)

standards
A basis of comparison for measuring the extent to which various kinds of organizational performance are satisfactory or unsatisfactory. (p. 275)

benchmarking
The process of identifying outstanding practices, processes, and standards in other companies and adapting them to your company. (p. 276)

cybernetic
The process of steering or keeping on course. (p. 276)

feedback control
A mechanism for gathering information about performance deficiencies after they occur. (p. 276)

concurrent control
A mechanism for gathering information about performance deficiencies as they occur, thereby eliminating or shortening the delay between performance and feedback. (p. 277)

feedforward control
A mechanism for monitoring performance inputs rather than outputs to prevent or minimize performance deficiencies before they occur. (p. 277)

control loss
The situation in which behaviour and work procedures do not conform to standards. (p. 277)

regulation costs
The costs associated with implementing or maintaining control. (p. 278)

cybernetic feasibility
The extent to which it is possible to implement each step in the control process. (p. 278)

LO2

bureaucratic control
The use of hierarchical authority to influence employee behaviour by rewarding or punishing employees for compliance or noncompliance with organizational policies, rules, and procedures. (p. 279)

objective control
The use of observable measures of worker behaviour or outputs to assess performance and influence behaviour. (p. 280)

behaviour control
The regulation of the behaviours and actions that employees perform on the job. (p. 280)

output control
The regulation of employees' results or outputs through rewards and incentives. (p. 280)

normative control
The regulation of employees' behaviour and decisions through widely shared organizational values and beliefs. (p. 280)

concertive control
The regulation of employees' behaviour and decisions through work group values and beliefs. (p. 281)

LO1 The Control Process

The control process begins by setting standards, measuring performance, and then comparing performance to the standards. The better a company's information and measurement systems, the easier it is to make these comparisons. The control process continues by identifying and analyzing performance deviations and then developing and implementing programs for corrective action. Control is a continuous, dynamic, cybernetic process, not a one-time achievement or result. Control requires frequent managerial attention. The three basic control methods are feedback control (after-the-fact performance information), concurrent control (simultaneous performance information), and feedforward control (preventive performance information). Control has regulation costs and unanticipated consequences and therefore isn't always worthwhile or possible.

Exhibit 16.1 Cybernetic Control Process

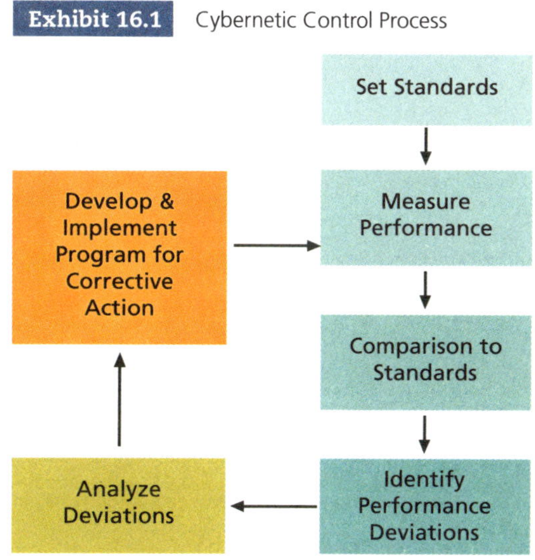

Source: Reprinted from H. Koontz & R. W. Bradspies, "Managing Through Feedforward Control: A Future Directed View," *Business Horizons*, June 1972, 25–36, with permission from Elsevier.

LO2 Control Methods

There are five methods of control: bureaucratic, objective, normative, concertive, and self-control (self-management). Bureaucratic and objective controls are top-down, management-based, and measurement-based. Normative and concertive controls represent shared forms of control because they evolve from company-wide or team-based beliefs and values. Self-control, or self-management, is a control system in which managers turn much, but not all, control over to the individuals themselves.

Bureaucratic control is based on organizational policies, rules, and procedures. Objective controls are based on reliable measures of behaviour or outputs. Normative control is based on strong corporate beliefs and careful hiring practices. Concertive control is based on the development of values, beliefs, and rules in autonomous work groups. Self-control is based on individuals' setting their own goals, monitoring themselves, and rewarding or punishing themselves with respect to goal achievement.

Bork/Shutterstock.com

self-control (self-management)
A control system in which managers and employees control their own behaviour by setting their own goals, monitoring their own progress, and rewarding themselves for goal achievement. (p. 281)

When to Use Different Methods of Control

BUREAUCRATIC CONTROL	• When it is necessary to standardize operating procedures • When it is necessary to establish limits
BEHAVIOUR CONTROL	• When it is easier to measure what workers do on the job than what they accomplish on the job • When cause–effect relationships are clear; that is, when companies know which behaviours will lead to success and which won't • When good measures of worker behaviour can be created
OUTPUT CONTROL	• When it is easier to measure what workers accomplish on the job than what they do on the job • When good measures of worker output can be created • When it is possible to set clear goals and standards for worker output • When cause–effect relationships are unclear
NORMATIVE CONTROL	• When organizational culture, values, and beliefs are strong • When it is difficult to create good measures of worker behaviour • When it is difficult to create good measures of worker output
CONCERTIVE CONTROL	• When responsibility for task accomplishment is given to autonomous work groups • When management wants workers to take ownership of their behaviour and outputs • When management desires a strong form of worker-based control
SELF-CONTROL	• When workers are intrinsically motivated to do their jobs well • When it is difficult to create good measures of worker behaviour • When it is difficult to create good measures of worker output • When workers have or are taught self-control and self-leadership skills

Sources: L. J. Kirsch, "The Management of Complex Tasks in Organizations: Controlling the Systems Development Process," *Organization Science* 7 (1996): 1–21; S. A. Snell, "Control Theory in Strategic Human Resource Management: The Mediating Effect of Administrative Information," *Academy of Management Journal* 35 (1992): 292–327.

We end this section by noting that each of these control methods may be more or less appropriate depending on the circumstances.

LO3 What to Control?

Deciding what to control is just as important as deciding whether to control or how to control. In most companies, performance is measured using financial measures alone. However, the balanced scorecard encourages managers to measure and control company performance from four perspectives: financial, customers, internal operations, and innovation and learning. Traditionally, financial control has been achieved through cash flow analysis, balance sheets, income statements, financial ratios, and budgets. (For a refresher on these traditional financial control tools, see the next card, which is a Financial Review card.) Another way to measure and control financial performance is through economic value added (EVA). Unlike traditional financial measures, EVA helps managers assess whether they are performing well enough to pay the cost of the capital needed to run the business. Instead of using customer satisfaction surveys to measure performance, companies should pay attention to customer defectors, who are more likely to speak up about what the company is doing wrong. Performance of internal operations is often measured in terms of quality, which is defined in three ways: excellence, value, and conformance to expectations. Minimizing waste has become an important part of innovation and learning in companies. The four levels of waste minimization are waste prevention and reduction, recycling and reuse, waste treatment, and waste disposal.

LO3

balanced scorecard
Measurement of organizational performance from four equally important perspectives: finances, customers, internal operations, and innovation and learning. (p. 282)

suboptimization
Performance improvement in one part of an organization at the expense of decreased performance in another part. (p. 282)

cash flow analysis
A type of analysis that predicts how changes in a business will affect its ability to take in more cash than it pays out. (p. 282)

balance sheets
Accounting statements that provide a snapshot of a company's financial position at a particular time. (p. 283)

income statements
Accounting statements, also called "profit and loss statements," that show what has happened to an organization's income, expenses, and net profit over a period of time. (p. 283)

financial ratios
Calculations typically used to track a business's liquidity (cash), efficiency, and profitability over time compared to other businesses in its industry. (p. 283)

budgets
Quantitative plans through which managers decide how to allocate available money to best accomplish company goals. (p. 283)

economic value added (EVA)
The amount by which company profits (revenues, minus expenses, minus taxes) exceed the cost of capital in a given year. (p. 284)

customer defections
A performance assessment in which companies identify which customers are leaving and measure the rate at which they are leaving. (p. 285)

value
Customer perception that the product quality is excellent for the price offered. (p. 287)

Bork/Shutterstock.com

Exhibit 16.7 Advantages and Disadvantages of Different Measures of Quality

Quality Measure	Advantages	Disadvantages
Excellence	Promotes clear organizational vision.	Provides little practical guidance for managers.
	Being/providing the "best" motivates and inspires managers and employees.	Excellence is ambiguous. What is it? Who defines it?
	Appeals to customers, who "know excellence when they see it."	Difficult to measure and control.
Value	Customers recognize differences in value.	Can be difficult to determine what factors influence whether a product/service is seen as having value.
	Easier to measure and compare whether products/services differ in value.	Controlling the balance between excellence and cost (i.e., affordable excellence) can be difficult.
Conformance to Specifications	If specifications can be written, conformance to specifications is usually measurable.	Many products/services cannot be easily evaluated in terms of conformance to specifications.
	Should lead to increased efficiency.	Promotes standardization, so may hurt performance when adapting to changes is more important.
	Promotes consistency in quality.	May be less appropriate for services, which are dependent on a high degree of human contact.

Source: C. A. Reeves and D. A. Bednar, "Defining Quality: Alternatives and Implications," *Academy of Management Review* 19 (1994): 419–445.

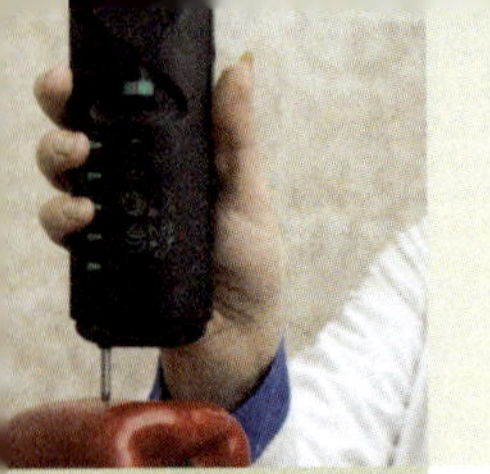
Bork/Shutterstock.com

Notes

FINANCIAL REVIEW CARD

Bork/Shutterstock.com

Basic Accounting Tools for Controlling Financial Performance

Steps for a Basic Cash Flow Analysis
1. Forecast sales (steady, up, or down).
2. Project changes in anticipated cash inflows (as a result of changes).
3. Project anticipated cash outflows (as a result of changes).
4. Project net cash flows by combining anticipated cash inflows and outflows.
Parts of a Basic Balance Sheet (Assets = Liabilities + Owner's Equity)
1. Assets a. Current Assets (cash, short-term investment, marketable securities, accounts receivable, etc.) b. Fixed Assets (land, buildings, machinery, equipment, etc.)
2. Liabilities a. Current Liabilities (accounts payable, notes payable, taxes payable, etc.) b. Long-Term Liabilities (long-term debt, deferred income taxes, etc.)
3. Owner's Equity a. Preferred stock and common stock b. Additional paid-in capital c. Retained earnings
Basic Income Statement
SALES REVENUE − sales returns and allowances + other income = NET REVENUE − cost of goods sold (beginning inventory, costs of goods purchased, ending inventory) = GROSS PROFIT − total operating expenses (selling, general, and administrative expenses) = INCOME FROM OPERATIONS − interest expense = PRETAX INCOME − income taxes = NET INCOME

Common Kinds of Budgets

Revenue Budgets—used to project or forecast future sales.	• Accuracy of projection depends on economy, competitors, sales force estimates, etc. • Determined by estimating future sales volume and sales prices for all products and services.
Expense Budgets—used within departments and divisions to determine how much will be spent on various supplies, projects, or activities.	• One of the first places that companies look for cuts when trying to lower expenses.
Profit Budgets—used by profit centres, which have "profit and loss" responsibility.	• Profit budgets combine revenue and expense budgets into one budget. • Typically used in large businesses with multiple plants and divisions.
Cash Budgets—used to forecast how much cash a company will have on hand to meet expenses.	• Similar to cash flow analyses. • Used to identify cash shortfalls, which must be covered to pay bills, or cash excesses, which should be invested for a higher return.

(Continued)

Bork/Shutterstock.com

Capital Expenditure Budgets—used to forecast large, long-lasting investments in equipment, buildings, and property.	• Help managers identify funding that will be needed to pay for future expansion or strategic moves designed to increase competitive advantage.
Variable Budgets—used to project costs across varying levels of sales and revenues.	• Important because it is difficult to accurately predict sales revenue and volume. • Lead to more accurate budgeting with respect to labour, materials, and administrative expenses, which vary with sales volume and revenues. • Build flexibility into the budgeting process.

Common Financial Ratios

Ratios	Formula	What It Means	When to Use
Liquidity Ratios Current Ratio	$\frac{\text{Current Assets}}{\text{Current Liabilities}}$	• Whether you have enough assets on hand to pay for short-term bills and obligations. • Higher is better. • Recommended level is two times as many current assets as current liabilities	• Track monthly and quarterly. • Basic measure of your company's health.
Quick (Acid Test) Ratio	$\frac{\text{(Current Assets} - \text{Inventories)}}{\text{Current Liabilities}}$	• Stricter than current ratio. • Whether you have enough (i.e., cash) to pay short-term bills and obligations. • Higher is better. • Recommended level is one or higher.	• Track monthly. • Also calculate quick ratio with potential customers to evaluate whether they're likely to pay you in a timely manner.
Leverage Ratios Debt to Equity	$\frac{\text{Total Liabilities}}{\text{Total Equity}}$	• Indicates how much the company is leveraged (in debt) by comparing what is owed (liabilities) to what is owned (equity). • Lower is better. A high debt-to-equity ratio could indicate that the company has too much debt. • Recommended level depends on industry.	• Track monthly. • Lenders often use this to determine the creditworthiness of a business (i.e., whether to approve additional loans).
Debt Coverage	$\frac{\text{(Net Profit + Noncash Expense)}}{\text{Debt}}$	• Indicates how well cash flow covers debt payments. • Higher is better.	• Track monthly. • Lenders look at this ratio to determine if there is adequate cash to make loan payment.
Efficiency Ratios Inventory Turnover	$\frac{\text{Cost of Goods Sold}}{\text{Average Value of Inventory}}$	• Whether you're making efficient use of inventory. • Higher is better, indicating that inventory (dollars) isn't purchased (spent) until needed. • Recommended level depends on industry.	• Track monthly by using a 12-month rolling average.
Average Collections Period	$\frac{\text{Accounts Receivable}}{\text{(Annual Net Credit Sales Divided by 365)}}$	• Shows on average how quickly your customers are paying their bills. • Recommended level is no more than 15 days longer than credit terms. If credit is net 30 days, then average should not be longer than 45 days.	• Track monthly. • Use to determine how long company's money is being tied up in customer credit.
Profitability Ratios Gross Profit Margin	$\frac{\text{Gross Profit}}{\text{Total Sales}}$	• Shows how efficiently a business is using its materials and labour in the production process. • Higher is better, indicating that a profit can be made if fixed costs are controlled.	• Track monthly. • Analyze when unsure about product or service pricing. • Low margin compared to competitors means you're underpricing.
Return on Equity	$\frac{\text{Net Income}}{\text{Owner's Equity}}$	• Shows what was earned on your investment in the business during a particular period. Often called "return on investment." • Higher is better.	• Track quarterly and annually. • Use to compare to what you might have earned on the stock market, bonds, or government Treasury bills during the same period.

Managing Information in a Global World

Hamara/Shutterstock.com

LO1

Moore's law
The prediction that the cost of computing will drop by 50 percent every 18 months as computer-processing power doubles. (p. 293)

raw data
Facts and figures. (p. 293)

information
Useful data that can influence people's choices and behaviour. (p. 293)

first-mover advantage
The strategic advantage that companies earn by being the first to use new information technology to substantially lower costs or to make a product or service different from that of competitors. (p. 294)

LO2

acquisition cost
The cost of obtaining data that you don't have. (p. 296)

processing cost
The cost of turning raw data into usable information. (p. 296)

storage cost
The cost of physically or electronically archiving information for later use and retrieval. (p. 296)

retrieval cost
The cost of accessing already-stored and processed information. (p. 296)

communication cost
The cost of transmitting information from one place to another. (p. 297)

LO3

bar code
A visual pattern that represents numerical data by varying the thickness and pattern of vertical bars. (p. 297)

radio frequency identification (RFID) tags
Tags containing minuscule microchips that transmit information via radio waves and can be used to track the number and location of the objects into which the tags have been inserted. (p. 298)

electronic scanner
An electronic device that converts printed text and pictures into digital images. (p. 298)

optical character recognition
The ability of software to convert digitized documents into ASCII (American Standard Code for Information Interchange) text or PDF documents that can be searched, read, and edited by word processing and other kinds of software. (p. 298)

processing information
Transforming raw data into meaningful information. (p. 298)

data mining
The process of discovering patterns and relationships in large amounts of data. (p. 298)

data warehouse
Stores huge amounts of data that have been prepared for data mining analysis by being cleaned of errors and redundancy. (p. 298)

supervised data mining
The process when the user tells the data mining software to look and test for specific patterns and relationships in a data set. (p. 298)

LO1 Strategic Importance of Information

The first company to use new information technology to substantially lower costs or differentiate products or services often gains first-mover advantage, higher profits, and larger market share. Creating a first-mover advantage can be difficult, expensive, and risky, however. According to the resource-based view of IT, sustainable competitive advantage occurs when IT adds value, is different across firms, and is difficult to create or acquire.

Exhibit 17.2 Using Information Technology to Sustain a Competitive Advantage

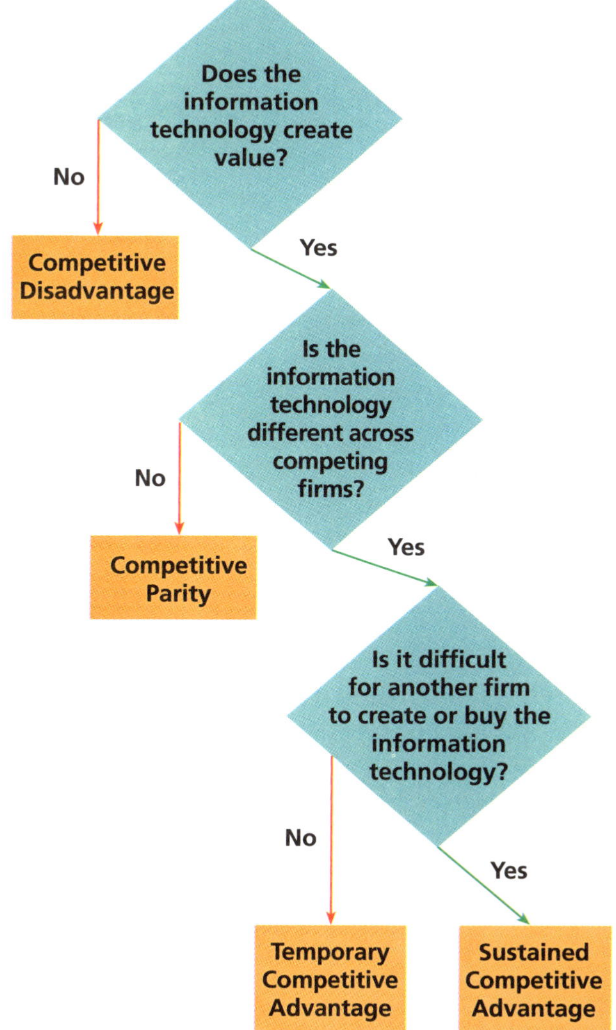

Source: Adapted from F. J. Mata, W. L. Fuerst, and J. B. Barney, "Information Technology and Sustained Competitive Advantage: A Resource-Based Analysis," *MIS Quarterly* 19, no. 4 (December 1995): 487–505. Copyright © 1995, Regents of the University of Minnesota. Reprinted by permission.

LO2 Characteristics and Costs of Useful Information

Raw data are facts and figures. Raw data do not become information until they are in a form that can affect decisions and behaviour. For information to be useful, it has to be reliable and valid (accurate), of sufficient quantity (complete), pertinent to the problems you're facing (relevant), and available when you need it (timely). Useful information does not come cheap. The five costs of obtaining good information are the costs of acquiring, processing, storing, retrieving, and communicating information.

Hamara/Shutterstock.com

unsupervised data mining
The process when the user simply tells the data mining software to uncover whatever uatterns and relationships it can find in a data set. (p. 299)

association or affinity patterns
When two or more database elements tend to occur together in a significant way. (p. 299)

sequence patterns
When two or more database elements occur together in a significant pattern, but one of the elements precedes the other. (p. 299)

predictive patterns
Patterns that help identify database elements that are different. (p. 299)

data clusters
When three or more database elements occur together (i.e., cluster) in a significant way. (p. 299)

protecting information
The process of ensuring that data are reliably and consistently retrievable in a usable format for authorized users but no one else. (p. 300)

authentication
Making sure potential users are who they claim to be. (p. 300)

authorization
Granting authenticated users approved access to data, software, and systems. (p. 300)

two-factor authentication
Authentication based on what users know, such as a password, and what they have in their possession, such as a secure ID card or key. (p. 301)

biometrics
Identifying users by unique, measurable body features, such as fingerprint recognition or iris scanning. (p. 301)

firewall
A protective hardware or software device that sits between the computers in an internal organizational network and outside networks, such as the Internet. (p. 301)

virus
A program or piece of code that, against your wishes, attaches itself to other programs on your computer and can trigger anything from a harmless flashing message to the reformatting of your hard drive to a system-wide network shutdown. (p. 301)

data encryption
The transformation of data into complex, scrambled digital codes that can be unencrypted only by authorized users who possess unique decryption keys. (p. 303)

virtual private network (VPN)
Software that securely encrypts data sent by employees outside the company network, decrypts the data when they arrive within the company computer network, and does the same when data are sent back to employees outside the network. (p. 303)

secure sockets layer (SSL) encryption
Internet browser–based encryption that provides secure off-site Web access to some data and programs. (p. 303)

LO3 Capturing, Processing, and Protecting Information

Electronic data capture (bar codes, radio frequency identification [RFID] tags, scanners, and optical character recognition) is much faster, easier, and cheaper than manual data capture. Processing information means transforming raw data into meaningful information that can be applied to business decision making. Data mining helps managers with this transformation by discovering unknown patterns and relationships in data. Supervised data mining looks for patterns specified by managers, while unsupervised data mining looks for four general kinds of data patterns: association/affinity patterns, sequence patterns, predictive patterns, and data clusters. Protecting information ensures that data are reliably and consistently retrievable in a usable format by authorized users but no one else. Authentication and authorization, firewalls, antivirus software for PCs and corporate e-mail and network servers, data encryption, virtual private networks (VPN), and Web-based secure sockets layer (SSL) encryption are some of the best ways to protect information. Be careful with wireless networks, which are easily compromised even when security and encryption protocols are in place.

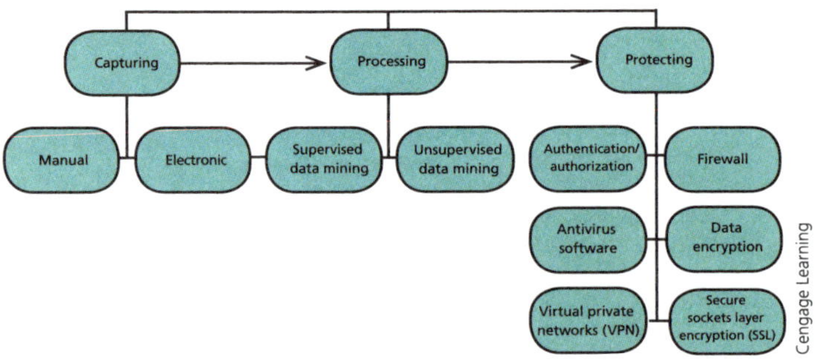

LO4 Accessing and Sharing Information and Knowledge

Executive information systems, intranets, and corporate portals facilitate internal sharing and access to company information and transactions. Electronic data interchange and the Internet allow external groups such as suppliers and customers to easily access company information. Both decrease costs by reducing or eliminating data entry, data errors, and paperwork and by speeding up communication. Organizations use decision support systems and expert systems to capture and share specialized knowledge with nonexpert employees.

LO4

executive information system (EIS)
A data processing system that uses internal and external data sources to provide the information needed to monitor and analyze organizational performance. (p. 304)

intranets
Private company networks that allow employees to easily access, share, and publish information using Internet software. (p. 304)

corporate portal
A hybrid of executive information systems and intranets that allows managers and employees to use a Web browser to gain access to customized company information and to complete specialized transactions. (p. 304)

electronic data interchange (EDI)
When two companies convert their purchase and ordering information to a standardized format to enable the direct electronic transmission of that information from one company's computer system to the other company's computer system. (p. 305)

extranets
Networks that allow companies to exchange information and conduct transactions with outsiders by providing them direct, Web-based access to authorized parts of a company's intranet or information system. (p. 305)

knowledge
The understanding that one gains from information. (p. 306)

decision support system (DSS)
An information system that helps managers understand specific kinds of problems and potential solutions and analyze the impact of different decision options using "what if" scenarios. (p. 306)

expert system
An information system that contains the specialized knowledge and decision rules used by experts and experienced decision makers so that nonexperts can draw on this knowledge base to make decisions. (p. 306)

CHAPTER IN REVIEW

Managing Service and Manufacturing Operations

The Canadian Press Images/ Bayne Stanley

LO1

productivity
A measure of performance that indicates how many inputs it takes to produce or create an output. (p. 309)

partial productivity
A measure of performance that indicates how much of a particular kind of input it takes to produce an output. (p. 310)

multifactor productivity
An overall measure of performance that indicates how much labour, capital, materials, and energy it takes to produce an output. (p. 311)

LO2

quality
A product or service free of deficiencies, or the characteristics of a product or service that satisfy customer needs. (p. 312)

ISO 9000
A series of five international standards, from ISO 9000 to ISO 9004, for achieving consistency in quality management and quality assurance in companies throughout the world. (p. 313)

ISO 14000
A series of international standards for managing, monitoring, and minimizing an organization's harmful effects on the environment. (p. 313)

total quality management (TQM)
An integrated, principle-based, organization-wide strategy for improving product and service quality. (p. 314)

customer focus
An organizational goal to concentrate on meeting customers' needs at all levels of the organization. (p. 314)

customer satisfaction
An organizational goal to provide products or services that meet or exceed customers' expectations. (p. 314)

continuous improvement
An organization's ongoing commitment to constantly assess and improve the processes and procedures used to create products and services. (p. 314)

variation
A deviation in the form, condition, or appearance of a product from the quality standard for that product. (p. 314)

teamwork
Collaboration between managers and non-managers, across business functions, and between companies, customers, and suppliers. (p. 315)

LO3

service recovery
Restoring customer satisfaction to strongly dissatisfied customers. (p. 316)

LO4

make-to-order operation
A manufacturing operation that does not start processing or assembling products until a customer order is received. (p. 317)

assemble-to-order operation
A manufacturing operation that divides manufacturing processes into separate parts or modules that are combined to create semicustomized products. (p. 317)

LO1 Productivity

Productivity is a measure of how many inputs it takes to produce or create an output. The greater the output from one input, or the fewer inputs it takes to create an output, the higher the productivity. Partial productivity measures how much of a single kind of input such as labour is needed to produce an output. Multifactor productivity is an overall measure of productivity that indicates how much labour, capital, materials, and energy are needed to produce an output.

$$\text{Partial productivity} = \frac{\text{Outputs}}{\text{Single kind of input}}$$

$$\text{Multifactor productivity} = \frac{\text{Outputs}}{(\text{Labour} + \text{Capital} + \text{Materials} + \text{Energy})}$$

LO2 Quality

Quality can mean a product or service free of deficiencies or the characteristics of a product or service that satisfies customer needs. Quality products usually possess three characteristics: reliability, serviceability, and durability. Quality service means reliability, tangibles, responsiveness, assurance, and empathy. ISO 9000 is a series of five international standards for achieving consistency in quality management and quality assurance, while ISO 14000 is a set of standards for minimizing an organization's harmful effects on the environment. The Baldrige National Quality Award recognizes U.S. companies for their achievements in quality and business performance. Each year, three Baldrige Awards may be given for manufacturing, service, small business, education, health care, and not-for-profit. Total quality management (TQM) is an integrated organization-wide strategy for improving product and service quality. TQM is based on three mutually reinforcing principles: customer focus and satisfaction, continuous improvement, and teamwork.

LO3 Service Operations

Services are different from goods. Goods are produced, tangible, and storable. Services are performed, intangible, and perishable. Likewise, managing service operations is different from managing production operations. The service–profit chain indicates that success begins with internal service quality, meaning how well management treats service employees. Internal service quality leads to employee satisfaction and service capability, which, in turn, lead to high-value service to customers, customer satisfaction, customer loyalty, and long-term profits and growth. Keeping existing customers is far more cost-effective than finding new ones. Consequently, to prevent disgruntled customers from leaving, some companies are empowering service employees to perform service recovery—restoring customer satisfaction to strongly dissatisfied customers—by giving them the authority and responsibility to immediately solve customer problems. The hope is that empowered service recovery will prevent customer defections.

Exhibit 18.3 Service-Profit Chain

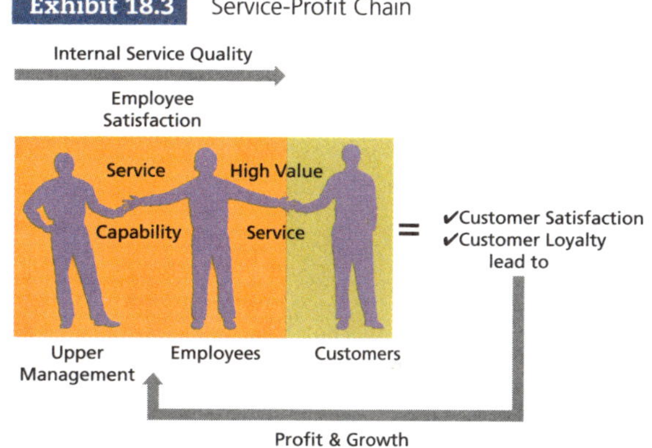

Sources: R. Hallowell, L.A. Schlesinger, and J. Zornitsky, "Internal Service Quality, Customer and Job Satisfaction: Linkages and Implications for Management," *Human Resource Planning* 19 (1996): 20–31; J.L. Heskett, T.O. Jones, G.W. Loveman, W.E. Sasser, Jr., and L.A. Schlesinger, "Putting the Service-Profit Chain to Work," *Harvard Business Review* (March-April 1994): 164–174.

The Canadian Press Images/
Bayne Stanley

make-to-stock operation
A manufacturing operation that orders parts and assembles standardized products before receiving customer orders. (p. 317)

manufacturing flexibility
The degree to which manufacturing operations can easily and quickly change the number, kind, and characteristics of products they produce. (p. 318)

continuous-flow production
A manufacturing operation that produces goods at a continuous, rather than a discrete, rate. (p. 318)

line-flow production
Manufacturing processes that are pre-established, occur in a serial or linear manner, and are dedicated to making one type of product. (p. 318)

batch production
A manufacturing operation that produces goods in large batches in standard lot sizes. (p. 318)

job shops
Manufacturing operations that handle custom orders or small batch jobs. (p. 318)

LO5

inventory
The amount and number of raw materials, parts, and finished products that a company has in its possession. (p. 319)

raw material inventories
The basic inputs in a manufacturing process. (p. 319)

component parts inventories
The basic parts used in manufacturing that are fabricated from raw materials. (p. 319)

work-in-process inventories
Partially finished goods consisting of assembled component parts. (p. 319)

finished goods inventories
The final outputs of manufacturing operations. (p. 319)

average aggregate inventory
Average overall inventory during a particular time period. (p. 320)

stockout
The situation when a company runs out of finished product. (p. 320)

inventory turnover
The number of times per year that a company sells or "turns over" its average inventory. (p. 321)

ordering cost
The costs associated with ordering inventory, including the cost of data entry, phone calls, obtaining bids, correcting mistakes, and determining when and how much inventory to order. (p. 321)

setup cost
The costs of downtime and lost efficiency that occur when a machine is changed or adjusted to produce a different kind of inventory. (p. 321)

holding cost
The cost of keeping inventory until it is used or sold, including storage, insurance, taxes, obsolescence, and opportunity costs. (p. 322)

stockout costs
The costs incurred when a company runs out of a product, including transaction costs to replace inventory and the loss of customers' goodwill. (p. 322)

LO4 Manufacturing Operations

Manufacturing operations produce physical goods. Manufacturing operations can be classified according to the amount of processing or assembly that occurs after receiving an order from a customer.

Manufacturing operations can also be classified in terms of flexibility, and the degree to which the number, kind, and characteristics of products can easily and quickly be changed. Flexibility allows companies to respond quickly to competitors and customers and to reduce order lead times, but it can also lead to higher unit costs.

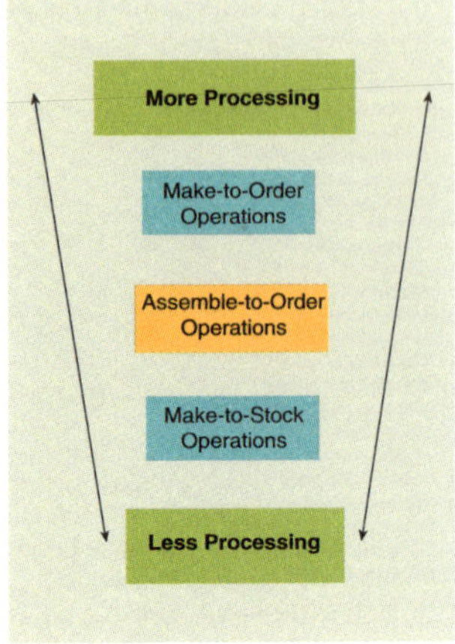

Cengage Learning

LEAST FLEXIBLE
Continuous-Flow Production
Line-Flow Production
Batch Production
Job Shops
MOST FLEXIBLE

Cengage Learning

LO5 Inventory

There are four kinds of inventory: raw materials, component parts, work-in-process, and finished goods. Because companies incur ordering, setup, holding, and stockout costs when handling inventory, inventory costs can be enormous. To control those costs, companies measure and track inventory in three ways: average aggregate inventory, weeks of supply, and turnover. Companies meet the basic goals of inventory management (avoiding stockouts and reducing inventory without hurting daily operations) through economic order quantity (EOQ) formulas, just-in-time (JIT) inventory systems, and materials requirement planning (MRP).

$$EOQ = \sqrt{\frac{2DO}{H}}$$

Use EOQ formulas when inventory levels are independent, and use JIT and MRP when inventory levels are dependent on the number of products to be produced.

economic order quantity (EOQ)
A system of formulas that minimizes ordering and holding costs and helps determine how much and how often inventory should be ordered. (p. 322)

just-in-time (JIT) inventory system
An inventory system in which component parts arrive from suppliers just as they are needed at each stage of production. (p. 322)

kanban
A ticket-based JIT system that indicates when to reorder inventory. (p. 322)

materials requirement planning (MRP)
A production and inventory system that determines the production schedule, production batch sizes, and inventory needed to complete final products. (p. 323)

independent demand system
An inventory system in which the level of one kind of inventory does not depend on another. (p. 323)

dependent demand system
An inventory system in which the level of inventory depends on the number of finished units to be produced. (p. 323)

Notes

Notes

Notes

Notes